The Forgotten Championships

The Forgotten Championships

Postseason Baseball, 1882–1981

by Jerry Lansche

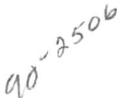

McFarland & Company, Inc., Publishers

Jefferson, North Carolina, and London

British Library Cataloguing-in-Publication data available

Library of Congress Cataloguing-in-Publication Data

Lansche, Jerry, 1951–
    The forgotten championships : postseason baseball, 1882-1981 / by
Jerry Lansche.
        p.   cm.
    Bibliography: p. 353.
    Includes index.
    ISBN 0-89950-414-0 (lib. bdg. : 50# alk. paper) ⊗
    1. Baseball—United States—History.   2. World series (Baseball)—
History.   I. Title.
    GV862.5.L36   1989
    796.357′782′0973 – dc 19   89-42584
                                                                    CIP

Printed in the United States of America.

McFarland & Company, Inc., Publishers
    Box 611, Jefferson, North Carolina 28640

This, my first book,
is dedicated with love
to my wife Sonia

Table of Contents

Acknowledgments

I would like to extend my deepest gratitude
to Steve Gietschier of *The Sporting News* for allowing me
to ruin so many of his days by camping in his offices;
to Lloyd Johnson of the Society for
American Baseball Research in Kansas City, Missouri;
to Tom Heintz of the Baseball Hall of Fame
in Cooperstown, New York;
to my mother, who proofread the book I didn't write;
and to the many individuals at the St. Louis County Library
who were so helpful when the microfilm copiers broke down,
as they often did;
special thanks go to Grace Laffey, my high school English teacher.
Very special thanks go to my three-year old son, Hunter,
without whose loving demands upon my time and attention
this project might have been completed months ago.
And a tip of the Redbird cap and much love to my wife, Sonia,
who will never comprehend what significance
we baseball fans attach to the game, but who was
exceedingly patient and understanding throughout the entire project.

Preface

This is my first book.

In the early stages of the project, I spent more than a little time brushing off friendly inquiries into why I was writing the book, what my qualifications were, and who died and made me a baseball authority. When I submitted the book to McFarland, they asked the same questions, but I couldn't very well brush them off. So I was forced to examine just what my qualifications were.

I have been an ardent baseball fan since my childhood. As a boy of ten, I—and every other child in America—had more insight into the game of baseball than, say, any one of the 55 million inhabitants of France, and I had acquired this information effortlessly, without ability, pain or study. My personal store of baseball knowledge increased through adulthood with the result that I—and every other child in America—was more qualified to write this book than approximately 4.7 billion people on the face of the earth.

Big deal, right?

A second qualification, however, placed me in the exclusive company of no more than a few thousand followers of baseball—an intimate knowledge of the rules of baseball as it was played a hundred years ago and a familiarity with the game's slang. This information often came in handy when I was trying to figure out what went on in some of the 19th century games. It is difficult to make heads or tails of an account which begins "Arlie Latham reached on a phantom," unless one knows "plantom" was slang for a base on balls.

A final qualification—and a prerequisite for all first-time authors—was, simply, an interest in the material and a willingness to do the book. It takes quite an investment of time and effort to research a book, to double-check the research, to write the manuscript, to rewrite it, and to rewrite it again. No one makes that kind of a commitment without interest and desire. I found in these games a wealth of material largely ignored or forgotten by baseball and assumed if it was of interest to me, it would be of interest to anyone who followed baseball.

A word or two on the accuracy of the box scores seems to be in order.

The newspapers of a century ago and, indeed, those of just forty years ago, placed no premium on accuracy. Box scores published in St. Louis often disagreed with those appearing in New York or Chicago, and even such a bulwark as *The Sporting News,* long considered the Bible of baseball, might carry a score slightly different from that in local newspapers. What was reported as an error in a local newspaper was often magically converted to a hit elsewhere and the opposite was true just as frequently. In a number of cases, two sources failed to agree on the most rudimentary matters — for example, how many runs and in which inning a team scored.

Well, what's a person to do?

I relied heavily upon the Macmillan *Baseball Encyclopedia,* a truly wonderful piece of work, but one that is hardly infallible. The current edition, for example, shows Cap Anson's birthdate as April 11, 1882. This would have the Chicago first baseman playing the first six years of his major league career from his mother's womb. Macmillan spells Charlie Getzien's last name with an "ie" even though every newspaper of the day showed the spelling as "ei." In the end, I took the *Baseball Encyclopedia* at face value on all spelling discrepancies.

The most valuable research publication of the time should have been the *Spalding Official Base Ball Guides.* They were not. In fact, of all the sources I used, the *Spaldings* were the least reliable. In 1888, the *Guide* left out the 12th contest of the 1887 World Series between the Detroit Wolverines and St. Louis Browns, listing only 14 of the 15 games. The next edition listed a 12th game, but the score and starting pitchers were those of the 11th game. As a statistical reference, the books were just useless.

But as a guided tour of baseball in the 19th century, the *Guide* reigns supreme. Baseball rules were printed in each edition along with advertisements for equipment, train schedules, and essays on player drunkenness and salary squabbles. Horton Publishing Company (P.O. Box 29234; St. Louis, Missouri 63126) has reprinted the 1880–1889 editions as of this writing, and I highly recommend these charming little books. They are a valuable and inexpensive addition to anyone's baseball library.

I spent hour upon hour comparing the same box scores from different publications for errors. All accounts were taken from at least two newspapers and, in case of discrepancies, a third or fourth source was consulted. Frequently, the "tie-breaker" additional source did nothing to clear up a mystery. Often it caused more. I did my best to reconstruct problem box scores from the accounts of the game. Any mistakes in the book are mine, and I take sole responsibility for my errors.

Introduction

There are over 400 box scores in *The Forgotten Championships*. The subject matter spans exactly one hundred years, from 1882 to 1981. Each of these games determined or helped determine a championship of something—a league division, a league, a city, a state, or the world. (Even in the early days of baseball, we Americans chauvinistically presumed the team which won the World Series was the best team in the world, a supposition which persists, but remains unproven, to this day.)

Most baseball fans are aware of the existence of the American Association, but few realize there were postseason championships between the pennant winners of the American Association and the National League. Even the Macmillan *Baseball Encyclopedia* disdains to make mention of the 19th century championships. For Macmillan and, by extension, for major league baseball hierarchy, these games did not exist. This line of reasoning fails to convince me.

The first section of *The Forgotten Championships* is about the World Series championships of the 19th century. There can be little argument that the postseason games between the American Association and National League pennant winners were the forerunners of the modern fall series. The Temple Cup games and the championship series of the 1892 season, although bastardized versions of the early World Series, are nonetheless worthy of inclusion.

The second section deals with the city and state championships. Ask someone in their thirties about the city championships and your reward will be a blank stare. Ask your father and he will squint and look off into the distance and eventually confess to a vague memory of the Cubs and White Sox playing back in the forties. But unless you're in your sixties or happen to be a member of the Society for American Baseball Research (SABR), this will probably be your first introduction to these games.

The final section of the book is a record of the league championship playoffs and the mini-playoffs of the 1981 strike-shortened season. These are the least forgotten of all the contests herein but, unless you have access to microfilmed newspapers, the box scores and descriptions of these games are exceedingly hard to come by.

Jerry Lansche
St. Louis, Missouri
October, 1988

1

The World Series
of the Nineteenth Century

Introduction

These postseason championships have been ignored and forgotten for four reasons. First, they failed to conform to the now familiar best-of-seven format. Secondly, they were often played under American Association rules. Third, they were not played under today's rules. And, finally, the office of the commissioner and the record books have a tendency to suppose that baseball — as we know it today — began in the 20th century, after the American League was born. Ignoring, for a moment, the Temple Cup series and the National League playoffs of 1892, let's look at these arguments one by one.

The games did not follow the best-of-seven format. It's true, they didn't. It's also true that they ranged from two games (in 1882) to 15 games (1887), but the club presidents of the American Association and National League had no commissioner to step in and set a standard. The championship series lasted as long as the club presidents decided it would last, the only motive being greed. When Barney Dreyfuss and Henry Killilea decided on a best-of-nine format for the first officially recognized series in 1903, not a soul in the country raised a voice against the idea. After 15 years of World Series play, major league baseball saw fit to return to the best-of-nine format for 1919, 1920, and 1921. And what was the motive? What else? Greed, pure and simple. Interest ran so high in the 1919 series — at least the gamblers were interested — that the series was expanded to a nine-game format for three years. Greed reared its head again in 1985 when Bowie Kuhn expanded the League Playoff Championships to seven games from five. To my knowledge, no one has suggested since then that the previous 16 years of LCS records should be thrown out.

The games were often played under American Association rules. Major league baseball has generally given more weight and consideration to the 19th century National League because of its seniority and because the American Association did not endure. And that would make a good argument, except that the American Association was, by any standard you would care to apply, much more forward-thinking than its older and somewhat stodgy rival. Just to cite two examples, the American Association played Sunday games while the National League did not. The American Association awarded a hit batsman first base. The National League, until 1887, did not.

The games were not played under today's rules. The game of baseball has undergone hundreds of changes since its birth. At what point should the line be drawn? The beginning of the 20th century seems as good a time as any, but in the 17 years immediately following the first World Series, there were 19 major scoring rule changes. A ballplayer in 1907 who drove in a run with a sacrifice fly was credited with a time at bat. In 1908, a pitcher or catcher was charged with an error if the runner reached first base on a wild pitch or passed ball. The spitball was legal until 1920. Until that same year, a batter who hit a game-winning home run in the bottom of the final inning was credited only with a single. The strike zone alone has been altered three times since 1963, but no one wants to take a second look at the called third strike on Dale Mitchell which put Don Larsen's perfect game in the record books. Even today's game is not played under today's rules. The American League has the Designated Hitter. The National League does not. What will future historians make of that?

Baseball truly began when the American League was formed. This is the least compelling of the arguments, especially when one considers that the Special Baseball Records Committee of the Major League Baseball Rules Committee has decreed six leagues as major: the National League, the American Association, the Union Association, the Players' League, the American League, and the Federal League.

If you were somehow magically transported to a ballgame in the year 1876, you wouldn't wonder what you had paid your 25 cents to watch. It wasn't cricket. It wasn't rounders. You might need to make some allowances for rule changes, but it was baseball. A child would recognize it as such. To ignore or reject the contests of a hundred years past because of an arbitrary and ultimately illogical line drawn in the record books or on a history dateline flies in the face of reason. In the 21st century, when the World Series is being played by teams of robots and managed by computer banks, today's records will be nonetheless valid.

Now having said that, let me say this. As far as the Temple Cup Games and the National League playoff series of 1892 are concerned, a different situation presents itself. A person can make a strong case against counting the Temple Cup games as anything substantial. Except for personal glory, these series meant little to the team which finished the season in second place, and absolutely nothing to the team which won the pennant. Neither club had anything to prove—the regular season had already determined the best club. The only appeal of the Temple Cup games, for players and owners alike, was found in the prospect of putting some extra cash in one's pocket.

Nonetheless, I have included the box scores and game accounts, all of which you would be hard pressed to find elsewhere.

A Summary of the 19th Century World Series

1882: Chicago White Stockings vs. Cincinnati Reds; 1–1, tie series.
1883: No championship series.
1884: Providence Grays defeat New York Metropolitans; 3–0.

1885: Chicago White Stockings vs. St. Louis Browns; 3–3–1, tie series.
1886: St. Louis Browns defeat Chicago White Stockings; 4–2.
1887: Detroit Wolverines defeat St. Louis Browns; 10–5.
1888: New York Giants defeat St. Louis Browns; 6–4.
1889: New York Giants defeat Brooklyn Bridegrooms; 6–3.
1890: Brooklyn Bridegrooms vs. Louisville Cyclones; 3–3–1, tie series.
1891: No championship series.
1892: Boston Beaneaters defeat Cleveland Spiders; 5–0.
1893: No championship series.
1894: New York Giants defeat Baltimore Orioles; 4–0.
1895: Cleveland Spiders defeat Baltimore Orioles; 4–1.
1896: Baltimore Orioles defeat Cleveland Spiders; 4–0.
1897: Baltimore Orioles defeat Boston Beaneaters; 4–1.

The 1882 Championship Series

Chicago White Stockings (NL) vs. Cincinnati Reds (AA); 1–1, tie series

The first attempt at a postseason series to determine the champions of baseball was little more than that — an attempt. The Cincinnati Reds, winner of the first American Association title, defied its own league rules and scheduled a series of exhibition games with the Cleveland Spiders, the Providence Grays, and the Chicago White Stockings of the National League. These were to be no more and no less than mere exhibition games. There was no hoopla, no fanfare, no pregame swarm of reporters. There were no tailgate parties.

Game One was played at Cincinnati's Bank Street Grounds on October 6th with the bespectacled Will White (40–12) shutting out the White Stockings and Larry Corcoran (27–13) 4–0 on seven hits. Will was the brother of Deacon White, and the first player to wear glasses in the history of the National League. Singles by Hick Carpenter, Dan Stearns and Chick Fulmer, a triple by Bid McPhee, and a wild pitch accounted for all four Cincinnati runs in the sixth inning.

Corcoran returned the favor the next day by shutting out Cincinnati and White 2–0 on three hits. Errors by Hick Carpenter and Harry Wheeler in the first scored George Gore and Ned Williamson with the only two runs of the game. Remarkable for the times, the White Stockings played a flawless defense.

When American Association president H.D. "Denny" McKnight learned of the games, he threatened Cincinnati with expulsion from the league if they continued play. At that time, the two leagues were anything but friendly competitors and it would be well over another year before they made peace. According to newspaper accounts, the Cincinnati ballplayers were ready to defy McKnight since, after all, the regular season was over and their contracts had expired, but Cap Anson, player-manager of the White Stockings, thought it would be in the best interests of baseball if the series ended. And so it did. Cincinnati was later fined and reprimanded by President McKnight.

1882 Championship Series

GAME ONE --- October 6

CHICAGO	AB	R	H	PO	A	E
Dalrymple, lf	4	0	2	3	0	0
Gore, cf	4	0	1	0	0	0
Williamson, 3b	4	0	2	1	2	0
Anson, 1b	4	0	1	12	0	0
Burns, 2b	3	0	0	3	4	0
Goldsmith, rf	3	0	0	1	7	0
Corcoran, p	3	0	0	0	1	1
Nichol, ss	3	0	0	1	0	0
Flint, c	3	0	1	3	1	1
	31	0	7	24	15	2

CINCINNATI	AB	R	H	PO	A	E
Sommers, lf	4	0	0	4	0	0
Wheeler, rf	4	0	0	4	0	0
Carpenter, 3b	4	1	2	2	0	0
Stearns, 1b	4	1	1	7	0	1
Fulmer, ss	4	1	1	1	4	1
McPhee, 2b	4	1	3	4	2	0
Macullar, cf	3	0	1	1	1	0
Powers, c	3	0	0	4	3	0
White, p	3	0	2	0	4	0
	33	4	10	27	14	2

```
CHI   0 0 0   0 0 0   0 0 0  -  0
CIN   0 0 0   0 0 0   4 0 x  -  4
```

Earned runs: Cin 3. 2B: Williamson. 3B: McPhee, Williamson. LOB: Cin 4, Chi 5. Struck out: by White 3, by Corcoran 4. WP: White, Goldsmith. Umpire: C.M. Smith. Att: 2,700. Time—1:40.

GAME TWO --- October 7

CHICAGO	AB	R	H	PO	A	E
Dalrymple, lf	4	0	1	0	1	0
Gore, cf	4	1	0	1	0	0
Williamson, 3b	4	1	2	1	3	0
Anson, 1b	3	0	1	13	0	0
Burns, 2b	3	0	0	1	4	0
Goldsmith, rf	3	0	0	1	0	0
Corcoran, p	3	0	0	0	12	0
Nichol, ss	3	0	0	1	0	0
Flint, c	3	0	0	9	1	0
	30	2	4	27	21	0

CINCINNATI	AB	R	H	PO	A	E
Sommers, lf	4	0	0	4	0	0
Wheeler, rf	4	0	2	0	1	0
Carpenter, 3b	3	0	0	3	1	1
Stearns, 1b	3	0	2	7	0	0
Fulmer, ss	3	0	0	1	3	0
McPhee, 2b	3	0	0	2	0	0
Macullar, cf	3	0	0	1	1	0
Powers, c	3	0	1	7	0	1
White, p	3	0	0	0	7	0
	29	0	3	27	12	3

```
CHI   2 0 0   0 0 0   0 0 0  -  2
CIN   0 0 0   0 0 0   0 0 0  -  0
```

LOB: Cin 2, Chi 1. Struck out: Corcoran 6, White 2. BB: White 1. DP: Cincinnati. Umpire: Smith. Att: 4,500. Time—1:55.

The American Association was considered a major league at the time of the aborted championship series and many fine National League players had jumped their contracts for Association clubs in 1882. Despite the fact that the championship series of 1882 ended in a tie and even though the games were for exhibition only, this was, nevertheless, the forerunner of the modern-day World Series.

The 1884 Championship Series

Providence Grays (NL) defeat the New York Metropolitans (AA); 3–0

The manager of the New York Metropolitans, James Mutrie, had challenged the National League Providence Grays to a championship game in the middle of the season. I've got the time, Mutrie said—August 15th, an off-day for both clubs—and the place—the Polo Grounds.

Thanks, but no thanks, said Providence.

Mutrie would not be put off, however, and sometime later wired Frank Bancroft, his Providence counterpart, challenging the National Leaguers to a postseason championship series of two games rather than one. The first game would be played at Providence, the second in New York.

Don't call me, I'll call you, said Bancroft.

By now, Mutrie had his dander up. He popped off to the newspapers that the Mets could beat the Grays, that Providence was afraid. When Bancroft read this, he felt he had to respond to the upstarts if only to avoid the charge of cowardice. The two managers agreed on a best-of-five series, the clubs posting $1,000 for the purse. The money was held by Alfred Wright, the baseball editor of *The New York Clipper* (now *Variety*). It was winner take all. Two of the games were to be played under American Association rules, two under National League rules, and if necessary, a decision would be made on the fifth game. The series never went that far.

Charles "Hoss" Radbourn (60–12) was the starting pitcher for Providence in the three games. Radbourn appeared in 75 games for the 1884 Grays, starting 73, with 73 complete games, and 11 shutouts. He allowed 528 hits and 216 runs in 629 and two-thirds innings pitched. Radbourn and Charlie Sweeney, the other Grays' pitcher, were bitter rivals and when Sweeney struck out 19 men in a game against Buffalo on June 7th, the situation worsened. Sweeney eventually jumped his contract and went to play for the St. Louis team of the Union Association, leaving all the pitching duties in Radbourn's capable hands. Hoss proved equal to the task as he pitched 36 of the next 39 games.

Radbourn proved equal to the Metropolitans as well, even though his opponent was the right-handed Tim Keefe (35–18). In their respective careers, Radbourn and Keefe would each break the 300 victory plateau and go on to be elected to the Hall of Fame.

Game One was played at the Polo Grounds on Thursday, October 23rd, a cold and windy day, before a crowd variously reported as between 1,800 and 3,000 people. Providence won the coin toss and elected to take the field in the top of the inning. Jack Nelson, the Mets' shortstop, became the first batter in the first truly close approximation of the modern-day World Series. Nelson, Steve Brady, and "Dude" Esterbrook went down 1-2-3. In the bottom of the inning, center-fielder Paul Hines was struck by a pitch and, since the games were being played under American Association rules, took first base. Left-fielder Cliff Carroll was the next batter and he, too, was struck by one of Keefe's deliveries. A wild pitch moved both runners up, another wild pitch scored Hines, and a passed ball by Mets' catcher Charlie Reipschlager scored Carroll. Keefe had allowed only one hit but entered the seventh inning losing 3–0. Providence second baseman Jack Farrell doubled and scored on shortstop Arthur Irwin's triple. The Grays eventually ran the score to 6–0 and that's how it ended. Radbourn was never in trouble and wound up with a two-hitter.

The weather for Game Two was even worse, but Radbourn and Keefe took the mound nonetheless before 1,000 paying spectators. The game was scoreless

1884 Championship Series

GAME ONE --- October 23

METROPOLITAN	AB	R	H	PO	A	E
Nelson, ss	4	0	0	2	2	0
Brady, rf	4	0	0	1	0	0
Esterbrook, 3b	4	0	0	1	3	0
Roseman, cf	3	0	0	0	0	0
Orr, 1b	3	0	0	13	0	0
Troy, 2b	3	0	1	0	5	0
Reipschlager, c	3	0	0	7	2	1
Kennedy, lf	3	0	0	0	0	0
Keefe, p	3	0	1	0	1	0
	30	0	2	24	13	1

PROVIDENCE	AB	R	H	PO	A	E
Hines, cf	4	2	1	1	0	0
Carroll, lf	4	1	0	1	0	0
Radbourn, p	4	0	0	0	1	0
Start, 1b	4	0	0	13	0	0
Farrell, 2b	3	1	1	2	2	0
Irwin, ss	3	1	1	0	6	1
Gilligan, c	3	1	1	8	2	0
Denny, 3b	3	0	1	0	2	1
Radford, rf	3	0	0	2	0	1
	31	6	5	27	13	3

```
MET   0  0  0    0  0  0    0  0  0  -  0
PRO   2  0  1    0  0  0    3  0  x  -  3
```

Earned runs: Providence 3. BB: Keefe 2. Struck out: Radbourn 9, Keefe 8. Umpire: Kelly. Att: 3,000. Time: 1:55.

GAME TWO --- October 24

METROPOLITAN	AB	R	H	PO	A	E
Nelson, ss	3	0	1	1	2	0
Brady, rf	3	0	0	3	0	0
Esterbrook, 3b	3	0	1	1	1	0
Roseman, cf	3	1	1	1	0	0
Orr, 1b	2	0	0	7	0	0
Troy, 2b	2	0	0	1	3	0
Reipschlager, c	2	0	0	5	1	0
Kennedy, lf	2	0	0	2	0	0
Keefe, p	2	0	0	0	1	0
	22	1	3	21	8	0

PROVIDENCE	AB	R	H	PO	A	E
Hines, cf	4	0	0	3	0	0
Carroll, lf	4	0	0	0	0	0
Radbourn, p	3	0	0	0	0	0
Start, 1b	3	0	1	7	0	0
Farrell, 2b	3	1	2	2	1	2
Irwin, ss	3	0	0	0	3	1
Gilligan, c	3	1	1	5	3	0
Denny, 3b	3	1	1	2	2	0
Radford, rf	3	0	0	2	0	0
	29	3	5	21	9	3

```
MET   0  0  0    0  1  0    0  -  0
PRO   0  0  0    0  3  0    0  -  3
```

Earned runs: Providence 2. BB: Keefe 2. Struck out: Keefe 4, Radbourn 6. Umpire: Remsen. Att: 1,000. Time—1:35.

GAME THREE --- October 25

METROPOLITAN	AB	R	H	PO	A	E
Nelson, ss	3	0	0	1	1	0
Brady, rf	3	1	0	2	0	0
Esterbrook, 3b	3	0	1	0	0	0
Roseman, cf	3	0	2	0	0	0
Orr, 1b	3	0	1	12	0	0
Foster, 2b	2	0	0	1	4	1
Reipschlager, c	2	1	0	1	2	0
Kennedy, lf	2	0	0	1	1	0
Becannon, p	2	0	1	0	4	1
	23	2	5	18	12	2

PROVIDENCE	AB	R	H	PO	A	E
Hines, cf	4	3	2	1	0	0
Carroll, lf	4	1	1	0	0	0
Radbourn, p	4	1	1	0	2	0
Start, 1b	3	0	0	6	1	1
Farrell, 2b	3	1	1	1	3	0
Irwin, ss	3	2	2	2	1	1
Gilligan, c	3	1	2	4	0	1
Denny, 3b	3	2	2	1	2	0
Radford, rf	3	1	2	3	0	1
	30	12	13	18	9	4

```
MET   0  0  0    0  1  1  -   2
PRO   1  2  0    1  4  4  -  12
```

Earned runs: Providence 2. BB: Becannon 2. Struck out: Radbourn 1, Becannon 1. Umpire: Keefe. Att: 300. Time—1:10.

until the fifth inning when Providence third baseman Jeremiah Dennis Eldridge—who played by the name of Jerry Denny—hit a home run with two men on base. The Mets scored an unearned run off Radbourn in the bottom of the same inning, but could score no more as Radbourn shut them down on three hits. The game was stopped at the end of seven innings because of the cold.

When between three and five hundred fans showed up for Game Three—partly because of the worsening weather, partly because Radbourn was pitching again and the issue seemed already to be settled—Providence refused to play. They finally consented to take the field when Mutrie said Providence could choose the umpire. Not surprisingly, they chose Tim Keefe. Rookie James "Buck" Becannon (1–0) became the starting pitcher in Keefe's stead. Providence pounded Becannon for 13 hits and 12 runs over the first six innings and the game ended by mutual consent on account of darkness in the sixth. The championship series was over, swept by Providence, three games to none.

1885 Championship Series

Chicago White Stockings (NL) vs. St. Louis Browns (AA); 3–3–1, tie series

The term "World Championship Series" was used for the first time in 1885. The phrase, which supposedly originated in St. Louis, was a misnomer of epic proportions. The Chicago White Stockings (87–25) and St. Louis Browns (79–33) played the first seven-game series—to no conclusion—and both teams actually took a little time off during the series to play some exhibition ball. All in all, it was one of the worst shows of postseason baseball.

Game One was played at Chicago's West Side Park on October 14th. The Browns, who scored once in the second and four times in the fourth, had a commanding 5–1 lead heading into the bottom of the eighth inning. Chicago scored one run, then second baseman Fred Pfeffer connected for a three run homer to tie the score at five all. The game was called on account of darkness before the ninth inning could be played. It remains a miracle that no more than ten runs were scored on the day—the Browns had seven hits, the White Stockings six, and the two clubs committed a total of 16 errors.

Game Two in St. Louis was, incredibly, even worse. With the Browns leading 4–2 behind Dave Foutz (33–14), Billy Sunday (yes, that Billy Sunday) led off the sixth with a double. Mike "King" Kelly hit a routine grounder to Bill Gleason at short. Gleason threw to first baseman Charlie Comiskey in time to nip Kelly, but umpire Dave Sullivan was watching the baserunner instead of the play at the bag. Sullivan called Kelly safe, Sunday came all the way around to score on the play, and a 15-minute argument ensued. The first batter when play resumed was Cap Anson. His RBI single tied the game. Shortstop Ned Williamson grounded to third and Sullivan took his time calling the ball fair. Comiskey took his team off the field in protest and the game was forfeited to Chicago.

1885 Championship Series

```
GAME ONE --- October 14

ST. LOUIS              AB  R  H PO  A  E      CHICAGO               AB  R  H PO  A  E
-------------------------------------------   -------------------------------------------
Gleason, ss             4  0  0  1  3  1      Dalrymple, lf          4  0  0  1  0  0
Welch, cf               4  0  1  1  0  0      Gore, cf               3  1  0  0  0  1
Barkley, 2b             4  0  0  3  4  0      Kelly, rf              4  2  1  1  0  0
Comiskey, 1b            4  1  1 11  0  1      Anson,1b               4  1  2  8  0  1
O'Neill, lf             4  1  1  0  0  0      Pfeffer, 2b            4  1  2  2  2  1
Robinson, rf            4  1  2  0  0  0      Williamson, 3b         3  0  0  2  2  2
Latham, 3b              4  1  1  2  0  0      Burns, ss              4  0  0  1  2  1
Caruthers, p            3  1  0  0  8  2      Clarkson, p            3  0  0  1 13  2
Bushong, c              3  0  1  6  0  1      Flint, c               3  0  1  8  4  3
                       ----------------                             ----------------
                       34  5  7 24 15  5                            32  5  6 24 23 11

STL    0   1   0     4   0   0     0   0   -   5
CHI    0   0   0     1   0   0     0   4   -   5
```

Earned runs: Chi 3. 2B: Welch. HR: Pfeffer. PB: Flint 1, Bushong 1. BB: Caruthers 2. Struck out: Clarkson 8, Caruthers 6. DP: Chi. Umpire: Sullivan.

```
GAME TWO --- October 15

CHICAGO               AB  R  H PO  A  E      ST. LOUIS             AB  R  H PO  A  E
-------------------------------------------   -------------------------------------------
Dalrymple, lf           3  0  0  3  0  0      Gleason, ss            3  1  1  1  2  1
Sunday, cf              2  2  3  0  0  0      Welch, cf              3  1  0  1  0  0
Kelly, rf               3  1  1  4  2  1      Barkley, 2b            2  0  0  3  3  0
Anson,1b                3  0  1  7  0  0      Comiskey, 1b           2  1  0  7  0  1
Pfeffer, 2b             3  2  1  0  2  2      Robinson, c            2  0  0  4  1  0
Williamson, 3b          2  0  0  0  4  1      O'Neill, lf            2  1  0  0  0  0
Burns, ss               2  0  0  0  1  1      Latham, 3b             2  0  1  0  1  0
McCormick, p            2  0  0  1  6  0      Foutz, p               2  0  0  0  2  1
Clarkson, rf            2  0  0  0  0  0      Nicol, rf              2  0  0  1  1  1
                       ----------------                             ----------------
                       22  5  6 15 15  5                            20  4  2 *16 10  4

* Only one man out in sixth inning

CHI    1   1   0     0   0   3     -   5
STL    3   0   0     1   0       -   4
```

Earned runs: Chi 1. 2B: Gleason, Latham, Sunday, Pfeffer. DP: STL. BB: Foutz 1. Struck out: Foutz 2, McCormick 3. PB: Robinson 3, Kelly 1. WP: Foutz 1. Umpire: Sullivan.

The next two games were also played in St. Louis with local men acting as umpires. John Clarkson (53–16) retired the first two men in the opening inning of Game Three when Charlie Comiskey reached on an error, Yank Robinson walked, Tip O'Neill singled, Arlie Latham doubled and Bob Caruthers tripled. Another Chicago error scored Caruthers and the Browns had a 5–1 lead. It was never close after that. "Parisian Bob" Caruthers (40–13) was the easy winner and Clarkson took the loss. The final score was 7–4.

The umpire for Game Four, played on the 17th of October, was a St. Louis fellow named William Medart who proved to be disconcertingly partial to his home team. The Browns won by a score of 3–2, but even Comiskey said his team had been outplayed. Chicago held their errors down to a mere three for

1885 Championship Series

GAME THREE --- October 16

CHICAGO	AB	R	H	PO	A	E		ST. LOUIS	AB	R	H	PO	A	E
Dalrymple, lf	4	0	1	1	0	1		Gleason, ss	4	0	1	1	4	1
Sunday, cf	3	1	0	3	0	0		Welch, cf	4	1	0	2	0	0
Kelly, rf	4	0	1	1	1	0		Barkley, 2b	4	0	0	4	1	0
Anson, 1b	4	1	1	9	1	1		Comiskey, 1b	4	1	0	9	0	0
Pfeffer, 2b	4	0	2	3	3	1		Robinson, rf	3	1	0	3	0	0
Williamson, 3b	4	0	0	0	2	2		O'Neill, lf	4	2	2	0	0	1
Burns, ss	4	1	1	1	1	2		Latham, 3b	4	2	3	0	1	0
Clarkson, p	4	1	2	1	7	2		Caruthers, p	4	0	2	0	8	1
Flint, c	4	0	0	5	4	3		Bushong, c	3	0	0	8	2	1
	35	4	8	24	19	12			34	7	8	27	16	4

```
CHI    1  1  1    0  0  0    0  0  1  -  4
STL    5  0  0    0  0  2    0  0  x  -  7
```

Earned runs: STL 2, Chi 2. 2B: Latham 2, Kelly, Clarkson. 3B: Caruthers, Burns. BB: Caruthers 1, Clarkson 1. Struck out: Caruthers 7, Clarkson 5. PB: Flint. WP: Clarkson 4. DP: Chi. Umpire: McCaffrey. Att: 3,000.

GAME FOUR --- October 17

CHICAGO	AB	R	H	PO	A	E		ST. LOUIS	AB	R	H	PO	A	E
Dalrymple, lf	4	1	1	1	0	0		Gleason, ss	4	1	0	1	1	0
Sunday, cf	4	0	1	1	0	0		Welch, cf	4	0	1	1	1	0
Kelly, c	4	0	1	3	1	1		Barkley, 2b	4	0	0	7	5	4
Anson, 1b	3	0	1	11	0	0		Comiskey, 1b	3	0	1	9	1	2
Pfeffer, 2b	4	0	1	4	3	1		Robinson, c	3	0	0	5	3	0
Williamson, 3b	3	0	1	3	5	0		O'Neill, lf	3	0	1	0	0	0
Burns, ss	4	0	1	0	1	0		Latham, 3b	3	2	2	4	0	1
McCormick, p	4	1	1	0	5	0		Foutz, p	3	0	0	0	5	0
Holliday, rf	4	0	0	1	0	1		Caruthers, rf	3	0	1	0	0	0
	34	2	8	24	15	3			30	3	6	27	16	7

```
CHI    0  0  0    0  2  0    0  0  0  -  2
STL    0  0  1    0  0  0    0  2  x  -  3
```

Earned runs: STL 1. 2B: Sunday. HR: Dalrymple. LOB: Chi 3, STL 7. BB: Foutz 1. Struck out: Foutz 4, McCormick 3. PB: Kelly 3, Robinson 2. DP: STL 1, Chi 2. Umpire: Medart. Att: 3,000. Time—1:50.

this game, but St. Louis picked up the slack with seven. The Browns broke on top in the third when Arlie Latham singled, stole second, went to third on a groundout by Foutz, and scored on Caruthers's grounder. The White Stockings took the lead in the fifth when Jim McCormick reached on an error and scored on Abner Dalrymple's home run over the right field fence. In the eighth, Latham reached on an infield single, went to second on a passed ball, to third on Foutz's ground out, and scored on Bob Caruthers's single. Caruthers was run down a moment later when Gleason reached on a fielder's choice. A wild throw sent Gleason to third where he scored on Curt Welch's single. Dave Foutz was the winner, beating the Scottish-born right-hander Jim McCormick (20–4 with Chicago, 21–7 on the year).

1885 Championship Series

```
GAME FIVE --- October 22 at Pittsburgh
```

ST. LOUIS	AB	R	H	PO	A	E		CHICAGO	AB	R	H	PO	A	E
Gleason, ss	4	0	2	0	3	1		Dalrymple, lf	3	2	3	1	0	0
Welch, cf	3	0	0	1	0	1		Sunday, cf	3	1	0	0	0	0
Barkley, 2b	4	0	0	4	2	1		Kelly, rf	4	2	1	0	0	0
Comiskey, 1b	3	2	2	8	0	1		Anson,1b	4	2	2	13	0	0
O'Neill, lf	3	0	0	1	0	0		Pfeffer, 2b	3	0	0	1	6	0
Robinson, c	3	0	0	4	3	1		Williamson, ss	2	1	0	1	1	0
Latham, 3b	3	0	0	1	2	1		Burns, 3b	3	1	0	1	3	0
Foutz, p	3	0	0	1	3	0		Clarkson, p	3	0	0	0	4	0
Caruthers, rf	3	0	0	1	0	1		Flint, c	3	0	0	4	0	1
	29	2	4	21	13	7			28	9	6	21	14	1

```
STL    0  1  0    0  0  0      1  -  2
CHI    4  0  0    1  1  0      3  -  9
```

Earned runs: Chi 1. 3B: Anson. DP: Chi. BB: Clarkson 2, Foutz 5. Struck out: Clarkson 4, Foutz 4. PB: Flint. WP: Foutz. Umpire: Kelly. Att: 500.

```
GAME SIX --- October 23 at Cincinnati
```

ST. LOUIS	AB	R	H	PO	A	E		CHICAGO	AB	R	H	PO	A	E
Gleason, ss	4	1	0	2	2	1		Dalrymple, lf	5	1	2	4	0	1
Welch, cf	4	0	0	2	2	2		Sunday, lf	4	0	1	1	0	0
Barkley, 2b	3	1	0	3	3	0		Kelly, c	5	2	2	7	3	2
Comiskey, 1b	4	0	1	8	2	0		Anson,1b	5	3	1	5	0	4
Robinson, rf	4	0	1	3	2	1		Pfeffer, 2b	4	2	3	3	3	1
O'Neill, lf	4	0	0	1	0	0		Williamson, ss	4	0	1	2	3	0
Latham, 3b	4	0	0	2	1	2		Burns, 3b	3	1	0	2	0	0
Caruthers, p	4	0	0	1	1	1		McCormick, p	4	0	1	0	2	0
Bushong, c	3	0	0	5	2	0		Clarkson, cf	4	0	0	3	0	2
	34	2	2	27	15	7			38	9	11	27	11	10

```
STL    0  0  2    0  0  0    0  0  0  -  2
CHI    2  0  0    1  1  1    0  4  x  -  9
```

Earned runs: Chi 4. 2B: Dalrymple 2, Anson. 3B: Kelly. BB: McCormick 1, Caruthers 2. Struck out: McCormick 6. DP: STL. PB: Kelly. Umpire: Kelly. Att: 1,500.

```
GAME SEVEN --- October 24 at Cincinnati
```

CHICAGO	AB	R	H	PO	A	E		ST. LOUIS	AB	R	H	PO	A	E
Dalrymple, lf	3	0	0	1	1	2		Gleason, ss	4	2	2	3	3	1
Sunday, cf	4	1	1	3	0	0		Welch, cf	5	3	2	2	0	0
Kelly, rf	4	2	2	2	0	1		Barkley, 2b	3	2	2	3	3	2
Anson,1b	4	1	2	7	2	4		Comiskey, 1b	4	1	1	10	0	1
Pfeffer, 2b	4	0	2	4	3	0		Robinson, rf	4	3	1	1	0	1
Williamson, ss	3	0	0	2	6	2		O'Neill, lf	4	0	1	0	0	0
Burns, 3b	4	0	0	0	1	2		Latham, 3b	3	0	0	1	3	0
McCormick, p	4	0	1	0	5	3		Foutz, p	4	1	2	0	6	2
Flint, c	3	0	1	2	3	3		Bushong, c	4	1	1	4	1	3
	33	4	9	21	21	17			35	13	12	24	16	10

```
CHI    2  0  0    0  2  0    0  0  -   4
STL    0  0  4    6  2  1    0  x  -  13
```

Earned runs: STL 4. 2B: Kelly 2. 3B: Welch, Robinson. DP: STL. BB: McCormick 3, Foutz 2. Struck out: McCormick 1, Foutz 4. PB: Flint 3, Bushong 2. Umpire: Kelly. Att: 1,200.

In the final inning of this game, umpire Medart got into a heated argument with Chicago's center-fielder Billy Sunday over a close call on the basepaths. McCormick, who had been called out at third, was the injured party and he refused to leave his base. Sunday argued the call, Medart called Sunday a liar and told him to shut up. The irreverent Mr. Sunday put up his fists and was about to take a poke at Medart when King Kelly intervened.

The series resumed on October 22nd as Game Five was played at Recreation Park in Pittsburgh before a mere 500 fans. Cap Anson brought in "Honest John" Kelly, the most respected umpire in the game, to do the officiating. With four runs in the first, Chicago's Clarkson beat Foutz, 9–2. The teams combined for a minuscule eight errors, the lowest amount of any game in the series.

Game Six, played at League Park in Cincinnati, was decided by the same score as McCormick shut down the Browns on two hits, one of them a scratch single. Tied 2–2 at the end of three, the White Stockings scored single runs in the fourth, fifth, and sixth, and then blasted Bob Caruthers for four runs in the eighth inning to put the game on ice.

Cap Anson was feeling a little cocky before Game Seven, played at League Park in Cincinnati, because he was quoted as saying, "We will not even claim the forfeited game. We each have two victories now and the winner of today's game will be the winner of the series." Look before you leap, Cap.

John Clarkson was due to be the seventh-game pitcher but Anson had to start Jim McCormick when Clarkson appeared on the field five minutes late. Cap must still have been feeling his oats when the third inning began. The White Stockings led by a score of 2–0 and McCormick had already won two games in the series. But how the mighty will fall, for the Browns scored 13 runs over the next four innings — four in the third, six in the fourth, two in the fifth, and one in the sixth. Although Chicago put two on the board in the fifth, they scored no more and went down to defeat, 13–4. Dave Foutz was the easy winner. There were 21 hits in the game — 12 for St. Louis and nine for Chicago — and a total of 27 errors. Anson made four errors of his own and his team made 13 more.

After the games ended, an owners' committee decided the forfeit would stand, declared the series a tie, and returned the $1,000 purse ($500 to each owner). Thus, not one member of either team made so much as a nickel for participating in the championship series of 1885 and perhaps rightfully so. Chicago finished the series with 59 errors against 55 hits. St. Louis made 43 errors against 41 hits. By no stretch of the imagination could these games have been called championship baseball.

1886 Championship Series

St. Louis Browns (AA) defeat Chicago White Stockings (NL); 4–2

It was quite a revolutionary move at the time. Chris Von Der Ahe, owner of the St Louis Browns, wrote a letter to Chicago White Stockings president Albert Spalding which said,

A.G. Spalding, President
Chicago League Club
Chicago

Dear Sir — The championship season is fast approaching an
end, and it now seems reasonably sure that the Chicago
White Stockings and St. Louis Brown Stockings will win the
championship of their respective associations. I therefore
take this opportunity of challenging your team, on behalf of
the Browns, for a series of contests to be known as the
World's Championship Series. It is immaterial to me
whether the series be composed of five, seven or nine
games. I would respectfully suggest, however, that it would
be better from a financial standpoint to play the entire
series on the two home grounds, and not travel around as we
did last season. I would like to hear from you at your
earliest convenience, in order that the dates and other
details may be arranged. I am yours respectfully,

C. Von Der Ahe
St. Louis
September 26, 1886

Spalding asked for a nine-game series, but requested it be of the winner-
take-all variety. Von Der Ahe accepted the winner-take-all concept, but asked
that the series be limited to seven games because his Browns would be playing
the National League Maroons in the city championship series. The 1886 series,
then, was to be the first best-four-of-seven format.

There were few changes on either club since their championship series
following the 1885 season. Mike "King" Kelly replaced Silver Flint as the
Chicago catcher and the rookie Jimmy Ryan took over Kelly's duties in right.
Sam Barkley had left to play for Pittsburgh, so the Browns' regular right-
fielder, William "Yank" Robinson, took over at second. Dave Foutz or Bob
Caruthers would play right field when not pitching. St. Louis had also added
a rare third starting pitcher, Nat Hudson (16-10).

The first game, played at Chicago's West Side Park on October 18 before
a crowd of 6,000, saw John Clarkson (35-17) best Dave Foutz (41-16). Chicago
scored all the runs they needed in the first inning on a walk to George Gore,
a forceout by Mike Kelly, Cap Anson's triple, and a single by Fred Pfeffer. The
White Stockings led 3-0 when they pushed across three insurance runs on the
board in the eighth. Anson singled, Pfeffer reached on an error by Yank Robinson and Ned Williamson's triple scored both runners. When the throw back to
the infield from center-fielder Curt Welch went wild, Williamson came home
to roost. The final score was 6-0.

The Browns came back the next day to deliver a defeat twice as bad as that
as Bob Caruthers (30-14) shut out Jim McCormick (31-11) and the White
Stockings on two hits, 12-0. St. Louis had a wild first inning. Arlie Latham
walked to lead off the game and went to second on a wild pitch. Bob Caruthers
struck out, but catcher King Kelly dropped the final strike. Instead of throwing
to first to retire Caruthers, Kelly fired the ball to Pfeffer at second and caught

1886 Championship Series

```
GAME ONE --- October 18
```

ST. LOUIS	R	H	PO	A	E		CHICAGO	R	H	PO	A	E
Latham, 3b	0	1	1	3	1		Gore, cf	0	0	0	0	1
Caruthers, rf	0	0	3	1	0		Kelly, c	1	1	8	3	2
O'Neill, lf	0	0	1	0	0		Anson, 1b	2	3	12	1	0
Gleason, ss	0	0	2	1	1		Pfeffer, 2b	2	3	4	4	1
Comiskey, 1b	0	2	4	0	0		Williamson, ss	1	1	1	2	0
Welch, cf	0	0	1	0	0		Burns, 3b	0	0	0	3	1
Foutz, p	0	0	0	4	2		Ryan, rf	0	1	0	0	0
Robinson, 2b	0	2	2	2	1		Dalrymple, lf	0	1	2	0	0
Bushong, c	0	0	10	1	0		Clarkson, p	0	0	0	12	1
	0	5	24	12	5			6	10	27	25	6

```
STL   0  0  0    0  0  0    0  0  0  -  0
CHI   2  0  0    0  0  1    3  0  x  -  6
```

Earned runs: Chicago 4. 2B: Dalrymple. 3B: Anson, Williamson, Robinson. SB: Pfeffer. BB: Clarkson 1, Foutz 2. LOB: Chi 6, STL 5. PB: Bushong. Struck out: Clarkson 10, Foutz 4. DP: Chicago. Umpire: McQuaid. Att: 6,000. Time—1:55.

```
GAME TWO --- October 19
```

ST. LOUIS	R	H	PO	A	E		CHICAGO	R	H	PO	A	E
Latham, 3b	1	0	2	0	2		Gore, cf	0	2	0	0	0
Caruthers, p	2	3	0	0	0		Kelly, c-ss	0	0	6	3	2
O'Neill, lf	2	3	1	0	0		Anson, 1b	0	0	8	1	0
Gleason, ss	1	1	0	1	0		Pfeffer, 2b	0	0	6	2	1
Comiskey, 1b	0	2	8	0	0		Williamson, ss	0	0	1	1	1
Welch, cf	2	1	0	0	0		Burns, 3b	0	0	1	2	3
Foutz, rf	2	2	3	0	0		Ryan, rf	0	0	1	0	0
Bushong, c	1	1	9	0	0		Dalrymple, lf	0	0	1	1	2
Robinson, 2b	1	1	1	5	0		McCormick, p	0	0	0	2	0
	12	14	24	6	2			0	2	24	12	9

```
STL   2  0  0    2  3  0    5  0  -  12
CHI   0  0  0    0  0  0    0  0  -   0
```

Earned runs: STL 8. 2B: Bushong, Caruthers. 3B: Foutz, Caruthers. HR: O'Neill (2). SH: Latham, Bushong, Pfeffer. LOB: STL 7, Chi 6. Struck out: McCormick 4, Caruthers 2. BB: Caruthers 2, McCormick 3. PB: Bushong. WP: McCormick 2. SB: Welch. Umpires: McQuaid and Quest. Referee: Kelly. Att: 5,000. Time—1:40.

Latham off base. Tip O'Neill followed this action with a home run—his first of two on the day—into some parked carriages outside of left field and the Browns led, 2-0. The Browns scored twice in the fourth on a single by Foutz, a double by Doc Bushong, and two groundouts. They added three more in the fifth when O'Neill homered, Gleason and Welch singled, and Foutz tripled. St. Louis then exploded for five insurance runs in the seventh and put the game away.

The final game at Chicago was played the next day. Clarkson won in his second time out, beating Caruthers and the Browns. Caruthers hit a wild streak in the first and the White Stockings scored two runs without benefit of a hit or an error. Gore and Kelly walked to lead off the inning, and advanced a base on

1886 Championship Series

GAME THREE --- October 20

ST. LOUIS	R	H	PO	A	E		CHICAGO	R	H	PO	A	E
Latham, 3b	0	1	3	0	0		Gore, cf	3	2	1	1	2
Caruthers, p	0	1	1	1	0		Kelly, c	3	3	6	2	0
O'Neill, lf	0	1	4	0	0		Anson, 1b	0	0	11	0	0
Gleason, ss	0	0	0	2	0		Pfeffer, 2b	1	0	3	2	0
Comiskey, 1b	0	0	6	2	1		Williamson, ss	0	1	1	1	0
Welch, cf	3	3	3	0	0		Burns, 3b	2	3	0	0	1
Robinson, 2b	1	2	2	3	1		Ryan, rf	1	2	1	1	0
Hudson, rf	0	0	3	0	0		Dalrymple, lf	1	1	1	0	1
Bushong, c	0	1	2	0	1		Clarkson, p	0	0	0	0	0
	4	9	24	8	3			11	12	24	7	4

```
STL    0  1  0    0  0  2    0  1  -   4
CHI    2  0  0    1  1  2    3  2  -  11
```

Earned runs: Chi 6, STL 1. 2B: Kelly, Ryan. 3B: Burns. HR: Kelly, Gore. LOB: STL 9, Chi 6. DP: STL. Struck out: Clarkson 7, Caruthers 1. BB: Clarkson 3, Caruthers 4. WP: Clarkson, Caruthers. PB: Kelly 2. Umpire: John Kelly. Att: 6,000. Time−2:00.

GAME FOUR --- October 21

CHICAGO	R	H	PO	A	E		ST. LOUIS	R	H	PO	A	E
Gore, cf	1	1	1	0	0		Latham, 3b	1	1	0	2	0
Kelly, c	1	0	6	1	0		Caruthers, rf	2	0	4	0	0
Anson, 1b	1	1	4	0	0		O'Neill, lf	1	1	1	0	0
Pfeffer, 2b	0	0	3	3	2		Gleason, ss	1	2	0	3	2
Williamson, ss	0	0	0	2	1		Comiskey, 1b	0	1	8	0	1
Burns, 3b	0	2	1	1	1		Welch, cf	0	0	2	0	1
Ryan, rf	1	0	3	1	0		Foutz, p	0	1	1	2	0
Dalrymple, lf	1	1	0	0	0		Robinson, 2b	1	0	2	0	0
Clarkson, p	0	1	0	1	0		Bushong, c	2	1	3	0	0
	5	6	18	9	4			8	7	21	7	4

```
CHI    3  0  0    0  0  2    0  -  5
STL    0  1  1    0  3  3    0  -  8
```

Earned runs: Chi 2. 2B: Foutz, Burns. 3B: Dalrymple, O'Neill. BB: Foutz 4, Clarkson 6. Struck out: Foutz 2, Clarkson 2. LOB: STL 4, Chi 5. SB: Anson, Robinson. Umpire: Quest. Att: 8,000. Time−1:50.

Anson's sacrifice bunt. Caruthers walked Pfeffer to load the bases and Williamson to force in a run. Kelly scored a moment later on Tom Burns's groundout. Chicago never relinquished the lead and won the game, 11–4.

The series shifted to St. Louis and Sportsman's Park for Game Four, played on the 21st. Chicago scored three times in their half of the first. Gore led off the game with a single, Kelly walked, and Anson singled on the infield to load the bases. Foutz walked Pfeffer to force in the first run of the game and leave the bases jammed. Williamson hit a long fly ball to Caruthers in right. Bob's throw to catcher Bushong was too late to get Kelly. When Pfeffer at-

1886 Championship Series

GAME FIVE --- October 22

CHICAGO	R	H	PO	A	E		ST. LOUIS	R	H	PO	A	E
Gore, cf	0	0	1	0	0		Latham, 3b	2	0	0	3	1
Kelly, ss	0	1	0	1	0		Caruthers, rf	2	3	1	0	0
Anson, 1b	0	1	6	0	1		O'Neill, lf	1	2	1	0	0
Pfeffer, 2b	1	0	6	0	0		Gleason, ss	1	2	0	3	1
Williamson, p-rf	0	0	0	2	0		Comiskey, 1b	1	1	12	0	0
Burns, 3b	0	0	1	2	0		Welch, cf	1	1	3	0	0
Ryan, rf-p	2	1	0	4	1		Robinson, 2b	1	2	1	2	1
Dalrymple, lf	0	0	1	1	0		Hudson, p	1	1	0	2	0
Flint, c	0	0	3	1	1		Bushong, c	0	0	3	0	0
	3	3	18	11	3			10	12	21	10	3

```
CHI    0  1  1    1  0  0  -  3
STL    2  1  4    0  0  3  - 10
```

Earned runs: STL 3. 2B: Comiskey, Welch, Anson. 3B: Caruthers, Hudson, Welch. BB: Hudson 3, Williamson 1, Ryan 3. Struck out: Hudson 3, Ryan 4. WP: Ryan 4. PB: Bushong, Flint 2. Umpires: Kelly, McQuaid, Quest. Att: 10,000. Time—1:45.

GAME SIX --- October 23

CHICAGO	AB	R	H	PO	A	E		ST. LOUIS	AB	R	H	PO	A	E
Gore, cf	5	0	0	2	0	0		Latham, 3b	4	0	1	1	2	0
Kelly, c	5	0	0	9	2	0		Caruthers, p	4	0	0	2	0	0
Anson, 1b	4	0	0	13	0	0		O'Neill, lf	3	0	1	5	0	0
Pfeffer, 2b	4	3	2	0	1	0		Gleason, ss	4	0	0	0	3	0
Williamson, ss	4	0	0	0	2	1		Comiskey, 1b	4	1	1	7	0	1
Burns, 3b	4	0	2	1	5	1		Welch, cf	4	2	2	5	0	0
Ryan, rf	4	0	1	3	1	0		Foutz, rf	4	0	0	3	0	1
Dalrymple, lf	4	0	1	0	0	0		Robinson, 2b	4	0	0	1	4	1
Clarkson, p	4	0	0	0	2	0		Bushong, c	2	1	0	6	0	0
	38	3	6	28	13	2			33	4	5	30	9	3

```
CHI    0  1  0    1  0  1    0  0  0    0  - 3
STL    0  0  0    0  0  0    0  3  0    1  - 4
```

Earned runs; Chi 2, STL 2. 2B: Burns. 3B: Latham, O'Neill. HR: Pfeffer. BB: Clarkson 2, Caruthers 2. Struck out: Clarkson 10, Caruthers 5. SH: Williamson, Ryan, Robinson. SB: Pfeffer. PB: Bushong, Kelly. WP: Caruthers, Clarkson. Umpire: Pierce. Att: 8,000. Time—2:15.

tempted to take second on the relay in, Bushong's throw to Robinson at second was wide of the bag and Anson scored.

The Browns closed to within one with single runs in the second and third and took the lead in the fifth. With one out, Bushong walked and Latham singled past third. Caruthers flied to right for the second out of the inning, but both runners moved up a base. Tip O'Neill was intentionally walked against manager Anson's wishes. Clarkson threw two quick strikes past Bill Gleason, but was unable to fool him a third time. His ground single up the middle put the Browns ahead, 4–3. Charlie Comiskey's hit past Burns at third scored the third run of the inning. Chicago battled back in the top of the sixth as a single by Burns, a forceout by Jimmy Ryan, a triple by Abner Dalrymple, and a single by Clarkson tied the score. The stalemate was short-lived, however, as St. Louis rang up three more runs in the bottom of the inning to win, 8–5. Robinson walked, Bushong singled to left, and Latham walked. Caruthers lifted a pop fly to Pfeffer on the infield and Pfeffer intentionally dropped the ball to make a double play. (This was in the days before the infield fly rule.) Pfeffer threw to Williamson covering second for the force, but Williamson's throw to third was dropped by Burns and Robinson scored the lead run. Clarkson once again walked O'Neill intentionally to load the bases and Gleason once again foiled the strategy by lining a two-run single. The game was called at the end of the seventh inning.

Clarkson and McCormick were both tired after pitching two games each in four days, and Anson attempted to start Mark Baldwin, a young man who had been signed for the 1887 season. Comiskey protested that Baldwin was ineligible and, when the umpire agreed, Anson had to throw shortstop Ned Williamson to the wolves. Why Anson did not start Jocko Flynn, 24–6 on the season, is a question for which I was unable to find an answer. Presumably, Flynn was not travelling with the club, a common enough occurrence in postseason games of the 19th century. Williamson had a 1–1 record over 18 innings in 1886 and wasn't a complete stranger to the pitcher's mound, but he wasn't on intimate terms with the position either. The Browns, on the other hand, had a fresh pitcher, the useful Mr. Nat Hudson. St. Louis knocked Williamson and his relief, Jimmy Ryan, all over the park, rapping out 11 hits to Chicago's three, and won the game, 10–3. St. Louis made an easy winner out of Hudson when they scored three runs in the sixth and put the final nails in the Chicago coffin. As seemed to be customary in this series, play was halted on account of darkness, this time in the sixth.

Game Six, played before 8,000 fans in Sportsman's Park on the following day, was the only truly interesting contest of the series and the only one to go extra innings. Chicago and Clarkson held a 3–0 lead through seven innings, but St. Louis scored three runs in the eighth to tie—the big blow a two-run triple by Arlie Latham, the "Freshest Man on Earth." Neither team scored in the ninth inning and Chicago failed to score in the top of the tenth. Curt Welch singled to center to start off the bottom of the inning for the Browns. Dave Foutz, playing right field, grounded to Ned Williamson and he booted the ball. After getting shelled the day before, the little shortstop was about to become the first series goat. Yank Robinson sacrificed the runners to second and third. With Doc Bushong batting, Welch broke for the plate—trying to steal home, the ball game, and the series for the Browns. No one will ever know if he would have been safe or out, because Clarkson's pitch sailed high over the heads of umpire Gracie Pearce, catcher King Kelly, and Bushong. Whether Welch slid or scored standing up has been lost in the mists of time, but the play has forever been known as Curt Welch's "$15,000 Slide."

Receipts for the series totaled $13,920.10. This amount was split evenly between Von Der Ahe, on the one hand, and all the players on the other. The 12 members of the Browns received $580 each for their efforts, a not insubstantial amount of money for the era.

1887 Championship Series

GAME ONE --- October 10

ST. LOUIS	AB	R	H	PO	A	E		DETROIT	AB	R	H	PO	A	E
Latham, 3b	6	1	3	2	1	0		Richardson, 3b	4	0	0	0	2	2
Gleason, ss	4	1	1	1	6	0		Twitchell, lf	4	0	1	2	0	0
O'Neill, lf	5	0	2	2	0	0		Rowe, ss	4	0	1	2	3	1
Comiskey, 1b	5	1	2	13	0	0		Thompson, rf	3	0	1	2	0	0
Caruthers, p	5	0	3	0	2	0		White, 1b	3	0	0	9	1	0
Foutz, rf	5	0	0	2	0	0		Dunlap, 2b	3	0	0	4	2	0
Welch, cf	5	1	0	2	0	0		Bennett, c	3	0	0	7	2	0
Robinson, 2b	5	1	2	2	7	0		Hanlon, cf	3	0	0	1	0	0
Bushong, c	5	1	3	3	0	0		Getzein, p	3	1	3	0	7	2
	45	6	16	27	16	0			30	1	5	27	17	5

```
STL   2 0 0   0 4 0   0 0 0  -  6
DET   0 0 0   0 0 0   0 0 1  -  1
```

Earned runs: Browns 5, Detroit 1. 2B: O'Neill, Getzein. 3B: Robinson. LOB: STL 12, Det 2. DP: Det 2, STL 2. BB: Getzein 4, Caruthers 2. Struck out: Caruthers 2, Getzein 2. WP: Getzein. Umpires: Kelly and Gaffney. Time—1:50.

The 1887 Dauvray Cup Championship Series

Detroit Wolverines (NL) beat St. Louis Browns (AA); 10–5

The 1887 championship between the Detroit Wolverines and the St. Louis Browns rivalled, and perhaps equalled, the 1885 championship series for pure silliness. The owner of the Wolverines, Fred K. Stearn, challenged Chris Von Der Ahe to a best-of-fifteen series—although exhibition tour would be more accurate—to determine the championship of the world. The teams would travel in a special train and play games in St. Louis, Detroit, Pittsburgh, Brooklyn, New York, Philadelphia, Boston, Washington, Baltimore, and Chicago. Not before 1887 and not after, thank God, would there ever be such an ambitious undertaking, or such a failure.

Admission prices were raised to $1.00 per game and two umpires, instead of the usual one, were employed for the series. "Honest John" Kelly would work the plate for the first half of each inning, with John Gaffney at second base, and the two would then switch places for the bottom of the inning.

The Dauvray Cup was the brainchild of Helen Dauvray, actress wife of John Montgomery Ward (yes, that Montgomery Ward), shortstop of the New York Giants. Dauvray persuaded Stearns and Von Der Ahe to spring for an elaborate silver trophy from Tiffany's and the trophy travelled by train with the two teams under its own special guard. It was to be presented to the first club that won three consecutive postseason championship series.

The series opened before 6,000 fans at Sportsman's Park in St. Louis on October 10th and the Browns surprised Detroit by winning, 6–1. Bob Caruthers (25–12) pitched a five-hitter and St. Louis collected 16 hits off Charlie Getzein (29–13). The Browns scored twice in the first as Arlie Latham singled and stole second. Bill Gleason walked and both runners moved up a base on Getzein's

1887 Championship Series

GAME TWO --- October 11 at St. Louis

DETROIT	AB	R	H	PO	A	E		ST. LOUIS	AB	R	H	PO	A	E
Richardson, lf	5	1	0	1	0	0		Latham, 3b	4	1	1	1	1	3
Ganzel, 1b	5	0	1	13	0	0		Gleason, ss	4	0	1	1	3	1
Rowe, ss	5	1	1	4	5	0		O'Neill, lf	4	0	1	2	0	0
Thompson, rf	4	2	3	1	0	0		Comiskey, 1b	4	1	1	10	1	0
White, 3b	4	1	2	2	2	1		Caruthers, rf	4	0	2	3	0	0
Dunlap, 2b	4	0	0	1	3	0		Foutz, p	4	0	1	3	4	0
Bennett, c	4	0	3	4	0	1		Welch, cf	4	1	1	2	0	1
Hanlon, cf	4	0	2	1	0	0		Robinson, 2b	4	0	2	1	3	0
Conway, p	4	0	0	0	4	0		Boyle, c	4	0	0	4	0	2
	39	5	12	27	14	2			36	3	10	27	12	7

```
DET     0  2  2    0  0  0    1  0  0  -  5
STL     0  0  0    0  0  0    1  2  0  -  3
```

Earned runs: STL 2, Det 1. 2B: Bennett, O'Neill, Foutz. 3B: Welch. SB: Latham, Comiskey, Richardson, Thompson, White, Hanlon 3. LOB: STL 6, Det 7. DP: STL 2, Det 1. BB: Conway 2, Foutz 2. Struck out: Foutz 2, Conway 2. WP: Foutz. Umpires: Kelly and Gaffney. Att: 6,408. Time—2:00.

GAME THREE --- October 12 at Detroit

ST. LOUIS	AB	R	H	PO	A	E		DETROIT	AB	R	H	PO	A	E
Latham, 3b	6	0	3	4	4	0		Richardson, lf	6	0	0	1	0	0
Gleason, ss	6	0	1	0	1	1		Ganzel, 1b	6	1	1	14	1	0
O'Neill, lf	6	0	0	3	0	0		Rowe, ss	6	0	2	2	4	0
Comiskey, 1b	6	1	2	21	1	2		Thompson, rf	5	0	0	3	0	0
Caruthers, p	6	0	2	1	7	2		White, 3b	5	0	0	3	7	0
Foutz, rf	6	0	1	2	1	1		Dunlap, 2b	5	0	0	7	2	0
Welch, cf	6	0	3	2	0	0		Bennett, c	5	0	1	3	1	0
Robinson, 2b	6	0	2	3	6	0		Hanlon, cf	5	0	1	6	0	1
Bushong, c	5	0	2	2	1	1		Getzein, p	5	1	2	0	4	0
	53	1	16*38	21	7				48	2	7	39	19	1

* Two out when winning run scored

```
STL     0  1  0    0  0  0    0  0  0    0  0  0    0  -  1
DET     0  0  0    0  0  0    0  1  0    0  0  0    1  -  2
```

Earned runs: Det 0, STL 1. 2B: Welch. DP: Det 1, STL 1. BB: Caruthers 1, Getzein 3. Struck out: Caruthers 3, Getzein 2. PB: Bushong. Umpires: Gaffney and Kelly. Att: 4,509.

wild pitch. Singles by Tip O'Neill and Charlie Comiskey scored Latham and Gleason. St. Louis scored four runs in the fifth and put the game away. Comiskey bunted for a single and went to second when Getzein threw wild to first. Caruthers singled and stole second. Dave Foutz fouled out to Sam Thompson in right, but Comiskey scored after the catch and Caruthers went to third. Curt Welch grounded to the Detroit shortstop, John Rowe. Rowe threw home and Detroit catcher Charlie Bennett put the tag on Caruthers but, inexplicably, Welch was able to get to third on the fielder's choice. Yank Robinson tripled to left, scoring Welch, and Robinson scored on Doc Bushong's infield single. Latham grounded to Hardy Richardson and Richardson's wild throw to first

1887 Championship Series

```
GAME FOUR --- October 13 at Pittsburgh
```

DETROIT	AB	R	H	PO	A	E
Richardson, lf	5	2	1	2	1	0
Ganzel, 1b	5	0	1	12	0	1
Rowe, ss	5	1	1	3	2	0
Thompson, rf	5	1	4	0	0	0
White, 3b	5	1	0	2	3	0
Dunlap, 2b	5	2	3	2	8	0
Bennett, c	5	0	1	4	0	0
Hanlon, cf	4	0	0	2	0	0
Baldwin, p	4	1	1	0	1	0
	43	8	12	27	15	1

ST. LOUIS	AB	R	H	PO	A	E
Latham, 3b	4	0	0	2	2	0
Gleason, ss	4	0	1	0	2	3
O'Neill, lf	4	0	1	1	0	0
Comiskey, 1b	4	0	0	11	0	0
Foutz, rf	4	0	1	1	0	0
Welch, cf	3	0	0	2	0	1
Robinson, 2b	3	0	1	4	6	1
Bushong, c	3	0	1	5	2	1
King, p	3	0	0	1	2	0
	32	0	5	27	14	6

```
DET    4  1  0    0  1  2    0  0  0  -  8
STL    0  0  0    0  0  0    0  0  0  -  0
```

Earned runs: DET 4. 2B: Richardson, Thompson, Robinson. 3B: Dunlap, Rowe. BB: Baldwin 3, King 1. Struck out: Baldwin 1, King 2. PB: Bushong 3. Umpires: Kelly, and Gaffney. Att: 2,447. Time—1:50.

```
GAME FIVE --- October 14
```

ST. LOUIS	AB	R	H	PO	A	E
Latham, 3b	5	2	1	1	2	0
Gleason, ss	5	1	1	2	3	2
O'Neill, lf	5	0	1	4	0	0
Comiskey, 1b	4	0	0	10	0	0
Caruthers, p	4	1	1	0	4	0
Foutz, rf	4	1	1	0	0	0
Welch, cf	4	0	1	2	0	0
Robinson, 2b	4	0	1	1	5	0
Boyle, c	4	0	0	4	1	2
	39	5	7	27	15	4

DETROIT	AB	R	H	PO	A	E
Richardson, lf	4	0	0	2	0	0
Ganzel, 1b	4	0	1	14	0	1
Rowe, ss	4	0	1	1	4	0
Thompson, rf	4	0	1	1	0	0
White, 3b	4	0	0	0	8	2
Dunlap, 2b	4	1	2	3	3	0
Bennett, c	4	1	2	3	0	2
Hanlon, cf	4	0	1	3	0	0
Conway, p	3	0	0	0	2	0
	35	2	8	27	17	5

```
STL    2  0  0    0  0  2    1  0  0  -  5
DET    0  0  0    0  2  0    0  0  0  -  2
```

Earned runs: STL 4, DET 2. DP: STL. BB: Conway 3, Caruthers 1. Struck out: Conway 2, Caruthers 2. PB: Boyle, Bennett. WP: Conway. Umpires: Gaffney, Kelly. Att: 6,796. Time—1:45.

allowed Bushong to score the fourth run of the inning. Detroit was held scoreless until the bottom of the ninth.

Both teams were right back at it the next day, but with a different result this time. Detroit scored two runs in the second and third, one more in the top of the seventh and had things pretty much go their way even though the Browns scored three runs in the late innings. Pete Conway (8-9) was the winning pitcher, while Dave Foutz (29-9) took the loss.

The series resumed at Recreation Park in Detroit the next day as the teams played their first close contest. Bob Caruthers pitched against Charlie Getzein and the game went into extra innings tied at one. In the eleventh, the Browns put two runners on base, but Getzein retired the next two batters on pop-ups

1887 Championship Series

GAME SIX --- October 15 at New York

DETROIT		R	H	PO	A	E	ST. LOUIS		R	H	PO	A	E
Richardson, lf		3	2	4	0	0	Latham, 3b		0	2	3	3	0
Ganzel, 1b		3	4	6	2	0	Gleason, ss		0	0	0	2	3
Rowe, ss		0	3	0	3	1	O'Neill, lf		0	1	3	1	0
Thompson, rf		1	1	3	0	0	Comiskey, 1b		0	1	9	0	0
White, 3b		0	1	3	2	0	Caruthers, rf		0	0	4	1	0
Dunlap, 2b		0	1	1	2	0	Foutz, p		0	1	1	1	0
Bennett, c		1	2	6	0	0	Welch, cf		0	0	2	0	0
Hanlon, cf		0	0	3	0	0	Robinson, 2b		0	0	4	5	2
Getzein, p		1	1	1	4	0	Bushong, c		0	0	3	2	2
		9	15	27	13	1			0	5	27	17	7

```
DET    3  3  0    0  0  0    0  0  3  -  9
STL    0  0  0    0  0  0    0  0  0  -  0
```

Earned runs: DET 2. 3B: Richardson. DP: STL 2, DET 1. BB: Foutz 3, Getzein 3. Struck out: Foutz 1, Getzein 4. PB: Bushong 1. Umpires: Gaffney and Kelly. Att: 5,797. Time—1:55.

GAME SEVEN --- October 17 at Philadelphia

ST. LOUIS	AB	R	H	PO	A	E	DETROIT	AB	R	H	PO	A	E
Latham, 3b	4	0	0	2	0	0	Richardson, lf	4	0	0	2	0	0
Lyons, ss	4	0	1	1	3	0	Ganzel, 1b	4	0	0	13	1	1
O'Neill, lf	4	1	1	1	0	0	Rowe, ss	4	0	1	1	4	0
Comiskey, 1b	4	0	3	8	0	0	Thompson, rf	3	1	3	2	0	0
Caruthers, p	4	0	1	1	3	0	White, 3b	3	1	1	2	4	0
Foutz, rf	4	0	2	2	1	0	Dunlap, 2b	3	0	0	5	3	0
Welch, cf	3	0	0	5	0	0	Bennett, c	3	1	0	1	2	0
Robinson, 2b	3	0	2	3	5	0	Hanlon, cf	3	0	2	1	1	0
Bushong, c	3	0	0	1	1	1	Baldwin, p	3	0	0	0	4	1
	33	1	10	24	13	1		30	3	7	27	19	2

```
STL    0  0  0    0  0  0    0  0  1  -  1
DET    0  3  0    0  0  0    0  0  x  -  3
```

Earned runs: DET 2. 2B: Comiskey 2, Robinson, Thompson. HR: O'Neill. DP: DET 2. BB: Baldwin 2, Caruthers 1. Struck out: Caruthers 2. WP: Caruthers, Baldwin 1. Umpires: Gaffney and Kelly. Att: 6,478. Time—1:35.

GAME EIGHT --- October 18 at Boston

DETROIT	AB	R	H	PO	A	E	ST. LOUIS	AB	R	H	PO	A	E
Richardson, lf	5	0	0	1	0	0	Latham, 3b	5	1	3	1	2	1
Ganzel, 1b	5	0	1	5	0	2	Gleason, ss	5	0	1	2	0	0
Rowe, ss	5	1	3	4	3	0	O'Neill, lf	4	0	1	2	0	1
Thompson, rf	5	2	3	4	0	0	Comiskey, 1b	4	0	1	9	1	0
White, 3b	5	1	3	1	3	0	Caruthers, p	4	1	1	4	6	1
Dunlap, 2b	5	2	0	5	1	0	Foutz, rf	4	0	1	1	1	0
Bennett, c	5	1	2	5	2	0	Welch, cf	4	0	1	1	1	0
Hanlon, cf	4	1	2	2	0	0	Robinson, 2b	4	0	3	1	6	1
Getzein, p	4	1	3	0	4	0	Bushong, c	4	0	0	6	2	1
	43	9	17	27	13	2		38	2	12	27	19	5

```
DET    0  3  1    0  0  3    2  0  0  -  9
STL    1  0  0    0  0  1    0  0  0  -  2
```

Earned runs: DET 5, STL 1. 2B: Rowe, White, Hanlon, Getzein, Robinson 3. 3B: Bennett. HR: Thompson 2. DP: STL. BB: Caruthers 4, Getzein 2. PB: Bennett 2. WP: Caruthers 1, Getzein 2. Umpires: Kelly and Gaffney. Time—1:55.

1887 Championship Series

```
GAME NINE --- October 19 at Philadelphia
```

ST. LOUIS	AB	R	H	PO	A	E
Latham, 3b	4	0	0	0	0	0
Gleason, ss	4	0	2	4	2	0
O'Neill, lf	4	0	0	0	0	0
Comiskey, 1b	4	1	2	7	1	0
Foutz, rf	4	0	1	1	0	0
Welch, cf	4	1	2	1	0	0
Robinson, 2b	4	0	1	0	3	0
Boyle, c	4	0	1	10	2	2
King, p	4	0	0	1	9	0
	36	2	9	24	17	2

DETROIT	AB	R	H	PO	A	E
Richardson, lf	4	1	1	2	2	0
Ganzel, 1b	4	0	0	5	0	1
Rowe, ss	3	1	2	2	2	0
Thompson, rf	3	1	1	1	0	0
White, 3b	3	0	0	3	6	0
Dunlap, 2b	3	0	0	2	0	2
Bennett, c	3	0	1	10	1	0
Hanlon, cf	3	1	1	1	0	0
Conway, p	3	0	0	1	7	0
	29	4	6	27	18	3

```
STL   0  0  0    1  0  1    0  0  0  -  2
DET   0  0  0    1  0  0    2  1  x  -  4
```

Earned runs: STL 1, DET 3. 2B: Richardson. 3B: Hanlon. Struck out: Conway 5, King 9. PB: Boyle. WP: King. SB: Thompson. Umpires: Gaffney and Kelly. Att. 2,389. Time—1:40.

and the third on a strikeout. In the bottom of the 13th, Detroit scored and won the game. After Charlie Getzein singled, Hardy Richardson grounded to Yank Robinson at second. Robinson bobbled the ball just long enough not to be able to turn the double play. Richardson was gone, but Getzein stood at second. Charlie Ganzel grounded out to Comiskey at first, Getzein advancing to third. Robinson booted John Rowe's grounder, recovered and threw to first, but Comiskey dropped his throw, and Getzein scored the winning run.

Game Four was played at Recreation Park in Pittsburgh as Charles Busted "Lady" Baldwin (13–10) shut out the Browns and Silver King (34–11) on five hits. The game was decided when Detroit scored four times in the first inning on doubles by Richardson and Thompson and singles by Deacon White, Fred Dunlap, and Charlie Bennett.

Game Five saw the teams move to Washington Park in Brooklyn with New York's Mayor Whitney in attendance. The Browns seemed to want to make a series out of it and beat Detroit 5–2. St. Louis broke on top in the first when Latham walked, Gleason was hit by a pitch, Latham going to third on the play. Gleason stole second and when O'Neill singled, the Browns had a 2–0 lead. The Wolverines tied the game in the fifth when Dunlap singled for the first Detroit hit of the game and, when the throw back to the infield went wild, he went to third. A double by Bennett and a single by Hanlon knotted the score. With Caruthers and Foutz on base in the sixth, Curt Welch's double put St. Louis on top to stay.

Game Six was played the next day at the Polo Grounds and Detroit served notice that they wouldn't put up with any more foolishness as they clobbered St. Louis, 9–0. The Wolverines jumped on top in the first on three consecutive singles as Richardson, Ganzel and Rowe hit safely to start the game. Rowe was thrown out trying to stretch his hit into a double, but Ganzel scored on Sam Thompson's single. When Gleason threw wildly past first on Deacon White's grounder, Thompson scored and Detroit led, 3–0. Detroit added three more in

1887 Championship Series

```
GAME TEN --- October 21 at Washington (morning)

DETROIT          AB  R  H PO  A  E       ST. LOUIS        AB  R  H PO  A  E
---------------------------------       ---------------------------------
Richardson, lf-2b 4  1  3  1  4  1       Latham, 3b        5  1  3  1  3  1
Ganzel, 1b-c      4  0  2  4  1  0       Gleason, ss       5  0  2  2  5  2
Rowe, ss          4  1  1  3  1  0       O'Neill, lf       5  2  2  3  0  1
Thompson, rf      4  0  0  0  1  0       Comiskey, 1b      5  3  3 11  0  0
White, 3b         4  0  1  3  1  2       Caruthers, p      5  1  2  0  3  0
Dunlap, 2b        2  0  0  2  1  0       Foutz, rf         5  1  2  0  0  0
Twitchell, lf     2  1  0  0  0  0       Welch, cf         5  2  2  2  0  0
Bennett, c-p      4  0  1  9  2  0       Robinson, 2b      4  0  1  3  3  0
Hanlon, cf        4  1  1  2  0  0       Boyle, c          4  1  1  5  2  1
Getzein, p        4  0  0  0  3  0                         ----------------
                  ----------------                        43 11 18 27 16  5
                 36  4  9 24 14  3

DET    2  0  0    0  1  0    0  0  1  -   4
STL    2  0  0    0  3  1    4  1  x  -  11
```

Earned runs: STL 9, DET 2. 3B: Foutz. HR: Richardson, Welch, Latham. Triple play: Gleason, Latham and Robinson. BB: Getzein 2, Caruthers 2. Struck out: Getzein 2, Caruthers 2. Umpires: Gaffney and Kelly. Time—2:10.

```
GAME ELEVEN --- October 21 at Baltimore, afternoon

ST. LOUIS        AB  R  H PO  A  E       DETROIT          AB  R  H PO  A  E
---------------------------------       ---------------------------------
Latham, 3b        5  0  1  0  2  0       Richardson, lf    5  3  4  2  5  1
Gleason, ss       3  1  0  1  2  3       Ganzel, 1b-c      5  1  0  7  2  0
O'Neill, lf       4  1  0  0  0  0       Rowe, ss          5  4  2  1  6  1
Comiskey, 1b      4  0  0 10  1  1       Thompson, rf      5  0  2  0  0  1
Caruthers, rf     4  0  1  2  0  1       White, 3b         5  2  2  2  0  2
Foutz, p          4  0  0  1  5  0       Twitchell, lf     4  2  3  1  0  0
Welch, cf         4  0  0  1  1       Bennett, c-1b     5  1  2  9  1  0
Robinson, 2b      3  1  2  4  6  0       Hanlon, cf        5  0  3  4  0  0
Boyle, c          4  0  0  6  1  1       Baldwin, p        5  0  0  1  6  1
                  ----------------                        ----------------
                 35  3  4 24 18  7                        44 13 18 27 20  7

STL    1  1  0    0  1  0    0  0  0  -   3
DET    1  0  0    3  4  4    1  0  x  -  13
```

Earned runs: DET 4, STL 0. 2B: Rowe, Twitchell, Richardson 2. HR: Twitchell. SB: Thompson, Richardson 2, Twitchell, Bennett 2, Hanlon, Latham, Caruthers, Robinson. DP: STL. BB: Foutz 4, Baldwin 2. HBP: Gleason and Welch (Baldwin); Twitchell (Foutz). Struck out: Foutz 2, Baldwin 2. PB: Boyle 3, Bennett 2. WP: Foutz. Umpires: Gaffney and Kelly. Att: 2,707. Time—2:00.

the second. Charlie Bennett singled to left, stole second, and went to third on Ned Hanlon's groundout. Getzein struck out, but Richardson tripled and Ganzel singled. With two out, Ganzel on second, Rowe singled through Comiskey at first and Detroit led, 6–0. The Wolverines added three more in the ninth, but those last six runs amounted to nothing more than overkill as St. Louis was only able to manage five hits on the day and no runs against Charlie Getzein. Dave Foutz took the loss.

After a day off, Game Seven and the series moved to Baseball Grounds in Philadelphia for a well-played game. It looked like it might be a replay of Game Six as Detroit scored three times in the bottom of the second inning. Sam Thompson singled, went to second on a wild pitch, and scored on Deacon

1887 Championship Series

```
GAME TWELVE --- October 22 at Brooklyn
```

DETROIT		R	H	PO	A	E
Richardson, lf		0	0	4	1	0
Brouthers, 1b		0	2	5	0	0
Rowe, ss		0	0	0	2	1
Thompson, rf		0	0	1	1	0
White, 3b		0	0	1	2	1
Twitchell, lf		0	0	1	0	0
Ganzel, c		1	3	4	1	1
Hanlon, cf		0	0	3	0	0
Conway, p		0	0	0	2	0
Getzein, p		0	0	0	0	0
		1	5	19	9	3

ST. LOUIS		R	H	PO	A	E
Latham, 3b		2	3	1	2	1
Gleason, ss		0	1	1	2	0
O'Neill, lf		1	2	3	2	0
Comiskey, rf		0	1	3	0	0
Foutz, 1b		1	0	6	0	0
Welch, cf		1	2	1	0	0
Robinson, 2b		0	0	1	0	1
Bushong, c		0	1	5	0	0
King, p		0	1	0	2	0
		5	11	21	8	2

```
DET    0  0  0    0  1  0    0  -  1
STL    4  1  0    0  0  0    0  -  5
```

Earned runs: STL 2. LOB: DET 3, STL 1. BB: Conway 2. Struck out: King 1, Conway 1. SB: Richardson, Ganzel 2, Latham 2, Foutz. 2B: Gleason. DP: DET. WP: King. PB: Ganzel 2. Umpires: Kelly and Gaffney. Att: 1,138. Time—1:20.

White's single to center. Dunlap grounded out, sending White to second, and Bennett reached when the St. Louis catcher, Bushong, let the fourth strike go past him (batters were allowed four strikes in 1887). White scored and Bennett went to third on Hanlon's single, and Bennett scored on a sacrifice fly by Lady Baldwin. St. Louis put Harry Lyons on third with one out in the first, but he was doubled off. Comiskey was in scoring position in the second with one out, but failed to score when he was thrown out stealing. Yank Robinson reached second in the third but he, too, was thrown out stealing. Comiskey doubled in the seventh, but died at second as Caruthers and Foutz both flied out. Robinson reached second in the eighth but was doubled off when Bushong's liner to center was caught. The Browns finally scored a run and mounted another scoring threat in the ninth as Tip O'Neill homered over the center field fence, Comiskey doubled, and Caruthers singled to center. Foutz, however, popped out to end the game. Caruthers took the loss, Baldwin the victory.

Game Eight, played on the 18th at South End Grounds in Boston, was no contest as Detroit racked up St. Louis by a 9–2 score. St. Louis had taken a 1–0 lead in the first but Detroit tied the game on their first at-bat of the second inning as Sam Thompson lined a home run over the left-field fence. Deacon White singled, but was forced by Dunlap. Consecutive singles by Charlie Bennett, Ned Hanlon, and Charlie Getzein netted Detroit two more runs. The Wolverines scored a single run in the third, three in the sixth, and two in the seventh to win going away. Getzein was the winning pitcher and, for the second day in a row, Caruthers took the loss.

It was back to Philadelphia on the 19th for another Detroit victory, this one by a considerably closer margin. Both teams scored a run in the fourth and the Browns took a short-lived lead in the bottom of the sixth on a double by Welch and a single by Robinson. Detroit got that run back and one more in the seventh. Rowe singled and went to third on Thompson's single. Thompson went to second when "Honest John" Boyle dropped the throw back in. Rowe

1887 Championship Series

```
GAME THIRTEEN --- October 24 at Detroit
```

ST. LOUIS	AB	R	H	PO	A	E		DETROIT	AB	R	H	PO	A	E
Latham, 3b	4	1	1	1	2	0		Richardson, 2b	5	0	1	1	5	0
Gleason, ss	4	0	0	2	3	1		Sutcliffe, 1b	5	0	1	16	0	1
O'Neill, lf	4	0	0	1	0	0		Rowe, ss	5	1	2	2	4	0
Comiskey, 1b	4	1	2	12	0	0		Thompson, rf	5	1	2	2	0	0
Caruthers, p	4	0	0	1	2	0		White, 3b	4	2	3	0	3	0
Foutz, rf	4	0	1	1	0	0		Twitchell, lf	4	1	1	0	0	1
Welch, cf	4	0	0	4	1	0		Ganzel,c	4	0	0	4	0	0
Robinson, 2b	3	1	0	0	8	1		Hanlon, cf	4	1	1	2	0	0
Bushong, c	3	0	1	5	2	3		Baldwin, p	4	0	3	0	1	1
	34	3	5	27	18	5			40	6	14	27	13	3

```
STL   1 0 0   0 1 0   0 0 1  -  3
DET   0 2 0   1 0 0   1 2 x  -  6
```

Earned runs: DET 3, STL 1. 2B: Baldwin, Foutz. 3B: White. DP: STL. BB: Caruthers 2, Baldwin 1. Struck out: Caruthers 2, Baldwin 1. PB: Ganzel 1, Bushong 2. WP: Caruthers. Umpires: Gaffney and Kelly. Att: 3,389. Time—1:55.

```
GAME FOURTEEN --- October 25 at Chicago
```

ST. LOUIS	AB	R	H	PO	A	E		DETROIT	AB	R	H	PO	A	E
Latham, 3b	4	1	2	0	3	3		Richardson, 2b	4	1	1	5	2	0
Gleason, ss	4	0	1	0	1	1		Sutcliffe, 1b	4	1	1	7	0	0
O'Neill, lf	4	1	0	0	0	0		Rowe, ss	4	1	1	1	3	3
Comiskey, 1b	4	0	1	9	0	0		Thompson, rf	4	0	1	1	0	0
Foutz, rf	4	0	0	2	0	0		White, 3b	4	0	0	0	1	0
Welch, cf	4	0	0	2	0	0		Twitchell, lf	3	0	0	2	2	0
Robinson, 2b	4	1	3	1	6	1		Ganzel, c	3	0	0	7	2	0
Boyle, c	4	0	3	10	1	0		Hanlon, cf	3	0	0	4	0	0
King, p	4	0	0	0	9	0		Getzein, p	3	1	0	0	7	1
	36	3	10	24	20	5			32	4	4	27	17	4

```
STL   0 0 0   0 0 2   1 0 0  -  3
DET   3 0 0   0 1 0   0 0 x  -  4
```

Earned runs: DET 1, STL 2. 3B: Richardson. Struck out: Getzein 4, King 9. PB: Ganzel 4, Boyle 1. Umpires: Kelly and Gaffney. Time—1:45.

scored on a squeeze bunt by Deacon White and Thompson scored on Charlie Bennett's two-out single. The Wolverines added an insurance run in the bottom of the eighth on Hanlon's triple and a wild pitch. Through the first nine games, Detroit held a 7–2 edge and needed but one victory to claim the championship.

Game Ten was played in the morning at Washington, D.C., after a day off due to rain. The Browns won for only the third time, solidly walloping Detroit by an 11–4 score. Both teams scored twice in the first inning, Detroit once in the fifth, but St. Louis went on top to stay in the bottom of the inning. Tip O'Neill singled and went to second on Comiskey's bunt single. Both runners advanced on Caruthers's sacrifice bunt and O'Neill scored on Foutz's groundout to third. Curt Welch's two-run homer decided the affair. St. Louis scored six more runs over the next three innings, but those were just icing on the cake. Caruthers was the winning pitcher, Getzein the loser.

1887 Championship Series

```
GAME FIFTEEN --- October 26 at St. Louis
```

DETROIT	AB	R	H	PO	A	E		ST. LOUIS	AB	R	H	PO	A	E
Richardson, lf	4	0	0	5	0	1		Latham, 3b	4	2	3	1	1	0
Sutcliffe, 1b-c	3	0	0	5	2	2		Lyons, ss	4	3	2	1	2	3
Rowe, ss	3	1	3	0	5	2		O'Neill, lf	4	1	1	1	0	0
Thompson, rf	3	0	2	2	0	0		Comiskey, 1b	4	0	1	4	1	0
White, 3b	3	1	2	0	0	0		Caruthers, p	4	0	0	1	4	0
Twitchell, lf	3	0	0	2	0	0		Foutz, rf	3	0	0	0	0	0
Ganzel, c-1b	3	0	1	3	0	1		Welch, cf	3	0	0	2	0	1
Hanlon, cf	3	0	1	1	0	0		Robinson, 2b	3	1	2	3	3	0
Baldwin, p	3	0	1	0	0	1		Boyle, c	3	2	2	5	1	0
	28	2	10	18	7	7			32	9	11	18	12	4

```
STL   3 4 0   1 1 0  -  9
DET   0 1 1   0 0 0  -  2
```

Earned runs: STL 6, DET 1. 2B: Latham. 3B: O'Neill. LOB: STL 5, DET 8. BB: Baldwin 2, Caruthers 1. Struck out: Caruthers 3. PB: Bushong 2. Umpires: Kelly and Gaffney. Time—1:30.

The teams immediately left for the depot to catch the train for Baltimore and an afternoon game. Detroit clinched the series in Union Park and left no doubt as to which team was the better. The Browns scored once in the top of the first, but Detroit matched that in the bottom of the frame. St. Louis scored in the top of the second and was leading going into the bottom of the fourth when Detroit struck for three runs to take a 4–2 lead. The damage started when Rowe singled and Twitchell blasted a two run homer. Bennett walked, stole second and third and, after Hanlon coaxed a base on balls, an error by Dave Foutz sent Bennett home. Four Detroit runs in the fifth, four in the sixth, and one in the seventh made the Wolverines champions of the world.

That the series should have ended in Baltimore goes without saying. But it didn't. The Browns won the next day in Brooklyn, 5–1; lost on the 24th in Detroit, 6–3; lost the next day in Chicago 4–3; and won the final game, played at Sportsman's Park in St. Louis on the 26th of October, 9–2. Attendance for the last two games was 378 and 659. Each member of the Detroit team received $500 from the gate receipts for his efforts. The St. Louis players took home unhappy memories, but no folding money.

After the series, St. Louis went to Chicago for three games with the White Stockings, then the two teams went on tour for 13 games in the South and three in San Francisco. In addition, the Browns played five more exhibition games out west.

The 1888 Dauvray Cup Championship Series

New York Giants (NL) defeat the St. Louis Browns (AA); 6–4

The New York Giants (84–47) won the National League pennant in 1888, the first of 17 flags the team would win before departing for the West Coast in

1888 Championship Series

GAME ONE --- October 16

ST. LOUIS	AB	R	H	PO	A	E		NEW YORK	AB	R	H	PO	A	E
Latham, 3b	3	1	0	2	3	0		Tiernan, rf	3	1	0	1	0	1
Robinson, 2b	4	0	1	0	2	0		Ewing, c	3	0	0	9	1	1
O'Neill, lf	4	0	1	2	0	0		Richardson, 2b	3	0	0	1	1	1
Comiskey, 1b	4	0	0	7	0	0		Connor, 1b	3	1	1	13	0	0
McCarthy, rf	4	0	0	2	0	1		Ward, ss	3	0	1	3	3	0
Lyons, cf	4	0	0	5	1	1		Slattery, cf	3	0	0	0	0	0
White, ss	4	0	0	3	2	1		O'Rourke, lf	3	0	1	0	0	0
Boyle, c	3	0	1	3	0	2		Whitney, 3b	3	0	0	0	2	0
King, p	3	0	0	0	3	0		Keefe, p	3	0	0	0	10	1
	33	1	3	24	11	5			27	2	3	27	17	4

```
STL    0  0  1    0  0  0    0  0  0  -  1
NY     0  1  1    0  0  0    0  0  x  -  2
```

Earned runs: none. SB: Robinson 2, Ewing 2, Tiernan, Latham. DP: St. Louis. BB: Keefe 1, King 1. Struck out: Keefe 9, King 3. PB: Boyle. WP: King. Umpires: Gaffney and Kelly. Att: 4,876. Time—2:00.

GAME TWO --- October 17

ST. LOUIS	AB	R	H	PO	A	E		NEW YORK	AB	R	H	PO	A	E
Latham, 3b	4	0	0	1	1	0		Tiernan, rf *	3	0	2	0	0	0
Robinson, 2b	2	0	0	3	2	0		Ewing, c	4	0	1	6	4	1
O'Neill, lf	4	1	1	3	0	1		Richardson, 2b	3	0	1	0	7	0
Comiskey, 1b	4	1	2	11	0	0		Connor, 1b	3	0	0	15	1	0
McCarthy, rf	4	1	2	0	0	0		Ward, ss	4	0	0	1	2	0
Lyons, cf	4	0	0	4	0	0		Slattery, cf	4	0	0	2	0	0
White, ss	3	0	0	2	5	2		O'Rourke, lf	4	0	1	2	0	0
Milligan, c	3	0	2	2	1	1		Whitney, 3b	3	0	0	1	1	0
Chamberlain, p	3	0	0	0	5	0		Welch, p	3	0	1	0	4	0
	31	3	7	26	14	4			31	0	6	27	19	1

* Tiernan declared out

```
STL    0  1  0    0  0  0    0  0  2  -  3
NY     0  0  0    0  0  0    0  0  0  -  0
```

Earned runs: St. Louis 2. 2B: Milligan 2. SB: Tiernan, Ewing, Richardson, Connor. DP: NY 2, STL 1. BB: Welch 3, Chamberlain 1. Struck out: Welch 3, Chamberlain 1. PB: Milligan 1, Ewing 2. WP: Chamberlain. Umpires: Kelly and Gaffney. Att: 5,575. Time: 1:40.

1958. Tim Keefe (35–20) and Jim Mutrie had moved to the team from the Metropolitans, and Keefe and "Smiling Mickey" Welch (23–15) were the two aces of the ballclub. New York coasted to an easy pennant with second-place Chicago a distant nine games back. The St. Louis Browns (92–43) captured their fourth consecutive American Association pennant but not without a fight, finishing six and a half games ahead of second-place Brooklyn. St. Louis won on the strength of the two fine arms possessed by Silver King (45–21) and Nat Hudson (25–10). During the 1888 series, however, the Browns were hampered by the loss of Hudson. A man of independent means, he had left the club to travel to Hot Springs, Arkansas.

The 1888 series was considerably shortened from the fiasco of 1887, with

1888 Championship Series

```
GAME THREE --- October 18
```

ST. LOUIS	AB	R	H	PO	A	E
Latham, 3b	5	0	1	2	0	0
Robinson, 2b	4	1	0	1	3	0
O'Neill, lf	4	0	2	3	0	0
Comiskey, 1b	4	0	0	11	0	0
McCarthy, rf	4	0	0	0	0	0
Lyons, cf	3	0	1	1	0	1
White, ss	4	0	0	1	3	1
Boyle, c	2	1	1	4	0	3
King, p	3	0	0	1	6	0
	33	2	5	24	12	5

NEW YORK	AB	R	H	PO	A	E
Tiernan, rf *	2	0	0	0	0	0
Ewing, c	4	1	1	11	0	0
Richardson, 2b	4	1	0	2	4	0
Connor, 1b	3	0	0	12	0	1
Ward, ss	3	1	2	0	3	0
Slattery, cf	3	1	1	0	0	0
O'Rourke, lf	3	0	0	1	0	0
Whitney, 3b	3	0	1	1	2	1
Keefe, p	3	0	0	0	12	0
	28	4	5	27	21	2

```
STL    0  0  0    0  0  0    0  1  1  -  2
NY     2  0  0    1  0  0    1  0  x  -  4
```

2B: O'Neill. DP: NY. SB: Ward 2, Tiernan, Ewing, Richardson, Slattery. BB: Keefe 4, King 2. Struck out: Keefe 10, King 2. PB: Ewing, Boyle. WP: Keefe. Umpires: Kelly and Gaffney. Att: 5,780. Time—2:05.

```
GAME FOUR --- October 19 at Brooklyn
```

ST. LOUIS	AB	H	PO	A	E
Latham, 3b	4	1	0	3	0
Robinson, 2b	4	1	1	3	1
O'Neill, lf	4	0	3	0	1
Comiskey, 1b	4	1	9	0	0
McCarthy, rf	4	0	0	0	0
Lyons, cf	3	1	4	0	0
White, ss	2	0	2	2	1
Milligan, c	3	2	7	2	1
Chamberlain, p	2	0	0	5	0
	30	6*26	15	4

NEW YORK	AB	H	PO	A	E
Tiernan, rf	4	1	0	0	0
Brown, c	5	1	11	4	0
Richardson, 2b	5	0	1	2	0
Connor, 1b	4	2	9	0	1
Ward, ss	4	2	3	2	1
Slattery, cf	4	0	0	0	0
O'Rourke, lf	2	1	2	0	0
Whitney, 3b	4	0	1	2	0
Crane, p	4	1	0	11	0
	36	8	27	21	2

* Brown declared out

```
NY     1  0  4    0  1  0    0  0  0  -  6
STL    0  0  1    0  0  0    0  2  0  -  3
```

Earned runs: NY 2. 3B: Connor, Comiskey. BB: Chamberlain 4, Crane 2. Struck out: Crane 7, Chamberlain 4. WP: Chamberlain 2, Crane 2. PB: Brown 2, Milligan. Umpires: Kelly and Gaffney. Att: 3,062. Time—2:00.

four games scheduled for New York and St. Louis and one game each in Brooklyn and Philadelphia. "Honest John" Kelly and John Gaffney returned as umpires. In addition to the challenge for the Dauvray Cup—which had to be won three years in a row—the teams were competing for the Hall Cup, donated by a Thomas Hall and valued at $1,000.

Game One took place at the Polo Grounds on October 16—Keefe vs. King. The Giants were leading 1-0 as the Browns came to bat in the third inning. Arlie Latham walked with one out and stole second. When catcher Buck Ewing's throw went into center field, Latham took third. Tip O'Neill's single to center tied the game. In the bottom of the inning, the Giants had two outs and no one

1888 Championship Series

GAME FIVE --- October 20

ST. LOUIS	AB	H	PO	A	E
Latham, 3b	3	1	1	1	0
Robinson, 2b	3	1	3	3	0
O'Neill, lf	3	0	1	0	0
Comiskey, 1b	3	1	9	2	1
McCarthy, rf	3	0	2	0	1
Lyons, cf	3	0	1	0	0
White, ss	3	0	3	3	2
Milligan, c	2	1	3	6	1
King, p	3	1	1	3	0
	26	5	24	18	5

NEW YORK	AB	H	PO	A	E
Tiernan, rf	4	2	0	0	0
Ewing, c	4	1	3	1	1
Richardson, 2b	4	1	2	1	0
Connor, 1b	4	2	12	0	0
Ward, ss	3	1	1	7	0
Slattery, cf	4	0	4	0	0
O'Rourke, lf	3	1	0	0	0
Whitney, 3b	2	1	1	1	0
Keefe, p	3	0	1	8	1
	31	9	24	18	2

```
NY    1 0 0   0 0 0   0 5  -  6
STL   0 0 3   0 0 1   0 0  -  4
```

Earned runs: STL 2, NY 2. 3B: Ewing, Connor. DP: NY. BB: Keefe 2, King 1. Struck out: King 2, Keefe 2. PB: Milligan 2, Ewing 1. WP: King. Umpires: Gaffney and Kelly. Att: 9,124. Time—1:50.

GAME SIX --- October 22 at Philadelphia

NEW YORK	AB	H	PO	A	E
Tiernan, rf	5	2	1	0	1
Ewing, c	5	3	4	3	0
Richardson, 2b	4	1	3	4	0
Connor, 1b	4	1	7	0	2
Ward, ss	4	1	2	1	1
Slattery, cf	4	0	4	0	1
O'Rourke, lf	4	3	0	0	0
Whitney, 3b	4	1	2	0	0
Welch, p	4	1	1	2	0
	38	13	24	10	5

ST. LOUIS	AB	H	PO	A	E
Latham, 3b	3	0	0	3	1
Robinson, 2b	3	1	1	5	2
O'Neill, lf	2	0	2	0	0
Comiskey, 1b	3	0	10	2	2
McCarthy, rf	3	2	0	0	1
Herr, cf	3	0	2	1	1
White, ss	3	0	3	1	0
Milligan, p	3	0	5	3	0
Chamberlain, p	3	0	1	6	0
	26	3	24	21	7

```
NY    0 0 0   1 0 3   3 5  -  12
STL   3 0 1   0 0 0   0 1  -   5
```

Earned runs: NY 7, STL 1. 2B: Ward. 3B: Richardson, Connor, Robinson. BB: Chamberlain 1, Welch, 6. Struck out: Chamberlain 3. WP: Welch 1, Chamberlain 1. Umpires: Gaffney and Kelly. Att: 3,281. Time—1:50.

on base, but "Silent Mike" Tiernan walked and stole second. When catcher John Boyle's throw went into center field and right through the legs of Harry Lyons, Tiernan came all the way around to score. Keefe wound up the victor, but both pitchers threw three-hitters.

Game Two, played the next day, was a tight affair. The Browns scored a single run in the second as Tommy McCarthy singled, went to second on a passed ball, and to third on a dropped strike three. After Bill White walked, St. Louis worked the double steal, McCarthy scoring. The Browns led 1–0 into the ninth behind "Icebox" Chamberlain (20–10, 11–2 with St. Louis), but two insurance runs off Welch put the game beyond reach for the Giants.

1888 Championship Series

```
GAME SEVEN --- October 24
```

ST. LOUIS	AB	H	PO	A	E		NEW YORK	AB	H	PO	A	E
Latham, 3b	4	0	4	4	1		Tiernan, rf	4	1	2	1	0
Robinson, 2b	3	0	2	2	0		Ward, ss	4	2	3	3	1
O'Neill, lf	2	0	2	0	0		Richardson, 2b	4	0	1	2	0
Comiskey, 1b	4	2	7	0	0		Connor, 1b	2	0	9	0	0
McCarthy, rf	4	1	1	1	0		O'Rourke, lf	3	1	1	0	0
Herr, cf	4	1	2	0	0		Slattery, cf	4	2	2	1	2
White, ss	2	2	0	2	1		Whitney, 3b	4	2	6	1	0
Milligan, c	4	2	6	1	1		Brown, c	3	2	0	3	0
King, p	4	0	0	10	0		Crane, p	3	0	0	0	0
							Ewing, 1b	1	1	0	0	0
	31	8	24	20	3		Murphy, c	1	0	0	0	0
								33	11	24	11	3

```
STL    0  0  4    3  0  0    0  0  -  7
NY     0  3  0    0  0  2    0  0  -  5
```

DP: STL 3. BB: Crane 3, King 5. Struck out: Crane 4, King 1. Umpires: Gaffney and Kelly. Att: 4,624. Time—2:00.

```
GAME EIGHT --- October 25
```

ST. LOUIS	AB	H	PO	A	E		NEW YORK	AB	H	PO	A	E
Latham, 3b	3	1	3	0	2		Tiernan, rf	4	1	3	0	0
Robinson, 2b	3	0	2	0	2		Ewing, c	5	2	11	1	1
O'Neill, lf	4	1	4	0	0		Richardson, 2b	5	0	2	0	0
Comiskey, 1b	4	1	8	0	0		Ward, ss	4	2	2	3	0
McCarthy, rf	4	1	2	1	0		O'Rourke, 1b	4	1	5	1	1
Herr, cf	4	0	1	0	1		Gore, lf	4	1	0	0	0
White, ss	4	0	0	2	0		Slattery, cf	4	2	3	0	0
Milligan, c	3	1	7	5	1		Whitney, 3b	4	2	1	1	0
Chamberlain, p	2	0	0	3	0		Keefe, p	2	1	0	11	0
	31	5	27	11	6			36	12	27	17	2

```
NY     1  0  3    1  0  0    0  0  6  -  11
STL    0  0  0    1  0  0    1  1  0  -   3
```

Earned runs: NY 9. 3B: Ewing. HR: Ewing, Tiernan. DP: STL 2, NY 1. BB: Chamberlain 3, Keefe 2. Struck out: Keefe 11, Chamberlain 3. PB: Ewing 4. WP: Chamberlain 2. HBP: Robinson (Keefe). Umpires: Gaffney and Kelly. Att: 4,865. Time—2:10.

Tim Keefe beat Silver King for the second time in Game Three. The Giants scored twice in the first. Mike Tiernan walked, stole second, went to third on Buck Ewing's single, and was thrown out at the plate as he attempted to score on Danny Richardson's groundout. Ewing and Richardson worked a double steal and when Roger Connor grounded out, it looked as if King might get out of the inning unscored upon. But Monte Ward singled home both men for the first runs of the day and gave New York a 2-0 lead. The Giants were never headed and won 4-2.

"Cannonball" Crane (5-6) beat Chamberlain in Game Four, played at Washington Park in Brooklyn. The Giants already led 1-0 when they exploded for four runs in the third inning. The Browns scored two in the eighth to make the score 6-3 and had Arlie Latham at second with two out, but the little third-sacker was thrown out trying to steal third. The Browns went out 1-2-3 in the ninth and the Giants took a three-to-one lead in games.

The series moved back to the Polo Grounds the next day as Keefe once again took the better of King. With a baserunner on first, the Browns attempted to turn a double play, but shortstop Bill White dropped the ball. A single by Tiernan, a triple by Ewing, a line drive off King's hands, a triple by Connor, and a fly ball which dropped between Robinson and Lyons accounted for five runs and the game. The final score was 6–4 Giants, and White was made the goat of the series by Von Der Ahe. After the season ended, he never played another major league game.

The Browns held a 4–0 lead after three innings in Game Six, played at the Baseball Grounds in Philadelphia, but New York rebounded with 12 runs over the final five innings as Welch beat Chamberlain, 12–5. With the game tied at four all, Welch drove in the lead run in the seventh inning. Needing but one victory for the title, the teams traveled to St. Louis. Their journey was anything but uneventful.

Stopping at Pittsburgh, everyone got off to stretch his legs and found the press and Curt Welch, the former St. Louis Brown, waiting. Welch had apparently lost a number of wagers on his ex-teammates and accused John Kelly of poor umpiring and of betting on the Giants. Chris Von Der Ahe got into the act at this point, standing four-square behind Welch, even going him one better by saying both umpires had bet on the Giants. Every close decision, he claimed, had gone in favor of New York. By the time the train arrived in St. Louis, the story had spread and it seemed likely the series would end then and there.

Umpires Gaffney and Kelly both stood their ground. "I don't care about anyone's opinion of my work," said Gaffney, "But I do object to being called crooked, and I will quit the business before taking any more of that."

Kelly echoed his partner's sentiments by adding, "If Gaffney won't umpire any more games, I won't either."

Von Der Ahe then resorted to the oldest dodge in the book and claimed he had been misquoted. But his left-handed apology seemed to mollify the two arbiters and the series continued.

Game Seven, played on the 24th at Sportsman's Park, was won by St. Louis, 7–5, as Silver King took his first victory of the series, beating "Cannonball" Crane. The Giants had taken a 3–0 lead in the second, two of the RBIs coming off the bat of Crane, but the Browns went ahead for good with four runs in the third and another three in the fourth.

Tim Keefe was on the job the next day and won his fourth straight start, beating Chamberlain 11–3. The game was not as lopsided as the final score makes it look. New York had a slim 5–3 lead at the end of eight innings, but exploded for six in the ninth, the big hit a grand-slam home run by Mike Tiernan. The series was over, won by the Giants six games to two. Ten games had been scheduled, however, and neither owner wanted to forgo the revenues from the final two games.

There was a sparse crowd of 711 spectators at Sportsman's Park as Jimmy Devlin (6–5) beat Bill George (2–1) of the Giants, 14–11, on the 26th. St. Louis

The 1888 Championship Series

```
GAME NINE --- October 26
```

ST. LOUIS	AB	H	PO	A	E		NEW YORK	AB	H	PO	A	E
Latham, 3b	5	1	2	7	0		Tiernan, rf	5	2	0	0	0
Robinson, 2b	5	3	4	3	1		O'Rourke, 1b	5	0	15	0	0
O'Neill, lf	5	1	0	0	0		Gore, lf	5	2	2	1	0
Comiskey, c-1b	6	3	8	0	0		Richardson, 2b	4	3	2	5	1
McCarthy, rf	5	2	3	0	2		Slattery, cf	5	2	0	0	0
Boyle, c-cf	5	3	3	0	0		Whitney, 3b	5	2	1	3	2
White, ss	5	1	0	4	1		Hatfield, ss	5	1	1	4	1
Milligan, c-1b	5	1	9	2	0		Murphy, c	5	1	7	0	1
King, p	2	0	0	2	0		George, p	5	1	2	5	0
Devlin, p	3	0	1	5	0							
	46	15	30	23	4			44	14	30	18	5

```
STL    1  4  0     0  2  0     2  0  2     3 - 14
NY     0  3  5     0  0  0     1  2  0     0 - 11
```

Earned runs: STL 8, NY 7. 2B: Robinson 2, Richardson 2, George. 3B: Boyle. HR: O'Neill. DP: STL. BB: George 3, King 2, Devlin 1. Struck out: George 4, King 5. PB: Murphy 1. Wild Pitch: King 1, Devlin 1. Umpire: Gaffney. Att: 711. Time—2:20.

```
GAME TEN --- October 27
```

ST. LOUIS	AB	H	PO	A	E		NEW YORK	AB	H	PO	A	E
Latham, 3b	6	4	0	2	0		Tiernan, rf	4	2	2	0	1
Robinson, 2b	5	2	6	2	0		O'Rourke, ss	5	1	1	6	0
O'Neill, lf	5	3	3	0	1		Gore, 3b	2	2	1	1	2
Comiskey, 1b	5	1	10	1	0		George, 1b	4	2	10	1	2
McCarthy, rf	6	2	2	0	0		Slattery, cf-2b	4	1	4	3	1
Boyle, cf	6	2	2	0	0		Whitney, lf	4	2	1	0	0
White, ss	4	2	1	4	1		Hatfield, 2b-p	3	1	2	4	1
Milligan, c	3	1	3	3	0		Murphy, c	4	0	4	1	1
Chamberlain, p	2	0	0	1	0		Titcomb, p-cf	4	2	1	3	0
	42	17	27	13	2			34	13	*26	19	8

```
STL    6  1  0     2  0  2     4  2  1  -  18        * Robinson declared out.
NY     3  1  0     0  0  0     0  2  1  -   7
```

Earned runs: STL 10, NY 7. 2B: Gore, Titcomb. HR: McCarthy, O'Neill, George. DP: NY. Struck out: Chamberlain 3, Titcomb 4. Umpire: Gaffney. Att: 412.

led 1–0, 5–0, 5–3, trailed 5–8, 7–8, led 9–8, were tied 9–9, trailed 9–11, and tied the game at 11 all in the top of the ninth. Three runs by the Browns won the game in the 12th inning. Even with substitutes in both lineups, the fans got their money's worth.

There were 412 people on hand as Chamberlain won his second game of the series the next day, beating Ledell "Cannonball" Titcomb, 18–7. Substitutes were again prevalent on both clubs. A "player's game" was won by the Browns before a home town crowd of 3,500 on the 28th by a score of 6–0. This was to be the last championship series played by a St. Louis team for the next 38 years, and it would take another 56 years before a team calling itself the St. Louis Browns would play in a World Series.

Tim Keefe was the undisputed hero of the series with four complete-game victories and no losses. He pitched 35 innings, allowed 18 hits and ten runs, and only five of the runs were earned. Jim Mutrie became the first manager to pilot

The 1888 Championship Series

```
GAME ELEVEN --- October 28 (exhibition game)
```

ST. LOUIS	AB	H	PO	A	E	NEW YORK	AB	H	PO	A	E
Latham, 3b	5	1	3	2	0	Tiernan, rf	4	1	1	0	1
Robinson, 2b	4	1	3	3	1	Gore, 1b	3	1	14	0	1
O'Neill, lf	4	0	1	0	0	Titcomb, lf-ss	3	0	2	0	1
Comiskey, 1b	4	1	11	0	0	Slattery, 2b	3	1	1	7	1
McCarthy, rf	3	0	0	0	0	George, ss-p	3	2	1	10	1
Boyle, cf	4	0	2	0	0	Hatfield, 3b	3	0	1	1	0
White, ss	4	2	1	3	0	Murphy, c	3	0	5	1	1
Dolan, c	3	0	6	3	0	Welch, cf-p	3	0	0	0	0
King, p	4	0	0	5	0	Keefe, p-cf	3	0	2	0	0
	35	5	27	16	1		28	5	27	19	6

```
STL    0  2  1    0  0  1    1  1  0  -  6
NY     0  0  0    0  0  0    0  0  0  -  0
```

Earned runs: STL 2. 2B: Robinson, Comiskey, White. DP: STL 2, NY 1. BB: Keefe 3. Struck out: Keefe 4, King 3. WP: George. PB: Murphy. Umpire: Devlin. Att: 3,500. Time—2:00.

two clubs from two different leagues in postseason competition. After the games ended, he set the standard for World Series to come when he said, "If I ever engage in another World Series, the ball will stop rolling just as soon as the series is decided. The games played after the series had been won were mere farces. Our boys did not care whether they won them or not."

The 1889 Dauvray Cup Championship Series

New York Giants (NL) defeat Brooklyn Bridegrooms (AA); 6–3

The long-time rivalry between the New York Giants and the Brooklyn Dodgers had its roots in this nine-game World Series. The Brooklyn Bridegrooms (93–44) won the American Association pennant by a narrow two-game margin over Von Der Ahe's Browns, mainly on the strength of pitcher Bob Caruthers's (40–11) arm. The St. Louis owner had sent Caruthers, Dave Foutz and catcher Doc Bushong to Brooklyn for cash at the end of the 1887 season, turning the Bridegrooms from an also-ran in 1887 (60–74, sixth place) to a contender in 1888 (88–52, second place) to a pennant winner in 1889. Caruthers won 69 games in his first two years with Brooklyn and Foutz won 12 games in 1888. He gave up pitching for the most part in 1889 and spent the rest of his time at first base where he batted .277. He did, however, appear in 12 games on the mound, compiling a 3–0 record.

The Boston Beaneaters and the New York Giants were tied up to the final day of the 1889 season, but Boston lost to Pittsburgh while New York defeated Cleveland. That made the Giants (83–43) the 1889 National League champions by an even narrower margin than that of the Bridegrooms. Jim Mutrie, faithful to his promise of 1888, decreed the first team to win six games would be declared the winner of the series. There would be no further games of exhibition.

Game One was played at the Polo Grounds on October 18 and was well-

1889 Championship Series

GAME ONE --- October 18

BROOKLYN	AB	R	H	PO	A	E
O'Brien, lf	5	2	1	2	0	2
Collins, 2b	5	4	3	2	2	1
Burns, rf	5	3	4	1	0	1
Foutz, 1b	5	0	2	5	1	0
Pinckney, 3b	4	0	0	5	1	0
Clarke, c	4	1	1	3	3	0
Terry, p	4	1	1	1	1	0
Visner, cf	2	1	1	1	0	0
Corkhill, cf	2	0	1	2	0	0
Smith, ss	4	0	0	2	3	0
	40	12	14	24	11	4

NEW YORK	AB	R	H	PO	A	E
Gore, cf	5	1	1	2	0	0
Tiernan, rf	5	1	2	0	0	0
Ewing, c	4	0	1	3	0	0
Ward, ss	2	1	2	3	2	1
Connor, 1b	3	3	0	10	0	0
Richardson, 2b	4	3	3	3	3	1
O'Rourke, lf	4	0	2	1	1	0
Whitney, 3b	4	0	0	1	2	0
Keefe, p	3	1	1	1	4	0
	34	10	12	24	12	2

```
BKN   5 1 0   0 0 0   2 4 -  12
NY    0 2 0   2 1 0   5 0 -  10
```

Earned runs: NY 1, BKN 6. LOB: NY 5, BKN 4. 2B: Ewing, Collins 2, Burns 2, Foutz. 3B: O'Rourke. HR: Richardson, Collins. BB: Terry 5. Struck out: Terry 3, Keefe 2. DP: NY 1. SH: O'Rourke, Foutz, Pinckney. PB: Clarke. Umpires: Gaffney and Ferguson. Att: 8,848. Time: 2:14.

GAME TWO --- October 19

NEW YORK	AB	R	H	PO	A	E
Gore, cf	4	2	3	2	1	0
Tiernan, rf	5	1	1	0	0	0
Ewing, c	5	0	0	3	2	1
Ward, ss	5	1	1	4	3	0
Connor, 1b	4	1	1	12	0	0
Richardson, 2b	4	0	1	2	9	3
O'Rourke, lf	4	1	2	2	0	0
Whitney, 3b	4	1	0	1	0	0
Crane, p	4	0	0	1	2	0
	39	7	9	27	17	4

BROOKLYN	AB	R	H	PO	A	E
O'Brien, lf	2	1	0	2	1	0
Collins, 2b	3	0	1	3	2	0
Burns, rf	4	0	0	2	0	0
Foutz, 1b	3	0	2	7	0	0
Pinckney, 3b	3	0	0	0	2	1
Visner, c	3	0	0	8	1	3
Caruthers, p	2	1	0	0	4	0
Corkhill, cf	4	0	0	1	0	0
Smith, ss	3	0	0	1	0	4
	27	2	3	27	10	8

```
NY    1 1 1   1 2 0   0 0 0 -  6
BKN   1 1 0   0 0 0   0 0 0 -  2
```

3B: Richardson. SB: Gore 2, Tiernan, Ward 2, O'Rourke 2, O'Brien. DP: NY 2, BKN 1. BB: Crane 7, Caruthers 1. Struck out: Crane 3, Caruthers 2. HBP: Pinckney. PB: Visner. WP: Crane, Caruthers. Umpires: Gaffney and Lynch. Att: 16,172. Time—1:53.

attended with nearly 9,000 fans in the stands. Brooklyn struck for five runs in the first off Tim Keefe (30–13) and at the end of three innings had a 6–2 lead. But three New York runs off Adonis Terry (21–16) in the third and fourth innings brought the Giants within one, 6–5. In the top of the seventh, the Giants scored five big runs and looked to be invincible with a 10–6 lead and only three innings to go. But Brooklyn scored twice in the seventh and four times off Cannonball Crane (14–10) in the bottom of the eighth to take a 12–10 lead. With darkness closing in, Brooklyn began stalling. Although there was a rule against this tactic, neither umpire seemed very eager to enforce it. Players talked to each other. Fans became angry, or bored, wandering onto the field, and eventually the game was called. Brooklyn had its 12–10 victory, but their hands were dirty. Keefe, who pitched poorly and took the loss, did not start another game in the series. Terry was the victor.

1889 Championship Series

GAME THREE --- October 22

BROOKLYN	AB	R	H	PO	A	E		NEW YORK	AB	R	H	PO	A	E
O'Brien, lf	4	1	1	2	0	0		Gore, cf	5	0	1	0	0	2
Collins, 2b	5	0	1	2	5	1		Tiernan, rf	5	1	2	2	0	1
Burns, rf	4	0	0	1	0	0		Ewing, c	5	0	1	7	1	0
Foutz, 1b	4	1	1	10	0	0		Ward, ss	5	1	3	0	6	1
Pinckney, 3b	3	0	1	2	1	0		Connor, 1b	5	3	3	7	1	0
Clarke, c	4	2	2	7	1	1		Richardson, 2b	4	0	2	1	3	0
Corkhill, cf	3	3	2	0	1	0		O'Rourke, lf	3	2	2	2	3	0
Smith, ss	4	0	2	0	1	1		Whitney, 3b	3	0	0	5	2	0
Hughes, p	3	1	1	0	1	0		O'Day, p	1	0	0	0	0	0
Caruthers, p	0	0	0	0	1	0		Welch, p	3	0	1	0	0	0
	34	8	11	24	11	3			39	7	15	24	16	4

```
BKN    0  2  3    1  2  0    0  0  -  8
NY     2  0  0    0  3  2    0  0  -  7
```

Earned runs: NY 4, BKN 2. 2B: Gore, Connor, Welch, Pinckney, Clarke. 3B: Tiernan, Smith 2, Hughes. HR: Corkhill, O'Rourke. SB: Tiernan, Ewing, Richardson. DP: BKN. BB: Welch 3, O'Day 2, Hughes 3, Caruthers 1. Struck out: Welch 1, O'Day 3, Hughes 3, Caruthers 3. SH: Tiernan, Collins, Corkhill. WP: Hughes 1, O'Day 1. PB: Clarke 1. Umpires: Gaffney and Lynch. Att: 5,181. Time—2:07.

GAME FOUR --- October 23

NEW YORK	AB	R	H	PO	A	E		BROOKLYN	AB	R	H	PO	A	E
Gore, cf	3	1	2	1	0	1		O'Brien, lf	3	2	1	0	0	0
Tiernan, rf	2	1	0	1	0	0		Collins, 2b	3	1	2	4	0	0
Ewing, c	4	1	1	4	3	2		Burns, rf	4	1	1	0	0	0
Ward, ss	4	1	1	3	1	0		Foutz, 1b	2	0	1	6	0	0
Connor, 1b	4	1	1	5	0	1		Pinckney, 3b	3	1	1	2	1	0
Richardson, 2b	2	0	0	1	1	1		Clarke, c	2	2	1	6	0	1
O'Rourke, lf	2	1	1	1	0	0		Terry, p	2	1	0	0	0	0
Whitney, 3b	3	1	2	1	2	2		Corkhill, cf	3	1	0	1	0	0
Crane, p	3	0	1	0	0	1		Smith, ss	3	1	0	1	5	0
	27	7	9	17	7	8			25	10	7	20	6	1

```
NY     0  0  1    1  0  5    -   7
BKN    2  0  2    0  3  3    -  10
```

Earned runs: NY 3, BKN 1. 2B: O'Rourke, Clarke. 3B: Gore, Crane. HR: Burns. SB: Connor, Ewing, O'Brien, Collins 2, Foutz, Pinckney, Smith. DP: NY. BB: Crane 5, Terry 5. Struck out: Crane 5, Terry 5. SH: Ewing, Pinckney. WP: Crane. PB: Ewing 3, Clarke 2. Umpires: Gaffney and Lynch. Att: 3,045. Time: 2:10.

    Game Two was played at Washington Park in Brooklyn and 16,000 fans showed up for the contest. Both clubs tallied single runs in the first and second, but New York just kept scoring. In the third, Gore singled, stole second, and scored on an error by Smith. In the fourth, O'Rourke singled, stole second, and scored on Crane's single. By the end of five, New York had a 6-2 lead. Crane shut down the Brooklyn offense on three hits and the series was tied up. Caruthers was the loser.

    Game Three was, by all accounts, a travesty. After two off-days, the series resumed at the Polo Grounds before an audience of over 5,000. New York

1889 Championship Series

```
GAME FIVE --- October 24
```

NEW YORK	AB	R	H	PO	A	E		BROOKLYN	AB	R	H	PO	A	E
Gore, cf	4	2	0	1	0	0		O'Brien, lf	4	1	0	1	0	0
Tiernan, rf	4	1	1	2	1	0		Collins, 2b	4	0	1	4	4	0
Brown, c	5	1	3	8	2	1		Burns, rf	4	0	1	0	0	1
Ward, ss	4	1	0	2	0	0		Foutz, 1b	5	1	1	12	0	0
Connor, 1b	4	1	1	10	0	0		Pinckney, 3b	4	0	2	1	1	0
Richardson, 2b	5	2	2	2	2	0		Clarke, c	2	0	1	1	0	0
O'Rourke, lf	5	1	0	1	0	1		Caruthers, p	4	0	2	3	3	0
Whitney, 3b	4	1	3	1	3	0		Corkhill, cf	2	1	0	0	0	1
Crane, p	4	1	2	0	1	0		Smith, ss	4	0	0	0	5	0
								Bushong, c	1	0	0	1	0	0
	39	11	12	27	9	2			34	3	8	23	13	2

```
NY    0  0  4    0  4  0    0  2  1  -  11
BKN   0  0  0    1  1  1    0  0  0  -   3
```

Earned runs: NY 7, BKN 1. 2B: Brown, Crane, Collins. 3B: Connor, Whitney. HR: Brown, Richardson, Crane. SB: Connor, Collins. DP: NY 1. BB: Crane 6, Caruthers 4. Struck out: Crane 7, Caruthers 1. SH: Ward, Richardson, Corkhill, Smith 2. WP: Crane 1. PB: Clarke 2. Umpires: Gaffney and Lynch. Att: 2,901. Time – 2:00.

jumped on top with two runs in the first off Hank O'Day (13–11), but that was the only lead they would hold. Brooklyn tied the game in the second off Mickey Welch (28–12), and went ahead 6–2 at the end of four. Trailing 8–4, New York scored three in the fifth and netted two more in the sixth to pull within one. The Giants looked as if they were about to tie or win the game in the bottom of the ninth when they loaded the bases with one out. Suddenly, umpire John Gaffney called the game on account of darkness. You can imagine the effect such a call had upon the Polo Grounds fans. Gaffney had to be escorted to the umpire's dressing room. The game was official, however, with Welch the winner and O'Day the loser.

Game Four, played at Brooklyn's Washington Park, was every bit as bizarre. New York argued with calls by Gaffney in the fourth, and both teams went at him in the sixth. Brooklyn led 7–2 into the top of the sixth but five New York runs tied the game. After Oscar Burns hit a three-run homer for the Bridegrooms in the bottom of the inning, Gaffney, for the second day in a row and seemingly right on cue, called the game on account of darkness.

The owner of the Giants, John Day, was furious. "Three times we have lost in this series through trickery and we shall do so no more. I don't mind losing games on their merits, but I do mind being robbed."

Whether some less oblique threat was levelled at Gaffney off the field is unknown, but the fact remains that the next five games were won by New York and all went a full nine innings.

Game Five was played before nearly 3,000 spectators at Washington Park. The Giants, behind "Cannonball" Crane, blasted Brooklyn and Bob Caruthers by a score of 11–3. New York scored four in the third and four more in the fifth and coasted to victory. Even more damaging to Brooklyn than the loss on the field was the loss of catcher Bob Clarke to a sprained ankle.

Game Six, at the Polo Grounds, was a pitcher's duel between Brooklyn's

1889 Championship Series

GAME SIX --- October 25

BROOKLYN	AB	R	H	PO	A	E		NEW YORK	AB	R	H	PO	A	E
O'Brien, lf	5	0	0	1	0	0		Slattery, cf	5	1	1	6	0	0
Collins, 2b	4	0	1	4	3	1		Tiernan, rf	5	0	2	0	0	0
Burns, rf	4	0	0	2	0	0		Ewing, c	4	0	1	5	2	1
Foutz, 1b	5	0	0	12	0	0		Ward, ss	2	1	2	2	3	0
Pinckney, 3b	4	0	2	2	4	0		Connor, 1b	3	0	0	11	0	0
Visner, c	2	1	1	5	0	2		Richardson, 2b	4	0	2	3	0	
Terry, p	4	0	1	1	2	0		O'Rourke, lf	4	0	1	4	1	0
Corkhill, cf	2	0	1	4	0	0		Whitney, 3b	4	0	1	1	3	0
Davis, ss	4	0	0	1	4	1		O'Day, p	3	0	0	2	0	0
	34	1	6	32	13	4			34	2	8	33	12	1

```
BKN   0  1  0    0  0  0    0  0  0   0 - 1
NY    0  0  0    0  0  0    0  1  0   0 - 2
```

Earned runs: BKN 1, NY 1. 2B: Ewing, Whitney, Pinckney. SH: Ewing, Brown. SB: Collins 2, Corkhill, Ward 2, Connor 2, Richardson. DP: BKN 2. HBP: Burns. BB: O'Day 4, Terry 1. Struck out: O'Day 4, Terry 4. WP: Terry 2. Umpires: Lynch and Gaffney. Att: 2,556. Time—2:00.

GAME SEVEN --- October 26

BROOKLYN	AB	R	H	PO	A	E		NEW YORK	AB	R	H	PO	A	E
O'Brien, lf	4	1	0	4	0	0		Slattery, cf	5	2	0	3	0	0
Collins, 2b	4	1	1	2	1	1		Tiernan, rf	5	2	1	1	0	0
Burns, rf	4	2	0	0	0	0		Ewing, c	5	1	3	4	2	1
Foutz, 1b	4	2	2	8	0	0		Ward, ss	5	0	1	4	3	1
Pinckney, 3b	4	0	1	3	1	1		Connor, 1b	4	1	2	14	0	1
Corkhill, cf	4	1	0	4	0	0		Richardson, 2b	4	1	2	1	4	0
Smith, ss	4	0	1	1	3	1		O'Rourke, lf	3	2	2	0	1	0
Bushong, c	4	0	0	2	2	0		Whitney, 3b	3	1	2	0	2	0
Lovett, p	4	0	0	0	1	0		Crane, p	1	1	0	0	1	1
Caruthers, p	4	0	0	0	1	0		Keefe, p	3	0	1	0	2	0
	40	7	5	24	9	3			38	11	14	27	15	4

```
BKN   0  0  4    0  3  0    0  0  0  -  7
NY    1  8  0    0  0  1    1  0  1  - 11
```

Earned runs: BKN 1, NY 7. LOB: BKN 9, NY 8. BB: Lovett 1, Caruthers 1, Crane 9, Keefe 2. Struck out: Lovett 1, Caruthers 1, Keefe 2. 2B: Connor, O'Rourke, Whitney, Keefe. 3B: Smith. HR: O'Rourke, Richardson. SB: O'Brien, Tiernan, Connor. SH: Burns, Smith, Slattery, Ward. HBP: Connor. PB: Ewing. Umpires: Lynch and Gaffney. Att: 3,312. Time: 2:15.

Adonis Terry and New York's Hank O'Day. The Bridegrooms scored one run in the second on hits by George Pinckney, Joe Visner, Adonis Terry and Pop Corkhill. They maintained that lead until, with two outs in the bottom of the ninth, Monte Ward practically tied the game single-handedly. He singled, stole second, stole third, and scored on Roger Connor's base hit through short. The game remained tied until the bottom of the 11th when Ward's bunt single drove in Mike Slattery with the winning run. Both pitchers went the distance, O'Day receiving the victory, Terry the heartbreaking loss.

Game Seven was played at the Polo Grounds on the 26th. Tom Lovett (18–10) started for Brooklyn and got bombed. Things looked innocent enough in the first as Mike Slattery reached on an error by George Pinckney, went to

1889 Championship Series

GAME EIGHT --- October 28

NEW YORK	AB	R	H	PO	A	E		BROOKLYN	AB	R	H	PO	A	E
Slattery, cf	3	2	1	0	0	0		O'Brien, lf	4	0	1	4	0	0
Tiernan, rf	5	2	2	2	0	1		Collins, 2b	3	1	0	6	1	0
Ewing, c	5	1	2	6	0	1		Burns, rf	4	1	1	0	0	0
Ward, ss	3	3	3	3	3	1		Foutz 1b-p	3	1	1	3	0	1
Connor, 1b	4	1	3	10	0	0		Pinckney, 3b	4	1	0	2	2	0
Richardson, 2b	5	2	1	3	4	1		Visner, c	3	1	0	5	3	3
O'Rourke, lf	5	1	2	2	0	0		Terry, p-1b	4	1	1	3	0	0
Whitney, 3b	5	1	0	1	4	0		Corkhill, cf	4	1	0	2	0	0
Crane, p	5	2	1	0	4	0		Smith, ss	3	0	1	2	2	1
	40	15	15	27	15	4			32	7	5	27	8	4

```
NY    5  4  1    2  0  3    0  0  1  -  16
BKN   2  0  0    0  0  0    0  2  3  -   7
```

Earned runs: NY 3, BKN 1. 2B: Ewing 2. 3B: Connor, O'Rourke, O'Brien, Burns. HR: Tiernan, Foutz, Ward, Connor, Richardson, O'Brien. SH: Ewing, Connor, O'Rourke, Whitney 2, Burns. BB: Crane 5, Foutz 2, Terry 2. Struck out: Crane 4, Terry 1, Foutz 2. WP: Terry, Foutz. Umpires: Gaffney and Lynch. Att: 2,584. Time: 1:57.

GAME NINE --- October 29

BROOKLYN	AB	R	H	PO	A	E		NEW YORK	AB	R	H	PO	A	E
O'Brien, lf	1	1	0	3	0	0		Slattery, cf	4	1	1	3	0	0
Collins, 2b	4	0	2	2	4	0		Tiernan, rf	3	1	1	1	0	0
Burns, rf	4	0	1	1	0	0		Ewing, c	3	1	0	4	3	2
Foutz, 1b	3	0	0	10	1	0		Ward, ss	3	0	2	3	6	1
Pinckney, 3b	3	0	0	1	0	0		Connor, 1b	4	0	1	7	2	0
Terry, p	4	0	1	1	2	0		Richardson, 2b	4	0	0	5	0	1
Visner, cf	4	0	1	4	0	0		O'Rourke, lf	4	0	2	1	0	0
Smith, ss	4	1	1	1	3	0		Whitney, 3b	4	0	0	3	2	0
Bushong, c	3	0	0	1	0	2		O'Day, p	2	0	1	0	0	1
	30	2	5	24	10	2			31	3	8	27	13	5

```
BKN   2  0  0    0  0  0    0  0  0  -  2
NY    1  0  0    0  0  1    0  1  0  -  3
```

Earned runs: BKN 1, NY 2. 2B: Burns, Tiernan. 3B: Ward. SB: Connor 2, O'Rourke 2, Slattery, Ward, O'Brien, Collins, Foutz, Pinckney, Smith. DP: NY 1, BKN 1. SH: Collins, Burns, Ewing, Connor, Richardson, O'Rourke, Whitney. BB: O'Day 2, Terry 2. Struck out: O'Day 5, Terry 1. WP: O'Day. PB: Bushong. Umpires: Lynch and Gaffney. Att: 3,067. Time: 2:05.

second on Mike Tiernan's sacrifice bunt, and scored on Buck Ewing's single. All hell broke loose for Lovett in the second inning. Jim O'Rourke doubled to lead off the inning and, one out later, Cannonball Crane drew a base on balls. Singles by Slattery and Tiernan drove in the Giants' second run. Slattery went to third when the relay throw bounced away from Lovett. Ewing singled Slattery home, Ward fouled out, and Roger Connor's double scored Ewing and Tiernan. Danny Richardson and O'Rourke then hit back-to-back home runs. When it was all over, the Giants had scored eight times and had a massive 9–0 lead. The Bridegrooms were game though, scoring four in the third and three more in the fifth to pull within two. That was all they could get, however, and they went down to their third straight defeat, 11–7.

If Brooklyn thought an off-day would help, they were mistaken. Game Eight, played at Washington Park, was a slaughter. New York scored five runs in the top of the first to Brooklyn's two. Four more runs for New York in the second, one in the third, two in the fourth, three in the sixth, and the Giants led 15–2 before Brooklyn was able to cross the plate again. The final score was 16–7. Crane got the victory, Terry the loss. The Giants had four straight victories in the bag and needed just one more to clinch the title.

In the final game, before 3,067 fans at the Polo Grounds, Terry again took the mound with O'Day his opponent. The Bridegrooms scored twice off O'Day in the top of the first, but New York cut their lead in half in the bottom of the inning. In the sixth, the Giants tied the game with a walk and two singles. In the bottom of the seventh, Connor scored all the way from first on Bushong's error. The Giants were champions for the second year in a row and were just one championship away from claiming the Dauvray Cup.

The 1890 Dauvray Cup Championship Series

Brooklyn Bridegrooms (NL) vs. the Louisville Cyclones (AA); 3–3–1, tie series

After the 1888 season, National League owners met and adopted a plan for grading ballplayers into classes from "A" to "E," with salaries ranging from $1,500 to $2,500. The ballplayer's skill was not the only basis for his grade—his personal habits, alcohol consumption, and attitude also went into the decision.

Chapters of the Players' Brotherhood met during the 1889 season and secured capital for starting a Players' League in existing National League cities. The players withdrew from the League in early November of 1889 and were able to build eight ballparks in as many cities prior to the opening of the 1890 season. Teams were fielded in Boston, Brooklyn, Buffalo, Chicago, Cleveland, New York, Philadelphia, and Pittsburgh. Such National League stars as Dan Brouthers, Harry Stovey, Monte Ward, "Cannonball" Crane, Hank O'Day, Tim Keefe, Roger Connor, Buck Ewing, Hugh Duffy, Silver King, Pud Galvin, Jake Beckley, Ed Delahanty, and Pete Browning jumped their National League and American Association contracts for Players' League teams.

It was a crisis of unequalled proportions for both major leagues. (There is some argument that the only major league that existed in 1890 was the Players' League.) National League and American Association attendance was down severely for the year although teams lied brazenly when reporting their paying crowds and, as a result, no one was breaking down the stadium doors to attend the 1890 Dauvray Cup Championship Series between the Louisville Cyclones and Brooklyn Bridegrooms. Attendance, in fact, ran perfectly downhill during the seven games from 5,600 to 2,860 to 2,500 to 1,050 to 1,000 to 600 to 300.

Each of the three leagues lost money, but all completed their respective schedules, so a World Series was planned. The Brooklyn ballclub (86–43), which just the year before had played its games under the banner of the American Association, was transplanted to the National League in 1890 and had escaped Players' League raids virtually untouched. The Louisville Cyclones (88–44) finished dead last in the 1889 pennant race with an eye-popping record of 27–111. New manager Jack Chapman cleaned house over the winter and started the 1890 season with new men at first, second, left field, and

1890 Championship Series

GAME ONE --- October 17

BROOKLYN	AB	R	H	PO	A	E		LOUISVILLE	AB	R	H	PO	A	E
Collins, 2b	5	3	2	1	1	0		Taylor, 1b	4	0	0	8	0	1
O'Brien, cf	4	1	0	2	0	0		Raymond, 3b	4	0	0	0	2	2
Burns, rf-1f	4	1	2	1	0	0		Weaver, cf	3	0	1	0	0	0
Pinckney, 3b	4	1	1	1	2	0		Wolf, rf	3	0	0	0	1	0
Foutz, 1b-1f	4	0	1	3	0	0		Hamburg, 1f	3	0	0	2	0	0
Terry, p	3	0	0	2	1	0		Shinnick, 2b	2	0	0	3	2	0
Daly, 1b-c	4	0	1	5	0	0		Tomney, ss	1	0	1	2	5	3
Smith, ss	4	1	1	6	4	0		Ryan, c	3	0	0	8	3	0
Clark, c	3	2	2	3	1	1		Stratton, p	3	0	0	0	1	0
Lovett, rf	1	0	1	0	0	0								
	36	9	11	24	9	1			26	0	2	23	14	6

```
BKN    3  0  0    0  3  0    0  3  0  -  9
LOU    0  0  0    0  0  0    0  0  0  -  0
```

Earned runs: BKN 1. 2B: Burns. 3B: Pinckney, Clark. SH: O'Brien, Burns. SB: Shinnick 2, Tomney, Collins 2. BB: Stratton 1, Terry 3. Struck out: Terry 3, Stratton 2. PB: Clark 2, Ryan 1. WP: Stratton. Umpires: Curry and McQuaid. Att: 5,600. Time: 1:45.

GAME TWO --- October 18

BROOKLYN	AB	R	H	PO	A	E		LOUISVILLE	AB	R	H	PO	A	E
Collins, 2b	4	0	2	3	0	0		Taylor, 1b	4	0	0	4	0	0
O'Brien, cf	4	0	1	0	0	0		Raymond, 3b	4	0	0	4	0	0
Burns, 1f	4	0	2	1	2	0		Weaver, cf	4	1	2	2	0	0
Pinckney, 3b	4	0	1	12	0	0		Wolf, rf	4	1	1	7	0	1
Foutz, 1b	3	0	0	3	4	0		Hamburg, 1f	4	1	1	1	4	1
Terry, rf	3	0	0	1	7	0		Shinnick, 2b	4	1	3	4	2	0
Daly, c	3	0	0	0	1	1		Tomney, ss	3	0	1	1	1	0
Smith, ss	3	0	0	1	0	0		Ryan, c	3	0	0	4	3	0
Lovett, p	3	0	1	3	1	1		Daily, p	3	0	2	0	4	0
	31	0	7	24	15	2			33	4	10	27	14	2

```
BKN    0  2  0    2  0  1    0  0  0  -  5
LOU    1  0  1    0  0  0    0  0  1  -  3
```

Earned runs; LOU 1. 2B: Foutz. 3B: Smith. SB: Taylor, Weaver 2, Daly. SH: Raymond 2, Wolf, Shinnick, Daly, Smith. BB: Lovett 4, Daily 2. Struck out: Lovett 6, Daily 3. PB: Daly, Ryan 2. WP: Daily, Lovett. Umpires: Curry and McQuaid. Att: 2,860. Time—1:45.

behind the plate. Two of the five starting pitchers from 1889 were also gone. The Cyclones' right-fielder, William "Chicken" Wolf, was still on the club, the only man who would appear in the American Association for the entire ten years it enjoyed major league status. The 1890 Cyclones finished ten games ahead of the second-place Columbus Solons.

The series, scaled down from 11 games to nine, began on October 17 — the first four games to be played in Louisville's Eclipse Park, the next three in Washington Park in Brooklyn.

Brooklyn was heavily favored to win and matters certainly went their way in Game One. George "Hub" Collins led off the game with a single and went

1890 Championship Series

```
GAME THREE --- October 20
```

BROOKLYN	AB	R	H	PO	A	E
Collins, 2b	5	1	3	0	1	0
O'Brien, cf	4	2	1	4	0	0
Burns, lf	4	0	0	0	1	0
Pinckney, 3b	4	0	1	2	3	0
Foutz, 1b	4	1	1	9	0	0
Terry, p	4	2	0	0	0	0
Daly, c	4	0	1	7	1	0
Smith, ss	4	0	2	2	3	2
Donovan, rf	4	1	1	0	0	0
	37	7	10	24	9	2

LOUISVILLE	AB	R	H	PO	A	E
Taylor, 1b	4	0	2	8	0	0
Raymond, 2b	3	0	0	1	4	0
Weaver, cf	3	0	0	1	0	0
Wolf, rf-3b	3	2	2	2	2	1
Hamburg, lf	3	2	2	4	0	0
Shinnick, 2b	3	2	2	4	2	0
Tomney, ss	1	0	0	1	1	2
Daily, rf	2	0	1	1	0	0
Ryan, c	1	0	0	0	2	0
Stratton, p	1	1	1	0	0	0
Bligh, c	2	0	0	2	0	0
Meakim, p	2	0	1	0	0	0
	28	7	11	24	11	3

```
BKN    0  0  1    1  0  2    0  3  -  7
LOU    0  2  0    1  3  0    0  1  -  7
```

Earned runs: BKN 3, LOU 3. 2B: Wolf, Shinnick 2, Daily, Stratton. 3B: Wolf, Hamburg, O'Brien, Smith. SH: Raymond, Weaver, Hamburg, Daily, Bligh, Donovan. Struck out: Meakim 2, Terry 3. BB: Meakim 2, Terry 2. PB: Ryan 2, Bligh. WP: Meakim, Terry. Umpires: McQuaid and Curry. Att: 2,500. Time—1:50.

to third when Harry Raymond booted Darby O'Brien's ground ball for his first of two errors on the day. Tommy Burns singled over second for the first Brooklyn run. George Pinckney grounded to Phil Tomney who failed to hold the ball, and O'Brien scored the second run of the inning. Dave Foutz grounded to Tim "Good Eye" Shinnick who tagged Pinckney coming into second and threw to first for the force on Foutz. Burns scored on the play. Those were the only runs Brooklyn needed as Adonis Terry (26–15) pitched a two-hit shutout and won by the not-so-close score of 9–0. The second worst shutout in postseason championship history matched the drubbing Detroit gave St. Louis in 1887, but fell short of the 12–0 whitewash the Browns administered to the Chicago White Stockings in 1886. Scott Stratton (34–15) was the loser.

The next day saw the Bridegrooms take a two-game lead before a crowd half the size of the previous afternoon as Tom Lovett (30–11) beat Ed Daily (18–18, 6–3 with Louisville). Louisville took an early lead in the first on a single by Harry Taylor, a sacrifice bunt by Raymond, and a single by William "Farmer" Weaver. But Brooklyn came back in the second, scoring twice with the help of some terrible Louisville fielding. Pinckney reached base when his pop fly fell between Tomney and Raymond. A passed ball sent him to second and, one out later, he went to third when Raymond booted Terry's grounder. Terry lit out for second and arrived safely when Shinnick dropped the throw from catcher John Ryan. Pinckney crossed the plate with the tying run on the play. Ed Daily's sacrifice sent Terry to third where he scored on a wild pitch. Louisville tied the game in the third, but more bad fielding proved to be their undoing in the fourth as Brooklyn took the lead for good. Pinckney walked and, one out later, Terry reached when Raymond kicked his ground ball. Tom Daly grounded into an apparent inning-ending double play, but Taylor juggled the ball at first. Daly then stole second and both runners scored when George

1890 Championship Series

GAME FOUR --- October 21

BROOKLYN	AB	R	H	PO	A	E	LOUISVILLE	AB	R	H	PO	A	E
Collins, 2b	4	1	1	2	0	1	Taylor, 1b	4	1	2	10	0	0
O'Brien, cf	4	0	0	2	0	0	Raymond, ss	4	1	1	0	1	0
Burns, 3b	4	0	1	1	1	0	Weaver, cf	4	1	1	2	0	1
Foutz, 1b	4	1	1	5	1	0	Wolf, 3b	4	1	2	2	3	1
Terry, lf	4	1	0	4	0	0	Daily, rf	4	0	0	6	0	0
Smith, ss	4	1	1	1	4	0	Hamburg, lf	4	0	1	0	0	0
Donovan, rf	4	0	3	1	0	0	Shinnick, 2b	4	1	1	2	3	0
Lovett, p	4	0	0	0	1	0	Ryan, c	4	0	0	5	2	0
Bushong, c	4	0	0	8	0	1	Ehret, p	3	0	1	0	0	0
	36	4	7	24	7	2		35	5	9	27	9	2

```
BKN   0 3 1   0 0 0   0 0 0  -  4
LOU   3 0 1   0 0 0   1 0 x  -  5
```

Earned runs: LOU 4, BKN 4. 2B: Weaver, Wolf. 3B: Shinnick. SH: Raymond, Weaver, O'Brien, Ryan. SB: Taylor. BB: Ehret 2. Struck out: Ehret 3, Lovett 5. PB: Bushong. Umpires: McQuaid and Curry. Att: 1,050. Time—1:45.

GAME FIVE --- October 25

LOUISVILLE	AB	R	H	PO	A	E	BROOKLYN	AB	R	H	PO	A	E
Taylor, 1b	4	0	0	13	1	1	Collins, 2b	5	2	1	2	3	0
Raymond, ss	4	0	1	2	6	1	Foutz, 1b	4	0	1	12	1	0
Weaver, cf	4	0	0	3	0	1	Burns, 3b	4	2	1	2	2	0
Wolf, 3b	4	0	0	0	2	1	Terry, cf	4	1	1	5	0	0
Stratton, rf	4	1	1	0	0	0	Daly, c	4	0	2	1	0	0
Hamburg, lf	3	0	2	1	0	0	Smith, ss	4	0	0	4	5	0
Shinnick, 2b	3	0	0	0	1	1	Caruthers, lf	4	0	0	0	0	0
Ryan, c	3	0	0	3	0	1	Donovan, rf	4	2	1	1	0	0
Daily, p	3	1	1	2	3	0	Lovett, p	4	0	0	0	2	0
	32	2	5	24	13	6		37	7	7	27	13	0

```
LOU   0 1 0   0 1 0   0 0 0  -  2
BKN   2 1 0   0 0 0   1 0 x  -  7
```

Earned runs: BKN 2, LOU 1. 2B: Terry, Daly 2, Raymond. 3B: Foutz, Daily. HR: Burns. BB: Daily 6, Lovett 1. Struck out: Daily 3. PB: Ryan. Umpires: McQuaid and Curry. Att: 1,000. Time—1:50.

"Germany" Smith singled to center. The Cyclones scored once in the ninth and had a man on second with the tying run at the plate but the two Harrys, Taylor and Raymond, failed to produce. The final score was 5–3.

After an off day, Terry and Stratton took the mound again. Brooklyn held a 7–4 lead into the bottom of the eighth, but three Louisville runs tied the score. The game was then called on account of darkness, a 7–7 tie.

Tom Lovett was the starting pitcher for Brooklyn in Game Four. He ran up against Phil "Red" Ehret (24–13). Louisville scored three runs in the first inning to take an early lead, but Brooklyn tied the game in the second. Both teams exchanged single runs in the third, but Ehret held Brooklyn to two hits after the fourth inning and Louisville scored the deciding run in the seventh on a Tim Shinnick triple and a groundout by Ryan.

After three days off because of rain, the series resumed at Washington Park. Tom Lovett put the Grooms ahead by a 3-to-1 margin in the series with

1890 Championship Series

GAME SIX --- October 27

LOUISVILLE	AB	R	H	PO	A	E		BROOKLYN	AB	R	H	PO	A	E
Taylor, 1b	5	1	2	10	1	0		Collins, 2b	5	0	0	4	3	0
Raymond, ss	5	3	1	2	5	0		O'Brien, cf	5	0	2	3	1	0
Weaver, cf	5	1	2	1	1	0		Burns, lf	5	2	1	0	0	0
Wolf, 3b	5	1	3	2	2	2		Pinckney, 3b	5	1	2	1	2	0
Daily, rf	5	0	0	2	0	0		Foutz, 1b	5	2	2	13	0	1
Hamburg, lf	5	1	2	2	0	0		Terry, p	5	1	0	0	4	0
Shinnick, 2b	5	0	0	2	0	0		Smith, ss	5	1	2	4	8	1
Ryan, c	5	0	3	6	0	1		Donovan, rf	4	1	3	1	1	0
Stratton, p-rf	4	2	0	0	3	0		Bushong, c	4	0	0	1	1	0
Ehret, p	4	0	0	0	1	0		Daly, c	4	0	0	1	1	1
	48	9	13	27	13	3			47	8	12	28	21	3

```
LOU   0 1 2   1 0 1   2 2 0  -  9
BKN   1 0 0   0 0 4   0 3 0  -  8
```

Earned runs: LOU 4, BKN 4. 2B: Wolf, Hamburg, Burns, Donovan. 3B: Pinckney. Umpires: Curry and McQuaid. Att: 600.

GAME SEVEN --- October 28

LOUISVILLE	AB	R	H	PO	A	E		BROOKLYN	AB	R	H	PO	A	E
Taylor, 1b	4	2	3	14	0	0		Collins, 2b	4	0	1	1	1	0
Raymond, ss	4	1	1	3	4	0		O'Brien, cf	4	0	0	0	0	0
Weaver, cf	4	2	0	3	1	1		Burns, 3b	4	1	1	5	5	0
Wolf, 3b	4	0	1	0	2	0		Foutz, 1b	4	1	2	13	0	1
Daily, rf	4	0	1	0	0	0		Smith, ss	4	0	0	1	6	0
Hamburg, lf	4	0	0	1	0	0		Daly, c	4	0	0	3	0	0
Shinnick, 2b	4	0	0	0	4	2		Donovan, rf	4	0	0	1	1	0
Bligh, c	2	0	0	0	0	0		Caruthers, lf	4	0	0	0	0	1
Weckbecker, c	2	0	0	6	0	0		Lovett, p	3	0	0	0	8	0
Ehret, p	4	1	2	0	1	0			35	2	4	24	21	2
	36	6	8	27	12	3								

```
LOU   1 0 3   0 0 0   0 2 0  -  6
BKN   2 0 0   0 0 0   0 0 0  -  2
```

Earned runs: LOU 1, BKN 1. 2B: Collins, Foutz, Taylor. 3B: Raymond, Ehret. Umpires: McQuaid and Curry. Att: 300.

a fine job of pitching as he shut down the Cyclones and Ed Daily, 7–2. A two-run homer by Oyster Burns in the first gave Brooklyn a lead it never relinquished.

　　After another off-day, Louisville won its second game of the series, but not without tribulation. Leading 5–1 in the sixth, the Cyclones watched helplessly as Brooklyn scored four times to tie the game. Louisville recovered and scored twice in both the seventh and eighth innings to regain their four-run lead. Three Brooklyn runs in the bottom of the eighth pulled the Bridegrooms within one, but no more offense was forthcoming for the home team. Red Ehret got the win in relief of Scott Stratton and Adonis Terry was the loser. The final score was Louisville 9, Brooklyn 8, and only eight of the 17 runs were earned.

　　Louisville tied the series at three games apiece before a very cold and very small crowd of 300 fans on the 28th. It was Ehret against Lovett, and Louisville had a 1–0 lead even before the fans were settled in their seats. Brooklyn struck for two in the bottom of the first, but scored no more as Ehret held the Bridegrooms to four hits. Louisville won the game, 6–2.

Because of the bad weather and sparse crowds, the managers agreed to dispense with the rest of the scheduled games, and the series ended in a tie. The Brotherhood collapsed after its brief fling with glory and its players returned to teams in the National League and American Association.

The 1892 Split-Season Championship Series

Boston Beaneaters (NL) defeat the Cleveland Spiders (NL); 5–0–1

The War Between the Leagues broke out again in 1891, making a postseason championship an impossibility. When the American Association disbanded at the end of the 1891 season, the National League expanded from eight teams to 12, taking the strongest AA ball clubs — Louisville, Washington, St. Louis, and Baltimore.

With 12 teams making the "new look" National League somewhat awkward, the owners hit upon the idea of a split season to revive fan interest in the teams. This plan, which was muddle-headed in 1892, worked every bit as well as it did in 1981 — which is to say it worked not at all.

The Boston Beaneaters (52–22, first half) met the Cleveland Spiders (53–22, second half) in a best-of-nine series after the conclusion of the regular season. The first three games were scheduled for Union Park in Cleveland, the next three for South End Grounds in Boston. The final three games, if necessary, were to be on a neutral ground.

Game One was played on October 17 before 6,000 Indians fans. Cy Young (36–11) shut out Boston on six hits, Jack Stivetts (35–16) shut out Cleveland on four, and the game was called after 11 innings on account of darkness. This was as close as Cleveland would come to a victory in the series. The series opener was marred by a bit of unsportsmanlike conduct on the part of Boston catcher King Kelly. In the ninth inning, Stivetts popped the ball up on the infield. As Cleveland catcher Charles "Chief" Zimmer circled under the ball, Kelly (who had been known to place a wager or two on his own team) called for the Cleveland second baseman, Jacob "Guesses" Virtue, to make the catch. Virtue and Zimmer collided and the ball dropped. The Spider bench emptied and manager Patsy Tebeau demanded that Kelly be ejected from the game. Kelly was fined ten dollars, but his mischef had no bearing on the outcome of the game.

The Beaneaters won Game Two by a score of 4–3 with Henry Staley (22–10) outpitching John Clarkson. Clarkson had been released from Boston earlier in the year despite compiling a 9–7 record and went 17–10 for the balance of the year with Cleveland. Boston took a lead in the first on singles by Herman Long and Tommy McCarthy and a sacrifice fly by Hugh Duffy. The teams traded single runs in the third and Cleveland tied the game in the fourth on an

1892 National League Championship Series

```
GAME ONE --- October 17
```

BOSTON	AB	R	H	PO	A	E		CLEVELAND	AB	R	H	PO	A	E
Long, ss	4	0	1	2	6	0		Childs, 2b	3	0	0	2	4	0
McCarthy, rf	4	0	1	1	0	0		Burkett, lf	4	0	2	0	0	0
Duffy, cf	4	0	2	1	0	0		Davis, 3b	4	0	1	1	3	0
Kelly, c	4	0	0	8	1	0		McKean, ss	3	0	1	2	1	0
Nash, 3b	4	0	1	1	2	0		Virtue, 1b	4	0	0	15	0	0
Lowe, lf	4	0	0	2	0	0		McAleer, cf	3	0	0	3	0	0
Tucker, 1b	4	0	0	15	0	0		O'Connor, rf	3	0	0	2	0	0
Quinn, 2b	4	0	1	3	5	0		Zimmer, c	4	0	0	8	3	1
Stivetts, p	4	0	0	1	4	0		Young, p	4	0	0	0	4	0
	36	0	6	34	18	0			32	0	4	33	15	1

```
BOS   0  0  0    0  0  0    0  0  0    0  0  -  0
CLE   0  0  0    0  0  0    0  0  0    0  0  -  0
```

SB: McAleer, Duffy. Struck out: Young 6, Stivetts 5. BB: Stivetts 4. DP: BOS. PB: Zimmer. SH: Virtue, Lowe, Tucker. Umpires: Snyder and Emslie. Att: 6,000. Time—2:00.

```
GAME TWO --- October 18
```

BOSTON	AB	R	H	PO	A	E		CLEVELAND	AB	R	H	PO	A	E
Long, ss	5	2	1	0	3	0		Childs, 2b	3	0	0	3	0	0
McCarthy, rf	5	1	2	2	1	0		Burkett, lf	4	0	1	1	0	0
Duffy, cf	5	1	3	2	1	0		Davis, 3b	1	0	0	0	0	0
Kelly, c	4	0	0	0	2	0		Tebeau, 3b	3	0	0	2	0	1
Nash, 3b	4	0	1	0	2	0		McKean, ss	4	1	2	2	5	0
Lowe, lf	4	0	1	1	0	1		Virtue, 1b	4	0	1	6	1	1
Tucker, 1b	4	0	2	15	0	0		McAleer, cf	3	0	1	2	0	0
Quinn, 2b	3	0	0	3	2	0		O'Connor, rf	4	1	1	2	1	0
Staley, p	4	0	1	4	4	0		Zimmer, c	4	1	2	8	0	0
								Clarkson, p	4	0	1	0	2	0
	38	4	11	27	15	1			34	3	9	26	9	2

* Kelly declared out for interference

```
BOS   1  0  1    0  1  0    0  1  0  -  4
CLE   0  0  1    1  0  0    0  0  1  -  3
```

Earned runs: CLE 2, BOS 2. LOB: CLE 5, BOS 9. 2B: Zimmer, Clarkson, Duffy. 3B: Duffy 2, Zimmer. SH: Burkett, Virtue, McAleer, O'Connor, Clarkson, Duffy. SB: Kelly. DP: Boston. BB: Clarkson 1, Staley 1. Struck out: Clarkson 5. Umpires: McQuaid and Gaffney. Time—1:35.

Ed McKean single, a Virtue sacrifice, and a Jimmy McAleer single. Boston took the lead for good in the next inning when McCarthy reached on an error by Patsy Tebeau and scored on a double by Duffy. Trailing 4–2 with two out in the ninth, Cleveland's Jack O'Connor singled and Chief Zimmer tripled him home. But John Clarkson, a .171 hitter for the year, grounded to Tommy Tucker at first who made the unassisted play.

Stivetts and Young were rematched for Game Three. This time Stivetts gave up eight hits and eight walks, but struck out six and came away a 4–3 winner. With the game tied 2–2 in the eighth, Boston scored the go-ahead run when Stivetts doubled and McCarthy singled him home.

Game Four of the series, the first played at Boston, was a tour de force for

1892 National League Championship Series

GAME THREE --- October 19

BOSTON	AB	R	H	PO	A	E		CLEVELAND	AB	R	H	PO	A	E
Long, ss	4	0	1	4	2	1		Childs, 2b	3	1	1	3	3	0
McCarthy, rf	4	1	2	1	0	0		Burkett, lf	4	1	2	1	0	0
Duffy, cf	4	0	1	2	1	0		Tebeau, 3b	4	0	0	0	0	0
Ganzel, c	4	0	2	7	1	0		McKean, ss	4	0	2	1	5	0
Nash, 3b	4	0	0	0	3	0		Virtue, 1b	4	0	1	11	0	0
Lowe, lf	4	1	1	2	0	0		McAleer, cf	4	0	1	3	0	0
Tucker, 1b	3	0	0	6	0	1		O'Connor, rf	4	0	1	2	0	0
Quinn, 2b	3	0	1	2	2	0		Zimmer, c	4	0	0	2	1	0
Stivetts, p	3	1	1	1	1	0		Young, p	3	0	0	0	1	0
								Davis *	1	0	0	0	0	0
	33	3	9	25	10	2			35	2	8	23	10	0

* batted for Young in the ninth

```
BOS   1 1 0   0 0 0   0 1 0  -  3
CLE   2 0 0   0 0 0   0 0 0  -  2
```

Earned runs: CLE 2, BOS 3. 2B: Burkett, Quinn, Stivetts. SB: McCarthy, McKean. SH: Tucker, Stivetts, Tebeau, McAleer, O'Connor, Zimmer. LOB: CLE 3, BOS 5. BB: Stivetts 1. Struck out: Stivetts 5. Umpires: Emslie and Snyder. Time—1:35.

GAME FOUR --- October 20

CLEVELAND	AB	R	H	PO	A	E		BOSTON	AB	R	H	PO	A	E
Childs, 2b	3	0	2	5	3	0		Long, ss	4	0	1	2	1	0
Burkett, cf	4	0	1	0	0	0		McCarthy, rf	1	1	0	2	1	0
Virtue, 1b	4	0	0	12	0	1		Duffy, cf	3	1	3	2	0	0
McKean, ss	4	0	2	1	4	0		Nash, 3b	4	1	0	2	2	0
McAleer, lf	4	0	2	2	1	0		Lowe, lf	3	1	1	0	0	0
O'Connor, rf	3	0	0	0	0	0		Tucker, 1b	3	0	0	8	1	0
Zimmer, c	3	0	0	2	5	0		Quinn, 2b	2	0	1	2	1	0
Tebeau, 3b	3	0	0	2	3	1		Bennett, c	3	0	0	8	3	0
Cuppy, p	3	0	0	0	3	0		Nichols, p	3	0	0	1	1	0
	31	0	7	24	19	2			26	4	6	27	10	0

```
CLE   0 0 0   0 0 0   0 0 0  -  0
BOS   0 0 2   0 0 2   0 0 x  -  4
```

Earned runs: BOS 1. 3B: Childs. HR: Duffy. SB: Duffy, Nash, Lowe. SH: Tucker, Quinn, Virtue. BB: Cuppy, Nichols 6. Umpires: McQuaid and Gaffney. Time—1:40.

Kid Nichols (35–16) who twirled a seven-hit shutout and won, 4–0. Boston scored the winning runs in the second when, with two outs, McCarthy walked and Duffy homered over the right field fence. They added two insurance tallies in the sixth when Billy Nash reached on an error and stole second. Bobby Lowe singled Nash to third, stole second, and both runners scored on Joe Quinn's single. Nig Cuppy (28–13) was the losing pitcher.

In Game Five, the Spiders and John Clarkson took a 6–0 lead in the second, partly on the strength of Clarkson's three-run homer. But John couldn't stand success. Boston cut the lead in half in the fourth. McCarthy singled and was sacrificed to second. Charlie Ganzel singled McCarthy to third and Ganzel

1892 National League Championship Series

GAME FIVE --- October 21

CLEVELAND	AB	R	H	PO	A	E		BOSTON	AB	R	H	PO	A	E
Childs, 2b	5	1	4	2	2	0		Long, ss	5	1	1	1	3	2
Burkett, lf	5	1	0	2	0	0		McCarthy, rf	4	3	2	1	0	1
Virtue, 1b	3	1	0	13	1	0		Duffy, cf	5	1	1	3	0	0
McKean, ss	5	1	2	2	2	1		Ganzel, c	4	1	2	5	0	0
McAleer, cf	4	0	0	1	0	1		Nash, 3b	4	1	1	3	3	0
O'Connor, rf	4	0	0	0	0	0		Lowe, lf	4	0	0	2	0	1
Zimmer, c	4	1	2	4	0	0		Tucker, 1b	5	1	3	10	0	0
Tebeau, 3b	4	1	0	0	5	2		Quinn, 2b	5	2	2	2	2	0
Clarkson, p	4	1	1	0	0	0		Stivetts, p	5	2	2	0	1	0
	38	7	9	24	10	4			41	12	14	27	9	4

```
CLE   0  6  0    0  1  0    0  0  0  -   7
BOS   0  0  0    3  2  4    3  0  x  -  12
```

Earned runs: BOS 6, CLE 1. 2B: McCarthy, Duffy. 3B: Stivetts, Childs. HR: Clarkson, Tucker. SH: Long, McCarthy, Duffy 2, Ganzel, Quinn 2, McAleer 1. SB: Burkett 2, Virtue, Tebeau. BB: Clarkson 4, Stivetts 2. Struck out: Clarkson 2, Stivetts 5. WP: Clarkson. PB: Zimmer. Umpires: Snyder and Emslie. Att: 3,466. Time—1:50.

GAME SIX --- October 24

CLEVELAND	AB	R	H	PO	A	E		BOSTON	AB	R	H	PO	A	E
Childs, 2b	5	1	2	3	3	0		Long, ss	5	1	1	3	4	1
Burkett, lf	4	1	2	1	0	0		McCarthy, rf	3	2	1	0	0	1
Virtue, 1b	5	0	1	13	1	0		Duffy, cf	5	0	2	1	0	0
McKean, ss	5	0	2	0	1	2		Nash, 3b	4	1	1	1	0	0
McAleer, cf	3	0	0	0	0	0		Lowe, lf	4	0	0	4	0	1
O'Connor, rf	3	0	1	2	0	0		Tucker, 1b	4	1	1	7	0	0
Zimmer, c	4	0	1	4	1	0		Quinn, 2b	4	0	1	3	0	0
Tebeau, 3b	4	0	0	1	4	2		Bennett, c	4	2	2	3	2	2
Young, p	4	1	1	0	3	0		Nichols, p	4	1	2	0	2	0
	37	3	10	24	13	4			37	8	11	22	8	5

```
BOS   0  0  2    1  1  1    1  1  1  -   8
CLE   0  0  3    0  0  0    0  0  0  -   3
```

Earned runs: BOS 6, CLE 2. 2B: Duffy, McCarthy. 3B: Quinn. HR: Bennett. SB: McCarthy, Nichols, Burkett, Zimmer, Tucker, Long. SH: McAleer, O'Connor, McCarthy, Lowe 2, Tucker 2. DP: BOS 1, CLE 1. BB: Young 3, Nichols 2. Struck out: Young 3, Nichols 8. PB: Bennett. WP: Young 3. Umpires: McQuaid and Gaffney. Time—1:55.

went to second on the throw to the plate. Billy Nash's single drove both men home. Lowe walked and Tucker singled Nash home for the third run of the inning. After Cleveland made the score 7–3 in the fifth, the Beaneaters pulled to within two in the bottom of the inning. Long reached on an error and McCarthy doubled him home for the first run of the inning. Duffy sacrificed him to third where he scored on Long's sacrifice fly. The Beaneaters took a two-run lead with four runs in the sixth. Quinn singled to lead off the inning and scored a moment later on pitcher Jack Stivetts' triple. Long singled to tie the game and McCarthy reached on an error by Tebeau. Second baseman Cupid Childs recovered Tebeau's wild throw and nailed Long at the plate. Duffy doubled home the lead run and Ganzel's single scored Duffy. Three more Boston tallies in the seventh put the game out of reach for Cleveland. Stivetts got the win and Clarkson took the loss. The Beaneaters needed one more win for the championship. After two days of rain, they got it.

Cleveland took an early lead in Game Six and again they failed to hold. Cy Young singled to lead off the third inning and scored when right fielder McCarthy dropped Cupid Childs' line drive. Jesse Burkett singled, stole second, and scored along with Childs on a single by McKean. Boston recovered two of those runs in the third on a Kid Nichols single, a walk to McCarthy, and a double by Hugh Duffy. Boston tied the game in the fourth on singles by Tucker, Charlie Bennett, and Nichols. The Beaneaters then went on to score single runs in the last five innings. Kid Nichols got the victory, his second of the series.

The 1894 Temple Cup Championship Series

New York Giants (NL) defeat the Baltimore Orioles (NL); 4–0

There was no postseason matchup in 1893, but at the winter meeting of the National League owners, businessman William Temple unfolded what he thought was a more workable plan for a National League postseason championship series. The team that won the pennant would play the team that finished second in a best-of-seven series. If the first-place team declined to play, the second-place and third-place teams would compete. If the second-place team declined to play, the pennant winner would play the third-place team. If the ... well, you get the idea.

Temple ordered a loving cup from New York jeweler A.E. Thrall. The $800 trophy stood 30 inches tall, was heavily ornamented, and featured a relief figure of a pitcher throwing a ball. In order to claim the prize, a team had to win the postseason championship series three consecutive years. On the financial side, the winning team would receive 65 percent of the receipts, the losing team, 35 percent.

The Baltimore Orioles (89–39) won the 1894 pennant by a margin of three games over the New York Giants (88–44). Manager Ned Hanlon objected to the terms of the split and suggested a winner-take-all plan. When Hanlon's idea was voted down, he suggested the receipts be split evenly—an even worse idea which would profit the players to drag out the series to a full seven games. A 65/35 split it was, then, but each Oriole paired up with a Giant and agreed before the games began to split their winnings fifty-fifty.

Baltimore had quite a scrappy team that year with Dan Brouthers (.347) at first, Heinie Reitz (.303) at second, John McGraw (.340) at third, Hughie Jennings (.335) at short, Wilbert Robinson (.353) behind the plate; and an outfield of Wee Willie Keeler (.371), Steve Brodie (.366), and Joe Kelley (.393). The Orioles' offense was stunning and their pitching staff, led by Sadie McMahon (25–8), Bill Hawke (16–9), and William "Kid" Gleason (15–5), was nothing to sneer at either. The Oriole teams of the 1890s were noted for playing

1894 Temple Cup Championship Series

```
GAME ONE --- October 4
```

NEW YORK	R	H	PO	A	E		BALTIMORE	R	H	PO	A	E
Burke, lf	0	4	0	0	0		Kelley, lf	0	1	3	0	1
Tiernan, rf	0	0	0	0	0		Keeler, rf	0	1	1	0	0
Davis, 3b	1	1	0	3	0		Brouthers, 1b	0	0	9	1	0
Doyle, 1b	1	2	11	5	0		McGraw, 3b	1	2	1	4	0
Ward, 2b	0	1	4	2	1		Brodie, cf	0	0	1	0	0
Van Haltren, cf	1	1	2	0	0		Reitz, 2b	0	1	4	1	0
Fuller, ss	0	1	3	1	1		Jennings, ss	0	1	0	3	0
Farrell, c	0	0	5	1	0		Robinson, c	0	1	7	1	0
Rusie, p	1	2	1	4	0		Esper, p	0	0	0	3	0
	4	12	26	16	2			1	7	26	13	1

```
NY    0  0  0    0  1  1    1  1  0  -  4
BAL   0  0  0    0  0  0    0  0  1  -  1
```

Earned runs: NY 4, BAL 1. 2B: Rusie. 3B: Davis, Doyle, Van Haltren. SB: McGraw, Reitz, Davis, Doyle, Van Haltren. DP: BAL 1, NY 1. SH: Brouthers, Keeler, Brodie, Jennings, Ward. LOB: BAL 7, NY 7. BB: Rusie 2, Esper 1. Struck out: Esper 3, Rusie 2. Umpires: Emslie and Hurst. Att: 12,000. Time—1:55.

dirty ball, but they were also the originators of the hit-and-run play and the "Baltimore Chop." No fewer than six players on the 1894 Baltimore Orioles are in baseball's Hall of Fame.

The Giants had an aging Monte Ward (.265) at second, "Dirty Jack" Doyle (.369) at first, George Davis (.346) at third, and that was about it. Their pitching staff, on the other hand, was something to be reckoned with. Amos Rusie (36–13) and Jouett Meekin (36–10) had stellar years and led the league in wins.

Game One was played on October 4th at Baltimore's Union Park. The 18,000-strong Baltimore crowd was shocked to see their hometown favorites take it on the chin by a 4–1 score. John McGraw and Monte Ward nearly fought with each other after a collision at second base and, later in the game, Steve Brodie and "Dirty Jack" Doyle did exchange blows. Neither team scored until the Giants tallied single runs in the fifth, sixth, seventh, and eighth innings. Baltimore's lone run was scored by McGraw in the ninth. Amos Rusie shut down the Oriole offense on seven hits while Duke Esper (10–2) allowed 13.

Game Two, the next day, resulted in a second victory for the Giants. New York trailed 6–5 into the ninth and scored once to tie the game when Hughie Jennings muffed an easy double play ball. With the bases loaded, Mike Tiernan's triple chased everone home and gave Jouett Meekin the victory over Kid Gleason (15–5).

The series moved to the Polo Grounds in New York for Game Three on the sixth. Amos Rusie started for the second time and faced Baltimore's George Hemming (17–19 on the year, 4–0 with Baltimore). The Giants broke on top in the first. Mike Tiernan grounded to Baltimore first baseman Dan Brouthers who flipped to the pitcher covering, but Hemming dropped the ball. George Davis' double scored Tiernan. Baltimore tied the game in the fourth when Brouthers bunted for a base hit and later scored on Hughie Jennings's groundout.

The 1894 Temple Cup Championship Series

GAME TWO --- October 5

NEW YORK	R	H	PO	A	E		BALTIMORE	R	H	PO	A	E
Burke, lf	1	0	1	0	0		Kelley, lf	1	1	2	0	0
Tiernan, rf	3	4	3	0	0		Keeler, rf	0	2	5	0	0
Davis, 3b	1	1	0	2	0		Brouthers, 1b	1	1	10	2	1
Doyle, 1b	1	1	9	1	1		McGraw, 3b	0	0	1	1	0
Ward, 2b	0	2	2	2	0		Brodie, cf	2	0	1	0	0
Van Haltren, cf	0	1	6	1	0		Reitz, 2b	1	2	2	3	0
Fuller, s	1	1	2	4	2		Jennings, ss	0	0	2	6	2
Farrell, c	1	1	3	0	0		Robinson, c	1	0	2	2	0
Meekin, p	1	1	1	1	0		Gleason, p	0	1	2	1	0
	9	12	27	11	3			6	7	27	15	3

```
NY    0  0  4    0  0  0    0  1  4  -  9
BAL   0  2  2    0  0  0    1  0  1  -  6
```

Earned runs: BAL 2, NY 2. 3B: Kelley, Gleason, Tiernan, Davis. SH: Jennings, Davis. SB: Kelley, Keeler, Brouthers, Brodie, Robinson, Tiernan, Doyle. DP: NY 1, BAL 1. LOB: BAL 8, NY 4. BB: Gleason 1, Meekin 2. Struck out: Gleason 3, Meekin 2. WP: Gleason, Meekin. Umpires: Hurst and Emslie. Att: 11,000. Time—2:00.

GAME THREE --- October 6

BALTIMORE	R	H	PO	A	E		NEW YORK	R	H	PO	A	E
Kelley, lf	0	1	1	0	1		Burke, lf	0	2	0	0	0
Keeler, rf	0	0	0	0	0		Tiernan, rf	1	0	0	1	1
Brouthers, 1b	1	2	6	1	1		Davis, 3b	1	2	1	2	0
McGraw, 3b	0	1	4	3	0		Doyle, 1b	1	2	12	1	2
Brodie, cf	0	0	2	1	0		Ward, 2b	0	2	3	0	1
Reitz, 2b	0	1	6	2	1		Van Haltren, cf	0	2	1	0	0
Jennings, ss	0	1	2	4	0		Fuller, s	0	0	4	6	0
Robinson, c	0	1	2	4	2		Farrell, c	1	0	6	1	1
Hemming, p	0	0	0	0	1		Rusie, p	0	1	0	2	0
	1	7	23	15	6			4	11	27	13	5

* Doyle declared out for being hit by batted ball

```
BAL   0  0  0    1  0  0    0  0  0  -  1
NY    1  0  0    0  1  2    0  0  x  -  4
```

LOB: BAL 9, NY 5. 2B: Kelley 1, Burke 2. SH: Ward, Rusie. DP: NY. HBP: Brodie. BB: Rusie 6, Hemming 3. Struck out: Rusie 6, Hemming 2. PB: Farrell 3. Umpires: Hurst and Emslie. Att: 20,000. Time—2:05.

In the fifth, New York moved ahead to stay. With Shorty Fuller on first, Duke Farrell grounded to McGraw at third. McGraw's throw to Heinie Reitz forced Fuller, but Reitz's throw to first went wild and Farrell wound up on third. The error was one of six for Baltimore on the day. With Rusie at the plate, the Giants worked the squeeze play successfully. Two more New York runs in the sixth put the game out of reach for the Orioles, who had seven hits for the third day in a row. Rusie got the victory, Hemming the loss.

The final game of the series, played at the Polo Grounds after an off-day, was won easily by the Giants. New York's Jouett Meekin was matched with Bill Hawke (16–9) before 12,000 fans eager to see the Giants take the first leg of the Temple Cup. They didn't have long to wait.

1894 Temple Cup Championship Series

```
GAME FOUR --- October 8
```

BALTIMORE	R	H	PO	A	E
Kelley, lf	1	1	0	1	3
Keeler, rf	1	0	2	1	0
Brouthers, 1b	0	0	5	0	0
McGraw, 3b	1	1	2	3	0
Brodie, cf	0	0	4	1	0
Reitz, 2b	0	1	4	2	0
Jennings, ss	0	0	1	1	0
Robinson, c	0	2	4	2	0
Hawke, p	0	0	0	0	1
Bonner, ss	0	0	2	0	1
Gleason, p	0	0	0	0	0
	3	5	24	11	5

NEW YORK	R	H	PO	A	E
Burke, lf	1	1	4	0	0
Tiernan, rf	1	1	1	0	0
Davis, 3b	2	1	1	1	2
Doyle, 1b	2	4	4	1	1
Ward, 2b	1	1	2	1	0
Van Haltren, cf	2	3	1	0	0
Fuller, s	3	1	2	4	2
Farrell, c	1	3	3	0	0
Meekin, p	3	3	6	1	0
Murphy, cf	0	0	0	5	0
	16	18	24	13	5

```
BAL   2 0 1   0 0 0   0 0  -  3
NY    1 0 1   3 5 1   5 1  -  16
```

Earned runs: NY 7. 2B: Davis, Doyle, Van Haltren. BB: Hawke, Gleason 4, Meekin 3. Struck out: Meekin 4. Umpires: Hurst and Emslie. Att: 12,000. Time—2:00.

The Orioles took the lead in the first. Kelley walked and Keeler hit a slow grounder that Fuller failed to stop. Brouthers sacrificed the runners to second and third where they scored on McGraw's bloop single to center. The Giants scored in the first and third, but it was 3–2 Baltimore when New York took their cuts in the fourth. With one out, George Van Haltren, Fuller and Farrell singled, Van Haltren scoring on Farrell's single and Fuller going to third. Meekin squeezed Fuller home and Farrell went to third. Eddie Burke's sacrifice fly made the score 5–3, Giants. New York added five more runs in the fifth off reliever Kid Gleason. George Davis walked and raced to second when ball four was a wild pitch. Doyle doubled, scoring Davis, and Ward grounded to Jennings at short who threw Doyle out at third. Van Haltren took a base on balls, Fuller singled to right, Ward scored and Val Haltren advanced to second. Farrell lifted a fly ball into left which Kelley dropped. One run scored, Fuller went to third and Farrell wound up on second. Meekin's third hit of the day drove in Fuller and Farrell, and the Giants had a 10–3 lead.

During the seventh inning, two horses escaped from the grasp of their owners behind the ropes in center field, delaying the game several minutes before they were caught. Five more Giant runs in the same inning added to the spirit of general merriment and made the final score 16–3. Meekin had the victory, his second in the series, and Hawke took the loss.

The 1895 Temple Cup Championship Series

Cleveland Spiders (NL) defeat the Baltimore Orioles (NL); 4–1

The Baltimore Orioles (87–43) finished the season three games ahead of Cleveland (84–46) and met the Spiders in the second playing of the Temple Cup Series.

1895 Temple Cup Championship Series

GAME ONE --- October 2

BALTIMORE	R	H	PO	A	E
McGraw, 3b	4	3	0	1	0
Keeler, rf	5	1	2	0	0
Jennings, ss	4	1	0	8	0
Kelley, lf	4	3	1	0	0
Brodie, cf	4	0	2	0	0
Gleason, 2b	4	2	3	1	0
Carey, 1b	4	0	10	1	0
Robinson, c	4	2	6	0	0
McMahon, p	4	0	2	3	0
	37	12	*26	14	0

CLEVELAND	R	H	PO	A	E
Burkett, lf	4	1	0	0	0
McKean, ss	4	3	4	5	1
Childs, 2b	5	1	3	3	1
McAleer, cf	5	1	2	0	0
P Tebeau, 1b	5	2	14	1	1
Zimmer, c	4	2	1	2	0
Blake, rf	4	2	3	0	0
McGarr, 3b	4	1	0	1	0
Young, p	4	1	0	6	0
	39	14	27	18	3

* Two out when winning run scored

```
BAL   0  0  0    0  0  1    0  2  1   -  4
CLE   0  0  0    0  1  1    0  1  2   -  5
```

Earned runs: CLE 5, BAL 4. LOB: CLE 3, BAL 6. 2B: Burkett, McKean, Tebeau, Blake, McGraw, Robinson. 3B: McKean. SH: Burkett. SB: McGarr 2, McGraw. DP: CLE. BB: Young 1. Struck out: McMahon 1. Umpires: McDonald and Keefe. Time – 2:17.

GAME TWO --- October 3

BALTIMORE	R	H	PO	A	E
McGraw, 3b	0	0	1	0	0
Keeler, rf	0	1	2	0	0
Jennings, ss	1	1	1	5	1
Kelley, lf	1	0	3	0	0
Brodie, cf	0	1	2	1	0
Gleason, 2b	0	0	3	2	0
Carey, 1b	0	2	10	1	1
Clarke, c	0	0	1	1	0
Hoffer, p	0	0	1	0	1
	2	5	24	10	3

CLEVELAND	R	H	PO	A	E
Burkett, lf	1	4	2	0	0
McKean, ss	1	1	4	8	1
Childs, 2b	1	0	3	2	0
McAleer, cf	1	0	1	0	1
P Tebeau, 1b	1	1	11	0	0
Zimmer, c	1	2	4	2	0
Blake, rf	0	0	2	1	1
McGarr, 3b	0	2	0	1	0
Cuppy, p	1	1	0	2	0
	7	11	27	16	3

```
BAL   0  1  0    0  0  1    0  0  0   -  2
CLE   3  0  0    0  1  2    1  0  x   -  7
```

Earned runs: CLE 3, BAL 1. 2B: Burkett, Zimmer, McGarr, Cuppy. SH: Childs, Cuppy. SB: Burkett, McKean 2, McAleer, Jennings. BB: Cuppy 2, Hoffer 2. Struck out: Cuppy 3, Hoffer 1. WP: Hoffer. PB: Clarke. Umpires: McDonald and Keefe. Att: 10,000.

Game One was held at League Park in Cleveland on October 2nd before an unruly crowd of Cleveland fans who heckled and threw garbage at the Orioles in the field. John McGraw was a favorite target. Heading into the ninth inning, John "Sadie" McMahon (10–4) had taken the measure of Cy Young (35–10) and was leading, 4–3, but Jesse Burkett, Ed McKean, and Cupid Childs singled to lead off the inning and tie the game. Two infield outs sent the winning run home and made Young a winner.

The Spiders won Game Two behind the strong pitching of Nig Cuppy (26–14). Trailing 3–0 in the second, Baltimore's Joe Kelley reached on an error. Steve Brodie and Kid Gleason both went out, but George "Scoops" Carey

1895 Temple Cup Championship Series

GAME THREE --- October 5

BALTIMORE	R	H	PO	A	E		CLEVELAND	R	H	PO	A	E
McGraw, 3b	0	1	0	0	1		Burkett, lf	0	2	0	0	0
Keeler, rf	1	0	3	0	0		McKean, ss	1	0	4	5	1
Jennings, ss	0	2	5	2	0		Childs, 2b	1	1	4	8	0
Kelley, lf	0	1	2	0	1		McAleer, cf	1	2	1	0	0
Brodie, cf	0	0	1	0	0		P Tebeau, 1b	0	1	13	0	0
Gleason, 2b	0	0	1	3	0		Zimmer, c	1	1	4	1	0
Carey, 1b	0	1	9	1	0		Blake, rf	1	1	0	0	0
Robinson, c	0	1	3	1	0		McGarr, 3b	1	2	1	1	0
McMahon, p	0	0	0	4	0		Young, p	1	1	0	2	1
	1	6	24	11	2			7	11	27	17	2

```
BAL   0 0 0   0 0 0   0 1 0  -  1
CLE   3 0 0   0 0 0   3 1 x  -  7
```

Earned runs: CLE 3, BAL 1. 2B: Childs, Zimmer, Blake, McGarr, Jennings. SB: McAleer, McGarr, Young. BB: Young, 1, McMahon 1. Struck out: Young 1, McMahon 1. Umpires: Hurst and McDonald. Att: 12,500.

GAME FOUR --- October 7

CLEVELAND	R	H	PO	A	E		BALTIMORE	R	H	PO	A	E
Burkett, lf	0	0	4	0	0		McGraw, 3b	1	1	1	2	0
McKean, ss	0	1	1	1	0		Keeler, rf	2	1	3	0	0
Childs, 2b	0	0	3	4	0		Jennings, ss	1	3	2	2	0
McAleer, cf	0	1	2	0	0		Kelley, lf	0	2	4	0	0
P Tebeau, 1b	0	1	6	1	0		Brodie, cf	1	1	3	0	0
Zimmer, c	0	0	3	0	1		Gleason, 2b	0	0	4	4	0
Blake, rf	0	1	4	0	0		Carey, 1b	0	1	6	1	0
McGarr, 3b	0	1	0	2	0		Robinson, c	0	0	3	0	0
Cuppy, p	0	0	1	0	0		Esper, p	0	0	1	0	0
	0	5	24	8	1			5	9	27	9	1

```
CLE   0 0 0   0 0 0   0 0 0  -  0
BAL   0 1 2   0 0 0   2 0 x  -  5
```

Earned runs; BAL 3. 2B: Carey, Jennings. SB: Jennings, Kelley. DP: BAL 1. BB: Cuppy 2. Struck out: Esper 3, Cuppy 3. PB: Zimmer. Umpires: Keefe and Hurst.

GAME FIVE --- October 8

CLEVELAND	R	H	PO	A	E		BALTIMORE	R	H	PO	A	E
Burkett, lf	1	3	2	0	0		McGraw, 3b	1	2	1	2	1
McKean, ss	0	1	1	5	0		Keeler, rf	0	1	1	0	1
Childs, 2b	1	1	2	0	1		Jennings, ss	0	0	3	4	0
McAleer, cf	0	1	5	0	0		Kelley, lf	0	1	1	1	1
P Tebeau, 1b	0	1	10	1	1		Brodie, cf	0	2	4	0	0
Zimmer, c	0	1	3	1	0		Gleason, 2b	0	0	3	0	0
Blake, rf	0	1	2	0	0		Carey, 1b	0	1	9	0	0
McGarr, 3b	1	1	1	1	1		Clarke, c	1	2	5	0	1
Young, p	2	1	1	3	0		Hoffer, p	0	0	0	2	1
	5	11	27	11	3			2	9	27	9	6

```
CLE   0 0 0   0 0 0   3 2 0  -  5
BAL   0 0 0   0 0 0   1 0 1  -  2
```

Earned runs: BAL 1, CLE 2. 2B: Blake, Young, McGraw. SH: Keeler, Gleason, Young. SB: Childs, McGraw, Clarke 2. BB: Hoffer 4, Young 2. Struck out: Hoffer 3, Young 1. Umpires: Hurst and Keefe. Att: 9,000.

grounded a single up the middle, sending Kelley to third where he scored on Jimmy McAleer's error. The Orioles' only other run came in the seventh, but by that time they were losing 6–1. William "Chick" Hoffer (30–7) was the loser. Jesse Burkett, with four hits on the day, was the batting star. The final score was 7–2.

Cy Young won his second game of the series on the 5th by beating McMahon again, this time by a slightly wider margin of 7–1. Cleveland jumped on top with three runs in the first inning for the second day in a row. Jesse Burkett continued his hot hitting, leading off the inning with a single. Ed McKean forced Burkett at second, but Childs, McAleer, and Patsy Tebeau all hit safely to drive in the first two runs of the game. McAleer stole third and scored on Chief Zimmer's groundout. Cleveland added three insurance runs in the seventh on a double by Harry Blake, singles by James "Chippy" Mc-Garr and Cy Young, Jesse Burkett's sacrifice bunt, and a sacrifice fly by McKean. A crowd of 12,500 watched a masterful pitching performance by Cy Young as the Orioles were unable to hit a ball out of the infield until the ninth inning.

The series continued at Baltimore's Union Park on October 7th. Baltimore residents exacted their revenge for what they considered shabby treatment of their boys in Cleveland. They pelted the Spiders with vegetables, eggs, rocks, and whatever else they could lay their hands on as the team made its way to the ballpark. Charles "Duke" Esper (10–12) threw a five-hit shutout against Cleveland, allowing hits in the fifth, seventh and ninth innings only, and Baltimore won their first and only game of the series, 5–0. Nig Cuppy took the loss.

Cy Young was back on the mound for Game Five facing Chick Hoffer for the finale. Neither team could mount a threat until the seventh inning when Young started an uprising with a double. Jesse Burkett followed with a single to center, sending Young to third. After Ed McKean went out, Cupid Childs hit an easy pop fly to Kelley in left. But Kelley dropped the ball, Young scored the first run of the game, and Burkett went to second. At this point, Hoffer blew up, allowing singles to McAleer and Tebeau which scored Burkett and Childs. Giving Cy Young a three run lead with nine outs to go was a dangerous thing and Denton True made those runs hold up. Baltimore scored once in the seventh, but Cleveland came back with two of their own in the eighth and the score was 5–1 heading into the final frame. Baltimore made some noise about getting back in the game after Clark and Hoffer were retired to start the ninth. Young hit a wild streak, walking McGraw and Willie Keeler, then he hit Jennings with a pitch. Kelley's single brought in McGraw, but Steve Brodie hit a little nubber right back to Young and the rest is history. Cleveland had won the series, four games to one. The batting star was Jesse Burkett, with a .500 batting average. Cy Young, with three wins in three starts, was the uncontested pitching star.

1896 Temple Cup Championship Series

```
GAME ONE --- October 2
```

CLEVELAND	AB	R	H	PO	A	E
Burkett, lf	3	0	1	1	0	1
McKean, ss	3	0	1	2	4	1
Childs, 2b	3	1	1	4	6	1
McAleer, cf	3	0	0	1	0	0
Zimmer, c	3	0	1	1	1	0
McGarr, 3b	4	0	0	2	5	1
Tebeau, 1b	1	0	0	4	0	0
O'Connor, 1b	3	0	1	10	0	0
Blake, rf	4	0	0	2	0	0
Young, p	3	0	0	0	2	0
Wallace, ph *	1	0	0	0	0	0
	31	1	5	27	18	4

BALTIMORE	AB	R	H	PO	A	E
McGraw, 3b	2	1	1	0	1	0
Quinn, 3b	3	1	0	1	1	0
Keeler, rf	5	1	2	1	0	0
Jennings, ss	5	2	3	3	5	1
Kelley, lf	5	0	2	2	0	0
Doyle, 1b	5	1	1	8	0	0
Reitz, 2b	4	0	1	4	1	0
Brodie, cf	4	1	0	1	0	0
Robinson, c	4	0	2	7	0	0
Hoffer, p	4	0	1	0	2	0
	41	7	13	27	10	1

```
* pinch-hit for Johnson in the ninth inning

CLE    0  0  0    0  0  1    0  0  0  -  1
BAL    0  0  2    0  0  1    3  1  0  -  7
```

Earned runs: BAL 6, CLE 1. LOB: BAL: 8, CLE 8. 2B: Zimmer, Jennings, Doyle. 3B: McKean, Hoffer, Keeler. SH: Childs. SB: Kelley 2, Brodie, McAleer. DP: BAL. BB: Hoffer 4, Young 1. Umpires: Sheridan and Emslie. Att: 4,000. Time—1:40.

```
GAME TWO --- October 3
```

CLEVELAND	AB	R	H	PO	A	E
Burkett, lf	3	0	2	2	0	0
McKean, ss	4	0	2	1	3	2
Childs, 2b	3	0	0	3	1	0
McAleer, cf	4	0	0	2	0	1
O'Connor, 1b	4	1	1	10	1	0
Zimmer, c	4	0	1	6	3	0
McGarr, 3b	4	0	0	0	3	0
Blake, rf	3	0	0	0	0	0
Wallace, p	3	1	1	0	2	0
	32	2	7	24	13	3

BALTIMORE	AB	R	H	PO	A	E
McGraw, 3b	5	1	1	0	1	0
Keeler, rf	4	1	2	1	3	0
Jennings, ss	2	2	1	4	4	3
Kelley, lf	4	2	3	3	0	0
Doyle, 1b	4	0	2	10	0	0
Reitz, 2b	2	1	0	1	5	0
Brodie, cf	4	0	0	0	0	0
Robinson, c	4	0	1	4	1	0
Corbett, p	3	0	0	1	1	0
	32	7	10	24	12	3

```
CLE    0  0  1    0  0  1    0  0  -  2
BAL    4  0  2    0  1  0    0  0  -  7
```

Earned runs: BAL 3, CLE 1. 2B: McKean. 3B: Keeler. SH: Reitz. SB: McGraw 2, Jennings, McGarr, Reitz, Kelley. BB: Corbett 2, Wallace 2. Struck out: Corbett 4, Wallace 4. WP: Wallace, Corbett 2. DP: BAL. Umpires: Emslie and Sheridan. Att: 3,100. Time—2:00.

The 1896 Temple Cup Championship Series

Baltimore Orioles (NL) defeat the Cleveland Spiders (NL); 4–0

The Baltimore Orioles (90–39) beat the Cleveland Spiders (80–48) to the pennant by an easy nine and one-half games and clinched the pennant on September 13. Seeking revenge for the previous year's Temple Cup loss, Baltimore prepared to meet the Spiders once again.

1896 Temple Cup Championship Series

```
GAME THREE --- October 5
```

CLEVELAND	AB	R	H	PO	A	E		BALTIMORE	AB	R	H	PO	A	E
Burkett, lf	5	1	2	7	0	0		McGraw, 3b	4	2	2	2	1	0
McKean, ss	5	0	1	3	3	0		Keeler, rf	4	1	1	1	0	0
Childs, 2b	4	1	1	2	0	0		Jennings, ss	4	0	0	2	7	1
McAleer, cf	4	0	2	3	0	0		Kelley, lf	4	0	2	4	0	0
O'Connor, 1b	4	0	2	5	0	0		Doyle, 1b	4	1	0	6	0	1
Zimmer, c	4	0	1	3	0	1		Reitz, 2b	4	0	0	5	0	0
McGarr, 3b	4	0	0	2	1	1		Brodie, cf	4	0	1	0	0	0
Blake, rf	4	0	1	2	0	0		Robinson, c	4	1	1	7	1	0
Young, p	4	0	0	0	1	0		Hoffer, p	3	1	1	0	1	0
	38	2	10	27	5	2			35	6	8	27	10	2

```
CLE   0  0  1    0  1  0    0  0  0  -  2
BAL   0  1  1    0  0  1    0  3  0  -  6
```

Earned runs: BAL 6, CLE 1. LOB: BAL 2, CLE 10. 2B: Robinson. 3B: Hoffer. SB: McGraw 2, Keeler, Doyle. BB: Hoffer. Struck out: Hoffer 5, Cuppy 2. Umpires: Sheridan and Emslie. Att: 6,000. Time—2:00.

```
GAME FOUR --- October 8
```

BALTIMORE	AB	R	H	PO	A	E		CLEVELAND	AB	R	H	PO	A	E
McGraw, 3b	4	0	0	0	1	0		Burkett, lf	4	0	0	3	0	0
Keeler, rf	4	1	3	0	0	0		McKean, ss	4	0	1	1	3	0
Jennings, ss	4	1	1	2	4	1		Childs, 2b	2	0	1	3	1	0
Kelley, lf	4	1	1	1	0	0		McAleer, cf	4	0	0	3	1	0
Doyle, 1b	4	1	2	9	2	0		O'Connor, 1b	4	0	0	9	0	0
Reitz, 2b	4	0	1	3	0	0		Zimmer, c	3	0	0	2	1	1
Brodie, cf	3	0	0	2	0	0		McGarr, 3b	4	0	1	0	2	0
Robinson, c	3	0	0	9	1	0		Blake, rf	3	0	0	3	0	0
Corbett, p	3	1	3	1	2	0		Cuppy, p	3	0	1	0	2	0
	33	5	11	27	10	1		Wallace, ph *	1	0	0	0	0	0
									32	0	4	24	10	1

```
*  pinch-hit for Cuppy in the ninth inning

BAL   0  0  0    0  0  0    0  0  0  -  0
CLE   0  0  0    0  0  0    2  3  x  -  5
```

Earned runs: BAL 5. 2B: Keeler, Jennings, Kelley, Corbett. SB: Burkett, Childs, McGarr, Blake, Doyle 2, Corbett. BB: Corbett 5. Struck out: Cuppy 2, Corbett 8. DP: CLE. Umpires: Sheridan and Emslie. Att: 1,200. Time—2:00.

Game One was played October 2nd before 4,000 spectators at Baltimore's Union Park, William "Chick" Hoffer (25–7) against Cy Young (29–16). The Orioles scored twice in the third for all the runs they needed. The teams traded single runs in the sixth before Baltimore reached Young for three in the seventh to take a commanding 6–1 lead. The final score was 7–1.

Joe Corbett (3–0), the younger brother of prize-fighter "Gentleman Jim" Corbett, won Game Two, beating Bobby Wallace (10–7). Corbett, a recent addition to the ball club, had been called up from the Tri-State League in September and had a 3–0 record in eight games. The Orioles scored four times in the first and were never in danger as they coasted to a 7–2 victory.

Game Three on the fifth of October was a rematch of Hoffer and Young and again Hoffer took the measure of the future Hall of Famer. Despite being outhit eight to ten, the Orioles beat the Spiders 6-2. Baltimore held a slim 3-2 lead until they exploded for three insurance runs in the eighth to put the game away.

The final game matched Joe Corbett against Nig Cuppy (25-14). Corbett was the batting and pitching star with two singles and a double and a four-hit shutout. The Orioles racked up 11 hits and five runs off Cuppy, but there was no scoring by either team until the seventh when Baltimore struck for two runs. Three more Oriole runs in the bottom of the eighth clinched the championship.

Two years after losing the Temple Cup to Baltimore, Cleveland owner Frank DeHaas Robinson bought the St. Louis franchise of the National League while still retaining ownership in the Spiders. (This was baseball as it was played before the commissioner system. A little thing like conflict of interest could be ignored.) Robinson sent Spider manager Patsy Tebeau to St. Louis along with his Cleveland stars — Cy Young, Nig Cuppy, "Chief" Zimmer, Cupid Childs, Ed McKean, Bobby Wallace, Jesse Burkett, Emmett Heidrick and Henry Blake. In the space of one year, the St. Louis team had replacements for seven of their starting eight positions, and three of their four starting pitchers. The 1899 version of the Cleveland Spiders — called the Exiles because they got so little fan support they wound up playing most of their games on the road — compiled a record of 20-134, the worst record in the history of baseball. St. Louis went from 39-111 to 84-67.

The 1897 Temple Cup Championship Series

Baltimore Orioles (NL) defeat the Boston Beaneaters (NL); 4-1

The 1897 pennant race came down to a three-game series in Baltimore between the Boston Beaneaters (93-39) and the Baltimore Orioles (90-40). Boston won the first and last games and left town a game and a half ahead of the Orioles. Three days later, they clinched the pennant. Boston, so the legend says, put everything they had into the season-ending series with Baltimore and had little left to give in the playoffs.

The first three games were played at South End Grounds in Boston. The Beaneaters won Game One on the fourth of October before 10,000 delighted Boston fans by a score of 13-12. Jery Nops (20-6) started against Kid Nichols (30-11) and neither pitcher displayed the form they showed throughout the season. Nichols were knocked out of the box and Ted "Parson" Lewis (24-12), got the victory in relief. Nops, inexplicably, was left in to take a fearful beating, giving up 12 hits, 7 walks, and 13 runs on the day. At that, he held a 12-11 lead after seven innings. But Boston scored twice in the eighth to win the game.

Game Two was another slugfest as Baltimore rebounded with a 13-11 victory. There were no ground rules for this game which saw an astonishing

1897 Temple Cup Championship Series

```
GAME ONE --- October 4
```

BALTIMORE	R	H	PO	A	E		BOSTON	R	H	PO	A	E
McGraw, 3b	3	3	0	1	1		Hamilton, cf	2	2	3	0	0
Keeler, rf	2	2	0	0	0		Tenney, 1b	3	0	8	1	1
Jennings, ss	2	5	2	6	1		Lowe, 2b	2	2	1	4	0
Kelley, lf	4	3	4	0	0		Stahl, rf	3	1	1	0	2
Stenzel, cf	1	1	1	0	0		Duffy, lf	2	3	3	0	0
Doyle, 1b	0	3	11	0	1		Collins, 3b	0	0	3	1	1
Reitz, 2b	0	1	3	2	1		Long, ss	1	2	2	3	0
Clarke, c	0	1	3	1	0		Bergen, c	0	2	5	0	0
Nops, p	0	1	0	1	0		Nichols, p	0	0	1	1	0
							Lewis, p	0	0	0	0	0
	12	20	24	11	4			13	12	27	10	4

```
BAL    4  0  1    0  2  3    2  0  0  -  12
BOS    3  0  0    1  2  5   .0  2  x  -  13
```

Earned runs: BOS 4, BAL 11. 2B: Lowe, Long, Jennings 2, Kelley 2, Reitz. SB: Hamilton, Stahl, Bergen. BB: Nops 7. Struck out: Nops 2, Nichols 3, Lewis 1. Umpires: Emslie and Hurst. Att: 10,000.

```
GAME TWO --- October 5
```

BALTIMORE	R	H	PO	A	E		BOSTON	R	H	PO	A	E
McGraw, 3b	1	1	1	1	2		Hamilton, cf	3	4	3	0	1
Keeler, rf	0	2	1	0	0		Tenney, 1b	0	0	13	1	0
Jennings, ss	1	1	3	2	0		Lowe, 2b	1	2	1	4	2
Kelley, lf	1	1	1	0	0		Stahl, rf	1	2	0	0	0
Stenzel, cf	1	1	9	0	0		Duffy, lf	1	2	4	0	0
Doyle, 1b	3	2	6	0	0		Collins, 3b	0	1	2	4	0
Reitz, 2b	2	2	3	3	0		Long, ss	1	1	3	6	0
Clarke, c	2	3	3	3	0		Yeager, c	1	2	1	1	0
Corbett, p	2	4	0	1	0		Klobedanz, p	2	2	0	2	0
							Stivetts, p	1	0	0	0	0
	13	17	27	10	2			11	16	27	18	3

```
BAL    1  3  0    1  6  0    1  1  0  -  13
BOS    0  0  2    6  2  0    1  0  0  -  11
```

Earned runs: BAL 8, BOS 7. 2B: Keeler, Kelley, Corbett, Hamilton, Duffy, Yeager. 3B: McGraw, Clark. HR: Reitz, Clark, Corbett, Long. SB: Doyle, Hamilton, Stivetts. DP: BOS. BB: Corbett 4, Klobedanz 4, Stivetts 1. Struck out: Corbett 3. Umpires: Emslie and Hurst Att: 6,000.

total of six doubles, two triples, and four home runs driven into the outfield crowds. Baltimore manager Ned Hanlon's sadistic streak emerged once again as Joe Corbett (24–8) was left stranded on the mound searching in vain for a way out of the ballpark. Corbett gave up four walks and 16 hits during his nine innings, but only four of the hits were for extra bases. Fred Klobedanz (26–7) and Jack Stivetts (12–5) gave up 17 hits between them and among those hits were three doubles, two triples, and three home runs. Apparently the two managers had some sort of wager going on the endurance of their respective pitching staffs.

Game Three saw Baltimore win in easier fashion as Chick Hoffer (22–11)

1897 Temple Cup Championship Series

```
GAME THREE --- October 6
```

BALTIMORE	R	H	PO	A	E		BOSTON	R	H	PO	A	E
McGraw, 3b	2	1	1	4	0		Hamilton, cf	1	2	2	0	0
Keeler, rf	1	1	0	0	0		Tenney, 1b	0	1	6	0	0
Jennings, ss	0	0	5	1	1		Lowe, 2b	1	0	3	2	0
Kelley, lf	0	1	3	0	0		Stahl, rf	0	1	2	0	0
Stenzel, cf	1	0	1	0	0		Duffy, lf	0	2	4	0	1
Doyle, 1b	2	2	5	1	0		Collins, 3b	0	1	2	1	0
Reitz, 2b	1	1	3	1	0		Long, ss	0	0	1	5	1
Clarke, c	0	2	3	1	0		Lake, c	0	0	1	2	1
Hoffer, p	1	1	0	0	1		Klobedanz, p	1	3	0	0	0
	8	9	21	8	2			3	10	21	10	3

```
BAL    0  4  4    0  0  0    0  -  8
BOS    0  0  3    0  0  0    0  -  3
```

Earned runs: BAL 2, BOS 2. 2B: Doyle. SB: Stenzel. DP: BOS. BB: Klobedanz 4, Hoffer 6. Struck out: Hoffer 1. Umpires: Hurst and Emslie. Att: 4,000.

took the measure of Klobedanz and Lewis. All the scoring came in just two innings as Baltimore scored four in the second and four in the third while Boston countered with three in the bottom of the third. Klobedanz had three of his team's ten hits.

Game Four, played in Baltimore's Union Park, saw the Orioles eke out another slugger's battle, this time by a score of 12–11. Baltimore scored six in the first and came right back with five in the second, but Nops was unable to keep the Beaneaters at bay. Boston racked up two in the fifth, four in the sixth, three in the seventh, two in the eighth, and threatened to tie the game in the ninth before reliever Joe Corbett finally shut the door. Nops got the victory, Stivetts the loss.

During the games, the rumor spread that the Orioles and Spiders had split the receipts fifty-fifty in 1896 and this year's teams were doing the same. William Temple, sponsor of the Temple Cup, angrily responded by asking that the players responsible be blacklisted. It must have been difficult to have discounted those rumors in view of the lackluster play in the first four games and harder still when Boston manager Frank Selee, trailing three-games-to-one in the series, trotted out rookie Charles "Piano Legs" Hickman (0–0) to start the fifth game. Hickman had been to the plate exactly three times during the 1897 season and had the lusty total of seven and two-thirds innings of major-league experience under his belt. Hanlon's men greeted him like an old friend, scoring two runs in the second and three more in the third. The final score was 9–3, Hickman taking the loss. Guy Hoffer, with a nifty 17-hitter, was the winning pitcher.

It's lucky no one got killed.

None of the players who were responsible for splitting the game receipts were ever disciplined, but when the National League owners held their winter meeting, the Temple Cup was abolished. Only Ned Hanlon, representing Baltimore, cast a vote in favor of continuing the series. The Temple Cup itself resides today in the Baseball Hall of Fame at Cooperstown.

1897 Temple Cup Championship Series

GAME FOUR --- October 9

BOSTON	AB	R	H	PO	A	E		BALTIMORE	AB	R	H	PO	A	E
Hamilton, cf		0	0	0	1	1		McGraw, 3b	0	1	1	0	0	0
Tenney, 1b		1	2	3	0	0		Keeler, rf	1	1	3	0	0
Lowe, 2b		2	2	3	2	0		Jennings, ss	1	0	3	5	0
Stahl, rf		2	3	3	1	0		Kelley, lf	2	0	1	0	0
Duffy, lf		2	2	3	0	1		Stenzel, cf	2	4	4	0	1
Collins, 3b		1	1	2	3	0		Doyle, 1b	3	3	6	1	0
Long, ss		2	2	6	0	0		Reitz, 2b	1	1	4	2	1
Yeager, c		0	1	4	5	1		Bowerman, c	2	3	5	0	1
Stivetts, p		0	0	0	2	0		Nops, p	0	1	0	0	0
Lewis, p		1	3	0	0	0		Corbett, p	0	0	0	0	0
		11	16	24	14	3			12	14	27	8	3

```
BOS   0 0 0   0 2 4   3 2 0  -  11
BAL   6 5 0   0 0 1   0 0 x  -  12
```

Earned runs: BAL 12, BOS 6. 2B: Stenzel, Doyle, Keeler, Lewis, Lowe, Stahl, Duffy. 3B: Long, Bowerman. SB: Stahl, Long, Tenney, Lowe, Stenzel. DP: BAL 1, BOS 1. BB: Nops 2, Corbett 3, Stivetts 6, Lewis 3. Struck out: Nops 1, Lewis 3, Corbett 2. PB: Bowerman 3. Umpires: Hurst and Emslie.

GAME FIVE --- October 11

BOSTON	AB	R	H	PO	A	E		BALTIMORE	AB	R	H	PO	A	E
Stivetts, p		0	0	1	0	1		McGraw, 3b	0	0	1	4	0
Tenney, 1b		0	3	10	0	1		Keeler, rf	1	3	1	0	0
Lowe, 2b		0	3	2	3	1		Jennings, ss	1	1	6	6	1
Stahl, rf		0	3	2	0	0		O'Brien, lf	2	2	1	0	0
Duffy, lf		1	2	2	0	0		Stenzel, cf	2	2	1	0	0
Collins, 3b		1	1	1	2	0		Bowerman, 1b	0	1	9	0	0
Long, ss		0	1	4	1	0		Reitz, 2b	0	0	5	6	1
Yeager, c		1	3	1	0	0		Clarke, c	2	3	3	0	0
Hickman, p-lf		0	1	1	3	0		Hoffer, p	1	1	0	1	0
Sullivan, p		0	0	0	0	0							
		3	17	24	9	3			9	13	27	17	2

```
BOS   0 2 0   0 0 0   0 0 1  -  3
BAL   0 2 3   0 0 0   2 2 x  -  9
```

Earned runs: BAL 2, BOS 3. 2B: O'Brien, Clarke, Hoffer, Hickman. 3B: Stenzel, Yeager. SB: Stenzel. DP: BAL 3. BB: Hickman 2. Struck out: Hoffer 1. Umpires: Hurst and Emslie.

The City and State Championships

Introduction

In the early days of baseball, the season usually ended in early October and player contracts expired around the middle of the month. Owners in two-team cities, frustrated at having to pay salaries in return for two weeks of player inactivity and sensing the opportunity for some extra ticket sales, staged these mini-championships for city and state titles. A classic case of something that seemed like a good idea at the time, the championships never really captured the fancy of the fans. Interest and attendance almost always ran high in Chicago. Fans in St. Louis generally turned out in good number, but the baseball-going public of Boston, New York, Philadelphia, and Ohio stayed away in droves. The city championships offered a pleasant and harmless diversion for the die-hard baseball fan, but even he wasn't fooled into thinking a championship for the state of Ohio really meant anything. After all, how much significance could you attach to a series between two fifth-place teams?

The city and state championships of the 1800s resembled barnstorming tours more than anything else except in one important respect: the teams that played postseason exhibitions were composed of the same men who played during the regular season because they were still under contract. A minor-leaguer might have joined the club and perhaps here and there was a man who had been signed for the coming season. A player or two may have jumped the club to go home for the winter, but these were not games between travelling all-stars. These clubs were the real McCoy.

The year of the first twentieth century World Series, 1903, offered championships for the cities of Chicago, Philadelphia and St. Louis, and for the state of Ohio. Boston held championships in 1905 and 1907; Philadelphia in 1903 and 1912; and New York in 1910 and 1914. The championships of Ohio were staged in 1903, 1910, 1911, and 1917. St. Louis championships took place from 1903–1907 and again from 1911–1917. But the most successful of all the city games were played in Chicago for the years 1903, 1905, 1909, 1911–1916, 1921–1926, 1928, 1930–1931, 1933, 1936–1937, and 1939–1942. The idea of a city championship had taken root in this great midwestern city even to the extent that the Chicago teams have played more than two dozen exhibition games during the regular season since the last city championship series was held in 1942. They do, indeed, take their baseball seriously in Chicago.

Until 1920, the contests were played purely for the enjoyment of the ballplayers. One gets the feeling from reading newspaper accounts and looking at box scores that the participants treated them almost like "pickup" games. Following the Black Sox scandal, however, teams could no longer play games merely "for exhibition"—they had to play to win, lest anyone raise the ugly specter of crookedness. By 1942, baseball had turned into the business it remains today and a large measure of the fun had gone out of the game. A Clarke Griffith would no longer feel comfortable fooling around on the pitcher's mound for an inning or two. An aging coach, such as Johnny Evers, could no longer go in and play third base for a lark. The stakes were just too high. The ballplayers had become too much like the owners. Baseball was a business, and a big business at that. Baseball fed a man's family year round. It was his career, his livelihood, his job. And people took their jobs seriously.

When the city championships finally passed away in Chicago in 1942, they had become nothing more than a relic of years gone by—a charming reminder of the past.

Summary of the City and State Championships

The St. Louis City Championships

1885: St. Louis Browns defeat St. Louis Maroons; 3–0.
1886: St. Louis Browns defeat St. Louis Maroons; 5–1.
1903: St. Louis Browns defeat St. Louis Cardinals; 5–2.
1904: St. Louis Cardinals vs. St. Louis Browns; 3–3, tie series.
1905: St. Louis Browns defeat St. Louis Cardinals; 4–3.
1906: St. Louis Browns defeat St. Louis Cardinals; 4–1.
1907: St. Louis Cardinals defeat St. Louis Browns; 5–2.
1911: St. Louis Browns defeat St. Louis Cardinals; 4–3.
1912: St. Louis Cardinals defeat St. Louis Browns; 4–3.
1913: St. Louis Cardinals vs. St. Louis Browns; 3–3–2, tie series.
1914: St. Louis Browns defeat St. Louis Cardinals; 4–1.
1915: St. Louis Browns defeat St. Louis Cardinals; 4–1.
1916: St. Louis Browns defeat St. Louis Cardinals; 4–1.
1917: St. Louis Cardinals defeat St. Louis Browns; 4–2.

The Chicago City Championships

1903: Chicago Cubs vs. Chicago White Sox; 7–7, tie series.
1905: Chicago Cubs defeat Chicago White Sox; 4–1.
1909: Chicago Cubs defeat Chicago White Sox; 4–1.
1911: Chicago White Sox defeat Chicago Cubs; 4–0.
1912: Chicago White Sox defeat Chicago Cubs; 4–3.
1913: Chicago White Sox defeat Chicago Cubs; 4–2.
1914: Chicago White Sox defeat Chicago Cubs; 4–3.
1915: Chicago White Sox defeat Chicago Cubs; 4–1.

1916: Chicago White Sox defeat Chicago Cubs; 4-0.
1921: Chicago White Sox defeat Chicago Cubs; 5-0.
1922: Chicago Cubs defeat Chicago White Sox; 4-3.
1923: Chicago White Sox defeat Chicago Cubs; 4-2.
1924: Chicago White Sox defeat Chicago Cubs; 4-2.
1925: Chicago Cubs defeat Chicago White Sox; 4-1.
1926: Chicago White Sox defeat Chicago Cubs; 4-3.
1928: Chicago Cubs defeat Chicago White Sox; 4-3.
1930: Chicago Cubs defeat Chicago White Sox; 4-2.
1931: Chicago White Sox defeat Chicago Cubs; 4-3.
1933: Chicago White Sox defeat Chicago Cubs; 4-0.
1936: Chicago White Sox defeat Chicago Cubs; 4-0.
1937: Chicago White Sox defeat Chicago Cubs; 4-3.
1939: Chicago White Sox defeat Chicago Cubs; 4-3.
1940: Chicago White Sox defeat Chicago Cubs; 4-2.
1941: Chicago White Sox defeat Chicago Cubs; 4-0.
1942: Chicago White Sox defeat Chicago Cubs; 4-2.

The Philadelphia City Championships

1883: Philadelphia Phillies defeat Philadelphia Athletics; 2-1.
1884: Philadelphia Phillies defeat Philadelphia Athletics; 3-0.
1885: Philadelphia Phillies defeat Philadelphia Athletics; 3-2.
1886: Philadelphia Phillies defeat Philadelphia Athletics; 1-0.
1887: Philadelphia Phillies defeat Philadelphia Athletics; 3-2.
1888: Philadelphia Phillies defeat Philadelphia Athletics; 2-1.
1889: Philadelphia Athletics defeat Philadelphia Phillies; 3-2.
1890: Philadelphia Phillies defeat Philadelphia Athletics; 1-0.
1903: Philadelphia Athletics defeat Philadelphia Phillies; 4-3.
1912: Philadelphia Athletics defeat Philadelphia Phillies; 4-1.

The Ohio State Championships

1882: Cleveland Spiders defeat Cincinnati Reds; 2-1.
1883: Cleveland Spiders defeat Cincinnati Reds; 2-0-1.
1889: Columbus Colts defeat Cleveland Spiders; 2-1.
1889: Cincinnati Reds defeat Cleveland Spiders; 3-2.
1889: Columbus Colts defeat Cincinnati Reds; 2-1.
1890: Cincinnati Reds defeat Cleveland Infants; 2-1.
1903: Cleveland Naps defeat Cincinnati Reds; 6-3.
1910: Cincinnati Reds defeat Cleveland Naps; 4-3.
1911: Cincinnati Reds defeat Cleveland Naps; 4-2.
1917: Cincinnati Reds defeat Cleveland Indians; 4-2.

The New York City Championships

1883: New York Metropolitans defeat New York Giants; 2–1.
1884: New York Giants vs. New York Metropolitans; 1–1–1, tie series.
1885: Brooklyn Trolley Dodgers defeat New York Metropolitans; 4–2.
1885: New York Giants defeat New York Metropolitans; 2–1.
1885: New York Giants defeat Brooklyn Trolley Dodgers; 1–0.
1886: New York Giants defeat New York Metropolitans; 3–0.
1886: Brooklyn Trolley Dodgers defeat New York Giants; 3–1.
1910: New York Giants defeat New York Yankees; 4–2.
1914: New York Giants defeat New York Yankees; 4–1.

The Boston City Championships

1905: Boston Pilgrims defeat Boston Beaneaters; 6–1.
1907: Boston Red Sox defeat Boston Doves; 6–0.

The Missouri State Championship

1889: St. Louis Browns defeat Kansas City Blues; 4–3.

The 1882 Ohio State Championship Series

Cleveland Spiders defeat Cincinnati Reds; 2–1

Before going on to play the Chicago White Stockings in the first World Series, the Cincinnati Reds (55–25) played three games with the fifth-place Cleveland Spiders (42–40) for the championship of Ohio. The Reds were led by pitcher Will White (40–12), who had finished first in the American Association in innings pitched (480), winning percentage, shutouts (8), complete games (52), and wins. The Spiders' premier hurler was Jim McCormick (36–29), the National League leader in games pitched (68), complete games (65), innings pitched (596), and victories. These guys were workhorses.

Game One, played in Cincinnati on the 8th of October, was the first interleague game between the National League and the American Association and resulted in the first victory for a National League team over an American Association team. Will White of the Reds went up against George Bradley (7–10) of the Spiders. Bradley had already become a part of history when he pitched the National League's first no-hitter, defeating the Hartford Grays 2–0 on July 15, 1876. Bill Phillips was the offensive star of this game as he tripled home one run and scored two others. The final score was 3–1, Cleveland.

Fans at the second game witnessed the first American Association victory over a National League team as White outpitched Dave Rowe (0–1) and the Spiders by a 5–2 score. Rowe had appeared in only one game for Cincinnati

1882 Ohio State Championship Series

GAME ONE --- October 3

CINCINNATI	AB	R	H	PO	A	E
Sommers, lf	4	0	1	3	0	0
Wheeler, rf	4	0	1	4	1	0
Carpenter, 3b	4	0	1	1	4	0
Snyder, c	4	0	0	7	1	1
Stearns, 1b	4	0	0	7	2	0
Fulmer, ss	3	0	0	1	1	1
McPhee, 2b	3	0	0	2	2	2
Macullar, cf	3	1	2	2	0	1
White, p	3	0	0	0	6	0
	32	1	5	27	17	5

CLEVELAND	AB	R	H	PO	A	E
Dunlap, 2b	4	0	2	4	4	0
Glasscock, ss	4	0	1	3	6	0
Phillips, 1b	4	2	1	14	1	0
Rowe, cf	4	0	0	2	0	0
Muldoon, 3b	4	0	0	0	3	2
Shaffer, rf	4	0	0	1	0	0
Bradley, p	4	0	0	1	2	0
Kelly, c	3	1	2	2	0	0
Tilley, lf	3	0	0	0	0	0
	34	3	6	27	16	2

```
CIN   0 0 1   0 0 0   0 0 0  -  1
CLE   0 0 1   1 0 1   0 0 x  -  3
```

3B: Phillips. LOB: CIN 3, CLE 3. BB: White 1. Struck out: White 3. PB: Snyder, Kelly 2. Umpire: Booth. Time—1:40.

GAME TWO --- October 4

CLEVELAND	AB	R	H	PO	A	E
Dunlap, 2b	4	0	0	3	6	2
Glasscock, ss	4	1	1	1	8	1
Phillips, 1b	4	1	1	14	0	0
Rowe, p-cf	4	0	0	1	2	0
Muldoon, cf-3b	4	0	0	0	1	1
Shaffer, lf	4	0	2	1	0	1
Bradley, 3b-p	4	0	1	1	3	0
Kelly, c	3	0	1	3	1	2
Tilley, lf	3	0	0	0	0	0
	34	2	6	24	21	7

CINCINNATI	AB	R	H	PO	A	E
Sommers, lf	4	1	1	2	0	0
Wheeler, rf	4	1	2	2	0	0
Carpenter, 3b	4	0	1	0	1	0
Snyder, c	4	0	0	5	2	1
Stearns, 1b	4	0	0	9	0	1
Fulmer, ss	4	1	3	2	2	2
McPhee, 2b	4	1	0	6	3	1
Macullar, cf	3	1	1	1	0	0
White, p	3	0	0	0	7	0
	34	5	8	27	15	5

```
CLE   0 0 0   0 0 0   0 0 2  -  2
CIN   1 3 0   0 0 0   0 1 x  -  5
```

2B: Phillips. LOB: CIN 2, CLE 5. BB: Rowe 3. Struck out: Rowe 1. PB: Snyder, Kelly. WP: Rowe 2, Bradley 1. Umpire: R. Crandall. Time—1:50.

GAME THREE --- October 5

CLEVELAND	AB	R	H	PO	A	E
Dunlap, 2b	5	2	3	3	4	0
Glasscock, ss	5	1	1	1	3	0
Phillips, 1b	4	1	2	10	0	0
Rowe, cf	4	0	0	2	0	0
Muldoon, 3b	4	1	1	2	1	0
Shaffer, rf	4	0	1	1	1	0
J. McCormick, p	4	1	1	1	9	0
Briody, c	4	1	0	7	3	1
Bradley, lf	4	1	0	0	0	0
	38	8	9	27	21	1

CINCINNATI	AB	R	H	PO	A	E
Sommers, lf	4	0	0	1	0	0
Wheeler, rf	4	0	0	4	1	0
Carpenter, 3b	3	0	0	2	0	2
Powers, c	3	0	0	3	3	2
Stearns, 1b	3	0	0	9	0	2
Fulmer, ss	3	0	0	1	4	1
McPhee, 2b	3	0	1	4	3	1
Macullar, cf	3	0	0	2	0	2
McCormick, p	3	0	2	1	4	0
	29	0	3	27	15	10

```
CLE   0 0 0   1 0 4   1 0 2  -  8
CIN   0 0 0   0 0 0   0 0 0  -  0
```

Earned runs: CLE 2. 2B: Dunlap. LOB: CIN 1, CLE 3. BB: McCormick 5. Struck out: McCormick 5. PB: Powers 1. WP: McCormick 2. Umpire: Riley. Time—1:40.

in the regular season of 1882, and in that dismal outing he allowed 29 hits, seven walks, and 12 earned runs over nine innings. His wildness hurt him in this game as he walked three Cincinnati batters and made two wild pitches before being replaced by Bradley in the third. None of the runs in the game were earned as the Spiders made seven errors, the Reds five. Cincinnati's Chick Fulmer was the batting star with three singles and a run scored in four times at bat.

The series finale took place on the 5th of October and marked the first shutout in interleague play. Jim McCormick, who pitched three shutouts in the regular season, shut down the Cincinnati offense by allowing three hits, all singles, and five walks. He also struck out five. Harry McCormick (14-11) started for the Reds and pitched credibly through the first five innings before he blew up in the sixth and allowed four Cleveland runners to cross the plate. Insurance runs by the Spiders in the seventh and ninth made the final score 8-0.

The 1883 Philadelphia City Championship

Philadelphia Phillies defeat Philadelphia Athletics; 2-1

There was no championship series between the two league champions of 1883 although the Boston Beaneaters (63-35) of the National League challenged the Philadelphia Athletics to a competition. The Athletics, perhaps somewhat fearful of the Boston club, declined the invitation. Thus it was that the last-place National League Phillies, with an incredibly poor record of 17-81, met the champion Athletics (66-32) in a city championship series which most people though would be no contest. Most people, however, did not include the Philadelphia Phillies.

There were 5,500 people in the stands at the Phillies' Recreation Park on the 3rd of October and everything went according to plan. Before the game, Harry Stovey was presented with a ball and bat, commemorating the past season. John "Cub" Stricker received a watch, and Bob Blakiston and George Bradley were given gold badges. Then the Athletics went out and mauled the Phillies, 13-3. The A's broke on top in the first on a walk and two wild pitches, but the Phillies tied the game in their half of the inning. A double by Fred Corey and a wild throw by left-fielder John Coleman put the A's up by a 2-1 score in the second, but the Phillies went ahead by one in the third on singles by Jack Manning and pitcher William "Blondie" Purcell (2-6), and throwing errors by Ed Rowen and Bradley. The Athletics took the lead for good in the fourth when they scored five times. Four runs in the sixth and a Stovey home run in the seventh capped the scoring for the Americans. The game featured 16 errors, 11 by the Phillies alone, and were it not for the wildness of winning pitcher George Bradley (16-7) and his teammates' poor defense, the Athletics would have won by a shutout. Nonetheless, Bradley wound up with a two-hitter.

1883 Philadelphia City Championship Series

GAME ONE --- October 3

ATHLETICS	AB	R	H	PO	A	E		PHILLIES	AB	R	H	PO	A	E
Birchall, lf	5	2	2	1	0	1		Manning, rf	3	1	1	0	0	0
Stovey, 1b	5	2	1	12	0	0		Purcell, p	3	2	1	0	3	1
Knight, rf	5	1	1	0	0	0		Gross, c	3	0	0	6	3	3
Moynahan, ss	5	1	1	1	2	0		Coleman, lf	3	0	0	0	0	1
Blakiston, cf	5	1	1	1	0	0		Farrar, 1b	3	0	0	8	0	0
Corey, 3b	4	3	2	1	2	0		McClellan, ss	3	0	0	2	2	2
Rowen, c	4	1	1	2	2	2		Mulvey, 3b	3	0	0	0	1	2
Bradley, p	4	1	1	0	2	2		Ferguson, 2b	2	0	0	3	0	2
Stricker, 2b	4	1	1	3	3	0		Harbidge, cf	2	0	0	2	1	0
	41	13	11	21	11	5			25	3	2	21	10	11

```
ATH   1 1 0   5 0 4   2 -  13
PHI   1 0 2   0 0 0   0 -   3
```

Earned runs: ATH 2. 2B: Birchall, Knight, Corey, Rowen. HR: Stovey, LOB: ATH 7, PHI 1. BB: Bradley 3, Purcell 2. Struck out: Purcell 8. WP: Purcell 2, Bradley 1. Umpire: John Kelly. Att: 5,500. Time—2:00.

GAME TWO --- October 8

PHILLIES	AB	R	H	PO	A	E		ATHLETICS	AB	R	H	PO	A	E
Manning, rf	5	2	1	1	0	0		Birchall, lf	4	1	0	3	0	0
Purcell, lf	5	1	2	0	1	0		Stovey, 1b	4	2	1	11	0	0
Gross, c	5	0	0	7	0	0		Knight, rf	4	0	1	0	0	0
Coleman, p	4	2	2	0	11	1		Moynahan, ss	4	1	1	2	2	0
Farrar, 1h	4	1	0	14	0	0		O'Brien, c	4	0	2	6	0	0
Harbidge, cf	4	1	2	1	1	0		Corey, 3b	4	0	0	1	6	1
Warner, 3b	4	0	2	1	0	1		Blakiston, cf	4	0	1	0	0	0
Ferguson, 2b	4	0	0	1	5	2		Bradley, p	4	0	0	1	2	2
Mulvey, ss	4	1	2	2	2	1		Stricker, 2b	4	0	0	3	3	1
	39	8	11	27	20	5			36	4	6	27	13	4

```
PHI   1 0 0   0 0 5   0 2 0 -  8
ATH   2 0 2   0 0 0   0 0 0 -  4
```

Earned runs: PHI 5, ATH 2. 2B: Coleman, O'Brien. 3B: Harbidge. LOB: PHI 4, ATH 5. BB: Bradley 1, Coleman 2. Struck out: Coleman 7, Bradley 5. PB: O'Brien 2. WP: Bradley 1. Umpire: Kelly. Time—1:55.

Things were still proceeding as expected in the early going of Game Two, played on the 8th of October at the Athletics' park, Jefferson Street Grounds. The A's jumped on John Coleman (12–48), National League leader in losses, for four runs over the first three innings, all on RBIs by Jack O'Brien. George Bradley was sailing along with a 4–1 lead and had allowed only one hit through the first five frames, but the Phillies exploded for six hits and five runs in the sixth to take a 6–4 lead. Coleman gave up only one hit over the final six innings and was the winning pitcher. Bradley took the loss.

It was back to Recreation Park for the series finale on the 15th. The Athletics took a brief 1–0 lead in the first inning off John Coleman, but the

1883 Philadelphia City Championship Series

```
GAME THREE --- October 15
```

ATHLETICS	AB	R	H	PO	A	E	PHILLIES	AB	R	H	PO	A	E
Birchall, lf	4	0	0	7	0	0	Manning, rf	4	0	1	1	0	0
Kenzil, cf	4	1	0	0	0	1	Purcell, lf	4	3	1	1	0	0
Knight, rf	4	1	1	1	0	0	Coleman, p	4	1	1	2	8	0
Moynahan, ss	4	1	2	2	5	2	Gross, c	4	1	1	5	2	0
Milligan, c	4	0	1	1	1	1	Harbidge, cf	4	0	1	2	0	1
Blakiston, 1b	4	0	0	10	1	0	Farrar, 1b	4	0	1	14	2	0
Bradley, 3b	4	0	0	0	3	0	Mulvey, ss	4	2	1	1	3	0
Strucker, 2b	3	0	0	3	1	1	Warner, 3b	4	0	2	0	2	1
Mathews, p	3	0	0	0	2	0	Ferguson, 2b	4	1	0	1	2	0
	34	3	4	24	13	5		36	8	9	27	19	2

```
ATH    1  0  0    0  0  0    2  0  0  -  3
PHI    2  1  1    2  0  0    2  0  x  -  8
```

Earned runs: ATH 2, PHI 2. 2B: Moynahan 2, Coleman, Gross, Milligan. LOB: ATH 2, PHI 4. DP: ATH. BB: Mathews 1, Coleman 4. Struck out: Coleman 5. Umpire: William McLean. Att: 1,500. Time—1:45.

Phillies scored in the first four innings against losing pitcher Bobby Mathews (30–13) and had a 6–1 lead by the time the Athletics scored their final two runs of the series in the seventh. Two more insurance runs by the Phils in the bottom of the same inning made the final score 8–3.

From here, the Athletics went on to lose their next six postseason exhibition games against National League competition so perhaps they were correct in being somewhat timid of playing the Boston Beaneaters.

The 1883 Ohio State Championship Series

Cleveland Spiders defeat Cincinnati Reds; 2-0-1

Playing out of tiny Bank Street Grounds, the American Association Cincinnati Reds led the major leagues in home runs in 1883 with the unbelievable total of 35 — the most home runs ever hit by a major-league team to that point in history. All those homers hadn't helped much, however, as the team finished five games off the pace set by the Philadelphia Athletics and in third place. The fourth-place Cleveland Spiders (55–42) had a few pretty fair home run hitters themselves — Fred Dunlap (4), Bill Phillips (2), and Tom York (2) accounted for all of their team's round-trippers. All three games took place at the Bank Street Grounds.

Game One, on the 15th of October, saw the Spiders run away and hide. Will Sawyer (4–10) started for Cleveland in place of Hugh "One Arm" Daily (23–19) who had hurt his hand. Sawyer proved equal to the task and, if not for Warren "Hick" Carpenter and Bid McPhee, the Reds would have had no hits at all. Cincinnati took a 1–0 lead in the first on a single by Carpenter and two passed balls, but the Spiders caught them in the third and seven Cleveland

1883 Ohio State Championship Series

```
GAME ONE --- October 15
```

CINCINNATI	AB	R	H	PO	A	E		CLEVELAND	AB	R	H	PO	A	E
Carpenter, 3b	4	1	3	1	2	0		Dunlap, 2b	4	0	0	3	2	2
Reilly, 1b	4	0	0	11	0	1		Hotaling, cf	4	0	0	1	0	0
Jones, cf	4	0	0	2	0	0		Gerhardt, ss	4	0	1	2	1	0
Weihe, lf	4	0	0	2	1	0		York, lf	4	2	2	3	0	0
Peoples, rf-ss	4	0	0	0	0	0		Phillips, 1b	4	0	0	6	0	0
McPhee, 2b	4	0	2	2	5	2		McCormick, rf	4	1	0	0	0	0
Fulmer, ss	2	0	0	0	1	0		Muldoon, 3b	4	2	2	0	0	0
Macullar, rf	1	0	0	2	1	0		Briody, c	4	2	3	12	1	0
Strauss, c	3	0	0	4	2	1		Sawyer, p	4	1	0	0	2	0
Deagle, p	3	0	0	0	0	0								
	33	1	5	24	12	4			36	8	8	27	6	2

```
CIN    1  0  0    0  0  0    0  0  0  -  1
CLE    0  0  1    1  2  3    1  0  x  -  8
```

Earned runs: CLE 2. 2B: York. 3B: York, Briody. Struck out: Sawyer 9, Deagle 3. PB: Briody 2, Strauss 5. WP. Deagle 2, Sawyer 1. Umpire: George W. Latham of the Louisville Eclipse club. Time—2:10.

runs over the middle four innings made the final score 8–1. Minor-leaguer Joe Strauss caught for the Reds in place of their regular catcher, Charles "Pop" Snyder, and he and losing pitcher Ren Deagle (10–8) were responsible for five passed balls and two wild pitches. In the fifth inning, Cincinnati shortstop Chick Fulmer batted a ball off his face, breaking the bridge of his nose and forcing his retirement from the series. Cincinnati right fielder John "Pop" Corkhill was out with a cold and, all things considered, it was a pretty bad day for the Reds. George "Juice" Latham of the Louisville club was passing through town on his way east, and was imposed upon to umpire the game. Jack Glasscock missed the train from Toledo so Louisville second baseman Joe Gerhardt played shortstop for the Spiders.

Game Two was played the next day and the Spiders were victorious again, although the score was much closer. Pop Snyder was back behind the plate for the Reds but, as it turned out, Joe Strauss couldn't have done much worse. With the Reds leading 4–2 in the seventh, Snyder's passed ball, dropped pop foul, and missed third strike, combined with a Cleveland triple and a single, sent three Spiders across the plate with what proved to be the winning runs. With a little more cautious baserunning, Cleveland might have won the game easily—five of their men were thrown out at the plate. One Arm Daily started for Cleveland and was the winning pitcher. Will White (43–22), who led the league in wins and earned run average (2.09) and tied for the league lead in shutouts (6), started for the Reds and suffered the loss. This game was also notable for the fact that White, Snyder, Glasscock, York, and Daily all hit triples.

The series' finale was played on the 17th and ended in a 3–3 tie. Will Sawyer was back on the mound for the Spiders. The Reds were still searching for a catcher and went with a battery of Phil "Grandmother" Powers and Billy Mountjoy (0–1). (No one nicknamed "Pop" figured in the scoring.) The Reds

1883 Ohio State Championship Series

GAME TWO --- October 16

CINCINNATI	AB	R	H	PO	A	E
Carpenter, 3b	4	1	2	2	3	0
Reilly, 1b	4	2	1	4	1	0
Jones, cf	4	0	0	0	1	1
Weihe, lf	4	0	0	2	0	0
Corkhill, rf	4	0	3	1	2	0
McPhee, 2b	4	0	1	5	2	0
Snyder, c	3	1	2	9	1	3
Peoples, ss	3	0	0	1	1	0
White, p	3	0	1	0	1	1
	33	4	10	24	12	5

CLEVELAND	AB	R	H	PO	A	E
Dunlap, 2b	4	1	1	6	3	0
Hotaling, cf	4	1	1	1	0	0
Glasscock, ss	4	1	2	0	5	0
York, lf	4	1	2	1	0	1
Phillips, 1b	4	0	2	7	1	0
McCormick, rf	4	0	0	0	0	0
Muldoon, 3b	4	0	1	0	0	0
Briody, c	4	0	2	9	2	2
Daily, p	4	1	1	0	2	0
	36	5	12	24	13	3

```
CIN   1 0 2   1 0 0   0 0 -  4
CLE   0 0 0   0 2 0   3 0 -  5
```

2B: Corkhill. 3B: White, Snyder, York, Glasscock, Daily. BB: Daily 3, White 2. WP: White. PB: Briody 1, Snyder 2. Umpire: Joe Gerhardt of the Louisville Eclipse club. Time—2:15.

GAME THREE --- October 17

CINCINNATI	AB	R	H	PO	A	E
Carpenter, 3b	4	1	2	1	0	0
Reilly, 1b	4	0	2	13	1	0
Jones, cf	4	1	2	1	0	0
Weihe, lf	4	0	1	0	0	1
Corkhill, rf	4	0	0	1	1	0
McPhee, 2b	4	0	1	1	1	1
Powers, c	4	1	1	7	1	1
Peoples, ss	3	0	0	0	6	1
Mountjoy, p	3	0	0	0	3	0
	34	3	9	24	13	4

CLEVELAND	AB	R	H	PO	A	E
Dunlap, 2b	4	0	2	2	6	0
Hotaling, cf	4	0	1	2	0	0
Glasscock, ss	4	0	0	0	4	0
York, lf	4	0	0	0	0	0
Phillips, 1b	4	0	2	15	0	0
Muldoon, 3b	4	1	1	1	2	0
Briody, c	3	0	0	4	2	0
McCormick, rf	3	1	1	0	0	0
Sawyer, p	3	1	1	0	1	0
	33	3	8	24	15	0

```
CIN   1 0 0   0 1 0   0 1 -  3
CLE   0 0 0   0 0 0   3 0 -  3
```

Earned runs: CLE 2, CIN 1. 2B: Reilly. 3B: McPhee. BB: Mountjoy 2. Struck out: Sawyer 4, Mountjoy 4. PB: Briody 2, Powers 1. WP: Mountjoy. Umpire: Joe Gerhardt of the Louisville Eclipse club. Time—1:50.

had a 2–0 lead until the Spiders bunched five hits, good for three runs, in the bottom of the seventh to go ahead 3–2. Charlie Jones's RBI single in the eighth tied the score. In the bottom of the ninth, the Spiders had a man on third with one out, Fred Dunlap at the plate, when umpire Joe Gerhardt of the Louisville Eclipse abruptly called the game on account of darkness. Gerhardt had played second for the Reds in 1878–1879 and perhaps personal loyalty to his former teammates was his motivation for taking away what seemed to be a sure victory for the Spiders.

1883 New York City Championship Series

GAME ONE --- October 15

NEW YORK GIANTS	AB	R	H	PO	A	E		METROPOLITANS	AB	R	H	PO	A	E
Ewing, c	4	0	0	2	0	0		Nelson, ss	4	0	1	3	5	0
Connor, 1b	4	0	0	16	0	0		Brady, rf	4	0	0	2	0	0
Ward, ss	4	0	1	2	3	0		Roseman, lf	4	0	0	3	0	0
Gillespie, lf	4	0	1	2	0	0		Esterbrook, 3b	4	0	1	3	0	0
Humphries, cf	4	1	1	0	0	0		Orr, 1b	4	0	0	12	0	0
Dorgan, rf	4	1	1	0	0	0		Holbert, c	4	1	0	6	3	0
Welch, p	4	0	1	1	3	2		Reipschlager, cf	4	2	3	0	0	0
Troy, 2b	4	0	1	3	7	0		Keefe, p	3	0	1	0	4	1
Hankinson, 3b	4	0	0	1	2	1		Crane, 2b	3	0	0	1	2	0
	36	2	6	27	15	3			34	3	6	30	14	1

```
NYG   0  0  0    0  2  0    0  0  0  -  2
MET   0  0  0    0  0  0    2  1  x  -  3
```

Earned runs: NY 2, MET 2. 2B: Reipschlager, Keefe. DP: NY. BB: Keefe 2, Welch 2. Struck out: Keefe 4. WP: Welch. Umpire: Quinn. Time 2:00.

GAME TWO --- October 16

NEW YORK GIANTS	AB	R	H	PO	A	E		METROPOLITANS	AB	R	H	PO	A	E
Ewing, ss	4	0	0	1	1	1		Nelson, ss	4	1	0	2	3	2
Connor, 1b	4	1	1	17	1	0		Brady, rf	4	1	2	3	1	0
Ward, p	4	2	3	2	4	0		Roseman, lf	4	0	0	0	0	0
Gillespie, lf	4	0	3	0	0	0		Esterbrook, 3b	4	0	1	0	0	0
Welch, cf	4	0	1	1	0	1		Orr, 1b	4	0	0	8	1	3
Dorgan, rf	4	0	1	0	0	0		Pierce, cf	4	1	0	1	0	0
Tracy, 2b	4	0	0	1	3	0		Reipschlager, c	4	0	1	10	1	1
Hankinson, 3b	4	0	0	0	4	0		Lynch, p	3	0	1	0	2	1
Humphries, c	3	0	0	3	2	1		Crane, 2b	3	0	0	3	3	0
	35	3	9	25	15	3			34	3	5	27	11	7

```
NYG   0  0  0    1  0  1    0  1  0  -  3
MET   1  0  0    0  0  1    0  0  1  -  3
```

Earned runs: NY 1. LOB: NY 6, MET 6. 2B: Esterbrook. 3B: Brady. DP: MET 3. BB: Lynch 1, Ward 1. Struck out: Lynch 7, Ward 4. PB: Humphries 3. Umpire: Buck Becannon. Time – 2:10.

The 1883 New York City Championship Series

New York Metropolitans defeat New York Giants; 2–1–1

The sixth-place New York Giants (46–50) met the fourth-place and more popular New York Metropolitans (54–42) at the Polo Grounds for a three-game series to decide the championship of New York City.

The opening game of the series, on the 15th of October, featured Mickey Welch (27–21) of the Giants against Tim Keefe (41–27) of the Metropolitans. Keefe led the American Association in strikeouts (361), innings pitched (619), and games pitched (68), finishing second in victories to Will White's 43. Both pitchers threw six-hitters, and the score was knotted at two all when Mets catcher Bill Holbert came to the plate to take his cuts leading off the ninth.

1883 New York City Championship Series

```
1883 NEW YORK CITY CHAMPIONSHIP SERIES (cont'd)
----------------------------------------
```

```
GAME THREE --- October 17
```

NEW YORK GIANTS	R	H	PO	A	E		METROPOLITANS	R	H	PO	A	E
Ewing, ss	0	2	6	0	2		Nelson, ss	2	2	4	1	0
Connor, 1b	2	1	8	1	1		Brady, rf	1	0	0	0	0
Ward, ss	0	1	0	3	0		Roseman, lf	1	2	0	0	0
Gillespie, lf	0	1	2	0	0		Esterbrook, 3b	1	1	3	1	2
O'Neill, cf	0	1	0	0	0		Orr, 1b	1	2	9	1	0
Dorgan, rf	1	2	1	0	0		Pierce, cf	1	0	0	0	0
Welch, p	1	0	1	0	6		Reipschlager, c	0	1	4	7	0
Troy, 2b	0	1	2	3	0		Keefe, p	1	1	1	1	2
Hankinson, 3b	1	0	1	2	0		Crane, 2b	2	2	3	2	0
	5	9	21	9	9			10	11	24	13	4

```
NY    1  0  0     0  0  1     3  0  -   5
MET   3  3  0     0  3  0     0  1  -  10
```

Earned runs: MET 2. LOB: NY 4, MET 6. DP: NY 2. BB: Welch 5, Keefe 2. Struck out: Keefe 3, Welch 2. WP: Keefe 2. PB: Reipschlager 2. 2B: Esterbrook, Roseman, Orr, Dorgan. Umpire: Quinn. Time—2:00.

```
GAME FOUR --- October 18
```

NEW YORK GIANTS	R	H	PO	A	E		METROPOLITANS	R	H	PO	A	E
O'Neill, cf	4	3	1	0	0		Nelson, ss	1	1	4	1	2
Connor, 1b	3	3	11	2	0		Brady, rf	1	1	2	0	0
Ward, p	3	1	2	2	0		Roseman, lf	1	2	2	0	0
Jones, ss	1	0	3	2	0		Esterbrook, 3b	0	1	2	3	1
Pierce, lf	1	0	1	1	1		Orr, 1b-p	0	2	3	2	0
Dorgan,, rf	1	3	2	1	0		Holbert, c	0	0	4	2	1
Troy, 2b	0	2	2	4	0		Reipschlager, cf	0	0	4	1	1
Hankinson, 3b	1	1	1	2	2		Lynch, p-1b	0	1	6	0	3
Humphries, c	1	2	4	1	0		Crane, 2b	0	1	0	4	2
	15	15	27	15	3			3	9	27	13	10

```
NY    6  3  3     0  2  0     1  0  0  -  15
MET   0  0  0     2  1  0     0  0  0  -   3
```

Earned runs: NY 4, MET 1. LOB: NY 5, MET 3. DP: MET 1, NY 1. Struck out: Lynch 3, Ward 1. 2B: Connor, Hankinson. 3B: Nelson, Brady, Ward, Roseman. WP: Ward 2, Orr 1. Umpire: Quinn. Time—1:40.

Holbert reached on an error and scored a moment later on rookie Charlie Reipschlager's double. Welch took the loss, Keefe the win.

The game of the 16th was called because of darkness at the end of nine innings with the scored tied 3–3. The details, however, make quite a story. The starting pitchers were Jack Lynch (13–15) for the Mets and John Montgomery Ward (12–14) for the Giants. Ward had pitched the second perfect game in National League history when he shut down the Buffalo Bisons by a 5–0 score on June 17, 1880. In this game, John Humphries was the catcher for the first seven innings, but was injured in the eighth and Buck Ewing took his place. With the Giants leading 3–2, Ewing refused to take the field in the bottom of the ninth, claiming it was too dark to play. John Clapp, captain of the New York team, ordered him to take his position. Ewing complied but, fearful of Monte Ward's delivery, stood a full 50 feet behind the batters. One out later, Pierce on second, Sam Crane struck out but the ball eluded Ewing and Pierce came in to score the tying run.

The Giants played rather indifferently in the third game of the series on the 17th of October. After watching the Nationals take a 1–0 lead, the Mets struck for three-run innings in the first, second and fifth to mount a 9–1 lead. The Giants scored a run in the seventh and three in the eighth, but the rally fell short as the Mets won the game easily, 10–5. Mickey Welch took the loss, his second of the series, and Tim Keefe won for the second time.

The series concluded the next day with a wretched game on the part of the Metropolitans. The Mets made 10 errors in the field and starting pitcher Jack Lynch was hit so freely that manager Jim Mutrie ceded the game and replaced Lynch with first baseman Dave Orr. Orr hadn't pitched at all during the regular season and gave up the final three New York runs in six innings pitched. The Giants broke on top with six runs in the first, scored three more in the second, three more in the third, and had a 12–0 lead by the time the Mets tallied their first runs in the fourth. The final score was 15–3, with Monte Ward the easy winner.

The 1884 Philadelphia City Championship Series

Philadelphia Phillies defeat Philadelphia Athletics; 3–0

The sixth-place National League Phillies, with a record of 39–73, did not plan on winning many games in the 1884 championship series from their cross-town rivals, the Philadelphia Athletics. The Athletics had finished a respectable seventh — respectable only in the bloated 13-team American Association of 1884 — and were led by pitchers Bobby Mathews (30–18) and Billy Taylor. Taylor compiled a 25–4 record with the St. Louis Maroons of the Union Association before finishing out the year and going 18–12 for Philadelphia.

The series opened at Jefferson Street Grounds, home of the Athletics, on the 14th of October and the Phillies surprised the A's with a 6–4 victory. Billy Taylor started against rookie Con Murphy (0–3). Murphy would not pitch again in the major leagues until 1890, and this game supplied ample evidence why. The Phillies scored the first run of the series in the third on a wild throw by Jack Taylor and a single by Tony Cusick. In the fourth, a single by Sid Farrar, an error by John Coleman, and a single by Jim Fogarty made the score 2–0, Phillies. The A's cut the lead in half in the sixth on a triple by Henry Larkin and an infield groundout, but the Phillies blew the game wide open in the sixth. An error by Fred Corey, singles by Ed Andrews, Joe Mulvey, and Murphy, and a passed ball by O'Brien put the Phillies ahead 6–1. The A's scored twice in the seventh and put on a strong rally in the ninth. Lon Knight doubled, Coleman and Jack O'Brien singled, but Murphy retired Taylor, Larkin — who already had two triples — and Cub Stricker to end the game.

1884 Philadelphia City Championship Series

```
GAME ONE --- October 14
```

ATHLETICS	AB	R	H	PO	A	E		PHILADELPHIA	AB	R	H	PO	A	E
Stovey, 1b	4	0	1	13	0	0		Manning, rf	4	0	1	0	0	0
Corey, 3b	3	0	0	1	1	1		McClellan, ss	4	0	2	1	2	0
Houck, ss	3	0	0	1	4	1		Lynch, lf	4	1	1	1	0	0
Knight, rf	3	1	1	1	0	0		Andrews, 2b	4	1	1	3	4	0
Coleman, cf	4	1	1	0	0	1		Farrar, 1b	4	2	1	9	1	0
O'Brien, c	4	1	1	3	6	0		Mulvey, 3b	4	0	1	3	1	0
Taylor, p	4	0	1	0	1	1		Fogarty, cf	3	1	1	0	0	1
Larkin, lf	4	1	2	0	0	0		Murphy, p	3	1	1	2	4	1
Stricker, 2b	4	0	0	5	6	1		Cusick, c	3	0	1	8	1	0
	33	4	7	24	18	5			33	6	10	27	13	2

```
ATH    0  0  0    0  0  1    2  0  1  -  4
PHI    0  0  1    1  0  4    0  0  x  -  6
```

Earned runs: ATH 2. 2B: Knight, Manning. 3B: Larkin 2. BB: Murphy 2. Struck out: Murphy 2, Taylor 3. WP: Murphy. PB: O'Brien, Cusick. LOB: ATH 5, PHI 3. Umpire: Cushman. Time—1:55.

At Recreation Park on the 16th, the Phillies prevailed once again after another hard-fought battle. Billy Taylor started for the Athletics but was gone after the Phillies raked his deliveries for three runs in the second. He managed to walk six men in his brief stint. Fred Corey relieved and pitched two innings, generously giving five runs to the Phillies, and was in turn relieved by Cub Stricker who went the rest of the way and allowed four more runs. One wonders if the hearts of the Athletics were really in this game. The Americans batted Con Murphy around freely for the second day in a row, but could muster no better than a 4–4 tie at the end of three. They were outscored by a margin of 8–5 over the final four innings of play before the game was called because of darkness. The Phillies made nine errors in the game, the Athletics 11. The Nationals' battery was responsible for four passed balls and three wild pitches; the A's, three passed balls and a wild pitch—altogether not the most professional example of baseball ever seen.

The series' finale was played on the 18th of October and was a benefit game for the Athletics' players. Given the caliber of their recent play, it was hardly surprising that only 350 people turned up for the game. The A's—not the fans—got their money's worth as the Phillies trounced them 13–5. Athletics' manager Bill Sharsig seemed to have lost his mind during the game, moving players around like checkers. Bobby Mathews started on the mound for the A's and was relieved by Cub Stricker in the second inning after giving up seven runs. Stricker was considerably more composed than Mathews and allowed a mere six runs of his own over the final four innings. The Phillies led 11–0 before the Athletics were able to score five runs in the fifth. Two more runs by the Nationals in the sixth made the score 13–5. The two teams took their places for the seventh, but the Phillies hit Stricker so hard that umpire Joe Simmons called the game before the half-inning could be concluded. The fans began leaving the park after the Phillies took their cuts in the first and most were gone by the end of the second inning. Rookie Charlie Ferguson (21–25) was the easy victor.

1884 Philadelphia City Championship Series

GAME TWO --- October 16

PHILADELPHIA	AB	R	H	PO	A	E		ATHLETIC	AB	R	H	PO	A	E
Clements, rf	4	2	0	1	0	3		Stovey, 1b	4	2	1	11	0	0
Fogarty, cf	3	1	2	2	0	1		Corey, 3b-p-2b	4	2	1	0	4	4
McClellan, ss	4	0	3	0	2	2		Houck, ss	3	2	2	0	2	1
Lynch, lf	3	0	0	0	0	0		Birchall, lf	4	0	0	1	0	0
Andrews, 2b	3	1	1	3	0	0		Coleman, cf	4	0	1	2	0	1
Farrar, 1b	3	2	2	12	0	0		O'Brien, c	3	0	1	4	1	1
Mulvey, 3b	4	3	1	1	3	0		Larkin, rf	4	0	0	1	0	0
Murphy, p	4	1	0	0	2	2		Stricker, 2b-p	3	1	1	1	2	0
Cusick, c	3	2	0	2	2	1		Taylor, p-3b	3	1	0	1	2	4
	31	12	9	21	9	9			32	8	7	21	11	11

```
PHI   0 3 1   4 4 0   0 - 12
ATH   2 0 2   2 0 2   1 -  9
```

Earned runs: PHI 1, ATH 1. 2B: Farrar, O'Brien, Stricker. 3B: Fogarty, Houck. HR: Stovey. BB: Taylor 6, Murphy 2. Struck out: Taylor 2, Murphy 2. LOB: PHI 7, ATH 4. DP: PHI. PB: Cusick 4, O'Brien 3. WP: Murphy 3, Taylor 1. Umpire: Curry. Time—1:50.

GAME THREE --- October 18

PHILADELPHIA	AB	R	H	PO	A	E		ATHLETICS	AB	R	H	PO	A	E
Manning, rf	4	2	3	2	0	0		O'Brien, 1b-ss-c	3	0	0	4	3	1
Purcell, lf	4	2	3	3	0	0		Birchall, 3b	3	0	0	0	1	2
McClellan, ss	4	0	1	0	0	0		Stricker, ss-p	3	0	0	0	2	0
Lynch, cf	3	0	0	1	0	0		Larkin, rf-1b	3	1	0	10	0	0
Ferguson, p	4	1	1	1	1	0		Coleman, 2b	3	1	1	0	5	0
Andrews, 2b	4	2	2	0	2	0		Milligan, c-ss	3	1	1	3	2	1
Farrar, 1b	3	2	1	4	0	0		Parker, lf	1	1	0	1	0	0
Mulvey, 3b	4	2	1	0	1	1		Ringo, cf	2	1	1	0	0	3
Cusick, c	3	2	1	7	0	2		Mathews, p-rf	2	0	1	0	0	0
	33	13	13	18	4	3			23	5	4	18	13	7

```
PHI   2 5 2   0 2 2 - 13
ATH   0 0 0   0 5 0 -  5
```

Earned runs: PHI 7, ATH 2. 2B; Manning 2, Farrar, Mulvey. HR: Purcell. HBP: Farrar. LOB: PHI 4, ATH 1. BB: Ferguson 1, Mathews 1. Struck out: McClellan, Ferguson, O'Brien, Coleman 2, Milligan, Parker, Ringo. WP: Stricker 4. PB: Cusick 2, Milligan 2. Umpire: Joseph Simmons. Att: 350. Time—1:20.

The 1884 New York City Championship Series

New York Giants vs. New York Metropolitans; 1-1-1, tie series

The year 1884 wasn't particularly a good one for city championships. The fifth-place National League New York Giants (62–50) and the American Association champion New York Metropolitans (75–32) met in what amounted to a tune-up for the Mets' games against the Providence Grays. The Giants were without the services of Frank Hankinson, Mike Dorgan, and Ed Caskin. Jack Remsen of the Brooklyn team filled in at center.

Game One saw the two aces of the staff go at each other—Tim Keefe

1884 New York City Championship Series

GAME ONE --- October 16

NEW YORK	AB	R	H	PO	A	E		METROPOLITANS	AB	R	H	PO	A	E
Ewing, c	3	1	0	4	2	1		Nelson, ss	3	0	0	1	4	0
Ward, 2b	3	0	0	0	0	0		Brady, rf	3	1	1	2	0	0
Connor, 3b	3	0	1	3	2	1		Esterbrook, 3b	3	1	1	1	0	0
Gillespie, lf	2	1	0	2	0	0		Roseman, cf	3	1	1	2	0	2
McKinnon, 1b	2	1	1	5	0	0		Orr, 1b	2	1	0	8	0	0
Richardson, ss	2	0	1	0	3	0		Troy, 2b	2	0	1	0	4	1
Griffin, rf	2	1	1	1	0	0		Holbert, c	2	0	0	1	2	0
Remsen, cf	2	1	0	0	0	1		Reipschlager, lf	2	1	0	0	0	0
Welch, p	2	0	1	0	1	0		Keefe, p	2	0	0	0	0	0
	21	5	5	15	8	3			22	5	5	15	10	3

```
NY    0  4  0    0  1  -  5
MET   4  0  0    1  0  -  5
```

Earned runs: NY 1. LOB: NY 1, MET 2. 2B: Reipschlager. 3B: Connor. HR: McKinnon. BB: Welch 1, Keefe 2. Struck out: Keefe 1, Welch 4. WP: Keefe 1, Welch 1. PB: Ewing. Umpire: Quinn. Time—1:15.

GAME TWO --- October 17

NEW YORK	AB	R	H	PO	A	E		METROPOLITANS	AB	R	H	PO	A	E
Ward, 2b	3	0	0	3	3	0		Reipschlager, lf	4	0	0	1	3	2
Connor, 3b	3	2	2	1	2	1		Brady, rf	3	2	1	0	0	0
Gillespie, lf	3	1	2	0	0	0		Esterbrook, 3b	3	3	3	2	4	0
Dorgan, rf	3	0	0	0	0	0		Roseman, cf	3	2	2	1	1	0
McKinnon, 1b	3	1	2	8	0	0		Orr, 1b	3	1	2	10	1	0
Begley, p	3	1	0	1	1	0		Troy, 2b	3	0	1	1	3	1
Richardson, cf	3	1	0	0	0	0		Murphy, c	3	0	0	2	0	3
Caskins, ss	3	1	0	1	2	0		Kennedy, lf	3	1	1	0	0	0
Humphries, c	2	1	2	4	2	1		Becannon, p	3	0	0	1	1	0
	26	8	8	18	10	2			28	9	10	18	13	6

```
NY    1  0  2    3  0  2  -  8
MET   4  0  2    0  2  1  -  9
```

Earned runs: NY 3, MET 2. LOB: NY 5, MET 2. 2B: Esterbrook 3. 3B: Roseman, Gillespie. HR: McKinnon. BB: Begley 1, Becannon 2. Struck out: Becannon 2, Begley 3. WP: Begley. PB: Humphries 1, Murphy 3. Umpire: Connolly. Time—1:45.

(41–27) of the Mets and Mickey Welch (39–21) of the Giants. Both pitchers threw five-hitters, both pitchers gave up five runs. The Mets jumped on Welch for four runs in their half of the first, but the Giants came right back with four off Keefe in their half of the second. This pattern was repeated a few innings later when the Mets scored once in the fourth and the Giants tied the game in the top of the fifth. At the end of five, the umpire called the game on account of darkness.

Indifferent playing in the series became the rule and not the exception in Game Two, played the next day. The Mets scored four times in the first to take a 4–1 lead, took a 6–3 lead at the end of three only to see the Giants tie the game with three runs in the fourth. The game was tied at 8 as the Mets came to the plate in the bottom of the sixth. Ed Kennedy singled, stole second, and came

1884 New York City Championship Series

```
GAME THREE --- October 18
```

NEW YORK	AB	R	H	PO	A	E		METROPOLITANS	AB	R	H	PO	A	E
Ewing, c	3	1	0	2	2	0		Nelson, ss	3	1	1	1	1	0
Ward, 2b	3	1	1	0	1	0		Brady, rf	3	1	1	1	0	1
Connor, 3b	3	1	1	2	0	1		Esterbrook, 3b	3	0	1	0	1	0
Gillespie, lf	3	2	0	1	0	0		Roseman, cf	3	2	0	1	0	1
Dorgan, rf	3	1	1	1	0	0		Orr, 1b	3	2	2	7	0	0
McKinnon, 1b	3	1	2	6	0	1		Troy, 2b	3	1	1	2	3	2
Richardson, cf	3	2	1	3	1	0		Holbert, c	2	0	0	3	1	3
Welch, p	2	0	1	0	0	0		Kennedy, lf	2	0	0	0	0	2
Caskins, ss	2	0	0	0	2	1		Keefe, p	2	0	1	0	1	2
	25	9	7	15	6	3			24	7	7	15	7	11

```
NY      1  2  2     1  3  -  9
MET     1  1  2     0  3  -  7
```

Earned runs: NY 2, MET 2. LOB: NY 3, MET 4. 2B: Orr, Troy, Richardson. 3B: McKinnon, Brady. BB: Welch 2. Struck out: Keefe 3, Welch 2. PB: Holbert 4. WP: Welch 1, Keefe 2. Umpire: Quinn. Time—1:30.

around to score the winning run on Steve Brady's single. At this point, Umpire Connolly called the game because of darkness. Rookie Buck Becannon (1–0) was the winning pitcher. Rookie Ed Begley (12–18) took the loss.

The final game was as silly as the first two. In just six innings, the Mets managed to make 11 errors and gave the Giants seven unearned runs. The Giants scored in every inning and were generous giving out unearned runs as well, though not as generous as the Mets. The final score was 9–7 with Welch the winning pitcher and Keefe the loser.

This game, like the two which went before, was also called because of darkness. In the three contests, the two teams had played a total of 16 innings. One can only speculate why the games were not scheduled for an earlier hour.

The 1885 St. Louis City Championship Series

St. Louis Browns defeat St. Louis Maroons; 3–0

The American Association champion St. Louis Browns (79–33) played the first game of the 1885 city championship against the last-place National League St. Louis Maroons (36–72) between games four and five of the World Series. The city championship resumed immediately following Game Seven between the Chicago White Stockings and the Browns. The Maroons had a terrific defensive infield with Alex McKinnon at first, Fred Dunlap at second, and Jack Glasscock at short, all leading the league at their respective positions in fielding percentage. Ed Caskin finished fourth in defense at third base, but only .009 off the leader's pace. The Maroons disbanded as a League team two days before the series started and reorganized as an independent nine so that they could circumvent the National League rule against Sunday games.

1885 St. Louis City Championship Series

```
GAME ONE --- October 19

BROWNS                 R  H PO  A  E     MAROONS             R  H PO  A  E
-------------------------------------    ---------------------------------
W. Gleason, ss         1  2  1  5  0     McKinnon, 1b        0  1 11  0  2
Welch, cf              1  0  0  1  0     Glasscock, 2b       1  1  1  2  0
Barkley, 2b            1  1  1  3  1     Rowe, cf            0  1  5  0  1
Comiskey, 1b           1  1 16  0  0     Gleason, 3b         0  0  0  3  2
Robinson, rf           0  0  3  0  0     Seery, lf           1  1  2  0  0
O'Neill, lf            0  0  3  0  0     Sweeney, p          0  0  1  8  0
Latham, 3b             1  0  0  1  0     Quinn, ss           0  0  1  2  0
Caruthers, p           0  0  0  3  0     Briody, c           0  0  4  0  3
Bushong, c             0  2  3  1  0     Dolan, rf           0  0  2  0  0
                      --------------                        --------------
                       5  6 27 14  1                        2  4 27 15  8

BRN    4  0  0    1  0  0    0  0  0  -  5
MAR    0  0  0    1  0  0    0  0  1  -  2
```

Earned runs: BRN 1, MAR 1. HR: Seery. LOB: BRN 5, MAR 4. BB: Sweeney 1. Struck out: Caruthers 2, Sweeney 3. PB: Bushong 1, Briody 1. WP: Sweeney. Umpire: Ed Cuthbert. Att: 10,000. Time—1:45.

```
GAME TWO --- October 25

MAROONS            AB  R  H PO  A  E     BROWNS             AB  R  H PO  A  E
-------------------------------------    ----------------------------------
Sweeney, lf         4  0  0  4  0  0     W. Gleason, ss      3  1  0  1  2  1
Glasscock, ss       4  0  0  0  2  1     Welch, cf           4  1  1  4  0  0
McKinnon, 1b        4  0  1 10  0  2     Barkley, 2b         4  1  0  2  1  1
Gleason, 3b         4  0  1  2  1  1     Comiskey, 1b        4  1  2  9  0  0
Quinn, 2b           4  0  1  2  2  0     O'Neill, lf         4  0  2  1  0  0
Seery, rf           3  0  0  0  0  1     Latham, 3b          4  1  0  2  2  0
Rowe, cf            4  0  0  1  0  0     Caruthers, p        3  0  1  1  7  2
Dolan, c            3  0  0  5  3  3     Nicol, rf           2  1  0  1  1  0
Boyle, p            3  0  1  0  8  3     Bushong, c          3  0  0  6  0  1
                   -----------------                        ----------------
                   33  0  4 24 16 11                        31  6  6 27 13  5

MAR    0  0  0    0  0  0    0  0  0  -  0
BRN    2  0  0    0  1  3    0  0  x  -  6
```

3B: Caruthers. LOB: MAR 7, BRN 3. BB: Caruthers 1, Boyle 3. Struck out: Caruthers 4, Boyle 5. PB: Dolan. WP: Caruthers 1, Boyle 1. Umpire: McSorley. Att: 10,000. Time—1:55.

The first game, played on Sunday the 19th of October at Sportsman's Park, saw the Browns jump on top with four runs in the first inning. Before many of the 10,000 fans had even taken their seats, Bill Gleason singled and stole second. Curt Welch was hit by a pitch and Sam Barkley drove in the first run of the day with a double. Charlie Comiskey's single brought home Welch and Barkley to make the score 3–0 and Comiskey scored when Yank Robinson grounded out. The Browns rang the bell again in the fourth when Arlie Latham singled, stole second and third, and scored on Doc Bushong's grounder. The Maroons scored a singleton in the fourth and their final run came on an Emmett Seery solo home run in the ninth. Bob Caruthers (40–13), the league leader in victories, was the easy winner. Charlie Sweeney (11–21) took the loss for the Maroons.

1885 St. Louis City Championship Series

```
GAME THREE --- October 27
```

BROWNS	AB	R	H	PO	A	E	MAROONS	AB	R	H	PO	A	E
W. Gleason, ss	4	3	2	1	3	0	Glasscock, ss	4	1	1	2	4	0
Welch, cf	3	2	1	2	0	1	McKinnon, 1b	4	0	0	12	0	0
Barkley, 2b	5	2	3	4	1	0	Sweeney, rf	3	0	0	1	0	0
Comiskey, 1b	5	2	2	11	1	1	Seery, lf	4	0	0	3	0	1
O'Neill, lf	5	1	1	1	0	1	Gleason, 3b	4	0	1	1	8	0
Latham, 3b	5	0	2	2	4	0	Quinn, 2b	3	0	0	0	4	2
Foutz, p	5	0	1	0	5	0	Rowe, cf	3	0	1	5	0	0
Nicol, rf	3	0	0	2	0	0	Dolan, c	3	0	0	3	1	3
Bushong, c	4	1	0	4	1	0	Kirby, p	3	0	0	0	2	0
	39	11	12	27	15	3		31	1	3	27	19	6

```
BRN    4  0  1    4  0  0    2  0  0  -  11
MAR    1  0  0    0  0  0    0  0  0  -   1
```

Earned runs: Browns 5. 2B: Latham 2, Barkley, O'Neill, Rowe, J. Gleason, Glasscock. LOB: BRN 7, MAR 5. BB: Foutz 2, Kirby 5. Struck out: Foutz 3, Kirby 2. DP: MAR. PB: Bushong 1, Dolan 1. WP: Foutz 1, Kirby 2. Umpire: Charles Krehmyer. Time—1:40.

Caruthers started the second game of the city series against Henry Boyle (16–24). Attendance was again excellent as 10,000 fans jammed Union Park only to be disappointed when Caruthers four-hit the home team and won by a score of 6–0. The game was delayed for 20 minutes until a suitable umpire, Dick McSorley, was chosen by Browns' manager Charlie Comiskey. The Browns again struck in the first inning, this time for two runs. Gleason walked, stole second, went to third on Welch's infield single and scored on a throwing error. Another wild throw sent Welch home. The Maroons were held hitless by Caruthers until the fourth inning when McKinnon singled. The Browns scored a single run in the fourth and three more in the fifth to win handily. Maroons' manager Henry Lucas said after the game, "Well, you can count me out of the baseball business. This game has sickened me." Lucas was a man of his word for, after the series ended, he never managed another major-league game.

The final game of the series, played on the 27th of October, was a blowout for the Browns as they pummelled the Maroons by a score of 11–1. In the first, Gleason started things off again by lining a single and advancing to third when center-fielder Dave Rowe's throw back to the infield went wild. Welch walked and stole second and Barkley's double scored both men. But the Browns weren't through with losing pitcher John Kirby (5–8) yet. Comiskey singled Barkley to third, then stole second. O'Neill's sacrifice fly scored Barkley and Comiskey went to third on the throw home. When catcher Tom Dolan's throw to third went wild, Comiskey trotted home with the fourth run of the inning. The Maroons made their only run of the game in the bottom of the inning when Jack Glasscock doubled, went to third on a wild pitch, and scored on a passed ball. Four runs by the Browns in the fourth and two more in the seventh only solidified the future plans of Mr. Lucas. Dave Foutz (33–14) started for the Browns and held the Maroons to three hits and two walks in recording the victory.

1885 Philadelphia City Championship Series

GAME ONE --- October 15

ATHLETICS	AB	R	H	PO	A	E		PHILLIES	AB	R	H	PO	A	E
Stovey, 1b	4	2	0	8	0	0		Manning, rf	4	1	0	1	0	1
Larkin, lf	5	2	2	1	0	0		Andrews, lf	4	1	1	3	0	1
Coleman, rf	4	1	0	2	0	0		Mulvey, 3b	4	0	0	1	1	0
Shaffer, cf	4	1	1	1	1	0		Farrar, 1b	4	0	1	8	0	1
O'Brien, 3b	3	0	1	0	1	1		Daily, p	4	0	1	0	1	0
Corey, ss	4	0	0	1	1	0		Fogarty, cf	3	0	0	0	0	0
Milligan, c	4	0	1	13	3	3		Myers, 2b	3	0	1	1	1	1
Stricker, 2b	4	0	0	1	1	0		Bastian, ss	3	0	0	1	4	1
Mathews, p	4	1	1	0	1	0		Clements, c	3	0	1	12	1	0
	36	7	6	27	8	4			32	2	5	27	8	5

```
ATH   2  0  0    0  5  0    0  0  0  -  7
PHI   2  0  0    0  0  0    0  0  0  -  2
```

Earned runs: ATH 2, PHI 1. 2B: Larkin, Andrews. 3B: O'Brien. BB: Daily 2. Struck out: Daily 7, Mathews 13. DP: PHI 2. PB: Clements 1. WP: Daily 1. Balk: Daily. Umpire: Fulmer. Time—1:55.

GAME TWO --- October 16

PHILLIES	AB	R	H	PO	A	E		ATHLETICS	AB	R	H	PO	A	E
Manning, rf	4	3	2	2	0	0		Stovey, 1b	4	0	0	10	0	2
Andrews, lf	5	2	1	2	0	0		Larkin, lf	3	1	1	0	0	0
Ferguson, p	3	3	1	0	9	0		Coleman, rf	3	0	0	0	0	0
Mulvey, 3b	5	2	4	0	0	0		Shaffer, cf	3	0	1	1	0	0
Farrar, 1b	4	1	0	5	0	0		O'Brien, 3b	3	1	2	2	0	1
Fogarty, cf	3	1	0	1	0	0		Corey, ss	3	0	0	1	2	1
Myers, 2b	3	2	1	1	3	0		Milligan, c	3	0	2	4	4	5
Bastian, ss	2	2	0	2	2	0		Stricker, 2b	3	0	0	3	3	1
Clements, c	4	1	1	8	1	1		Knouff, p	1	0	0	0	0	3
								Hughes, p	2	0	0	0	7	8
	33	17	10	21	15	1			28	2	6	21	16	21

```
PHI   2  5  0    0  3  1    6  -  17
ATH   0  1  0    0  0  1    0  -   2
```

Earned runs: PHI 4, ATH 1. 2B: Mulvey. 3B: Mulvey. HR: O'Brien. BB: Manning, Ferguson 2, Farrar, Fogarty, Myers, Bastian 2. Struck out: Manning, Fogarty, Bastian, Clements, Stovey, Coleman 2, Shaffer, Corey, Stricker 2, Hughes. LOB: PHI 4, ATH 5. DP: ATH. PB: Milligan 3. WP: Hughes 3. Umpire: Fulmer. Time—2:00.

The 1885 Philadelphia City Championship Series

Philadelphia Phillies defeat Philadelphia Athletics; 3–2

The third-place National League Philadelphia Phillies (56–54) met the fourth-place Philadelphia Athletics (55–57) in the 1885 Philadelphia city championship series. The A's were a hard-hitting team which led the league in runs scored, doubles, home runs, batting average, and slugging average, and were the favorites to win the series.

The series opened on the 15th of October at Jefferson Street Grounds and

1885 Philadelphia City Championship Series

```
GAME THREE --- October 17
```

ATHLETICS	AB	R	H	PO	A	E
Stovey, 1b	4	2	2	11	0	0
Larkin, lf	3	1	2	0	0	0
Coleman, rf	4	1	2	1	0	0
Shaffer, cf	4	0	2	2	0	1
O'Brien, 3b	3	1	0	0	1	1
Corey, ss	4	0	1	1	9	0
Milligan, c	4	0	0	8	2	0
Stricker, 2b	3	1	0	4	1	1
Mathews, p	4	1	1	0	2	0
	33	7	10	27	15	3

PHILLIES	AB	R	H	PO	A	E
Manning, rf	4	0	0	3	1	1
Andrews, lf	4	0	0	2	0	1
Mulvey, 3b	4	0	0	2	0	1
Farrar, 1b	4	1	3	7	0	0
Daily, p	4	0	0	1	0	0
Fogarty, cf	3	0	0	1	0	1
Myers, 2b	3	0	1	4	3	0
Bastian, ss	3	0	0	2	5	1
Clements, c	3	0	0	5	3	0
	32	1	4	27	12	5

```
ATH    3  0  0     0  0  1     3  0  0  -  7
PHI    0  0  0     1  0  0     0  0  0  -  1
```

Earned runs: ATH 4. 2B: Stovey, Farrar. BB: Daily 3. Struck out: Daily 4, Mathews 6. DP: PHI 3. PB: Milligan 2, Clements 2. LOB: ATH 3, PHI 4. Umpire. Carlin. Time—1:40.

```
GAME FOUR --- October 19
```

PHILLIES	AB	R	H	PO	A	E
Daily, p	3	1	2	0	7	2
Andrews, lf	5	0	0	1	0	1
Ferguson, rf	5	1	2	2	0	0
Mulvey, 3b	4	0	0	1	1	0
Farrar, 1b	4	1	2	13	0	1
Fogarty, cf	5	1	1	1	0	0
Myers, 2b	4	1	1	3	1	0
Bastian, ss	4	0	0	1	4	0
Clements, c	4	1	1	5	4	1
	38	6	9	27	17	5

ATHLETICS	AB	R	H	PO	A	E
Stovey, 1b	4	1	3	11	0	1
Larkin, lf	4	0	1	3	0	0
Coleman, rf	4	1	1	3	1	0
Shaffer, cf	4	0	2	3	0	0
O'Brien, 3b	4	1	0	1	2	0
Corey, ss	4	0	0	1	3	1
Stricker, 2b	3	0	1	3	2	1
Siffel, c	3	0	0	2	0	3
Brown, p	3	0	0	0	3	6
	33	3	8	27	11	12

```
PHI    0  1  0     2  0  0     2  1  0  -  6
ATH    1  0  0     0  0  0     1  1  0  -  3
```

Earned runs: PHI 1, ATH 1. 2B: Clements, Shaffer. HR: Stovey. BB: Daily 2. Struck out: Brown 2, Daily 7. LOB: PHI 10, ATH 3. DP: ATH. WP: Daily 2, Brown 1. PB: Clements 1, Siffel 3. Umpire: Carlin. Time—1:50.

featured Bobby Mathews (30–17) for the Athletics against Ed Daily (26–23). Mathews gave up three hits and two runs in the first on a missed third strike, a double by Ed Andrews and singles by Sid Farrar and Daily. But after that, Mathews was untouchable. He gave up only two hits, no walks, and struck out 13 over the final eight innings. The Athletics scored twice off Daily in their half of the first on an error by Farrar, a single by Henry Larkin, John Coleman's groundout, and Orator Shaffer's single. The A's took the lead for good in the fifth when they scored five times. Mathews singled, Harry Stovey walked and Larkin singled Mathews home. Daily balked Stovey home, Coleman walked, and when Charlie Bastian fumbled Shaffer's grounder, the bases were loaded. Jack O'Brien's triple cleared the bases and made an easy winner of Mathews.

Game Two at Recreation Park saw the Phillies jump all over rookies Ed

1885 Philadelphia City Championship Series

```
GAME FIVE --- October 20
```

ATHLETICS	AB	R	H	PO	A	E		PHILLIES	AB	R	H	PO	A	E
Stovey, 1b	4	0	2	3	1	0		Daily, rf	4	3	1	2	1	0
Larkin, lf	3	1	1	2	1	1		Andrews, lf	4	1	3	2	0	0
Coleman, rf	3	0	0	4	0	0		Ferguson, p	3	0	0	0	2	0
Shaffer, cf	3	0	0	4	1	0		Mulvey, 3b	4	0	0	0	3	0
O'Brien, 3b	3	1	2	2	0	4		Farrar, 1b	4	1	3	8	0	0
Corey, ss	3	0	1	0	2	1		Fogarty, cf	4	1	0	1	0	0
Milligan, c	3	0	0	4	3	3		Myers, 2b	4	2	2	2	1	2
Stricker, 2b	3	1	1	1	2	1		Bastian, ss	3	1	1	1	2	0
Mathews, p	3	1	0	0	3	1		Clements, c	3	0	1	5	3	1
	28	4	7	*20	13	11			33	9	11	21	12	3

```
*  One man out when game was called

ATH    1  1  0    0  2  0    0  -  4
PHI    0  0  2    0  1  4    2  -  9
```

Earned runs: ATH 2, PHI 2. 2B: O'Brien, Stricker. 3B: Myers. BB: Ferguson 1. Struck out: Ferguson 5, Mathews 3. LOB: ATH 3, PHI 5. PB: Milligan 1, Clements 1. WP: Mathews. Umpire: Carlin. Time—1:55.

Knouff (7–6) and Bill Hughes (0–2). Hughes had just spent his first and only season in the major leagues. The Phils batted Knouff around figuratively and literally in the early frames, scoring twice in the first and five times in the second before Knouff had to leave the game after being hit by a batted ball. Hughes fared little better, giving up ten runs over the final five innings. All eight Phillies who were given walks came around to score. Charlie Ferguson (26–20) started for the Phillies and was an easy winner. The hitting star of the game was Joe Mulvey with a double, triple, and two singles in five trips to the plate.

The third game featured some more fine work by Bobby Mathews as he allowed one less hit and one less run than in Game One. The Athletics broke on top with three runs in the first and were never headed. The only Phillies' run came in the fourth and was disputed at that. Farrar doubled, stole third, and came home on a passed ball. Mathews was at the plate to take the throw from catcher Jocko Milligan and tagged Farrar before he reached home, but then dropped the ball.

Game Four saw the Phillies bounce back behind the pitching of Ed Daily who had been blasted in Game One. Daily gave up two walks and eight hits, among them a home run by Harry Stovey, but was tough with men on base, striking out seven. He began weakening in the late innings, but a 5–1 lead saved him. The final score was 6–3 with Jim Brown, recently from the Union Association St. Paul Saints, taking the loss.

The series' finale took place on the 20th at Jefferson Street Grounds. Bobby Mathews was back on the mound going for his third win, but his teammates' defense let him down. The A's took a 2–0 lead with single runs in the first and second, but the Phillies tied the game with two of their own in the third. Two more runs in the fifth gave the Athletics their original two-run lead, but the

Phillies scored once in the bottom of the fifth and four times in the sixth to pull ahead to stay. Eleven errors by the Athletics let in seven unearned runs and made a loser of Mathews. Charlie Ferguson was the winning pitcher.

The 1885 New York City Championship Series I

Brooklyn Trolley Dodgers defeat New York Metropolitans; 4–2

The fifth-place Brooklyn Trolley Dodgers (53–59) improved on their ninth-place 40–64 record of 1884 and prepared to play in the first New York City championship series of 1885 against the New York Metropolitans, a team headed in the opposite direction. After winning the American Association pennant in 1884 with a 75–32 record, the Mets plummeted to a seventh-place 44–64 season in 1885.

1885 New York City Championship Series I

GAME ONE --- October 3

METROPOLITANS	AB	R	H	PO	A	E		BROOKLYN	AB	R	H	PO	A	E
Nelson, ss	3	1	0	0	2	0		Pinckney, 3b	4	0	0	1	2	0
Roseman, cf	5	1	1	0	0	0		McClellan, 2b	4	0	2	3	3	0
Orr, 1b	4	1	2	10	0	0		Swartwood, 1b	4	0	1	6	1	0
Brady, rf	4	2	3	2	0	0		Hotaling, cf	3	0	0	3	0	0
Foster, 2b	3	0	0	1	4	1		McTamany, lf	4	0	0	2	0	0
Hankinson, 3b	4	1	1	4	2	0		Smith, ss	3	0	1	2	0	0
Reipschlager, c	4	0	0	8	4	0		Peoples, c	3	0	1	1	2	0
Kennedy, lf	4	1	1	1	0	0		Terry, rf	3	0	1	9	1	2
Lynch, p	4	1	1	1	1	0		Porter, p	3	0	0	0	0	1
	35	8	9	27	13	1			31	0	6	27	9	3

```
MET   0  0  0   0  6  0   0  2  0  -  8
BKN   0  0  0   0  0  0   0  0  0  -  0
```

Earned runs: MET 4. 2B: Brady, Kennedy, Lynch, Terry. DP: BKN. BB: Porter 3, Lynch 1. Struck out: Porter 7, Lynch 7. WP: Porter. LOB: MET 3, BKN 5. Umpire: Connolly. Time—2:00.

The series opened at the Polo Grounds on October 3rd with Brooklyn the "home" club and the Mets shut out the Dodgers behind the four-hit pitching of Jack Lynch (23–21). Lynch walked only one and struck out seven in recording the easy win. The Mets enjoyed a six-run fifth inning and added two more runs in the eighth. Henry Porter (33–21) took the loss.

The second game, played on the seventh, was a reversal of the first. John Harkins (14–20) pitched a superlative game for the Dodgers, striking out ten and holding the Mets hitless through the first eight innings until a ninth-inning single by Dave Orr broke the string. Jack Lynch was the losing pitcher. The Mets used three catchers in the game. Charlie Reipschlager started behind the plate but had to leave when he received word that his wife was seriously ill. He was replaced by Bill Holbert who retired because of sore hands. Elmer Foster, who would play for the Mets during the 1886 season, caught the final innings.

1885 New York City Championship Series I

GAME TWO --- October 7

METROPOLITANS	AB	R	H	PO	A	E		BROOKLYN	AB	R	H	PO	A	E
Nelson, ss	2	0	0	0	2	0		Pinckney, 3b	4	0	1	0	3	1
Roseman, cf	4	0	0	2	0	0		McClellan, 2b	4	1	0	1	3	0
Orr, 1b	4	0	1	8	0	0		Swartwood, 1b	4	2	1	11	0	2
Brady, rf	4	0	0	2	0	1		Hotaling, cf	3	0	1	3	0	0
Foster, 2b-c	4	0	0	3	6	1		McTamany, lf	4	1	0	0	0	0
Hankinson, 3b	3	0	0	1	0	1		Harkins, p	3	1	1	0	0	0
Reipschlager, c	1	0	0	4	0	0		Smith, ss	3	0	1	0	2	0
Holbert, c-lf	2	0	0	0	0	0		Terry, rf	3	0	1	2	0	0
Kennedy, lf-2b	3	0	0	4	2	0		Oldfield, c	3	0	1	10	2	0
Lynch, p	3	0	0	0	1	0								
	30	0	1	24	11	3			31	5	7	27	10	3

```
MET    0  0  0    0  0  0    0  0  0  -  0
BKN    0  0  1    2  0  1    0  1  x  -  5
```

LOB: MET 3, BKN 2. BB: Harkins 2, Lynch 1. Struck out: Harkins 10, Lynch 4. WP: Lynch 3. PB: Foster 3. Umpire: Connell. Time—2:00.

GAME THREE --- October 8

METROPOLITANS	AB	R	H	PO	A	E		BROOKLYN	AB	R	H	PO	A	E
Nelson, ss	2	0	0	1	2	1		Pinckney, 3b	3	0	1	0	0	0
Roseman, cf	4	0	0	1	0	0		McClellan, 2b	3	0	0	3	2	1
Orr, 1b	4	1	1	11	0	0		Swartwood, 1b	2	1	0	9	0	1
Brady, rf	4	0	0	1	0	0		Hotaling, cf	3	0	0	0	0	0
Foster, 2b	3	0	1	0	4	1		McTamany, lf	3	0	0	2	0	0
Hankinson, 3b	3	0	0	0	1	0		Harkins, p	3	0	0	0	7	1
Reipschlager, c	3	0	2	6	3	0		Smith, ss	3	0	0	0	1	0
Kennedy, lf	3	0	0	1	0	0		Terry, rf	2	0	0	4	0	0
Lynch, p	2	0	0	0	3	0		Oldfield, c	2	1	1	6	3	1
Cushman, p	1	0	0	0	4	0								
	29	1	4	21	17	2			24	2	2	24	13	4

```
MET    0  0  0    0  0  0    0  1  -  1
BKN    0  0  1    0  0  0    1  x  -  2
```

Earned runs: MET 1. LOB: MET 5, BKN 2. HR: Orr. BB: MET 2, BKN 1. Struck out: MET 6, BKN 7. WP: Lynch 1. Umpire: Connell. Time—1:50.

GAME FOUR --- October 10

METROPOLITANS	AB	R	H	PO	A	E		BROOKLYN	AB	R	H	PO	A	E
Nelson, ss	4	0	1	2	2	2		Pinckney, 3b	3	2	1	1	2	0
Roseman, cf	4	0	0	0	0	1		McClellan, 2b	4	0	1	3	3	2
Orr, 1b	4	0	0	9	0	0		Smith, ss	4	0	0	1	6	2
Brady, rf	4	0	0	0	0	0		McTamany, lf	4	1	1	1	0	0
Foster, 2b	4	0	0	3	2	0		Peoples, c	2	0	1	3	1	0
Hankinson, 3b	4	0	3	2	1	0		Terry, rf	4	0	1	1	1	0
Reipschlager, c	4	0	0	6	4	1		Swartwood, 1b	4	0	0	15	0	1
Kennedy, lf	2	0	0	2	0	0		Hotaling, cf	3	0	0	2	0	0
Cushman, p	3	0	1	0	1	0		Porter, p	3	1	1	0	2	1
	33	0	5	24	10	4			31	4	6	27	15	6

```
MET    0  0  0    0  0  0    0  0  0  -  0
BKN    1  0  3    0  0  0    0  0  x  -  4
```

LOB: MET 6, BKN 6. DP: MET. 3B: McTamany. BB: Porter 1, Cushman 3. Struck out: Cushman 7, Porter 3. PB: Peoples 1, Reipschlager 1. WP: Cushman 2. Umpire: Connell. Time—1:45.

1885 New York City Championship Series I

GAME FIVE --- October 12

METROPOLITANS	AB	R	H	PO	A	E		BROOKLYN	AB	R	H	PO	A	E
Nelson, ss	3	0	0	1	2	1		Pinckney, 3b	3	1	1	0	1	0
Roseman, cf	3	0	0	2	0	0		McClellan, 2b	3	0	1	2	6	0
Orr, 1b	4	0	0	7	0	0		Swartwood, rf	3	0	0	2	0	0
Brady, rf	3	0	0	0	0	0		Phillips, 1b	3	0	0	10	0	0
Foster, 2b	3	1	1	2	2	0		Hotaling, cf	3	0	0	2	0	0
Hankinson, 3b	3	0	0	2	3	1		McTamany, lf	3	1	1	2	0	0
Reipschlager, c	3	0	1	6	2	2		Harkins, p	3	0	1	0	1	0
Kennedy, lf	3	0	0	1	0	1		Smith, ss	3	0	0	0	1	1
Cushman, p	3	0	0	0	2	0		Oldfield, c	2	0	0	6	1	3
	28	1	2	21	11	5			26	2	4	24	10	4

```
MET   0  0  0    0  0  0    1  0  -  1
BKN   0  1  1    0  0  0    0  x  -  2
```

Earned runs: MET 1, BKN 1. LOB: MET 2, BKN 2. DP: MET. 2B: Pinckney. BB: Cushman 4, Harkins 1. Struck out: Harkins 7, Cushman 6. WP: Cushman 2. PB: Reipschlager 3, Oldfield 1. Umpire: Connolly. Time—1:30.

Game Three at the Polo Grounds was a rematch of Lynch and Harkins. Lynch gave up one run through the first five innings but had to leave because of a knee injury. He was replaced by Ed Cushman (8–14) who went the rest of the way. Cushman gave a walk to Ed Swartwood in the seventh and Elmer Foster's wild throw brought him around for a 2–0 Brooklyn lead. Dave Orr's home run in the eighth off winning pitcher John Harkins accounted for the Mets' only run.

Game Four featured Cushman against Henry Porter. Porter was on the wrong end of an 8–0 shutout in the first game, but delivered one of his own in this 4–0 whitewash. He scattered five Met singles, walked one and struck out three in going the distance. George Pinckney scored the initial run of the game in the first inning for all the offense Porter needed. Three Brooklyn runs in the third provided enough insurance as Cushman went down to defeat.

The fifth game of the series was played at Washington Park on the 12th of October, Cushman against Harkins. Brooklyn took a 1–0 lead in the second when Jim McTamany singled and scored on errors by Reipschlager and Cushman. The Dodgers increased their lead in the third when George Pinckney doubled and scored on Bill McClellan's single. The Mets scored their only run of the game in the eighth when Elmer Foster singled, stole second, and scored on Reipschlager's single. Harkins was the victor, Cushman took the loss.

The series' finale took place ten days later at Washington Park. The Mets took a 2–0 lead in the first, Brooklyn scored four times to go ahead in the second, and the Mets came back with two in the third to tie. A double by Connie Mack—who would play his first professional season with Washington in the 1886 season—a missed third strike, and a throwing error by Pinckney accounted for the final two runs of the Mets in their fourth. The final score was 6–4 Mets with Cushman taking the win. Harkins was the losing pitcher.

1885 New York City Championship Series I

GAME SIX --- October 22

METROPOLITANS	AB	R	H	PO	A	E
Nelson, ss	3	2	1	1	1	1
Roseman, cf	4	1	3	0	0	0
Orr, 1b	4	1	0	8	0	1
Brady, rf	4	0	1	2	0	0
Foster, 2b	3	0	1	2	4	0
Hankinson, 3b	3	0	0	1	0	0
Mack, c	3	1	1	6	2	2
Kennedy, lf	3	1	0	0	0	0
Cushman, p	3	0	0	1	1	0
	30	6	7	21	8	4

BROOKLYN	AB	R	H	PO	A	E
Pinckney, 3b	4	0	0	0	2	2
McClellan, 2b	4	0	3	2	0	0
Swartwood, 1b	1	0	0	9	0	0
Peoples, cf	3	0	0	2	0	0
McTamany, lf	3	1	1	0	0	0
Harkins, p	3	1	1	2	4	0
Smith, ss	3	1	1	0	4	1
Terry, rf	3	0	0	3	0	0
Oldfield, c	3	1	1	3	0	2
	27	4	7	21	10	5

```
MET    2  0  2    2  0  0    0  -  6
BKN    0  4  0    0  0  0    0  -  4
```

Earned runs: MET 3, BKN 1. LOB: MET 4, BKN 4. DP: MET. 2B: Roseman, Mack, Harkins. BB: Harkins 1, Cushman 1. Struck out: Harkins 3, Cushman 5. WP: Cushman. PB: Mack 4. Umpire: West. Time—1:25.

The 1885 New York City Championship Series II

New York Giants defeat New York Metropolitans; 2–1

The New York Giants (85–27) improved considerably from their 62–50 record in 1884 and just narrowly missed taking the pennant from the Chicago White Stockings (87–25). The second city championship looked to be a lock for the Giants as they met the 44–64 Metropolitans.

Game One was played at the Polo Grounds on the 19th of October with the Giants' Tim Keefe (32–13) going against Jack Lynch (23–21). The Giants were without the services of Orator Jim O'Rourke, Pete Gillespie, and Joe Gerhardt, but Pat Deasley, Larry Corcoran, and Danny Richardson filled in at their positions. The Giants and Keefe jumped off to an early 4–0 lead, held on to withstand a three-run third by the Mets, and added an insurance run in the fifth to win the game. Umpire Quinn called the game at the end of six innings because of darkness.

Game Two was played in cold weather and for less than 100 fans and was called at the end of thirty minutes' play with the Metropolitans leading 2–0. The Mets scored all their runs in the first on an error by Roger Connor which allowed James "Chief" Roseman to reach base, a double by Dave Orr and a single by Steve Brady. Losing pitcher Mickey Welch (44–11) only gave up two hits over the next four innings, but the damage was done. Buck Becannon (2–8) took the victory.

As in the first game, the Giants took an early lead in Game Three behind Keefe then held on to withstand an assault by the Mets. The Giants scored two in the second, one in the third, and three in the fourth for a 6–0 lead, but the Mets came back with three in their half of the fourth and two more in the fifth to pull within one. The game was called because of darkness after play in

1885 New York City Championship Series II

GAME ONE --- October 19

NEW YORK	AB	R	H	PO	A	E
Connor, 1b	3	2	2	6	0	0
Ewing, c	3	2	1	8	0	0
Richardson, cf	3	1	2	0	6	1
Dorgan, rf	3	0	1	2	0	0
Esterbrook, 3b	3	0	0	0	0	0
Corcoran, cf	2	0	0	2	0	0
Deasley, lf	3	0	1	0	0	0
Keefe, p	3	0	0	0	7	2
Ward, ss	2	0	0	0	1	0
	25	5	7	18	14	3

METROPOLITANS	AB	R	H	PO	A	E
Nelson, ss	4	1	2	4	2	0
Roseman, cf	3	0	1	1	0	0
Orr, 1b	3	1	2	7	0	0
Brady, rf	3	1	1	0	0	0
Foster, 2b	3	0	1	2	2	1
Hankinson, 3b	3	0	0	0	1	1
Mack, c	3	0	0	3	2	1
Kennedy, lf	3	0	1	1	0	0
Lynch, p	2	0	1	0	2	3
	27	3	9	18	9	6

```
NY    1 0 3   0 1 0  -  5
MET   0 0 3   0 0 0  -  3
```

Earned runs: NY 2, MET 2. LOB: NY 10, MET 7. 2B: Connor, Kennedy, Lynch. 3B: Ewing. BB: Lynch 1, Keefe 1. Struck out: Lynch 2, Keefe 5. WP: Lynch 2, Keefe 1. PB: Mack 1. Umpire: Quinn. Time—1:33.

GAME TWO --- October 21

METROPOLITANS	AB	R	H	PO	A	E
Nelson, ss	2	0	0	1	5	0
Roseman, cf	2	1	0	0	0	0
Orr, 1b	2	1	2	7	0	1
Brady, 2b-rf	2	0	1	3	2	0
Foster, c-2b	2	0	1	1	2	1
Hankinson, 3b	2	0	0	0	2	0
Re'schlager, rf-c	2	0	0	2	0	1
Kennedy, lf	2	0	0	1	0	0
Becannon, p	2	0	0	0	1	1
	18	2	4	15	12	4

NEW YORK	AB	R	H	PO	A	E
Connor, 1b	3	0	1	8	0	1
Ewing, rf	3	0	1	0	1	0
Gillespie, lf	3	0	0	1	0	0
Richardson, 3b	2	0	1	1	2	0
Welch, p	1	0	1	1	2	0
Corcoran, ss	2	0	1	1	1	0
Keefe, cf	2	0	0	1	0	0
Crane, 2b	2	0	0	0	2	1
Schriner, c	2	0	0	2	2	0
	20	0	5	15	9	2

```
MET   2 0 0   0 0  -  2
NY    0 0 0   0 0  -  0
```

Earned runs: MET 1. 2B: Orr 2, Connor. BB: Becannon 1. Struck out: Becannon 1. Umpire: Blank. Time—30 min.

GAME THREE --- October 23

NEW YORK	AB	R	H	PO	A	E
Connor, 1b	4	1	1	8	1	0
Ewing, c	4	1	1	2	0	0
Gillespie, lf	4	0	1	2	0	1
Dorgann, rf	4	1	1	3	0	0
Esterbrook, 3b	3	1	1	0	0	0
Richardson, cf	3	0	0	1	0	0
Keefe, p	3	2	2	0	3	0
Gerhardt, 2b	3	0	0	2	3	0
Ward, ss	3	0	1	3	3	2
	31	6	8	21	10	3

METROPOLITANS	AB	R	H	PO	A	E
Nelson, ss	4	0	1	0	1	0
Roseman, cf	4	0	1	1	0	0
Orr, 1b	4	0	1	14	0	1
Brady, rf	3	2	1	2	0	1
Foster, 2b	3	2	1	0	3	1
Hankinson, 3b	3	0	1	1	2	0
Mack, c	3	1	0	3	1	0
Kennedy, lf	3	0	0	0	0	0
Conley, p	3	0	2	0	2	1
	30	5	8	21	9	4

```
NY    0 2 1   3 0 0   0  -  6
MET   0 0 0   3 2 0   0  -  5
```

Earned runs: NY 3, MET 2. LOB: NY 4, MET 6. DP: MY 2. 2B: Esterbrook, Hankinson. 3B: Gillespie. BB: Keefe 2. Struck out: Conley 4, Keefe 2. PB: Mack 1. Umpire: West. Time—1:15.

the seventh. Ed Conley of the Providence Grays was the pitcher for the Mets and took the loss. The two pitchers were hitting stars in this game, Keefe with a 2-for-3 performance and two runs scored, and Conley with two singles.

The 1885 New York City Championship Series III
New York Giants defeat Brooklyn Trolley Dodgers; 1–0–1

The Giants finally got around to playing the Dodgers for the final New York City championship, a hodge-podge of games that dragged on into the cold of November.

1885 New York City Championship Series III

GAME ONE --- October 20

NEW YORK	AB	R	H	PO	A	E		BROOKLYN	AB	R	H	PO	A	E
Richardson, cf	2	2	2	0	0	1		Pinckney, 3b	3	1	0	1	0	1
Connor, 1b	2	2	1	9	0	0		McClellan, 2b	2	1	0	3	7	1
Gillespie, lf	3	0	0	0	0	0		Swartwood, 1b	3	0	1	10	0	0
Dorgan, rf	3	0	0	2	0	0		Hotaling, cf	2	0	0	0	0	0
Esterbrook,, 3b	3	0	0	1	0	0		McTamany, lf	3	0	1	1	0	0
Deasley, c	2	0	0	5	3	1		Smith, ss	3	0	0	4	0	0
Welch, p	3	0	1	0	0	0		Peoples, c	2	0	0	4	1	0
Gerhardt, 2b	3	0	0	3	5	1		Terry, rf	3	0	1	2	0	0
Ward, ss	3	0	0	1	3	1		Porter, p	3	0	0	0	1	0
	24	4	4	21	11	4			24	2	3	21	13	3

```
NY    2  0  0    0  0  2    0  -  4
BKN   0  0  0    0  0  2    0  -  2
```

   LOB: NY 1, BKN 1. DP: BKN 2. 2B: Swartwood, Richardson. 3B: Welch. BB: Porter 3, Welch 3. Struck out: Porter 3, Welch 5. PB: Peoples 1. Umpire: Connell. Time—1:40.

GAME TWO --- October 24

NEW YORK	AB	R	H	PO	A	E		BROOKLYN	AB	R	H	PO	A	E
Connor, 1b	3	0	1	6	0	0		Pinckney, 3b	3	0	0	0	0	1
Gillespie, lf	2	0	0	0	0	1		McClellan, 2b	3	1	1	4	3	1
Richardson, cf	3	1	1	1	0	1		Swartwood, 1b	2	0	2	8	0	0
Esterbrook, 3b	3	1	2	1	4	2		Hotaling, cf	3	0	0	0	0	0
Corcoran, rf	3	0	1	0	0	0		McTamany, lf	3	1	0	0	0	0
Deasley, c	3	0	0	6	2	0		Smith, ss	3	0	2	1	2	0
Welch, p	2	0	1	0	0	0		Peoples, c	2	1	0	4	3	0
Gerhardt, 2b	2	0	0	4	2	0		Terry, rf	2	0	0	1	0	1
Ward, ss	2	1	0	0	1	0		Porter, p	2	0	1	0	2	0
	23	3	6	18	9	4			23	3	6	18	10	3

```
NY    2  0  0    0  1  0    -  3
BKN   0  1  1    1  0  0    -  3
```

   Earned runs: NY 2, BKN 1. LOB: NY 3, BKN 5. DP: NY 1, BKN 1. 2B: Gillespie, Esterbrook, Swartwood, McClellan. 3B: Connor. BB: Porter 1, Welch 1. Struck out: Welch 3, Porter 2. PB: Peoples. WP: Welch 1, Porter 1. Umpire: Bunce. Time—1:30.

The series opened on October 20 at the Brooklyn grounds, Washington Park, with the Giants jumping out to a 2-0 lead off Henry Porter (33-21) on a hit, two walks, and a wild pitch. For the next four innings, the only offense was a scratch single by New York's Joe Gerhardt and a double by Brooklyn's Ed Swartwood. The Giants took a 4-0 lead in the sixth on a single by Roger Connor, a double by Danny Richardson, and a Brooklyn error. Brooklyn negated those runs with a two-run sixth on two walks and two Giant errors. The Giants scored a single run in the top of the eighth and the Dodgers scored twice in the bottom of the inning. The tying run was on third with no one out when umpire Connell suddenly decided it was too dark to continue play. Porter was the losing pitcher while Welch (44-11) took the victory.

The second and final game took place on the 24th of October and ended in a 3-3 tie after six full innings had been played. The Giants opened the first with two earned runs as Richardson singled, stole second, and scored on Thomas "Dude" Esterbrook's double. Larry Corcoran's single scored Esterbrook. Brooklyn cut the lead in half in the second and back-to-back doubles by Swartwood and Bill McClellan tied the score in the third. The Dodgers pulled ahead 3-2 in the fourth when Jimmy Peoples reached on a forceout, stole second, and scored on a wild pitch. The Giants knotted the score in the fifth when Monte Ward reached on an error and scored on Roger Connor's triple. Part of the seventh inning was played before the umpire called the game because of darkness.

The deciding game was to be played on the 27th of October, but Brooklyn had disbanded a few days earlier and so a picked nine was chosen. None of the Brooklyn ballplayers represented the "Brooklyn" club and the Giants won by a score of 6-3. Several New York ballplayers appeared for the "Brooklyn" team. A final game between "New York" and "Brooklyn" picked nines was played on the 3rd of November, the New Yorks winning by the same 6-3 score.

The 1886 St. Louis City Championship Series

St. Louis Browns defeat St. Louis Maroons; 5-1

The 1886 St. Louis Maroons (43-79) had just suffered through their last year in the National League, prevented from a lower finish than sixth place only because of Kansas City and Washington teams which won 30 and 29 games respectively. The Maroons' place in the National League would be taken in 1892 by the American Association St. Louis Browns, their opponent in the 1886 St. Louis city championship series. The Browns, with a 93-46 record, played the first four games of the city championship series before meeting the Chicago White Stockings in the 1886 World Series, then resumed these games the day after they had knocked off the Chicagos four-games-to-two. This year marked the second of four consecutive pennants for the AA Browns.

The series opened on October 14th at the Palace Park of America (sometimes known as Union Association Park), the home field of the Maroons.

1886 St. Louis City Championship Series

GAME ONE --- October 14

BROWNS	AB	R	H	PO	A	E		MAROONS	AB	R	H	PO	A	E
Latham, 3b	4	1	1	0	3	0		Glasscock, ss	4	0	1	0	4	0
O'Neill, lf	4	0	0	1	0	2		McKinnon, 1b	4	0	0	10	0	0
Caruthers, rf	4	1	1	1	0	0		Denny, 3b	4	0	1	1	5	2
Gleason, ss	4	0	0	0	3	0		Myers, c	4	0	1	8	0	2
Comiskey, 1b	4	1	0	13	0	0		McGeachy, cf	4	0	0	2	0	0
Welch, cf	4	0	1	1	0	0		Seery, lf	4	0	1	0	0	0
Foutz, p	4	0	1	1	4	0		Cahill, rf	4	0	1	1	0	0
Robinson, 2b	3	0	0	1	0	0		Quinn, 2b	4	0	0	3	2	1
Bushong, c	2	0	1	8	2	0		Healey, p	4	0	0	2	3	2
Kemmler, rf	0	0	0	1	0	0								
	33	3	5	27	12	2			36	0	5	27	14	7

```
MAR   0  0  0    0  0  0    0  0  0  -  0
BRN   0  0  0    0  3  0    0  0  x  -  3
```

2B: Latham. LOB: MAR 5, BRN 3. Struck out: Healey 8, Foutz 8. BB: Healey 2. PB: Myers. WP: Healey. Umpire: McQuaid. Time—1:45.

GAME TWO --- October 15

BROWNS	R	H	PO	A	E		MAROONS	R	H	PO	A	E
Latham, 3b	0	0	0	3	0		Glasscock, ss	0	2	2	5	1
O'Neill, lf	2	2	2	0	0		McKinnon, 1b	0	0	10	1	0
Gleason, ss	1	1	0	0	1		Denny, 3b	0	0	2	0	0
Comiskey, 1b	2	1	8	0	0		Myers, c	0	0	3	3	0
Welch, cf	1	3	3	1	0		McGeachy, cf	1	0	4	0	0
Foutz, rf	1	1	1	0	0		Seery, lf	0	1	0	0	0
Robinson, 2b	1	0	2	5	0		Quinn, 2b	0	0	2	1	0
Hudson, p	1	1	0	0	0		Cahill, rf	0	0	3	0	0
Bushong, c	1	1	11	1	1		Crothers, p	0	0	1	0	1
	10	10	27	10	2			1	3	27	10	2

```
BRN   0  0  0    0  0  0    10  0  0  -  10
MAR   0  1  0    0  0  0     0  0  0  -   1
```

Earned runs: BRN 7. 2B: O'Neill, Hudson, Gleason. SB: McKinnon, Welch 2, Comiskey, Bushong, Gleason. LOB: BRN 1, MAR 2. BB: Crothers 3. Struck out: Hudson 1, Crothers 3. PB: Myers, Bushong. Umpire: McQuaid. Time—1:45.

GAME THREE --- October 16

BROWNS	R	H	PO	A	E		MAROONS	R	H	PO	A	E
Latham, 3b	2	0	2	0	2		Glasscock, ss	0	1	1	5	1
O'Neill, lf	1	0	3	0	0		McKinnon, 1b	0	1	10	0	0
Gleason, ss	0	1	1	1	0		Denny, 3b	1	1	2	2	1
Comiskey, 1b	1	1	10	0	0		Myers, c	0	0	6	1	0
Welch, cf	1	2	2	1	0		McGeachy, cf	0	0	3	0	0
Foutz, p	1	1	1	3	1		Seery, lf	0	0	1	1	0
Robinson, 2b	1	0	3	3	1		Quinn, 2b	0	1	1	2	2
Hudson, rf	0	0	1	0	0		Cahill, rf	1	1	1	0	0
Bushong, c	0	0	4	1	0		Kirby, p	0	0	0	1	3
	7	5	27	9	4			2	5	24	12	8

```
BRN   3  0  0    0  0  0    4  0  0  -  7
MAR   0  0  0    0  1  0    0  0  1  -  2
```

2B: Foutz, Welch, McKinnon. SH: Hudson. LOB: MAR 6, BRN 3. BB: Foutz 1, Kirby 1. Struck out: Kirby 6, Foutz 4. PB: Myers 3, Bushong 1. WP: Kirby. Umpire: McQuaid. Time—1:40.

1886 St. Louis City Championship Series

GAME FOUR --- October 17

BROWNS	R	H	PO	A	E		MAROONS	R	H	PO	A	E
Latham, 3b	0	0	1	2	0		Seery, lf	1	1	1	0	0
Caruthers, rf	0	1	1	0	0		Glasscock, ss	1	0	1	2	0
O'Neill, lf	0	1	1	2	1		McKinnon, 1b	0	1	5	0	0
Gleason, ss	1	0	2	4	0		Denny, 3b	0	1	1	3	0
Comiskey, 1b	2	2	9	0	1		McGeachy, cf	0	0	2	0	0
Welch, cf	1	1	1	0	0		Cahill, rf	0	1	2	0	0
Robinson, 2b	0	2	2	4	1		Mappis, c	0	0	5	2	1
Hudson, p	0	0	1	1	2		Crane, 2b	0	0	4	2	0
Bushong, c	0	0	3	3	0		Healy, p	0	0	0	1	4
	4	7	21	16	5			2	4	21	10	5

```
BRN   0 2 0   0 0 2   0 - 4
MAR   0 0 2   0 0 0   0 - 2
```

Earned runs: BRN 1. 2B: Seery, Comiskey, Welch. LOB: MAR 3, BRN 4. SB: Cahill, Glasscock, Bushong. DP: MAR 1, BRN 2. Struck out: Hudson 3, Healy 4. PB: Mappis, Bushong. Umpire: McQuaid. Time—2:00.

All the offense came in the fifth inning when the Browns scored three times. Arlie Latham doubled, Tip O'Neill reached on an error, and both runners moved up on a passed ball. Bob Caruthers grounded out, Latham scoring, then Charlie Comiskey grounded to Healey who threw O'Neill out at the plate. Comiskey kept running on the play and catcher Al Myers threw to Joe Quinn at second. Quinn muffed the ball and Caruthers came in to score. Comiskey scored a moment later on a single by Curt Welch. Caruthers injured himself while running the bases in the seventh and was lost for the next two games of the series. Dave Foutz (41–16), who led the American Association in victories, winning percentage, and earned run average, pitched a five-hit shutout, walking no one and striking out eight for the victory. John "Egyptian" Healey (17–23) took the loss. (Healey was so named because he was born in Cairo, Illinois.)

Game Two was played the next day at Sportsman's Park with Browns' rookie Nat Hudson (16–10) going against Dug Crothers, recently of the New York Metropolitans and the Syracuse club. The Maroons took a 1–0 lead in the second when Jack McGeachy reached on an error by Bill Gleason, went to second on Emmett Seery's single, and scored after two groundouts. Crothers was rolling along and had given up only one hit through the first six innings when disaster struck in the seventh. O'Neill doubled, Comiskey, Welch, and Dave Foutz singled. Yank Robinson drew a base on balls and Hudson doubled. Doc Bushong, O'Neill, and Welch singled and Bill Gleason doubled. The only two men in the lineup who failed to get a hit in the inning were Latham, who made two outs, and Robinson, who walked and scored a run. When the carnage ended, the Browns had racked up ten runs.

The third game was played the next day and resulted in another easy victory for the Browns. The Americans scored three runs off John Kirby (11–25) in the first inning on a walk, errors by Jack Glasscock, Jerry Denny, and

1886 St. Louis City Championship Series

```
GAME FIVE --- October 24

BROWNS                    R  H PO  A  E     MAROONS              R  H PO  A  E
------------------------------------       ------------------------------------
Latham, 3b                2  1  5  7  2     Seery, lf            3  1  2  0  0
Caruthers, rf-p           0  0  0  2  0     Glasscock, ss        0  1  2  5  0
O'Neill, lf               1  2  0  0  0     McKinnon, 1b         0  1 13  0  0
Gleason, ss               0  1  0  2  0     Denny, 2b            1  0  1  6  0
Comiskey, 1b              1  1 14  0  0     McGeachy, cf         1  2  2  0  1
Welch, cf                 0  0  0  1  0     Myers, c             0  1  6  0  2
Foutz, p-rf               1  1  2  1  0     O'Brien, 3b          0  0  1  0  3
Robinson, 3b              0  0  1  4  2     Cahill, rf           0  1  0  0  0
Kemmler, c                1  0  5  3  2     Boyle, p             0  2  0  2  0
                         --------------                        --------------
                          6  6 27 20  6                         5  9 27 13  6

BRN    0  0  0    2  2  0    0  2  0  -  6
MAR    1  0  1    0  1  0    0  2  0  -  5
```

Earned runs: MAR 1. 2B: Boyle, Glasscock. LOB: BRN 6, MAR 5. SB: Comiskey 2, Seery 2, Myers, Cahill. BB: Foutz 2, Boyle 3, Caruthers 1. Struck out: Foutz 5, Boyle 7. HBP: Comiskey (Boyle). WP: Boyle, Foutz. Umpire: McQuaid. Time—2:00.

Quinn, a passed ball, a single by Comiskey, and Dave Foutz's double. The Maroons scored once in the fifth when John Cahill hit into a forceout, went to second on a passed ball, and scored on Glasscock's single. The Browns broke the game wide open in the seventh. A Curt Welch single and errors by Quinn and Kirby filled the bases with no one out. Welch scored on a Yank Robinson forceout and Cahill made a fine one-handed running catch of Nat Hudson's fly ball for the second out of the inning. But Arlie Latham made first when he swung and missed at a wild pitch third strike. A throwing error sent two runs home and Latham scored on a passed ball. The Maroons scored their final run in the ninth on a single by Denny, an error by Latham, and a Joe Quinn single. Foutz was the easy victor, Kirby took the loss.

The fourth game was played at Union Park on the 17th of October and the Browns won again by superior batting. The Americans broke on top with two in the second on Comiskey's single, a base on balls to Welch, a passed ball and two outs. The Maroons tied the score in the third on a double by Seery, an error by Comiskey, and Alex McKinnon's triple. The Browns closed out the scoring in the sixth when Gleason walked, Comiskey doubled, George Mappis threw wild and Yank Robinson singled. Nat Hudson took the victory. Egyptian Healey took the loss.

The fifth game was a closely contested victory for the Browns at Sportsman's Park. The Maroons scored first when Emmett Seery went to second on a wild pitch ball four. A throwing error by Kemmler sent Seery to third where he scored on Denny's groundout. The Maroons increased their lead to 2–0 in the third when Seery singled, stole second, and scored on McKinnon's single to right. Henry Boyle (9–15) set the Browns down 1-2-3 in the first three innings but in the fourth Arlie Latham went all the way to second on an errant throw by O'Brien, to third on a wild pitch, and home on O'Neill's single. Gleason walked and Comiskey filled the bases with a looping single to left. Curt Welch's

1886 St. Louis City Championship Series

GAME SIX --- October 31

MAROONS	R	H	PO	A	E		BROWNS	R	H	PO	A	E
Seery, lf	1	1	0	0	0		Latham, 3b-c	0	0	3	0	0
McKinnon, 1b	0	2	11	0	1		O'Neill, lf	0	0	2	0	0
Denny, 3b	0	0	1	2	1		Caruthers, rf-3b	0	1	2	0	1
Myers, c	0	1	9	1	2		Gleason, ss	0	0	1	4	0
McGeachy, cf	0	1	2	0	0		Comiskey, 2b	0	0	3	2	0
Cahill, rf	0	2	3	0	0		Welch, cf	0	0	2	0	0
Quinn, ss	0	0	1	2	1		Foutz, 1b	1	2	6	0	1
Crane, 2b	1	2	0	3	0		Hudson, p	0	0	1	1	3
Healy, p	0	1	0	2	2		Bushong, c-rf	0	0	7	2	2
	2	10	27	10	7			1	3	27	9	7

```
MAR   0  1  0    0  0  0    1  0  1  -  2
BRN   0  0  0    0  0  0    1  0  0  -  1
```

Earned runs: MAR 1. 2B: McGeachy, Crane, Healy, Caruthers, Foutz. SH: Denny, Gleason, Hudson 2. BB: Healy 2, Hudson 3. Struck out: Healy 7, Hudson 7. DP: BRN. PB: Bushong 1, Myers 1. WP: Hudson. Umpire: McQuaid. Time—1:55.

sacrifice fly tied the game. The Browns pulled ahead 4–2 in the next inning when Kemmler walked and Latham reached on a wild strike three. O'Neill walked and Gleason's single sent Kemmler and Latham home. In the bottom of the inning, Seery reached on a forceout and scored on Glasscock's double. The Browns widened the gap to 6–3 in the eighth when Comiskey reached on an error, stole second, and scored on Dave Foutz's single. Foutz went to steal second and Myers's throw was so wild it eluded center-fielder McGeachy and Dave came all the way around. In the eighth, with two out, Maroons' second baseman Denny reached on an error by Latham, McGeachy singled, and Myers singled Denny home and McGeachy to third. Myers lit out for second and when Latham dropped the ball for his second error of the inning, McGeachy scored. The Maroons wasted an opportunity to win the game in the ninth when Boyle doubled with one out and Seery walked. Glasscock flew out to Foutz, now playing right, but his throw back to the infield went wild and Boyle moved up to third. A moment later, Seery stole second. A single would have won the game, but Alex McKinnon grounded out to Comiskey at first to end the contest. Boyle took the loss, Foutz the win. Bob Caruthers (30–14) worked for the Browns in relief.

The two teams met a week later at Union Park for the final game and the National Leaguers won their only game of the series. The Maroons took a 1–0 lead in the second on back-to-back doubles by Sam Crane and Healey, then went up 2–0 in the seventh on singles by Seery and McKinnon and an error by Foutz. The Browns scored their only run of the game in the bottom of the inning when Foutz doubled, went to second on Hudson's sacrifice, and scored on Myers's error. Healey took the victory, Nat Hudson the loss.

1886 Philadelphia City Championship

```
GAME ONE --- October 16
```

PHILLIES	AB	R	H	PO	A	E
Fogarty, rf	4	0	1	3	0	0
Andrews, cf	4	1	1	2	0	0
Wood, lf	4	1	1	1	0	0
Mulvey, 3b	4	2	2	0	2	1
Ferguson, p	4	1	1	2	9	0
A. Irwin, ss	4	0	0	3	2	0
Bastian, 2b	3	0	1	1	1	1
Farrar, 1b	4	0	0	7	1	0
Clements, c	4	0	0	8	2	2
	35	5	7	27	17	4

ATHLETICS	AB	R	H	PO	A	E
Stovey, rf	4	0	1	4	0	0
Larkin, lf	4	0	0	2	0	0
Lyons, 3b	4	0	0	1	3	1
Robinson, c	3	0	0	3	0	0
McGarr, ss	3	0	2	0	5	0
Bierbauer, 2b	3	0	0	3	4	1
Fields, 1b	3	0	0	11	0	1
Greer, cf	3	0	0	3	0	0
Miller, p	3	0	0	0	2	1
	30	0	3	27	14	4

```
PHI   0  0  0   3  2  0   0  0  0  -  5
ATH   0  0  0   0  0  0   0  0  0  -  0
```

Earned runs: PHI 2. 3B: Mulvey. SB: McGarr, Andrews, Ferguson, Bastian. LOB: PHI 4, ATH 3. BB: Miller 1. Struck out: Miller 2, Ferguson 7. PB: Robinson 2. WP: Miller 3. Umpire: Fulmer. Time—1:35.

```
GAME TWO --- October 18
```

ATHLETICS	AB	R	H	PO	A	E
Larkin, lf	3	1	2	1	0	0
Lyons, 3b	3	0	1	0	1	0
Milligan, c	3	1	1	7	4	1
O'Brien, rf	2	0	0	1	0	0
McGarr, ss	3	1	1	2	1	0
Fields, 1b	3	1	1	8	0	2
Bierbauer, 2b	3	1	1	2	4	2
Greer, cf	2	0	1	0	0	0
Mathews, p	2	1	0	0	3	0
	24	6	8	21	13	5

PHILLIES	AB	R	H	PO	A	E
Fogarty, rf	1	0	1	2	0	1
Andrews, cf	3	1	0	0	0	1
Wood, lf	3	1	2	0	0	0
Mulvey, 3b	3	0	1	1	1	2
Ferguson, p	3	1	2	0	10	0
A. Irwin, ss	3	1	1	1	3	0
Bastian, 2b	3	0	0	1	2	0
J. Irwin, 1b	3	0	0	6	0	0
Clements, c	2	2	2	10	0	0
	24	6	9	21	16	4

```
ATH   0  0  6   0  0  0   0  -  6
PHI   0  0  2   3  0  0   1  -  6
```

Earned runs: PHI 1. 2B: Fogarty, Ferguson, A. Irwin, Clements. 3B: Greer, Wood. DP: PHI 1, ATH 2. LOB: ATH 4, PHI 5. SB: Andrews. BB: Mathews 1, Ferguson 1. Struck out: Mathews 2, Ferguson 9. PB: Clements 1. WP: Mathews 1. Umpire: Fulmer. Att: 2,000. Time—1:30.

The 1886 Philadelphia City Championship Series

Philadelphia Phillies defeat Philadelphia Athletics; 1-0-1

Amidst the postseason exhibition season, the second-place American Association Athletics (75–48) met the sixth-place National League Phillies (63–72) for a brief and generally unsatisfactory two-game series.

Game One saw Joseph "Cyclone" Miller (10–8) of the Athletics square off against Charlie Ferguson (30–9), coming off his best year in majors. The Phillies scored the first run of the series in the fourth when three singles, an error by third baseman Denny Lyons, and a passed ball sent three men across the plate. In the fifth, a single by Ed Andrews, a Joe Mulvey triple, and a wild pitch by Miller accounted for two more. The nearest the Athletics came to scoring was in the second when Jim McGarr singled, stole second, and went to third on a groundout. His teammates stranded him there. Ferguson scattered three singles, walked no one and struck out seven in recording the shutout. Jimmy Fields of the Savannah club played first base for the Athletics. Former major-leaguer Chick Fulmer was the umpire.

The second game was played two days later on the 18th of October with Bobby Mathews (13–9) against Ferguson. The Athletics pounded Ferguson for a six-run second inning, but Mathews failed to hold the big lead. The Phils scored twice in the third, three times in the fourth and once in the bottom of the sixth. After the Phillies took their cuts in the sixth, the game was called because of darkness. Harry Stovey and Sid Farrar had gone home for the winter, so Jack O'Brien filled in at right field and John Irwin at first base.

The 1886 New York Championship Series I

New York Giants defeat New York Metropolitans; 3–0

The New York Giants (75–44) finished a distant third behind the Chicago White Stockings (90–34) despite having the best pitcher in the league on their staff—Tim Keefe (42–20). Keefe led the National League in victories, innings pitched (540), games pitched (64), and complete games (62). Keefe and Mickey Welch (33–22) combined to win all the Giants games in 1886. The trouble was, the day of the two-man pitching staff had ended. Jim Mutrie's Giants just hadn't made the transition yet. The New York Metropolitans (52–82) had made the transition to a three-man staff—trouble was, their three starters just weren't very good. The Mets finished a dismal seventh place, 38 games behind the American Association league leading St. Louis Browns.

In a short series, the one-two punch of Keefe and Welch could be devastating to a lesser club and this was proven in the first of two New York city championships. The Giants trotted out Keefe against John Schaffer (5–3) for Game One on the 16th of October played, oddly enough, at the new Ridgewood Park, home of the Brooklyn Dodgers. Schaffer limited the Giants to only four hits, all singles, but the New Yorks bunched theirs well, scoring single runs in the first and third and two in the fifth. The only run the Mets could manage, although they had eight hits off Keefe, came in the first as John "Candy" Nelson doubled and came around to score on Dave Orr's single. The game was called because of darkness at the end of five innings and one wonders just how long it would take the New York clubs to realize they might get a full game in if they just started a little earlier than 3:15 in the afternoon. It is a mystery why any fans at all came out to the games, knowing in advance that they were paying full admission to see only five or six innings.

The second game of the series was played the next day before a large gathering of 4,000 fans, also at Ridgewood. Mickey Welch and Jack Lynch (20–30) were the two starting pitchers and it didn't take long for the fun to begin. The Mets scored twice in the top of the first on hits by Nelson and rookie John

1886 New York City Championship Series I

GAME ONE --- October 16

METROPOLITANS	AB	R	H	PO	A	E		NEW YORK	AB	R	H	PO	A	E
Nelson, ss	3	1	1	0	1	1		Ewing, c	3	1	2	3	1	0
Roseman, lf	3	0	0	1	0	0		Ward, ss	3	1	1	1	2	2
Meister, 2b	3	0	0	2	2	0		Connor, 1b	2	0	0	5	0	0
Orr, 1b	2	0	1	7	0	0		Gillespie, lf	2	0	0	1	0	0
Hankinson, 3b	2	0	0	2	1	0		Dorgan, rf	2	0	0	1	0	0
Donahue, cf	2	0	1	0	0	1		Esterbrook, 3b	2	0	0	1	1	1
McLaughlin, ss	2	0	1	0	2	1		Finley, rf	2	0	0	0	0	0
Holbert, c	2	0	1	3	2	0		Keefe, p	2	1	0	1	3	1
Schaffer, p	2	0	0	0	4	1		Richardson, 2b	2	1	1	2	2	0
	21	1	5	15	12	4			20	4	4	15	9	4

```
MET     1  0  0    0  0  -  1
NY      1  0  1    0  2  -  4
```

Earned runs: MET 1, NY 2. LOB: MET 6, NY 1. 2B: Nelson. 3B: Orr. BB: Keefe 1, Schaffer 1. Struck out: Keefe 3, Schaffer 2. DP: NY. PB: Ewing. Umpire: Connelly. Time—1:20.

GAME TWO --- October 17

METROPOLITANS	AB	R	H	PO	A	E		NEW YORK	AB	R	H	PO	A	E
Nelson, rf	3	1	1	2	0	0		Ewing, c	3	1	0	0	7	0
Roseman, lf	4	0	1	1	0	0		Connor, 1b	4	0	0	16	1	0
Meister, 2b	4	2	2	3	0	0		Gillespie, lf	4	0	0	4	0	0
Orr, 1b	4	0	1	11	0	1		Richardson, 3b	3	2	1	2	3	1
Hankinson, 3b	4	0	1	2	6	0		Finley, rf	4	1	2	0	0	0
Donahue, cf	4	0	0	3	0	1		Keefe, cf	4	0	3	0	0	0
McLaughlin, ss	3	0	0	0	4	0		Wilson, c	4	0	1	1	1	2
Reipschlager, c	4	0	0	2	2	0		Welch, p	3	0	1	1	0	0
Lynch, p	4	0	2	0	0	0		Gerhardt, 2b	3	1	1	3	3	0
	34	3	8	24	12	2			32	5	9	27	15	3

```
MET     2  0  0    0  0  1    0  0  0  -  3
NY      3  0  0    0  0  0    1  1  x  -  5
```

Earned run: MET. LOB: MET 3, NY 5. 2B: Richardson, Keefe, Meister, Lynch. DP: NY 1. BB: Welch 3, Lynch 2. Struck out: Lynch 3, Welch 2. PB: Wilson 2. WP: Lynch 2, Welch 1. Umpire: Mathews. Att: 4,000. Time—1:35.

Meister and a wild throw. The Giants came back in their half of the inning with walks to Buck Ewing and Danny Richardson, a single by rookie Bill Finley, and a double by Keefe (playing center field). The Mets tied the game in the sixth on Meister's double and a single by Frank Hankinson. The Giants took the lead for good with two hits and a wild throw in the seventh and scored an insurance run in the eighth on Richardson's double and Keefe's single. The starting pitchers got the decisions. After being the pitching star on the previous day, Tim Keefe was the batting star of this game with a 3-for-4 performance, including two singles, a double, and three RBIs.

The series moved to the Polo Grounds for the finale on the 19th, Welch against Ed Cushman (17–20). Welch pitched a four-hit shutout, walked one, and struck out two in an abbreviated five-inning game which took under an

1886 New York City Championship Series I

```
GAME THREE --- October 19
```

METROPOLITANS	AB	R	H	PO	A	E		NEW YORK	AB	R	H	PO	A	E
Nelson, ss	1	0	0	0	0	0		Ewing, c	3	0	1	1	2	0
Scheffelin, cf	2	0	1	1	0	0		Connor, 1b	3	1	0	7	0	0
Meister, 2b	2	0	0	5	4	1		Gillespie, lf	3	0	2	2	0	0
Orr, 1b	2	0	0	7	1	1		Dorgan, rf	2	0	1	0	0	0
Brady, rf	2	0	1	0	1	0		Esterbrook, 3b	2	1	0	0	3	0
Donahue, lf	2	0	0	0	0	0		Richardson, cf	1	0	0	1	0	0
McLaughlin, 3b	2	0	0	0	2	1		Finley, c	2	0	0	2	2	0
Holbert, c	2	0	2	2	1	0		Welch, p	1	1	1	0	1	0
Cushman, p	1	0	0	0	1	0		Gerhardt, 2b	2	0	0	2	2	0
	16	0	4	15	10	3			19	3	5	15	10	0

```
NY    0  2  1    0  0  -  3
MET   0  0  0    0  0  -  0
```

Earned run: NY. LOB: MET 2, NY 3. DP: NY 1, MET 1. 2B: Welch. SB: Connor. BB: Welch 1, Cushman 2. Struck out: Cushman 2, Welch 2. WP: Cushman. Umpire: West. Time—55 min.

hour to play. He also helped himself at the plate, doubling and scoring a run. Errors hurt the Mets as only one of the Giant runs was earned.

The 1886 New York Championship Series II

Brooklyn Trolley Dodgers defeat New York Giants; 3–1

The Giants were less fortunate in the second 1886 New York city championship series, going down to defeat to the Brooklyn Trolley Dodgers three-games-to-one. The third-place Dodgers (76–61) were a much improved team from their 53–59 finish of 1885.

Game One was played on the 18th of October at Washington Park with Brooklyn's Steve Toole (6–6) matched against Tim Keefe (42–20). The game was scoreless until the third when a walk to George Pinckney and successive singles by Bill McClellan, Ed Swartwood, Bill Phillips, Jim McTamany, and Ernie Burch pushed across five Brooklyn runs. The Dodgers tallied two insurance runs in the fifth and the Giants scored their only two runs in the bottom of the inning on a base on balls to Buck Ewing, a double by Monte Ward, and a wild pitch. The game could only be played five innings because of, guess what, darkness.

The Giants returned the 7–2 victory two days later at the Polo Grounds. Adonis Terry (18–16) took the hill against Tim Keefe and was rocked for all seven New York runs in the first four innings. Each team had seven hits, all singles, but the Giants bunched theirs somewhat better than the Dodgers. Umpire West called the game at the end of six because of darkness.

The third game of the series saw a come-from-behind victory for the Dodgers in the last game of the year at the Polo Grounds. The Giants took an

1886 New York City Championship Series II

```
GAME ONE --- October 18
```

BROOKLYN	AB	R	H	PO	A	E
Pinckney, 3b	1	1	0	2	1	1
McClellan, 2b	3	1	2	0	2	1
Swartwood, rf	2	1	0	1	0	0
Phillips, 1b	3	1	1	7	0	2
McTamany, cf	3	2	2	2	0	1
Burch, lf	3	1	1	0	0	0
Smith, ss	3	0	1	0	1	0
Toole, p	3	0	0	1	4	1
Clarke, c	2	0	0	2	0	1
	23	7	7	15	8	7

NEW YORK	AB	R	H	PO	A	E
Ewing, 1b	2	1	1	4	0	0
Ward, ss	3	1	1	2	3	0
Finley, cf	3	0	0	0	0	0
Gillespie, lf	3	0	0	0	0	0
Dorgan, rf	2	0	1	1	0	0
Richardson, 3b	2	0	0	0	0	0
Deasley, c	2	0	0	5	1	1
Keefe, p	2	0	0	0	0	0
Gerhardt, 2b	2	0	0	3	3	1
	21	2	3	15	7	2

```
BKN   0  0  5   0  2  -  7
NY    0  0  0   0  2  -  2
```

Earned runs: BKN 3. LOB: BKN 4, NY 6. DP: NY. 2B: Ward. BB: Keefe 3, Toole 2. Struck out: Toole 1. WP: Keefe, Toole. Umpire: Gill. Time—1:28.

```
GAME TWO --- October 20
```

NEW YORK	AB	R	H	PO	A	E
Ewing, c	4	1	1	3	0	0
Connor, 1b	3	2	1	6	0	0
Gillespie, lf	1	0	0	1	0	0
Dorgan, rf	3	1	1	0	0	0
Esterbrook, 3b	3	0	1	0	0	0
Richardson, ss	2	1	1	3	6	1
Deasley, cf	2	1	0	0	0	1
Keefe, p	3	0	1	0	0	0
Gerhardt, 2b	3	1	1	5	5	1
	24	7	7	18	11	3

BROOKLYN	AB	R	H	PO	A	E
Pinckney, 3b	3	0	0	0	1	0
McClellan, 2b	3	0	2	2	0	2
Swartwood, rf	2	0	0	0	0	0
Phillips, 1b	3	1	1	6	0	0
McTamany, cf	3	0	1	0	0	0
Burch, lf	3	1	2	2	0	0
Smith, ss	3	0	1	0	3	0
Peoples, c	2	0	0	8	1	1
Terry, p	2	0	0	0	2	0
	24	2	7	18	7	3

```
NY    1  4  1   1  0  0  -  7
BKN   0  1  0   1  0  0  -  2
```

Earned run: NY. LOB: NY 3, BKN 5. DP: NY 3. BB: Terry 5, Keefe 1. Struck out: Terry 5, Keefe 3. PB: Peoples 2. WP: Terry 1, Keefe 2. Umpire: West. Time—1:25.

early 6–1 lead against Henry Porter (27–19) and with Mickey Welch (33–22) on the mound things seemed to be in hand. But Welch faltered, giving up single runs to the Dodgers in the third, fourth, and fifth. He still held a 6–4 lead when the Dodgers came to the plate in the bottom of the sixth, but an error by Dude Esterbrook, walks to Porter, Pinckney, and McClellan, a single by Swartwood, and a sacrifice fly by Phillips sent across four runs and gave the Dodgers an 8–6 lead. Coitus interruptus struck again, and the game was called because of darkness.

The final game of the series took place at Washington Park before 2,500 spectators on the 23rd of October, Tim Keefe against Adonis Terry. The Dodgers struck for three runs in the third when Jimmy Peoples walked, stole second, and scored on a double by Pinckney. McClellan singled, scoring Pinckney, stole second, and scored on a double by Swartwood. The Dodgers scored

1886 New York Championship Series II

GAME THREE --- October 22

NEW YORK	AB	R	H	PO	A	E
Ewing, c	4	0	0	5	1	0
Connor, 1b	3	0	0	5	1	1
Gillespie, lf	3	2	3	3	0	0
Dorgan, rf	3	2	2	0	2	0
Esterbrook, 3b	3	2	2	2	2	2
Richardson, ss	3	0	1	0	1	0
Begley, cf	3	0	0	0	0	0
Welch, p	2	0	0	1	3	7
Gerhardt, 2b	3	0	1	2	3	1
	27	6	9	18	13	11

BROOKLYN	AB	R	H	PO	A	E
Pinckney, 3b	2	1	0	1	0	0
McClellan, 2b	3	2	2	0	6	1
Swartwood, rf	2	0	1	1	1	0
Phillips, 1b	4	0	2	11	0	0
McTamany, cf	3	2	2	1	1	0
Burch, lf	3	0	0	1	0	0
Smith, ss	3	1	1	1	4	0
Clark, c	3	0	0	2	0	3
Porter, p	2	2	0	0	3	1
	25	8	8	18	15	5

```
NY    3  0  3    0  0  0  -  6
BKN   0  1  1    1  1  4  -  8
```

Earned runs: NY 3. LOB: NY 4, BKN 6. 2B: Dorgan, McTamany. BB: Porter 1, Welch 7. Struck out: Porter 2, Welch 3. PB: Ewing 3, Clark 1. WP: Porter 2. Umpire: Connell. Time—1:30.

GAME FOUR --- October 23

NEW YORK	R	H	PO	A	E
Ewing, cf	0	0	2	0	2
Connor, 1b	0	0	8	0	0
Gillespie, lf	0	0	0	0	0
Ward, ss	0	2	1	3	0
Esterbrook, 3b	0	0	0	2	0
Richardson, rf	0	0	2	0	0
Deasley, c	0	0	3	2	0
Keefe, p	0	0	0	1	0
Gerhardt, 2b	0	0	2	2	0
	0	2	18	10	2

BROOKLYN	R	H	PO	A	E
Pinckney, 3b	1	1	0	1	0
McClellan, 2b	1	2	1	0	0
Swartwood, rf	0	1	1	0	0
Phillips, 1b	0	0	4	0	0
McTamany, cf	0	1	3	0	0
Burch, lf	0	1	1	0	0
Smith, ss	0	0	1	3	0
Terry, p	0	0	1	0	0
Peoples, c	2	0	6	3	0
	4	6	18	7	0

```
BKN   0  0  3    0  1  0  -  4
NY    0  0  0    0  0  0  -  0
```

Earned runs: BKN 2. 2B: Pinckney, Swartwood. BB: Terry 1, Keefe 1. Struck out: Terry 6, Keefe 3. PB: Peoples. DP: BKN. Umpire: Connell. Att: 2,500. Time—1:35.

the final run of the game in the fifth, courtesy of Giants' center-fielder Buck Ewing. Peoples hit a fly ball to Ewing which he dropped for an error. George Pinckney then flew out to Ewing and Buck, in an ineffectual attempt to throw Peoples out at third, heaved the ball over the head of Dude Esterbrook and Peoples scored. Tim Keefe took the loss. Terry pitched a two-hit shutout, walked one and struck out six, and would have had a no-hitter if Monte Ward had taken the day off. Ward had the only two hits for the Giants, both singles.

The umpires, still scratching their heads at how the evening followed the day, called the game at the end of six innings.

1887 Philadelphia City Championship Series

```
GAME ONE --- October 12
```

ATHLETICS	AB	R	H	PO	A	E		PHILLIES	AB	R	H	PO	A	E
Poorman, rf	5	1	1	3	0	0		Wood, lf	5	1	2	1	0	1
Lyons, 3b	5	0	4	5	1	0		Andrews, cf	5	0	1	2	0	1
Milligan, 1b	5	0	1	10	1	1		Fogarty, rf	5	0	2	0	0	1
Stovey, lf	5	0	2	2	0	0		Mulvey, 3b	5	1	1	3	4	1
Larkin, 2b	5	1	2	1	5	0		Ferguson, 2b	4	1	1	2	2	0
Mann, cf	5	0	1	2	0	0		Farrar, 1b	4	0	1	10	1	0
Robinson, c	5	0	1	5	1	1		Irwin, ss	4	0	1	3	2	0
McGarr, ss	4	0	2	1	3	0		Buffinton, p	4	0	1	0	5	0
Seward, p	4	1	0	1	3	0		Clements, c	4	0	1	9	5	1
	43	3	14	30	14	2			40	3	11	30	19	5

```
PHI   1 0 0   0 0 0    0 0 2   0 - 3
ATH   0 0 1   0 0 1    1 0 0   0 - 3
```
Earned run: ATH 1. DP: PHI 1, ATH 2. 2B: Fogarty 2, Milligan. SB: Andrews, Ferguson, Robinson, McGarr. BB: Seward 4, Buffinton 4. Struck out: Seward 1, Buffinton 4. WP: Seward. PB: Robinson. Umpire: Ferguson.

The 1887 Philadelphia City Championship Series

Philadelphia Phillies defeat Philadelphia Athletics; 3–2–1

The second-place National League Philadelphia Phillies (75–48), managed by Harry Wright, were narrowly beaten out for the 1887 pennant by the Detroit Wolverines. They met the fifth-place American Association Philadelphia Athletics (64–69) in a postseason series for the 1887 championship of the city of Philadelphia. All six games were played at the National League park, the Philadelphia Baseball Grounds, and the Phillies expected to dispatch the Athletics without any difficulty.

Game One was scheduled for the 11th of October, but cold and rain delayed the series' opener until the 12th. Charlie Buffinton (21–17) and Ed Seward (25–25) were the starting pitchers. The Phillies got off to a fast start in the top of the first when leadoff batter George "Dandy" Wood walked, stole second, and came around to score on Jocko Milligan's error. The Athletics tied the game in the third on errors by Joe Mulvey, Ed Andrews, and Jim Fogarty, and Denny Lyons's single. The Athletics went up 2–1 in the sixth when Henry Larkin walked, moved to second on an out, and scored on Wilbert Robinson's single. Singles by Tom Poorman and Lyons in the seventh and a wild throw by Jack Clements accounted for their final run. The Phillies were one out away from going down to a 3–1 defeat in the ninth when Mulvey and Charlie Ferguson singled. Ferguson lit out to steal second and Mulvey bluffed a steal from third. Wilbert Robinson fired the ball over Lyons' head at third and both runners scored to tie the game. Neither side did anything in the tenth inning and the game was called because of darkness.

The second game featured rookie Gus Weyhing (26–28) against Charlie Ferguson (22–10) of the Phillies. This was Ferguson's fourth and last year in the major leagues after compiling a 99–64 lifetime record. If Weyhing had been

1887 Philadelphia City Championship Series

GAME TWO --- October 13

ATHLETICS	AB	R	H	PO	A	E
Poorman, rf	5	0	0	1	0	0
Lyons, 3b	5	2	1	2	1	0
Milligan, c	4	1	3	4	1	2
Stovey, lf	4	1	2	0	1	0
Larkin, 1b	4	0	1	11	0	0
Mann, cf	4	0	1	2	0	0
Bierbauer, 2b	4	0	1	4	3	0
McGarr, ss	4	1	2	2	3	1
Weyhing, p	4	0	0	0	3	0
	38	5	11	*26	12	3

PHILLIES	AB	R	H	PO	A	E
Wood, lf	5	2	2	1	0	0
Andrews, cf	5	1	2	1	1	0
Fogarty, rf	5	0	3	1	0	0
Mulvey, 3b	4	1	2	2	4	1
Ferguson, 2b	4	1	2	1	3	0
Buffinton, 1b	4	0	0	11	0	0
Irwin, ss	4	0	0	1	6	1
Clements, c	4	0	1	5	2	0
Bastian, 2b	4	1	1	4	2	0
	39	6	13	27	18	2

* Two men out when winning run scored

```
ATH    0   0   2     0   0   3     0   0   0   -   5
PHI    0   1   2     0   1   0     1   0   1   -   6
```

Earned runs: ATH 3, PHI 5. DP: PHI 3. 2B: McGarr, Mulvey, Andrews. 3B: Clements. BB: Weyhing 6. Struck out: Weyhing 3, Ferguson 3. LOB: ATH 3, PHI 6. PB: Milligan 2. Umpire: Ferguson. Time—1:45.

GAME THREE --- October 14

ATHLETICS	AB	R	H	PO	A	E
Poorman, rf	5	3	3	0	0	0
Lyons, 3b	5	0	1	1	4	0
Milligan, 1b	5	1	2	11	0	1
Stovey, lf	5	1	2	2	0	0
Larkin, 2b	5	2	3	1	4	2
Mann, cf	5	1	3	2	0	0
Robinson, c	4	1	1	6	0	0
McGarr, ss	4	1	0	1	2	2
Seward, p	4	1	0	0	6	0
	42	11	15	24	16	5

PHILLIES	AB	R	H	PO	A	E
Wood, lf	5	1	2	1	0	0
Andrews, cf	5	1	3	1	0	0
Fogarty, rf	5	1	1	3	0	0
Mulvey, 3b	4	0	0	3	2	0
Ferguson, 2b	4	0	1	2	0	2
Buffinton, 1b	4	1	2	7	0	0
Irwin, ss	4	1	0	3	8	2
Maul, p	4	0	1	0	1	0
Clements, c	4	1	1	2	0	2
	39	6	11	*22	11	6

* One man out when game was called

```
PHI    0   2   0     1   0   0     3   0   -   6
ATH    1   0   0     2   0   7     0   1   -   11
```

Earned runs: PHI 4, ATH 2. LOB: ATH 5, PHI 9. DP: ATH. 2B: Maul, Milligan, Larkin 2. 3B: Clements. BB: Seward 3, Maul 3. Struck out: Seward 3, Maul 1. PB: Robinson 2, Clements 2. WP: Maul 1, Seward 2. Umpire: Ferguson. Time—1:50.

able to control his wildness, he might have won the game. Gus gave up six bases on balls during the contest and it was a free pass that eventually spelled his doom. The lead changed hands four times before the Phillies mounted their final assault against Weyhing in the bottom of the ninth. Charlie Bastian walked and stole second, and Jim Fogarty's two-out single brought him in with the winning run. The final score was 6–5.

Game Three was a wild contest which saw 17 runs, 25 hits, 11 errors, six walks, five stolen bases, four passed balls, and three wild pitches. Ed Seward of the Athletics and the much-travelled Al Maul (4–2) were the two starting

1887 Philadelphia City Championship Series

GAME FOUR --- October 15

ATHLETICS	R	H	PO	A	E		PHILLIES	R	H	PO	A	E
Poorman, rf	2	2	0	1	1		Wood, lf	1	3	0	1	0
Lyons, 3b	2	1	4	2	2		Andrews, cf	2	0	3	0	0
Milligan, 1b	1	2	5	0	0		Fogarty, rf	2	1	0	0	0
Stovey, lf	1	1	4	0	0		Mulvey, 3b	1	2	1	2	0
Larkin, 2b	2	2	5	2	0		Ferguson, 2b	1	2	3	0	1
Mann, cf	1	1	0	1	0		Farrar, 1b	0	2	13	0	1
Townsend, c	0	1	4	4	0		Irwin, ss	0	0	1	2	0
McGarr, ss	0	0	1	2	1		McGuire, c	2	2	3	0	1
Weyhing, p	1	1	1	3	0		Casey, p	0	1	0	6	1
	10	11	24	15	4			9	13	24	11	4

```
ATH    4  6  0    0  0  0    0  0  -  10
PHI    3  1  0    0  2  2    0  1  -   9
```

Earned runs: ATH 7, PHI 3. DP: ATH 1. SB: Poorman, Larkin, Andrews 3, Fogarty. BB: Casey 1, Weyhing 5. Struck out: Casey 1, Weyhing 2. PB: Townsend 3, McGuire 1. WP: Weyhing 1, Casey 1. Umpire: Ferguson. Time—1:45.

pitchers. Maul would spend time with ten teams in his 15-year major league career, including two tours of duty with the Phillies. The game was tied at three all until the bottom of the sixth. Errors by Ferguson, Art Irwin, and Clements, combined with six hits, sent across seven runs for the A's, only one of which was earned. The Phillies scored three times in the seventh, but still lost by the wide margin of 11–6. The game was called at the end of eight innings because of darkness. Seward got the win, Maul the loss. Every man in the Athletics' lineup got a hit except the pitcher and shortstop James "Chippy" McGarr.

The fourth game was played on the 15th and resulted in a contest not unlike the day before. This game saw 19 runs, 24 hits, ten errors, six walks, five stolen bases, five passed balls, two hit batsmen, a wild pitch, and a partridge in a pear tree. The Athletics started off with a rush against losing pitcher Dan Casey (24–18) when they banged out ten hits and scored ten runs in the first two innings, nine of them earned. In one of the most unbelievable turnarounds in the history of baseball, Casey then retired 18 of the next 19 batters he faced, allowing only one hit. (He lost his touch in the ninth, however. The Athletics struck for three singles, a double, and a base on balls, good for three runs, but the inning was unplayed and the score reverted to the end of the eighth.) The Phillies, meanwhile, were doing a little pounding of their own against Gus Weyhing. Weyhing, suffering from wildness in his second start, gave up five walks, hit two batters and allowed 12 hits, but managed to hold on for a 10–9 victory. The Phillies scored in five of the eight innings played, and might even have won the game, but darkness called a halt to the proceedings in the ninth. For the second day in a row, Chippy McGarr failed to get a hit even though every other batter in the Athletic's lineup hit safely.

Some semblance of sanity returned to the series in Game Five, at least from the point of view of the Phillies. Charlie Buffinton returned to the mound for the Nationals and gave up 11 hits, but held the Athletics to two runs over

1887 Philadelphia City Championship Series

```
GAME FIVE --- October 18
```

PHILLIES	AB	R	H	PO	A	E		ATHLETICS	AB	R	H	PO	A	E
Wood, lf	5	0	1	0	1	0		Poorman, rf	5	1	2	3	1	0
Andrews, cf	5	1	1	0	0	0		Lyons, 3b	4	0	2	1	0	0
Fogarty, rf	5	2	2	1	0	0		Milligan, 1b	4	0	2	7	0	1
Mulvey, 3b	5	2	2	0	3	1		Stovey, lf	4	0	0	0	0	0
Ferguson, 2b	5	2	3	5	3	0		Larkin, 2b	4	0	1	4	6	1
Farrar, 1b	4	1	2	6	0	0		Mann, cf	4	0	1	1	0	0
Bastian, ss	4	1	2	3	3	0		Robinson, c	4	0	1	4	2	2
Buffinton, p	4	0	1	0	1	0		McGarr, ss	4	0	1	1	1	0
Clements, c	4	0	1	6	4	0		Seward, p	4	1	1	0	4	0
	41	9	15	21	15	1			37	2	11	21	14	4

```
PHI   0  1  0    4  1  0    3  -  9
ATH   0  0  0    0  0  2    0  -  2
```

Earned runs: PHI 4. 2B: Fogarty, Mulvey 2, Bastian, Lyons, Seward. SB: Andrews, Fogarty, Poorman, Robinson. DP: PHI 2, ATH 1. BB: Seward 4, Buffinton 2. Struck out: Seward 3. WP: Seward 3. Umpire: Ferguson.

```
GAME SIX --- October 21
```

ATHLETICS	AB	R	H	PO	A	E		PHILLIES	AB	R	H	PO	A	E
Poorman, rf	5	1	1	0	0	0		Wood, lf	6	2	4	1	0	0
Lyons, 3b	5	0	3	2	4	0		Andrews, cf	6	3	4	1	1	0
Milligan, 1b	4	0	1	11	0	1		Maul, rf	6	2	0	1	0	0
Stovey, lf	4	0	0	0	1	0		Mulvey, 3b	5	3	3	0	2	0
Larkin, 2b	4	0	0	1	5	0		Ferguson, 2b	5	1	4	1	3	0
Mann, cf	4	0	1	1	1	0		Farrar, 1b	5	1	1	7	0	0
Townsend, c	4	0	1	3	0	0		Irwin, ss	5	1	2	2	2	0
McGarr, ss	4	1	1	3	5	0		McGuire, c	5	2	2	7	1	1
Weyhing, p	4	0	1	0	2	0		Casey, p	5	2	3	1	6	0
	38	2	9	21	19	1			48	17	23	21	15	1

```
ATH   0  0  1    0  1  0    0  -  2
PHI   2  2  3    3  6  0    1  - 17
```

Earned runs: ATH 2, PHI 15. 2B: Lyons, Milligan, Wood, Irwin, Casey. 3B: Mulvey, McGuire. DP: ATH 2. HBP: Maul and Farrar (Weyhing). Struck out: Casey 6, Weyhing 1. PB: Townsend 5, McGuire 1. Umpire: Ferguson.

the seven innings played. Two double plays bailed him out of any more serious trouble. The only runs the A's scored were unearned and came as a result of Joe Mulvey dropping the ball after making a tag for the final out of the sixth inning. The Phillies belted Ed Seward all around the park to the tune of 15 base hits, among them four doubles and two triples. Every man hit safely in the game except for the Athletics' left fielder, Harry Stovey.

Rain postponed the game scheduled for the 20th so the series finale was played on the 21st. Gus Weyhing, who by now must have been carrying on some lively conversations with imaginary playmates, was clubbed all about the head and shoulders by the Phillies. He gave up 23 hits and 17 runs and one shudders to think what might have happened if he had suffered a recurrence of his previous wildness. (He walked no one.) The Phillies scored twice in the first and second, three times in the third and fourth, six times in the fifth, took a brief rest in the sixth, then scored their final run of the day in the bottom of the seventh. Umpire Ferguson mercifully called the game at this point. Fifteen of the 17 Philadelphia runs were earned. The Athletics, meanwhile, were getting nowhere fast with the deliveries of Dan Casey and could only manage single runs in the third and fifth.

A fifth game was scheduled for the 22nd of October, but because of extremely cold temperatures, the contest was cancelled.

In the three games he started, Gus Weyhing pitched a total of 24 innings, allowed 49 hits, 32 runs, 27 earned runs, 11 walks, and he struck out six. His earned run average was a lofty 10.13. But rather than leave the impression that Weyhing was a sort of 19th century George Frazier (the pitcher), let me mention some of his lifetime statistics. In a 14-year career which saw him don 11 different uniforms — in the middle of his career, he played for eight teams in six years — Weyhing won 264 games and lost 235, a career winning percentage of .529, better than some Hall of Famers. He worked in four leagues — the National League, the American Association, the Players' League, and the American League. Weyhing appeared in 538 games, started 503, and completed 448. He pitched 4325 innings which was 441 more than Bob Gibson and 2101 more than Sandy Koufax. His career ERA was 3.89. In his first seven years in the majors, he won 20 or more games, and in four of those years, won 30 or more. He never led the league in any category during his career, but his wildness earned him an eighth-place finish on the all-time walks list with 1566.

Gus Weyhing was no pushover. But he clearly didn't care a fig about the 1887 Philadelphia city championship series.

The 1888 Philadelphia City Championship Series

Philadelphia Phillies defeat Philadelphia Athletics; 2–1

The third-place Philadelphia Phillies (69–61) met the third-place American Association Philadelphia Athletics (81–52) for the 1888 city championship series. The Athletics finished a distant third behind the champion St. Louis Browns but led the AA in runs scored, doubles, triples, batting average and slugging average and were a formidable team.

Game One, on October 18th, was played at the Philadelphia Baseball Grounds, home of the Phillies and future site of the Baker Bowl. Ben Sanders (19–10) got off to a good start when he struck out the side in the first, but the Athletics touched him for two runs in the second. The Phillies held a 4–3 lead into the bottom of the eighth when the A's struck for six hits and five runs to go ahead 8–4. A final rally by the Nationals fell three runs short in the ninth. Harry Decker, catcher for the Toronto team, was the fielding star of the game, making a fine one-handed running catch of a ball off the bat of winning pitcher Ed Seward (35–19). Decker went on to catch for the Phillies in 1889.

1888 Philadelphia City Championship Series

GAME ONE --- October 18

PHILLIES	AB	R	H	PO	A	E		ATHLETICS	AB	R	H	PO	A	E
Delahanty, rf	5	1	4	0	0	0		Mattimore, cf	5	1	2	1	0	0
Andrews, cf	4	1	0	1	1	1		Stovey, lf	5	0	2	3	0	0
Sanders, p	5	0	1	0	10	0		Lyons, 3b	4	1	1	1	1	0
Farrar, 1b	5	0	0	8	0	0		Larkin, 1b	5	1	1	8	0	2
Clements, c	5	0	2	9	1	0		Purcell, rf	5	2	2	3	2	0
Decker, c	4	0	0	1	0	1		Bierbauer, 2b	5	2	2	1	2	0
Mulvey, 3b	4	2	3	2	3	0		Fennelly, ss	4	1	2	1	2	0
Irwin, ss	3	0	1	1	1	2		Robinson, c	4	0	1	9	1	0
Bastian, 2b	4	1	1	2	2	1		Seward, p	4	0	0	0	7	0
	39	5	12	24	18	5			41	8	13	27	15	2

```
PHI    0   0   1     0   0   0     3   0   1   -   5
ATH    0   2   0     0   1   0     0   5   x   -   8
```

Earned runs: PHI 3, ATH 5. DP: ATH. LOB: ATH 6, PHI 7. 2B: Delahanty, Mulvey 2, Lyons, Larkin, Fennelly. 3B: Irwin. SB: Delahanty, Andrews 2, Mulvey, Mattimore. BB: Seward 2, Sanders 1. Struck out: Seward 4, Sanders 8. WP: Seward 2. PB: Clements 2, Robinson 3. Umpire: Ferguson. Time—2:00.

GAME TWO --- October 19

ATHLETICS	AB	R	H	PO	A	E		PHILLIES	AB	R	H	PO	A	E
Welch, cf	2	0	0	0	0	0		Delahanty, rf	4	1	1	1	0	0
Stovey, lf	3	0	1	2	0	0		Andrews, cf	5	1	1	1	0	0
Lyons, 3b	4	0	1	1	3	1		Farrar, 1b	5	1	1	7	0	0
Larkin, 1b	4	0	0	12	1	0		Decker, lf	4	0	1	2	0	0
Purcell, rf	3	0	0	1	0	0		Irwin, ss	4	2	2	2	1	0
Bierbauer, 2b	3	0	1	3	3	1		Mulvey, 3b	4	2	2	1	4	1
Fennelly, ss	3	0	1	1	4	0		Hallman, c	4	1	1	9	2	0
Townsend, c	3	0	0	3	1	1		Bastian, 2b	4	0	1	4	1	0
Weyhing, p	3	0	0	1	6	0		Casey, p	4	0	0	0	7	0
	28	0	4	24	18	3			38	8	10	27	15	1

```
ATH    0   0   0     0   0   0     0   0   0   -   0
PHI    4   1   2     0   0   0     0   1   x   -   8
```

Earned runs: PHI 2. DP: PHI. LOB: ATH 4, PHI 4. 2B: Mulvey. 3B: Farrar. SB: Delahanty, Decker, Irwin, Mulvey, Hallman 2. BB: Casey 2, Weyhing 1. Struck out: Casey 6, Weyhing 1. HBP: Welch (Casey). WP: Weyhing. PB: Hallman. Umpire: Ferguson. Time—1:35.

The series moved to Gloucester Point Grounds, the home of the Athletics, for Game Two on the 19th of October. Dan Casey (14–18) of the Phillies and the A's Gus Weyhing (28–18) were the starters. Weyhing had just won 20 games for the second year in a row and would go on to win 20 or more in the next five consecutive seasons. But today he just didn't have it. The Phillies scored seven runs in the first three innings and went on to an 8–0 victory. Casey scattered four singles, walked two, and struck out six batters for the easy win. Only one Athletic runner made it as far as third base.

The rubber game of the series was played at the Philadelphia Baseball Grounds and was a complete blowout. The Phillies duplicated their performance

1888 Philadelphia City Championship Series

GAME THREE --- October 20

PHILLIES	AB	R	H	PO	A	E		ATHLETICS	AB	R	H	PO	A	E
Delahanty, rf	4	1	0	0	0	0		Welch, cf	4	0	1	0	0	0
Gleason, rf	1	0	0	0	0	0		Stovey, lf	4	0	0	0	0	0
Andrews, cf	5	2	2	1	0	0		Lyons, 3b	4	0	0	1	7	1
Farrar, 1b	3	3	2	10	0	0		Larkin, 1b	4	0	1	15	1	2
Schriver, 1b	1	0	1	3	0	0		Purcell, rf	3	0	0	1	0	1
Clements, c	5	1	1	8	0	1		Bierbauer, 2b	3	0	1	2	9	2
Irwin, ss	5	1	1	1	2	0		Gleason, ss	3	0	0	0	2	1
Decker, lf	5	2	1	1	0	0		Robinson, c	2	0	0	7	6	2
Mulvey, 3b	5	0	2	0	4	1		Townsend, c	1	0	0	0	1	0
Buffinton, p	4	1	3	0	12	1		Smith, p	3	0	0	1	4	2
Bastian, 2b	4	1	1	3	0	0			31	0	3	27	30	11
	42	12	14	27	18	3								

```
PHI   4  1  2     3  0  1     0  1  0  -  12
ATH   0  0  0     0  0  0     0  0  0  -   0
```

Earned runs: PHI 5. LOB: PHI 7, ATH 4. 2B: Mulvey, Schriver. 3B: Farrar, Bierbauer. SB: Delahanty, Farrar, Buffinton 2, Robinson. BB: Smith 2. Struck out: Smith 3, Buffinton 7. HBP: Buffinton (Smith). PB: Robinson 2, Clements 1. Umpire: Ferguson. Time—1:35.

of the previous day by jumping out to the same 7–0 lead after three innings, then went on to score five more runs in this 12–0 shellacking. Charlie Buffinton (28–17) retired the Athletics in order through the first five innings and was so tough that the A's were unable to score even when Sid Farrar tripled to lead off the eighth. The Phillies just manhandled losing pitcher John "Phenomenal" Smith (2–1) for 14 hits. Only five of their 12 runs were earned, due to the staggering total of 11 errors on the part of the Athletics.

The 1889 Missouri State Championship Series

St. Louis Browns defeat Kansas City Blues; 4–3

Judging by the quality of play, it is hard to imagine either of these two teams placed much importance upon these games and, rightfully, they should be treated as nothing more than a tour. Nonetheless, the St. Louis Browns (90–45) and the Kansas City Blues (55–82) of the American Association were the only two Missouri teams in 1889 and the local papers touted the series as the championship of Missouri. The Blues (sometimes called the Cowboys after the National League team of 1886) were an awful team and spent only two years in the league before reclaiming their minor league status. They finished last in 1888 and seventh in 1889. The Browns, on the other hand, had just won four straight league pennants and had narrowly missed a fifth, finishing two games behind the Brooklyn Trolley Dodgers (93–44).

The first game was played at Sedalia, Missouri on the 19th of October. The umpire was Joe Gunson of the Kansas City club and the starting pitchers were Elton "Icebox" Chamberlain (32–15) for the Browns and rookie Frank Pears

1889 Missouri State Championship Series

GAME ONE --- October 19 at Sedalia

KANSAS CITY	AB	R	H	PO	A	E
Long, ss	5	1	3	2	2	0
Hamilton, rf	4	0	0	1	0	0
Burns, cf	4	1	0	4	0	0
Stearns, 1b	4	0	0	10	0	1
Manning, lf	4	0	0	1	0	0
Alvorde, 3b	4	0	1	1	1	2
Pickett, 2b	4	1	2	2	2	1
Donahue, c	4	0	1	2	1	2
Pears, p	4	0	0	1	6	0
	37	3	7	24	12	6

ST. LOUIS	AB	R	H	PO	A	E
McCarthy, 2b	5	1	2	8	2	0
O'Neill, lf	5	1	1	2	1	0
Comiskey, rf	5	1	0	1	0	0
Duffee, 3b	4	0	0	1	3	1
Fuller, ss	4	0	0	1	2	2
Milligan, 1b	4	1	1	8	1	1
Gettinger, cf	4	0	1	0	0	0
Chamberlain, p	4	0	0	1	1	0
Meek, c	4	0	1	5	1	0
	39	4	6	27	11	4

```
KC    2 0 0   0 0 0   1 0 0  -  3
STL   1 0 0   2 0 1   0 0 x  -  4
```

2B: Meek, Pickett. 3B: Milligan. Struck out: Pears 1, Chamberlain 5. Umpire: Gunson. Time—1:45.

GAME TWO --- October 20 at St. Louis

ST. LOUIS	AB	R	H	PO	A	E
McCarthy, 2b	4	0	0	3	0	0
O'Neill, lf	4	0	0	2	0	0
Comiskey, rf	3	1	0	1	0	0
Milligan, 1b	4	1	2	7	0	0
Duffee, 3b	3	0	1	4	2	1
Gettinger, cf	4	0	2	2	0	0
Fuller, ss	3	0	1	4	3	0
King, p	3	1	1	0	4	0
Meek, c	3	0	0	4	1	1
	31	3	7	27	10	2

KANSAS CITY	AB	R	H	PO	A	E
Long, ss	4	1	1	2	6	0
Hamilton, rf	3	0	0	2	0	0
Burns, cf	4	0	0	2	0	0
Stearns, 1b	4	0	1	9	0	0
Manning, lf	4	0	0	4	0	1
Pickett, 2b	4	0	1	2	1	0
Alvorde, 3b	3	0	1	1	3	0
Gunson, c	3	0	0	5	1	1
Swartzel, p	3	0	0	0	2	0
	32	1	4	27	13	2

```
STL   2 0 0   0 1 0   0 0 0  -  3
KC    0 0 0   0 0 1   0 0 0  -  1
```

Earned runs: STL 2. 3B: King. BB: Swartzel 2, King 1. Struck out: King 4, Swartzel 2. Umpire: McGinnis. Att: 2,000. Time—1:08.

GAME THREE --- October 21 at Quincy

KANSAS CITY	AB	R	H	PO	A	E
Long, ss	4	1	1	3	4	0
Hamilton, rf	3	0	0	0	0	0
Burns, cf	4	3	3	6	0	0
Stearns, 1b	4	2	2	4	0	0
Manning, lf	4	1	1	3	0	0
Pickett, 2b	4	1	1	1	1	0
Alvorde, 3b	4	1	2	0	2	0
Donahue, c	4	1	0	3	0	1
Bell, p	3	1	0	1	1	0
	34	11	10	21	8	1

ST. LOUIS	AB	R	H	PO	A	E
McCarthy, rf	3	0	0	0	1	3
O'Neill, lf	4	1	1	4	1	0
Comiskey, 2b	3	0	1	3	0	0
Milligan, 1b	3	1	1	7	2	0
Duffee, 3b	3	1	1	9	1	2
Gettinger, cf	3	1	2	2	0	0
Fuller, ss	3	0	0	2	5	0
King, p	3	1	1	4	4	0
Ramsey, p	3	0	1	0	0	0
	28	5	8	31	14	5

```
KC    0 1 1   4 1 1   3  -  11
STL   0 0 3   0 1 1   0  -   5
```

Earned runs: KC 2, STL 2. 2B: Burns, Pickett. 3B: Burns, Stearns, O'Neill. HR: Duffee. SB: Comiskey, Burns, Bell 2. BB: Bell 1, Ramsey 1. Struck out: Long 2, Bell 1, Ramsey 3. PB: Boyle 6, Donahue 1. Umpire: Gunson. Att: 2,000. Time—1:15.

1889 Missouri State Championship Series

```
GAME FOUR --- October 23 at Omaha
```

ST. LOUIS	AB	R	H	PO	A	E		KANSAS CITY	AB	R	H	PO	A	E
McCarthy, 2b	4	3	2	1	0	0		Long, ss	4	2	2	0	2	0
O'Neill, lf	4	1	2	1	0	0		Hamilton, rf	4	1	3	2	0	0
Comiskey, rf	4	2	1	3	2	0		Burns, cf	4	2	0	2	0	0
Milligan, 1b	3	1	1	11	0	0		Stearns, 1b	4	2	2	4	0	1
Duffee, 3b	3	1	2	0	3	0		Manning, lf	4	1	1	4	0	0
Gettinger, cf	3	0	1	0	0	0		Pickett, 2b	4	2	1	2	3	0
Fuller, ss	3	0	1	1	2	0		Alvorde, 3b	4	2	1	1	0	0
Meek, c	3	0	0	4	1	2		Gunson, c	4	1	3	5	1	0
Stivetts, p	3	0	1	0	2	0		Pears, p	3	1	1	1	0	0
	30	8	11	21	10	2			35	14	14	21	6	1

```
STL    1  0  6    1  0  0    0  -  8
KC     5  0  1    1  7  0    0  -  14
```

Earned runs: STL 4, KC 9. 2B: McCarthy, Milligan, O'Neill. 3B: McCarthy, Long, Manning. HR: O'Neill, Gettinger, Stearns, Long. SB: Hamilton 2, Pickett 2, Stearns, Manning, Fuller, Comiskey. BB: Pears 2, Stivetts 3. Struck out: Stivetts 4, Pears 5. Umpire: Ramsey. Time—2:00.

```
GAME FIVE --- October 25 at Kansas City
```

KANSAS CITY	AB	R	H	PO	A	E		ST. LOUIS	AB	R	H	PO	A	E
Long, ss	5	0	0	4	2	0		McCarthy, rf	6	1	0	1	0	1
Hamilton, rf	4	0	0	3	0	1		O'Neill, lf	6	0	1	0	0	0
Burns, cf	4	0	1	1	0	0		Comiskey, 1b	5	1	2	11	0	0
Stearns, 1b	4	0	0	10	1	0		Milligan, c	6	2	2	5	2	0
Manning, lf	4	2	2	2	1	0		Duffee, 2b	4	2	3	1	0	0
Pickett, 2b	4	0	0	1	5	0		Gettinger, cf	5	2	2	4	0	1
Donahue, c	4	1	3	3	0	0		W. Fuller, ss	5	2	3	5	3	4
Gunson, 3b	4	0	0	0	0	2		H. Fuller, 3b	5	2	2	0	3	0
Swartzel, p	4	1	0	0	5	3		Ramsey, p	4	0	2	0	0	1
	37	4	6	24	14	6			46	12	17	27	8	7

```
KC     0  0  1    1  0  2    0  0  0  -  4
STL    0  4  3    1  3  0    1  0  x  -  12
```

Earned runs: KC 3, STL 9. 2B: Manning, H. Fuller. 3B: Manning, H. Fuller, Milligan. HR: Duffee, Donahue. SB: Gunson, McCarthy. SH: Long, Ramsey, Gettinger, O'Neill, Comiskey. DP: STL. BB: Swartzel 3. Struck out: Ramsey 3, Swartzel 2. WP: Ramsey. Umpire: Stivetts. Time—1:30.

(0–2) for the Blues. Pears would spend a brief two years in the major leagues, this one and 1893 with the National League St. Louis Browns, but all of his decisions came in 1889. The Blues took a 2–0 first-inning lead, but the Browns caught up and took the lead in the fourth, then held on for a 4–3 victory. The starting pitchers took the decisions and the offensive star of the game was Kansas City's Long with three singles in five times at bat.

The second game was played the next day at Sportsman's Park in St. Louis in bitterly cold weather before 4,000 fans. The Browns scored all the runs they needed in the first when Charlie Comiskey walked and Jocko Milligan singled him to third. Milligan, at 195 pounds, then shocked everyone in the park by stealing second base. Charlie Duffee's single brought both runners home to

1889 Missouri State Championship Series

GAME SIX --- October 26 at Kansas City

ST. LOUIS	AB	R	H	PO	A	E	KANSAS CITY	AB	R	H	PO	A	E
McCarthy, rf	7	1	2	2	0	0	Long, ss	5	1	1	4	0	1
O'Neill, lf	5	2	2	2	0	0	Hamilton, rf	5	1	2	0	0
Comiskey, 1b	6	2	2	8	0	1	Burns, cf	5	1	1	2	0	3
Milligan, c	6	3	3	6	0	1	Stearns, 1b	5	0	1	11	0	0
Duffee, 2b	6	2	2	4	3	0	Manning, 2b	4	2	2	3	4	1
Gettinger, cf	6	3	3	0	1	1	Pickett, 2b	4	1	0	2	1	1
W. Fuller, ss	6	1	2	3	5	1	Donahue, 3b	4	0	1	0	2	0
H. Fuller, 3b	6	2	2	2	1	0	Gunson, c	4	0	0	3	1	2
Stivetts, p	6	2	2	0	2	2	Bell, p	4	0	0	0	3	0
	54	18	20	27	12	6		40	6	7	27	11	8

STL	5	2	1	6	0	0	2	2	0	-	18
KC	0	1	2	0	0	3	0	0	0	-	6

Earned runs: KC 2, STL 8. 2B: Long, Donahue, O'Neill, Comiskey, W. Fuller. 3B: Duffee, Stivetts, Gettinger. HR: Stivetts. SB: Long, Hamilton, Manning, O'Neill, Comiskey, W. Fuller. BB: Bell 2, Stivetts 3. Struck out: Stivetts 6, Bell 1. WP: Bell 2. PB: Milligan 2. Umpire: McCarthy. Att: 50. Time—1:30.

GAME SEVEN --- October 27 at Kansas City

KANSAS CITY	AB	H	PO	A	E	ST. LOUIS	AB	H	PO	A	E
Long, lf	5	2	4	0	0	McCarthy, rf	5	1	0	0	0
Hamilton, rf	4	1	1	0	0	O'Neill, lf	3	0	1	0	0
Swartzel, cf	5	1	2	1	0	Comiskey, 1b	5	3	5	1	0
Stearns, 1b	5	0	16	0	0	Milligan, c	5	1	15	2	0
Manning, ss	3	2	1	3	1	Duffee, 2b	5	2	1	2	0
Pickett, 2b	4	1	2	3	0	Gettinger, cf	5	2	3	0	0
Donahue, c	5	2	1	1	1	W. Fuller, ss	5	1	2	6	2
Gunson, 3b	4	1	0	2	1	H. Fuller, 3b	2	0	0	1	2
pears, p	5	3	0	3	0	Ramsey, p	4	1	0	1	1
	40	13	27	13	3		39	11	27	13	5

KC	2	4	0	0	1	0	2	4	0	-	13
STL	0	1	1	0	0	4	0	1	2	-	9

Earned runs: KC 7, STL 3. 2B: Ramsey. 3B: Manning, Donahue, Gettinger. HR: Duffee. SB: Long, Hamilton, Swartzel, Manning 2, Pears, McCarthy, Comiskey, W. Fuller. DP: KC 2. BB: Pears 3, Ramsey 5. Struck out: Pears 2, Ramsey 2. HBP: H. Fuller (Pears). Umpire: Hoover. Att: 2,500. Time—2:00.

roost. Long scored the only run of the day for the Blues in the sixth when he singled, stole second, and came around on Duffee's error. Silver King (33–17) pitched a four-hitter and helped his own cause when he tripled and scored an insurance run in the sixth. Parke Swartzel (19–27), pitching for his only year in the majors, was the loser.

The Browns, having proved to themselves that they were the superior team, took the next two days off, figuratively speaking. Game Three was played at Quincy, Illinois, before 2,000 fans who gave Jim Burns—a local boy—a standing ovation when he stroked the first hit of the game in the opening half-inning. Burns was popular all day long when he later doubled, tripled, stole a base, and scored three runs. The Blues failed to break on board in the first, but tallied runs in each of the next six innings and won easily, 11–5. Only two of their runs were earned. Rookie Charlie Bell (1–0) was the winning pitcher and Thomas "Toad" Ramsey (3–1), who had only appeared in five games for St. Louis that year, was the loser. The game was halted in the last half of the eighth inning because of rain.

The fourth game was to have been held in Burlington, Iowa, the next day, but rain prevented play. The Browns spent the day playing poker in their Pullman car and left that evening for Omaha, Nebraska, where Game Four was played on the 23rd of October in an open field. Because of the lack of fences, the teams rapped out three doubles, three triples, and four home runs among a total of 25 hits. The Browns scored a measly little run in the first and the Blues answered with five of their own in the bottom of the inning. St. Louis got the idea and came back with a six-run third. They led 8–7 until the Blues exploded for seven in the bottom of the fifth. That ended the scoring on the day. Jack Stivetts (13–7) took the loss, Frank Pears the victory.

The teams trained to Kansas City's Exposition Park and the Browns decided to give the Blues a lesson in how good they really were. In Game Five, played on the 25th, St. Louis banged out 17 hits and won going away, 12–4. Every man in the Browns's lineup had two hits or more except Tip O'Neill with one, and leadoff batter Tommy McCarthy who inexplicably went 0-for-6. The extreme cold weather forced the ballplayers to wear extra clothes under their uniforms which accounts for the elevated total of 13 errors in what had been a rather well-played defensive series. Toad Ramsey pitched a six-hitter, although giving up four runs, and won the game. Parke Swartzel was the losing pitcher for the second time in the series.

If the fifth game was a runaway for the Browns, it was only a poor indicator of what was to come in Game Six. St. Louis scored five times off Charlie Bell in the first inning, twice in the second, once in the third, and six times in the fourth by which time they led 14–3. Among their 20 hits, the Browns had three doubles, three triples, and a home run. The final score was 18–6 and the weather was so cold (how cold was it?) that some of the fielders wore overcoats. A total of 14 errors were made and only 10 of the 24 runs were earned. The ballplayers were barely outnumbered by the 50 fans in attendance.

The final game of the series was Blues' pitcher Frank Pears's first and only appearance before the local fans. Fair weather greeted the teams and 2,500 fans turned out. Kansas City took a 6–0 lead after an inning and a half, then watched while the Browns came back to close to 7–6 at the end of six. This turn of events seemed to spur the Blues on and they scored six runs in the next two innings. The final score was 13–9. The only noteworthy aspect of the contest was that it featured six stolen bases by the Blues and three by the Browns. Pears went the distance for the victory and Toad Ramsey lost his second game of the series. Ramsey had the further distinction of handling the ball three times in the series and making two errors.

1889 Philadelphia City Championship Series

GAME ONE --- October 16

PHILLIES	AB	R	H	PO	A	E		ATHLETICS	AB	R	H	PO	A	E
Delahanty, lf	5	0	1	2	0	1		Welch, cf	5	0	0	5	1	0
Myers, 2b	5	1	1	1	3	0		Larkin, 1b	4	0	0	7	1	0
Fogarty, cf	5	1	2	6	0	0		Lyons, 3b	4	1	2	0	1	0
Thompson, rf	5	1	0	1	0	0		Stovey, lf	4	0	1	2	0	0
Mulvey, 3b	4	0	0	0	2	0		Bierbauer, 2b	4	1	1	2	0	0
Farrar, 1b	4	0	2	12	0	1		Purcell, rf	4	1	2	2	0	1
Decker, c	4	0	2	1	3	0		Fennelly, ss	4	0	0	2	0	0
Hallman, ss	4	0	1	0	3	3		Robinson, c	4	0	1	6	1	0
Gleason, p	4	0	2	1	2	0		Seward, p	4	1	0	1	1	1
	40	3	11	*24	13	5			37	4	7	27	5	2

* None out in ninth when winning run scored

```
PHI   0  0  0    0  0  0    0  0  3  -  3
ATH   0  0  0    0  1  0    1  1  1  -  4
```

2B: Gleason 2, Lyons, Bierbauer. SH: Myers, Welch, Fennelly. SB: Delahanty 2, Fogarty, Stovall 2, Purcell 2. BB: Seward 5, Gleason 3. Struck out: Seward 2, Gleason 1. PB: Decker 4. WP: Seward. Umpires: Curry and Connell. Time—1:45.

The 1889 Philadelphia City Championship Series

Philadelphia Athletics defeat Philadelphia Phillies; 3–2

The fourth-place National League Phillies (63–64) and third-place American Association Athletics (75–78) fought a closely contested 1889 city championship which ended after five games because of inclement weather.

The series opened on October 16th at Gloucester Point Grounds, the home park of the Athletics, with the Phillies' Kid Gleason (9–15) going against Ed Seward (21–15). The game was scoreless until the fifth inning when the Athletics tallied the first run of the series. The A's added single runs in the seventh and eighth, but the Phillies tied the game in the ninth when they finally got to Seward for three runs. Gleason failed to retire anyone in the bottom of the ninth as the Athletics pushed across a run to win the game 4–3. The Phillies, with five errors in the field and four runners thrown out at the plate, contributed heavily to their loss.

Game Two was played on the 17th at the Philadelphia Baseball Grounds, a stadium which would burn down in August of 1894. Ben Sanders (19–18) took the mound against the ace of the Athletics' staff, Gus Weyhing (30–21). The A's beat up on Sanders as if he were pitching batting practice, scoring three in the third, two in the fifth, and four in the sixth. Rookie Dave Anderson (0–1) relieved for the Phils in the seventh and held the hard-hitting A's to a single run over the final three innings. The Phillies might have held the score a little closer were it not for six errors which accounted for eight unearned Athletic runs. The difference probably would have been negligible, however — the A's banged out 15 hits, with Henry Larkin and Lou Bierbauer accounting for three each, and William "Blondie" Purcell, Frank Fennelly, and Weyhing enjoying two-hit

1889 Philadelphia City Championship Series

GAME TWO --- October 17

PHILLIES	AB	R	H	PO	A	E		ATHLETICS	AB	R	H	PO	A	E
Delahanty, 3b	4	0	0	1	2	2		Welch, cf	5	0	0	1	0	0
Myers, 2b	4	1	3	2	4	1		Larkin, 1b	5	3	3	8	0	0
Fogarty, cf	4	0	1	3	0	0		Lyons, 3b	5	0	1	1	0	0
Thompson, rf	4	0	1	0	0	0		Stovey, lf	5	2	1	0	1	0
Gleason, lf	4	0	1	1	1	1		Bierbauer, 2b	5	3	3	4	3	1
Clements, c	4	0	0	8	0	2		Purcell, rf	5	1	2	0	0	0
Sanders, p	2	0	1	0	0	0		Fennelly, ss	5	1	2	0	3	0
Anderson, p	2	0	0	0	1	0		Cross, c	5	0	1	9	2	1
Farrar, 1b	4	0	0	7	0	0		Weyhing, p	5	0	2	1	2	0
Hallman, ss	4	0	0	2	4	0								
	36	1	7	24	12	6			45	10	15	24	11	2

```
PHI   0  0  0    0  0  0    0  0  1  -   1
ATH   0  0  3    0  2  4    1  0  x  -  10
```

Earned runs: ATH 2, PHI 1. 2B: Thompson, Fogarty, Cross. SH: Stovey, Cross, Weyhing, Fogarty. SB: Stovey, Bierbauer, Fogarty. BB: Larkins, Lyons 2, Thompson, Farrar, Fogarty. Struck out: Lyons 2, Stovey 2, Purcell, Fennelly 2, Delahanty 2, Thompson, Clements 2, Anderson, Hallman. PB: Clements. Umpires: Curry and Connell. Time—1:40.

GAME THREE --- October 19

PHILLIES	AB	R	H	PO	A	E		ATHLETICS	AB	R	H	PO	A	E
Fogarty, cf	6	2	2	4	0	0		Welch, cf	5	0	0	1	1	0
Myers, 2b	5	1	0	3	2	0		Larkin, 1b	5	0	2	8	1	0
Delahanty, lf	5	2	3	2	0	0		Lyons, 3b	5	0	2	0	4	0
Thompson, rf	5	2	5	1	1	1		Stovey, lf	5	1	1	0	0	0
Gleason, 3b	5	2	1	1	1	1		Bierbauer, 2b	5	0	1	4	4	0
Clements, c	5	1	2	6	0	0		Purcell, rf	3	1	3	1	0	0
Farrar, 1b	5	0	2	8	0	0		Fennelly, ss	4	0	2	0	3	2
Hallman, ss	5	1	1	2	5	0		Robinson, c	4	0	1	9	1	0
Buffinton, p	5	1	1	0	1	0		McMahon, p	4	0	0	0	0	0
	46	12	17	27	10	2			40	2	12	24	14	2

```
PHI   1  2  1    0  2  3    0  0  3  -  12
ATH   0  1  0    0  0  1    0  0  0  -   2
```

Earned runs: ATH 1, PHI 6. 2B: Lyons, Robinson, Thompson, Hallman. 3B: Farrar. BB: Buffinton 2, McMahon 3. Struck out: Buffinton 3, McMahon 5. WP: McMahon 2. PB: Robinson. Umpires: Curry and Connell. Time—1:30.

days. Weyhing scored an easy victory by scattering seven hits and pitching shutout ball until the Phillies scored a lone run in the ninth. The final score was 10–1.

The series continued at the home park of the Phillies on the 19th of October when Charlie Buffinton (27–17) met rookie John "Sadie" McMahon (16–12) of the Athletics. The Phils avenged their big loss of two days earlier by jumping all over the youngster McMahon and coasting to an easy victory. Buffinton, because of arm troubles, hadn't pitched in several weeks, and the Athletics solved him for 12. But the veteran, with a career record of 231–151 and a winning percentage (.605) higher than many members of the Hall of

1889 Philadelphia City Championship Series

GAME FOUR --- October 21

PHILLIES	AB	R	H	PO	A	E		ATHLETICS	AB	R	H	PO	A	E
Fogarty, cf	4	0	0	2	0	0		Welch, cf	5	0	1	1	0	0
Myers, 2b	4	0	0	4	2	0		Larkin, 1b	5	3	2	12	0	0
Delahanty, lf	4	0	0	2	1	1		Lyons, 3b	5	2	2	0	3	0
Thompson, rf	4	0	0	1	0	0		Stovey, lf	5	1	2	1	0	0
Sanders, p	4	0	0	0	2	0		Bierbauer, 2b	3	1	1	2	2	1
Farrar, 1b	3	0	1	9	2	0		Purcell, rf	3	1	1	0	0	0
Decker, c	3	0	0	3	0	0		Fennelly, ss	3	1	1	0	4	1
Gleason, 2b	3	0	1	3	5	1		Robinson, c	3	0	0	8	2	0
Hallman, ss	3	0	0	0	4	1		Seward, p	3	0	1	0	1	1
	32	0	2	24	16	3			35	9	11	24	12	3

```
PHI   0  0  0    0  0  0    0  0  -  0
ATH   0  0  1    0  0  5    3  0  -  9
```

Earned runs: ATH 7. 2B: Larkin, Fennelly, Seward. 3B: Stovey. SH: Delahanty, Bierbauer. SB: Bierbauer. LOB: PHI 4, ATH 6. BB: Sanders 4. Struck out: Seward 8, Sanders 3. DP: PHI. WP: Seward. PB: Decker. Umpires: Curry and Connell. Time—1:20.

GAME FIVE --- October 22

PHILLIES	AB	R	H	PO	A	E		ATHLETICS	AB	R	H	PO	A	E
Fogarty, cf	4	0	2	0	0	0		Welch, cf	4	0	1	1	0	0
Sanders, p	1	0	0	1	0	0		Larkin, 1b	4	0	0	7	0	3
Myers, 2b	4	1	0	2	1	1		Lyons, 3b	4	1	1	1	1	0
Delahanty, lf	4	0	0	3	0	0		Stovey, lf	4	0	0	0	0	1
Thompson, rf	4	1	0	0	0	0		Bierbauer, 2b	5	0	2	0	0	0
Farrar, 1b	4	0	1	7	1	0		Purcell, rf	4	0	0	0	0	1
Decker, c	4	0	0	2	0	0		Fennelly, ss	4	0	1	2	0	0
Gleason, 3b	4	0	0	1	1	0		Cross, c	3	0	0	7	2	0
Hallman, ss	4	1	1	1	3	0		McMahon, p	3	0	1	0	10	0
Anderson, p	3	0	0	1	4	0			35	1	6	18	13	5
	36	3	4	18	10	1								

```
PHI   2  1  0    0  0  0    -  3
ATH   0  0  0    0  0  1    -  1
```

Earned runs: PHI 1, ATH 1. 2B: Lyons. 3B: Fogarty, Hallman. BB: McMahon 1, Anderson. Struck out: Anderson 2, McMahon 7. PB: Decker. Umpires: Connell and Curry. Time—1:10.

Fame, was extraordinarily hard on the A's with men on base and the best the Americans could do was score single runs in the second and sixth. The Phillies, meanwhile, banged out 14 singles, two doubles, and a triple, scored in five of the first six innings, and finished with an easy 12-2 victory.

Two days later, the clubs met for Game Four at Gloucester Point Grounds as the home-field fans watched the most lopsided game of the series. Ben Sanders held the Athletics to one run on three hits through the first five innings, but four singles, two doubles, and a triple combined with two Philadelphia errors in the sixth and seventh to net eight Athletic runs. On the other side of the ledger, Ed Seward pitched a masterful game, giving up hits to Sid Farrar and Kid Gleason only, walking no one and striking out eight.

For the fourth time in five games, the home team won as the Phillies squeaked by the A's 5–4 in the series finale on the 23rd of October. Cold weather prevented the game from going past six innings and the Phillies won by a score of 3–1. The Phils scored two unearned runs in the first and Bill Hallman's triple coupled with Jim Fogarty's RBI single netted an insurance run in the second. Dave Anderson was the winning pitcher, Sadie McMahon took the loss.

The series' finale was played at Mt. Gretna, Pennsylvania, before nearly a thousand people in what must have been some of the worst playing conditions of all time. It snowed all morning prior to the game and as much as two inches of the white stuff covered the playing surface. The ballplayers had a snowball fight before the game, then went out and played a close contest before their hands went numb and they were forced to quit after seven innings. The Phillies, behind rookie Bill Day (0–3), took a 3–0 lead in the first and saw the A's tie with three of their own in the fourth. The Nationals then scored single runs in the fifth and sixth and withstood an assault by the A's to hold on to a 5–4 victory. Rookie George Baueswine (1–4), who had just spent his only year in the major leagues, took the loss.

The 1889 Ohio State Championship Series I

Columbus Colts defeat Cleveland Spiders; 2–1

The fifth-place Cleveland Spiders (61–72) and the sixth-place Columbus Colts (60–78) met for the first time in postseason play following the 1889 championship season. The Colts had just spent their first year in the American Association and would spend two more there before the AA closed its doors. This was the first in a series of three postseason series for the championship of the state of Ohio.

The series' opener was played at Cleveland's League Park on the 15th of October and the Colts struck for three early runs off Ed Beatin (20–15). Jack "Peach Pie" O'Connor scored the first run in the second and doubled home Charles "Lefty" Marr and Jack Crooks in the third for a 3–0 lead. That was all the offense on the day for the Colts as Beatin settled down and pitched shutout ball for the final six innings. The Spiders, meanwhile, tied the game in the fourth off Hank Gastright (10–16) and went ahead to stay in the eighth when Ed McKean doubled, went to third on a wild pitch, and scored on an out. The final score was 5–3, Cleveland.

Game Two was played the next day with Colts' pitcher Edward "Jersey" Bakely (12–22) going against Frank Knauss. Knauss wouldn't actually reach the majors with Columbus until 1890. This was a wild affair which featured heavy batting on the part of the Colts as they banged out 12 hits in seven innings, among them a double by Jim McTamany, and a double and triple by Lefty Marr. Cleveland took a 3–0 lead in the first, but Columbus came back with two in their half of the inning. The Spiders increased their lead to 5–2 in the top of the third, but a throwing error by Jay Faatz (who would go on to be player-manager of the Players' League Buffalo Bisons in 1890) let in three runs and tied

1889 Ohio State Championship Series I

GAME ONE --- October 15

CLEVELAND	AB	R	H	PO	A	E		COLUMBUS	AB	R	H	PO	A	E
Radford, rf	4	1	0	0	0	0		McTamany, cf	4	0	0	2	0	0
Stricker, 2b	5	0	1	3	2	0		Marr, ss	4	1	1	1	4	0
McKean, ss	2	2	2	2	6	0		Daily, lf	4	0	1	1	0	0
Twitchell, lf	4	0	0	1	0	2		Crooks, 2b	3	1	1	5	2	0
Zimmer, 3b	4	1	1	0	1	1		O'Connor, rf	4	1	2	2	1	0
Faatz, 1b	4	1	3	11	0	0		Orr, 1b	4	0	0	9	0	0
McAleer, cf	3	0	0	1	0	0		Reilly, 2b	3	0	1	1	2	2
Sutcliffe, c	4	0	2	9	2	0		Doyle, c	3	0	0	5	2	0
Beatin, p	4	0	1	0	1	0		Gastright, p	3	0	0	1	2	0
	34	5	10	27	12	3			32	3	6	27	13	2

```
CLE   0 0 0   3 0 0   0 1 1  -  5
COL   0 1 2   0 0 0   0 0 0  -  3
```

Earned runs: CLE 2, COL 2. 2B: McKean, O'Connor. BB: Gastright 3, Beatin 1. Struck out: Gastright 5, Beatin 9. WP: Gastright. Umpire: McDermott. Time—2:00.

GAME TWO --- October 16

COLUMBUS	AB	R	H	PO	A	E		CLEVELAND	AB	R	H	PO	A	E
McTamany, cf	3	1	1	3	0	0		Radford, rf	4	1	1	1	0	0
Marr, ss	4	2	3	2	0	0		Stricker, 2b	3	2	0	3	5	0
Daily, lf	3	1	0	1	0	0		McKean, ss	4	1	1	1	5	0
Crooks, 2b	4	2	2	1	1	0		Twitchell, lf	3	1	2	1	0	2
Johnson, 3b	4	1	3	0	3	1		Gilks, 3b	4	1	0	0	2	0
Orr, 1b	4	1	1	8	0	0		Faatz, 1b	3	0	0	8	0	1
O'Connor, rf	4	1	1	1	0	0		McAleer, cf	3	0	1	2	0	0
Doyle, c	3	0	1	6	0	1		Zimmer, c	2	0	0	4	1	2
Knauss, p	3	0	0	1	0	1		Bakely, p	1	0	0	0	0	0
								Gruber, p	1	0	0	0	0	0
	32	9	12	21	7	3			28	6	5	*20	13	5

* Two out when game was called.

```
CLE   3 0 2   0 1 0   0  -  6
COL   2 0 3   1 1 0   2  -  9
```

Earned runs: CLE 2, COL 2. 2B: McTamany, Marr. 3B: Twitchell, Marr. BB: Knauss 3, Gruber 2. Struck out: Knauss 6, Gruber 4. PB: Zimmer. WP: Gruber. Umpire: McDermott. Time—2:15.

the game in the bottom of the inning. That seemed to set the Colts free as they scored in three of the next four innings and won the game. Henry Gruber (7–16), pitching in relief of Bakely, took the loss. Knauss went the distance in the seven-inning game and gave up only five hits, but the Spiders made the most of those and scored six runs. The final score was 9–6.

A third game had been scheduled for the 22nd, but inclement weather prevented play, so the finale took place on the 23rd at the home field of the Colts, Recreation Park. Ed Beatin started for the Spiders against Mark Baldwin (27–34) of the Colts. The game was tied until the seventh when the Colts climbed all over Beatin and scored four runs. Batting stars of the day were Ed Daily with a 3-for-5 performance including a double and two stolen bases, and John "Spud" Johnson with a 3-for-5 including a double and triple.

1889 Ohio State Championship I

```
GAME THREE --- October 23
```

CLEVELAND	AB	R	H	PO	A	E		COLUMBUS	AB	R	H	PO	A	E
Radford, rf	4	0	0	0	0	0		McTamany, cf	3	1	0	0	0	0
Stricker, 2b	4	0	1	6	2	0		Marr, ss	4	1	1	3	3	0
McKean, ss	4	1	2	0	5	1		Daily, lf	5	1	3	1	0	1
Twitchell, lf	4	0	0	2	0	1		Crooks, 2b	4	1	1	2	3	1
Gilks, 3b	4	0	0	0	1	0		Johnson, 3b	3	2	3	0	0	0
Faatz, 1b	3	0	0	7	0	0		Orr, 1b	4	0	1	9	0	0
Zimmer, 1b	1	0	0	0	0	0		Reilly, 3b	3	0	0	0	3	0
McAleer, cf	3	0	1	2	0	0		O'Connor, c	3	0	0	6	2	1
Sutcliffe, c	3	1	1	4	1	0		Baldwin, p	3	0	0	0	2	1
Beatin, p	3	0	0	0	2	0			32	6	9	21	13	4
	33	2	5	21	11	2								

```
CLE     0  0  0     0  1  1     0  -  2
COL     1  0  0     0  0  1     4  -  6
```

Earned runs: COL 4, CLE 1. 2B: Marr, Johnson, Daily, Sutcliffe. 3B: Johnson. SB: McTamany, Daily 2. LOB: COL 5, CLE 6. DP: COL 1, CLE 1. BB: Baldwin 1, Beatin 5. Struck out: Beatin 5, Baldwin 6. HBP: Faatz (Baldwin); McTamany and Johnson (Beatin). WP: Beatin 1, Baldwin 1. Umpires: McDermott, Butler, Bauer. Time — 2:00.

The 1889 Ohio State Championship Series II

Cincinnati Reds defeat Cleveland Spiders; 3–2

The Cleveland Spiders (61–72) finished in sixth place, a distant 25½ games behind the league-leading New York Giants, and met the fourth-place American Association Cincinnati Reds (76–63) in the second of three Ohio state championships to be held in 1889.

The series opener was played on the 17th of October at Cleveland's National League Park with Ed Beatin (20–15) going against Cincinnati's Lee Viau (22–20). Had Hugh Nicol not been in the lineup, Beatin would have no-hit the Reds. The Scottish-born right fielder had a single and a double, both scratch hits, but the Reds were unable to score on either. The Spiders, meanwhile, tallied single runs in every other inning starting with the second and finished up with a 4–0 shutout.

Game Two was played at Akron, Ohio, on the next day. Edward "Jersey" Bakely (12–22) took the hill against Cincinnati's Tony Mullane (11–9), the well-travelled pitcher who spent time with eight teams in his 13-year major league career. The teams traded runs in the third, but Cincinnati rang up three-run innings in the sixth and seventh off Bakely to take a commanding 7–2 lead. The Spiders retaliated with three of their own in the seventh, but an insurance run in the eighth made Cincinnati an 8–5 winner. Every man in the Cincinnati lineup except Bid McPhee hit safely as the Reds finished with 13 hits. The Spiders weren't exactly mystified by Mullane and wound up with 12 hits of their own.

The third game was played at National League Park on the 19th of October. Ed Beatin and Jesse Duryea were the starting pitchers. Duryea was just

1889 Ohio State Championship Series II

GAME ONE --- October 17

CLEVELAND	AB	R	H	PO	A	E		CINCINNATI	AB	R	H	PO	A	E
Radford, rf	5	0	2	1	0	0		Tebeau, lf	3	0	0	2	0	0
Stricker, 2b	4	0	1	4	3	0		McPhee, 2b	4	0	0	3	3	1
McKean, ss	5	0	2	1	6	0		Holliday, cf	4	0	0	2	0	0
Twitchell, lf	3	0	0	1	0	1		Nicol, rf	3	0	2	4	0	0
Gilks, 3b	5	1	1	0	3	0		Mullane, 1b	3	0	0	7	0	0
Faatz, 1b	5	0	0	12	0	0		Carpenter, 3b	3	0	0	2	1	0
McAleer, cf	4	2	1	6	0	0		Beard, ss	3	0	0	2	0	2
Sutcliffe, c	4	0	4	2	1	0		Viau, p	3	0	0	0	3	0
Beatin, p	3	1	0	0	1	0		Earle, c	2	0	0	5	2	0
	38	4	11	27	14	1			28	0	2	27	9	3

```
CLE   0  1  0    1  0  1    0  1  0  -  4
CIN   0  0  0    0  0  0    0  0  0  -  0
```

Earned runs: CLE 2. 2B: Nicol. 3B: McKean. BB: Viau 2, Beatin 2. Struck out: Beatin 2, Viau 4. PB: Earle. WP: Viau 2. Umpire: McDermott. Time—1:35.

GAME TWO --- October 18 at Akron

CINCINNATI	AB	R	H	PO	A	E		CLEVELAND	AB	R	H	PO	A	E
Tebeau, lf	5	1	1	2	0	0		Radford, rf	4	1	1	2	1	1
McPhee, 2b	5	0	0	1	3	0		Stricker, 2b	5	1	2	3	0	0
Holliday, cf	4	1	3	1	0	2		McKean, ss	4	1	3	1	5	1
Nicol, rf	5	2	2	1	0	1		Twitchell, lf	4	0	0	2	1	1
Reilly, 1b	5	1	1	10	0	0		Gilks, 3b	4	0	2	1	1	1
Carpenter, 3b	5	1	2	1	0	0		Faatz, 1b	4	0	1	9	1	0
Beard, ss	4	0	2	1	3	2		McAleer, cf	4	0	1	2	0	0
Earle, c	4	1	1	10	2	1		Snyder, c	4	2	2	6	0	2
Mullane, p	3	1	1	0	3	0		Bakely, p	4	0	0	1	2	0
	40	0	13	27	11	6			37	5	12	27	11	6

```
CIN   0  0  1    0  0  3    3  1  0  -  8
CLE   0  0  1    0  0  1    3  0  0  -  5
```

Earned runs: CIN 2, CLE 2. 2B: Gilks 2, Nicol. 3B: Stricker, McKean, Reilly. HR: Earle. BB: Bakely 2, Mullane 1. Struck out: Bakely 4, Mullane 10. PB: Snyder 2, Earle 1. Umpire: McDermott. Time—2:00.

coming off a fine rookie season in which he ran up a record of 32–19 and he showed why for the first seven innings as he held the Spiders to two hits and no runs. But hits by Beatin, Cub Stricker, Ed McKean, Larry Twitchell, and Bob Gilks accounted for four Cleveland runs in the seventh. The Reds scored once in the bottom of the inning before the game was called because of darkness.

Game Four was the first to be played at the Cincinnati Base Ball Grounds—also known as League Park—and featured a triple play. The Reds had James "Bug" Holliday on third and Hugh Nicol on second when Tony Mullane grounded to Cub Stricker. Holliday got a slow start off third and was run down between third and home. Stricker threw the ball to catcher Chief Zimmer who threw to Bob Gilks for the tag. Nicol, attempting to sneak into

1889 Ohio State Championship Series II

GAME THREE --- October 19

CLEVELAND	AB	R	H	PO	A	E		CINCINNATI	AB	R	H	PO	A	E
Radford, rf	3	1	0	0	0	0		Tebeau, lf	3	0	1	3	0	0
Stricker, 2b	4	1	2	3	2	0		McPhee, 2b	4	0	2	4	3	0
McKean, ss	4	1	2	1	3	0		Holliday, cf	4	0	1	0	0	0
Twitchell, lf	4	1	1	0	1	0		Nicol, rf	4	0	0	2	0	0
Gilks, 3b	4	0	1	3	2	0		Mullane, 1b	2	0	0	7	0	0
Faatz, 1b	4	0	0	8	1	0		Carpenter, 3b	3	0	0	0	0	0
McAleer, cf	3	0	0	0	0	0		Beard, ss	2	0	0	2	3	0
Sutcliffe, c	4	0	0	8	1	1		Earle, c	3	0	1	5	1	0
Beatin, p	3	0	1	1	2	0		Duryea, p	3	1	1	1	0	0
	33	4	7	24	12	1			28	1	6	24	7	0

```
CLE   0 0 0   0 0 0   0 4 - 4
CIN   0 0 0   0 0 0   0 1 - 1
```

Earned runs: CLE 4, CIN 1. 2B: McPhee. 3B: Stricker, Gilks. SB: Radford. SH: Carpenter, Beatin, McPhee, Twitchell. BB: Duryea 2, Beatin 3. Struck out: Duryea 2, Beatin 8. PB: Earle. Umpire: McDermott.

GAME FOUR --- October 24

CINCINNATI	AB	R	H	PO	A	E		CLEVELAND	AB	R	H	PO	A	E
Tebeau, lf	5	0	2	1	0	0		Radford, rf	3	1	0	0	0	0
McPhee, 2b	6	2	2	5	4	0		Stricker, 2b	4	0	1	3	4	0
Holliday, cf	5	1	3	4	0	1		McKean, ss	4	1	0	0	1	0
Nicol, rf	5	0	3	1	0	0		Twitchell, lf	4	0	0	2	0	0
Mullane, 1b	4	1	1	10	0	0		Sutcliffe, 1b	3	0	1	10	0	0
Carpenter, 3b	4	2	1	0	1	0		Gilks, 3b	3	0	0	1	1	0
Beard, ss	3	1	1	2	1	0		McAleer, cf	3	0	1	3	0	1
Keenan, c	4	0	0	3	0	0		Zimmer, c	3	0	0	5	2	1
Duryea, p	4	0	1	0	6	0		O'Brien, p	3	0	0	0	3	0
	40	7	14	*26	12	1			30	2	3	24	11	2

* Sutcliffe out for batting out of turn

```
CIN   0 2 0   2 0 0   1 0 2 - 7
CLE   1 0 0   0 0 0   0 0 1 - 2
```

Earned runs: CIN 4. 2B: McPhee. 3B: Tebeau. SH: Holliday, Mullane, Twitchell. SB: Nicol, Holliday, Mulane. BB: Duryea 3, O'Brien 3. Struck out: Duryea 3, O'Brien 6. WP: Duryea 2. Triple play: Stricker to Zimmer to Gilks to Sutcliffe. Umpire: McDermott.

third, was tagged out by Gilks. Gilks fired the ball across the diamond to Sy Sutcliffe who tagged out Mullane diving back into first. This was Sutcliffe's only claim to fame in a lackluster major league career which included seven teams in seven years and games played at each position except pitcher. Even this game included a clue to the caliber of his play—he was called out by umpire McDermott for batting out of turn. The Reds had no trouble with Darby O'Brien (22–17) and made a winner of Jesse Duryea. The final score was 7–2.

The Reds took the city championship at Cincinnati on the 26th behind the strong pitching of Tony Mullane. Mullane was in trouble only in the third when Paul Radford doubled and later scored. (Radford moved around pretty well

1889 Ohio State Championship Series II

GAME FIVE --- October 26

CINCINNATI	AB	R	H	PO	A	E		CLEVELAND	AB	R	H	PO	A	E
Tebeau, lf	4	1	1	3	0	0		Radford, rf	4	1	2	0	0	1
McPhee, 2b	4	1	2	4	4	0		Stricker, 2b	4	0	0	7	3	0
Holliday, cf	4	0	2	5	0	0		McKean, ss	3	0	0	1	6	2
Nicol, rf	3	0	0	2	0	0		Twitchell, lf	4	0	0	1	0	0
Reilly, 1b	4	0	1	3	0	0		Sutcliffe, c	4	0	0	5	3	0
Carpenter, 3b	4	0	1	0	0	0		Gilks, 3b	3	0	1	2	1	1
Beard, ss	4	0	1	1	0	0		McAleer, cf	3	0	0	3	2	0
Earle, c	4	1	4	4	1	0		Zimmer, 1b	2	0	1	8	0	0
Mullane, p	4	0	0	0	1	0		Beatin, p	3	0	0	0	3	0
	35	3	12	22	6	0			30	1	4	27	18	4

```
CIN    0  0  2    1  0  0    0  0  0  -  3
CLE    0  0  1    0  0  0    0  0  0  -  1
```

Earned runs: CIN 2, CLE 1. 2B: Reilly, Beard, Zimmer, Radford. BB: Mullane 1, Beatin 1. SB: Tebeau, McPhee 2, Earle, Radford. PB: Earle, Sutcliffe. Umpire: McDermott. Time—1:30.

himself—nine teams in 12 years.) The Reds tallied two in the top of the third and one more in the fourth and Mullane held on for a 3–1 victory. Billy "The Little Globetrotter" Earle—five teams in five years—was the hitting star of the day with four singles in four times at bat.

The 1889 Ohio State Championship Series III

Columbus Colts defeat Cincinnati Reds; 2–0

The sixth-place Columbus Colts (60–78) and fourth-place Cincinnati Reds (79–63) met in the third and last championship for the state of Ohio, one of two postseason championships played in 1889 between teams of the same league. Both games were held at the home field of the Columbus team, Recreation Park.

Game One was played during a snowstorm on the 20th of October with Cincinnati's Tony Mullane (11–9) against Mark Baldwin (27–39). Baldwin was the workhorse of the American Association, leading the league in games pitched (63), games started (59), innings pitched (513.2), walks (274), and strikeouts (368). Playing for this weak Columbus team, unfortunately, he also led the league in losses. He was no pushover for the Reds on this day as the Colts easily defeated their opponent by a score of 5–2. The Colts struck for two runs in the first and three more in the fifth and held that 5–0 lead until the Reds scored their only two runs of the game in the seventh. The batting star of the day was Lefty Marr with a perfect 3-for-3, two singles and a double.

The Colts won the next day by the same 5–2 score. Lee Viau (22–20) was wild in the first, walking Lefty Marr and Ed Daily, both of whom scored on a single by Jack Crooks. The Reds tied the game in the fifth on a single by Mullane, a walk to Warren "Hick" Carpenter, a groundout, and an error by

1889 Ohio State Championship Series III

```
GAME ONE --- October 20
```

COLUMBUS	AB	R	H	PO	A	E	CINCINNATI	AB	R	H	PO	A	E
McTamany, cf	4	0	1	2	1	1	Tebeau, lf	2	1	1	1	0	1
Marr, ss	3	2	3	1	4	1	McPhee, 2b	3	0	0	2	6	0
Daily, lf	4	1	0	1	0	0	Holiday, cf	4	0	1	0	0	0
Crooks, 2b	3	1	1	4	1	1	Nicol, rf	4	0	1	0	0	1
Johnson, rf	3	1	0	2	0	0	Duryea, 1b	3	0	0	12	0	1
Orr, 1b	4	0	2	11	0	0	Carpenter, 3b	4	0	0	3	4	0
Reilly, 3b	4	0	0	0	3	0	Beard, ss	4	0	0	1	0	0
O'Connor, c	3	0	0	3	0	1	Earle, c	4	0	0	5	1	1
Baldwin, p	4	0	1	0	1	1	Mullane, p	3	1	1	0	2	0
	32	5	8	24	10	5		31	2	4	24	13	4

```
COL    2 0 0    0 3 0    0 0 0  -  5
CIN    0 0 0    0 0 0    2 0 0  -  2
```

Earned runs: COL 1. 2B: Holliday, Tebeau, Marr. SH: Carpenter, Beard, Reilly, Daily, Crooks, Johnson. BB: Baldwin 3, Mullane 3. Struck out: Baldwin 3, Mullane 5. PB: O'Connor. SB: Marr, Crooks 2. Umpire: McDermott.

```
GAME TWO --- October 21
```

COLUMBUS	AB	R	H	PO	A	E	CINCINNATI	AB	R	H	PO	A	E
McTamany, cf	4	0	0	4	0	0	Tebeau, lf	4	0	0	2	0	0
Marr, ss	3	1	1	1	6	0	McPhee, 2b	4	0	0	2	5	0
Daily, lf	3	2	0	2	0	0	Holiday, cf	4	0	0	1	0	0
Crooks, 2b	4	1	2	0	0	1	Nicol, rf	3	0	0	1	1	0
Johnson, rf	4	0	0	0	0	0	Mullane, 1b	4	1	2	12	0	1
Orr, 1b	4	1	2	7	1	0	Carpenter, 3b	3	1	0	1	5	2
Reilly, 3b	4	0	0	2	1	0	Beard, ss	3	0	1	3	4	0
O'Connor, c	4	0	0	9	2	2	Baldwin, c	3	0	0	5	0	0
Gastright, p	4	0	0	2	0	0	Viau, p	3	0	0	0	0	0
	34	5	5	27	10	3		31	2	3	27	15	3

```
COL    2 0 0    0 0 0    0 3 0  -  5
CIN    0 0 0    0 2 0    0 0 0  -  2  .
```

Earned runs: COL 2. 3B: Orr. BB: Viau 2, Gastright 1. Struck out: Viau 5, Gastright 9. PB: Baldwin 2. SB: Daily, Nicol 2, Mullane 2. Umpire: McDermott. Time—1:45.

Crooks. The Colts scored three runs in the eighth on an error by Carpenter, singles by Marr and Crooks, and a triple by Dave Orr. Hank Gastright (10–16) went the distance for the Colts, pitched a three-hitter, walked one, and struck out nine for the win.

The 1890 Philadelphia City Championship Game

Philadelphia Quakers defeat Philadelphia Athletics; 1–0

About 3,000 fans showed up at Forepaugh Park, home of the Players' League Philadelphia Quakers, to watch a game between the Quakers and the

1890 Philadelphia City Championship Benefit Game

```
October 18

PHILADELPHIA      AB  R  H PO  A  E    ATHLETICS        AB  R  H PO  A  E
-----------------------------------    ----------------------------------
Fogarty, cf        4  0  2  2  0  0    O'Neill, cf       3  0  0  0  0  0
Shindle, ss        4  1  1  3  4  0    Kappel, lf        3  1  0  0  0  1
Wood, 3b           4  1  1  0  1  0    Bierbauer, 2b     3  1  3  3  1  0
Knell, p           4  1  1  1  1  0    O'Brien, 3b       3  0  1  0  1  0
Milligan, c        3  1  1  4  0  0    Robinson, c       3  0  2 12  3  1
Myers, lf          3  0  0  0  0  1    Fields, 1b        3  0  0  4  0  0
Hardie, 1b         3  0  1  7  2  0    Carman, ss        3  0  0  1  1  0
Brooks, rf         3  0  0  0  0  0    McMahon, p        3  0  0  0  2  1
Bradley, 2b        3  0  0  3  0  0    Esper, rf         3  0  0  1  0  0
                  --------------                        --------------
                  31  4  7 20  8  1                     27  2  6 21  8  3

PHI    0  0  0    0  0  3    1  -  4
ATH    1  0  1    0  0  0    0  -  2
```

Earned runs: PHI 1, ATH 1. 2B: Milligan. 3B: Shindle, Robinson. SH: Brooks, Bradley. SB: Wood, Milligan, Hardie. Struck out: McMahon 9, Knell 4. Umpire: Mathews. Att: 3,000. Time—1:00.

American Association Athletics, the receipts of which would be shared by the players on the two ball clubs. The Athletics (54–78) had suffered through a terrible season under manager Bill Sharsig. The Quakers, who would merge with the A's at the end of the season when the Players' League folded, fared somewhat better, finishing in fifth place with a 68–63 record. Most of the Quaker players were transplants from the Philadelphia Phillies club.

The game was played on the 18th of October and the A's jumped out to a 2–0 lead on the strong batting of Lou Bierbauer and Wilbert Robinson. But the Quakers scored three times in the third when Bill Shindle's triple got their offense moving. The Quakers added an insurance run in the seventh and the game was called at the end of that inning because of darkness. John "Sadie" McMahon (36–21) went down to defeat to Phil Knell (22–11) despite the fact that McMahon had led the American Association in victories, games (60), games started (57), complete games (55), innings pitched (509), hits (498), and strikeouts (291)—all in his second year in the majors!

The 1890 Ohio State Championship Series

Cincinnati Reds defeat Cleveland Infants; 2–1

The fourth-place Cincinnati Reds (77–55), coming off their first year back in the National League, met the seventh-place Players' League Cleveland Infants (55–75) in the 1889 Ohio state championship series. By the time the 1891 season started, most of the players on the Brotherhood teams would be back in the American Association or National League. But for this one year, there was little doubt that the Players' League was the only major league in existence.

1890 Ohio State Championship Series

GAME ONE --- October 6

CINCINNATI	AB	R	H	PO	A	E
McPhee, 2b	5	0	0	0	2	0
Latham,, 3b	4	2	1	4	1	0
Marr, rf	5	2	3	0	0	1
Reilly, 1b	5	2	2	13	0	0
Beard, ss	5	1	2	2	5	0
Holliday, cf	5	1	4	0	1	0
Knight, lf	5	1	1	1	0	0
Harrington, c	4	1	3	7	1	0
Mullane, p	3	1	1	0	2	0
	41	11	17	27	12	1

CLEVELAND	AB	R	H	PO	A	E
Radford, ss	4	0	0	0	9	1
Delahanty, 3b	4	1	2	3	2	0
Browning, lf	4	0	1	1	0	0
Larkin, 1b	3	1	2	13	1	0
McAleer, cf	4	1	1	0	2	0
Stricker, 2b	4	0	0	8	3	0
Carney, rf	3	0	1	0	0	1
Brennan, c	4	0	0	1	1	0
O'Brien, p	3	1	1	1	1	1
	33	4	8	27	19	3

```
CIN   0 1 4   2 0 0   4 0 0  -  11
CLE   0 0 0   0 0 2   0 0 2  -  4
```

Earned runs: CIN 8, CLE 4. DP: CLE 2, CIN 1. LOB: CIN 3, CLE 4. 2B: Holliday 2, Beard, Latham, Delahanty, Carney. 3B: Reilly. SH: McPhee, Latham, Marr, Beard, Browning 2. SB: Latham, Holliday. BB: O'Brien 2, Mullane 2. Struck out: Mullane 6. PB: Harrington. WP: Mullane 2. Umpire: Sheridan. Time—1:20.

GAME TWO --- October 7

CINCINNATI	AB	R	H	PO	A	E
McPhee, 2b	3	1	1	1	0	0
Latham,, 3b	4	0	1	0	5	1
Marr, rf	4	0	0	1	1	0
Reilly, 1b	4	0	1	12	1	0
Beard, ss	4	0	0	1	1	0
Holliday, cf	4	0	1	1	0	1
Mullane, lf	2	1	0	2	0	0
Harrington, c	3	0	0	6	3	1
Rhines, p	3	0	0	0	0	0
	31	2	4	24	11	3

CLEVELAND	AB	R	H	PO	A	E
Radford, ss	4	0	0	2	2	0
Delahanty, 3b	4	2	2	0	2	0
Browning, lf	4	2	2	3	1	0
Larkin, 1b	4	1	2	10	0	0
McAleer, cf	4	1	1	4	0	0
Stricker, 2b	4	1	1	2	4	0
Carney, rf	3	1	1	0	0	0
Brennan, c	4	0	0	6	0	1
McGill, p	3	0	0	0	1	0
	34	8	9	27	10	2

```
CIN   0 0 0   0 0 2   0 0 0  -  2
CLE   0 0 0   0 2 2   0 4 x  -  8
```

Earned runs: CLE 6. LOB: CIN 4, CLE 3. 2B: Stricker, Larkin 2. SH: Rhines, Latham, Brennan 2, Stricker. SB: McPhee, Mullane. BB: Rhines 1, McGill 1. Struck out: Rhines 6, McGill 4. HBP: Mullane (McGill). Umpire: Sheridan. Time—1:30.

All three games took place in Cincinnati's League Park and Game One saw Tony Mullane (12–10) start against the Infants' Darby O'Brien (8–16). Cincinnati got on the board first when James "Bug" Holliday doubled and Jerry Harrington singled for a 1–0 lead. The Reds struck for four runs in the third, all after two were out. Arlie Latham walked, Charles "Lefty" Marr singled, Long John Reilly tripled, Ollie Beard singled, and Holliday doubled. A single, a walk, two putouts, and an error pushed across two more Cincinnati runs in the fourth for a 7–0 lead. The Infants scored twice in the sixth to close the gap to 7–2, but six hits in the seventh put the Reds up 11–2. Two Cleveland runs in the ninth closed out the scoring. Mullane was the winning pitcher, O'Brien the

1890 Ohio State Championship Series

GAME THREE --- October 8

CINCINNATI	AB	R	H	PO	A	E		CLEVELAND	AB	R	H	PO	A	E
McPhee, 2b	2	1	0	4	2	0		Radford, ss	4	1	2	2	4	1
Latham,, 3b	3	3	1	1	2	1		Delahanty, 3b	4	0	0	2	2	1
Marr, rf	4	3	3	0	0	0		Browning, lf	4	0	2	2	0	0
Reilly, 1b	4	2	2	7	0	0		Larkin, 1b	3	0	1	13	0	0
Beard, ss	5	2	3	1	3	1		McAleer, cf	4	0	0	0	0	0
Holliday, cf	5	0	2	2	1	0		Stricker, 2b	3	0	0	0	3	0
Mullane, lf	5	2	3	2	1	1		Carney, rf	4	0	0	2	1	0
Keenan, c	5	0	0	7	1	0		Brennan, c	2	0	1	2	4	1
Dolan, p	4	0	0	0	1	0		Gruber, p	3	0	0	1	0	0
	37	13	14	24	11	3			31	1	6	24	14	3

```
CIN   2 1 0   1 3 0   0 0 7  -  14
CLE   0 0 1   0 0 0   0 0 0  -   1
```

Earned runs: CIN 7. DP: CIN 3, CLE 2. 2B: Beard, Larkin. HR: Beard. SB: Latham 2, Marr 2, Reilly, Dolan, Radford, Browning. BB: Gruber 7, Dolan 4. Struck out: Gruber 2, Dolan 7. PB: Brennan 5. Umpire: Sheridan. Att: 300.

loser. The hitting star of the day was Holliday with four hits, two of them doubles, in five times at bat.

Game Two was played the next day, October 7. Willie McGill (11–9) of the Infants would have hurled a shutout were it not for errors by catcher Jim Brennan and second sacker John "Cub" Stricker which accounted for the two Reds' runs in the sixth. Billy Rhines (28–17) was batted around freely after the fourth, the Infants scoring twice in the fifth and sixth and four times in the eighth to put the game on ice.

The final game gave no indication of superiority of the Players' League as the Reds trounced Cleveland 14–1. Cincinnati jumped on losing pitcher Henry Gruber (21–23) for two runs in the first, one in the second and fourth, and three in the fifth. A resounding seven-run ninth for Cincinnati capped the scoring. The Reds also ran wild on the base paths, stealing a total of six bases. Cincinnati's John Dolan (1–1) was the winning pitcher.

The 1903 St. Louis City Championship Series

St. Louis Browns defeat St. Louis Cardinals; 5–2

The St. Louis Browns (65–74) met the St. Louis Cardinals (43–94) in the first city championship series between American and National League clubs of that city. The Browns had dropped to fifth from a second-place finish in 1902, and the Cardinals had dropped down two notches to the National League cellar. The Cardinals had no pitcher who won more than nine games and the team featured the worst won-loss record of the young century. To make matters worse, there was dissension on the club, many of the ballplayers refusing to give their best effort for manager Patsy Donovan. The Browns were odds-

1903 St. Louis City Championship Series

GAME ONE --- October 3

BROWNS	AB	H	PO	A	E		CARDINALS	AB	H	PO	A	E
Burkett, lf	3	1	1	0	0		Farrell, 2b	4	0	3	3	0
Swander, rf	4	1	1	0	0		Dunleavy, rf	4	1	1	0	0
Heidrick, cf	4	1	0	0	0		Smoot, cf	4	1	1	0	1
Anderson, 1b	4	0	14	0	0		Brain, ss	4	0	2	4	2
Wallace, ss	4	2	1	3	0		Burke, 3b	4	0	1	2	1
Martin, 3b	4	1	2	4	0		Barclay, lf	3	0	0	2	0
Bowcock, 2b	3	1	0	3	1		Ryan, 1b	3	0	16	0	0
Sugden, c	1	0	8	1	1		O'Neill, c	2	0	3	2	0
Powell, p	2	0	0	2	0		McFarland, p	3	1	0	4	1
	29	7	27	13	2			31	3	27	17	5

```
STA   2 0 0   0 1 0   2 0 0 - 5
STN   0 0 0   0 0 0   0 0 0 - 0
```

DP: STN. SB: Burkett, Bowcock, Dunleavy. PB: O'Neill. WP: McFarland. BB: McFarland 4, Powell 1. Struck out: Powell 6. Umpire: Frank Pears.

GAME TWO --- October 4

BROWNS	AB	H	PO	A	E		CARDINALS	AB	H	PO	A	E
Burkett, lf	5	1	1	0	0		Farrell, 2b	4	1	1	3	1
Swander, rf	5	0	1	0	0		Dunleavy, rf	4	1	1	0	0
Heidrick, cf	4	1	1	0	1		Smoot, cf	4	1	2	2	0
Anderson, 1b	5	3	10	1	0		Brain, ss	3	1	4	6	0
Wallace, ss	4	3	2	2	0		Moran, 3b	4	1	1	1	2
Hill, 3b	4	1	2	0	0		Barclay, lf	4	0	0	0	0
Bowcock, 2b	4	1	0	6	0		Ryan, 1b	4	0	7	1	1
Sugden, c	2	0	8	1	0		O'Neill, c	3	1	10	2	1
Sudhoff, p	1	1	2	2	0		Brown, p	3	1	1	0	0
	34	11	27	12	1			33	7	27	15	5

```
STA   0 3 1   0 0 2   0 0 3 - 9
STN   0 0 1   0 1 0   0 0 0 - 2
```

2B: Wallace, Hill, Sudhoff. 3B: Anderson. DP: STN 2, STA 1. BB: Brown 3, Sudhoff 1. Struck out: Brown 6, Sudhoff 4. WP: Brown. Umpire: Frank Pears.

GAME THREE --- October 6

CARDINALS	AB	H	PO	A	E		BROWNS	AB	H	PO	A	E
Farrell, 2b	2	0	3	4	0		Burkett, lf	5	4	1	0	0
Dunleavy, rf	4	0	2	3	0		Swander, rf	4	1	2	0	0
Smoot, cf	4	2	1	0	0		Heidrick, cf	5	3	3	0	0
Brain, 3b	4	0	1	4	2		Anderson, 1b	5	2	14	1	1
Murphy, cf	4	0	2	0	1		Hill, ss	4	0	0	1	1
Barclay, lf	4	2	0	0	0		Friel, 3b	4	3	1	6	0
Ryan, 1b	4	1	12	0	0		Bowcock, 2b	4	1	1	0	0
Coveney, c	4	0	3	2	0		Sugden, c	4	0	4	2	0
Hackett, p	4	2	0	0	2		Siever, p	4	1	1	3	0
	34	7	24	13	5			39	15	27	13	2

```
STN   0 0 1   0 0 0   0 0 1 -  2
STA   2 0 1   3 0 2   1 1 x - 10
```

2B: Heidrick, Anderson 2, Bowcock, Barclay, Burkett, Hackett. 3B: Swander. DP: STN 2. BB: Siever 2, Hackett 1. Struck out: Siever 4, Hackett 2. WP: Hackett 2. Umpire: Pears.

1903 St. Louis City Championship Series

```
GAME FOUR --- October 8
```

BROWNS	AB	H	PO	A	E		CARDINALS	AB	H	PO	A	E
Burkett, lf	5	4	1	0	1		Farrell, 2b	5	2	3	4	2
Swander, rf	4	1	1	0	0		Dunleavy, rf	3	0	2	0	0
Heidrick, cf	5	1	1	1	0		Smoot, cf	4	1	1	0	1
Anderson, 1b	5	3	7	0	0		Brain, 3b	4	1	2	0	0
Hill, ss	5	4	0	1	0		Barclay, lf	3	0	1	0	0
Friel, 3b	5	2	1	3	0		Moran, ss	4	0	1	3	2
Bowcock, 2b	5	1	0	1	1		Hackett, 1b	4	0	11	0	1
Sugden, c	4	0	16	0	0		Ryan, c	4	0	5	1	0
Powell, p	5	1	0	1	0		O'Neill, p	1	1	0	4	0
							Sanders, p	2	2	0	1	0
	43	17	27	7	2			34	7	*26	13	6

```
* Swander out, hit by batted ball
```

STA	2	5	1	0	2	1	0	0	0	-	11
STN	0	0	0	0	0	3	0	0	0	-	3

2B: Anderson, O'Neill, Friel, Brain. 3B: Powell, Smoot. HR: Anderson. DP: STN 2. BB: O'Neill 1, Powell 4. Struck out: Powell 15, O'Neill 2, Sanders 1. Hits: O'Neill 14 in 5 innings; Sanders 3 in 4 innings. WP: Powell. Umpire: Frank Pears.

on favorites to win the postseason series and they had little trouble doing just that.

Game One opened at the American League Sportsman's Park on October 3rd and the Cardinals were unable to do anything with the deliveries of Browns' pitcher Jack Powell (15–19). Powell held the Cardinals to three hits, all singles, and struck out six in recording a complete game victory. No Cardinal runner passed second base after the first inning. The Americans scored all the runs they needed in the first inning. Jesse Burkett led the inning off with a walk and was sacrificed to second by Pinky Swander. Cardinal center-fielder Homer Smoot — there's a name to reckon with — dropped a line drive off the bat of R. Emmett "Snags" Heidrick and Burkett came around to score. Heidrick went to third on a passed ball and scored on Bobby Wallace's single. The Browns added insurance runs in the fifth and seventh and won the game, 5–0. Chappie McFarland (9–18) took the loss for the Cardinals.

Game Two matched Willie Sudhoff (21–15) against Cardinal rookie Mordecai "Three Finger" Brown (9–13). Brown displayed little of the talent which would eventually land him in the Hall of Fame, giving up 11 hits, walking three, and sending home a wild pitch. The Browns broke on top in the second on a John Anderson triple, singles by Wallace and Benny Bowcock and a double by Sudhoff. The Cardinals closed to 4–2 at the end of five, but a throwing error by Charlie Moran let two Browns' runners cross the plate in the sixth. The Nationals were incompetence personified in the ninth as the Browns scored their final three runs of the game. Joe Sugden walked and Sudhoff hit a slow roller off Brown's glove to second baseman John Farrell. Farrell picked the ball up and threw wild past first. First baseman Jack Ryan retrieved the hot potato and threw to third trying to nail Sugden. When the ball bounded into left field, both runners scored. The next batter, Jesse Burkett, bunted and went all the

1903 St. Louis City Championship Series

GAME FIVE --- October 10

CARDINALS	AB	H	PO	A	E		BROWNS	AB	H	PO	A	E
Farrell, 2b	4	1	2	8	0		Burkett, lf	4	0	2	0	0
Dunleavy, rf	4	0	1	0	1		Swander, rf	4	1	0	0	2
Smoot, cf	5	2	0	0	0		Heidrick, cf	4	3	2	2	0
Brain, ss	4	3	3	4	1		Anderson, 1b	4	1	11	0	0
Barclay, lf	5	1	0	0	0		Hill, ss	4	0	0	5	2
Burke, 3b	5	1	3	0	0		Friel, 3b	4	3	1	3	0
Hackett, 1b	4	2	14	0	0		Bowcock, 2b	4	0	1	2	0
Ryan, c	4	3	4	1	0		Shannon, c	3	1	6	2	0
Murphy, p	5	2	0	3	0		Sudhoff, p	0	0	3	1	0
							Morgan, p	2	0	1	2	0
	40	15	27	16	2		Martin, ph	1	0	0	0	0
								34	9	27	17	4

```
STN  0 0 7   2 0 0   3 0 0 - 12
STA  0 0 0   0 0 0   0 0 1 -  1
```

2B: Smoot, Barclay, Hackett, Heidrick. SB: Brain, Barclay. DP: STN 3. BB: Morgan 5. Struck out: Sudhoff 1, Morgan 3, Murphy 3. Hits: Sudhoff 7, Morgan 6. Umpire: Frank Pears.

GAME SIX --- October 10 (second game)

BROWNS	AB	H	PO	A	E		CARDINALS	AB	H	PO	A	E
Burkett, lf	3	1	2	1	0		Farrell, 2b	4	2	1	4	0
Swander, rf	4	1	1	0	0		Dunleavy, rf	4	2	1	0	0
Heidrick, cf	5	2	3	1	0		Smoot, cf	4	0	3	0	0
Anderson, 1b	4	1	9	1	0		Brain, ss	4	1	4	1	0
Hill, ss	4	1	3	3	1		Barclay, lf	3	2	1	1	0
Friel, 3b	3	0	2	2	0		Burke, 3b	4	0	2	1	1
Bowcock, 2b	4	2	0	1	0		Hackett, 1b	4	1	7	0	0
Sugden, c	3	0	7	0	0		Ryan, c	3	0	3	0	0
Siever, p	4	3	0	4	0		McFarland, p	3	0	2	4	0
	34	11	27	13	1			33	8	24	11	1

```
STN  0 0 1   0 0 0   0 0 1 - 2
STA  0 0 2   0 0 0   3 1 x - 6
```

2B: Siever. 3B: Hackett, Farrell. HR: Heidrick. SB: Dunleavy, Barclay. WP: McFarland. BB: Siever 1, McFarland 3. Struck out: Siever 7, McFarland 3. Umpire: Pears.

GAME SEVEN --- October 11

BROWNS	AB	H	PO	A	E		CARDINALS	AB	H	PO	A	E
Burkett, lf	4	3	4	0	0		Demontreville, 2b	4	1	2	4	0
Swander, rf	5	3	3	1	0		Dunleavy, rf	4	2	0	1	0
Heidrick, cf	5	2	3	0	0		Smoot, cf	5	2	2	1	0
Anderson, 1b	4	0	8	0	1		Brain, ss	4	2	2	3	0
Hill, ss	4	1	2	3	1		Barclay, lf	4	1	3	1	0
Friel, 2b	4	0	1	4	0		Burke, 3b	4	1	2	2	0
Bowcock, 3b	4	0	1	3	0		Hackett, 1b	3	0	11	0	0
Shannon, c	4	2	2	2	1		Ryan, c	4	1	4	1	0
Pelty, p	4	3	0	3	0		Brown, p	4	2	1	5	0
	38	14	24	16	3			36	12	27	18	0

```
STA  0 0 4   0 0 0   0 0 1 - 5
STN  0 0 4   1 2 0   0 2 x - 9
```

Earned runs: STN 6, STA 5. 2B: Ryan. SB: Smoot 2, Barclay, Demontreville 2, Burke. DP: STN 2. BB: Brown 1, Pelty 3. Struck out: Brown 1. LOB: STN 4, STA 9. Umpire: Pears. Time—1:30.

way to third when catcher Jack O'Neill's throw to first went into right field. Burkett scored on Heidrick's groundout. In the end, it was Sudhoff's second inning double which provided the margin of victory as the Cardinals went down to defeat 9–2.

All lumped up, the Cardinals dropped the next two games in convincing fashion. On the sixth, Ed Siever (13–14) scattered seven Cardinal hits and two runs and won easily. The Browns savaged Cards' starter Jim Hackett (1–4) for nine singles, five doubles, a triple, and ten runs. For the third day in a row, the Cardinals aided in their own defeat with five errors. Jesse Burkett was the hitting star of the game with a 4-for-5 performance.

The fourth game was more of the same, only more so. Cardinal starter Mike O'Neill (4–13) was hammered from the very call of "Play Ball!" The Browns scored twice in the first, five times in the second, once in the third, and by the end of five and a half innings had an 11–0 lead. A bases-loaded sixth-inning triple by Homer Smoot in the bottom of the inning accounted for all the Cardinal runs. Browns' winner Jack Powell struck out 15 Redbirds in the game which was more strikeouts than any pitcher in either league had managed in the 1902 season. The Cardinals, who had made five errors in each of the first three games, added to their totals with six in this fiasco. Moran and Brain were leading the team with errors, both men having fumbled the ball four times.

The teams split a doubleheader on the tenth of October. In the first game, the Cardinals surprised their American League opponents by racking up nine hits and seven runs in the third inning off Willie Sudhoff. Five more runs off reliever Cy Morgan (0–2) and the Cards had a 12–0 lead before the Browns were able to push across a solitary run in the ninth. Ed Murphy (4–8) scattered nine hits for an easy victory and even had a little fun with the Browns, delivering the ball underhanded several times. Perhaps not entirely by coincidence, the Cardinals won for the first time when manager Patsy Donovan had to stay away from the park because of illness.

Ed Siever pitched the nightcap for the Browns against Chappie McFarland as the Browns clinched the city series, winning the game by a score of 6–2. The big hit came in the seventh inning. With the Browns already holding a 2–1 lead, Snags Heidrick belted a three run homer over the right field fence. Heidrick wound up 5-for-9 on the day.

With manager Donovan still under the weather, the Cardinals won for the second time in three tries as the series concluded on the 11th of October. The two starting pitchers, Mordecai Brown and Barney Pelty (3–3), were both roughed up for four runs in the third inning, but Brown surrendered no more runs until the ninth. By then, the Cardinals had the game well in hand. The final score was 9–5.

The 1903 Chicago City Championship Series

Chicago Cubs and Chicago White Sox; tie series, 7–7

At the end of the 1903 regular season, president Barney Dreyfuss of the Pittsburgh Pirates and president Matt Killilea of the Boston Pilgrims agreed

1903 Chicago City Championship Series

GAME ONE --- October 1

WHITE SOX	AB	H	PO	A	E		CUBS	AB	H	PO	A	E
Holmes, 3b	4	0	0	0	1		Slagle, cf	5	4	3	0	0
F.Jones, cf	4	1	4	0	0		McCarthy, lf	4	0	3	0	0
Callahan, lf	4	0	1	0	0		Chance, 1b	2	2	7	0	0
Green, rf	4	0	0	0	0		Jones, rf	4	1	3	3	0
Tannehill, ss	4	1	6	5	1		Tinker, ss	3	0	0	2	0
Slattery, 1b	3	0	11	2	1		Kling, c	4	0	7	2	0
Magoon, 2b	3	2	1	2	0		Evers, 2b	5	3	3	0	1
Sullivan, c	3	0	1	1	0		Casey, 3b	4	0	1	0	0
Flaherty, p	3	0	0	2	0		Taylor, p	3	0	0	2	0
	32	4	24	12	3			34	10	27	9	1

```
SOX   0  0  0    0  0  0    0  0  0  -   0
CUB   0  1  1    6  0  2    1  0  x  -  11
```

2B: Chance. 3B: Slagle, Evers. SB: Kling, Casey, Callahan. DP: Sox. BB: Flaherty 1. Struck out: Taylor 6, Flaherty 1. Umpires: Sheridan and James Johnstone.

GAME TWO --- October 2

CUBS	·AB	H	PO	A	E		WHITE SOX	AB	H	PO	A	E
Slagle, cf	5	3	1	0	0		Holmes, 3b	4	0	4	1	0
McCarthy, lf	3	0	2	0	0		F.Jones, cf	4	1	1	0	0
Chance, 1b	4	2	10	0	0		Callahan, lf	4	1	1	0	0
Jones, rf	4	0	3	0	0		Green, rf	4	0	0	0	0
Tinker, ss	4	3	0	4	0		Tannehill, ss	3	0	1	5	0
Kling, c	3	0	7	0	0		Isbell, 1b	4	0	13	2	1
Evers, 2b	2	0	1	2	0		Magoon, 2b	2	0	1	0	0
Casey, 3b	4	0	1	2	1		Sullivan, c	3	1	4	3	0
Weimer, p	4	2	2	0	0		White, p	3	0	2	5	0
	33	10	27	8	1			31	3	27	16	1

```
CUB   2  0  3    0  0  0    0  0  0  -  5
SOX   0  0  0    0  0  0    1  0  0  -  1
```

2B: Tinker. 3B: Chance. SB: Tinker, Evers. BB: White 2, Weimer 1. Struck out: White 3, Weimer 7. Umpires: Sheridan and Johnstone. Att: 3,100.

GAME THREE --- October 3

CUBS	AB	H	PO	A	E		WHITE SOX	AB	H	PO	A	E
Slagle, cf	5	0	2	0	0		Holmes, 3b	3	0	1	0	0
McCarthy, lf	5	2	0	0	0		F.Jones, cf	4	0	2	0	1
Chance, 1b	5	0	15	0	0		Callahan, lf	4	0	2	0	0
Jones, rf	5	1	0	0	0		Green, rf	0	0	0	0	0
Tinker, ss	5	1	1	2	0		White, rf	3	1	0	0	0
Kling, c	5	2	3	3	0		Tannehill, ss	4	1	2	4	4
Evers, 2b	4	1	4	7	1		Isbell, 1b	4	0	12	0	0
Casey, 3b	4	2	2	6	0		Magoon, 2b	4	0	3	2	0
Wicker, p	4	0	0	1	1		Sullivan, c	3	1	5	1	0
							Patterson, p	2	1	0	5	0
	38	9	27	18	1			31	4	27	12	5

```
CUB   0  2  0    2  0  1    1  0  0  -  6
SOX   0  0  0    0  0  0    0  0  0  -  0
```

2B: Casey, Tinker, McCarthy. SB: Chance, Tinker. DP: Cubs. BB: Patterson 2, Wicker 2. Struck out: Patterson 4, Wicker 3. WP: Patterson 2. Umpires: Johnstone and Sheridan A: 7,008.

1903 Chicago City Championship Series

GAME FOUR --- October 4

WHITE SOX	AB	H	PO	A	E		CUBS	AB	H	PO	A	E
Holmes, 3b	6	0	0	2	0		Slagle, cf	4	1	2	0	0
F.Jones, cf	5	2	3	0	0		McCarthy, lf	4	0	3	0	0
Callahan, lf	5	3	2	0	0		Chance, 1b	4	2	11	1	0
White, rf	3	2	3	0	0		Jones, rf	4	1	3	1	0
Tannehill, ss	2	0	5	5	1		Tinker, ss	4	0	2	3	1
Isbell, 1b	3	2	11	2	0		Kling, c	4	1	2	1	0
Magoon, 2b	4	3	2	7	0		Evers, 2b	4	1	3	2	0
Sullivan, c	5	0	1	1	0		Casey, 3b	4	2	1	3	0
Owen, p	5	2	0	0	0		Taylor, p	3	0	0	0	2
	38	14	27	17	1			35	8	27	11	3

```
SOX    2  0  1    0  2  0    1  0  4  -  10
CUB    0  0  1    1  0  0    0  0  0  -   2
```

2B: D. Jones, Kling, F. Jones, Callahan, Isbell. BB: Taylor 2, Owen 1. Struck out: Taylor 2, Owen 1. WP: Taylor. Umpires: Johnstone and Sheridan. Att: 1,700.

to meet in a nine-game series to determine the champions of baseball. (Please note that this "system" differed not at all from the approach which prevailed between championship clubs of the 19th century. Why, then, does major-league baseball continue to ignore the early World Series championships?) Postseason confrontations were also hastily arranged in the cities of Philadelphia, St. Louis, and Chicago, and an Ohio state series was planned for the Cleveland Indians and Cincinnati Reds. These became the first city championships of the 20th century.

Each of the postseason series was to go nine games, but Sox president Charles A. Comiskey and Cubs president James A. Hart went everyone one better by scheduling a 15-game set between their two clubs. Even at the time, it was a clear case of overkill, particularly considering the apparent superiority of the National League team.

The Chicago Cubs (82–56) were a year away from acquiring Mordecai "Three Finger" Brown, two years away from acquiring Ed Reulbach, and just three years from becoming one of the strongest and most dominating teams in the history of baseball. The Cubs won 100 or more games each year from 1906 through 1910 with the exception of 1908 when they could muster only 99. The only year in which they failed to win the pennant was 1909 when they finished six and a half games behind the Pittsburgh Pirates, despite winning 104 games. Even without Brown and Reulbach, the Cubs had two 20-game winners in Jack Taylor (21–14) and Jake Weimer (21–9) to go with Bob Wicker (19–10) — not bad for a third-place ballclub. This was a strong team and an obvious favorite to roll over the White Sox (60–77) who finished in seventh place. That they did not is a tribute to the Sox's refusal to believe everything they read in the newspapers.

The Cubs, to no one's surprise, dominated the first three games of the series, holding the White Sox to a single run while winning by scores of 11–0, 5–1, and 6–0.

1903 Chicago City Championship Series

```
GAME FIVE --- October 5
```

WHITE SOX	AB	H	PO	A	E		CUBS	AB	H	PO	A	E
Holmes, 3b	5	1	1	0	0		Slagle, cf	4	1	1	0	0
F.Jones, cf	5	1	0	0	0		McCarthy, lf	4	0	1	0	0
Callahan, lf	4	2	3	0	0		Chance, 1b	5	0	10	0	1
White, rf	5	3	1	2	0		D.Jones, rf	3	1	1	1	0
Tannehill, ss	5	4	3	7	0		Tinker, ss	3	1	4	2	1
Isbell, 1b	5	3	9	2	0		Kling, c	3	1	10	1	0
Magoon, 2b	5	0	3	6	0		Evers, 2b	4	0	1	4	1
Sullivan, c	4	0	9	2	0		Casey, 3b	4	3	2	0	1
Altrock, p	4	0	1	2	0		Wicker, p	4	2	0	5	0
	42	14	30	21	0			34	9	30	13	4

```
SOX    0  0  0    2  0  0    1  0  0    1  -  4
CUB    1  0  0    0  0  0    1  0  1    0  -  3
```

2B: Tannehill. 3B: Tinker, Kling. SB: McCarthy, Evers, Holmes, White. DP: Cubs. BB: Altrock 2. Struck out: Altrock 6, Wicker 8. PB: Kling. Umpires: Johnstone and Sheridan. Att: 2,500 (estimated).

```
GAME SIX --- October 6
```

CUBS	R	H	PO	A	E		WHITE SOX	R	H	PO	A	E
Slagle, cf	1	1	4	0	0		Holmes, 3b	0	2	0	1	0
McCarthy, lf	0	0	1	0	0		F.Jones, cf	0	1	4	0	0
Chance, 1b	2	1	10	1	0		Callahan, lf	0	0	4	0	0
Jones, rf	0	1	4	0	0		Green, rf	0	1	2	1	1
Tinker, ss	1	1	3	1	1		Tannehill, ss	0	0	2	2	0
Kling, c	0	1	4	1	0		Isbell, 1b	0	0	6	0	2
Evers, 2b	1	2	1	4	0		Magoon, 2b	1	1	2	1	0
Casey, 3b	0	1	0	1	0		Sullivan, c	1	2	6	1	1
Weimer, p	0	1	0	3	0		Patterson, p	0	0	2	2	0
							Slattery, ph	0	1	0	0	0
	5	9	27	11	1			2	8	*26	8	4

```
*  Evers out, hit by batted ball

CUB    1  1  1    0  0  1    1  0  0    -  5
SOX    0  0  0    1  0  0    0  0  1    -  2
```

2B: Holmes, Sullivan 2, Evers. 3B: Tinker, Chance. SB: Chance. DP: Sox. BB: Patterson 1, Weimer 1. Struck out: Patterson 4, Weimer 2. WP: Patterson. Umpires: Johnstone and Sheridan. Att: 2,500 (estimated).

Game One, played on October 1st at West Side Park, saw Jack Taylor shut out the Sox on four singles while his teammates rang up 10 hits and 11 runs against Patsy Flaherty (11–25). In a time when relief pitchers were exceedingly rare, Flaherty went the distance although allowing runs in every inning but the first, fifth, and eighth. (Indeed, there were no relief pitchers used in the entire series except for Game 13.) Jimmy Slagle was the batting star of the game with four hits in five times at bat.

In Game Two, Jake Weimer did not allow the Sox a hit until the sixth inning, nor a run until the seventh. The Cubs, meanwhile, had scored twice in the first and three times in the third to decide the game. Weimer helped his own

1903 Chicago City Championship Series

```
GAME SEVEN --- October 8
```

CUBS	AB	H	PO	A	E		WHITE SOX	AB	H	PO	A	E
Slagle, cf	5	1	2	1	0		Holmes, 3b	4	1	0	2	0
McCarthy, lf	4	2	3	0	0		F.Jones, cf	4	1	1	0	0
Chance, 1b	3	0	6	0	0		Callahan, lf	4	2	2	0	0
Jones, rf	4	1	2	0	0		Green, rf	5	3	0	0	0
Tinker, ss	5	1	1	2	1		Tannehill, ss	5	1	2	2	0
Kling, c	5	2	5	2	0		Slattery, 1b	3	2	10	0	2
Evers, 2b	5	1	4	1	1		Magoon, 2b	4	0	5	2	0
Casey, 3b	3	1	1	2	0		Sullivan, c	4	3	6	1	0
Taylor, p	4	3	0	1	0		White, p	3	1	1	5	0
	38	12	24	9	2			36	14	27	12	2

```
CUB   2  0  0    1  0  0    0  0  0  -  3
SOX   0  1  2    1  0  0    0  5  x  -  9
```

2B: Green, Kling, F. Jones, McCarthy. 3B: Green. BB: Taylor 4, White 2. Struck out: Taylor 3, White 6. Umpires: Johnstone and Sheridan.

```
GAME EIGHT --- October 9
```

WHITE SOX	AB	H	PO	A	E		CUBS	AB	H	PO	A	E
Holmes, 3b	4	1	0	4	0		Slagle, cf	4	1	3	1	0
F.Jones, cf	4	0	3	0	0		McCarthy, lf	3	0	2	1	0
Callahan, lf	3	0	0	0	0		Chance, 1b	4	1	11	0	0
Green, rf	4	2	3	0	0		Jones, rf	2	0	1	0	0
Tannehill, ss	4	1	2	3	0		Tinker, ss	3	0	2	5	1
Slattery, 1b	3	0	15	1	0		Kling, c	3	1	4	0	0
Magoon, 2b	3	1	1	4	0		Evers, 2b	3	0	1	3	0
Sullivan, c	3	0	0	2	0		Casey, 3b	3	0	2	1	0
Owen, p	3	0	1	2	0		Lundgren, p	3	0	1	2	0
	31	5	*25	16	0			28	3	27	13	1

```
*  One out when winning run scored

SOX   0  0  0    0  0  0    0  0  0  -  0
CUB   0  0  0    0  0  0    0  0  1  -  1
```

BB: Lundgren 1, Owen 2. Struck out: Lundgren 3. Balk: Lundgren. Umpires: Johnstone and Sheridan. Att: 2,500 (estimated).

cause with two hits, Joe Tinker had three, and Jimmy Slagle ran his batting average for the two games to .700 with a 3-for-5 performance. Frank Owen (8–12), youngest of the White Sox pitchers, went the distance and took the loss.

Game Three was played at South Side Park (also known as White Stocking Park) on the 3rd of October. The Sox were once again helpless, unable to get their first hit off Bob Wicker until two were out in the fifth. Wicker wound up with a four-hit shutout as the Cubs blasted Roy Patterson (15–15) for nine hits and six runs.

Trailing three-games-to-none in the series and seemingly down for the

1903 Chicago City Championship Series

```
GAME NINE --- October 10
```

WHITE SOX	AB	H	PO	A	E
Holmes, 3b	4	0	0	0	1
F.Jones, cf	3	1	7	0	0
Callahan, lf	4	1	2	0	0
Green, rf	4	1	1	0	0
Tannehill, ss	4	0	1	4	0
Slattery, 1b	4	2	8	2	1
Magoon, 2b	3	0	1	2	0
Sullivan, c	3	0	1	2	0
Altrock, p	3	0	3	3	0
White, ph	1	0	0	0	0
	33	5	24	13	2

CUBS	AB	H	PO	A	E
Slagle, cf	4	1	3	0	0
McCarthy, lf	4	1	1	0	0
Chance, 1b	4	1	10	0	0
Jones, rf	4	1	2	0	0
Tinker, ss	3	1	0	1	0
Kling, c	4	1	10	1	0
Evers, 2b	4	2	0	5	0
Casey, 3b	2	1	1	0	1
Weimer, p	3	0	0	0	0
Taylor, pr	0	0	0	0	0
	32	9	27	7	1

```
SOX    0  0  0    0  0  1    0  1  0  -  2
CUB    0  4  0    0  0  0    0  0  x  -  4
```

2B: Evers, Chance. 3B: Tinker. DP: Sox. BB: Weimer 3. Struck out: Altrock 1, Weimer 9. Umpires: Johnstone and Sheridan. Att: 6,000 (estimated).

count, the White Sox went on record as nobody's patsies in Game Four. Frank Owen gave up eight hits and a walk but only two runs, and was ably supported by his American League teammates. The Sox banged out 14 hits and scored 10 runs off Jack Taylor, the shutout pitcher of Game One. Two errors by Taylor added to the general fun.

Nick Altrock (4–3) and Bob Wicker dueled to a 3–3 tie through nine innings in Game Five before the White Sox pushed across a run against Wicker in the tenth for the victory. Wicker struck out eight men in the game, but 14 hits proved his undoing. Lee Tannehill was 4-for-5 at the plate in the game, with three singles and a double.

The Cubs took a 4–2 lead in the series the next day behind Jake Weimer who won his second game of the series. Weimer scattered eight hits and two runs over his nine innings and got all the support he needed when the Cubs scored single runs in the first three innings.

It rained all the next day and Game Seven was not played until the 8th of October. The Nationals struck for two runs in the first but by the end of four the White Sox held a 4–3 lead. Five Sox runs in the bottom of the eighth inning quelled any hopes of a late-inning Cubs rally. Winning pitcher Doc White (17–16) gave up 12 hits and two walks but worked out of trouble after a shaky first four innings. Jack Taylor was the loser. The batting star was Danny Green with a 3-for-5 performance, including a single, double, and triple.

Frank Owen lost a heartbreaker to the Cubs' Carl Lundgren (10–9) the next day. The game was scoreless into the bottom of the ninth inning and the Sox had been held to five hits. Through eight, Owen had handcuffed the Cubs on a walk and a Johnny Kling single. But with one out in the ninth, Jimmy Slagle singled and Jack McCarthy walked. A wild pitch by Owen moved both runners up and Frank Chance got a scratch hit on the infield to win the game. Lundgren went the distance for the five-hit shutout.

GAME TEN --- October 11

CUBS	R	H	PO	A	E
Slagle, cf	0	0	1	0	0
McCarthy, lf	0	1	2	0	0
Chance, 1b	0	3	9	0	0
Jones, rf	0	0	0	0	0
Tinker, ss	0	0	2	5	0
Kling, c	0	1	8	1	0
Evers, 2b	0	1	1	1	0
Casey, 3b	0	0	1	2	0
Lundgren, p	0	0	0	2	0
	0	6	24	11	0

WHITE SOX	R	H	PO	A	E
Holmes, 3b	1	2	0	3	0
F.Jones, cf	0	1	2	0	0
Callahan, lf	0	1	3	0	0
Green, rf	0	1	1	0	0
Tannehill, ss	0	0	5	2	0
Isbell, 1b	0	0	7	0	0
Magoon, 2b	0	0	1	1	1
Sullivan, c	1	1	8	1	1
White, p	0	0	0	1	0
	2	6	27	8	2

```
CUB   0  0  0    0  0  0    0  0  0  -  0
SOX   0  0  2    0  0  0    0  0  x  -  2
```

2B: Chance, Holmes. 3B: McCarthy, Sullivan. SB: Tinker. BB: White 1. Struck out: White 7, Lundgren 7. WP: White. Umpires: Sheridan and Johnstone. Att: 11,500 (estimated).

GAME ELEVEN --- October 12

CUBS	AB	H	PO	A	E
Slagle, cf	4	1	6	0	0
McCarthy, lf	4	0	4	0	0
Chance, 1b	3	0	6	0	0
Jones, rf	3	1	1	1	0
Tinker, ss	4	0	1	2	0
Kling, c	4	0	4	1	0
Evers, 2b	4	1	2	0	1
Casey, 3b	4	1	0	2	0
Taylor, p	3	0	0	1	0
Harley, ph	1	0	0	0	0
	34	4	24	7	1

WHITE SOX	AB	H	PO	A	E
Holmes, 3b	4	1	1	2	1
F.Jones, cf	4	2	4	1	0
Callahan, lf	3	0	3	0	0
Green, rf	3	1	1	0	0
Tannehill, ss	4	1	1	3	2
Isbell, 1b	4	3	10	1	0
Magoon, 2b	3	1	2	3	0
Sullivan, c	4	2	4	0	0
Owen, p	4	0	1	4	0
	33	11	27	14	3

```
CUB   0  1  0    0  0  0    0  0  1  -  2
SOX   0  0  0    2  1  0    0  1  x  -  4
```

2B: Sullivan, F. Jones, Casey, Evers. 3B: Isbell. SB: Tinker, Green 2. BB: Owen 1. Struck out: Owen 3, Taylor 3. WP: Taylor. Umpires: Johnstone and Sheridan. Att: 2,000.

GAME TWELVE --- October 13

WHITE SOX	R	H	PO	A	E
Holmes, 3b	0	0	1	0	0
F.Jones, cf	0	2	2	0	0
Callahan, lf	0	0	1	0	0
Green, rf	0	2	2	0	0
Tannehill, ss	0	0	2	1	0
Isbell, 1b	0	0	6	1	0
Magoon, 2b	0	0	2	2	0
Sullivan, c	1	2	7	0	0
White, p	0	1	1	3	1
	1	7	24	7	1

CUBS	R	H	PO	A	E
Slagle, cf	1	1	2	0	0
McCarthy, lf	1	1	2	0	0
Chance, 1b	2	1	9	0	0
Jones, rf	1	0	0	0	0
Tinker, ss	0	2	4	2	0
Kling, c	0	2	3	2	0
Evers, 2b	0	0	5	4	0
Casey, 3b	0	0	2	2	0
Wicker, p	0	1	0	1	1
	5	9	27	11	1

```
SOX   0  0  0    0  1  0    0  0  0  -  1
CUB   2  0  0    0  0  1    2  0  x  -  5
```

2B: McCarthy, Green, Chance. SB: Chance. BB: White 2, Wicker 1. Struck out: White 6, Wicker 3. WP: White. Umpires: Sheridan and Johnstone. Att: 3,500.

1903 Chicago City Championship Series

GAME THIRTEEN --- October 14

CUBS	AB	H	PO	A	E	WHITE SOX	AB	H	PO	A	E
Slagle, cf	4	0	2	0	0	Holmes, 3b	4	1	1	1	0
McCarthy, lf	3	1	0	0	0	F. Jones, cf	4	1	4	0	0
Chance, 1b	4	0	8	0	0	Callahan, lf	3	0	4	0	0
D. Jones, rf	4	1	1	0	0	Green, rf	3	2	0	0	0
Tinker, ss	4	0	1	1	0	Tannehill, ss	3	0	1	6	0
Kling, c	4	1	9	1	1	Isbell, 1b	4	1	9	0	0
Evers, 2b	4	0	2	2	0	Magoon, 2b	4	1	4	1	0
Casey, 3b	3	2	0	3	0	Sullivan, c	3	2	3	1	2
Weimer, p	3	0	1	3	0	Owen, p	3	0	1	1	0
Lundgren, p	0	0	0	3	0						
	33	5	24	13	1		31	8	27	10	2

```
CUB    0  0  0    0  0  0    0  0  0  -  0
SOX    1  0  0    1  0  0    0  0  x  -  2
```

2B: Isbell, Magoon, D. Jones. SB: Holmes. HBP: Tannehill (Lundgren). BB: Weimer 1, Owen 1. Struck out: Weimer 7, Lundgren 1, Owen 3. PB: Sullivan. Umpires: Johnstone and Sheridan.

GAME FOURTEEN --- October 15

CUBS	AB	H	PO	A	E	WHITE SOX	AB	H	PO	A	E
Slagle, cf	4	2	1	0	0	Holmes, 3b	2	0	0	1	0
McCarthy, lf	3	0	5	0	0	F. Jones, cf	2	0	3	0	0
Chance, 1b	4	0	10	0	0	Callahan, lf	2	0	5	0	0
D. Jones, rf	3	1	0	0	0	Green, rf	3	1	1	0	0
Tinker, ss	3	0	3	5	0	Sullivan, c	4	0	2	0	0
Kling, c	3	0	4	1	0	Tannehill, ss	3	1	1	5	1
Evers, 2b	3	0	1	1	0	Isbell, 1b	3	2	11	1	0
Casey, 3b	3	1	0	2	1	Magoon, 2b	2	0	3	1	0
Lundgren, p	3	0	0	3	0	Altrock, p	3	0	1	4	0
Williams, ph	1	0	0	0	0						
	30	4	24	12	1		24	4	27	12	1

```
CUB    0  0  0    0  0  0    0  0  0  -  0
SOX    2  0  0    0  0  0    0  0  0  -  2
```

2B: Green. DP: Sox. BB: Lundgren 4. Struck out: Lundgren 3, Altrock 2. Umpires: Johnstone and Sheridan. Att: 3,500 (estimated).

The Cubs went up six games to three the next day as they scored all four of their runs off loser Nick Altrock in the second inning. Jake Weimer allowed five hits, all singles, and even though he weakened in the final innings, held on for his third win of the series.

Doc White pitched a six-hitter and struck out seven in Game Ten as did his opponent, Carl Lundgren. Unfortunately for Lundgren, a triple by Billy Sullivan, a double by Ducky Holmes, and a single accounted for all the runs in the game as the Sox scored twice in the third. Despite a three-hit performance at the plate by Frank Chance, the Cubs were unable to push anyone across the plate.

The White Sox closed to within one game on the 12th behind Frank Owen who threw a four-hitter at the West Siders. Carl Taylor lost his third game of the series. Lee Tannehill made his seventh and eighth errors of the series, but despite his remarkable inability with the glove, the Sox won the game, 4–2. Owen took the victory, Taylor the loss.

The Cubs tallied their seventh victory and were within one game of winning the 1903 city series with a 5–1 victory in Game Twelve. Bob Wicker scattered seven hits through the Sox lineup and was never seriously threatened. Doc White took the loss.

The Sox wrapped up the series with 2–0 shutouts in the final two games. It was Jake Weimer against Frank Owen in the thirteenth game, but Weimer was no match for the White Sox hurler. The Sox struck for a first inning run, the only offense Owen needed as he scattered five hits and shut down the Cub offense completely.

The series' finale on the 15th of October saw Nick Altrock whitewash the Cubs and Carl Lundgren by the same score. The Cubs had one less hit than the previous day, and all four of their hits were singles. The Sox scored early again—two runs in the first due to Lundren's wildness—and sailed along to an easy victory despite being held to four hits.

Player contracts expired October 15th so the series ended at this point. Sox president Charles Comiskey had offered to play a doubleheader on the 15th, but Cubs' manager Frank Selee declined. Selee also declined an offer to pay the players for the final game because he didn't want to do without the services of his shortstop, Joe Tinker. Tinker had to travel to Kansas City for his wedding. Don't let anybody tell you the old-time ballplayers didn't take their game seriously.

The 1903 Philadelphia City Championship Series

Philadelphia Athletics defeat Philadelphia Phillies; 4–3

The 1903 Philadelphia Athletics (75–60) were a fair team which had won the 1902 American League pennant and which would win again just two years later. The Big Three on the pitching staff—Eddie Plank (23–16), Rube Waddell (22–16), and Chief Bender (17–15)—would all improve their records from 1903 to 1905, but the catalyst to that pennant drive would prove to be young Andy Coakley. In 1903, the 21-year-old youngster had a mark of 0–3 with an earned run average of 5.45. He improved upon this (how could he not?) in 1904 and in the pennant-winning year of 1905 shaved three and a half runs off his ERA and wound up leading the league in winning percentage with a 20–7 record. The 1903 Athletics finished a distant 14 and a half games behind the Boston Pilgrims.

The 1903 Philadelphia Phillies (49–86), on the other hand, were in the third year of a four-year decline. When the National League schedule expanded from 140 games to 154 games in 1904, the Phillies promptly responded by losing 100 of their games and dropping an already miserable .363 winning percentage

1903 Philadelphia City Championship Series

GAME ONE --- September 30

PHILLIES	AB	H	PO	A	E
Thomas, cf	3	0	4	0	0
Gleason, 2b	5	1	0	3	0
Wolverton, 3b	3	1	1	1	1
Barry, lf	4	0	4	0	0
Titus, rf	2	1	2	0	0
Douglass, 1b	4	1	9	0	0
Hulswitt, ss	4	0	2	2	0
Dooin, c	3	0	2	1	1
Duggleby, p	3	1	0	2	0
Keister, ph	1	0	0	0	0
	32	5	24	9	2

ATHLETICS	AB	H	PO	A	E
Hartsel, lf	5	2	1	0	1
Pickering, cf	5	0	1	0	0
Davis, 1b	4	2	9	0	0
L.Cross, 3b	4	2	2	2	0
Seybold, rf	4	3	1	0	0
Murphy, 2b	4	2	0	7	1
M.Cross, ss	3	0	4	0	0
Powers, c	4	1	9	2	0
Bender, p	4	1	0	3	1
	37	13	27	14	3

```
PHI    0  0  0    0  2  0    1  0  0  -  3
ATH    0  0  0    0  1  1    0  5  x  -  7
```

2B: Duggleby, Hartsel, Davis, Bender. 3B: Wolverton, Hartsel, Murphy 2, DP: ATH. BB: Bender 5, Duggleby 1. Struck out: Bender 7, Duggleby 1. HBP: Titus. SB: Wolverton. Umpire: Billy Smith.

GAME TWO --- October 1

ATHLETICS	AB	H	PO	A	E
Hartsel, lf	5	2	1	0	0
Pickering, cf	3	0	2	0	0
Davis, 1b	3	1	10	0	0
L.Cross, 3b	4	0	1	0	0
Seybold, rf	5	0	1	2	0
Murphy, 2b	4	0	1	4	0
M.Cross, ss	4	3	6	3	0
Powers, c	3	1	5	1	0
Henley, p	4	1	0	0	0
	35	8	27	10	0

PHILLIES	AB	H	PO	A	E
Thomas, cf	2	0	2	0	0
Gleason, 2b	4	2	3	5	0
Wolverton, 3b	3	0	2	1	0
Barry, lf	4	1	1	0	1
Titus, rf	3	0	2	0	0
Douglass, 1b	4	0	10	0	0
Hulswitt, ss	3	0	1	2	0
Roth, c	4	1	6	0	1
Mitchell, p	3	0	0	3	0
Dooin, ph	1	0	0	0	0
	31	4	27	11	2

```
ATH    1  2  0    3  0  0  ·   0  0  0  -  6
PHI    0  0  0    0  0  0      0  0  0  -  0
```

2B: M. Cross, Powers. 3B: Hartsel. SB: Thomas. BB: Mitchell 5, Henley 5. Struck out: Mitchell 5, Henley 4. HBP: Titus. WP: Henley, Mitchell 2. Umpire: Billy Smith.

to .342. Needless to say, no one gave much consideration to the idea that the National League entry might win this 1903 city championship.

All the games were played at the Athletics' home field, Columbia Park, a wooden stadium which had no dugouts. Players used benches on the field sidelines. On August 8th, the third-base stands at the Phillies' home field, the Baker Bowl, had collapsed into the street and the park would not be ready for use until opening day of 1904.

The series opened on September 30. The game was scoreless until the fifth when the Phillies struck for two runs off a surprised Chief Bender. The Athletics tied the game with single runs in the fifth and sixth, but the Phillies

1903 Philadelphia City Championship Series

GAME THREE --- October 2

PHILLIES	AB	H	PO	A	E		ATHLETICS	AB	H	PO	A	E
Thomas, cf	4	1	4	0	0		Hartsel, lf	3	1	0	0	0
Gleason, 2b	4	1	1	1	0		Pickering, cf	4	1	4	0	0
Wolverton, 3b	3	0	2	1	0		Davis, 1b	4	0	6	1	1
Barry, lf	3	0	1	0	0		L.Cross, 3b	4	1	1	0	0
Keister, rf	3	2	1	0	0		Seybold, rf	3	0	3	0	1
Douglass, 1b	4	1	10	0	0		Murphy, 2b	3	1	4	2	0
Hulswitt, ss	4	1	1	4	0		M.Cross, ss	4	0	3	4	0
Dooin, c	4	1	7	0	0		Powers, c	3	0	5	4	0
Sparks, p	3	0	0	4	0		Plank, p	2	0	1	3	0
							Pinnance, p	1	0	0	1	0
	32	7	27	10	0		Hoffman, ph	1	0	0	0	0
							Schreck, ph	1	1	0	0	0
								33	5	27	15	2

```
PHI   1  2  1    0  1  0    0  0  0  -  5
ATH   0  0  0    0  0  0    0  0  1  -  1
```

2B: Hartsel, Murphy, L. Cross. DP: ATH. BB: Plank 2, Pinnance 1, Sparks 3. Struck out: Plank 1, Pinnance 2, Sparks 6. WP: Plank. Umpire: Billy Smith.

GAME FOUR --- October 3

ATHLETICS	AB	H	PO	A	E		PHILLIES	AB	H	PO	A	E
Hartsel, lf	3	1	3	0	0		Thomas, cf	4	2	1	0	0
Pickering, cf	3	0	2	0	0		Gleason, 2b	4	1	9	4	0
Davis, 1b	4	1	7	0	0		Wolverton, 3b	4	2	0	3	0
L.Cross, 3b	4	1	1	0	0		Barry, lf	4	0	1	0	0
Seybold, rf	3	1	1	0	0		Keister, rf	4	0	0	0	0
Murphy, 2b	4	2	3	3	0		Douglass, 1b	4	0	10	1	0
M.Cross, ss	2	0	2	2	0		Hulswitt, ss	4	2	1	2	0
Schreck, c	4	1	8	0	0		Zimmer, c	3	0	5	3	0
Bender, p	4	2	0	4	0		Fraser, p	3	0	0	5	1
	31	9	27	9	0			34	7	27	18	1

```
ATH   0  0  0    2  0  0    0  1  2  -  5
PHI   0  0  0    0  0  0    0  0  0  -  0
```

2B: Murphy. 3B: L. Cross. HR: Hartsel. SB: Bender, Wolverton. DP: PHI. BB: Fraser 4. Struck out: Fraser 5, Bender 7. Umpire: Billy Smith.

GAME FIVE --- October 5

PHILLIES	AB	H	PO	A	E		ATHLETICS	AB	H	PO	A	E
Thomas, cf	4	0	5	0	0		Hartsel, lf	4	1	2	0	0
Gleason, 2b	4	0	0	1	0		Pickering, cf	5	1	2	0	0
Wolverton, 3b	4	1	1	2	0		Davis, 1b	5	0	14	1	0
Barry, lf	3	0	4	0	0		L.Cross, 3b	4	1	0	1	0
Keister, rf	3	1	1	0	0		Seybold, rf	3	1	2	3	0
Douglass, 1b	3	1	6	2	1		Murphy, 2b	4	2	1	2	0
Hulswitt, ss	3	0	4	4	2		M.Cross, ss	4	3	1	4	0
Roth, c	3	0	3	0	0		Powers, c	4	2	5	1	1
Duggleby, p	3	0	0	2	0		Plank, p	4	1	0	5	0
	30	3	24	11	3			37	12	27	17	1

```
PHI   0  1  0    0  0  0    0  0  0  -  1
ATH   0  3  0    1  1  0    1  0  x  -  6
```

2B: Pickering, L. Cross, Powers. 3B: Hartsel, SB: Wolverton, Murphy, DP: ATH. BB: Plank 2, Duggleby 2. Struck out: Plank 5, Duggleby 1. PB: Powers 2. Umpire: Billy Smith.

1903 Philadelphia City Championship Series

```
GAME SIX --- October 6
```

ATHLETICS	AB	H	PO	A	E
Hartsel, lf	4	1	1	0	0
Pickering, cf	4	1	1	0	0
Davis, 1b	4	2	6	3	0
L.Cross, 3b	4	0	2	2	0
Seybold, rf	4	0	3	0	1
Murphy, 2b	3	1	2	0	1
M.Cross, ss	3	0	0	2	2
Schreck, c	3	0	5	1	1
Henley, p	0	0	0	0	1
Pinnance, p	2	0	1	3	0
	31	5	24	11	6

PHILLIES	AB	H	PO	A	E
Thomas, cf	3	0	4	0	1
Gleason, 2b	3	1	2	2	1
Wolverton, 3b	4	2	1	0	0
Barry, lf	5	2	1	0	0
Titus, rf	5	4	1	0	0
Douglass, 1b	5	4	8	0	0
Hulswitt, ss	5	1	1	4	1
Dooin, c	5	2	6	2	0
Mitchell, p	5	1	0	0	1
	40	17	24	8	4

```
ATH   0  0  2   0  0  0    0  0  -   2
PHI   3  1  2   2  0  5    1  x  -  14
```

2B: Davis, Murphy, Wolverton, Barry, Douglass. 3B: Dooin. SH: Wolverton. SB: Hulswitt. DP: ATH 2. BB: Henley 1, Pinnance 2, Mitchell 1. Struck out: Henley, Pinnance 1, Mitchell 3. PB: Schreck. Umpire: Billy Smith.

regained the lead in the seventh. The A's finally righted themselves and pounded Phillies' starter Bill Duggleby (13–18) for five eighth-inning runs to win, 7–3. Bender only allowed five hits in the game, but five free passes and three errors by his teammates kept him in trouble all day long. He managed to quell most of the rallies with strikeouts and finished with seven for the day. The A's pounded Duggleby hard. Five members of the team had two hits or more and Danny Murphy belted out two triples in the game.

Game Two featured more of the same as the Athletics struck early and often and beat the Phillies handily, 6–0. The A's tallied one run in the first, two in the second, and ended the day's scoring with three in the fourth. Weldon Henley (12–9) shut out the Nationals on four hits, two of those by Kid Gleason, but had to work out of trouble most of the day because of five walks. Fred Mitchell (11–15) allowed only eight hits, but the five walks, two wild pitches, and errors by Frank Roth and Shad Barry contributed to his undoing.

The Phillies got on the board in Game Three behind a fine pitching performance by Tully Sparks (11–15) who stifled the A's offense on five hits, all singles, while striking out six. The Athletics were unable to mount any kind of a scoring threat until the ninth when they pushed a solitary run across. By that time, the Phils had matters well in hand with a 5–0 lead. Eddie Plank and Ed Pinnance (0–1) allowed only seven hits, but doubles by Topsy Hartsel, Danny Murphy, and Lave Cross did the two hurlers in.

Game Four saw the Athletics get back on track as Chief Bender scattered seven hits, walked no one, and struck out seven for his second win of the series. The big man had a pretty good day at the plate also, with two hits in four times at bat and a stolen base. Topsy Hartsel's home run provided all the runs Bender needed. Chick Fraser (12–17) took the loss.

1903 Philadelphia City Championship Series

```
GAME SEVEN --- October 7
```

PHILLIES	AB	H	PO	A	E		ATHLETICS	AB	H	PO	A	E
Thomas, cf	5	1	4	0	0		Hartsel, lf	3	3	1	0	0
Gleason, 2b	6	2	0	3	0		Pickering, cf	5	0	2	0	0
Wolverton, 3b	5	2	0	2	0		Davis, 1b	5	0	7	1	1
Barry, lf	5	0	6	0	0		L.Cross, 3b	5	0	1	1	0
Titus, rf	4	2	1	0	0		Seybold, rf	3	1	3	1	0
Douglass, 1b	5	1	7	1	0		Murphy, 2b	4	2	6	2	1
Hulswitt, ss	5	3	3	1	1		M.Cross, ss	4	1	1	2	2
Roth, c	4	1	6	0	0		Powers, c	4	2	6	1	0
Sparks, p	4	1	0	2	0		Bender, p	3	0	0	2	1
	43	13	27	9	1			36	9	27	10	5

```
PHI   0  0  1    3  2  5    0  0  2  -  13
ATH   0  1  0    0  0  2    0  0  0  -   3
```

2B: Titus, Hulswitt, Hartsel, Murphy 2. 3B: Titus. SB: Gleason, Sparks, Hartsel, L. Cross. HR: Thomas, Seybold. DP: PHI. HBP: Wolverton and Roth (Bender). BB: Bender 3, Sparks 4. Struck out: Bender 4, Sparks 5. Umpire: Billy Smith.

Bill Duggleby and Eddie Plank were matched for the first time in Game Five and Duggleby, who had nothing, suffered through his second loss of the series as the A's defeated him by a 6-1 score. Every member of the Athletic lineup hit safely except first baseman Harry Davis. The Phillies took an early 1-0 lead in the second, but the Americans responded with three runs of their own in the bottom of the inning and the contest was never in doubt from there on. Plank evened his record in the series at 1-1.

The Phillies showed a spark of life in Game Six as they pounded Weldon Henley and Ed Pinnance for 17 hits, among them three doubles and a triple. The Phils scored three in the first, one in the second, two in the third, and two in the fourth before exploding for five runs in the sixth. Ironically everyone except Roy Thomas, who led the team during the season with a .327 batting average, hit safely. John Titus and William "Klondike" Douglass were 4-for-5 at the dish. Fred Mitchell went the distance for the easy 14-2 victory. Questionable fielding was the hallmark of this game, the A's making six errors, the Phillies four.

With a little momentum on their side, the Phillies came back in Game Seven with a similar pounding as they walloped the Athletics by a 13-3 score, racking up 10 of their runs in the middle innings. Seven players had two hits or more in the game and there were a total of five doubles, a triple, and two home runs. The Athletics continued their miserable fielding, with errors by Davis, Bender, and Danny Murphy. For the second day in a row, Monte Cross chipped in with two.

Heavy rains and cold weather prevented any further games from being played, and the postseason championship ended with the Athletics leading, four games to three. The Phillies had acquitted themselves very well in the series.

1903 Ohio State Championship Series

GAME ONE --- October 3 at Cleveland

CINCINNATI	AB	H	PO	A	E		CLEVELAND	AB	H	PO	A	E
Donlin, 1b	4	1	13	0	0		Flick, rf	4	2	1	0	0
Seymour, cf	4	1	2	0	0		Bay, lf	3	0	3	0	0
Dolan, rf	4	0	2	0	0		Bradley, 3b	4	2	1	4	0
Kerwin, lf	2	0	0	0	1		Lajoie, ss	3	0	1	3	0
Daly, 2b	3	1	1	5	1		Hickman, 2b	3	1	2	4	0
Corcoran, ss	3	0	2	8	1		Bemis, 1b	2	0	11	1	0
DeArmond, 3b	3	0	0	2	0		Abbott, c	2	1	2	0	0
Peitz, c	2	0	4	0	0		Thoney, cf	3	0	4	0	0
Sutthoff, p	3	0	0	2	0		Donahue, p	3	0	2	0	0
	28	3	24	17	3			27	6	27	12	0

```
CIN    0  0  0    0  0  0    1  0  0  -  1
CLE    1  0  0    0  0  1    0  0  x  -  2
```

2B: Flick. 3B: Flick. SB: Bay. DP: CLE 2, CIN 2. BB: Donahue 2. Struck out: Donahue 2, Sutthoff 3. Umpire: Tim Hurst. Att: 5,546.

GAME TWO --- October 4 at Cincinnati

CLEVELAND	AB	H	PO	A	E		CINCINNATI	AB	H	PO	A	E
Flick, rf	4	2	2	0	0		Donlin, 1b	4	1	9	1	0
Bay, lf	5	0	2	1	0		Seymour, cf	5	0	3	0	0
Bradley, 3b	5	4	3	4	0		Dolan, rf	4	2	1	0	0
Lajoie, 2b	4	0	4	1	0		Kerwin, lf	5	0	0	0	1
Hickman, 1b	4	2	4	0	0		DeArmond, 3b	4	2	0	2	1
Bemis, c	4	0	4	0	0		Daly, 2b	4	3	3	4	0
Gochnaur, ss	3	1	1	2	1		Corcoran, ss	4	3	5	4	0
Thoney, cf	4	1	3	0	1		Peitz, c	3	0	4	0	0
Moore, p	3	1	1	0	0		Ewing, p	4	1	0	1	0
Abbott, ph	1	0	0	0	0			37	12	27	10	2
	37	11	24	8	2							

```
CLE    0  0  0    0  1  0    0  2  0  -  3
CIN    4  0  1    0  2  0    0  0  x  -  7
```

2B: Flick. 3B: Donlin, DeArmond, Hickman. DP: CIN 3, CLE 1. BB: Ewing 2, Moore 3. Struck out: Ewing 2, Moore 4. PB: Peitz. Umpire: Tim Hurst. Att: 5,678.

The 1903 Ohio State Championship Series

Cleveland Naps beat Cincinnati Reds; 6–3

In the first of four sporadically held 20th century postseason series for the championship of Ohio, the fourth-place Cincinnati Reds (74–65) and the third-place Cleveland Naps (77–63) proved to be evenly matched for the first four games before Cleveland pulled away to win.

Game One was played at Cleveland's League Park on the 3rd of October. Cincinnati's Jack Sutthoff (16–10) took the mound against Red Donahue (7–9) in a pitcher's duel which featured light hitting on both sides. Sutthoff held Cleveland to only six hits, but those were good enough for two runs, due in

1903 Ohio State Championship Series

GAME THREE --- October 6 at Columbus

CLEVELAND	AB	H	PO	A	E
Flick, rf	2	0	2	0	0
Bay, lf	3	0	2	1	0
Bradley, 3b	4	1	2	5	0
Lajoie, 2b	4	2	1	1	0
Hickman, 1b	4	0	10	1	0
Bemis, c	4	0	1	1	0
Gochnaur, ss	4	1	2	0	2
Thoney, cf	3	0	3	2	0
Bernhard, p	3	1	1	2	0
	31	5	24	13	2

CINCINNATI	AB	H	PO	A	E
Donlin, 1b	3	1	9	0	0
Seymour, cf	4	2	2	0	0
Dolan, rf	3	1	2	0	0
Kerwin, lf	2	0	4	0	0
DeArmond, 3b	3	2	1	4	0
Daly, 2b	3	0	3	1	1
Corcoran, ss	3	0	2	0	0
Peitz, c	3	0	4	0	0
Hahn, p	3	0	0	2	0
	27	6	27	7	1

```
CLE  1 0 0   0 0 0   0 0 0  -  1
CIN  0 0 0   0 0 2   0 0 x  -  2
```

2B: Seymour, Lajoie. SB: DeArmond. DP: CLE. BB: Hahn 1, Bernhard 2. Struck out: Hahn 3. Umpire: Tim Hurst.

GAME FOUR --- October 7 at Newark

CINCINNATI	AB	H	PO	A	E
Donlin, 1b	4	1	11	1	2
Seymour, cf	4	2	1	0	2
Kelley, lf	3	2	1	0	0
Kerwin, rf	3	1	1	0	0
DeArmond, 3b	3	1	1	4	0
Daly, 2b	4	2	2	2	1
Corcoran, ss	4	0	2	2	0
Peitz, c	4	0	2	1	0
Harper, p	3	0	0	3	0
	32	9	21	13	7

CLEVELAND	AB	H	PO	A	E
Flick, rf	5	2	0	0	0
Bay, lf	5	3	1	0	0
Bradley, 3b	4	0	1	0	0
Lajoie, ss	4	2	6	2	0
Hickman, 2b	4	1	1	3	0
Bemis, 1b	4	3	6	1	0
Abbott, c	4	2	6	1	1
Thoney, cf	4	0	2	1	0
Rhoades, p	4	2	1	1	0
	38	15	24	9	1

```
CIN  0 0 0   0 0 0   1 2  -   3
CLE  0 0 0   0 2 2   7 x  -  11
```

2B: Bay, Seymour, DeArmond, Lajoie, Bemis, Daly, Flick. 3B: Kelley. HR: Rhoades, Bemis. DP: CIN 4. SB: Bemis. BB: Harper 2, Rhoades 2. Struck out: Rhoades, 7, Harper 2. PB: Peitz. Umpire: Tim Hurst. Att: 1,207.

large measure to right fielder Elmer Flick's double and triple in four times at bat. Cincinnati, which was held to three hits by Donahue, could muster only a single seventh inning run and went down to defeat, 2–1.

Game Two was played at the home field of the Reds, the Palace of the Fans, the next day. Cleveland ace Earl Moore (19–9) and Bob Ewing (14–13) were both hit hard, but Cincinnati bunched its hits in the first and scored four runs off Moore for a lead they never relinquished. The Naps squandered most of their opportunities as they hit into three double plays. Both pitchers went the distance as Cincinnati tied the series with a 7–3 victory.

Game Three was played at Columbus, Ohio, on the 6th and Cincinnati took their first and only lead in the series in another light-hitting contest. The Reds overcame a first inning run by Cleveland with two of their own in the sixth

1903 Ohio State Championship Series

GAME FIVE --- October 9 at Cleveland

CINCINNATI	AB	H	PO	A	E		CLEVELAND	AB	H	PO	A	E
Donlin, 1b	4	1	5	1	0		Flick, rf	4	0	2	0	0
Seymour, cf	4	2	4	2	2		Bay, lf	3	1	2	0	1
Kelley, lf	3	0	1	0	0		Bradley, 3b	4	1	4	1	0
Kerwin, rf	3	1	0	0	0		Lajoie, ss	4	0	1	4	0
DeArmond, 3b	4	0	2	1	1		Hickman, 2b	2	2	2	2	2
Daly, 2b	4	0	6	2	0		Bemis, 1b	4	1	9	0	0
Corcoran, ss	3	1	2	2	3		Abbott, c	3	1	5	0	0
Peitz, c	3	0	3	2	0		Thoney, cf	3	0	2	1	0
Sutthoff, p	2	0	1	5	0		Donahue, p	3	0	0	6	0
Dolan, ph	1	0	0	0	0							
	31	5	24	15	6			30	6	27	14	3

```
CIN   0  0  1    0  2  0    0  0  0  -  3
CLE   0  1  0    1  0  1    0  2  x  -  5
```

3B: Donlin. SB: Hickman. DP: CIN 3, CLE 1. BB: Sutthoff 1, Donahue 6. Struck out: Sutthoff 3, Donahue 4. WP: Sutthoff. Umpire: Tim Hurst. Att: 3,586.

GAME SIX --- October 10 at Cleveland

CINCINNATI	AB	H	PO	A	E		CLEVELAND	AB	H	PO	A	E
Donlin, 1b	5	2	12	1	0		Flick, rf	3	1	0	0	0
Seymour, cf	4	1	1	0	0		Bay, lf	4	1	0	0	0
Dolan, rf	3	1	1	0	2		Bradley, 3b	4	0	1	4	0
Kerwin, lf	1	0	0	0	0		Lajoie, ss	4	2	8	3	0
DeArmond, 3b	3	0	1	4	0		Hickman, 2b	3	2	2	2	1
Daly, 2b	3	1	0	3	0		Bemis, 1b	4	2	10	0	0
Corcoran, ss	4	1	3	2	0		Abbott, c	3	1	5	3	0
Peitz, c	2	0	5	2	0		Thoney, cf	3	2	1	0	0
Hahn, p	2	0	1	3	0		Moore, p	3	0	0	0	0
Kelley, ph	1	0	0	0	0							
	28	6	24	15	2			31	11	27	12	1

```
CIN   0  0  0    0  1  0    0  0  0  -  1
CLE   0  1  0    2  0  0    1  1  x  -  4
```

SB: Bay. DP: CIN 1, CLE 2. BB: Hahn 1, Moore 8. Struck out: Moore 6, Hahn 3. WP: Moore 2. PB: Peitz. Umpire: Tim Hurst.

GAME SEVEN --- October 10 (second game) at Cleveland

CINCINNATI	AB	H	PO	A	E		CLEVELAND	AB	H	PO	A	E
Donlin, 1b	4	0	7	0	2		Flick, rf	4	2	2	0	0
Seymour, cf	3	0	1	1	1		Bay, lf	3	1	2	0	0
Dolan, rf	4	0	1	1	0		Bradley, 3b	4	1	1	2	0
Kerwin, lf	4	0	1	0	0		Lajoie, ss	3	1	1	2	1
DeArmond, 3b	4	0	3	2	0		Hickman, 2b	4	1	0	5	1
Daly, 2b	4	0	3	1	2		Bemis, 1b	4	0	13	1	0
Corcoran, ss	2	0	4	1	0		Abbott, c	3	0	3	0	0
Peitz, c	2	0	4	1	0		Thoney, cf	3	0	5	0	0
Ewing, p	3	1	0	4	0		Bernhard, p	3	1	0	1	0
	30	1	24	11	5			31	7	27	11	2

```
CIN   0  0  0    0  0  0    1  0  0  -  1
CLE   1  0  0    2  0  0    0  3  x  -  6
```

2B: Bernhard, Flick. SB: Hickman. BB: Bernhard 3. Struck out: Ewing 4, Bernhard 3. PB: Peitz. Umpire: Tim Hurst. Att: 2,807.

and Cincinnati ace Frank "Noodles" Hahn (22–12) held the Naps at bay for the balance of the game. Bill Bernhard (14–6) went all the way for Cleveland and took the loss.

The fourth game of the series was played at Newark and featured Bob Rhoades (2–3 with Cleveland) against Jack Harper (6–8). The game was scoreless for the first four innings until all hell broke loose. The Naps tagged Harper for two runs in the fifth, two more in the sixth, and exploded for a touchdown in the seventh. Harry Bemis, making a rare start at first base, was the hitting star of the day with a single, double, and home run in four times at bat. The Naps knocked out 15 hits against Harper, among them four doubles and two home runs. Cincinnati finally got untracked with three runs in the final two innings, but it wasn't enough. The final score was 11–3.

The teams journeyed back to Cleveland for Game Five, the most exciting game of the series so far. Cleveland took a 1–0 lead in the second, but Cincinnati tied the game in the third. A third-inning run by the Naps was countered with two in the fifth by the Reds, but Cleveland tied the game in the sixth and broke on top to stay with two in the eighth. Six walks by Cleveland starter Red Donahue and three errors by his teammates kept him in hot water for much of the game, but four strikeouts and three double plays took him off the hook time and again. The final score was 5–3.

The teams played a doubleheader on the 10th of October and Cleveland wrapped up the series by winning both games, 4–1 and 6–1. In the first game, Earl Moore kept the Reds guessing at the plate as he struck out six and walked eight, pitching a complete game. The Reds could manage only six hits and a lone fifth-inning run as Cleveland won to take a 4–2 lead in the series. Noodles Hahn suffered his first loss.

In the nightcap, Bill Bernhard pitched a masterful one-hitter, the lone safety a single by opposing pitcher Bob Ewing, as the Naps coasted to a 6–1 victory.

The next two games were scheduled for Cincinnati although the series was officially over. The games were played so Reds' management could garner some additional revenues. The first game of a doubleheader on the 11th was the most exciting by far. Cincinnati starter Jack Sutthoff was knocked from the box after only one inning and the Naps held a 6–2 lead into the bottom of the eighth. But the Reds struck for four runs off Bob Rhoades to tie the game and pushed the deciding run across with one out in the bottom of the ninth. Jack Harper, who worked the final eight innings in relief of Sutthoff, was the victor.

In the nightcap, the Naps couldn't do anything against the curveballs of rookie Rip Reagan (0–2) who shut them out for the first seven innings. It was so dark by the eighth inning that spectators swarmed onto the field, setting fire to their scorecards and pleading with umpire Tim Hurst to halt the game and give Reagan the win. Hurst refused to be swayed and called for the police to push the crowd back. When order was finally restored, Reagan's curveballs apparently became easier to see. Cleveland tallied two runs in the eighth and one in the ninth to win the finale for Red Donahue, 6–3.

1903 Ohio State Championship Series

GAME EIGHT --- October 11 at Cincinnati

CLEVELAND	AB	H	PO	A	E
Flick, rf	5	3	2	0	1
Bay, lf	4	2	3	0	0
Bradley, 3b	4	2	1	1	0
Lajoie, ss	4	0	3	2	0
Hickman, 2b	4	2	0	4	0
Bemis, 1b	4	0	10	0	0
Abbott, c	4	1	3	2	0
Thoney, cf	1	0	2	0	0
Bernhard, cf	3	0	2	0	1
Rhoades, p	4	0	0	2	1
	37	10	*26	11	3

CINCINNATI	AB	H	PO	A	E
Donlin, 1b	5	2	9	0	0
Seymour, cf	5	4	2	0	0
Dolan, rf	5	1	1	0	0
Kerwin, lf	5	1	1	0	1
DeArmond, 3b	4	1	1	1	1
Daly, 2b	4	1	1	3	1
Corcoran, ss	4	1	2	1	1
Schlei, c	3	0	10	4	1
Sutthoff, p	0	0	0	0	1
Harper, p	4	2	0	2	0
	39	13	27	11	6

* One out when winning run scored

```
CLE    2  0  1    0  3  0    0  0  0  -  6
CIN    1  1  0    0  0  0    0  4  1  -  7
```

2B: DeArmond. 3B: Flick. SB: Donlin, Seymour 2, Daly, Corcoran 2, Bay. DP: CIN 2. IP: Sutthoff 1, Harper 8. Hits: Sutthoff 2, Harper 8. Umpire: Tim Hurst.

GAME NINE --- October 11 (second game) at Cincinnati

CINCINNATI	AB	H	PO	A	E
Donlin, 1b	3	1	6	1	0
Seymour, cf	4	0	7	1	0
Dolan, rf	3	1	1	0	0
Kerwin, lf	4	0	2	0	0
DeArmond, 3b	4	3	0	3	1
Daly, 2b	4	0	1	0	0
Corcoran, ss	4	1	3	1	0
Schlei, c	4	1	6	1	0
Reagan, p	3	0	1	2	0
	33	7	27	9	1

CLEVELAND	AB	H	PO	A	E
Flick, rf	4	2	2	1	0
Bay, lf	3	0	1	1	0
Bradley, 3b	4	1	3	1	0
Lajoie, ss	4	2	5	5	0
Hickman, 2b	4	1	5	3	1
Bemis, c	2	1	2	0	0
Abbott, 1b	4	0	6	1	1
Bernhard, cf	4	0	2	0	0
Donahue, p	4	0	1	3	0
	33	7	27	15	2

```
CLE    0  0  0    0  0  0    0  2  1  -  3
CIN    1  0  0    0  0  0    0  0  0  -  1
```

2B: Dolan, DeArmond, Lajoie. 3B: Flick, Bemis. SB: Flick. DP: CLE 1, CIN 1. WP: Reagan. Umpire: Tim Hurst. Att: 5,743.

The 1904 St. Louis City Championship Series

St. Louis Cardinals v. St. Louis Browns; tie series, 3–3

The 1904 St. Louis Cardinals (75–79) had the unusual distinction of being headed by a player-manager who was a pitcher—Kid Nichols. The Redbirds improved in the wins column by 33, and 21 of those could be attributed to Nichols (21–13) himself. The ought-four Browns (65–87) had the same number of victories as the previous year, but with the expanded schedule they were able to play 13 more games. They lost them all. Both teams were looking forward to postseason exhibitions that might help them salvage something from their lost seasons. Neither team got its wish.

1904 St. Louis City Championship Series

```
GAME ONE --- October 10
```

CARDINALS	AB	H	PO	A	E		BROWNS	AB	H	PO	A	E
Farrell, 2b	4	1	2	6	1		Burkett, lf	2	0	1	0	0
Shannon, lf	3	1	2	0	0		Heidrick, cf	3	0	6	0	0
Beckley, 1b	4	1	16	0	0		Wallace, ss	4	2	4	2	0
Brain, 3b	4	0	1	0	1		Hines, rf	4	0	0	0	0
Smoot, cf	4	2	3	3	0		Jones, 1b	4	1	8	1	0
Dunleavy, rf	4	0	2	1	0		Padden, 2b	4	0	4	3	0
Shay, ss	3	0	2	4	0		Moran, 3b	4	1	1	4	0
Grady, c	4	1	2	0	1		Kahoe, c	4	0	5	1	0
Taylor, p	3	0	0	4	0		Pelty, p	3	0	1	1	0
	33	6	30	18	3			32	4	30	12	0

```
STN   0  0  0    1  0  0    0  0  0    2  -  3
STA   0  0  1    0  0  0    0  0  0    0  -  1
```

2B: Beckley, Moran. 3B: Wallace. HR: Grady. DP: STN 1, STA 1. BB: Taylor 2, Pelty 3. Struck out: Pelty 5, Taylor 1. Umpire: Hart.

Game One, on the 10th of October, was sensational. Barney Pelty (15–18) and Cardinal ace Jack Taylor (21–19) assumed the pitching duties. The Browns broke on top in the third when Jesse Burkett drew a walk and scored on short-stop Bobby Wallace's triple to the left-field bleachers. The Cardinals evened matters in the next half-inning. Jake Beckley doubled, went to third on Dave Brain's groundout, and scored on Homer Smoot's single. That's where the score stayed until the tenth, the Browns failing to put another man on base against Taylor. After Cardinal outfielders Homer Smoot and Jack Dunleavy grounded out to start the final inning, Danny Shay worked Pelty for a base on balls. Mike Grady was the next batter and he crashed Pelty's second delivery into the left-field bleachers, bringing the affair to a rapid conclusion.

The second game made the spectators wonder if these were the same two teams which had played the first contest. It was Mike O'Neill (10–14) of the Cards against Ed Siever (10–15) and the Browns took a two run lead in the first inning on three hits and an error. Two infield singles, an error, and a single by Jesse Burkett added three more to the Browns' ledger in the fourth. Three Cardinal errors and a squeeze bunt by Siever brought in the final American League run in the fifth. The Cardinals finally got on the board in the sixth when Dave Brain's single was followed by walks to Dunleavy and Shay, and a two-run single by pitcher O'Neill. A triple by Jake Beckley and an error by Kahoe scored the final Cardinal run. All told, the Redbirds made eight errors on the day, Danny Shay making three of those by himself. The final score was 6–3 in favor of the Browns.

Manager Kid Nichols elected to start Game Three, taking the mound against the Browns' Harry Howell (13–21). The Cardinals went out in order in the top of the first, but Jesse Burkett led off the bottom of the inning with a single. After Snags Heidrick flied out, Bobby Wallace hit a grounder to Farrell who flipped to the base to force Burkett. But shortstop Danny Shay bobbled the ball and Burkett was safe, despite oversliding the bag. One out later, Tom

1904 St. Louis City Championship Series

GAME TWO --- October 11

BROWNS	AB	H	PO	A	E
Burkett, lf	5	1	2	0	0
Heidrick, cf	5	2	4	2	0
Wallace, ss	5	2	1	5	0
Hines, rf	2	1	0	0	0
Jones, 1b	4	1	8	0	0
Padden, 2b	5	3	3	2	0
Moran, 3b	5	2	2	0	0
Kahoe, c	4	2	7	0	1
Siever, p	2	0	0	3	0
Howell, rf	3	0	0	0	0
	40	14	27	12	1

CARDINALS	AB	H	PO	A	E
Farrell, 2b	4	1	2	6	0
Shannon, lf	4	1	0	1	0
Beckley, 1b	5	2	12	1	1
Brain, 3b	5	1	3	4	1
Smoot, cf	4	0	1	0	0
Dunleavy, rf	2	2	3	4	1
Shay, ss	2	0	1	3	0
Grady, c	4	1	5	2	1
O'Neill, p	4	2	0	1	1
	34	10	27	22	8

```
STA   2 0 0   3 1 0   0 0 0  -  6
STN   0 0 0   0 0 2   1 0 0  -  3
```

2B: Moran, Farrell. 3B: Beckley. SB: Heidrick, Kahoe, Siever, Grady. DP: STN 1. BB: off Siever 5. Struck out: Siever 3, O'Neill 3. Umpire: Hart.

GAME THREE --- October 12

CARDINALS	AB	H	PO	A	E
Farrell, 2b	4	1	2	1	0
Shannon, lf	3	0	2	0	0
Beckley, 1b	4	0	10	0	0
Brain, 3b	3	0	1	2	0
Smoot, cf	3	0	2	0	0
Dunleavy, rf	3	1	2	0	0
Shay, ss	0	0	1	3	1
Grady, c	3	0	4	1	1
Nichols, p	3	0	0	3	0
	26	2	24	10	2

BROWNS	AB	H	PO	A	E
Burkett, lf	4	1	1	0	0
Heidrick, cf	4	0	1	0	0
Wallace, ss	3	0	2	2	0
Hines, rf	3	1	0	0	0
Jones, 1b	2	1	11	1	0
Padden, 2b	3	0	3	3	0
Moran, 3b	3	0	1	1	0
Kahoe, c	3	1	7	2	0
Howell, p	2	0	1	2	0
	27	4	27	11	0

```
STN   0 0 1   0 0 0   0 0 0  -  1
STA   2 0 0   0 0 0   0 0 x  -  2
```

SB: Shay. DP: STA. BB: Howell 2. Struck out: Howell 6, Nichols 2. Umpire: Hart.

GAME FOUR --- October 13

BROWNS	AB	H	1	A	E
Burkett, lf	4	1	1	0	0
Heidrick, cf	4	2	0	0	0
Wallace, ss	4	2	2	3	0
Hines, rf	4	2	3	0	0
Jones, 1b	3	0	9	0	0
Padden, 2b	4	0	7	2	0
Moran, 3b	4	0	1	2	1
Kahoe, c	3	0	4	1	0
Glade, p	3	0	0	3	0
	33	7	27	11	1

CARDINALS	AB	H	PO	A	E
Farrell, 2b	4	1	1	2	1
Shannon, lf	3	0	3	0	0
Beckley, 1b	4	1	12	0	0
Brain, ss	4	2	1	6	0
Smoot, cf	4	1	2	0	0
Dunleavy, rf	4	0	3	0	1
Burke, 3b	4	1	1	3	0
Grady, c	3	1	4	0	0
McFarland, p	3	0	0	1	0
Hill, ph	0	0	0	0	0
	33	7	27	12	2

```
STA   0 0 0   0 3 0   0 0 0  -  3
STN   2 0 0   0 0 0   0 0 0  -  2
```

2B: Hines, Grady, Beckley. 3B: Heidrick. SB: Heidrick, Wallace, Brain. DP: STN 1. BB: Glade 3. Struck out: Glade 4, McFarland 2. PB: Kahoe. Umpires: Zearfoss (Cardinals) and Sudhoff (Browns).

1904 St. Louis City Championship Series

GAME FIVE --- October 14

CARDINALS	AB	H	PO	A	E		BROWNS	AB	H	PO	A	E
Farrell, 2b	5	2	5	5	0		Burkett, lf	2	0	1	0	0
Shannon, lf	5	0	2	0	0		Heidrick, cf	4	0	1	1	0
Beckley, 1b	4	2	10	0	0		Wallace, ss	3	0	7	3	0
Brain, 3b	4	2	1	2	1		Hines, rf	4	1	0	0	1
Smoot, cf	4	0	1	0	0		Jones, 1b	4	0	5	2	0
Dunleavy, rf	4	2	3	0	1		Padden, 2b	4	1	6	1	0
Shay, ss	3	2	2	4	1		Moran, 3b	4	3	2	2	0
Butler, c	3	1	2	1	0		Kahoe, c	4	0	4	0	0
Taylor, p	4	2	1	2	1		Pelty, p	4	1	1	1	0
	36	13	27	14	4			33	6	27	10	1

```
STN   0  0  0   2  0  0   1  0  5  -  8
STA   0  0  0   2  0  0   0  0  0  -  2
```

2B: Beckley, Brain 2. HR: Butler. SB: Brain, Shay, Hines. DP: STN. BB: Taylor 3, Pelty 2. Struck out: Taylor 2, Pelty 4. Umpires: Zearfoss (Cardinals) and Sudhoff (Browns).

Jones singled to left and Burkett scored in a bone-crushing collision with catcher Mike Grady. Spike Shannon's throw to the plate caromed past the reeling Grady and Wallace also scored. Nichols pitched nearly perfect ball the rest of the way, allowing singles to Pat Hines and Mike Kahoe and walking no one, but the damage had been done. The Cardinals' only run came in the third as Shay atoned somewhat for his error with a leadoff walk, stole second, and scored on John Farrell's single to center. Howell pitched a masterful two-hitter, the only other hit a single off the bat of Jack Dunleavy.

Game Four saw Chappie McFarland (14–17) take on Browns' ace Fred Glade (18–15). Glade got off to a rocky start, giving two runs in the first inning when Farrell singled to lead off the game and Shannon walked. After Beckley rolled out, advancing both runners, Dave Brain's single made the score 2–0 in favor of the Cards. Those two runs looked like they might hold up, but the Browns got to McFarland in the fifth. With one out, Cardinal right fielder Dunleavy dropped an easy fly ball off the bat of Mike Kahoe. Kahoe scored on Jesse Burkett's single. Snags Heidrick's triple and a single by Bobby Wallace put the Browns on top to stay. The Cardinals made a bid to tie the game in the ninth when, with Jimmy Burke on first, Glade weakened and gave free passes to Mike Grady and pinch-hitter Hugh Hill. But light-hitting second baseman John Farrell grounded into a forceout to end the game. An interesting feature of this game and the next was that Cardinals' reserve catcher Dave Zearfoss and Browns' pitcher Willie Sudhoff umpired. Neither team had been altogether pleased with Hart's work in the first three games.

Jack Taylor won his second game of the series by shutting down the Browns on six hits and two runs in Game Five. The Cardinals scored twice in the fourth on three errors, but the Browns tied the game in the bottom of the inning on a walk, a single, an error, and an infield out. The Cards took a slim one run lead in the seventh when Brain doubled, Shay singled, and the two runners worked the double steal successfully. When Cardinal umpire Zearfoss

1904 St. Louis City Championship Series

GAME SIX --- October 15

BROWNS	AB	H	PO	A	E		CARDINALS	AB	H	PO	A	E
Burkett, lf	5	1	1	3	0		Farrell, 2b	4	2	5	3	0
Heidrick, cf	5	2	0	0	0		Shannon, lf	5	1	0	1	0
Wallace, ss	4	2	2	3	2		Beckley, 1b	5	1	8	0	0
Hines, rf	3	1	3	0	0		Brain, 3b	5	2	1	4	0
Jones, 1b	2	0	4	1	0		Smoot, cf	4	1	2	0	0
Powell, 1b	2	2	6	0	0		Dunleavy, rf	4	0	1	0	1
Padden, 2b	2	1	1	2	0		Shay, ss	4	0	3	3	1
Gleason, 2b	2	0	1	4	0		Grady, c	4	1	7	1	0
Moran, 3b	4	1	1	2	0		Nichols, p	4	3	0	1	0
Kahoe, c	4	0	5	1	0							
Sudhoff, p	2	0	0	1	1			39	11	27	13	3
Morgan, p	2	1	0	0	0							
	37	11	24	17	3							

```
STA    2  0  2    0  0  2    0  0  0  -  6
STN    0  0  9    0  0  0    1  0  x  - 10
```

2B: Heidrick, Howell. SB: Jones. Struck out: Nichols 4, Sudhoff 1, Morgan 2. PB: Kahoe. Umpires: Pears and Genins.

called Brain safe at the plate, the Browns made a fearful row. Harsh words were again exchanged in the eighth when Jesse Burkett tried to score from third on a passed ball and Zearfoss rulled him out. In the ninth, Pelty's arm gave out and he was hammered for six hits and five runs. John Butler started the fun by driving a ball to deep center for an inside-the-park home run. Browns' catcher Mike Kahoe slammed a shoulder into Butler as he reached the plate. When Butler was able to catch his breath, he launched himself at Kahoe and the two men had to be restrained. Fighting broke out in the stands at this point and everyone had a good time.

When Browns' manager Jimmy McAleer called upon the Cardinals' front office after the game to make arrangements for impartial umpires, he was ordered to leave. The Cardinals relented, however, and Zearfoss and Sudhoff retired their indicators.

The final game of the series turned out to be a laugher for the National League after a shaky start. The Browns looked like they were going to roll over the Redbirds when they hit Nichols freely in the first and third to take a 4–0 lead. The Cardinals went wild in their half of the third. Nichols and Farrell singled to open the inning and Shannon reached on a wide throw to first by Bobby Wallace, Nichols scoring. Beckley grounded to pitcher Willie Sudhoff (8–15) who threw to third for the forceout on Farrell. Unfortunately for Willie, the man standing on the bag was none other than Cardinal third-base coach Danny Shay who was pretty amused at pulling such a fast one. Umpire Frank Pears should have called the runner out and when he failed to do so, Browns' left-fielder Jesse Burkett came in to pass a few friendly remarks with the arbiter. At this juncture of the game, Sudhoff came completely apart. When the inning was over, the Cardinals had sent 14 men to the plate, made nine runs on seven hits, and were aided by four Brownie errors. The final score was 10–6, Cardinals.

Cardinal ballplayers, whose contracts expired at the end of the next day, had announced they would play no more games unless allowed to split Sunday's gate receipts with the Browns. This was unacceptable to the management of both clubs. A alternate solution, that the teams play a doubleheader on Saturday the 15th, had also been rejected so the series ended in a 3-3 tie.

The 1905 St. Louis City Championship Series

St. Louis Browns defeat St. Louis Cardinals; 4-3-1

The St. Louis Browns (54-99), with a declining record for the third straight year, averted the 100-loss plateau only by not playing out the full season. This was the first last-place finish for the Browns in their illustrious history. Their starting five included two 20-game losers — Harry Howell (15-22) and Fred Glade (6-25). Willie Sudhoff (10-19) narrowly missed being the third. The sixth-place Cardinals (58-96), with a record nearly as dreadful, could only manage one 20-game loser on their staff — Jack Taylor (15-21).

1905 St. Louis City Championship Series

```
GAME ONE --- October 9

CARDINALS            AB   H   PO   A   E      BROWNS               AB   H   PO   A   E
--------------------------------------      --------------------------------------
Dunleavy, rf          4   0   1    0   0      Stone, lf             4   0   2    0   0
Shannon, lf           4   1   4    0   0      Rockenfield, 2b       4   0   2    6   0
Smoot, cf             3   1   3    0   0      Frisk, rf             3   0   2    0   0
Beckley, 1b           3   1   7    0   0      Wallace, ss           4   0   3    3   0
Grady, c              3   1   4    2   0      Jones, 1b             4   1   12   1   1
Shay, 2b              3   0   5    1   0      Gleason, 3b           3   1   1    2   0
Hoelskoetter, 3b      4   1   3    0   0      Koehler, cf           3   1   1    0   0
McBride, ss           3   0   0    3   3      Spencer, c            3   0   3    2   0
Taylor, p             3   1   0    1   0      Howell, p             3   2   1    4   0
                     -----------------                           -----------------
                     30   6   27   7   3                         31   5   27   18  1

STN      0  0  0     0  0  0    4  0  0  -  4
STA      0  0  0     0  1  0    0  0  0  -  1
```

SH: Gleason, Grady. DP: STA. BB: Howell 4, Taylor 1. Struck out: Howell 2, Taylor 3. LOB: STA 3, STN 1. SB: Shay. Umpire: William Klem.

Game One was played at Sportsman's Park on the 9th of October, Taylor taking the mound against Howell. In the early going, it looked as though the team that scored first would win the game as neither club could get a man past first base through four innings. In the bottom of the fifth, Browns' first baseman Tom Jones singled on the infield and went to second when shortstop George McBride threw low to first. Harry Gleason sacrificed Jones to third where he scored on Ben Koehler's single. Nothing doing for either team until the Cardinals scored all four of their runs in the seventh. Homer Smoot led off the inning with a single, Jake Beckley walked, and both runners moved up on Mike Grady's sacrifice bunt. Smoot was tagged out at the plate on Danny Shay's grounder to Ike Rockenfield, but Beckley went to third and Shay to

1905 St. Louis City Championship Series

GAME TWO --- October 10

CARDINALS	AB	H	PO	A	E		BROWNS	AB	H	PO	A	E
Dunleavy, rf	3	1	1	0	0		Stone, lf	5	3	3	0	0
Shannon, lf	4	3	3	0	0		Rockenfield, 2b	4	1	3	4	0
Smoot, cf	4	0	3	0	0		Frisk, rf	4	0	3	0	0
Beckley, 1b	4	0	9	0	0		Wallace, ss	5	3	2	2	0
Grady, c	4	3	5	1	0		Jones, 1b	4	1	8	1	0
Shay, 2b	4	1	3	2	2		Gleason, 3b	4	0	0	3	0
Hoelskoetter, 3b	4	0	1	3	0		Koehler, cf	3	1	4	0	0
McBride, ss	4	0	2	3	0		Spencer, c	2	0	4	0	1
Brown, p	3	0	0	1	0		Glade, p	3	0	0	2	0
	34	8	27	10	2			34	9	27	12	1

```
STA   0 0 0   0 0 0   0 6 2  -  8
STN   2 0 0   1 0 0   0 0 0  -  3
```

2B: Stone. 3B: Koehler, Dunleavy. HR: Grady. DP: STN 2. BB: Brown 4, Glade 1. Struck out: Brown 3, Glade 4. Umpire: William Klem.

GAME THREE --- October 11

CARDINALS	AB	H	PO	A	E		BROWNS	AB	H	PO	A	E
Dunleavy, rf	4	1	3	1	0		Stone, lf	3	1	1	0	0
Shannon, lf	1	1	1	0	0		Rockenfield, 2b	2	1	0	3	0
Smoot, cf	4	1	3	0	0		Frisk, rf	4	2	3	0	1
Beckley, 1b	4	2	10	2	0		Wallace, ss	4	0	3	2	1
Grady, c	4	1	3	0	0		Jones, 1b	3	0	7	0	0
Shay, 2b	4	3	2	5	0		Gleason, 3b	4	0	5	1	0
Hoelskoetter, 3b	5	1	1	0	0		Koehler, cf	2	0	2	1	0
McBride, ss	3	0	2	2	0		Spencer, c	3	0	4	3	0
Taylor, p	4	1	2	3	0		Sudhoff, p	0	0	0	1	0
							Pelty, p	3	0	2	2	1
	33	11	27	13	0			28	4	27	13	3

```
STN   0 0 4   0 1 0   0 4 0  -  9
STA   1 0 0   0 0 0   0 0 0  -  1
```

2B: Shay. SB: Koehler, Beckley 2, Shay 2. DP: STN 1, STA 1. BB: Sudhoff 3, Taylor 4, Pelty 1. Struck out: Sudhoff 1, Pelty 3, Taylor 4. Hits: Sudhoff 3 in 2.1 innings Umpire: Klem.

GAME FOUR --- October 12

CARDINALS	AB	H	PO	A	E		BROWNS	AB	H	PO	A	E
Dunleavy, rf	4	0	0	0	0		Stone, lf	5	2	0	0	0
Shannon, lf	4	1	1	0	0		Rockenfield, 2b	4	0	2	3	0
Smoot, cf	4	0	4	0	0		Frisk, rf	4	2	1	0	0
Beckley, 1b	4	1	20	1	0		Wallace, ss	3	0	2	5	1
Grady, c	4	0	3	3	0		Jones, 1b	3	2	13	2	1
Shay, 2b	3	0	1	5	0		Gleason, 3b	3	0	2	3	0
Hoelskoetter, 3b	4	1	1	3	0		Koehler, cf	4	0	1	0	0
McBride, ss	4	0	0	4	1		Spencer, c	4	0	9	2	0
McFarland, p	3	0	0	6	0		Powell, p	3	0	0	2	1
	34	3	30	22	1			33	6	30	17	3

```
STN   0 0 0   0 0 0   1 0 0   0  -  1
STA   1 0 0   0 0 0   0 0 0   0  -  1
```

2B: Stone, Hoelskoetter. SB: Jones, Beckley. BB: McFarland 1, Powell 1. Struck out: McFarland 2, Powell 9. WP: McFarland. Umpire: Klem.

1905 St. Louis City Championship Series

GAME FIVE --- October 13

CARDINALS	AB	H	PO	A	E	BROWNS	AB	H	PO	A	E
Dunleavy, rf	4	1	0	0	0	Stone, lf	4	1	0	0	0
Shannon, lf	4	0	2	0	0	Rockenfield, 2b	3	0	3	3	0
Smoot, cf	4	1	3	0	0	Frisk, rf	4	2	0	0	0
Beckley, 1b	4	1	10	0	0	Wallace, ss	4	0	3	2	0
Grady, c	3	1	3	1	0	Jones, 1b	3	1	10	2	0
Shay, 2b	3	1	2	5	0	Gleason, 3b	3	1	0	1	0
Hoelskoetter, 3b	3	1	3	1	0	Koehler, cf	2	0	2	0	0
McBride, ss	2	0	1	1	0	Spencer, c	2	0	8	2	0
Taylor, p	3	0	0	2	0	Howell, p	3	0	1	5	0
	30	6	24	10	0		28	5	27	15	0

```
STN    0  0  0    0  0  0    0  1  0  -  1
STA    0  0  0    0  0  0    1  1  x  -  2
```

2B: Jones, Hoelskoetter, Frisk. SB: Beckley. BB: Taylor 2. Struck out: Howell 8, Taylor 3. Umpire: Klem.

second. Art Hoelskoetter's single put the Cards on top, 2–1. George McBride walked and Taylor reached on an infield single to load the bases. Jack Dunleavy smashed a ball through Tom Jones's legs and the Cardinals added two more runs. A light rain began to fall in the eighth but the game was played to a conclusion, the Cardinals winning, 4–1.

Fred Glade led the American League in losses in 1905 and he showed why in the first four innings of Game Two. Dunleavy walked to lead off the Cardinal first and went to second on Shannon's bunt single. Two outs later, with the runners on second and third, Mike Grady's single put the Cardinals up 2–0. Grady's solo home run in the fourth gave the Cards a three-run lead. It looked as if the Browns were going to suffer their second straight defeat as two Cardinal double plays and the effective work of Buster Brown (8–11) kept the American Leaguers away from the plate through the first seven innings. But in the eighth, Brown fell apart. With one out, Koehler tripled down the left field line and scored when rookie Edward "Tubby" Spencer reached on Shay's error. Brown committed the unpardonable sin of walking the opposing pitcher and when George Stone reached on an infield single, the bases were loaded. Rockenfield struck out and Brown began to believe he might escape the inning with his lead intact. But a walk to Emil Frisk and a double by Bobby Wallace put the Browns in the van, 4–3. Tom Jones, the ninth man to bat in the inning, singled Frisk and Wallace home and the Browns had increased their margin to 6–3. Harry Gleason fanned, earning the honor of making two of the three outs in the inning. The Browns scored two more runs in the ninth and the final score was 8–3.

Jack Taylor returned to the mound for Game Three and took his second victory of the series. Willie Sudhoff was knocked from the hill with a Cardinal uprising of four runs in the third inning and his relief, Barney Pelty (14–14) was roughed up for five more runs as the Cardinals won in a walk, 9–1.

Game Four went ten innings and resulted in a 1–1 tie when darkness halted

1905 St. Louis City Championship Series

```
GAME SIX --- October 14

CARDINALS          AB   H   PO   A   E      BROWNS             AB   H   PO   A   E
-----------------------------------------   ------------------------------------------
Dunleavy, rf        4   0    2   0   0      Stone, lf           4   1    2   0   0
Shannon, lf         4   1    0   0   0      Rockenfield, 2b     4   0    2   3   1
Smoot, cf           4   1    4   0   0      Frisk, rf           2   0    1   0   0
Beckley, 1b         3   0    9   1   0      Wallace, ss         3   0    3   3   1
Grady, c            3   0    1   3   0      Jones, 1b           4   1   13   0   0
Shay, 2b            2   0    4   1   0      Gleason, 3b         4   0    0   3   0
Hoelskoetter, 3b    2   1    2   0   0      Koehler, cf         2   0    1   0   0
McBride, ss         3   0    5   5   1      Spencer, c          3   1    5   3   0
Brown, p            3   0    0   3   0      Glade, p            3   2    0   1   0
                   -------------------                         --------------------
                   28   3   27  13   1                         29   5   27  13   2

STN     0   0   0      0   0   0      0   0   1   -   1
STA     0   0   0      0   0   0      0   0   0   -   0
```

2B: Hoelskoetter. 3B: Shannon. BB: Glade 2, Brown 2. Struck out: Glade 5, Brown 2. Umpire: Klem.

play. Both runs scored as the result of errors. Chappie McFarland (8–18) and Jack Powell (2–1 with the Browns) pitched terrific ball, Powell striking out nine and allowing only three hits — singles by Shannon and Beckley and a double by Hoelskoetter. The Browns got on the board in the first inning when leadoff batter George Stone singled, went to second on a groundout, and to third on an error by George McBride. He scored on Bobby Wallace's sacrifice fly. In the seventh, Beckley singled, stole second, and scored on a Tom Jones throwing error. The Cardinals failed to put a man on base for the remainder of the game and the Browns were unable to mount any kind of a scoring threat.

Game Five was a tour de force by spitballer Harry Howell as the Browns handed Jack Taylor his first loss of the series. Taylor, who had started four games in the last seven days, held the Americans to one hit and a base on balls through the first six innings but weakened in the final two frames. He gave up a run in the seventh on an infield safety, a hit batsman, and an RBI single by Harry Gleason. Taylor got that run back in the next half-inning when his fielder's choice scored Art Hoelskoetter who had doubled and was sacrificed to third. But the Browns scored the deciding run in the eighth on a George Stone single and a double by Emil Frisk.

The sixth game was a corker. The contest was scoreless for eight innings, Buster Brown twirling a five-hitter and Fred Glade a one-hitter. Glade, in fact, had made more hits than he had allowed. But in the top of the ninth, Spike Shannon tripled with two out and scored on Homer Smoot's infield single when no one covered first base.

It seemed unlikely the Browns would win the city championship since they had to sweep the doubleheader scheduled for the 15th. But sweep they did, in a day marred by squabbles on the field.

Barney Pelty started the first game for the Browns and got slammed for a run in the fourth and two in the fifth. With just four innings to go, it looked as if the Cardinals were going to take the championship. The Browns pulled

1905 St. Louis City Championship Series

GAME SEVEN --- October 15

BROWNS	AB	H	PO	A	E		CARDINALS	AB	H	PO	A	E
Stone, lf	5	2	1	0	0		Dunleavy, rf	5	0	2	0	0
Rockenfield, 2b	4	2	3	1	0		Shannon, lf	5	2	2	0	0
Frisk, rf	5	3	1	0	0		Smoot, cf	4	1	1	0	0
Wallace, ss	5	1	4	4	2		Beckley, 1b	4	1	9	1	1
Jones, 1b	5	2	8	0	0		Grady, c	4	1	5	0	0
Gleason, 3b	5	0	0	3	0		Shay, 2b	1	0	1	3	0
Koehler, cf	4	1	3	0	0		Hoelskoetter, 3b	4	2	2	1	0
Sugden, c	2	0	2	2	0		McBride, ss	3	0	4	5	2
Van Zandt, ph	1	0	0	0	0		Brown, p	2	1	1	0	0
Spencer, c	2	0	3	0	0		Taylor, p	2	0	0	0	0
Pelty, p	2	1	2	1	0		Arndt, ph	0	0	0	0	0
Roth, ph	0	0	0	0	0							
Howell, p	1	1	0	0	0			34	8	27	10	3
Sudhoff, p	1	0	0	0	0							
	42	13	27	11	2							

```
STA   0  0  0    0  0  2    0  5  0  -  7
STN   0  0  0    1  2  3    0  0  0  -  6
```

2B: Howell, Frisk. 3B: Shannon, Frisk, Wallace. SB: Shay, Hoelskoetter, Gleason. DP: STA. BB: Brown 1, Howell 1. Struck out: Pelty 2, Brown 2, Howell 1, Taylor 2. Hits: Brown 8 in 5 innings; Taylor 5 in 4 innings; Pelty 4 in 5 innings; Howell 4 in 4.1 innings. Sudhoff 0 in 0.2 innings. Umpire: Klem.

GAME EIGHT --- October 15 (second game)

BROWNS	AB	H	PO	A	E		CARDINALS	AB	H	PO	A	E
Stone, lf	3	0	2	0	0		Dunleavy, rf	3	2	0	0	0
Rockenfield, 2b	2	2	2	1	0		Shannon, lf	2	0	4	0	0
Frisk, rf	3	0	1	0	0		Smoot, cf	3	0	2	0	1
Wallace, ss	3	0	1	3	0		Beckley, 1b	2	0	5	0	1
Jones, 1b	3	1	6	0	0		Grady, c	2	0	3	0	0
Gleason, 3b	3	0	0	0	1		Arndt, 2b	3	2	1	1	0
Koehler, cf	3	1	0	1	0		Hoelskoetter, 3b	2	0	2	0	0
Spencer, c	2	0	6	1	0		McBride, ss	2	0	1	1	1
Howell, p	2	0	0	3	1		Taylor, p	1	0	0	4	0
	24	4	18	9	2			20	4	18	6	3

```
STA   0  0  0    0  3  0  -  3
STN   0  0  0    0  0  0  -  0
```

2B: Koehler, Rockenfield. SH: Shannon, Rockenfield, Grady. BB: Howell 3. Struck out: Taylor 3, Howell 4. LOB: STN 7, STA 4. Umpire: Klem. Time—1:10.

within one in the next half-frame on a double by Frisk, a triple by Wallace and a Tom Jones single. Jack Taylor came on in relief of Brown and retired the side without further incident. Fortune seemed to be smiling upon the Cardinals when they struck for three runs off reliever Harry Howell to take a 6–2 lead at the end of six. Singles by Shannon and Smoot and an error by Bobby Wallace on Jake Beckley's grounder filled the bases. Shannon was out at the plate but Shay walked, forcing in a run. Hoelskoetter flied to left and George Stone's throw home hit Beckley in the back and glanced off rookie umpire Bill Klem.

What followed next almost had to be seen to be believed. Beckley, holding Spencer's leg in a death grip to prevent him from retrieving the ball, struggled to touch home. Spencer finally got away, but before he could make a tag, Beckley had crawled to the plate. Klem, who either hadn't seen Beckley's holding penalty or who wasn't quite the legend he was going to become, motioned the runner in from third as a result of his own unintentional interference. The game was delayed for the next few minutes while the Browns crowded around Klem in a vain attempt to make him see reason. When the furor finally died down, Howell took his place on the mound and retired the last two batters. Neither team scored in the seventh, but the Browns batted Taylor all around the park for five runs in the eighth, the big blow a bases-loaded triple by Emil Frisk which gave the Browns a 7–6 lead. In the eighth inning, Howell came inside to Danny Shay and the ball ticked off his bat for an apparent foul. Shay fell down, pretending he had been hit, and Klem awarded him first base. Howell argued loud and long and was eventually dismissed for the balance of the game by Klem. The Cardinals threatened to tie the game in the ninth but George Stone's brilliant tumbling catch in left field ended the game. Taylor took the loss while Howell was the victor.

The nightcap was limited to seven innings by agreement, but darkness prevented the final inning from being played. A weary Harry Howell and an equally weary Jack Taylor were the starters and both men pitched on nothing but fumes. With one out in the fifth, Ben Koehler doubled and Tubby Spencer reached on an error. Spencer was forced by Howell with Koehler holding at third. Center fielder Homer Smoot misjudged Stone's line drive for an error, Koehler scored, Howell went to third and Stone to second. Ike Rockenfield's single made the final score 3–0 and the American Leaguers had won their second city series in three years.

1905 Chicago City Championship Series

Chicago Cubs defeat Chicago White Sox; 4–1

The 1905 city championship between the Cubs (92–61) and White Sox (92–60) was one of the two most evenly matched series played, although one wouldn't guess so by the box scores. Both clubs had led their respective leagues in team earned run average — the Cubs with 2.04, the Sox with an even more astounding 1.99 — and both had allowed the fewest opponents' runs in their leagues.

The series opened on October 11th at South Side Park, home of the Sox, as the Cubs won behind the arm of Carl Lundgren (13–4). The Nationals took a 5–0 lead, then held on to withstand four runs by the Sox in the sixth inning to win 5–4. Frank Owen (21–13) took the loss.

Game Two was played at West Side Park, home of the Cubs, as Nick Altrock (22–12) squared off against Ed Reulbach (18–13). The Sox put four runs on the scoreboard in the first inning, knocking Reulbach out of the box, and were never headed. Mordecai Brown (18–12) pitched credibly the rest of the

1905 Chicago City Championship Series

GAME ONE --- October 11

CUBS	AB	H	PO	A	E
Slagle, cf	5	1	2	0	0
Casey, 3b	5	2	1	2	0
Chance, 1b	5	1	14	0	0
McCarthy, lf	3	0	0	0	0
Tinker, ss	3	0	2	3	0
Maloney, rf	3	0	0	1	0
Evers, 2b	3	0	0	2	0
Hoffman, 2b	1	0	1	3	0
Kling, c	3	1	7	1	0
Lundgren, p	3	2	0	1	0
	34	7	27	13	0

WHITE SOX	AB	H	PO	A	E
Jones, cf	5	2	4	0	0
Green, rf	4	0	2	1	0
G.Davis, ss	4	1	1	2	0
Callahan, lf	4	0	1	0	0
Donahue, 1b	3	0	14	1	0
Isbell, 2b	3	2	2	0	0
Sullivan, c	4	1	3	2	0
Tannehill, 3b	3	0	0	3	0
McFarland, ph	1	1	0	0	0
Owen, p	3	0	0	4	0
Rohe, ph	1	1	0	0	0
	35	8	27	17	2

```
CUB   0  0  2    1  0  2    0  0  0  -  5
SOX   0  0  0    0  0  4    0  0  0  -  4
```

2B: Davis, Isbell, Sullivan, Rohe. BB: Owen 4, Lundgren 4. 3B: Lundgren, Casey. HBP: Isbell (Lundgren). Struck out: Owen 2, Lundgren 4. Umpires: Connolly and Johnstone.

GAME TWO --- October 12

WHITE SOX	AB	H	PO	A	E
Jones, cf	4	2	2	0	0
Green, rf	5	0	1	0	0
G.Davis, ss	4	0	1	2	0
Callahan, lf	4	0	1	0	0
Donahue, 1b	3	1	10	0	0
Isbell, 2b	3	1	6	2	0
McFarland, c	4	3	5	1	0
Tannehill, 3b	3	0	0	4	1
Altrock, p	4	1	0	3	0
	34	8	*26	12	1

CUBS	AB	H	PO	A	E
Slagle, cf	5	1	3	0	0
Casey, 3b	5	0	0	3	0
Chance, 1b	3	3	11	1	0
McCarthy, rf	2	0	1	0	0
Hoffman, lf	2	1	0	0	0
Tinker, ss	4	2	0	2	1
Maloney, rf	4	2	1	0	0
Evers, 2b	3	0	2	3	1
Kling, c	4	2	9	0	1
Reulbach, p	0	0	0	1	0
Brown, p	4	0	0	1	0
	36	11	27	11	3

* Maloney out, hit by batted ball.

```
SOX   4  1  1    0  0  0    0  0  1  -  7
CUB   1  0  0    0  0  0    3  0  0  -  4
```

2B: McFarland 2, Chance. 3B: Chance. HR: Donohue. SB: Davis. BB: Brown 2, Altrock 1. Struck out: Reulbach 1, Brown 5, Altrock 3. Umpires: Johnstone and Connolly.

way but Altrock kept the Cubs at bay until the seventh by which time he already held a 6-1 lead. The Cubs rallied for three in the seventh, but an insurance run by the Sox in the ninth made the final score 7–4.

It was Doctor's Day at South Side Park as Sox manager Fielder Jones selected Doc White (18-14) to pitch against Jake Weimer (18-12) in Game Three. White pitched a three-hitter and walked no one, but one of the three hits was a second inning triple by Doc Casey which provided all the runs the Cubs needed. The heart of the White Sox lineup went 8-for-16 but no one else produced and the Americans were able to muster only two runs. Frank Smith (19-13) and Ed Walsh (8-3) pitched in relief of White.

1905 Chicago City Championship Series

GAME THREE --- October 13

CUBS	AB	H	PO	A	E		WHITE SOX	AB	H	PO	A	E
Slagle, cf	4	2	4	0	0		Jones, cf	4	0	0	0	0
Casey, 3b	3	1	2	0	0		Green, rf	4	0	1	0	0
Chance, 1b	2	0	5	0	0		G.Davis, ss	4	3	1	1	0
Hoffman, lf	3	0	4	0	0		Callahan, lf	4	1	2	0	0
Tinker, ss	3	0	1	1	0		Donahue, 1b	4	2	12	0	1
Maloney, rf	4	0	2	0	0		Isbell, 2b	4	2	4	5	1
Evers, 2b	2	0	1	3	2		Sullivan, c	3	0	4	2	0
Kling, c	3	0	8	0	0		McFarland, c	1	0	1	0	0
Weimer, p	3	0	0	0	0		Tannehill, 3b	3	0	1	3	0
							White, p	1	0	1	3	0
	27	3	27	4	2		Rohe, ph	1	0	0	0	0
							Smith, ph-p	1	0	0	0	0
							Walsh, ph-p	1	0	0	0	0
								35	8	27	14	2

```
CUB    0  3  0    0  0  0    0  0  0  -  3
SOX    0  0  1    0  0  0    0  1  0  -  2
```

3B: Casey. DP: SOX. Struck out: White 5, Weimer 6. WP: White. Umpires Connolly and Johnstone.

GAME FOUR --- October 14

WHITE SOX	R	H	PO	A	E		CUBS	R	H	PO	A	E
Jones, cf	0	1	3	0	0		Slagle, cf	1	1	3	0	0
Isbell, 2b	1	1	3	4	2		Casey, 3b	1	1	0	1	0
G.Davis, ss	1	1	1	1	1		Chance, 1b	1	1	7	0	0
Callahan, lf	1	2	2	1	0		Hoffman, lf	0	0	1	1	0
Donahue, 1b	1	2	10	1	0		Tinker, ss	2	1	1	4	1
Green, rf	1	2	1	0	0		Maloney, rf	0	2	2	0	0
Sullivan, c	0	1	2	2	1		Evers, 2b	1	1	3	3	0
Smith, p	0	0	0	0	0		Kling, c	0	1	9	1	1
Tannehill, 3b	0	0	1	1	0		Lundgren, p	0	0	0	0	0
Rohe, 3b	0	0	0	0	0		Reulbach, p	0	0	1	1	0
Owen, p	0	0	0	3	1			6	8	27	11	2
White, p	0	0	0	1	0							
McFarland, c	0	0	1	1	0							
	5	10	24	15	5							

```
SOX    5  0  0    0  0  0    0  0  0  -  5
CUB    0  0  0    0  0  3    3  0  x  -  6
```

2B: Chance, Slagle. SB: Tinker, Evers, Maloney. BB: Lundgren 2, Reulbach 3, Owen 1, Smith 1. Struck out: Reulbach 5, Owen 1, White 1, Smith 1. Hits: Lundgren 6 in 2 innings; Owen 7 in 6.1 innings; White 1 in 0.2 innings. Umpires: Johnstone and Connolly.

Game Four saw the White Sox tear into Carl Lundgren as if there were no tomorrow. Five runs in the first were reason enough for Lundgren's early dismissal after two innings of play. Ed Reulbach pitched the rest of the way and held the Sox at bay while his teammates chipped away at the lead with three runs in the sixth and three more in the seventh to pull out a 6–5 victory. Frank Owen took his second loss of the series.

The final game started out to be a romp for the Cubs as they scored five runs in the first off Frank Smith only to see the Sox score three in the bottom of the inning. The Sox trailed by only one after six innings, but three Cub runs

1905 Chicago City Championship Series

```
GAME FIVE --- October 15
```

CUBS	R	H	PO	A	E		WHITE SOX	R	H	PO	A	E
Slagle, cf	2	0	2	0	0		Jones, cf	5	2	1	0	0
Casey, 3b	5	0	2	3	0		Isbell, 2b	5	2	0	3	1
Chance, 1b	4	2	11	1	0		G.Davis, ss	4	0	5	2	0
Hoffman, lf	4	1	2	0	0		Callahan, lf	5	2	1	0	0
Tinker, ss	5	4	2	2	0		Donahue, 1b	3	0	13	0	0
Maloney, rf	4	1	2	1	0		Green, rf	4	2	0	0	0
Evers, 2b	4	1	5	5	0		McFarland, c	4	2	0	3	0
Kling, c	4	3	1	0	0		Rohe, 3b	3	0	4	4	0
Weimer, p	3	0	0	0	0		Smith, p	0	0	3	0	0
Brown, p	2	0	0	1	0		Altrock, p	3	1	0	7	0
							Holmes, ph	1	0	0	0	0
	37	12	27	13	0			37	11	27	19	1

```
CUB   5  1  0    0  0  0    3  0  1  -  10
SOX   3  0  0    1  1  0    0  0  0  -   5
```

2B: Tinker 2. 3B: Chance, Green. SB: Tinker. BB: Smith 3, Altrock 4, Weimer 2. Struck out: Brown 2, Altrock 3. WP: Altrock. DP: SOX. Umpires: Connolly and Johnstone.

in the seventh and one in the ninth put the game and the championship away for the National Leaguers as they won 10–5 behind Weimer and Brown. Joe Tinker was the hitting star for the Cubs with four hits, two of them doubles, in five times at bat.

The 1905 Boston City Championship Series

Boston Pilgrims defeat Boston Beaneaters; 6–1

After winning the American League pennant the previous two years, the 1905 Boston Pilgrims (78–74) collapsed and finished fourth, 16 games behind a much improved Philadelphia team. It would be another seven years before they took top honors again. The Boston Beaneaters (51–103) were suffering through the third of five seasons which would feature at least one 20-game loser on each club. The 1903 and 1907 clubs had one 20-game loser each; the 1904 club had three; this club and the 1906 entry had a whopping four. Irv Young (20–21), Irvin "Kaiser" Wilhelm (4–23), and Chick Fraser (14–21) all competed for the league lead in losses, but in the end they had to tip their hats to Vic Willis (11–29) who had led all American League pitchers in losses for three of the past four years. In fairness to Willis, he had won 20 games four times in his career and, after an off-season trade to the Pittsburgh Pirates, would win 20 games four more times. Considering how bad the teams were in his last few years at Boston, his career won-loss record of 247–206 doesn't look half bad.

The Pilgrims figured to have an easy time of it in the series and, to no one's surprise, they did. The Beaneaters won Game One behind the strong pitching of Willis and lost the next six games in convincing fashion.

1905 Boston City Championship Series

GAME ONE --- October 9

BEANEATERS	R	H	PO	A	E
Abbaticchio, ss	1	0	3	2	0
Tenney, 1b	0	1	9	1	0
Dolan, rf	1	1	2	0	0
Delahanty, lf	0	2	0	0	0
Wolverton, 3b	1	0	1	1	0
Cannell, cf	1	2	3	0	0
Raymer, 2b	0	0	2	1	1
Moran, c	1	3	6	2	1
Willis, p	0	0	1	6	0
	5	9	27	13	2

PILGRIMS	R	H	PO	A	E
Parent, ss	0	0	1	3	0
Stahl, cf	0	0	1	0	0
Unglaub, 3b	0	0	0	2	0
Burkett, lf	1	1	4	0	0
Grimshaw, 1b	1	2	14	0	0
Selbach, rf	0	3	2	0	0
Ferris, 2b	0	1	2	1	1
Criger, c	0	0	1	1	0
Dineen, p	0	0	2	4	1
Freeman, ph	0	0	0	0	0
	2	7	27	11	2

```
BOSN   1 0 0   0 0 1   0 0 3 - 5
BOSA   0 0 0   0 0 0   1 0 1 - 2
```

    2B: Moran 2, Selbach. 3B: Dolan, Burkett. SB: Abbaticchio. BB: Willis 4, Dineen 3. Struck out: Willis 6, Dineen 2. DP: BOSA 2. Umpires: O'Loughlin and Emslie.

GAME TWO --- October 10

PILGRIMS	AB	H	PO	A	E
Parent, ss	4	0	0	3	0
Stahl, cf	3	0	0	0	1
Unglaub, 3b	4	1	1	2	1
Burkett, lf	3	1	0	0	0
Grimshaw, 1b	4	2	9	0	0
Selbach, rf	4	0	1	0	0
Ferris, 2b	4	0	1	3	0
Criger, c	3	0	15	1	1
C.Young, p	3	1	0	1	0
	32	5	27	10	3

BEANEATERS	AB	H	PO	A	E
Abbaticchio, ss	4	1	1	6	0
Tenney, 1b	4	0	14	2	0
Dolan, rf	4	0	4	1	1
Delahanty, lf	3	0	0	0	0
Wolverton, 3b	3	1	0	1	0
Cannell, cf	3	0	2	0	1
Raymer, 2b	3	0	1	2	0
Needham, c	3	0	4	1	0
I.Young, p	3	0	1	1	0
	30	2	27	14	2

```
BOSA   2 0 0   0 0 0   1 0 0 - 3
BOSN   0 0 0   0 1 0   0 0 0 - 1
```

    BB: I. Young 1. Struck out: C. Young 15, I. Young 4. DP: BOSN. Umpires: O'Loughlin and Emslie.

GAME THREE --- October 11

BEANEATERS	AB	H	PO	A	E
Abbaticchio, ss	3	0	2	2	2
Tenney, 1b	2	1	8	0	0
Dolan, rf	4	1	1	0	0
Delahanty, lf	4	0	5	0	0
Wolverton, 3b	4	0	2	2	0
Cannell, cf	4	2	2	0	0
Raymer, 2b	3	0	1	1	0
Needham, c	3	1	3	1	0
Wilhelm, p	3	0	0	3	0
	30	5	24	9	2

PILGRIMS	AB	H	PO	A	E
Parent, ss	5	3	1	1	0
Stahl, cf	4	0	2	0	0
Unglaub, 3b	4	2	1	1	0
Burkett, lf	3	0	1	0	0
Grimshaw, 1b	4	1	10	0	0
Selbach, rf	3	0	2	0	0
Ferris, 2b	4	1	2	4	0
Armbruster, c	3	0	7	3	1
Harris, p	4	2	1	3	0
	34	9	27	12	1

```
BOSN   1 0 0   0 0 0   0 0 0 - 1
BOSA   0 1 0   1 0 0   0 3 x - 5
```

    3B: Grimshaw, Parent. HR: Unglaub. SB: Tenney, Cannell, Burkett, Dolan, Needham. BB: Harris 3, Wilhelm 3. Struck out: Harris 6, Wilhelm 3. DP: BOSA. PB: Armbruster. WP: Wilhelm. HBP: Raymer (Harris). Umpires: O'Loughlin and Emslie

1905 Boston City Championship Series

GAME FOUR - October 12

PILGRIMS	AB	H	PO	A	E		BEANEATERS	AB	H	PO	A	E
Parent, ss	6	2	2	3	0		Abbaticchio, ss	4	0	3	2	0
Stahl, cf	5	1	1	0	0		Tenney, 1b	4	1	9	0	0
Unglaub, 3b	4	0	1	2	1		Dolan, rf	4	0	1	0	0
Burkett, lf	5	1	1	0	1		Delahanty, lf	4	1	4	0	0
Grimshaw, 1b	5	2	13	0	1		Wolverton, 3b	4	1	1	1	1
Freeman, rf	4	2	3	0	0		Cannell, cf	3	1	4	0	1
Ferris, 2b	5	4	2	4	0		Raymer, 2b	3	0	0	2	0
Criger, c	4	2	4	2	0		Moran, c	3	1	5	1	1
Winter, p	3	0	0	3	0		Fraser, p	3	0	0	2	1
	41	14	27	14	3			32	5	27	8	4

```
BOSA    0  1  1     2  4  0     3  0  1   -  12
BOSN    0  0  0     0  0  0     0  0  0   -   0
```

2B: Grimshaw, Ferris, Criger, Delahanty. 3B: Ferris. HR: Ferris. SB: Burkett. BB: Fraser 5, Winter 3. DP: BOSA. WP: Fraser. HBP: Freeman (Fraser). Umpires: Emslie and O'Loughlin.

GAME FIVE --- October 13

BEANEATERS	R	H	PO	A	E		PILGRIMS	R	H	PO	A	E
Abbaticchio, ss	1	2	4	3	1		Parent, ss	1	0	2	2	0
Tenney, 1b	1	4	7	2	1		Selbach, cf	1	0	2	0	0
Dolan, rf	0	1	0	0	1		Unglaub, 3b	1	2	0	5	0
Delahanty, lf	0	0	1	0	0		Burkett, lf	2	1	2	0	0
Wolverton, 3b	0	1	2	0	0		Grimshaw, 1b	0	1	12	0	0
Cannell, cf	0	0	3	0	0		Freeman, rf	0	1	3	0	0
Raymer, 2b	0	1	2	2	0		Ferris, 2b	0	1	2	3	0
Moran, c	0	0	3	1	0		Armbruster, c	0	0	4	1	0
Willis, p	0	0	2	2	0		Tannehill, p	0	0	0	2	0
	2	9	24	10	3			5	6	27	13	0

```
BOSN    0  0  0     0  0  0     0  2  0   -  2
BOSA    4  0  1     0  0  0     0  0  x   -  5
```

2B: Freeman, Grimshaw, Abbaticchio, Burkett. 3B: Unglaub, Dolan. BB: Willis 2. Struck out: Willis 1, Tannehill 3. DP: BOSN. WP: Tannehill. Umpires: O'Loughlin and Emslie.

Game One opened at the Huntington Avenue Baseball Grounds, home of the Pilgrims, on the 9th of October. Willis scattered seven hits and four walks in the first game and shut down the Pilgrims' offense until he weakened in the final three innings. The Beaneaters scored single runs in the first and sixth and three insurance runs in the top of the ninth put the game on ice. Bill Dinneen (12–15) went the distance for the Pilgrims and took the loss.

Game Two shifted to the Beaneaters' South End Grounds and featured Denton True Young (18–19) against the Beaneater's Irv Young. Old Cy had failed to win 20 games or more for the first time since he was a rookie in 1890. On this day, he pitched as if he were 28 years old instead of 38 and took care of the Beaneaters with a superlative two-hitter — the only singles coming off the bats of Ed Abbaticchio and Harry Wolverton — and struck out 15 men. The final score was 3–1.

1905 Boston City Championship Series

```
GAME SIX --- October 14
```

PILGRIMS	R	H	PO	A	E		BEANEATERS	R	H	PO	A	E
Parent, ss	2	2	2	4	0		Abbaticchio, ss	0	0	2	3	0
Selbach, cf	2	2	0	0	0		Tenney, 1b	1	2	13	0	0
Unglaub, 3b	1	3	3	1	0		Dolan, rf	1	0	2	1	0
Burkett, lf	0	1	0	1	0		Delahanty, lf	0	1	2	0	0
Freeman, 1b	0	0	12	1	0		Wolverton, 3b	0	2	1	1	0
Godwin, rf	1	1	1	1	1		Cannell, cf	0	1	2	1	0
Ferris, 2b	2	2	4	2	0		Raymer, 2b	0	0	2	7	0
Armbruster, c	0	1	5	1	0		Needham, c	0	1	2	2	0
Gibson, c	0	1	0	3	0		I.Young, p	0	0	1	0	0
	8	13	27	14	1			2	7	27	15	2

```
BOSA   2 1 0   1 1 0   1 2 0  -  8
BOSN   0 0 1   0 0 0   0 1 0  -  2
```

2B: Needham, Parent, Selbach, Burkett, Godwin, Ferris, Armbruster. 3B: Ferris. BB: Young 1, Gibson 2. Struck out: Young 2, Gibson 4. HBP: Dolan (Gibson). DP: BOSA, BOSN 2. WP: Young 1, Gibson 1. PB: Needham. Umpires: Emslie and O'Loughlin.

```
SEVENTH GAME --- October 14 (second game)
```

BEANEATERS	R	H	PO	A	E		PILGRIMS	R	H	PO	A	E
Abbaticchio, ss	0	0	0	5	0		Parent, ss	1	2	1	2	0
Tenney, 1b	1	1	14	2	0		Selbach, cf	0	0	1	0	0
Dolan, rf	1	1	0	1	0		Unglaub, 3b	1	2	1	1	0
Delahanty, lf	0	1	2	0	0		Burkett, lf	0	1	4	0	0
Wolverton, 3b	1	0	1	2	0		Grimshaw, 1b	2	1	11	1	0
Cannell, cf	0	1	1	0	0		Godwin, cf	0	1	1	0	1
Raymer, 2b	0	1	1	4	0		Ferris, 2b	0	0	2	3	0
Moran, c	0	1	4	0	0		McGovern, c	0	0	4	0	0
Fraser, p	0	1	1	1	1		C.Young, p	0	0	1	2	0
	3	7	24	15	1		Harris, p	0	1	1	0	0
								4	8	27	9	1

```
BOSN   2 1 0   0 0 0   0 0 0  -  3
BOSA   1 0 0   0 1 1   0 1 x  -  4
```

2B: Grimshaw, Godwin. 3B: Dolan. HR: Parent, Unglaub. BB: Fraser 3. Struck out: Fraser 1, Harris 1, Young 2. WP: Young 2. DP: BOSA. Umpires: O'Loughlin and Emslie.

Joe Harris (1–2) pitched for the Americans in Game Three and took the measure of Kaiser Wilhelm, 5–1. The Pilgrims overcame an early 1–0 Beaneater lead and led 2–1 in the eighth when they struck for three insurance runs. Triples by Moose Grimshaw and Freddy Parent and a home run by reserve infielder Bob Unglaub proved the margin of difference in the game.

Game Four was the 1905 version of the Boston Massacre as the Pilgrims mauled the Beaneaters behind the five-hit shutout pitching of George Winter (16–16). Second baseman Hobe Ferris hit for the cycle and the American Leaguers converted nine singles, three doubles, a triple, a home run, four walks, a wild pitch, and a stolen base into 12 runs. Beaneaters' manager Fred Tenney left Chick Fraser on the mound to take the entire terrible pounding.

The Pilgrims jumped on Willis early in Game Five, scoring four runs in the first and their final run in the third. The Americans were outhit, 10-6, but four of their six hits went for extra bases. The Beaneaters scored two eighth-inning runs off Jesse Tannehill (22-9), but he breezed through the ninth for his only victory of the series.

Game Six was another slaughter as the Pilgrims scored in six of the nine innings and won easily behind Norwood Gibson (4-7). Irv Young lost his second game of the series. Heavy hitting again marked the Pilgrims' attack, seven of their 13 hits going for extra bases. The final score was 8-2.

The Beaneaters took a last gasp with three runs in the first two innings of the finale, but that was all they could muster off Cy Young and reliever Joe Harris. Bob Unglaub's homer in the eighth was the margin of victory. Chick Fraser went the distance and absorbed the loss.

The 1906 St. Louis City Championship Series

St. Louis Browns defeat St. Louis Cardinals; 4-1-3

The 1906 Browns (76-73) had improved considerably from the year before — this team had no 20-game losers — but the Cardinals (52-98) only got worse. A best-of-seven exhibition series was scheduled and the Browns looked forward to an easy time of defeating the Redbirds, maybe even a sweep. That it would take eight games to wrap up the championship never occurred to anyone. This series featured some of the most exciting baseball of any of the various city championships.

Game One featured a matchup of Ed Karger (5-16) for the Cards against the Browns' Harry Howell (15-14). The Cardinals' starting lineup featured not one man from the previous fall's city series and the Redbirds looked as though they might make a series out of it as they struck for two third-inning runs off Howell. Eddie Zimmerman tripled and scored when one of Howell's spitters bounced past Browns' catcher Tubby Spencer. Pete Noonan followed with another triple and scored on Tom O'Hara's groundout. Both teams traded runs in the next two half-innings and the Cardinals held a 3-1 lead into the bottom of the sixth. A walk to Ike Rockenfield, and singles by Howell, Tom Jones, and George Stone tied the game. The Browns scored the deciding run in the eighth when Spencer walked, was sacrificed to second, and came home when center-fielder Al Burch fumbled Harry Niles' single. The Cardinals made a bid to tie the game in the ninth when Eddie Holly singled, was sacrificed to second, and went to third on a groundout. Howell hit Karger with a pitch, but leadoff batter O'Hara grounded to third for the final out of the game.

The two teams were right back at it on October 9th, battling to a 4-4 tie until darkness and the cold forced a halt to the proceedings after nine innings. This was the first of three ties in the series. Fred Beebe (9-9) and Barney Pelty (16-11) were both rough around the edges in the first three frames, but then settled down to pitch shutout ball over the last six innings. The Cards got all their runs in the first. O'Hara lined the ball into center for a safety and Burch

1906 St. Louis City Championship Series

GAME ONE --- October 8

BROWNS	AB	H	PO	A	E		CARDINALS	AB	H	PO	A	E
Niles, rf	5	2	1	1	1		O'Hara, lf	5	2	1	0	0
T.Jones, 1b	5	3	14	3	0		Burch, cf	3	0	1	0	0
Stone, lf	3	2	0	0	0		Bennett, 2b	2	1	6	1	0
Hemphill, cf	4	0	2	0	0		Barry, 1b	4	0	6	2	0
Wallace, ss	3	0	3	7	0		Murray, rf	3	0	2	0	0
O'Brien, 3b	3	0	1	3	1		Holly, ss	4	2	1	3	1
Rockenfield, 2b	3	2	1	2	0		Zimmerman, 3b	3	1	1	0	1
Spencer, c	2	0	3	2	0		Noonan, c	4	1	6	1	0
Howell, p	3	1	2	6	0		Karger, p	2	0	0	3	1
	31	10	27	24	2			30	7	24	10	3

```
STN   0  0  2    1  0  0    0  0  0  -  3
STA   0  0  1    0  0  2    0  1  x  -  4
```

3B: Zimmerman, Noonan. SB: Stone, Bennett, O'Hara 2. DP: STA. BB: Howell 2, Karger 3. Struck out: Howell 1, Karger 3. Umpires: Carpenter and Evans.

GAME TWO --- October 9

CARDINALS	AB	H	PO	A	E		BROWNS	AB	H	PO	A	E
O'Hara, lf	3	1	4	1	0		Niles, rf	5	3	2	1	0
Burch, cf	4	2	2	1	0		T.Jones, 1b	5	2	7	0	0
Bennett, 2b	2	0	0	1	0		Stone, lf	5	2	1	0	0
Barry, 1b	2	1	4	0	0		Hemphill, cf	3	1	1	0	0
Murray, rf	4	1	0	0	0		Wallace, ss	4	2	6	3	0
Holly, ss	4	1	0	1	0		O'Brien, 3b	3	0	1	3	0
Zimmerman, 3b	4	1	2	2	0		Rockenfield, 2b	5	0	3	3	0
Noonan, c	4	0	14	1	0		Spencer, c	3	1	6	2	0
Beebe, p	3	0	1	0	0		Pelty, p	4	0	0	3	0
	30	7	27	7	0			37	11	27	15	0

```
STN   4  0  0    0  0  0    0  0  0  -  4
STA   0  3  1    0  0  0    0  0  0  -  4
```

2B: Jones, Stone. 3B: Jones. HR: Spencer. SB: O'Hara, Niles 2, Wallace. DP: STA. BB: Pelty 5, Beebe 1. Struck out: Pelty 6, Beebe 9. Umpires: Carpenter and Evans.

GAME THREE --- October 11

BROWNS	AB	H	PO	A	E		CARDINALS	AB	H	PO	A	E
Niles, rf	4	1	3	0	0		O'Hara, lf	4	0	1	0	0
T.Jones, 1b	3	0	10	0	0		Burch, cf	4	1	2	1	0
Stone, lf	3	1	1	0	0		Bennett, 2b	3	1	1	3	1
Hemphill, cf	4	1	1	0	0		Barry, 1b	4	1	10	0	0
Wallace, ss	4	1	2	2	0		Murray, rf	3	0	2	0	1
O'Brien, 3b	4	1	0	2	0		Holly, ss	3	0	0	2	0
Rockenfield, 2b	3	0	1	3	0		Zimmerman, 3b	4	1	4	0	0
O'Connor, c	4	0	8	0	0		Noonan, c	3	0	7	1	1
Powell, p	3	1	1	4	0		McGlynn, p	3	0	0	3	1
	32	6	27	11	0			31	4	27	10	4

```
STA   0  0  0    2  0  0    0  0  0  -  2
STN   0  0  0    0  0  0    0  1  0  -  1
```

3B: Barry. SB: Burch, Noonan, Stone. BB: McGlynn 4, Powell 4. Struck out: McGlynn 6, Powell 6. Umpires: Evans and Carpenter.

1906 St. Louis City Championship Series

GAME FOUR --- October 12

CARDINALS	AB	H	PO	A	E
O'Hara, lf	5	2	4	0	2
Burch, cf	3	1	2	0	0
Bennett, 2b	4	0	2	2	0
Barry, 1b	5	1	16	1	2
Murray, rf	5	0	0	1	0
Holly, ss	4	2	3	7	1
Zimmerman, 3b	4	0	1	1	0
Noonan, c	4	0	4	1	1
Fromme, p	4	3	0	2	1
	38	9	*32	15	7

BROWNS	AB	H	PO	A	E
Niles, rf	5	0	1	0	0
T.Jones, 1b	6	1	17	0	0
Stone, lf	5	2	1	0	0
Hemphill, cf	5	2	2	0	0
Wallace, ss	4	0	4	5	0
O'Brien, 3b	4	1	0	4	0
Rockenfield, 2b	4	1	4	4	0
Spencer, c	2	0	4	2	1
Glade, p	4	1	0	5	0
Koehler, pr	0	1	0	0	0
	39	9	33	20	1

* Two out when winning run scored

```
STN  0 1 0   0 0 0   2 0 0   0 0 - 3
STA  0 1 0   0 2 0   0 0 0   0 1 - 4
```

2B: Hemphill, Fromme. SB: Holly. DP: STN. BB: Glade 4, Fromme 4. Struck out: Glade 4, Fromme 3. PB: Noonan. Umpires: Carpenter and Evans.

GAME FIVE --- October 13

CARDINALS	AB	H	PO	A	E
O'Hara, lf	4	0	2	0	0
Burch, cf	4	0	1	0	0
Bennett, 2b	4	2	0	3	1
Beckley, 1b	4	0	14	2	0
Murray, rf	4	0	1	0	0
Holly, ss	2	0	2	3	0
Zimmerman, 3b	3	1	0	0	0
Marshall, c	3	0	4	1	0
Karger, p	3	0	0	8	0
	31	3	24	17	1

BROWNS	AB	H	PO	A	E
Niles, rf	4	0	2	0	0
T.Jones, 1b	4	2	9	0	1
Stone, lf	4	1	1	0	0
Hemphill, cf	3	2	2	0	0
Wallace, ss	3	1	3	3	0
O'Brien, 3b	2	0	1	3	1
Rockenfield, 2b	3	0	3	1	0
Spencer, c	3	1	5	2	0
Howell, p	3	0	1	0	0
	29	7	27	9	2

```
STN  0 0 0   1 0 0   0 0 0 - 1
STA  0 0 3   0 0 0   0 0 x - 3
```

2B: Bennett, Wallace. SB: Hemphill. BB: Karger 2, Howell 1. WP: Howell. PB: Spencer. Umpires: Carpenter and Evans.

GAME SIX --- October 13 (second game)

CARDINALS	AB	H	PO	A	E
O'Hara, lf	1	0	0	0	0
Burch, cf	2	0	1	0	0
Bennett, 2b	2	0	1	3	0
Beckley, 1b	2	1	5	1	0
Murray, rf	2	0	2	1	0
Holly, ss	2	0	1	0	0
Zimmerman, 3b	2	0	1	0	1
Noonan, c	2	0	5	0	0
Beebe, p	1	0	0	1	1
	16	1	15	7	2

BROWNS	AB	H	PO	A	E
Niles, rf	3	0	0	0	0
T.Jones, 1b	3	1	8	0	0
Stone, lf	2	1	0	0	0
Hemphill, cf	2	0	0	0	0
Wallace, ss	2	0	1	3	0
O'Brien, 3b	2	0	1	3	1
Rockenfield, 2b	1	0	0	4	0
Spencer, c	1	1	5	1	0
Pelty, p	1	1	0	0	0
	17	4	15	11	1

```
STN  0 0 0   0 0 - 0
STA  0 0 0   0 0 - 0
```

3B: Beckley. SB: Holly, O'Hara, Jones, Rockenfield, Stone, Hemphill. DP: STN 2. BB: Beebe 1. Struck out: Beebe 3, Pelty 4. Hit by pitch: Rockenfield (Beebe). Umpires: Evans and Carpenter.

1906 St. Louis City Championship Series

GAME SEVEN --- October 14

CARDINALS	AB	H	PO	A	E	BROWNS	AB	H	PO	A	E
O'Hara, lf	4	0	1	0	0	Niles, rf	4	1	0	1	0
Burch, cf	2	1	1	0	0	Rockenfield, 2b	4	0	0	3	0
Bennett, 2b	3	1	1	3	0	Stone, lf	3	1	3	0	0
Barry, 1b	3	1	10	1	1	Hemphill, cf	4	2	3	0	0
Murray, rf	2	0	1	0	0	Wallace, ss	3	0	4	2	0
Holly, ss	3	0	1	2	1	O'Brien, 3b	2	1	0	1	0
Zimmerman, 3b	3	0	2	1	0	Koehler, 1b	2	0	9	0	0
Marshall, c	3	1	10	1	0	O'Connor, c	3	0	5	2	0
McGlynn, p	3	0	0	4	0	Powell, p	3	0	0	1	0
	26	4	27	12	2		28	5	24	10	0

```
STN    1 0 0    0 0 0    0 0 0  -  1
STA    0 0 0    0 0 0    0 0 x  -  0
```

SB: Burch, Bennett, Barry. BB: Powell 2, McGlynn 1. Struck out: Powell 3, McGlynn 6. PB: Marshall. Umpires: Evans and Carpenter.

bunted for a single. Pug Bennett was hit by a pitch to load the bases. Shad Barry's single through a drawn-in infield scored two runs and Red Murray's single to right scored Bennett. Eddie Holly's base knock accounted for the fourth run of the inning. From that point on, the Cardinals failed to advance a man past first base against Pelty. In the second, after Pete O'Brien had walked, Spencer's home run cut the Cardinals' lead in half. With two outs, Niles singled and scored just before Tom Jones was thrown out at the plate trying to stretch a triple into an inside-the-park home run. The Americans tied the game in the third on a bunt single by Stone, a walk to Charlie Hemphill, and a Bobby Wallace single.

Game Three was a pitcher's duel between Jack Powell (13–14) and Cardinal rookie Stony McGlynn (2–2). The Browns got after McGlynn for two runs in the fourth. After Jones popped out, Stone walked and Hemphill singled. Right-fielder Murray's throw to third rolled past Zimmerman and to the stands, Stone scoring and Hemphill advancing to third. Bobby Wallace's single scored the final American League run of the day. Through seven innings, the Cardinals had made only two hits off Powell, one of them a bunt single. A Pug Bennett single and a Shad Barry triple made things interesting, but Powell retired the Cardinals in order in the ninth for a four-hit complete game.

For the second day in a row, the Cardinals started a rookie on the mound. Art Fromme (1–2) faced Fred Glade (15–14) in this tense contest. After the teams exchanged single runs in the second, the Browns broke on top in the fifth. Singles by Jones and Stone were followed by a Charlie Hemphill double to put the Browns ahead, 2–0. The Cardinals tied the game in their half of the seventh. With two out and a man on first, Fromme got the Cardinals' first extra base hit when his wind-blown double scored Pete Noonan. Spencer threw the relay back to second, trying to catch Fromme off the bag, but the throw went into center field and the rookie came home to tie the game. The game rolled along into extra innings. Umpire William Evans had already announced that

1906 St. Louis City Championship Series

GAME EIGHT --- October 14 (second game)

CARDINALS	AB	H	PO	A	E		BROWNS	AB	H	PO	A	E
O'Hara, lf	1	0	1	0	0		Niles, rf	2	0	1	0	0
Burch, cf	1	1	1	0	0		Rockenfield, 2b	3	0	0	2	0
Bennett, 2b	2	0	1	0	0		Stone, lf	3	1	0	0	0
Beckley, 1b	2	0	3	0	0		Hemphill, cf	0	0	0	0	0
Murray, rf	2	0	0	0	0		Wallace, ss	3	0	4	3	0
Holly, ss	2	0	2	3	1		O'Brien, 3b	3	0	0	2	0
Zimmerman, 3b	2	1	1	0	0		Koehler, 1b	1	0	6	0	0
Marshall, c	2	1	5	0	0		Spencer, c	2	1	2	1	0
Hoelskoetter, p	2	0	1	1	0		Pelty, p	2	0	2	1	0
	16	3	15	4	1			19	2	15	9	0

```
STN    0  0  0    0  0  -  0
STA    0  0  0    0  0  -  0
```

SB: Hemphill. BB: Hoelskoetter 2, Pelty 1. Struck out: Pelty 3, Hoelskoetter 1. PB: Marshall 2. Umpires: Evans and Carpenter.

he was going to call the game after the eleventh because of darkness. Glade opened the inning with a walk and Koehler was sent in as a pinch-runner. Niles sacrificed Koehler to second where he stayed when Jones popped out. George Stone then sent a high fly to left-fielder Tom O'Hara. O'Hara camped under the ball, caught it, then dropped it. Koehler had veered off for the dugout and hastily returned to the field to touch home plate. O'Hara's explanation that he was just getting ready to throw the ball to Al Burch in center didn't hold much water and umpire Evans allowed the run to stand.

A doubleheader was scheduled for the 13th of October, and the Browns clinched the city series with a victory in the first game. Ed Karger and Harry Howell were rematched for this game, the only contest in which the winning team won by more than one run. In the bottom of the third, the Browns opened up on Karger when Niles reached on an error and went to second when Tom Jones's groundball to second baseman Bennett took a bad hop. Bennett quickly recovered and threw to second to get Jones, but the throw was wild and both runners moved up a base. A groundout by Stone scored Niles and Charlie Hemphill's single scored Jones. Hemphill then stole second and scored on Bobby Wallace's double. The Cardinals' only run came in the fourth through the courtesy of two Browns errors. Al Burch grounded to Pete O'Brien who threw wild past first. Jones scrambled after the errant baseball, but when he cocked his arm to throw home, the ball slipped out of his hand and Burch came in to score.

The second game of the doubleheader went only five innings before being called because of darkness. Browns' hurler Barney Pelty allowed only one hit, a triple by Jake Beckley in the fourth when Niles attempted a shoetop catch. Beckley was caught in a rundown when the next batter, Red Murray, grounded to short. Red made it to second on the rundown and was then picked off base. The Browns had several scoring opportunities against Fred Beebe and made the least of them all. In the second, they loaded the bases with two out, but Niles grounded out. In the third, they had Stone at third with one out, but he was thrown out at the plate on Hemphill's grounder. Rockenfield was hit by a pitch and stole second in the fourth, but was thrown out at the plate attempting to score on Spencer's single to right.

One day before the players' contracts expired, the two teams played another doubleheader on the 14th. Stony McGlynn made his second start of the series and for the second time the Cardinals saw fit to give him only one run of offensive support. This time, however, McGlynn made that run stand up as he shut out the Browns on five hits, striking out six, for the only Cardinal victory of the series. Jack Powell pitched a four-hitter but was the losing pitcher.

The second game of the doubleheader featured Barney Pelty against the useful Art Hoelskoetter (2–4). Hoelskoetter had played the outfield, three infield positions, and pitched 58⅓ innings for the Cardinals in the 1906 season. Through six innings, he shut out the Browns on two singles, two walks, and three strikeouts. Pelty matched him pitch for pitch though, and the game ended in a scoreless tie.

The 1907 St. Louis City Championship Series

St. Louis Cardinals defeat St. Louis Browns; 5–2

Jimmy McAleer's Browns (69–83) had dropped from a fifth-place finish to sixth in 1907 with a considerably worse record than the 76–73 they had managed in 1906. But if the 1907 Browns were a bad team, one only had to look a little further for how low a ballclub could sink. If you lived in St. Louis, you only had to look a little further down the front page of the newspaper. The Cardinals (52–101) dropped from seventh in 1906 to last in 1907 and had their first 100-loss season of the century. Stony McGlynn (14–25) led the major leagues in losses, with Ed Karger (15–19) and Fred Beebe (7–19) not far behind. The highest batting average among the team's starting eight was .262 by left-fielder Red Murray. Ed Holly led the majors in errors at shortstop with the staggering total of 62. Bobby Byrne led all third basemen in errors with 49, Murray all left fielders with 18, and Doc Marshall all catchers with 26.

This was a team whose pitchers couldn't pitch, whose hitters couldn't hit, whose fielders couldn't field — in short, a well-rounded ballclub. Then they surprised everyone and trimmed the Browns five games to two in the postseason championship. The Cardinal hallmark in five of the first six games was the ability to score runs in bunches.

The series opened at Sportsman's Park on the 7th of October with Fred Glade (13–9) and Johnny Lush (7–10) the starting pitchers. The game was scoreless until the fifth when the Cardinals struck for five runs off Glade. Byrne singled, leading off, and was sacrificed to second. Art Hoelskoetter's single put the Cardinals up 1–0. Doc Marshall singled and Lush walked to load the bases, giving reserve outfielder Al Shaw an opportunity to do some damage. His single made the score 2–0, Cardinals. In a wild turn of events, right fielder Ollie

1907 St. Louis City Championship Series

GAME ONE --- October 7

CARDINALS		AB	H	PO	A	E		BROWNS		AB	H	PO	A	E
Shaw, rf		5	1	0	0	1		Niles, 2b		4	3	1	4	0
Barry, cf		5	3	0	0	0		Hemphill, cf		4	0	1	0	0
Delahanty, lf		3	1	0	0	0		Stone, lf		4	1	1	0	0
Konetchy, 1b		4	0	14	0	0		Pickering, rf		3	0	0	1	0
Byrne, 3b		4	3	1	5	0		Wallace, ss		3	0	5	6	0
Holly, ss		2	1	4	8	1		Yeager, 3b		3	1	4	3	0
Hoelskoetter, 2b		4	1	4	5	0		Spencer, c		2	0	3	0	0
Marshall, c		3	1	4	2	0		Jones, 1b		3	1	12	0	0
Lush, p		3	0	0	0	0		Glade, p		1	0	0	1	0
								Pelty, p		2	1	0	1	0
		33	11	27	20	2				29	7	27	16	0

```
STN   0  0  0    0  5  0    0  1  0  -  6
STA   0  0  0    0  1  0    0  0  0  -  1
```

2B: Stone, Holly. 3B: Delahanty. SH: Holly 2. SB: Barry. DP: STN 4, STA 3. BB: Glade 1, Pelty 2, Lush 2. Struck out: Glade 1, Pelty 1, Lush 3. Hits: Glade 8 and 5 runs in 5 innings; Pelty 3 hits and 1 run in 4 innings. LOB: STN 5, STA 4. Umpires: Johnstone and Evans. Time— 1:35.

GAME TWO --- October 8

CARDINALS		AB	H	PO	A	E		BROWNS		AB	H	PO	A	E
Shaw, cf		4	0	1	0	0		Niles, 2b		4	0	3	4	0
Barry, rf		4	3	1	0	0		Jones, 1b		4	1	7	1	1
Delahanty, lf		4	0	2	0	0		Stone, lf		4	1	2	0	0
Konetchy, 1b		3	0	10	0	0		Wallace, ss		4	0	4	2	0
Byrne, 3b		3	0	4	4	1		Pickering, rf		4	2	2	0	0
Holly, ss		2	0	1	3	0		Yeager, 3b		4	0	1	2	0
Hoelskoetter, 2b		3	0	3	4	0		Spencer, c		3	1	7	1	0
Marshall, c		3	0	5	1	1		Hemphill, cf		2	0	1	0	0
Karger, p		3	1	0	2	0		Powell, p		3	0	0	0	0
		29	4	27	14	2				32	5	27	10	1

```
STA   0  0  0    0  0  0    0  0  1  -  1
STN   0  0  0    0  0  0    0  0  0  -  0
```

DP: STN 1, STA 1. PB: Marshall. SB: Pickering. WP: Karger. Struck out: Karger 6, Powell 6. LOB: STN 3, STA 5. Umpires: Johnstone and Evans. Time—1:50.

Pickering's throw came into third base which was occupied by both Marshall and Lush, but third sacker Joe Yeager failed to notice the extra man and threw down to second for the out on Shaw who had attempted to advance on the throw in. Shaw was out, but Marshall scored on the play. Shad Barry's single scored Lush and Joe Delahanty's triple scored Barry. Lush gave up seven hits and two walks, but the Browns could manage to put two hits together in only one of the nine innings. Four double plays took the Cardinals out of trouble in every inning but the fifth when the Browns scored once. The final score was 6–1.

Game Two was a superlative pitcher's battle between Ed Karger of the

1907 St. Louis City Championship Series

GAME THREE --- October 9

BROWNS	AB	H	PO	A	E	CARDINALS	AB	H	PO	A	E
Niles, 2b	6	2	3	4	0	Barry, rf	5	4	1	0	0
Jones, 1b	3	0	10	1	0	Shaw, cf	3	0	1	0	0
Stone, lf	4	1	1	1	0	Delahanty, lf	4	3	2	0	0
Wallace, ss	4	1	1	3	2	Konetchy, 1b	5	0	9	1	1
Pickering, rf	3	0	1	0	0	Byrne, 3b	4	1	1	3	0
Hartzell, 3b	3	0	0	1	1	Holly, ss	4	1	1	2	0
Spencer, c	3	1	9	1	0	Hoelskoetter, 2b	4	0	3	1	0
Hemphill, cf	3	2	1	0	1	Noonan, c	1	0	1	0	0
Howell, p	3	0	1	2	0	Marshall, c	3	0	7	2	0
Glade, p	0	0	0	0	0	Raymond, p	1	0	0	1	0
Yeager, ph	0	0	0	0	0	McGlynn, p	1	1	1	2	0
						Bennett, ph	1	0	0	0	0
	32	7	27	13	4	Murray, cf	2	1	0	0	0
						Fromme, p	0	0	0	0	0
							38	11	27	12	1

```
STN   0  0  0    0  0  0    0  2  6  -  8
STA   0  0  5    0  0  0    0  0  0  -  5
```

2B: Wallace, Barry, Delahanty. SB: Hartzell. DP: STA 1, STN 1. BB: Raymond 2, Howell 1, McGlynn 3, Fromme 1. Struck out: Raymond 2, Howell 6, McGlynn 4, Fromme 1, Glade 1. Hits: Raymond 4 in 2.2 innings: McGlynn 3 in 5.1 innings; Howell 10 in 8.1 innings. WP: Raymond. Umpires: Johnstone and Evans.

GAME FOUR --- October 10

BROWNS	AB	H	PO	A	E	CARDINALS	AB	H	PO	A	E
Niles, 2b	4	2	3	3	2	Barry, rf	5	1	3	0	0
T.Jones, 1b	4	1	7	0	1	Murray, cf	5	2	6	0	2
Stone, lf	4	2	2	0	0	Delahanty, lf	4	1	3	1	0
Wallace, ss	4	0	3	5	0	Konetchy, 1b	5	1	6	2	0
Pickering, rf	5	2	2	0	0	Byrne, 3b	4	1	0	0	0
Yeager, 3b	5	4	1	1	0	Holly, ss	4	1	3	5	0
Spencer, c	5	0	7	0	0	Hoelskoetter, 3b	4	1	2	1	0
Hemphill, cf	5	1	1	1	0	Marshall, c	3	0	2	1	3
Pelty, p	4	0	1	0	0	Lush, p	1	0	0	0	1
Bailey, p	0	0	0	0	1	McGlynn, p	1	0	1	0	1
						Raymond, p	1	0	1	0	1
	40	12	27	10	4	Bennett, ph	1	1	0	0	0
						Noonan, ph	1	1	0	0	0
							39	10	27	10	8

```
STA   0  0  4    4  0  0    0  2  1  -  11
STN   0  0  0    0  2  0    0  0  5  -  7
```

2B: Holly, Pickering, Noonan. HR: Murray. DP: STN. SB: Stone. BB: Lush 1, McGlynn 2, Raymond 1, Pelty 3. Struck out: Lush 1, Raymond 1, Pelty 6. Hits. Lush 6 in 3 innings; McGlynn 3 in 2 innings; Pelty 10 in 8.1 innings. PB: Marshall. Umpires: Johnstone and Evans.

Cardinals and Jack Powell (13–16). Neither pitcher was guilty of giving up any bases on balls, both men struck out six, and the game was scoreless after eight innings. Karger had a three-hitter going into the top of the ninth when George Stone beat out an infield hit with one out. After advancing to second on a groundout and third on a passed ball, Stone came home when Pickering's grounder sneaked between Holly and Hoelskoetter into center field. Powell gave up a two-out single in the ninth, but retired Delahanty for a five-hit shutout.

The Browns looked to take a two-to-one edge in the series in Game Three

1907 St. Louis City Championship Series

```
GAME FIVE --- October 11
```

BROWNS	AB	H	PO	A	E	CARDINALS	AB	H	PO	A	E
Niles, 2b	4	1	3	1	0	Barry, rf	4	2	2	0	0
T.Jones, 1b	4	0	8	1	1	Murray, cf	3	0	3	0	0
Stone, lf	4	1	5	0	0	Delahanty, lf	4	1	3	0	1
Wallace, ss	4	1	0	6	1	Konetchy, 1b	3	1	8	0	0
Pickering, rf	4	2	2	1	0	Bennett, 2b	4	0	6	2	0
Yeager, 3b	4	1	4	0	0	Holly, ss	4	1	1	5	0
Spencer, c	3	1	2	0	0	Hoelskoetter, 3b	2	0	0	2	0
Hemphill, cf	4	0	0	0	0	Noonan, c	3	1	4	0	0
Powell, p	2	0	0	1	1	Karger, p	2	2	0	2	0
	33	7	24	10	3		29	8	27	11	1

```
STA   0  0  0    0  0  0    2  0  0  -  2
STN   1  0  0    0  2  0    0  4  x  -  7
```

2B: Karger, Holly. HR: Delahanty, Konetchy. SH: Karger, Hoelsketter. SB: Yeager. DP: STN. LOB: STN 2, STA 6. BB: Karger 2, Powell 2. Struck out: Karger 4, Powell 1. Umpires: Evans and Johnstone. Time—1:29.

as they got after Arthur "Bugs" Raymond (2–4) for five runs in the third inning. Tubby Spencer led off with a single, Charlie Hemphill walked, and after Howell struck out, Harry Niles beat out an infield tap to load the bases. Tom Jones walked to force in the first run of the day. With Stone at the plate, Cardinals' catcher Doc Marshall tried to pick Hemphill off at third, but his throw went wild into left field. Hemphill scored and the other two men moved up a notch. Stone's single made the score 4–0. Bobby Wallace grounded to Konetchy, but his throw to second was too late to force Stone. Pickering moved both runners up with a groundout and Stone scored on a wild pitch. That's where the score remained until the Cardinals struck for two in the eighth. Harry Howell (16–15) seemed to have matters in hand until the ninth. Byrne and Holly singled and Hoelskoetter grounded a sure double play ball to short. But Wallace bobbled the ball for an error and the bases were loaded with no one out. Pinch-hitter Bennett grounded the ball behind second. Wallace got to the ball only to fall down, Byrne scoring. Pete Noonan's grounder forced Holly at the plate and the Browns narrowly missed their second double play of the inning. Barry's Texas Leaguer dropped in behind short, Hoelskoetter and Bennett scoring to tie the game. Fred Glade came on in relief and fanned Murray for the second out of the inning, but Delahanty's double scored Noonan and Roy Hartzell's wild throw on Ed Konetchy's groundball brought in Barry and Delahanty. Konetchy, the old rally-killer, was thrown out stealing second and the inning came to a close. But the Cardinals had scored six times to take an 8–5 lead. Art Fromme (5–13) came on in relief for the Cardinals and pitched a scoreless ninth.

The Browns made short work of Johnny Lush in Game Four, striking for four runs in the third and four more in the fourth, breezing to an 11–7 victory. Barney Pelty (12–21) weakened in the ninth and gave up four runs before rookie

1907 St. Louis City Championship Series

```
GAME SIX --- October 12
```

CARDINALS	AB	H	PO	A	E		BROWNS	AB	H	PO	A	E
Barry, rf	3	0	0	0	0		Niles, 2b	5	2	4	1	1
Murray, cf	5	1	3	0	0		T.Jones, 1b	5	2	5	2	0
Delahanty, lf	4	2	4	0	0		Stone, lf	4	2	3	1	0
Konetchy, 1b	4	1	12	1	0		Wallace, ss	4	0	7	0	0
Bennett, 2b	4	1	2	6	0		Pickering, rf	4	1	1	0	0
Holly, ss	4	2	0	3	0		Hartzell, 3b	4	1	0	2	0
Hoelskoetter, 3b	3	0	0	1	1		Stephens, c	4	1	5	3	1
Noonan, c	4	2	5	0	0		Hemphill, cf	4	1	1	0	0
Fromme, p	2	1	0	0	0		Howell, p	0	0	1	0	0
Karger, p	2	0	1	2	0		Bailey, p	3	0	0	2	0
							Yeager, ph	1	1	0	0	0
	35	10	27	13	1			38	11	27	11	2

```
STN    1  6  0    0  0  0    0  2  0  -  9
STA    0  0  1    1  0  0    0  0  0  -  2
```

2B: Pickering, Holly, Noonan. 3B: Konetchy. DP: STN. BB: Howell 1, Bailey 4. Struck out: Howell 2, Fromme 1, Karger 4, Bailey 3. Hits: Howell 4 in 1.2 innings; Fromme 7 in 3.1 innings. WP: Howell. PB: Stephens 3. Umpires: Johnstone and Evans.

```
GAME SEVEN --- October 13
```

BROWNS	AB	H	PO	A	E		CARDINALS	AB	H	PO	A	E
Niles, 2b	4	1	4	2	1		Barry, rf	3	0	1	0	0
T.Jones, 1b	3	1	11	0	0		Murray, cf	4	1	3	0	0
Stone, lf	4	0	2	2	0		Delahanty, lf	4	0	1	0	0
Wallace, ss	4	1	0	0	1		Konetchy, 1b	4	1	9	2	0
Pickering, rf	4	1	0	0	0		Bennett, 2b	4	2	3	1	0
Hartzell, 3b	3	0	0	3	1		Holly, ss	4	2	1	3	0
Stephens, c	3	0	4	3	0		Hoelskoetter, 3b	3	1	2	2	1
Hemphill, cf	3	0	2	1	0		Noonan, c	3	2	5	1	0
Glade, p	3	1	1	2	0		McGlynn, p	3	0	2	2	0
	31	5	24	13	3			32	9	27	11	1

```
STA    0  0  0    0  0  0    0  0  1  -  1
STN    1  2  0    0  0  0    0  0  x  -  3
```

2B: Konetchy, Holly. SH: Hoelskoetter, Hartzell. DP: STN. PB: Noonan 2. SB: Noonan, Barry, Murray, Jones. BB: McGlynn 1. Struck out: McGlynn 4, Glade 4. LOB: STN 7, STA 5. Umpires: Johnstone and Evans. Time—1:22.

reliever Bill Bailey (4–1) was called upon. The youngster retired Konetchy and Byrne for the save, the Cardinals' fifth run of the inning scoring on Konetchy's out.

Game Five was a reprise of Jack Powell and Ed Karger and was a lot closer than the 7–2 score would seem to indicate. The Cardinals scored a singleton in the first when Joe Delahanty legged out an inside-the-park home run. Two more National League runs came home in the fifth before the Browns tallied their only two runs of the game in the seventh as a result of a dropped line drive by Delahanty in left. The score stood at 3–2 Cardinals when Ed Karger lined the ball over center-fielder Charlie Hemphill's head for an apparent inside-the-park home run. But Karger stumbled rounding second, missed the bag entirely, and had to settle for a 450-foot double. Barry attempted to sacrifice but bunted the ball back to Powell. Karger would have been a dead duck at third if Roy Hartzell had been there to cover the bag. Both men eventually scored. The capper on the scoring was supplied by Ed Konetchy's two-run homer later in the inning.

Art Fromme and Harry Howell squared off for Game Six as the Cardinals moved toward clinching the best-of-nine series. Leading 1–0 into the second, the Redbirds produced their second six-run inning of the series and the issue was never in doubt thereafter. Holly led off the second with a single and was forced by Hoelskoetter, the Browns barely missing the double play. Hoelskoetter took second on a wild pitch, but Noonan fanned and it looked like Howell would escape the inning untouched. But Fromme singled and Barry walked to load the bases. Red Murray's single made the score 3–0. Browns' manager McAleer called upon young Bill Bailey to duplicate his game-saving efforts of the fourth contest. Bailey wasn't up to the pressure today. A walk to Delahanty loaded the bases and a triple by Konetchy emptied them. Pug Bennett's single made the score 7–0. Fromme got into some minor trouble and gave up a run in the third before being relieved by Karger with one out and a run home in the fourth. Karger held the Browns in check the rest of the way and, under today's standards, would have been given the victory. The final score was 9–2, Cardinals.

The National Leaguers and Stony McGlynn again had an easy time of it in the seventh game, winning handily 3–1. The Cards broke on top in the first as Shad Barry scored on Ed Konetchy's double. In the second, Holly singled, was sacrificed to second, and went to third on Noonan's scratch single. Barry grounded to Hartzell who threw low to first, Holly scoring. Red Murray's single brought Noonan home with the Cardinals' third run of the game. No American Leaguer made it as far as second base through the first eight innings and McGlynn had a three-hit shutout until the Browns scored an unearned run in the ninth on two singles and an error by Hoelskoetter.

The 1907 Boston City Championship Series

Boston Red Sox defeat Boston Doves; 6-0-1

The Boston Doves (58–90) — so named after owner John Dovey — improved upon their dreadful 1906 finish (49–102), but had not yet managed to cross the .400 threshold in winning percentage and escaped last place only by dint of the 1907 Cardinals, an even worse team than their own. They were evenly matched, or so it appeared, with the seventh-place Boston Red Sox (59–90). But the Sox must have taken confidence from the drubbing they gave their National League rivals in 1905 and beat the Doves in resounding fashion, six games to none.

The series opened at Huntington Avenue Baseball Grounds on the 7th of October and the home team Red Sox won behind the four-hit pitching of the ageless Cy Young (22–15). Young, who blew out 40 candles just a few

1907 Boston City Championship Series

```
GAME ONE --- October 7

DOVES                   AB  H PO  A  E      RED SOX                 AB  H PO  A  E
------------------------------------       ------------------------------------
Hoffman, rf              4  1  3  0  0      Barrett, lf              4  1  4  0  0
Tenney, 1b               3  1  9  0  0      Sullivan, cf             5  4  1  0  0
Sweeney, ss              4  0  0  3  0      Congalton, rf            3  2  0  0  0
Beaumont, cf             3  1  1  0  0      Grimshaw, 1b             4  1  9  0  0
Bates, lf                3  0  2  0  1      Ferris, 2b               4  0  3  3  0
Ritchey, 2b              3  0  5  6  1      Knight, 3b               4  0  1  2  0
Brain, 3b                4  1  2  1  0      Wagner, ss               4  1  2  3  0
Needham, c               2  0  1  0  0      Shaw, c                  3  0  7  0  0
Dorner, p                3  0  1  3  0      Young, p                 3  1  0  0  0
                        -------------                               -------------
                        29  4 24 13  2                              34 10 27  8  0

BOSN    0  0  0     0  0  1     0  0  0  -  1
BOSA    0  0  1     0  1  0     1  1  x  -- 4
```

2B: Congalton 2. 3B: Brain. BB: Young 3, Dorner 2. Struck out: Young 5, Dorner 1. HBP: Barrett (Young). Umpires: Connolly and Emslie.

```
GAME TWO --- October 9

RED SOX                 AB  H PO  A  E      DOVES                   AB  H PO  A  E
------------------------------------       ------------------------------------
Sullivan, cf             3  1  4  0  0      Hoffman, lf              5  0  4  0  0
Parent, lf               2  0  2  2  0      Tenney, 1b               4  0 12  0  1
Congalton, rf            4  2  1  1  0      Sweeney, ss              3  1  3  5  0
Unglaub, 1b              5  1 13  0  1      Beaumont, cf             4  2  3  0  0
Carrigan, c              5  0  5  4  1      Bates, rf                4  1  1  0  0
Ferris, 1b               5  0  4  1  0      Ritchey, 2b              4  2  5  1  0
Knight, 3b               3  1  3  0  0      Brain, 3b                4  1  2  3  3
Wagner, ss               3  1  1  1  0      Ball, c                  3  1  3  6  0
Winter, p                4  0  0  3  0      Needham, c               0  0  0  0  1
Burchell, p              0  0  0  1  0      Brown, c                 0  0  0  0  1
                        -------------       Frock, p                 0  0  0  0  1
                        34  6 33 13  2      Flaherty, p              3  0  0  6  1
                                                                    -------------
                                                                    34  8 33 21  7

BOSA    0  0  2     0  0  0     0  0  0     0  2  -  4
BOSN    0  1  0     0  0  0     0  0  1     0  0  -  2
```

2B: Sweeney, Ritchie, Brain, Ball. 3B: Wagner. DP: BOSA 1, BOSN 1. BB: Winter 2, Burchell 2, Flaherty 2, Frock 4. Struck out: Winter 3, Burchell 2, Flaherty 4. Hits: Winter 8 in 9.1 innings; Flaherty 5 in 10 innings; Frock 1 in 1 inning. Umpires: Emslie and Connolly.

weeks before the season began, struck out five and walked three in going the distance. Bunk Congalton, with two doubles in three times at bat, and Denny Sullivan, with four singles in five plate appearances, provided all the offense the Red Sox needed. Gus Dorner (12–16) took the 4–1 loss.

Game Two saw Red Sox pitcher Patsy Flaherty (12–15) matched with George Winter (12–15) at the Beaneaters' South End Grounds. Both men pitched well, but Flaherty was undermined by a lack of defense on the part of his team-mates who made seven errors in the game. The Doves tied the game at two with a run in the bottom of the ninth, but two Sox runs off rookie reliever Sam Frock (1–2) in the top of the tenth decided the issue. Winter retired in favor of reliever

1907 Boston City Championship Series

GAME THREE --- October 10

DOVES	AB	H	PO	A	E		RED SOX	AB	H	PO	A	E
Hoffman, lf	4	1	0	0	0		Sullivan, cf	4	1	1	0	0
Tenney, 1b	4	1	9	2	1		Parent, lf	2	0	1	0	0
Sweeney, ss	4	0	3	4	0		Congalton, rf	3	0	0	0	0
Beaumont, cf	3	1	4	0	0		Donahue, 1b	3	2	10	1	0
Bates, rf	4	2	0	0	0		Shaw, c	2	0	6	3	1
Ritchey, 2b	2	1	4	2	0		Wagner, ss	3	0	3	3	0
Brain, 3b	3	0	1	2	0		Knight, 3b	3	1	0	4	0
Needham, c	2	0	2	1	0		Ferris, 2b	3	0	6	1	0
Young, p	3	0	1	2	0		Morgan, p	3	0	0	3	1
	29	6	24	13	1			26	4	27	15	2

```
BOSN    0  0  0    0  0  0    1  0  0  -  1
BOSA    1  0  0    0  0  0    1  0  x  -  2
```

2B: Hoffman, Ritchey. SB: Bates. BB: Morgan 2, Young 1. Struck out: Morgan 6, Young 2. WP: Morgan. Umpires: Emslie and Connolly.

GAME FOUR --- October 10 (second game)

DOVES	AB	H	PO	A	E		RED SOX	AB	H	PO	A	E
Hoffman, rf	3	2	0	0	0		Sullivan, cf	3	0	2	0	0
Tenney, 1b	3	0	13	0	1		Parent, lf	4	1	3	0	0
Sweeney, ss	3	1	2	4	1		Congalton, rf	4	1	0	0	0
Beaumont, cf	4	0	2	0	0		Grimshaw, 1b	4	0	11	1	0
Randall, lf	3	1	4	1	1		Carrigan, c	3	0	4	2	0
Ritchey, 2b	3	1	0	6	0		Wagner, ss	4	1	4	3	0
Brain, 3b	4	1	2	4	0		Knight, 3b	4	1	1	0	0
Ball, c	4	0	3	1	0		Ferris, 2b	4	0	2	4	1
Frock, p	3	0	0	0	0		Young, p	3	1	0	4	0
	30	6	*26	16	3			33	5	27	14	1

* Two out when winning run scored

```
BOSN    0  0  0    2  2  0    0  0  0  -  4
BOSA    0  4  0    0  0  0    0  0  1  -  5
```

2B: Hoffman, Sweeney. SB: Carrigan, Wagner. BB: Young 4, Frock 3. Struck out: Young 5, Frock 4. PB: Ball. WP: Frock. Umpires: Emslie and Connolly.

Fred Burchell (0–1) when he got into trouble with one out in the tenth inning, and Burchell got the final two outs.

The third game was another squeaker as the Red Sox took a first-inning 1–0 lead which they held until the Doves tied the game in the top of the seventh. The Sox struck for one of their own in the bottom of the frame and won the game, 2–1. Cy Morgan (6–6) pitched a six-hitter, walked two and struck out six, and was the victor. Irv Young (10–23) gave up one walk and only four Red Sox hits, all singles, but the Americans used their limited offense to good advantage by bunching hits in the two innings they scored.

Game Five was yet another close contest, although it didn't look to be that

1907 Boston City Championship Series

```
GAME FIVE --- October 11
```

RED SOX	AB	H	PO	A	E		DOVES	AB	H	PO	A	E
Sullivan, cf	5	1	2	0	0		Hoffman, rf	3	1	2	0	0
Parent, lf	4	0	3	0	0		Tenney, 1b	4	0	9	3	0
Congalton, rf	4	2	0	0	0		Sweeney, ss	2	1	2	3	1
Grimshaw, 1b	4	1	13	0	1		Beaumont, cf	4	1	0	0	0
Carrigan, c	4	3	4	3	0		Randall, lf	4	2	2	0	1
Wagner, ss	4	0	3	2	0		Ritchey, 2b	4	1	4	3	1
Knight, 3b	3	0	0	2	0		Brain, 3b	4	2	0	3	1
Ferris, 2b	4	2	2	7	1		Ball, c	0	0	1	2	0
Harris, p	3	0	0	1	0		Needham, c	3	0	4	3	1
Glaze, p	0	0	0	0	0		Bates, ph	1	1	0	0	0
							Lindaman, p	3	0	3	3	2
	35	9	27	15	2		Bridwell, ph	1	0	0	0	0
								33	9	27	20	7

```
BOSA    1  0  0    0  1  1    1  2  0  -  6
BOSN    0  0  0    2  0  0    0  0  2  -  4
```

HR: Carrigan. SB: Congalton, Wagner, Sweeney. BB: Harris 4, Lindaman 1. Struck out: Harris 6, Lindaman 4. WP: Lindaman 2. PB: Needham. DP: BOSN. Umpires: Emslie and Connolly.

way at the outset. The Sox continued to have the upper hand on young Mr. Sam Frock as they struck for four runs in the second inning. But the Doves tied the score with two in the fourth and two more in the fifth. That's where the score stayed until the bottom of the ninth when the Americans pushed across the deciding run against Frock. Cy Young went the distance for the Red Sox, giving up six hits, walking four, and striking out five.

The Americans scored early and late in Game Five, then held on as the Doves continued to pull close. The Red Sox took a 1–0 lead in the first only to see the Doves pull ahead with two in the fourth. Single runs in the fifth, sixth, and seventh, and two more in the eighth put the Sox up 6–2. The Doves tallied two in the ninth, but reliever Ralph Glaze (8–13) finally got the last out, preserving the victory. The hitting star of the day was catcher Bill Carrigan with two singles and a home run. Vive Lindaman (11–15) took the loss for the Doves.

Game Six was the first game of a doubleheader on the 12th and featured a come-from-behind rally for the Red Sox as Fred Burchell was matched against the Doves' Jake Boultes (5–9). The Red Sox jumped on Boultes for two runs in the first, but the Doves came back with three in the fifth and one in the seventh to take a 4–2 lead. Single runs for the Sox over each of the final three innings brought Ralph Glaze home a winner.

In the final game of what must have been a very long series for the Doves, the Nationals struck for a first-inning run only to see the Red Sox tie the game and take the lead when they scored three times in the next half-inning. The Doves refused to quit, however, and scored single runs in the fourth and fifth to tie. The game was finally halted due to darkness at the end of nine innings. Irv Young went the distance for the Doves, giving up seven hits and two walks, and striking out seven. Tex Pruiett (3–11) held the Doves to four hits, all singles, but five free passes kept him in trouble along the way.

1907 Boston City Championship Series

GAME SIX --- October 12

RED SOX	AB	H	PO	A	E		DOVES	AB	H	PO	A	E
Sullivan, cf	4	1	1	0	0		Hoffman, rf	4	1	3	0	0
Hoey, lf	4	1	2	0	0		Tenney, 1b	3	2	15	3	1
Congalton, rf	4	1	1	0	0		Sweeney, ss	4	1	2	9	0
Grimshaw, 1b	3	1	8	1	0		Beaumont, cf	4	2	0	0	1
Carrigan, c	4	3	8	2	0		Randall, lf	5	0	1	0	0
Wagner, ss	4	0	1	1	0		Ritchey, 2b	4	1	1	4	0
Knight, 3b	4	1	3	2	0		Brain, 3b	4	2	1	1	0
Ferris, 2b	3	0	3	3	0		Needham, c	2	0	3	1	0
Burchell, p	1	0	0	1	0		Boultes, p	3	0	3	1	0
Glaze, p	2	0	0	1	0			33	9	*26	21	2
	33	8	27	11	0							

* Two out when winning run scored

```
BOSN    0  0  0    0  3  0    1  0  0  -  4
BOSA    2  0  0    0  0  0    1  1  1  -  5
```

2B: Knight. 3B: Carrigan. SB: Brain. DP: BOSA. BB: Burchell 4, Glaze 3, Boultes 1. Struck out: Burchell 1, Glaze 4. Umpires: Emslie and Connolly.

GAME SEVEN --- October 12 (second game)

RED SOX	AB	H	PO	A	E		DOVES	AB	H	PO	A	E
Sullivan, cf	5	1	2	0	0		Hoffman, rf	4	0	1	0	0
Hoey, lf	3	0	1	0	0		Tenney, 1b	3	0	11	0	0
Barrett, rf	4	1	4	0	3		Sweeney, ss	4	1	0	3	1
Grimshaw, ss	4	0	4	3	1		Beaumont, cf	2	1	3	0	0
Carrigan, c	4	0	3	1	0		Randall, lf	3	0	0	0	0
Donahue, 1b	3	2	10	3	0		Ritchey, 2b	4	1	2	4	0
Knight, 3b	3	0	1	2	0		Brain, 3b	4	0	2	2	0
Ferris, 2b	4	2	2	3	1		Brown, c	4	0	7	3	0
Pruiett, p	4	1	0	4	0		Young, p	3	1	1	3	0
	34	7	27	16	5			31	4	27	15	1

```
BOSA    0  3  0    0  0  0    0  0  0  -  3
BOSN    1  0  0    1  1  0    0  0  0  -  3
```

2B: Unglaub. 3B: Barrett, Ferris, Beaumont. BB: Pruiett 5, Young 2. Struck out: Pruiett 3, Young 7. Umpires: Emslie and Connolly.

The idea of a city championship never quite caught on in Boston, perhaps due to the early and complete dominance of the American League team, and even though this was only the second series between the two teams, it was also the last. The Red Sox had won both championships with a convincing 11-1-1 record in games played.

The 1909 Chicago City Championship Series

Chicago Cubs defeat Chicago White Sox; 4–1

Because the Chicago Cubs won pennants in 1907 and 1908, the city championship did not resume until 1909. The Cubs (104–49) lost out to an improved

1909 Chicago City Championship Series

GAME ONE --- October 8

WHITE SOX	AB	H	PO	A	E
Altizer, rf	4	1	0	0	0
Isbell, 1b	3	1	7	2	0
Cole, cf	4	0	1	1	0
Dougherty, lf	4	0	0	0	0
Purtell, 2b	4	1	3	6	2
Parent, ss	3	1	3	3	0
Tannehill, 3b	3	0	2	0	1
Sullivan, c	3	0	8	3	0
Walsh, p	3	0	0	4	1
	31	4	24	19	4

CUBS	AB	H	PO	A	E
Evers, 2b	4	3	1	3	0
Sheckard, lf	4	0	0	0	0
Schulte, rf	2	0	1	0	0
Chance, 1b	3	1	7	0	0
Steinfeldt, 3b	2	1	1	1	1
Hofman, cf	3	1	9	0	0
Tinker, ss	3	0	2	1	1
Archer, c	2	0	6	3	0
Overall, p	3	0	0	1	0
	26	6	27	9	2

```
SOX   0  0  0    0  0  0    0  0  0  -  0
CUB   2  0  0    1  0  0    0  1  x  -  4
```

2B: Isbell, Evers. SH: Steinfeldt 2. SB: Schulte, Isbell, Evers. DP: SOX. LOB: Sox 6, Cubs 2. Runs: Evers 2, Schulte, Chance. BB: Walsh 2, Overall 1. Struck out: Walsh 7, Overall 5. WP: Overall, Walsh. Umpires: O'Day and Sheridan. Att: 16,762. Time—1:40.

GAME TWO --- October 9

CUBS	AB	H	PO	A	E
Evers, 2b	4	0	4	4	0
Sheckard, lf	3	0	2	0	0
Schulte, rf	4	2	1	0	0
Chance, 1b	5	1	8	2	0
Steinfeldt, 3b	3	1	0	1	0
Hofman, cf	3	0	4	0	0
Tinker, ss	4	0	3	1	2
Archer, c	3	1	5	1	0
Brown, p	3	0	0	3	0
	32	5	27	12	2

WHITE SOX	AB	H	PO	A	E
Altizer, rf	3	0	3	0	0
Isbell, 1b	4	0	14	0	0
Cole, cf	4	0	1	0	0
Dougherty, lf	4	3	0	0	0
Purtell, 2b	3	1	0	3	0
Parent, ss	4	1	0	0	0
Tannehill, 3b	4	0	2	2	1
Sullivan, c	3	1	7	0	0
Smith, p	4	0	0	4	0
	33	6	27	9	1

```
CUB   1  0  0    0  0  0    0  2  2  -  5
SOX   0  0  1    1  0  0    0  0  0  -  2
```

2B: Schulte 2, Chance. HR: Purtell. SH: Altizer, Brown. SB: Evers, Schulte, Steinfeldt, Chance, Isbell, Sheckard. Runs: Sheckard 2, Evers, Schulte, Archer, Purtell, Sullivan. DP: Cubs. BB: Smith 7, Brown 1. Struck out: Smith 7, Brown 4. Umpires: Sheridan and O'Day. Att: 20,657. Time—2:08.

Pirates team in 1909 and prepared to meet the fourth-place White Sox (78–74) in the city series. Cubs' ace Mordecai Brown (27–9) led the National League in starts (50) and innings pitched (343) as did his counterpart, White Sox ace Frank Smith (25–17) with 51 starts and 365 innings. In addition, the National League pitching staff led the majors in ERA with a microscopic 1.75. Cubs' pitching figured to win the day in the series.

It was Ed Walsh (15–11) for the Sox against Orval Overall (20–11) in Game One, played on the eighth of October at the home of the Cubs, West Side Park. A small fire, which started in one of the upper boxes of the grandstand and was quickly extinguished, did nothing to prevent Cub fans from enjoying the

1909 Chicago City Championship Series

GAME THREE --- October 10

WHITE SOX	AB	H	PO	A	E		CUBS	AB	H	PO	A	E
Altizer, rf	4	1	3	1	0		Evers, 2b	3	1	3	3	0
Isbell, 1b	4	1	13	2	0		Sheckard, lf	3	0	2	0	0
Cole, cf	4	2	1	1	0		Schulte, rf	3	1	2	0	0
Dougherty, lf	4	3	1	0	0		Chance, 1b	3	1	7	1	1
Purtell, 2b	5	0	0	1	0		Steinfeldt, 3b	4	1	2	3	0
Parent, ss	4	1	2	2	0		Hofman, cf	4	1	2	0	0
Tannehill, 3b	2	0	0	2	0		Tinker, ss	3	0	3	2	0
Sullivan, c	2	0	6	1	0		Archer, c	3	1	6	1	0
Walsh, p	4	1	1	4	0		Reulbach, c	3	0	0	1	1
	33	9	27	14	0			29	6	27	11	2

```
SOX   0  1  0    0  0  0    0  0  1  -  2
CUB   1  0  0    0  0  0    0  0  0  -  1
```

2B: Hofman. SF: Sullivan. SH: Isbell, Schulte. SB: Evers 2, Cole, Parent. Runs: Altizer, Dougherty, Sheckard. LOB: Cubs 5, Sox 12. DP: Sox. BB: Walsh 3, Reulbach 6. Struck out: Walsh 6, Reulbach 4. Balk: Reulbach. Umpires: O'Day and Sheridan. Att: 24,034. Time—1:58.

masterful work of Overall as he shut out the Sox on four hits and a walk, striking out five. Four White Sox errors aided the Nationals' cause as the Cubs scored twice in the first and were never headed. The final score was 4–0.

Game Two was played the next day at South Side Park with the two aces of the clubs, Brown and Smith, going against each other. The Cubs took a one-run lead in the first on a walk, an infield out, and an error, but the Sox bunched three hits in the third to tie the game. Billy Purtell's solo home run in the fourth gave the Sox the lead for the next three innings, but a walk to Jimmy Sheckard and back-to-back doubles from Frank "Wildfire" Schulte and Frank Chance put the Cubs ahead in the eighth. Two walks and another Schulte double in the ninth provided the final two runs in this 5–2 Cubs' victory. Smith wound up with a five-hitter, only because he was too busy issuing seven bases on balls. Brown got stronger as the game progressed and finished with a six-hitter.

The series resumed at West Side Park for Game Three and the only White Sox victory. The Cubs took a first inning lead off Ed Walsh on walks to Johnny Evers and Sheckard and a Frank Chance single. The White Sox loaded the bases and scored the tying run on Billy Sullivan's sacrifice fly in the second. The game remained a 1–1 stalemate until the ninth inning when, with two out and Altizer on first, Willis Cole singled and Patsy Dougherty walked to load the bases. With Purtell at the plate, Altizer broke for the plate. Ed Reulbach (19–10) failed to deliver the ball after going into his windup and Umpire Hank O'Day called a balk. Altizer scored, Walsh retired the Cubs without incident in the ninth, and the Sox had a 2–1 victory. After his shaky start, Walsh scattered five hits over the final eight innings for the decision.

Rain and cold weather prevented play for the next two days and the Cubs took a three-games-to-one lead in Game Four on the 14th. In the first, Evers walked and stole second, went to third on Sheckard's infield out, and scored on Frank Schulte's grounder. The Cubs widened their margin to 2–0 in the third

1909 Chicago City Championship Series

GAME FOUR --- October 14

CUBS	AB	H	PO	A	E	WHITE SOX	AB	H	PO	A	E
Evers, 2b	2	2	4	1	0	Altizer, rf	3	1	1	0	0
Sheckard, lf	2	0	1	0	0	Isbell, 1b	3	1	14	0	0
Schulte, rf	4	1	3	0	1	Cole, cf	4	1	1	0	0
Chance, 1b	4	0	6	1	0	Dougherty, lf	1	0	0	0	0
Steinfeldt, 3b	3	0	1	1	0	Messenger, lf	2	0	1	0	1
Hofman, cf	3	0	3	0	0	Purtell, 2b	2	0	0	4	0
Tinker, ss	4	1	0	3	1	Tannehill, 3b	4	0	1	4	0
Archer, c	3	1	9	1	0	Sullivan, c	2	0	5	0	0
Overall, p	3	0	0	1	0	Payne, c	2	0	2	1	0
						Parent, ss	4	1	2	1	0
						Walsh, p	3	1	0	4	1
	28	5	27	8	2		30	5	27	14	2

```
CUB    1  0  1    0  0  0    0  0  0  -  2
SOX    0  0  0    1  0  0    0  0  0  -  1
```

2B: Archer. SH: Hofman, Purtell, Sheckard, Evers. SB: Evers, Parent, Altizer, Cole. LOB: Sox 7, Cubs 7. BB: Walsh 4, Overall 2. Struck out: Overall 9, Walsh 6. Umpires: Sheridan and O'Day. Att: 9,917. Time—1:45.

GAME FIVE --- October 15

WHITE SOX	AB	H	PO	A	E	CUBS	AB	H	PO	A	E
Altizer, rf	3	0	3	0	0	Evers, 2b	4	2	0	6	0
Isbell, 1b	4	0	10	0	0	Sheckard, lf	4	1	0	0	0
Cole, cf	4	0	1	0	0	Schulte, rf	4	0	3	0	0
Dougherty, lf	3	0	1	0	0	Chance, 1b	2	1	12	0	0
Purtell, 3b	3	0	2	1	1	Steinfeldt, 3b	2	0	2	2	0
Parent, ss	3	1	1	3	0	Hofman, cf	3	0	2	0	0
Atz, 2b	3	0	0	1	0	Tinker, ss	3	1	0	1	0
Payne, c	3	0	6	2	0	Moran, c	2	0	8	0	0
White, p	2	0	0	5	0	Brown, p	3	1	0	2	0
	28	1	24	12	1		27	6	27	11	0

```
SOX    0  0  0    0  0  0    0  0  0  -  0
CUB    0  0  1    0  0  0    0  0  x  -  1
```

Run: Brown. SH: Moran, Steinfeldt. SB: Parent, Evers. LOB: Cubs 5, Sox 3. BB: White 1, Brown 2. Struck out: White 5, Brown 3. Umpires: O'Day and Sheridan. Att: 3,142. Time: 1:33.

on a single by Evers, a walk to Sheckard, a single by Schulte, and a Harry Steinfeldt infield out. The Sox made their only run of the game in the fourth. Willis Cole singled. When Patsy Dougherty protested a strike call a little too vigorously, umpire Sheridan ejected him from the game. Bob Messenger finished Dougherty's at-bat and drew a base on balls. Purtell sacrificed and Cole scored on Freddy Parent's groundout. Overall went the distance for the victory and Ed Walsh, the previous game's winner, pitched the complete game loss. After drawing a total of 61,453 for the first three games, the cold weather kept the attendance for this game to 9,917.

A tiny crowd of 3,142 turned out to see the finale at South Side Park the next day, but they were rewarded for braving the cold by seeing the best pitched game of the series. The Cubs bunched their hits in the third to score the only run of the game. Joe Tinker singled and was sacrificed to second, but was out stealing third. Consecutive singles by Mordecai Brown, Johnny Evers and Jimmy Sheckard put the Cubs on top 1–0. That was all Brown got to work with, but that was all he needed. Mordecai retired the first 12 men he faced before Freddy Parent got the Sox's only hit in the fifth. Brown encountered some difficulty when he walked two men in the ninth, but he recovered and got the final two outs of the game. Sox starter Doc White (11–9) gave the Cubs only two hits after allowing the one run in the third, but his effort wasn't enough.

The 1910 Ohio State Championship Series

Cincinnati Reds defeat Cleveland Naps; 4–3

There wasn't a lot to recommend this series between two fifth-place clubs, the Cleveland Naps (71–81) and the Cincinnati Reds (75–79). With the exception of a few scattered innings here and there, none of the games was even close. The only interesting feature of this series was that the home team won every game — a feat which wasn't accomplished in the World Series until 1987.

1910 Ohio State Championship Series

GAME ONE --- October 11

CLEVELAND NAPS	AB	H	PO	A	E	CINCINNATI	AB	H	PO	A	E
Turner, 3b	5	2	2	1	0	Miller, cf	5	2	3	0	1
Hohnhorst, 1b	4	1	11	2	1	Alitzer, ss	3	2	2	4	1
Jackson, cf	4	2	1	0	0	Hoblitzell, 1b	6	2	13	0	0
Lajoie, 2b	4	1	2	1	0	M.Mitchell, rf	3	1	0	0	0
Easterly, rf	4	1	2	0	0	Paskert, lf	5	2	4	0	0
Graney, lf	4	0	0	0	0	Lobert, 3b	3	0	0	3	1
Smith, c	0	0	2	1	0	McLean, c	5	4	3	2	0
Clarke, c	3	0	3	0	1	Egan, 2b	3	2	2	4	0
Ball, ss	4	0	1	3	0	Suggs, p	3	2	0	1	1
W.Mitchell, p	1	0	0	2	0		36	17	27	14	4
Koestner, p	1	1	0	0	0						
Kahler, p	1	0	0	0	0						
Stovall, ph	1	1	0	0	0						
	36	9	24	10	2						

```
CLE    0  0  0    0  0  5    2  0  0  -   7
CIN    0  0  4    4  0  4    0  2  x  -  14
```

2B: Turner, Stovall, McLean. 3B: Hoblitzell, Koestner. HR: Paskert. SB: Graney, Lobert, M. Mitchell, Alitzer. DP: CIN. BB: W. Mitchell 3, Koestner 3, Kahler 2, Suggs 3. Struck out: Mitchell 3, Suggs 3. PB: Clarke 2. Umpires: Brennan and Frank O'Loughlin.

The Reds won the series opener, played on the 11th of October at their home park, the Palace of the Fans. The Reds took an early 8–0 lead behind George Suggs (19–11) with four more in the third and four in the fourth. Cleveland struck back with five runs in the sixth, but another Cincinnati four-run inning in the bottom of the frame left the Naps somewhat dispirited. Suggs stayed on the mound for the entire game and was roughed up for seven runs

1910 Ohio State Championship Series

GAME TWO --- October 12

CINCINNATI	AB	H	PO	A	E		CLEVELAND NAPS	AB	H	PO	A	E
Miller, cf	4	1	5	0	0		Turner, 3b	5	1	1	0	0
Alitzer, ss	4	1	1	1	1		Stovall, 1b	4	1	8	1	0
Hoblitzell, 1b	3	0	6	1	0		Jackson, cf	4	2	4	0	0
M.Mitchell, rf	4	2	1	0	0		Lajoie, 2b	4	1	5	2	0
Paskert, lf	4	1	3	0	0		Easterly, rf	3	3	0	0	0
Lobert, 3b	4	1	3	1	0		Birmingham, cf	1	0	0	0	0
McLean, c	4	1	3	1	0		Graney, lf	3	0	2	0	1
Egan, 2b	4	0	2	1	0		Peckinpaugh, ss	4	2	2	3	2
Gaspar, p	1	0	0	1	1		Adams, c	3	0	4	2	0
Fromme, p	1	0	0	1	0		Joss, p	2	0	1	4	0
Burns, p	0	0	0	1	0		Kahler, p	0	0	0	1	0
Downey, ph	1	0	0	0	0		Hohnhorst, ph	1	1	0	0	0
Phelan, pr	0	0	0	0	0							
	34	7	24	8	2			34	11	27	13	3

```
CIN   0  0  0     0  0  2     0  0  1  -  3
CLE   0  2  1     0  0  2     0  0  x  -  5
```

2B: Lajoie, Miller, Lobert. 3B: Mitchell. SB: Peckinpaugh, Phelan, Paskert. DP: CLE. BB: Joss 1, Burns 1. Struck out: Kahler 2, Joss 2. PB: Adams. Umpires: O'Loughlin and Brennan.

GAME THREE --- October 15

CINCINNATI	AB	H	PO	A	E		CLEVELAND NAPS	AB	H	PO	A	E
Miller, cf	4	1	4	0	0		Turner, 3b	4	1	2	8	0
Alitzer, ss	4	0	1	5	0		Stovall, 1b	4	2	18	0	0
Hoblitzell, 1b	4	3	12	0	0		Jackson, cf	3	1	1	0	0
M.Mitchell, rf	4	1	2	0	0		Lajoie, 2b	4	2	3	7	0
Paskert, lf	4	0	0	0	0		Easterly, rf	3	1	0	1	0
Lobert, 3b	3	0	0	2	0		Birmingham, rf	1	0	0	0	0
McLean, c	3	0	2	1	0		Graney, lf	4	2	1	0	0
Egan, 2b	3	1	3	5	0		Ball, ss	4	2	1	2	2
Beebe, p	1	0	0	1	0		Adams, c	4	3	1	0	0
Burns, p	1	0	0	0	0		Falkenberg, p	3	0	0	5	0
Rowan, p	0	0	0	0	0							
Downey, ph	1	0	0	0	0			34	14	27	23	2
	32	6	24	14	0							

```
CIN   0  0  0     1  0  0     0  0  0  -  1
CLE   0  0  6     0  0  0     1  0  x  -  7
```

2B: Graney, Miller, Ball, Lajoie. DP: CLE 2, CIN 2. BB: Beebe 1. Struck out: Beebe 1, Burns 1, Falkenberg 1. WP: Falkenberg. Umpires: Brennan and O'Loughlin.

on nine hits and three walks, but 14 runs by his teammates made him an easy winner nonetheless. Cleveland starter Willie Mitchell (12–8) took the loss. Hit equally hard were relievers Elmer Koestner (5–10) and George Kahler (6–4). McLean was the batting star with a 4-for-5 day, but his hitting was nearly forgotten in a robust Cincinnati performance that saw six other men garner two hits each.

Game Two moved to Cleveland's League Park on the following day. Addie Joss (5–5) was the starter and the Naps gave him a 3-0 lead after three innings. The teams exchanged two-run innings in the sixth, but Joss hung on for

1910 Ohio State Championship Series

GAME FOUR --- October 16

CLEVELAND NAPS	AB	H	PO	A	E		CINCINNATI	AB	H	PO	A	E
Turner, 3b	5	1	3	1	0		Miller, cf	5	4	4	0	0
Stovall, 1b	4	0	8	1	0		Alitzer, ss	5	2	3	4	0
Jackson, cf	4	2	2	0	0		Hoblitzell, 1b	4	2	7	0	0
Lajoie, 2b	4	3	3	3	0		M.Mitchell, rf	3	1	2	1	0
Easterly, rf	3	1	2	0	0		Paskert, lf	4	1	3	1	0
Graney, lf	4	0	1	1	0		Lobert, 3b	4	2	0	0	0
Ball, ss	3	1	3	4	0		McLean, c	2	1	6	0	0
Adams, c	4	0	2	3	0		Clarke, c	0	0	0	0	0
Kahler, p	0	0	0	1	0		Egan, 2b	4	2	2	4	0
Fanwell, p	0	0	0	0	0		Gaspar, p	3	0	0	0	0
W.Mitchell, p	2	1	0	0	0							
Hohnhorst, ph	1	0	0	0	0			34	15	27	10	0
	34	9	24	14	0							

```
CLE   0 0 0   0 0 0   0 1 0  -  1
CIN   3 0 2   0 0 0   1 2 x  -  8
```

2B: Egan, Miller, W. Mitchell. 3B: Alitzer, Jackson. SB: Hoblitzell, M. Mitchell. DP: CIN 1, CLE 1. BB: Fanwell 2, Mitchell 2, Gaspar 2. Struck out: W. Mitchell 2, Gaspar 4. WP: Kahler. Umpires: Brennan and O'Loughlin.

GAME FIVE --- October 16 (second game)

CLEVELAND NAPS	AB	H	PO	A	E		CINCINNATI	AB	H	PO	A	E
Turner, 3b	4	1	0	1	0		Miller, cf	4	2	2	0	0
Stovall, 1b	4	1	10	0	0		Alitzer, ss	4	2	2	1	0
Jackson, cf	4	1	0	0	0		Hoblitzell, 1b	4	1	6	0	0
Lajoie, 2b	3	1	1	0	0		M.Mitchell, rf	4	1	3	0	0
Easterly, rf	2	1	2	0	0		Paskert, lf	4	1	2	0	0
Graney, lf	3	2	2	0	1		Lobert, 3b	4	0	1	2	0
Ball, ss	3	0	1	2	0		McLean, c	3	2	4	0	1
Adams, c	3	0	5	1	1		Clarke, c	1	1	0	0	0
Young, p	3	1	0	2	1		Egan, 2b	3	3	1	2	1
Fanwell, p	0	0	0	0	0		Suggs, p	2	1	0	0	0
	29	8	21	6	3		Burns, p	1	0	0	0	0
							Phelan, pr	0	0	0	0	0
								34	14	21	5	2

```
CLE   0 1 0   1 0 0   0  -  2
CIN   0 0 0   0 0 5   0  -  5
```

SB: Turner, Lajoie, Miller 2, Hoblitzell, Paskert, Egan, Mitchell. Struck out: Young 4, Fanwell 1, Suggs 4. WP: Fanwell. Umpires: Brennan and O'Loughlin.

a 5–3 victory. Harry Gaspar (15–17) started the game for the Reds and took the loss. Art Fromme (3–4) and Bill Burns (8–13) worked in relief.

The Naps racked up 14 hits and seven runs off Cincinnati pitchers Fred Beebe (12–15), Bill Burns, and Jack Rowan (14–13) in the third game, winning by a 7–1 score. A six-run third provided all the runs Cy Falkenberg (14–13) needed as he held the Reds to six hits and a run in pitching a complete game.

Game Four saw Cincinnati win by another seven-run margin in the first game of a doubleheader on the 16th of October. The Reds jumped on George Kahler for five early runs as they won easily, 8–1. The Nationals belted out 15

1910 Ohio State Championship Series

GAME SIX --- October 17

CINCINNATI	AB	H	PO	A	E		CLEVELAND NAPS	AB	H	PO	A	E
Miller, cf	5	1	1	0	0		Turner, 3b	4	3	1	3	0
Alitzer, ss	5	0	1	3	0		Stovall, 1b	4	2	12	0	0
Hoblitzell, 1b	4	2	3	0	0		Jackson, cf	4	1	1	0	0
M.Mitchell, rf	3	2	2	0	0		Lajoie, 2b	3	1	4	3	0
Paskert, lf	3	0	3	0	0		Easterly, rf	3	0	0	0	0
Lobert, 3b	4	2	5	3	2		Birmingham, lf	3	2	1	0	0
McLean, c	4	2	4	2	0		Graney, lf	3	2	4	0	0
Egan, 2b	3	1	1	2	0		Ball, ss	4	2	2	4	1
Fromme, p	0	0	0	0	0		Adams, c	4	0	1	2	1
Burns, p	1	0	2	3	0		Blanding, p	2	1	1	3	0
Beebe, p	1	0	0	0	0							
Rowan, p	0	0	0	0	0			34	14	27	15	2
Clarke, ph	1	1	0	0	0							
Griffith, p	0	0	0	0	0							
	34	11	22	13	2							

```
CIN    0  2  0    1  0  0    2  0  0  -  5
CLE    0  0  5    0  3  0    1  0  x  -  9
```

2B: Lobert, Jackson. 3B: Mitchell. HR: Birmingham. SB: Paskert. DP: CIN. BB: Beebe 2, Rowan 2, Blanding 3. Struck out: Blanding 2, Rowan 3. Umpires: O'Loughlin and Brennan.

GAME SEVEN --- October 18

CLEVELAND NAPS	AB	H	PO	A	E		CINCINNATI	AB	H	PO	A	E
Turner, 3b	5	3	0	3	0		Miller, cf	3	0	3	0	0
Stovall, 1b	5	3	13	0	0		Alitzer, ss	3	1	1	2	0
Jackson, cf	5	1	1	0	0		Downey, ss	1	1	1	0	0
Lajoie, 2b	4	1	2	7	0		Hoblitzell, 1b	3	1	9	0	0
Easterly, lf	3	2	2	0	0		M.Mitchell, rf	4	1	1	0	0
Birmingham, cf	0	0	0	0	0		Paskert, lf	3	2	2	0	0
Graney, rf	3	1	1	0	0		Lobert, 3b	2	1	2	1	0
Ball, ss	4	1	1	6	0		McLean, c	2	0	8	1	0
Adams, c	4	0	4	2	1		Egan, 2b	2	1	0	4	1
Falkenberg, p	2	0	0	1	0		Suggs, p	1	0	0	2	0
Kahler, p	1	0	0	0	0		Gaspar, p	1	0	0	1	0
W.Mitchell, p	0	0	0	0	0		Clarke, ph	1	0	0	0	0
Hohnhorst, ph	1	0	0	0	0			26	8	27	11	1
	37	12	24	19	1							

```
CLE    0  0  0    4  0  0    1  0  0  -  5
CIN    0  0  0    0  0  5    2  1  x  -  8
```

2B: Egan, Easterly. 3B: Lobert, Jackson. SB: Lobert. DP: CLE. BB: Falkenberg 2, Kahler 3, Mitchell 1, Suggs 1. Struck out: Falkenberg 1, Mitchell 1, Suggs 4, Gaspar 2. WP: Mitchell. Umpires: Brennan and O'Loughlin.

hits against Kahler and relievers Harry Fanwell (2-9) and Willie Mitchell. Harry Gaspar went all the way for the Reds and scattered nine hits and two walks.

The nightcap game featured the first start in the series by the 43-year old youngster, Cy Young (7-10). During the past season, Cy crested the 500-victory mark and the ageless one cruised along for the first five innings, leading 2-0, until the Reds batted him around in the sixth for five runs. Young was knocked from the box, a more frequent occurrence than in years past, and Harry Fanwell came on in relief. George Suggs started for the Reds, but the victory went to reliever Bill Burns.

The sixth game was yet another runaway which featured yet another big inning. This time it was the Naps who kept the scoreboard operator busy. Trailing 2–0 into the bottom of the third, Cleveland put five runs in their column, then scored three more in the fifth to win easily, 9–5. Cleveland rookie Fred Blanding (2–2) went the distance for the Naps, giving up the five runs on 11 hits. When the game was all but lost, Cincinnati manager Clarke Griffith inserted himself into the contest as pitcher. Griffith, who pitching career had effectively ended in 1906, enjoyed making an occasional appearance in lost causes during the season and would continue to do so through 1914 when he was 45 years old.

Tied 3–3 in the series, Cleveland hoped to defeat the visiting team jinx in Game Seven by racking up four runs in the fourth inning against Cincinnati starter George Suggs. Cy Falkenberg rolled along with this lead for the next two innings until the Reds pounded him for five runs in the sixth. (During the series, Cleveland scored three or more runs in an inning five times; Cincinnati did so six times.) The Naps tied the score in the next half-inning, but Cincinnati captured the free-hitting championship with two runs in the bottom of the seventh and an insurance run in the eighth. Falkenberg, Kahler, and Mitchell worked for the Naps in the finale; Suggs and Gaspar were the Cincinnati pitchers.

The 1910 New York City Championship Series

New York Giants defeat New York Yankees; 4–2–1

The 1910 New York Giants (91–63) had won 90 or more games for the third year in a row, failing to win the pennant each year, when they met the New

1910 New York City Championship Series

GAME ONE --- October 13

YANKEES	AB	H	PO	A	E		GIANTS	AB	H	PO	A	E
Daniels, lf	4	0	1	0	0		Devore, rf	3	3	1	0	0
Hamphill, rf	4	0	1	0	0		Doyle, 2b	3	1	2	0	0
Chase, 1b	4	2	3	2	0		Snodgrass, cf	4	0	0	0	0
Knight, ss	4	1	4	1	0		Murray, rf	4	1	3	1	0
LaPorte, 2b	4	1	1	1	0		Bridwell, ss	2	2	0	0	1
Cree, cf	4	1	5	0	0		Fletcher, ss	0	0	0	0	0
Sweeney, c	1	0	4	1	0		Devlin, 3b	3	1	0	2	1
Mitchell, c	3	2	3	3	0		Merkle, 3b	4	2	5	0	2
Ford, p	4	0	0	2	0		Meyers, c	4	1	15	1	0
Austin, 3b	4	1	2	1	1		Mathewson, p	4	1	1	1	0
	36	8	24	11	1			31	12	27	5	4

```
NYA    0  1  0    0  0  0    0  0  0  -  1
NYN    0  0  0    0  1  0    0  4  x  -  5
```

2B: Cree, Chase. SB: Devore 2, Bridwell, Austin, LaPorte. DP: NYN. BB: Ford 1. Struck out: Mathewson 14, Ford 6. PB: Mitchell. Umpires: William Klem and Kane.

1910 New York City Championship Series

GAME TWO --- October 14

GIANTS	AB	H	PO	A	E
Devore, rf	4	1	1	1	0
Doyle, 2b	4	1	2	2	0
Snodgrass, cf	2	1	3	0	1
Murray, rf	4	1	0	0	0
Merkle, 1b	4	0	14	0	0
Devlin, 3b	3	2	1	4	0
Fletcher, ss	4	0	2	6	0
Meyers, c	2	0	2	2	0
Wiltse	3	0	1	1	0
	30	6*26	16	1	

YANKEES	AB	H	PO	A	E
Daniels, lf	4	1	2	0	0
Hamphill, rf	4	3	1	0	0
Chase, 1b	4	1	11	0	0
Knight, ss	3	1	0	2	1
Cree, cf	4	0	3	0	0
Gardner, 2b	3	0	4	2	1
Mitchell, c	2	1	1	1	1
Warhop, p	3	0	1	4	0
Roach, ph	0	0	0	0	0
Austin, 3b	4	1	4	3	0
	31	8	27	12	3

* Two out when winning run scored

```
NYN    0  2  1    0  0  0    0  0  1  -  4
NYA    0  0  0    1  0  0    0  2  2  -  5
```

2B: Doyle, Devlin. HR: Devlin. DP: NYA 1, NYN 1. BB: Wiltse 5, Warhop 1. Struck out: Wiltse 2, Warhop 1. Umpires: William Evans and William Klem.

GAME THREE --- October 15

YANKEES	AB	H	PO	A	E
Daniels, lf	3	0	0	0	1
Hamphill, rf	4	2	0	0	0
Chase, 1b	4	3	11	2	0
Knight, ss	2	0	1	3	0
Cree, cf	3	0	3	1	0
Gardner, 2b	3	1	1	3	0
Roach, 2b	1	0	0	0	0
Mitchell, c	2	0	5	2	0
Vaughn, p	1	0	0	2	2
Quinn, p	1	0	0	1	0
Austin, 3b	4	0	3	1	0
Wolter, ph	1	1	0	0	0
	29	7	24	15	3

GIANTS	AB	H	PO	A	E
Devore, rf	4	2	2	1	0
Doyle, 2b	3	2	2	0	0
Snodgrass, cf	3	0	0	0	0
Murray, rf	3	0	0	0	0
Merkle, 1b	4	2	7	0	0
Devlin, 3b	3	1	2	0	0
Fletcher, ss	3	0	4	1	0
Schafer, ss	0	0	0	2	0
Meyers, c	2	0	10	1	0
Drucke, p	2	0	0	2	0
Mathewson, p	1	0	0	1	0
	28	7	27	8	0

```
NYA    0  0  0    0  0  1    3  0  0  -  4
NYN    1  0  0    1  0  3    1  0  x  -  6
```

2B: Hamphill 2, Chase, Merkle 2, Devlin. SB: Devore 2, Knight. DP: NYA. BB: Vaughn 1, Quinn 1, Drucke 4. Struck out: Vaughn 3, Quinn 1, Drucke 6, Mathewson 4. PB: Mitchell. Umpires: William Klem and William Evans.

York Yankees (88–63) in the 1910 city championship series. The Yankees were not yet the powerhouse team they would become and, in fact, had just finished over .500 for the first time since 1906. The team hadn't even settled on a name yet, sometimes being referred to as the Highlanders, sometimes as the Yankees.

Game One saw Russ Ford (26–6) against Christy Mathewson (27–9). Mathewson had led the National League in victories in 1910 and had won 20 games or more for the eighth consecutive season and nine of the last ten. The Yankees scored first in the second when Jack Knight singled, went to second on a wild throw, and came home when Fred Merkle dropped Ed Sweeney's pop fly. The Nationals tied the game in the sixth and struck for four runs off Ford

1910 New York City Championship Series

GAME FOUR --- October 17

GIANTS	AB	H	PO	A	E		YANKEES	AB	H	PO	A	E
Devore, rf	5	2	2	1	0		Wolter, lf	5	3	2	0	0
Doyle, 2b	5	1	0	1	0		Hamphill, rf	5	0	0	0	1
Becker, cf	5	0	5	0	1		Chase, 1b	5	1	6	3	0
Murray, rf	4	1	0	0	0		Knight, ss	4	0	5	3	0
Bridwell, ss	4	1	5	1	0		Cree, cf	3	1	1	1	1
Devlin, 3b	4	2	2	6	1		Roach, 2b	4	0	5	1	0
Merkle, 1b	4	3	11	0	0		Mitchell, c	4	1	9	2	0
Meyers, c	4	2	3	0	2		Ford, p	2	0	1	3	0
Wilson, c	0	0	2	0	0		LaPorte, ph	1	0	0	0	0
Crandall, p	3	1	0	1	0		Hughey, p	0	0	0	2	0
Snodgrass, ph	1	0	0	0	0		Warhop, p	1	0	0	0	0
Ames, p	0	0	0	1	0		Austin, 3b	4	0	1	1	0
	39	13	30	11	4			38	6	30	16	2

```
NYN    0  1  0    0  1  0    2  0  1    0  -  5
NYA    0  1  0    0  0  1    0  3  0    0  -  5
```

2B: Devlin, Cree. 3B: Merkle, Wolter, Myers. SB: Cree 2, Mitchell, Wolter, Hemphill, Devore, Knight, Merkle, Myers. LOB: NYN 5, NYA 4. DP: NYN. BB: Crandall 1, Hughes 1. Struck out: Ford 7, Crandall 3, Warhop 1, Ames 2. HBP: Knight (Crandall). WP: Ford 1, Crandall 1. Hits: Ford 9 in 7 innings; Hughes 0 in 1 innings; Warhop 4 in 2 innings; Crandall 6 in 8 innings; Ames 0 in 2 innings. Umpires: Evans and Klem. Time—2:24.

GAME FIVE --- October 18

YANKEES	AB	H	PO	A	E		GIANTS	AB	H	PO	A	E
Wolter, lf	4	0	1	0	0		Devore, rf	4	2	1	1	0
Hamphill, rf	4	1	1	0	0		Doyle, 2b	4	2	2	1	1
Chase, 1b	4	1	7	1	0		Becker, cf	4	0	1	0	0
Knight, ss	4	2	6	2	0		Murray, rf	3	0	1	0	0
Cree, cf	4	0	1	0	0		Bridwell, ss	3	0	3	3	0
Roach, 2b	2	0	0	2	0		Devlin, 3b	4	0	2	0	0
Mitchell, c	3	1	8	1	0		Merkle, 1b	3	1	7	1	0
Fisher, p	0	0	0	4	0		Meyers, c	2	1	10	2	1
Austin, 3b	3	1	0	0	0		Mathewson, p	1	0	2	0	0
	28	6	24	10	0			28	6	27	10	2

```
NYA    0  0  0    0  0  0    1  0  0    -  1
NYN    1  4  0    0  0  0    0  0  x    -  5
```

2B: Hamphill, Devore. HR: Devore, Doyle. SB: Doyle 2, Merkle, Austin, Murray 2. DP: NYN. BB: Mathewson 1, Fisher 4. Struck out: Mathewson 3, Fisher 7. WP: Mathewson. Umpires: William Klem and William Evans.

in the eighth. Mathewson singled and Josh Devore reached on an error when Ford misplayed his bunt. Larry Doyle bunted and slick-fielding first baseman Hal Chase fired the ball to Jimmy Austin at third. But Austin dropped the ball and the Giants had the bases loaded with nobody out. After hitting Al Bridwell with a pitch, Ford gave up singles to Art Devlin, Merkle, and Chief Meyers for the final three runs of the inning. Both pitchers went the distance and Mathewson wound up with 14 strikeouts.

Game Two looked to be a duplicate of the first as the Giants jumped on

1910 New York City Championship Series

GAME SIX --- October 19

GIANTS	AB	H	PO	A	E
Devore, rf	5	1	1	2	0
Doyle, 2b	5	2	3	0	1
Snodgrass, cf	4	1	3	0	0
Murray, rf	5	2	1	1	0
Bridwell, ss	3	0	2	2	1
Devlin, 3b	3	2	1	2	0
Merkle, 1b	2	1	7	2	0
Meyers, c	2	0	1	3	0
Wilson, c	2	0	4	0	0
Ames, p	1	0	0	4	0
Wiltse, p	3	1	1	0	0
	35	10	24	16	2

YANKEES	AB	H	PO	A	E
Wolter, lf	5	1	0	0	0
Hamphill, rf	5	3	1	1	0
Chase, 1b	4	2	13	2	1
Knight, ss	3	2	3	4	0
Cree, cf	3	1	0	0	0
Roach, 2b	3	1	3	5	0
Criger, c	3	1	6	1	0
Vaughn, p	0	0	0	1	0
Quinn, p	3	0	1	5	0
Austin, 3b	4	3	0	1	0
	33	14	27	20	1

```
NYN    0  0  2     0  0  0     0  0  0  -  2
NYA    0  3  0     0  1  1     5  0  x  - 10
```

2B: Knight, Cree, Roach, Chase, Snodgrass, Devlin, Murray, Merkle. 3B: Chase. BB: Vaughn 3, Ames 1, Wiltse 1, Quinn 2. Struck out: Vaughn 3, Wiltse 5, Quinn 2. Umpires: William Klem and William Evans.

GAME SEVEN --- October 21

YANKEES	AB	H	PO	A	E
Wolter, lf	4	2	2	0	0
Hamphill, rf	4	1	1	0	0
Chase, 1b	4	0	1	1	2
Knight, ss	4	1	1	1	1
Cree, cf	4	1	0	0	0
Roach, 2b	3	1	2	1	1
Criger, c	2	0	2	0	0
Mitchell, c	2	0	6	0	0
Warhop, p	2	1	9	2	0
Ford, p	1	0	0	2	0
Daniels, ph	1	1	0	0	0
Austin, 3b	4	2	0	4	0
	35	10	24	11	4

GIANTS	AB	H	PO	A	E
Devore, rf	4	1	0	0	0
Doyle, 2b	5	2	1	2	1
Becker, cf-rf	3	1	0	0	0
Murray, rf	1	0	1	0	0
Snodgrass, cf	0	0	0	0	0
Bridwell, ss	4	1	1	2	0
Devlin, 3b	4	1	1	4	0
Merkle, 1b	3	0	13	1	0
Meyers, c	3	1	9	3	0
Mathewson, p	3	1	1	3	0
	30	8	27	15	1

```
NYA    0  0  1     0  0  0     2  0  0  -  3
NYN    0  0  3     0  2  0     1  0  x  -  6
```

2B: Hamphill. HR: Doyle. SB: Wolter, Becker, Murray, Doyle, Devlin. BB: Warhop 1, Ford 2. Struck out: Warhop 2, Mathewson 8, Ford 4. WP: Mathewson. PB: Evans. Umpires: William Klem and William Evans.

Jack Warhop (14–14) in the second and third innings to take a 3–0 lead. The Yankees scored once off George "Hooks" Wiltse (14–12) in the fourth and broke through for two runs in the eighth to tie. The Giants seemed to put the lid on the coffin when they scored a run in the top of the ninth to take a 4–3 lead. But the Yankees rebounded with two off Wiltse in the bottom of the inning and won their first game of the series.

The Giants were eager to avenge the loss of the previous day and held a 5–1 lead after scoring three runs off Yankees starter Hippo Vaughn (13–11) in the sixth inning of Game Three. Three Yankee runs in the next half-inning off

Louis Drucke (12–10) made the game interesting, but the Giants tallied an insurance run in the bottom of the seventh and won, 6–4. Jack Quinn (18–12), pitching in relief of Vaughn, took the win.

Game Four saw Doc Crandall (17–4) for the Giants hook up with Russ Ford. Unlike his namesake of the 1950s, this Ford was an Edsel as he failed to win for the second time in as many outings. The Yankees used three pitchers in the game — Ford, Tom Hughes (7–9) and Jack Warhop — none of whom were effective, as the Giants belted out 13 hits. Crandall and Red Ames (12–11) held the Yanks to only six hits, but the end result was the same. The contest ended in a 5–5 tie, called after ten innings because of darkness.

Yankee rookie Ray Fisher (5–3) was thrown to the wolves for Game Five, the wolf pack in this case a small one, numbering only one — Christy Mathewson. The Giants struck for one in the first and four more in the second. Mathewson threw nothing but fastballs the rest of the way and won easily, 5–1. The big blows were home runs by Josh Devore and Larry Doyle.

The Yankees suited up in their hitting clothes for Game Six and pounded Red Ames and Hooks Wiltse to the tune of 10–2. The Americans broke on top with three in the second. Hippo Vaughn started the game in fine fashion for the Yankees, but was relieved by Jack Quinn after he walked three men in the third. Two Giants' runs made the score 3–2, but that was the closest they would come. The Yankees scored single runs in the fourth and fifth and pushed across five insurance runs in the seventh.

In the series finale the Giants, as had been their fashion, struck in the early innings again. Three third-inning runs proved the margin of victory as Christy Mathewson gave up ten hits but walked no one and struck out eight for the 6–3 victory. Jack Warhop took the loss.

The 1911 St. Louis City Championship Series

St. Louis Browns defeat St. Louis Cardinals; 4–3–1

By 1911, the St. Louis Browns (45–107) had become comfortably mired in the second division, finishing last for the second year in a row. The St. Louis Cardinals (75–74) had just broken the .500 mark for the first time since 1901 and the outlook was somewhat rosy for the 1912 season. The National Leaguers miscalculated by looking for the Browns to be an easy mark in the postseason championship.

Game One opened on the 11th of October at Sportsman's Park and was the most interesting contest of the series, going nine scoreless innings before darkness halted proceedings. Lou Lowdermilk (0–1) squared off against rookie Earl Hamilton (5–12) and although Lowdermilk pitched the better game, the end result was the same. The Cards outhit the Browns by a two-to-one margin, but four of their eight hits were of the infield variety. The Redbirds had the best scoring opportunity of the day in the first inning when Miller Huggins singled and Oakes bunted for a base hit, but the next three men in the order failed at the plate.

1911 St. Louis City Championship Series

```
GAME ONE --- October 11
```

CARDINALS	AB	H	PO	A	E		BROWNS	AB	H	PO	A	E
Huggins, 2b	4	1	3	3	0		Shotton, cf	3	2	2	0	0
Oakes, cf	4	2	1	0	0		Austin, 3b	4	0	1	3	0
Konetchy, 1b	4	1	14	1	0		Hogan, 1f	3	0	1	0	0
Evans, rf	4	1	5	0	0		LaPorte, 2b	3	0	0	2	0
Ellis, 1f	4	0	2	0	0		Compton, rf	2	0	2	0	0
Hauser, ss	4	0	1	1	0		Kutina, 1b	4	0	9	1	0
Mowrey, 3b	3	1	0	4	1		Hallinan, ss	4	0	6	1	0
Bliss, c	3	2	1	2	0		Stephens, c	3	1	6	1	0
Lowdermilk, p	3	0	0	3	2		Hamilton, p	3	1	0	1	0
							Schweitzer, ph	1	0	0	0	0
	33	8	27	14	3			30	4	27	9	0

```
STN   0  0  0    0  0  0     0  0  0  -  0
STA   0  0  0    0  0  0     0  0  0  -  0
```

SB: Huggins, Oakes, Konetchy, Kutina. DP: STN. BB: Lowdermilk 2. Struck out: Lowdermilk 2, Hamilton 6. Umpires: Perine and James Johnstone.

Game Two saw the Cardinals open up on Barney Pelty (7–15) for two runs in the first inning on singles by Huggins and Ed Konetchy and a double by Steve Evans. The Browns couldn't do anything until the fourth when Cardinal ace Bob Harmon (23–16) hit one of his characteristic wild streaks. (Harmon led the major leagues in walks with 181, eclipsing the American League leader, Gene Krapp, by a whopping 45 free passes.) Harmon walked Jimmy Austin who went to second on Willie Hogan's sacrifice bunt. A wild pitch sent Austin to third and walks to Frank LaPorte and Pete Compton loaded the bases. Joe Kutina's single tied the game. The Nationals scored the deciding run in the sixth when Mike Mowrey walked, stole second, and went to third on catcher Jim Stephens' wild throw. He scored on Miller Huggins's ground double to right.

The third game was a massacre, the home team Browns scoring in every inning but the second and winning easily, 10–2. The game-winning RBI, had their been such a silly statistic in 1911, came when Willie Hogan's sacrifice fly scored Burt Shotton in the third. Rookie Thomas "Lefty" George (4–9) had an easy time of it, scattering seven hits throughout the game. The Cardinals used Jacob "Rube" Geyer (9–6) and Roy Golden (4–9). A former member of the Negro League St. Louis Giants, an Indian named Watkins, pitched the final four innings for the Nationals.

The Browns again made short work of the Cardinals in Game Four, the first game of a doubleheader on the 15th. The Americans struck for five runs in the first three innings and won the game behind Joe Lake (10–15) by a 6–2 score. Lake gave up seven hits and three walks but was tough in the clutch, striking out eight. Bill Steele (18–19) started for the Cardinals and was knocked out in the four-run third after allowing five walks and two hits. Bob Harmon pitched the final six innings in relief.

The second game of the doubleheader was a wild affair. Lowdermilk and Hamilton were the starters, but were these the same two men who had pitched shutout ball in the first game of the series? In the top of the first, the Browns

1911 St. Louis City Championship Series

GAME TWO --- October 12

BROWNS	AB	H	PO	A	E		CARDINALS	AB	H	PO	A	E
Shotton, cf	4	0	2	0	0		Huggins, 2b	5	3	1	2	0
Austin, 3b	2	1	3	1	0		Oakes, cf	4	1	4	0	0
Hogan, lf	2	0	1	0	0		Konetchy, 1b	4	1	10	0	0
LaPorte, 2b	3	0	1	2	0		Evans, rf	4	2	2	0	0
Compton, rf	3	0	3	0	0		Ellis, lf	4	0	2	1	0
Kutina, 1b	4	3	6	0	0		Hauser, ss	3	0	2	4	0
Hallinan, ss	2	0	0	3	0		Mowrey, 3b	3	0	1	1	0
Stephens, c	3	1	8	0	1		Bliss, c	2	0	4	1	0
Pelty, p	3	0	0	1	0		Harmon, p	4	2	1	5	0
	26	5	24	7	1			33	9	27	14	0

```
STA   0  0  0    2  0  0    0  0  0  -  2
STN   2  0  0    0  0  1    0  0  x  -  3
```

2B: Evans, Huggins, Stephens. SB: Austin, Huggins, Oakes, Evans, Mowrey. DP: STN. BB: Pelty 3, Harmon 5. Struck out: Harmon 3, Pelty 6. WP: Harmon 2. Umpires: Johnstone and Perine.

GAME THREE --- October 14

CARDINALS	AB	H	PO	A	E		BROWNS	AB	H	PO	A	E
Huggins, 2b	5	2	4	3	0		Shotton, cf	5	4	2	0	0
Oakes, cf	5	0	2	0	0		Austin, 3b	4	0	2	4	0
Konetchy, 1b	5	2	7	0	0		Hogan, lf	3	2	1	0	1
Evans, rf	2	0	1	0	0		LaPorte, 2b	3	2	3	7	0
Ellis, lf	4	3	5	0	0		Compton, rf	4	1	2	0	0
Hauser, ss	4	0	1	5	1		Kutina, 1b	4	3	15	1	0
Mowrey, 3b	2	0	1	1	0		Hallinan, ss	3	0	0	2	1
Bliss, c	2	0	3	1	0		Krichell, c	3	1	0	2	0
Geyer, p	2	0	0	2	0		George, p	4	1	2	3	0
Golden, p	0	0	0	0	0							
Watkins, p	2	0	0	0	0			33	14	27	19	2
	33	7	24	12	1							

```
STN   1  0  0    0  1  0    0  0  0  -   2
STA   1  0  1    2  1  1    3  1  x  -  10
```

2B: Konetchy. 3B: Kutina. SB: Shotton 2, Konetchy, Mowrey, Hogan. DP: STA 1. BB: George 6, Geyer 1, Watkins 1, Golden 2. Struck out: Geyer 1, Watkins 1. WP: Geyer. Umpires: Johnstone and Perine.

scored once on a Willie Hogan double that scored Jimmy Austin. The Cardinals responded with four off Hamilton in the bottom of the inning. Huggins led off with a single and one out later found himself trapped off first base. Stephens's throw to Kutina went wild, however, and Huggins went all the way around to third. Konetchy and McIvor walked to load the bases and Arnold Hauser's single scored two. Hamilton's throwing error on Mowrey's grounder scored two more. The Browns scored once in the second and when the Cardinals netted two runs in the bottom of the inning, Lowdermilk went to the hill in the third with a 6–2 lead. LaPorte doubled and scored when Lowdermilk threw wild trying to retire Compton. Kutina's single scored Compton. Ed Hallinan beat out a hit and Paul Krichell walked to load the bases. In came

1911 St. Louis City Championship Series

GAME FOUR --- October 15

BROWNS	AB	H	PO	A	E		CARDINALS	AB	H	PO	A	E
Shotton, cf	5	0	0	0	0		Huggins, 2b	3	1	4	2	1
Austin, 3b	5	1	1	1	0		Oakes, cf	4	2	2	0	0
Hogan, lf	2	0	2	0	0		Konetchy, 1b	3	0	9	0	0
LaPorte, 2b	4	1	2	5	0		Evans, rf	3	1	0	0	0
Compton, rf	1	0	1	0	0		Ellis, lf	4	1	3	0	0
Kutina, 1b	3	1	12	0	0		Hauser, ss	4	0	0	6	0
Hallinan, ss	3	0	1	6	0		Mowrey, 3b	4	0	1	3	0
Stephens, c	3	1	8	1	0		Bliss, c	4	1	8	1	0
Lake, p	4	1	0	1	0		Steele, p	0	0	0	0	0
							Harmon, p	3	1	0	0	0
	30	5	27	14	0		Magee, ph	1	0	0	0	0
								33	7	27	12	1

```
STA   0  1  4    0  1  0    0  0  0  -  6
STN   0  0  2    0  0  0    0  0  0  -  2
```

2B: Kutina. BB: Steele 5, Harmon 2, Lake 3. Struck out: Steele 3, Harmon 4, Lake 8. Hits: Steele 2 in 2 innings. Umpires: Perine and Johnstone.

Rube Geyer to protect what was now a two-run lead. Pinch-hitter Jim Stephens singled to tie the game and after Shotton fanned, Jimmy Austin's single scored Krichell to put the Browns ahead, 7–6.

But the Cardinals were undaunted. With one out in the third, Hauser singled off reliever Roy Mitchell (4–8) and stole second. Mowrey singled to right and came around to score when Compton threw the ball into left field. After an uneventful inning in which both clubs paused to catch their breath, the Browns rallied again for three runs in the fifth. With Krichell on second, Shotton doubled home the tying run, Al Schweitzer singled, and LaPorte doubled for the final run of the game. The 90-minute ballgame was called at the end of five on account of darkness. Both teams, presumably, slept well that evening.

Game Six saw the Browns' lead in the series dwindle to one as Bill Steele and the Cardinals beat Lefty George, 9–5. George couldn't locate the plate in his only inning of work, walking Huggins and Oakes to start the game. Ed Konetchy's single put the Cards on the board and a walk to Evans loaded the bases. Player-manager Bobby Wallace had seen enough and replaced George with Jack Powell (8–19). Rube Ellis singled to right but Evans, who thought the ball was going to be caught, was forced at second. Konetchy scored a moment later on a passed ball. The Browns pecked away all afternoon long and had closed to within two in the ninth when the Cardinals scored three times off reliever Al "Red" Nelson (3–9) to go ahead 9–4. Six men had three hits in the game—Huggins, Oakes, Ellis, Jack Bliss, Austin, and Kutina—the Browns making a total of 10 safeties, the Cardinals 16. The final score was 9–5.

The Americans won the first game of a doubleheader played on the 17th of October by a 5–1 score. The game was a 1–1 pitcher's duel until the eighth inning when the Browns broke through against Bob Harmon for three runs and claimed the city championship. Pitcher Joe Lake started the fun with a one-out single and went to second on Shotton's base knock. Jimmy Austin's triple over

1911 St. Louis City Championship Series

GAME FIVE --- October 15 (second game)

BROWNS	AB	H	PO	A	E
Shotton, cf	3	2	2	0	0
Austin, 3b	4	1	1	1	1
Hogan, lf	2	1	0	0	0
Schweitzer, lf	2	1	0	0	0
LaPorte, 2b	4	2	1	3	0
Compton, rf	3	0	0	0	1
Kutina, 1b	3	2	8	0	0
Hallinan, ss	3	1	0	1	0
Krichell, c	1	1	3	2	1
Hamilton, p	1	0	0	0	1
Stephens, ph	1	1	0	0	0
Mitchell, p	1	0	0	1	0
	28	12	15	8	4

CARDINALS	AB	H	PO	A	E
Huggins, 2b	3	2	2	1	0
Oakes, cf	3	1	2	0	0
Konetchy, 1b	2	2	4	0	0
Evans, rf	1	0	0	1	1
Ellis, lf	2	0	2	0	0
Hauser, ss	3	2	0	1	0
Mowrey, 3b	3	1	1	1	0
Bliss, c	3	0	4	0	0
Lowdermilk, p	1	0	0	0	1
Geyer, p	1	0	0	0	0
	22	8	15	4	2

```
STA    1  1  5    0  3  - 10
STN    4  2  2    0  0  -  8
```

2B: Hogan, Oakes, LaPorte 2. SB: Austin 2, Konetchy 2, Stephens, Hauser, Schweitzer. BB: Hamilton 3, Lowdermilk 3. Struck out: Hamilton 2, Mitchell 1, Geyer 3. Hits: Hamilton 5 in 2 innings; Lowdermilk in 7 in 2 innings. PB: Bliss. Umpires: Perine and Johnstone.

GAME SIX --- October 16

BROWNS	AB	H	PO	A	E
Shotton, cf	4	0	2	0	1
Austin, 3b	5	3	4	2	0
Schweitzer, lf	4	2	0	1	1
LaPorte, 2b	5	1	1	2	0
Compton, rf	4	1	0	1	0
Kutina, 1b	5	3	10	1	0
Hallinan, ss	4	0	5	2	2
Stephens, c	1	0	5	5	0
George, p	0	0	0	0	0
Powell, p	2	0	0	3	0
Nelson, p	1	0	0	1	0
	35	10	27	18	4

CARDINALS	AB	H	PO	A	E
Huggins, 2b	4	2	2	5	0
Oakes, cf	4	2	1	0	0
Konetchy, 1b	5	2	14	0	0
Evans, rf	2	0	1	0	0
Wilie, rf	1	0	0	0	0
Ellis, lf	4	1	2	0	1
Hauser, ss	4	0	0	1	1
Mowrey, 3b	4	0	1	3	0
Bliss, c	5	1	6	0	0
Steele, p	3	1	0	4	0
	36	9	27	13	2

```
STN    3  2  0    1  0  0    0  0  3  - 9
STA    0  1  1    0  0  1    1  0  1  - 5
```

2B: Kutina, Konetchy. 3B: Kutina, Austin, Schweitzer. DP: STN 1, STA 1. BB: George 3, Nelson 2, Steele 5. Struck out: Steele 5, Powell 1, Nelson 2. WP: Powell. Umpires: Johnstone and Perine.

the head of center-fielder Oakes scored the go-ahead runs and LaPorte's single drove in Austin. The Browns tallied an insurance run in the ninth off reliever Rube Geyer. Lake went all the way, scattering seven hits and two walks and striking out seven.

In the nightcap, the Cardinals returned the compliment with a 5–1 victory of their own as Lowdermilk and Hamilton faced each other for the third time in the series. Lowdermilk had regained his form, but Hamilton was still searching for his. After the Browns struck for a first-inning run, the Cardinals took a lead they never relinquished in the bottom of the second. Hauser beat

1911 St. Louis City Championship Series

GAME SEVEN --- October 17

BROWNS	AB	H	PO	A	E		CARDINALS	AB	H	PO	A	E
Shotton, cf	4	3	1	0	0		Huggins, 2b	4	0	3	1	0
Austin, 3b	4	2	1	2	0		Oakes, cf	4	2	6	0	0
Schweitzer, lf	3	0	2	0	0		Konetchy, 1b	4	1	7	0	0
LaPorte, 2b	4	1	1	6	0		Evans, rf	4	0	0	0	1
Compton, rf	4	0	0	0	0		Ellis, lf	4	1	4	0	0
Kutina, 1b	4	1	13	0	0		Hauser, ss	4	0	1	4	0
Hallinan, ss	4	1	1	3	1		Mowrey, 3b	2	1	1	2	0
Stephens, c	4	1	8	2	0		Bliss, c	3	1	5	1	1
Lake, p	4	2	0	2	0		Harmon, p	2	1	0	2	0
							Geyer, p	0	0	0	0	0
	35	11	27	15	1		Magee, ph	1	0	0	0	0
								32	7	27	10	2

```
STA   0  1  0    0  0  0    0  3  1  -  5
STN   0  0  0    1  0  0    0  0  0  -  1
```

3B: Oakes, Austin. DP: STN. BB: Lake 2, Harmon 4. Struck out: Lake 7, Harmon 4, Geyer 1. Hits: Harmon 8 in 8 innings. Umpires: Perine and Johnstone.

GAME EIGHT --- October 17 (second game)

BROWNS	AB	H	PO	A	E		CARDINALS	AB	H	PO	A	E
Shotton, cf	3	0	4	0	0		Huggins, 2b	4	1	4	2	0
Austin, 3b	4	3	1	1	0		Oakes, cf	4	3	2	0	0
Schweitzer, lf	2	0	2	0	0		Konetchy, 1b	4	1	7	0	1
LaPorte, 2b	4	0	1	1	0		Evans, rf	4	0	1	0	0
Compton, rf	4	0	1	0	0		Ellis, lf	4	1	5	1	1
Kutina, 1b	4	0	9	0	0		Hauser, ss	4	1	3	4	0
Hallinan, ss	4	0	0	4	0		Magee, 3b	4	1	2	4	0
Krichell, c	4	2	6	0	0		Wingo, c	4	2	3	1	0
Hamilton, p	3	0	0	0	0		Lowdermilk, p	3	1	0	2	0
	32	5	24	6	0			35	11	27	14	2

```
STA   1  0  0    0  0  0    0  0  0  -  1
STN   0  2  0    3  0  0    0  0  x  -  5
```

2B: Austin, Ellis. 3B: Wingo, Austin, Lowdermilk. HR: Magee. SB: Compton. PB: Krichell. WP: Hamilton. BB: Lowdermilk 2. Struck out: Lowdermilk 2, Hamilton 2. Umpires: Johnstone and Perine.

out an infield hit and with two gone, Ivy Wingo's triple tied the game. Wingo scored on a passed ball. The Cardinals scored the last three runs of the series in the fourth on an inside-the-park home run by Lee Magee, a Wingo single, a Lowdermilk triple, and a wild pitch.

Joe Kutina was the undisputed hitting star of the series with 13 hits in 31 times at bat for a .419 batting average. The Cardinals' leading batter was Evans with a .406 batting average and 13 hits in 32 times at the plate.

1911 Chicago City Championship Series

GAME ONE --- October 13

CUBS	AB	H	PO	A	E
Evers, 2b	4	1	3	5	0
Sheckard, lf	3	1	2	0	0
Tinker, ss	3	1	5	5	0
Schulte, rf	4	2	1	0	0
Doyle, 3b	4	0	0	0	0
Saier, 1b	3	0	11	1	0
Hofman, cf	2	0	1	0	0
Archer, c	3	0	3	0	0
Brown, p	3	0	0	3	0
	29	5	*26	14	0

WHITE SOX	AB	H	PO	A	E
McConnell, 2b	4	2	4	2	0
Lord, 3b	4	1	0	1	0
McIntyre, rf	4	1	2	0	0
Bodie, cf	4	1	0	0	0
Callahan, lf	4	1	2	0	0
Tannnehill, ss	4	0	0	7	1
Zeider, 1b	4	2	13	0	0
Sullivan, c	1	1	4	0	0
Walsh, p	4	2	0	5	0
Dougherty, ph	1	0	0	0	0
Kreitz, c	1	1	1	0	0
	35	12	#26	15	1

* One out when winning run scored
\# Hofman out for interference

```
CUB   0  0  0    1  0  2    0  0  0  -  3
SOX   0  0  0    0  0  0    0  1  3  -  4
```

2B: Evers. 3B: Walsh. DP: Cubs 2. BB: Walsh 2. Struck out: Walsh 4, Brown 3. Umpires: Frank O'Loughlin and Hank O'Day.

1911 Chicago City Championship Series

Chicago White Sox defeat Chicago Cubs; 4–0

The 1911 Cubs (92–62) failed to repeat as pennant winners, losing out to the New York Giants by seven and a half games. As if the season hadn't ended on a low enough note, the Cubs then went out and got mauled four straight by the fourth-place White Sox (77–74) in the city championship series. After losing two hard-fought battles in the first games, the Nationals seemed to lose heart and went down to defeat easily in the final two contests.

Game One opened on the 13th of October at White Sox Park (later known as Comiskey Park) with Mordecai Brown (21–11) for the Cubs going against White Sox ace Ed Walsh (27–18). Had Walsh won one more game during the regular season he would have led the American League in wins and losses. A pretty amazing accomplishment — to be the best and the worst in the same year. The Cubs touched Big Ed for a run in the fourth and two in the sixth, but the White Sox scored once in the bottom of the eighth and rallied to drive home the winning run with one out in the ninth. Walsh took the victory, Brown the loss.

Game Two was played the next day at the home of the Cubs, West Side Park, and was a wild affair featuring 15 runs, 29 hits (12 for extra bases), ten strikeouts, nine bases on balls, and three double plays. The Cubs took a 1–0 lead in their half of the first, but the Sox went ahead with two in the second and increased their margin to 3–1 in the third. Five Cub runs in the bottom of the third put the Nationals up 6–3, but the Sox tied the game with one in the fifth and two in the sixth. The Cubs pulled ahead again with a solo run in the bottom of the sixth, but the Sox caught them and went ahead to stay with two in the

1911 Chicago City Championship Series

GAME TWO --- October 14

WHITE SOX	AB	H	PO	A	E		CUBS	AB	H	PO	A	E
McConnell, 2b	3	4	5	2	0		Evers, 2b	3	3	3	2	0
Lord, 3b	5	1	1	0	0		Sheckard, lf	5	1	4	0	0
McIntyre, rf	5	3	1	0	0		Tinker, ss	5	2	1	5	0
Bodie, cf	5	3	0	0	0		Schulte, rf	5	2	2	0	0
Callahan, lf	4	1	1	0	0		Doyle, 3b	2	0	1	1	0
Tannnehill, ss	3	0	3	1	0		Saier, 1b	4	1	10	0	2
Zeider, 1b	4	1	7	2	0		Hofman, cf	5	2	2	1	0
Sullivan, c	3	1	7	1	0		Archer, c	4	1	4	0	0
Scott, p	1	1	1	0	0		Richie, p	0	0	0	0	0
White, p	0	0	0	0	0		Reulbach, p	1	0	0	2	0
Benz, p	3	0	1	3	0		Smith, p	1	1	0	1	0
Walsh, p	0	0	0	1	0		Cheney, p	0	0	0	1	0
							Good, ph	1	0	0	0	0
	36	15	27	10	0		Zimmerman, ph	1	1	0	0	0
								37	14	27	13	2

```
SOX   0 2 1   0 1 2   0 2 0  -  8
CUB   1 0 5   0 0 1   0 0 0  -  7
```

2B: Evers 2, Schulte 2, Zeider, Hofman 2, Archer, Bodie, McIntyre, McConnell. 3B: McIntyre. DP: Cubs 2, Sox 1. BB: Richie 2, Scott 2, Benz 3, Reulbach 1, Cheney 1. Struck out: White 1, Benz 4, Smith 3, Walsh 2. SB: Callahan. Umpires: Frank O'Loughlin and Hank O'Day.

GAME THREE --- October 15

CUBS	AB	H	PO	A	E		WHITE SOX	AB	H	PO	A	E
Evers, 2b	4	0	1	1	0		McConnell, 2b	4	3	2	3	2
Sheckard, lf	3	2	0	0	0		Lord, 3b	4	1	1	0	0
Tinker, ss	4	1	2	5	0		McIntyre, rf	4	0	0	0	0
Schulte, rf	3	0	1	0	0		Bodie, cf	3	1	1	0	0
Doyle, 3b	3	1	3	4	0		Callahan, lf	3	0	4	0	0
Saier, 1b	2	0	8	1	0		Tannnehill, ss	4	2	2	5	0
Zimmerman, 2b	1	0	1	0	0		Zeider, 1b	4	1	10	1	0
Hoffman, cf	4	1	3	1	0		Sullivan, c	2	0	6	1	0
Archer, c	4	1	4	3	0		White, p	3	2	1	3	0
Cole, p	1	0	0	1	0			31	10	27	13	2
Graham, ph	1	0	0	0	0							
H.McIntyre, p	1	0	1	1	0							
Bransfield, ph	1	0	0	0	0							
	32	6	24	17	0							

```
CUB   0 0 0   1 0 0   0 1 0  -  2
SOX   0 0 2   0 0 1   1 0 x  -  4
```

2B: Sheckard, McConnell 2, Tannehill 2. BB: McIntyre 3, White 4. Struck out: Cole 2, McIntyre 1, White 5. Hits: Cole 4 in 3 innings. WP: McIntyre. PB: Archer. Umpires: Frank O'Loughlin and Hank O'Day. Att: 36,208.

eighth. Sox manager Hugh Duffy used four pitchers in the game—Jim Scott (14-11), Doc White (10-14), rookie Joe Benz (3-2), and Ed Walsh—and Cubs manager Frank Chance made an equal number of trips to the mound, using Lew Richie (15-11), Ed Reulbach (16-9), Charlie Smith (3-2), and Larry Cheney (1-0).

Game Three was played on the 15th at White Sox Park. Leonard "King" Cole (18-7) started for the Cubs and Doc White for the Sox. Cole was gone at the end of three, having given up four hits and two runs and a lead the White

1911 Chicago City Championship Series

GAME FOUR --- October 18

WHITE SOX	AB	H	PO	A	E		CUBS	AB	H	PO	A	E
McConnell, 2b	3	1	2	2	0		Evers, 2b	3	2	3	2	0
Lord, 3b	4	1	0	1	0		Sheckard, lf	4	0	3	0	0
McIntyre, rf	4	1	1	0	0		Tinker, ss	4	0	2	4	1
Bodie, cf	3	0	1	0	0		Schulte, rf	4	1	3	0	0
Callahan, lf	5	2	1	0	0		Doyle, 3b	3	1	2	0	0
Tannnehill, ss	5	2	3	5	1		Saier, 1b	2	0	7	0	0
Zeider, 1b	4	1	11	1	0		Hofman, cf	4	0	3	0	0
Sullivan, c	4	2	7	0	0		Archer, c	4	0	4	4	0
Walsh, p	4	2	1	2	0		Brown, p	1	0	0	1	0
							Good, ph	1	1	0	0	0
	36	12	27	11	1		Cheney, p	1	0	1	0	0
							Zimmerman, ph	1	0	0	0	0
								32	5	28	11	1

```
SOX    2  0  2    0  2  1    0  0  0  -  7
CUB    1  0  0    0  1  0    0  0  0  -  2
```

2B: McIntyre, Tannehill. SB: Schulte, Saier, Evers, Bodie. DP: Cubs. BB: Walsh 3, Brown 2, Cheney 3. Struck out: Brown 1, Walsh 7, Cheney 3. Hits: Brown 11 in 5 innings. Umpires: Frank O'Loughlin and Hank O'Day.

Sox never relinquished. White allowed six hits and four walks, but the Cubs were never able to string together a sustained offense and scored only single runs in the fourth and eighth. The attendance for the game was 36,208, the largest crowd ever to watch a baseball game in Chicago to that point. In fact, the four games drew a total of 99,359, which was a very healthy figure for a four-game series 77 years ago.

The White Sox closed out the 1911 city championship with an easy 7–2 win behind Ed Walsh on the 18th of October at West Side Park. Mordecai Brown started for the Cubs, but was relieved by Larry Cheney after giving up 11 hits and six runs in five innings. Walsh held the Cubs to five hits and single runs in the first and fifth in recording the victory. Every man in the White Sox lineup hit safely, except for center-fielder Ping Bodie.

1911 Ohio State Championship Series

Cincinnati Reds defeat Cleveland Naps; 4–2

The sixth-place Cincinnati Reds (70–83) sported a starting lineup which featured no .300 hitters and a thoroughly unremarkable pitching staff. The third-place Cleveland Naps (80–73), on the other hand, had "Shoeless Joe" Jackson and Napoleon Lajoie. Jackson twirled the bat well enough to compile a .408 batting average, yet didn't even win the batting title. That honor went to Tyrus Raymond Cobb who abused the beleaguered pitching staffs of seven American League clubs for a .420 mark. From 1903 through 1911, the Cleveland team was nicknamed the Naps, after their popular star second baseman. They eventually settled on the "Indians," a nickname taken from Louis Francis Sockalexis, the first American Indian to reach the major leagues.

1911 Ohio State Championship Series

GAME ONE --- October 10

CLEVELAND NAPS	AB	H	PO	A	E		CINCINNATI	AB	H	PO	A	E
Graney, lf	2	1	1	0	0		Bescher, lf	3	2	0	0	0
Olson, ss	4	0	1	3	0		Hoblitzell, 1b	3	1	12	0	0
Jackson, rf	4	0	1	0	0		Bates, cf	4	3	3	0	0
Lajoie, 1b	4	1	10	0	0		Mitchell, rf	4	2	2	1	0
Birmingham, cf	4	0	3	0	0		Egan, 2b	3	0	3	4	0
Ball, 2b	4	2	2	1	0		Esmond, ss	4	1	2	4	0
Turner, 3b	4	2	2	0	0		Grant, 3b	3	0	1	2	0
O'Neill, c	2	0	4	5	0		Clarke, c	2	0	4	1	0
Blanding, p	2	0	0	2	0		Suggs, p	2	0	0	2	0
Falkenberg, p	0	0	0	0	0							
Easterly, ph	1	0	0	0	0			28	9	27	14	0
	31	6	24	11	0							

```
CLE    0  0  0    0  0  0    0  0  0  -  0
CIN    2  0  0    0  1  1    0  0  x  -  4
```

2B: Bescher 2, Mitchell, Bates. DP: CIN 1, CLE 1. BB: Suggs 3, Blanding 3. Hits: Blanding 8 in 7 innings. Balk: Blanding. WP: Blanding 2. Umpires: Charles Rigler and William Evans.

GAME TWO --- October 13

CINCINNATI	AB	H	PO	A	E		CLEVELAND NAPS	AB	H	PO	A	E
Bescher, lf	5	2	1	0	0		Butcher, lf	4	1	3	0	0
Hoblitzell, 1b	4	2	10	0	0		Olson, ss	4	1	1	3	0
Bates, cf	4	0	1	0	0		Jackson, rf	4	3	0	0	2
Mitchell, rf	3	1	3	2	0		Lajoie, 1b	3	0	14	2	0
Marsans, rf	0	0	0	0	0		Birmingham, cf	3	1	2	1	0
Egan, 2b	3	0	3	1	0		Ball, 2b	3	0	0	3	0
Esmond, ss	4	1	4	5	0		Turner, 3b	4	1	0	3	0
Grant, 3b	4	2	1	1	0		O'Neill, c	2	1	5	0	0
Clarke, c	5	3	4	0	0		Kahler, p	2	0	1	4	0
Benton, p	5	1	0	3	0		Stovall, ph	1	0	0	0	0
	37	12	27	12	0		W.Mitchell, p	0	0	0	0	0
							Falkenberg, p	0	0	1	0	0
							Hendrix, ph	1	0	0	0	0
								31	8	27	16	2

```
CIN    0  0  0    0  0  0    2  8  0  -  10
CLE    0  0  0    0  0  0    1  1  0  -   2
```

2B: Hobitzell. 3B: Grant. SB: Bates. DP: CIN 2, CLE 1. BB: Benton 2, Kahler, 2, Mitchell 2, Falkenberg 1. Struck out: Benton 4, Kahler 4. Hits: Kahler 6 in 7 innings; Falkenberg 4 in 2 innings. PB: Clarke. Umpires: William Evans and Charles Rigler.

The Naps clearly had the better team in 1911 and oddsmakers favored them in the series.

Game One was held on the 10th of October at Cincinnati's Palace of the Fans, only the second ballpark in the major leagues to use iron and cement in its foundation and superstructure. (The first was the Baker Bowl in Philadelphia.) The Palace of the Fans had the lowest number of box seats in the major leagues and was razed after the 1911 season to make way for the more spacious Redland Field (Crosley Field). The Reds hit Fred Blanding (7–11) for two runs in the first inning and that proved to be all they needed as George Suggs (15–13) went on to post a six-hit shutout. Cincinnati scored insurance

1911 Ohio State Championship Series

```
GAME THREE --- October 14
```

CINCINNATI	AB	H	PO	A	E
Bescher, lf	4	1	6	1	0
Hoblitzell, 1b	3	2	6	0	0
Bates, cf	4	1	5	0	0
Marsans, rf	5	3	2	0	0
Egan, 2b	6	2	4	0	0
Esmond, ss	5	1	4	3	0
Grant, 3b	5	2	0	3	1
McLean, c	2	0	3	0	0
Almeida, ph	1	0	0	0	0
Gaspar, p	3	3	0	1	0
Downey, ph	1	0	0	0	0
Clarke, c	1	0	3	0	0
Fromme, p	1	0	0	0	0
	41	15	33	8	1

CLEVELAND NAPS	AB	H	PO	A	E
Butcher, lf	4	0	2	0	0
Olson, ss	5	1	6	4	2
Jackson, rf	5	1	3	1	1
Lajoie, 1b	5	1	12	2	0
Birmingham, cf	5	1	1	0	0
Ball, 2b	4	1	2	2	0
Turner, 3b	5	1	1	5	0
Easterly, c	4	1	6	5	0
Krapp, p	2	1	0	4	0
Baskette, p	1	0	0	1	0
	40	8	33	24	3

```
CIN   0  0  0    0  1  0    0  0  4    0  2  -  7
CLE   0  0  0    0  0  2    2  1  0    0  0  -  5
```

2B: Krapp, Birmingham, Jackson, Lajoie, Gaspar, Bates, Hoblitzell. SB: Jackson, Ball. BB: Gaspar 3, Krapp 9. Struck out: Krapp 7, Gaspar 2, Fromme 3. Hits: Gaspar 6 in 8 innings; Krapp 10 in 8.1 innings. HBP: Bescher (Krapp). Umpires: William Evans and Charles Rigler.

```
GAME FOUR --- October 14 (second game)
```

CINCINNATI	AB	H	PO	A	E
Bescher, lf	3	1	2	0	0
Hoblitzell, 1b	3	2	7	0	1
Bates, cf	3	0	0	0	0
Marsans, rf	3	0	1	0	0
Egan, 2b	3	2	2	1	0
Esmond, ss	3	0	0	2	0
Grant, 3b	1	1	0	0	0
Clarke, c	2	0	3	2	0
Humphries, p	2	0	0	1	0
Boyd, p	0	0	0	1	0
	23	6	15	7	1

CLEVELAND NAPS	AB	H	PO	A	E
Butcher, lf	3	1	1	0	0
Olson, ss	3	2	2	1	0
Jackson, rf	3	2	0	0	0
Lajoie, 1b	2	1	6	0	0
Birmingham, cf	3	1	2	0	0
Ball, 2b	2	1	2	1	0
Turner, 3b	3	1	0	0	0
Easterly, c	3	0	5	2	0
James, p	2	0	0	3	0
	24	9	18	7	0

```
CIN   0  0  0    0  0  1  -  1
CLE   0  1  1    0  3  x  -  5
```

2B: Lajoie, Hoblitzell, Egan. SB: Ball, Jackson, Easterly, Egan. BB: Humphries 1, Boyd 1, James 1. Struck out: James 6, Humphries 1. Hits: Humphries 6 in 5 innings. PB: Easterly, Clarke. WP: Boyd 2. DP: CIN. Umpires: William Evans and Charles Rigler.

runs in the fifth and sixth and struck for eight hits off Blanding in his seven innings of work and one hit off Cy Falkenberg (8–5) in the eighth.

The second game, played three days later, was a nail-biter for the first six innings. The game was scoreless until Cincinnati came to the plate in the seventh and scored two runs off losing pitcher George Kahler (9–8). The Naps cut the lead in half in the bottom of the inning with a run off Rube Benton (3–3), but Cincinnati exploded for eight runs against Cy Falkenberg in the eighth. Benton went all the way in notching the victory.

Games Three and Four were scheduled as a doubleheader on the 14th of

1911 Ohio State Championship Series

GAME FIVE --- October 15

CINCINNATI	AB	H	PO	A	E		CLEVELAND NAPS	AB	H	PO	A	E
Bescher, lf	4	0	6	0	2		Butcher, lf	4	0	4	0	0
Hoblitzell, 1b	4	1	2	0	0		Olson, ss	4	1	1	1	2
Bates, cf	3	0	1	0	1		Jackson, rf	3	1	1	0	0
Marsans, rf	3	0	1	0	0		Lajoie, 1b	3	1	9	1	1
Egan, 2b	4	1	0	1	0		Birmingham, cf	4	1	1	0	0
Esmond, ss	4	1	1	0	0		Ball, 2b	4	0	1	1	0
Grant, 3b	4	1	2	1	0		Turner, 3b	2	1	0	6	0
Clarke, c	3	0	11	1	0		O'Neill, c	3	1	9	1	0
Keefe, p	1	1	0	0	0		Kahler, p	3	2	1	1	0
Fromme, p	1	0	0	0	0							
Severeid, ph	1	0	0	0	0			30	8	27	1i	3
	32	5	24	3	3							

```
CIN   0  1  0    0  0  0    1  0  0  -  2
CLE   0  2  0    2  0  0    0  0  x  -  4
```

2B: Esmond, Grant, Birmingham. SB: Marsans. BB: Kahler 1, Keefe 2. Struck out: Kahler 6, Keefe 4, Fromme 6. Hits: Keefe 8 in 3.2 innings. PB: O'Neill, Clarke. Umpires: William Evans and Charles Rigler.

GAME SIX --- October 15 (second game)

CINCINNATI	AB	H	PO	A	E		CLEVELAND NAPS	AB	H	PO	A	E
Bescher, lf	5	1	1	0	0		Butcher, lf	4	1	2	0	0
Hoblitzell, 1b	2	1	13	0	0		Olson, ss	4	1	0	4	0
Bates, cf	3	0	1	0	0		Jackson, rf	2	0	2	0	0
Marsans, rf	2	1	2	0	0		Lajoie, 1b	3	1	14	0	0
Egan, 2b	3	1	1	4	0		Birmingham, cf	2	0	4	0	0
Esmond, ss	4	0	2	2	0		Ball, 2b	3	1	1	1	0
Grant, 3b	2	1	2	4	0		Turner, 3b	3	0	0	1	0
Clarke, c	2	1	2	1	0		O'Neill, c	3	0	0	0	0
Suggs, p	4	0	0	2	0		Blanding, p	0	0	0	1	0
	27	6	24	13	0		Mitchell, p	0	0	1	1	0
							James, p	1	0	0	0	0
							Baskette, p	1	0	0	1	0
							Easterly, ph	1	0	0	0	0
								27	4	24	9	0

```
CIN   4  0  2    0  0  0    1  0  -  7
CLE   0  0  0    0  0  0    0  0  -  0
```

SB: Bescher, Egan 2, Marsans, Hoblitzell 2. BB: Mitchell 6, James 1, Suggs 1, Baskette 3. Struck out: Suggs 2. Hits: Blanding 5 in 0.2 innings; Baskette 1 in 3 innings. WP: James. Umpires: Charles Rigler and William Evans.

October. The third game was the most exciting of the series. The Reds took a 1–0 lead in the fifth, but the Naps went ahead 5–1 with two runs in the sixth, two in the seventh, and one in the eighth. But Cincinnati wouldn't give up, scoring four in the ninth to pull even with a surprised Cleveland bunch. Two more runs in the eleventh, and the Reds had won their third game in a row. Rookie Gene Krapp (13–9) started on the hill for the Naps and looked like he might take home a victory until the Reds knocked him out of the box with one out in the ninth. Rookie Jim Baskette (1–2) worked the final two and two-thirds innings in relief and took the loss. Harry Gaspar (10–17) started for the Reds, but gave way in the ninth to Art Fromme (10–11), who was the winning pitcher.

The nightcap was abbreviated because of darkness but Cleveland captured their first game of the series, beating Bert Humphries (4–3) by a score of 5–1.

Games Five and Six were a doubleheader played the next day. In the first game, Cincinnati's Bob Keefe (12–13) went against George Kahler. The Reds scored first when they took a 1–0 lead in the second inning, but Cleveland came back with two of their own in their half to go ahead 2–1. The Naps tallied two more in the fourth off Keefe and reliever Art Fromme. Kahler was never in danger from there on as he finished with a five-hitter, striking out six and walking only one.

The Reds took the championship in the nightcap as they blasted Fred Blanding off the mound in the first. Blanding gave up five hits and four runs in two-thirds of an inning and the issue was never in doubt. Cincinnati scored two runs when reliever Willie Mitchell (7–14) failed to retire anyone in the third and an insurance run off Jim Baskette in the seventh. In between Mitchell and Baskette, rookie Bill James (2–4) pitched a scoreless, hitless three innings. Winning pitcher George Suggs went the distance in this eight-inning game, allowing four hits and a walk, and striking out two.

The 1912 St. Louis City Championship Series

St. Louis Cardinals defeat St. Louis Browns; 4–3–1

The bad St. Louis Cardinals (63–90) and the worse St. Louis Browns (53–101), two deep-dish second division clubs, met after the 1912 season to determine the championship of St. Louis. Despite the obvious shortcomings of the two teams, this championship turned out to be one of the best ever, with the Cardinals ultimately enjoying the distinction of winning the only 1912 postseason series for the National League. American League entries had won city championships in Chicago and Philadelphia, and the Giants had been vanquished by the Boston Braves in the World Series.

Cardinal pitcher Bob Harmon (18–18) faced off against Earl Hamilton (11–14) in Game One. Hamilton was trailing 3–1 when Browns manager George Stovall lifted him for a pinch-hitter in the sixth. The Browns rallied for four runs and a 5–3 lead. A run in the seventh increased their margin to three, but reliever Mack Allison (6–17) couldn't stand prosperity. Three Cardinal runs in the eighth tied the game and a two-out bases-loaded walk in the bottom of the tenth won it. Rube Geyer (7–14) pitched in relief of Hamilton and got the victory.

Sandy Burk (1–3 with the Cardinals) and George Baumgardner (11–14) took the mound for Game Two, another close contest. Baumgardner pitched five innings and hit the showers after the Browns tied the game at two all. His relief, Roy Mitchell (3–4), allowed just two hits over the next four innings, but one of those resulted in the eighth-inning run that decided the game. Light hitting marked this contest as the Browns had six hits, the Cardinals only five.

1912 St. Louis City Championship Series

GAME ONE --- October 9

BROWNS	AB	R	H	PO	A	E		CARDINALS	AB	R	H	PO	A	E
Shotton, cf	6	0	2	3	0	0		Huggins, 2b	3	1	0	2	4	0
Williams, rf	3	0	0	0	0	0		Magee, lf	4	0	1	0	0	1
Brief, ss	5	0	1	4	0	0		Mowrey, 3b	4	1	1	1	0	0
Pratt, 2b	3	1	0	1	4	0		Konetchy, 1b	3	2	2	10	1	0
Stovall, 1b	4	2	2	12	1	0		Evans, rf	5	3	3	2	1	0
Wallace, ss	4	1	3	1	2	0		Hauser, ss	4	0	0	4	4	1
Austin, 3b	4	0	0	3	4	1		Oakes, cf	4	0	0	1	0	0
Alexander, c	1	0	0	1	0	0		Bresnahan, c	1	0	0	5	3	0
Stephens, c	3	1	0	3	2	0		Wingo, c	3	0	1	4	0	1
Hamilton, p	2	0	1	0	1	0		Harmon, p	1	0	0	1	2	0
Allison, p	2	0	1	1	0	0		Geyer, p	1	0	0	0	1	0
Hogan, ph	1	1	1	0	0	0		Ellis, ph	1	0	0	0	0	0
								Bliss, ph	0	0	0	0	0	0
	38	6	11	*29	14	1			34	7	8	30	16	3

*　Two out when winning run scored

```
STA    0  0  0    1  0  4    1  0  0    0  -  6
STN    1  0  2    0  0  0    0  3  0    1  -  7
```

　　2B: Evans. 3B: Evans. SH: Magee, Hauser. SB: Austin, Konetchy. LOB: STA 12, STN 9. DP: STA 2, STN 1. BB: Hamilton 4, Geyer 1, Harmon 8, Allison 5. Struck out: Harmon 5, Geyer 2, Hamilton 2. Umpires: Finneran and O'Brien. Time—2:30.

GAME TWO --- October 10

CARDINALS	AB	R	H	PO	A	E		BROWNS	AB	R	H	PO	A	E
Huggins, 2b	1	0	0	3	3	0		Shotton, cf	2	0	0	1	0	0
Magee, lf	4	0	1	3	0	0		Hogan, rf	4	0	0	4	0	0
Mowrey, 3b	3	1	0	3	0			Brief, ss	4	0	1	1	0	0
Konetchy, 1b	4	0	1	15	0	0		Pratt, 2b	4	0	0	3	4	0
Evans, rf	3	0	2	1	0	0		Stovall, 1b	4	0	1	10	2	1
Hauser, ss	3	1	0	2	3	1		Wallace, ss	4	1	0	2	1	0
Oakes, cf	3	1	0	1	0	0		Austin, 3b	4	1	2	1	3	0
Wingo, c	4	0	0	1	1	0		Stephens, c	3	0	0	4	3	0
Burk, p	4	0	0	1	4	0		Baumgardner, p	1	0	1	1	0	0
								Mitchell, p	1	0	1	0	2	0
	29	3	5	27	14	1		Compton, ph	1	0	0	0	0	0
									32	2	6	27	15	1

```
STN    0  0  0    0  2  0    0  1  0  -  3
STA    0  1  0    0  1  0    0  0  0  -  2
```

　　2B: Austin, Brief. LOB: STN 6, STA 6. DP: STN 2. BB: Burk 3, Mitchell 1, Baumgardner 6. Hits: Baumgardner 3 in 5 innings; Mitchell 2 in 4 innings. WP: Burk. Umpires: O'Brien and Finneran. Time—2:00.

　　Rookie Carl Weilman (2–4) threw a masterful one-hit shutout against the Cardinals in Game Three. In years to come, Weilman would exert a mastery over his National League rivals the likes of which has rarely been seen, and this game got him off to a rousing start. The only Cardinal hit was a single by right-fielder Steve Evans. The Browns, meanwhile, batted out ten hits and four runs against Cardinal pitchers Bob Harmon and Rube Geyer. Single runs in the third and fifth, and two runs in the eighth, decided the game.

1912 St. Louis City Championship Series

GAME THREE --- October 12

CARDINALS	AB	R	H	PO	A	E
Huggins, 2b	3	0	0	4	1	0
Magee, lf	2	0	0	0	0	0
Mowrey, 3b	4	0	0	1	4	0
Konetchy, 1b	4	0	0	12	1	0
Evans, rf	3	0	1	0	0	0
Hauser, ss	3	0	0	1	5	0
Oakes, cf	2	0	0	4	0	0
Bresnahan, c	3	0	0	4	5	0
Harmon, p	2	0	0	1	2	0
Geyer, p	0	0	0	0	0	0
Bliss, ph	1	0	0	0	0	0
	27	0	1	27	18	0

BROWNS	AB	R	H	PO	A	E
Shotton, cf	4	1	3	1	0	0
Hogan, rf	3	0	0	1	0	0
Brief, lf	4	0	1	4	0	0
Pratt, 2b	4	0	1	1	1	0
Stovall, 1b	4	1	1	7	2	0
Wallace, ss	4	0	0	2	4	0
Austin, 3b	3	0	1	1	0	0
Alexander, c	3	1	1	8	0	0
Weilman, p	3	1	2	2	2	0
	32	4	10	27	9	0

```
STN   0 0 0   0 0 0   0 0 0  -  0
STA   0 0 1   0 1 0   0 2 0  -  4
```

2B: Alexander, Stovall, Evans, Shotton. LOB: STA 3, STN 4. DP: STN. BB: Weilman 4, Harmon 2. Struck out: Weilman 6, Harmon 5. Hits: Harmon 10 in 8 innings. Umpires: Finneran and O'Brien. Time.1:45.

GAME FOUR --- October 13

BROWNS	AB	R	H	PO	A	E
Shotton, cf	4	0	0	0	0	1
Hogan, rf	3	0	0	4	0	0
Brief, lf	3	0	0	3	0	0
Pratt, 2b	3	1	0	1	4	0
Stovall, 1b	4	1	1	12	1	1
Wallace, ss	4	0	0	2	2	0
Austin, 3b	4	0	2	1	1	0
Alexander, c	2	0	0	6	1	1
Hamilton, p	3	0	0	1	3	0
Compton, ph	1	0	0	0	0	0
	31	2	3	30	12	3

CARDINALS	AB	R	H	PO	A	E
Huggins, 2b	3	0	0	4	2	0
Magee, lf	4	0	0	0	1	1
Mowrey, 3b	4	0	0	0	2	0
Konetchy, 1b	5	0	3	14	1	0
Evans, rf	4	1	1	1	1	0
Hauser, ss	3	0	0	0	3	1
Oakes, cf	4	0	1	2	0	0
Bresnahan, c	3	0	1	9	3	0
Steele, p	3	1	1	0	4	0
	33	2	7	30	17	2

```
STA   0 0 1   1 0 0   0 0 0   0  -  2
STN   0 0 0   2 0 0   0 0 0   0  -  2
```

2B: Oakes, Evans, Konetchy. SH: Alexander, Huggins, Magee, Hauser, Evans, Steele. SB: Pratt. LOB: STA 3, STN 9. DP: STN 1. BB: Hamilton 3, Steele 3. Struck out: Hamilton 5, Steele 9. WP: Steele, Hamilton. PB: Bresnahan. Umpires: O'Brien and Finnerman. Time—2:10.

Game Four was a pitcher's duel as spitballer Bill Steele (9–13) and Earl Hamilton stood toe-to-toe for ten innings to no resolution. Steele pitched the stronger game, giving up just three singles, three walks, and striking out nine men in his ten innings. But Hamilton, who gave up seven hits, three walks and struck out five, matched him where it counted—the runs column. The Cardinals scored singletons in the third and fourth, but the Browns tied the game with a two-run fourth of their own. The game stayed deadlocked for the next six innings until called because of darkness.

Game Five was not a pitcher's duel. After the Browns took a brief one-run

1912 St. Louis City Championship Series

GAME FIVE --- October 14

BROWNS	AB	R	H	PO	A	E		CARDINALS	AB	R	H	PO	A	E
Shotton, cf	4	2	1	2	0	1		Huggins, 2b	4	1	1	2	6	0
Williams, rf	4	1	2	0	0	1		Magee, lf	4	2	1	4	0	0
Brief, lf	4	1	1	1	1	1		Mowrey, 3b	4	1	1	0	2	0
Pratt, 2b	5	0	2	1	4	1		Konetchy, 1b	2	1	1	10	0	0
Stovall, 1b	5	0	0	7	0	0		Evans, rf	4	2	2	2	0	0
Wallace, ss	4	0	3	5	5	0		Hauser, ss	4	0	1	2	3	0
Austin, 3b	4	0	0	3	1	0		Oakes, cf	3	2	2	1	0	0
Stephens, c	3	0	0	4	1	0		Wingo, c	4	1	2	6	0	0
Powell, p	0	0	0	0	1	0		Burk, p	1	0	0	0	1	0
Mitchell, p	1	0	1	0	2	0		Griner, p	3	0	1	0	0	0
Napier, p	2	0	0	0	2	0			33	10	12	27	12	0
	36	4	10	*23	17	4								

* Huggins out, hit by batted ball

```
STA    1  0  0    0  2  0    0  0  1   -   4
STN    5  0  3    1  0  1    0  0  x   -  10
```

2B: Pratt, Evans, Oakes. SH: Brief, Konetchy. SB: Shotton, Pratt. LOB: STA 10, STN 5. BB: Powell 1, Griner 1, Burk 3, Napier 3, Mitchell 2. Struck out: Burk 1, Napier 2, Griner 4. Hits: Powell 5 in ⅔ inning; Mitchell 6 in 3.1 innings; Napier 1 in 4 innings; Burk 2 in 1.1 innings; Griner 8 in 7.2 innings. Umpires: Finneran and O'Brien. Time—2:05.

GAME SIX --- October 15

CARDINALS	AB	R	H	PO	A	E		BROWNS	AB	R	H	PO	A	E
Huggins, 2b	5	0	0	0	4	0		Shotton, cf	4	1	3	3	0	0
Magee, lf	5	0	1	2	0	0		Williams, rf	4	1	2	0	0	1
Mowrey, 3b	3	0	0	2	4	0		Brief, lf	3	0	0	2	0	0
Konetchy, 1b	3	1	1	10	0	0		Pratt, 2b	3	0	0	2	3	0
Evans, rf	3	0	2	2	1	0		Stovall, 1b	3	0	0	5	0	0
Hauser, ss	4	0	1	2	4	0		Wallace, ss	3	0	0	4	1	1
Oakes, cf	3	0	2	2	0	0		Austin, 3b	3	0	0	1	0	0
Wingo, c	4	0	0	4	0	0		Alexander, c	2	1	1	10	1	0
Sallee, p	3	0	0	0	1	0		Baumgardner, p	2	0	0	0	2	0
Ellis, ph	1	0	1	0	0	0			27	3	6	27	7	2
	34	1	8	24	14	0								

```
STN    0  0  0    1  0  0    0  0  0   -  1
STA    0  0  0    0  1  0    0  2  x   -  3
```

2B: Magee, Ellis. 3B: Shotton. HR: Williams. SH: Brief. LOB: STN: 10, STA 4. DP: STA 1, STN 1. BB: Baumgardner 4, Sallee 3. Struck out: Baumgardner 10, Sallee 3. Umpires: Finnerman and O'Brien. Time—1:40.

lead in the top of the first, the Cardinals struck for five runs on five hits off Jack Powell (9–16) in their half of the frame and were never headed. The 38-year-old Powell was pitching his last game for a major league club and lasted only two-thirds of an inning. The Nationals continued their hot hitting with five more runs off relievers Roy Mitchell and rookie Buddy Napier (1–2) and won the game, 10–4. Staked to the big lead, Cardinal starting pitcher Sandy Burk was saved for another day and pitched only the first inning and a third. His relief, Dan Griner (3–4), finished the game.

1912 St. Louis City Championship Series

GAME SEVEN --- October 15 (second game)

BROWNS	AB	R	H	PO	A	E		CARDINALS	AB	R	H	PO	A	E
Shotton, cf	4	2	2	3	0	0		Huggins, 2b	4	0	2	3	4	0
Williams, rf	4	0	2	1	0	0		Magee, lf	4	0	1	2	0	0
Brief, lf	4	0	2	1	0	0		Mowrey, 3b	4	0	0	1	2	0
Pratt, 2b	4	0	1	4	0	0		Konetchy, 1b	4	0	3	9	0	0
Stovall, 1b	4	0	0	12	1	0		Evans, rf	3	0	0	1	0	0
Wallace, ss	4	0	3	1	8	0		Hauser, ss	3	0	0	1	2	0
Austin, 3b	2	0	0	0	4	0		Oakes, cf	3	0	0	0	0	1
Alexander, c	3	0	0	3	0	0		Bresnahan, c	3	0	0	6	0	0
Weilman, p	3	0	0	2	4	0		Harmon, p	2	0	0	1	2	0
								Burk, p	0	0	0	0	0	0
	32	2	10	27	17	0		Bliss, ph	1	0	0	0	0	0
									31	0	6	24	10	1

STN	0	0	0	0	0	0	0	0	0	-	0
STA	1	0	0	0	0	0	1	0	x	-	2

2B: Williams. SH: Austin, Evans. SB: Shotton. LOB: STA 7, STN 5. DP: STA 1, STN 1. Struck out: Harmon 6, Weilman 2. WP: Harmon. Hits: Harmon 10 in 7 innings. Umpires: O'Brien and Finnerman. Time—1:40.

GAME EIGHT --- October 16

BROWNS	AB	R	H	PO	A	E		CARDINALS	AB	R	H	PO	A	E
Shotton, cf	4	0	1	3	0	0		Huggins, 2b	4	1	0	2	3	0
Williams, rf	4	0	1	0	0	0		Magee, lf	4	0	0	3	0	0
Brief, lf	4	0	0	2	0	0		Mowrey, 3b	3	1	1	1	2	0
Pratt, 2b	4	0	0	2	3	1		Konetchy, 1b	3	2	1	14	1	0
Stovall, 1b	4	0	0	14	0	1		Evans, rf	3	2	1	1	0	0
Wallace, ss	2	0	1	0	4	0		Hauser, ss	3	0	1	1	6	1
Austin, 3b	2	0	0	1	2	0		Oakes, cf	3	0	2	1	0	0
Alexander, c	2	1	0	3	0	0		Wingo, c	3	0	0	4	2	0
Compton, ph	0	0	0	0	1	0		Steele, p	4	0	1	0	3	0
Hamilton, p	2	0	1	0	2	0			30	6	7	27	17	1
Hogan, ph	1	0	0	0	0	0								
Stephens, c	0	0	0	0	0	0								
Allison, p	0	0	0	0	0	0								
	29	1	4	27	12	2								

STN	1	0	0	1	0	3	0	1	0	-	6
STA	0	0	1	0	0	0	0	0	0	-	1

2B: Steele. 3B: Shotton. SH: Hauser, Magee, Oakes, Wingo, Austin. DP: STA 2, STN 1. SB: Konetchy, Evans, Oakes. BB: Hamilton 3, Steele 2. Struck out: Steele 5, Hamilton 3. Hits: Hamilton 7 in 8 innings. LOB: STN 5, STA 4. Umpires: O'Brien and Finnerman. Time—1:35.

Slim Sallee (16–17) got his first start of the series against George Baumgardner in Game Six, another pitcher's duel. The Cardinals struck first, with a run in the fourth, but Gus Williams tied the score with a solo home run in the fifth. Both pitchers were on their game and the score was tied 1–1 into the bottom of the eighth when the Browns scored twice off Sallee for the victory. Baumgardner shut down the Cardinal offense on eight hits, striking out ten.

The Browns squared the series in Game Seven as Carl Weilman pitched his second shutout in his second start, winning 2–0. Weilman was a little freer with the hits this time, giving up six hits, all singles. Burt Shotton scored in the first to give the rookie all the offensive support he needed. Bob Harmon lost his second game of the series, pitching the first seven innings before being relieved by Burk in the eighth.

Bill Steele was rematched with Earl Hamilton for the deciding game of the championship. Unlike Game Four, this contest was a pitcher's duel only through five innings. The Cards had a 2–1 lead when they struck for three runs off Hamilton in the sixth. The final score was 6–1. Steele went the distance, giving up four hits, two walks, and striking out five for the victory. One gets the feeling that had manager George Stovall given Weilman three starts instead of two, the Browns might have won the series.

The 1912 Chicago City Championship Series

Chicago White Sox defeat Chicago Cubs; 4–3–2

The 1912 third-place Chicago Cubs (91–59) had a better record than in the previous year, but dropped one place in the standings nevertheless. The mediocre White Sox (78–76) were underdogs in this unusual series which took nine games to complete because of ties in the first two games. Despite taking a three-games-to-none lead, the Cubs saw the Sox deliver four stunning defeats in a row to win the series. This championship marked the only time in any postseason competition that a team battled back from a three-games-to-none deficit to win a series.

1912 Chicago City Championship Series

GAME ONE --- October 9

WHITE SOX	AB	R	H	PO	A	E	CUBS	AB	R	H	PO	A	E
Rath, 2b	4	0	0	0	3	1	Sheckard, lf	4	0	0	2	0	0
Lord, lf	4	0	1	4	0	0	Miller, cf	3	0	0	2	0	0
Collins, rf	4	0	2	2	0	0	Tinker, ss	3	0	1	2	4	0
Bodie, cf	3	0	1	0	0	0	Zimmerman, 3b	3	0	0	0	3	0
Borton, 1b	2	0	0	10	0	0	Schulte, rf	3	0	0	1	0	0
Zeider, 3b	3	0	0	2	1	0	Saier, 1b	3	0	0	12	0	0
Weaver, ss	3	0	0	1	2	0	Evers, 2b	3	0	0	4	1	1
Sullivan, c	3	0	0	8	0	0	Archer, c	3	0	0	4	4	0
Walsh, p	3	0	2	0	4	0	Lavender, p	3	0	0	0	4	0
	29	0	6	27	10	1		28	0	1	27	16	1

```
SOX     0  0  0     0  0  0     0  0  0   -  0
CUB     0  0  0     0  0  0     0  0  0   -  0
```

2B: Bodie, Tinker, Walsh. SH: Bodie, Borton. LOB: Sox 4, Cub 1. Struck out: Walsh 7, Lavender 1. Umpires: Dineen and Brennan. Time—1:56.

Before the series began, the Cubs released pitcher Mordecai "Three Finger" Brown, just a week before his 36th birthday. Mordecai had been with the Cubs since 1904 and his record during the previous season was a mediocre 5–6 although his ERA of 2.63 was second on the club only to Lefty Leifield

1912 Chicago City Championship Series

GAME TWO --- October 11

CUBS	AB	R	H	PO	A	E		WHITE SOX	AB	R	H	PO	A	E
Sheckard, lf	5	0	0	1	0	0		Rath, 2b	5	1	0	3	4	0
Miller, cf	5	1	3	4	0	0		Lord, lf	3	0	1	1	0	0
Tinker, ss	3	1	2	4	6	0		Mattick, lf	3	0	0	1	0	0
Zimmerman, 3b	5	0	1	3	3	0		Collins, rf	6	0	2	1	0	0
Schulte, rf	5	0	1	0	0	0		Bodie, cf	6	0	1	2	1	0
Saier, 1b	5	0	0	18	0	1		Borton, 1b	4	1	1	10	1	1
Evers, 2b	4	1	1	0	4	0		Zeider, 3b	5	0	0	1	1	0
Archer, c	5	0	2	6	3	0		Weaver, ss	3	0	0	5	3	1
Cheney, p	5	0	1	0	4	0		Johnson, ss	2	1	2	0	1	0
								Easterly, c	4	0	4	9	2	0
	42	3	11	36	20	1		Kuhn, pr *	0	0	0	0	0	0
								Sullivan, c	1	0	0	2	0	0
								Cicotte, p	3	0	1	1	1	0
								Callahan, ph +	1	0	0	0	0	0
								Walsh, p	1	0	1	0	3	0
									47	3	13	36	17	2

```
* ran for Easterly in ninth inning
+ batted for Cicotte in ninth inning
```

```
CUB   0 0 0   0 1 0   0 2 0   0 0 0 - 3
SOX   1 0 0   0 0 0   0 0 2   0 0 0 - 3
```

2B: Archer 2, Easterly. 3B: Miller, Johnson. SH: Sheckard. SB: Schulte. LOB: Sox 10, Cub 6. DP: Sox 2, Cub 2. BB: Cicotte 3, Cheney 2. Struck out: Cicotte 6, Cheney 6, Walsh 1. Hits: Cicotte 9 in 9 innings; Walsh 2 in 3 innings. Umpires: Dineen, home; Brennan on bases; Connolly, left field; Owens, right field. Time—2:44.

GAME THREE --- October 12

WHITE SOX	AB	R	H	PO	A	E		CUBS	AB	R	H	PO	A	E
Rath, 2b	2	0	0	0	1	0		Sheckard, lf	5	1	1	1	0	0
Lord, lf	5	0	2	2	0	1		Leach, cf	5	0	1	1	0	0
Collins, rf	4	2	3	0	0	0		Tinker, ss	5	0	0	5	5	0
Bodie, cf	3	1	2	1	0	0		Zimmerman, 3b	3	1	1	1	1	0
Mattick, cf	2	0	1	0	0	0		Schulte, rf	4	0	1	1	0	0
Easterly, c	4	0	3	8	3	0		Saier, 1b	2	1	1	9	1	0
Borton, 1b	4	0	1	11	1	1		Evers, 2b	2	1	0	2	2	1
Johnson, ss	3	0	0	3	5	1		Archer, c	4	0	3	7	6	0
Zeider, 3b	4	0	1	2	3	0		Lavender, p	3	1	1	0	2	0
White, p	3	0	1	0	1	0								
Callahan, pr	0	1	0	0	0	0			33	5	9	27	17	1
	34	4	14	27	14	3								

```
SOX   0 0 0   2 0 1   0 0 1 - 4
CUB   0 1 0   0 2 1   1 0 0 - 5
```

2B: Archer 2, White, Easterly, Mattick. SH: Rath, Borton, Lavender. LOB: Sox 11, Cub 8. DP: Sox 1, Cub 4. BB: White 5, Lavender 6. Struck out: White 5, Lavender 5. WP: Lavender. Umpires: Brennan and Dineen. Field umpires: Owens and Connolly. Time—2:00.

(2.41). Had the Cubs' management waited until the conclusion of the city series before making such a move, Brown's experience might have aided the team's fortunes in Games Six, Seven or Eight.

Game One saw the two rivals battle for nine innings on a muddy field only to end up with a scoreless tie. Jimmy Lavender (16–13) pitched nine magnificent innings and gave the White Sox a mere six hits. Ed Walsh (27–17) was even

1912 Chicago City Championship Series

GAME FOUR --- October 13

WHITE SOX	AB	R	H	PO	A	E		CUBS	AB	R	H	PO	A	E
Rath, 2b	4	0	1	2	3	1		Sheckard, lf	2	1	0	3	0	0
Lord, lf	3	0	1	1	0	0		Leach, cf	3	0	0	2	0	0
Collins, rf	3	0	1	1	0	0		Tinker, ss	4	0	1	0	5	0
Bodie, cf	3	0	1	0	0	0		Zimmerman, 3b	4	0	1	1	0	0
Borton, 1b	3	0	1	11	2	0		Schulte, rf	4	1	2	1	0	0
Johnson, ss	4	0	0	1	3	0		Saier, 1b	3	0	0	12	0	0
Zeider, 3b	3	1	1	0	0	0		Evers, 2b	3	1	1	3	5	0
Easterly, ph	1	0	1	0	0	0		Archer, c	2	1	1	4	1	0
Callahan, pr	0	0	0	0	0	0		Reulbach, p	3	0	1	1	3	0
Sullivan, c	3	0	0	8	2	1								
Mattick, ph	1	0	0	0	0	0			28	4	7	27	14	0
Walsh, p	3	1	1	0	4	0								
	31	2	8	24	14	2								

```
SOX   0 0 0   0 0 1   1 0 0  -  2
CUB   0 0 0   0 0 1   3 0 x  -  4
```

2B: Schulte, Lord, Walsh, Zeider, Archer, Collins. HR: Schulte. LOB: Cub 4, Sox 6. DP: Cub BB: Walsh 2, Reulbach 2. Struck out: Walsh 6, Reulbach 3. WP: Reulbach. Umpires: Owens and Connolly. Field Umpires: Dineen and Brennan. Time—2:12.

GAME FIVE --- October 14

CUBS	AB	R	H	PO	A	E		WHITE SOX	AB	R	H	PO	A	E
Sheckard, lf	2	1	0	2	0	0		Rath, 2b	4	0	2	3	2	0
Leach, cf	3	2	1	0	0	0		Lord, lf	4	0	0	1	1	0
Tinker, ss	3	1	1	2	6	1		Collins, rf	4	0	1	1	0	1
Zimmerman, 3b	5	2	3	1	2	0		Bodie, cf	4	1	2	0	1	0
Schulte, rf	4	2	1	1	0	0		Borton, 1b	4	0	0	6	2	0
Saier, 1b	3	0	3	9	1	0		Johnson, ss	4	0	1	2	4	0
Evers, 2b	4	0	0	2	4	1		Zeider, 3b	4	0	2	1	0	0
Archer, c	4	0	2	10	1	0		Kuhn, c	2	0	0	12	2	1
Cheney, p	4	0	1	0	4	0		Cicotte, p	0	0	0	0	0	0
								Lange, p	3	0	0	1	2	0
	32	8	12	27	18	2		Barrows, ph	1	0	0	0	0	0
									34	1	8	27	14	2

```
CUB   3 0 3   0 0 0   0 0 2  -  8
SOX   0 0 0   0 0 1   0 0 0  -  1
```

3B: Schulte, Saier 2, Bodie. SH: Tinker 2. DP: Cub 1, Sox 2. BB: Cicotte 2, Lange 5, Cheney 1. Struck out: Cicotte 2, Cheney 8, Lange 9. Umpires: Connolly and Owens. Field umpires: Brennan and Dineen. Time—2:00.

better than that, giving up nothing to the Cubs but a Joe Tinker double. Walsh had seven strikeouts, Lavender one.

Game Two was a virtual replay of Game One, only longer, and Comiskey Park was in even worse shape than the Cubs' West Side Park. Eddie Cicotte (9–7) of the Sox went eight innings against Larry Cheney (26–10) and left trailing 3–1, but his teammates rallied for two in the ninth to send the game into overtime. Three more innings failed to produce a winner and the game was called because of darkness. Twenty-one innings had been played so far, and to no result.

Lavender held on to defeat Doc White (8–10) and the Sox in Game Three.

1912 Chicago City Championship Series

GAME SIX --- October 15

WHITE SOX	AB	R	H	PO	A	E		CUBS	AB	R	H	PO	A	E
Rath, 2b	6	0	2	3	6	0		Sheckard, lf	5	0	1	1	0	0
Lord, lf	6	1	2	1	0	0		Leach, cf	3	0	1	4	0	0
Collins, rf	4	0	1	2	0	0		Tinker, ss	4	0	0	2	4	1
Bodie, cf	2	0	0	0	0	0		Zimmerman, 3b	5	1	2	1	5	1
Mattick, cf	3	0	0	4	0	0		Schulte, rf	5	2	2	0	0	0
Borton, 1b	3	2	2	14	1	0		Saier, 1b	5	0	0	15	1	0
Johnson, ss	4	1	1	4	2	0		Evers, 2b	5	0	0	3	6	0
Zeider, 3b	4	1	1	2	2	1		Archer, c	4	1	2	6	0	0
Schalk, c	4	0	1	3	1	1		Lavender, p	3	0	1	0	0	0
Easterly, ph	0	0	0	0	0	0		Miller, ph	1	0	0	0	0	0
Walsh, p	5	0	1	0	3	0								
Sullivan c	1	0	0	0	1	0			40	4	8	33	16	2
	42	5	11	33	16	2								

```
SOX   0 3 0   0 0 0   0 1 0   0 1 - 5
CUB   0 0 0   2 0 0   1 1 0   0 0 - 4
```

2B: Zeider, Sheckard, Walsh, Zimmerman, Archer, Lord, Borton, Leach, Schulte. HR: Schulte. SH: Mattick, Borton, Lavender, Collins. DP: Cub 2, Sox 2. BB: Walsh 5, Lavender 5. Umpires: Brennan, Dineen, Owens, Connolly. Time—2:15.

Jimmy Archer was the big gun for the Cubs with two doubles and a single, while Eddie Collins and Ted Easterly both had three hits for the Sox. The Cubs won the game 5–4, despite being outhit 14–9, and withstood a Sox rally which saw rookie first baseman Babe Borton at the plate with a 3–2 count and the bases loaded in the ninth inning. Lavender came through with a strikeout, however, and the Cubs had their first victory of the series after 30 innings of play.

The Nationals took a 2–0 lead in games in Game Four as Ed Reulbach (10–6) outdueled Ed Walsh. Reulbach got the win, holding the White Sox to eight hits and two runs, while Walsh took the loss. Trailing 2–1, the Cubs tallied three runs in the seventh to win, 4–2. RBIs by Evers, Jimmy Archer, and Ed Reulbach iced the game for the Nationals.

The Cubs won Game Five as they batted around Eddie Cicotte and Frank Lange (10–10). Three runs in the first and three more in the third helped give Cubs ace Larry Cheney an easy 8–1 victory. Third baseman Heinie Zimmerman was 3-for-5 and teammate Vic Saier a perfect 3-for-3.

Leading three-games-to-none and needing only one victory to clinch the series, the Cubs gave up the ghost. Or maybe, as the papers suggested, they celebrated their imminent fourth victory a little too early and a little too often. Game Six saw Ed Walsh outlast Jimmy Lavender in an eleven-inning affair. The Sox scored three runs in the second and had a 3–2 lead into the bottom of the seventh only to see the Cubs tie the score. Both teams scored single runs in the eighth and at the end of regulation time the game was tied. The White Sox scored once in the eleventh and won the game, their first victory of the series. Ten of the 19 hits made in the game went for extra bases.

Game Seven saw the Cubs holding onto a 4–3 lead into the bottom of the eighth inning. They looked to put the series away until the Sox struck for four

1912 Chicago City Championship Series

```
GAME SEVEN --- October 16
```

WHITE SOX	AB	R	H	PO	A	E
Rath, 2b	3	2	2	1	4	0
Lord, lf	4	1	1	3	0	1
Mattick, cf	4	1	1	1	1	0
Collins, rf	4	1	1	2	0	0
Borton, 1b	4	0	1	10	0	0
Johnson, ss	3	0	0	5	2	0
Zeider, 3b	3	1	1	1	2	0
Schalk, c	4	0	1	4	2	0
White, p	0	0	0	0	0	0
Harrows, ph	1	0	0	0	0	0
Benz, p	2	1	1	0	1	0
	32	7	9	27	12	1

CUBS	AB	R	H	PO	A	E
Sheckard, lf	4	1	0	4	0	0
Leach, cf	4	0	0	3	0	1
Tinker, ss	4	0	1	2	3	0
Zimmerman, 3b	3	1	1	0	0	1
Schulte, rf	2	0	0	1	0	0
Saier, 1b	1	2	0	7	0	0
Downs, 2b	3	0	0	2	3	0
Goode, ph	1	0	1	0	0	0
Archer, c	4	1	1	5	1	0
Reulbach, p	1	0	0	0	1	0
Cheney, p	0	0	0	0	0	0
Smith, p	0	0	0	0	0	0
Miller	1	0	1	0	0	0
	28	5	5	24	8	2

```
CUB   1  2  0    0  0  1    0  0  1  -  5
SOX   0  0  1    0  0  2    0  4  x  -  7
```

LOB: Cub 5, Sox 4. 2B: Archer, Rath. SH: Reulbach, Zeider. SB: Schulte. DP: Cub 1, Sox 2. BB: Reulbach 1, Smith 1, White 2, Benz 6. Struck out: Reulbach 6, White 1, Benz 2. Umpires: Dineen and Eason. Field umpires: Owens and Connolly. Time—2:10.

```
GAME EIGHT --- October 17
```

WHITE SOX	AB	R	H	PO	A	E
Rath, 2b	3	0	1	0	4	0
Lord, lf	4	1	0	2	0	0
Mattick, cf	5	1	1	1	0	0
Collins, rf	5	1	1	1	0	0
Borton, 1b	5	2	3	13	0	0
Zeider, 3b	2	0	1	1	1	0
Weaver, ss	4	1	2	1	5	0
Schalk, c	4	1	3	8	0	0
Lange, p	3	0	1	0	1	0
Easterly, ph	0	0	0	0	0	0
Johnson, pr	0	1	0	0	0	0
Walsh, p	0	0	0	0	1	0
	35	8	13	27	12	0

CUBS	AB	R	H	PO	A	E
Sheckard, lf	4	0	0	2	0	0
Miller, cf	4	2	2	1	1	0
Tinker, ss	4	1	2	3	4	0
Zimmerman, 3b	3	1	2	0	2	0
Schulte, rf	4	0	0	2	0	0
Saier, 1b	4	0	0	10	0	0
Evers, 2b	4	0	1	3	1	0
Archer, c	4	0	0	6	3	0
Cheney, p	2	0	1	0	2	0
Goode, ph	0	1	0	0	0	0
Richie, p	0	0	0	0	1	0
Lavender, p	0	0	0	0	0	0
Downey, ph	1	0	0	0	0	0
	34	5	8	27	14	0

```
SOX   0  1  0    0  0  3    0  0  4  -  8
CUB   1  0  0    2  0  0    0  2  0  -  5
```

2B: Tinker, Borton, Zimmerman. 3B: Mattick, Miller. HR: Zimmerman, Collins, Weaver. SH: Zimmerman, Rath, Zeider. LOB: Cub 4, Sox 7. BB: Cheney 2, Richie 2. Struck out: Lange 7, Cheney 5, Walsh 1. WP: Cheney. Hits: Lange 7 in 8 innings; Walsh 1 in 1 inning; Cheney 10 in 8 innings, Richie 1 in ⅓ inning; Lavender 2 in ⅔ inning. Umpires: Owens, Connolly, and Eason. Time—2:00.

runs to take a 7–4 lead. The Cubs responded with one of their own in the ninth, but the rally fell short of tying the game. Doc White started for the Sox and Joe Benz (13–17) got the victory. Ed Reulbach was the Cubs' starter and was relieved by Larry Cheney and Charley Smith (7–4), the loser.

　　The White Sox staged another stunning comeback in Game Eight. The Cubs held a 3–1 lead as late as the sixth inning and still led by one after eight, but the Sox scored four runs in the ninth to win the game, 8–5. Frank Lange

1912 Chicago City Championship Series

```
GAME NINE --- October 18
```

CUBS	AB	R	H	PO	A	E	WHITE SOX	AB	R	H	PO	A	E
Sheckard, lf	3	0	0	1	0	0	Rath, 2b	5	2	2	0	4	0
Miller, cf	4	0	0	0	0	3	Lord, lf	5	2	2	0	0	0
Tinker, ss	4	0	1	0	4	1	Bodie, lf	1	0	0	0	0	0
Zimmerman, 3b	4	0	1	1	2	0	Mattick,cf	4	2	0	3	0	0
Schulte, rf	3	0	0	0	0	0	Collins, rf	3	3	3	0	0	0
Saier, 1b	4	0	1	13	0	0	Borton, 1b	5	1	3	11	2	0
Evers, 2b	4	0	1	2	5	0	Zeider, 3b	5	1	1	0	4	0
Archer, c	2	0	0	3	0	0	Weaver, ss	4	3	2	2	4	0
Cotter, c	0	0	0	4	0	0	Schalk, c	5	2	3	9	0	0
Lavender, p	0	0	0	0	2	0	Walsh, p	5	0	1	2	1	0
Goode, ph	1	0	0	0	0	0							
Smith, p	0	0	0	0	0	0		42	16	17	27	15	0
Reulbach, p	0	0	0	0	0	0							
Leifield, p	1	0	1	0	3	0							
Toney, p	1	0	0	0	0	0							
	31	0	5	24	16	4							

```
CUB   0  0  0    0  0  0    0  0  0  -   0
SOX   1  2  8    2  3  0    0  0  x  -  16
```

2B: Weaver. 3B: Lord, Weaver, Borton, Schalk. SB: Mattick, Collins 2, Borton. LOB: Sox 7, Cub 7. DP: Cubs. BB: Walsh 3, Lavender 1, Leifield 2. Struck out: Walsh 5, Reulbach 1, Leifield 2, Toney 1. WP: Lavender, Leifield. Hits: Lavender 4 in 2 innings; Smith 3 (none out) in third inning; Reulbach 6 in 1 inning; Leifield 3 in 2 innings; Toney 1 in 3 innings. Umpires: Connolly, Owens, Dineen, Eason. Time—2:15.

started and went the first eight innings, taking the victory for the Sox, and Ed Walsh pitched a scoreless ninth for the save. Larry Cheney would have won the game for the Cubs, but his bullpen betrayed him. Lew Richie (16–8), the losing pitcher, started the ninth and had to be relieved by Jimmy Lavender.

Behind by a seemingly insurmountable margin, the White Sox had forced the series to go the distance. To say the Cubs made a run for the money in Game Nine would be stretching the truth to a distance the law of physics would not allow. The White Sox battered five Cub pitchers for 17 hits and 16 runs while Ed Walsh pitched a complete game, five-hit shutout. Nothing less than a gunshot wound could have prevented him from winning. Eddie Collins, Ray Schalk, and Babe Borton each had three hits; Morrie Rath, Bris Lord, and Buck Weaver all had two. The Sox offense included a double, four triples, and four stolen bases. Lavender gave up four hits and three runs in the first two innings. Charley Smith didn't get anybody out in the third and gave up three runs. Ed Reulbach relieved Smith but allowed five runs of his own in the same inning. Lefty Leifield pitched the fourth and fifth as the Sox racked up another three hits and five runs. Fred Toney was the Cubs pitcher for the last three innings and held the Sox to one hit and no runs, probably because they were winded from running the bases. The final score was 16–0. Cubs manager Frank Chance was so disgusted he left the ballpark at the end of five innings.

The memory of such a devastating loss in the series and the loss of this game in particular was, perhaps, one of the reasons the White Sox would win the next five city championships.

1912 Philadelphia City Championship Series

GAME ONE --- October 7

PHILLIES	AB	R	H	PO	A	E	ATHLETICS	AB	R	H	PO	A	E
Paskert, cf	4	2	2	5	0	0	Murphy, rf	5	0	1	3	0	0
Dolan, 3b	4	2	2	2	2	0	Oldring, lf	3	0	1	2	0	0
Magee, lf	4	1	2	2	0	0	Collins, 2b	5	1	1	3	3	0
Miller, rf	5	0	1	2	0	0	Baker, 3b	4	0	1	0	0	0
Luderus, 1b	1	1	0	7	1	0	McInnis, 1b	4	0	2	9	1	0
Walsh, 2b	4	0	1	3	1	0	Strunk, cf	4	1	2	2	0	0
Doolan, ss	4	1	2	1	3	0	Barry, ss	4	1	3	3	2	0
Killefer, c	4	0	2	5	4	0	Lapp, c	4	1	1	5	3	0
Alexander, p	1	0	0	0	0	0	Coombs, p	2	0	1	0	1	0
Moore, p	1	1	0	0	0	0	Maggert, ph	1	0	0	0	0	0
Cravath, ph	1	0	0	0	0	0	Brown, p	0	0	0	0	2	0
							J. Walsh, pr	1	0	0	0	0	0
	33	8	12	27	11	0	Crabb, p	0	0	0	0	2	0
								37	4	13	27	14	0

```
PHI    0  1  0    0  0  3    0  1  3  -  8
ATH    1  0  0    3  0  0    0  0  0  -  4
```

2B: Doolan, McInnis, Walsh, Barry. 3B: Dolan 2, Paskert, Lapp. SB: Collins, Baker, Magee. DP: PHI 1, ATH 2. HBP: Luderus (Coombs), Moore (Coombs). WP: Coombs. BB: Alexander 1, Moore 2, Coombs 3, Brown 3. Struck out: Alexander 1, Moore 2, Coombs 2. Umpires: Hart and Johnstone. Time—1:45.

The 1912 Philadelphia City Championship Series

Philadelphia Athletics defeat Philadelphia Phillies; 4–1

Although he disliked the meaningless city championships, Philadelphia Athletics manager Connie Mack promised club president Horace Fogel that the Athletics (90–62) would play the Philadelphia Phillies (73–79) if neither club won the pennant. Connie figured a pennant was a pretty safe bet since his team had won the World Series in 1910 and 1911. But the A's suffered through a disappointing third-place finish and Mack had to make good on his promise. The Nationals got their feet wet by winning the first game, then took a dunking as the Athletics rebounded to sweep the next four games.

Grover Cleveland Alexander (19–17) squared off against Jack Coombs (21–10) in Game One, but neither pitcher was around for the finish. Ol' Pete lasted only five innings, gave up four runs, and left trailing 4–1. Coombs went six for the A's but was relieved after he was touched for three sixth-inning runs. Losing pitcher Carroll "Boardwalk" Brown (13–11) allowed one run in the eighth and Jim Crabb (2–4 with the Phillies and making his last appearance with a major-league club) gave up three more in the ninth to put the game out of reach for the Athletics. Earl Moore (9–14), who pitched the last four innings in relief of Alexander, was the winner. The final score was 8–4.

Game Two saw Athletics ace Eddie Plank (26–6) limit the Phillies' offense to six hits and a lone seventh-inning run. The A's scored twice in the third, sixth, and ninth innings, the last pair of runs coming off reliever Ad Brennan (11–9). Only half of the Athletics' runs were earned and everyone in the lineup hit safely except Amos Strunk. Starter Tom Seaton (16–12) took the loss for the Phillies.

1912 Philadelphia City Championship Series

GAME TWO --- October 8

ATHLETICS	AB	R	H	PO	A	E		PHILLIES	AB	R	H	PO	A	E
Murphy, rf	5	1	1	0	1	0		Paskert, cf	4	0	0	3	0	0
Oldring, lf	4	2	2	3	1	0		Dolan, 3b	4	0	0	1	4	1
Collins, 2b	4	3	2	1	1	0		Magee, lf	4	1	2	1	0	0
Baker, 3b	5	0	2	1	1	1		Luderus, 1b	4	0	0	15	0	2
McInnis, 1b	5	0	2	9	0	0		Cravath, rf	3	0	1	0	0	1
Strunk, cf	5	0	0	2	0	0		Walsh, 2b	2	0	0	3	6	0
Barry, ss	5	0	1	4	4	1		Doolan, ss	3	0	0	2	6	2
Lapp, c	4	0	1	7	1	0		Killefer, c	3	0	2	2	0	0
Plank, p	4	0	1	0	2	0		Seaton, p	2	0	1	0	1	0
								Brennan, p	0	0	0	0	0	0
	41	6	12	27	11	2		Lobert, ph	1	0	0	0	0	0
									30	1	6	27	17	6

```
ATH   0 0 2   0 2 0   0 0 2  -  6
PHI   0 0 0   0 0 0   1 0 0  -  1
```

Earned runs: ATH 3. 2B: Oldring, Killefer. 3B: Murphy. SF: Walsh. LOB: ATH 10, PHI 4. BB: Seaton 1, Plank 1. Struck out: Seaton 2, Plank 7. DP: ATH 2, PHI 2. Hits: Seaton 9 and 4 runs in 8 innings; Brennan 3 and 2 runs in 1 inning. PB: Lapp. Umpires: Johnstone and Hart. Time—1:54

GAME THREE --- October 9

PHILLIES	AB	R	H	PO	A	E		ATHLETICS	AB	R	H	PO	A	E
Paskert, cf	3	0	0	2	0	0		Murphy, rf	4	1	1	0	0	0
Dolan, 3b	4	0	0	2	2	1		Oldring, lf	3	0	0	2	0	0
Magee, lf	3	0	1	6	0	0		Collins, 2b	3	1	2	4	5	0
Miller, rf	3	0	0	1	1	0		Baker, 3b	4	1	2	0	0	0
Luderus, 1b	2	0	1	5	2	0		McInnis, 1b	4	0	0	12	0	0
Walsh, 2b	2	0	1	2	3	0		Strunk, cf	2	0	0	4	0	0
Doolan, ss	3	0	0	2	1	1		Barry, ss	2	0	0	3	3	0
Killefer, c	3	0	0	4	1	0		Lapp, c	3	0	0	5	1	0
Chalmers, p	2	0	0	0	0	1		Houck, p	3	1	1	0	4	0
Cravath, ph	1	0	0	0	0	0								
	26	0	3	24	10	3			28	4	6	27	13	0

```
PHI   0 0 0   0 0 0   0 0 0  -  0
ATH   0 0 1   0 0 0   0 3 x  -  4
```

Earned runs: ATH 2. 2B: Baker. LOB: ATH 5, PHI: 2. SB: Collins, Baker, Magee. SH: Walsh, Oldring, Barry. DP: ATH 2. BB: Collins, Strunk 2, Paskert, Luderus. Struck out: Baker, Houck, Dolan 2, Miller, Chalmers, Cravath. Umpires: Hart and Johnstone. Time—1:30.

The American Leaguers were right back at it in the next game, this victory a 90 minute three-hit shutout by Byron Houck (8–8). George Chalmers (3–4) did good work for the Phillies, holding the A's close on one run through seven innings, but then blew up in the eighth as three Athletics runners crossed the plate.

Game Four was the most exciting of the series. The A's took a one-run lead in the second, but the Phillies tied and went ahead with two in the third. Two Athletics runs in the fourth and one in the fifth settled the contest as the Phillies were able to muster only one more run. The final score was 4–3, Athletics. Boardwalk Brown started for the Americans and worked the first three innings

1912 Philadelphia City Championship Series

GAME FOUR --- October 10

ATHLETICS	AB	R	H	PO	A	E	PHILLIES	AB	R	H	PO	A	E
Murphy, rf	5	0	1	0	0	0	Paskert, cf	4	1	1	3	0	0
Oldring, lf	5	0	1	4	0	0	Dolan, 3b	5	0	4	4	0	0
Collins, 2b	5	1	3	2	1	0	Magee, lf	1	0	0	0	0	1
Baker, 3b	4	0	1	3	1	0	Lobert, lf	3	0	1	1	0	0
McInnis, 1b	5	2	3	9	0	0	Miller, rf	4	0	1	3	0	0
Strunk, cf	4	1	0	2	0	0	Luderus, 1b	2	0	0	10	3	0
Barry, ss	3	0	2	1	3	1	Walsh, 2b	4	0	0	1	4	0
Lapp, c	2	0	0	6	1	0	Doolan, ss	4	1	2	1	3	0
Brown, p	1	0	0	0	0	0	Killefer, c	1	0	0	2	0	0
Bender, p	2	0	0	0	1	0	Moran, c	3	0	0	2	1	0
Maggert, ph	0	0	0	0	0	0	Moore, p	2	1	2	0	2	0
							Seaton, p	1	0	0	0	2	1
	36	4	11	27	7	1	Cravath, ph	1	0	1	0	0	0
								35	3	8	27	19	2

```
ATH    0  1  0    2  1  0    0  0  0  -  4
PHI    0  0  2    0  0  1    0  0  0  -  3
```

Earned runs: ATH 3, PHI 1. 2B: McInnis, Barry, Paskert, Miller, Doolan. SB: Collins, Strunk, Paskert. SH: Barry. LOB: ATH 10, PHI 9. DP: PHI 4. HBP: Magee (Brown). BB: Moore 3, Seaton 1, Brown 2, Bender 1. Struck out: Moore 1, Seaton 1, Bender 6. Hits: Brown 3 and 2 runs in 3 innings; Bender 5 and 1 run in 6 innings; Moore 7 and 4 runs in 6 innings; Seaton 4 and no runs in 3 innings. WP: Bender, Brown. Umpires: Johnstone and Hart. Time—2:05.

GAME FIVE --- October 11

ATHLETICS	AB	R	H	PO	A	E	PHILLIES	AB	R	H	PO	A	E
Murphy, rf	3	0	1	0	0	0	Paskert, cf	3	1	0	2	0	0
Oldring, lf	4	1	0	4	0	0	Lobert, lf	4	0	1	1	0	0
Collins, 2b	3	1	2	3	4	0	Luderus, 1b	3	0	0	10	1	0
Baker, 3b	4	1	1	0	3	0	Cravath, rf	4	0	1	0	1	0
McInnis, 1b	3	2	2	13	0	0	Dolan, 3b	2	0	1	1	4	0
J. Walsh, lf	3	0	2	1	1	0	R. Walsh, c	1	0	0	0	1	0
Barry, ss	3	0	0	1	2	0	Moran, c	3	0	0	3	3	0
Thomas, c	2	0	0	5	2	0	Doolan, ss	3	1	2	2	2	2
Brown, p	3	0	0	0	2	0	Dodge, 2b	2	0	1	4	3	0
	28	5	8	27	14	0	Rixey, p	1	0	0	0	0	0
							Chalmers, p	1	0	0	0	0	0
							Miller, ph	1	0	1	0	0	0
								28	2	7	*23	15	2

* Collins out for interference

```
PHI    1  0  0    0  1  0    0  0  0  -  2
ATH    0  1  1    0  0  3    0  0  x  -  5
```

Earned runs: ATH 1, PHI 1. 2B: Collins, Doolan. SF: J. Walsh, Luderus. SH: Barry, Dodge. SB: Baker, Doolan. LOB: ATH 5, PHI 4. DP: ATH 1. BB: Rixey 1, Chalmers 3, Brown 3. Struck out: Rixey 2, Chalmers 2, Brown 4. Hits: Rixey 6 and 2 runs in 4 innings; Chalmers 2 and 3 runs in 4 innings. PB: R. Walsh 2, Moran 1. Umpires: Hart and Johnstone. Time—1:50.

before being knocked out when the Phillies rallied in the third. Chief Bender (13–8) went the final six for the victory. Tom Seaton (16–12) worked in relief of Earl Moore who took the loss.

Boardwalk Brown was the starting pitcher for the second consecutive game in the series' finale. Eppa Rixey (10–10), his opponent, went four innings and left trailing 2–1. The Phillies took him off the hook when they scored once in the top of the fifth. Reliever George Chalmers was touched for three runs in his second inning of work and was the loser in this 5–2 game.

Each member of the Athletics received $82 for winning the series and each Phillie $54. The receipts were so pitifully small that Connie Mack said never again would he allow his team to play in another such championship. True to his word, this was the last city series played in Philadelphia. The Athletics had won both championships and finished with an 8-4 record in games played.

The 1913 St. Louis City Championship Series

St. Louis Cardinals vs. St. Louis Browns; tie series, 3-3-2

The last-place National League Cardinals (51-99) played the last-place American League Browns (57-96) in a postseason matchup which might easily have been called the "Worst Series." Two teams and their long-suffering fans were made to endure eight games in five days only to have the series end in a tie.

1913 St. Louis City Championship Series

GAME ONE --- October 9

CARDINALS	AB	R	H	PO	A	E		BROWNS	AB	R	H	PO	A	E
Huggins, 2b	2	0	0	2	1	0		Austin, 3b	4	0	0	0	2	0
Magee, lf	4	0	0	3	1	0		Wares, 2b	3	0	1	2	2	0
Mowrey, 3b	4	0	1	3	3	0		Pratt, 1b	4	0	1	12	2	0
Oakes, cf	3	0	0	0	0	0		Walker, lf	4	0	0	4	0	0
Konetchy, 1b	3	0	0	13	0	0		Williams, cf	3	0	0	1	0	0
Whitted, rf	2	1	0	0	0	0		Sloan, rf	3	0	0	0	0	0
O'Leary, ss	3	0	0	0	0	0		Bisland, ss	3	0	2	2	4	0
Wingo, c	3	0	0	6	1	0		Agnew, c	2	0	0	6	2	0
Sallee, p	3	0	0	0	3	0		Weilman, p	2	0	0	0	2	1
								McAllister, ph	1	0	0	0	0	0
	27	1	1	27	9	0			29	0	4	27	14	1

```
STN    0  1  0    0  0  0    0  0  0  -  1
STA    0  0  0    0  0  0    0  0  0  -  0
```

SH: Agnew. SB: Huggins. DP: STN 1, STA 1. LOB: STN 2, STA 4. BB: Sallee 1, Weilman 3. Struck out: Sallee 2, Weilman 5. Umpires: Hildebrand, Brennan. Time—1:35.

Game One, on October 9, saw the Browns shut out on the strength of a lone Cardinal run in the second inning—the very minimum effort required for one team to beat another. The Browns could manage only four hits off Slim Sallee (18-15), and the Cardinals were unable to mount even that much offense. The Redbirds' lone hit was a single by third baseman Mike Mowrey. Browns pitcher Carl Weilman (10-20) completely dominated the Cardinals, although taking the loss.

Tied 1-1, the Cardinals won the second game of the series with three runs in the top of the seventh. After the Browns scored once in the bottom of the inning to make the score 4-2, umpires Brennan and Hildebrand called the game on account of darkness. The winning pitcher was Pol Perritt (6-14); the losing pitcher, George Baumgardner (10-19).

1913 St. Louis City Championship Series

GAME TWO --- October 10

CARDINALS	AB	R	H	PO	A	E		BROWNS	AB	R	H	PO	A	E
Huggins, 2b	4	0	0	4	1	0		Williams, cf	2	0	1	1	0	0
Magee, lf	3	0	1	1	1	0		Austin, 3b	3	0	0	3	1	2
Mowrey, 3b	3	0	0	0	2	0		Pratt, 1b	3	0	2	5	2	0
Oakes, cf	3	0	0	0	0	0		Walker, lf	2	0	0	4	0	0
Konetchy, 1b	3	2	2	8	0	0		Sloan, rf	3	0	1	1	0	0
Whitted, rf	2	1	1	4	0	0		Bisland, ss	3	0	0	1	1	0
O'Leary, ss	3	0	0	0	0	0		Wares, 2b	3	1	3	0	1	0
Wingo, c	3	1	1	4	1	0		Agnew, c	2	0	1	6	1	0
Perritt, p	3	0	1	0	2	0		Baumgardner, p	3	0	0	0	1	0
	27	4	6	21	7	0			24	1	8	21	7	2

```
STN    0  0  0    0  1  0    3  -  4
STA    0  0  0    0  0  0    1  -  1
```

2B: Magee, Evans. 3B: Konetchy. SH: Walker, Austin. SF: Agnew. SB: Perritt, Williams. LOB: STA 7, STN 3. DP: STN. BB: Perritt 2. Struck out: Baumgardner 5, Perritt 4. HBP: Evans (Baumgardner). Umpires: Brennan, Hildebrand. Time—1:30.

GAME THREE --- October 11

CARDINALS	AB	R	H	PO	A	E		BROWNS	AB	R	H	PO	A	E
Huggins, 2b	4	0	0	1	0	0		Shotton, cf	3	1	1	4	0	0
Magee, lf	3	1	2	3	0	0		Austin, 3b	5	1	3	0	2	1
Mowrey, 3b	1	0	0	1	0	0		Pratt, 1b	5	2	3	11	0	1
Evans, rf	2	1	2	1	0	0		Walker, lf	5	2	3	3	0	0
Oakes, cf	4	0	2	2	0	0		Williams, rf	3	1	1	0	0	0
Konetchy, 1b	4	0	2	7	1	0		Bisland, ss	5	0	2	1	2	0
Whitted, rf-ss	4	0	0	0	0	0		Wares, 2b	3	1	1	2	4	0
O'Leary, ss	4	1	2	2	1	0		Agnew, c	3	0	1	4	1	0
Wingo, c	2	1	1	4	2	0		Hamilton, p	1	0	0	1	4	0
Snyder, c	2	0	0	3	3	1		Mitchell, p	2	0	0	1	0	0
Doak, p	1	1	0	0	2	0		Sloan, ph	1	0	0	0	0	0
Trekell, p	0	0	0	0	0	0			36	8	15	27	13	2
Griner, p	2	0	0	0	0	0								
	33	5	9	24	9	1								

```
STN    0  0  3    0  0  1    0  1  0  -  5
STA    0  0  0    1  3  4    0  0  x  -  8
```

2B: Agnew, Austin, Pratt, Evans. 3B: Magee. HR: Evans. SF: Mowrey. SB: Shotton 2, Pratt, Williams. DP: STA 2. LOB: STA 10, STN 4. BB: Hamilton 2, Doak 4, Trekell 1, Griner 1. Struck out: Hamilton 1, Mitchell 3, Doak 3, Griner 1. Hits: Hamilton 4 in 4 innings; Mitchell 5 in 5 innings; Doak 8 in 4.1 innings; Trekell 3 in 1.1 innings; Griner 4 in 2.1 innings. WP: Hamilton. Umpires: Hildebrand, Brennan. Time—2:15.

In the first game of a double-header the next day, the Cardinals took a 3–0 lead but Harry Trekell (0–1), pitching in relief of Bill Doak (2–8), failed to hold the Browns. The Americans scored once in the fourth, three times in the fifth to go ahead, and four times in the sixth to go on top to stay. Earl Hamilton (13–12) started for the Browns, but left the game in the fifth. Roy Mitchell (13–16) pitched the next inning and a third for the win

1913 St. Louis City Championship Series

GAME FOUR --- October 11 (second game)

CARDINALS	AB	R	H	PO	A	E		BROWNS	AB	R	H	PO	A	E
Huggins, 2b	2	0	2	1	1	1		Shotton, cf	2	1	0	1	0	0
Magee, lf	3	0	0	2	0	0		Austin, 3b	3	1	1	1	0	0
Mowrey, 3b	3	1	0	0	4	0		Pratt, 1b	3	0	0	3	0	0
Oakes, cf	3	0	0	0	1	0		Walker, lf	3	0	2	1	0	0
Konetchy, 1b	3	0	1	11	1	0		Williams, rf	1	0	0	3	0	0
Evans, rf	2	1	1	0	0	0		Bisland, ss	2	0	1	0	1	1
O'Leary, ss	3	0	1	0	0	0		Wares, 2b	2	0	0	1	0	1
Snyder, c	3	0	1	4	0	0		Agnew, c	2	0	0	8	1	0
Harmon, p	2	0	0	0	3	0		Taylor, p	1	0	0	0	2	0
								Sloan, ph	1	0	0	0	0	0
	24	2	6	18	10	1			20	2	4	18	4	2

```
STN   0  1  1    0  0  0  -  2
STA   0  0  0    0  0  2  -  2
```

SF: Williams. SB: Austin, Huggins. DP: STN 1. LOB: STN 6, STA 2. BB: Taylor 1, Harmon 1. Struck out: Taylor 7, Harmon 2. HBP: Huggins (Taylor). PB: Agnew. WP: Harmon, Taylor. Umpires: Brennan, Hildebrand. Time—1:05.

GAME FIVE --- October 12

BROWNS	AB	R	H	PO	A	E		CARDINALS	AB	R	H	PO	A	E
Shotton, cf	5	2	4	2	0	0		Huggins, 2b	4	0	0	3	2	0
Austin, 3b	5	1	3	1	1	0		Magee, lf	3	1	1	1	0	1
Pratt, 1b	4	0	1	7	0	0		Beck, 3b	4	0	0	2	0	0
Walker, lf	4	1	2	3	0	0		Oakes, cf	4	0	2	4	0	0
Williams, rf	3	1	1	3	0	0		Konetchy, 1b	4	2	1	9	0	0
Bisland, ss	4	0	0	3	2	0		Whitted, rf	3	1	2	3	1	0
Wares, 2b	4	1	2	4	3	0		O'Leary, ss	4	1	1	2	3	0
Agnew, c	4	0	0	4	3	0		Snyder, c	3	1	1	3	1	0
Weilman, p	3	0	0	0	1	0		Sallee, p	3	0	2	0	3	0
McAllister, ph	0	0	0	0	0	0		Evans, ph	0	0	0	0	0	0
Sloan, pr	0	1	0	0	0	0		Mowrey, ph	1	0	0	0	0	0
Baumgardner, p	0	0	0	0	0	0		Harmon, pr	0	0	0	0	0	0
	36	7	13	27	10	0			33	6	10	27	10	1

```
STA   0  0  1    2  0  0    0  2  2  -  7
STN   0  0  0    5  0  1    0  0  0  -  6
```

2B: Wares, Sallee, Walker. 3B: Magee, Whitted. SH: Williams. SF: Pratt. SB: Konetchy, Magee. DP: STA 1, STN 1. LOB: STA 5, STN 2. BB: Weilman 1, Sallee 1, Baumgardner 1. Struck out: Sallee 3, Weilman 4. Hits: Weilman 10 in 8 innings; Baumgardner 0 in 1 inning. WP: Weilman. Umpires: Hildebrand, Brennan. Time—2:10.

In the nightcap, the Cardinals tallied single runs in the second and third and the Browns scored twice in the bottom of the sixth. The game was called at that point because of darkness. Starting pitchers were Bob Harmon (8–21) for the Cardinals and Wiley Taylor (0–2) for the Browns.

Games Five and Six were played on October 12. Carl Weilman started for the Browns against Slim Sallee and, for once, was unable to contain the Cardinals. Rolling along with a 3–0 lead, Weilman blew up in the fourth when the Cardinals scored five runs to take the lead. The Redbirds padded their lead to 6–3 but the Browns exploded for two runs in the eighth and two more in the

1913 St. Louis City Championship Series

GAME SIX --- October 12 (second game)

BROWNS	AB	R	H	PO	A	E		CARDINALS	AB	R	H	PO	A	E
Shotton, cf	3	1	0	3	0	0		Huggins, 2b	3	1	1	1	4	1
Austin, 3b	3	2	3	1	1	1		Magee, lf	3	0	1	2	1	0
Pratt, 1b	3	1	2	4	1	0		Beck, 3b	1	0	0	1	2	1
Walker, lf	3	0	0	0	0	0		Oakes, cf	3	1	1	0	0	0
Williams, rf	3	1	0	0	0	0		Konetchy, 1b	3	0	1	9	1	0
Bisland, ss	3	0	2	3	2	0		Whitted, rf	3	0	2	0	1	1
Wares, 2b	3	0	2	2	1	0		O'Leary, ss	3	0	1	1	2	0
Agnew, c	3	0	1	4	0	0		Snyder, c	3	0	1	4	0	0
Leverenz, p	3	1	1	1	2	0		Perritt, p	2	0	0	0	3	0
								Mowrey, ph	1	0	0	0	0	0
	27	6	11	18	7	1			25	2	8	18	14	3

```
STA    3 3 0    0 0 0  -  6
STN    0 0 0    0 2 0  -  2
```

2B: Bisland. 3B: Pratt. SB: Wares. LOB: STN 8, STA 4. DP: STA 1. BB: Leverenz 3, Perritt 1. Struck out: Leverenz 3, Perritt 2. PB: Snyder 2. Umpires: Brennan, Hildebrand. Time—1:30.

GAME SEVEN --- October 13

BROWNS	AB	R	H	PO	A	E		CARDINALS	AB	R	H	PO	A	E
Shotton, cf	4	1	2	3	0	1		Huggins, 2b	3	0	0	0	5	0
Austin, 3b	3	0	0	3	1	0		Magee, lf	4	1	1	1	0	0
Pratt, 1b	2	0	0	3	1	0		Whitted, 3b	4	0	0	2	3	0
Crossin, 1b	1	0	0	6	1	0		Oakes, cf	4	0	1	2	0	0
Walker, lf	3	0	1	1	0	0		Konetchy, 1b	4	2	2	15	0	1
Williams, rf	3	0	1	0	0	0		Evans, rf	1	1	0	2	0	0
Bisland, ss	4	0	0	1	1	0		O'Leary, ss	3	1	1	1	2	1
Wares, 2b	4	0	0	4	5	0		Snyder, c	2	0	1	3	1	0
Agnew, c	4	0	0	3	1	0		Harmon, p	3	0	0	1	3	0
Baumgardner, p	0	0	0	0	0	0		Mowrey, rf	1	0	1	0	0	0
Taylor, p	0	0	0	0	1	1								
Leverenz, p	1	1	0	0	1	0			29	5	7	27	14	2
Sloan, ph	1	0	0	0	0	0								
Rickey, ph	1	0	1	0	0	0								
	31	2	5	24	12	2								

```
STA    0 0 0    0 0 0    0 2 0  -  2
STN    1 0 0    2 0 1    0 1 x  -  5
```

2B: O'Leary. 3B: Konetchy. SH: O'Leary, Snyder, Austin. SF: Crossin. SB: Williams, Evans. LOB: STN 5, STA 7. DP: STA 2, STN 1. HBP: Baumgardner (Harmon). BB: Baumgardner 2, Taylor 1, Harmon 2. Struck out: Baumgardner 3, Harmon 2. Hits: Baumgardner 5 in 4 innings; Taylor 0 in 3 innings; Leverenz 2 in 1 inning. Umpires: Hildebrand, Brennan. Time—2:05.

ninth to win. Weilman, who left the game in favor of pinch-hitter Bill McAllester in the ninth, got the win. George Baumgardner pitched the final inning for the Browns. Sallee went the distance for the loss.

    After a brief interval, Game Six began with Walt Leverenz (6–17) on the mound for the Browns against Pol Perrit. With darkness fast approaching, the Americans made short work of Perritt, scoring three runs in the first and three more in the second. The game was called at the end of six innings with the Browns leading, 6–2.

1913 St. Louis City Championship Series

```
GAME EIGHT --- October 13 (second game)
```

BROWNS	AB	R	H	PO	A	E	CARDINALS	AB	R	H	PO	A	E
Shotton, cf	3	1	2	1	0	0	Huggins, 2b	3	0	1	1	0	0
Austin, 3b	3	0	0	0	2	0	Magee, lf	2	0	0	1	0	0
Wares, 2b	3	0	0	2	3	0	Whitted, 3b	2	0	0	0	2	1
Walker, lf	3	0	0	1	0	0	Oakes, cf	2	0	0	0	0	0
Williams, rf	2	0	1	1	0	0	Konetchy, 1b	1	0	0	7	1	0
Bisland, ss	1	0	0	0	1	1	Evans, rf	2	0	0	1	0	0
Crossin, 1b	2	0	0	7	0	1	O'Leary, ss	2	1	0	0	4	2
Agnew, c	2	0	0	3	0	0	Snyder, c	2	0	0	4	0	0
Leverenz, p	2	0	1	0	0	0	Harmon, p	1	0	0	1	1	0
							Mowrey, ph	1	0	0	0	0	0
	21	1	4	15	6	2		18	1	1	15	8	3

```
STA   0  0  1    0  0  -  1
STN   0  0  0    0  1  -  1
```

SH: Bisland. SB: Shotton, Konetchy. LOB: STN 4, STA 6. BB: Leverenz 2. Struck out: Harmon 3, Leverenz 2. Umpires: Brennan and Hildebrand. Time—1:10.

Games Seven and Eight were scheduled as a double-header on Monday, October 13. The Cardinals and Bob Harmon easily won the first game, 5–2, and George Baumgardner, who gave up the first three Cardinal runs, was the loser. Derrill Pratt of the Browns and Zinn Beck, a utility infielder with the Cardinals, got into an argument over some imaginative name-calling on Beck's part and Pratt was ejected from the game by umpire George Hildebrand.

The Cardinals objected when Pratt took his position at first base for the nightcap. Browns manager Branch Rickey refused to let his team take their positions unless Pratt was allowed to play. Cardinals manager Miller Huggins appealed to umpires Hildebrand and Brennan who ruled that Pratt must leave. Rickey continued to argue with the two arbiters until, out of exasperation, they deserted the field. After a short delay, the umpires and both teams re-emerged from their respective hideouts – Frank Crossin on first base for the Browns – and the game began. At the end of five, the contest was called on account of darkness, tied 1–1.

Because of the lack of discipline and prevalence of bad feeling between the two clubs, Rickey and Huggins decided to end the series with three wins apiece. One can easily imagine the residents of St. Louis – National and American League fans alike – extending their gratitude for an act of such thoughtfulness.

The 1913 Chicago City Championship Series

Chicago White Sox defeat the Chicago Cubs; 4–2

The Chicago Cubs (88–65) finished a distant third in 1913 behind the New York Giants (101–51). The White Sox fared even worse than the Cubs, finishing fifth with a 78–74 record. Yet despite the apparent superiority of the Cubs, it was the White Sox who won their third consecutive city championship, four games to two.

1913 Chicago City Championship Series

GAME ONE --- October 8

WHITE SOX	AB	R	H	PO	A	E	CUBS	AB	R	H	PO	A	E
Weaver, ss	5	0	2	0	3	1	Leach, cf	5	0	3	0	1	0
Lord, 3b	4	1	1	0	0	0	Evers, 2b	5	0	1	5	3	0
Chase, 1b	3	1	0	10	0	1	Schulte, lf	4	0	0	0	0	0
Bodie, cf	3	1	1	2	0	0	Zimmerman, 3b	5	0	1	2	2	0
Collins, rf	4	1	2	1	0	0	Saier, 1b	5	2	2	13	2	0
Chappelle, lf	3	0	1	3	0	0	Good, rf	4	2	2	1	0	0
Schalk, c	4	2	2	9	0	0	Bridwell, ss	3	0	1	1	5	3
Berger, 2b	3	0	1	1	3	0	Archer, c	3	0	2	5	4	0
Russell, p	4	0	1	1	2	0	Cheney, p	3	0	0	0	2	0
Scott, p	0	0	0	0	1	0	Lavender, p	0	0	0	0	0	0
							Williams, ph	1	0	0	0	0	0
	33	6	11	27	9	2		38	4	12	27	19	3

```
SOX   2 0 0   1 0 2   1 0 0 - 6
CUB   0 0 0   1 0 2   0 1 0 - 4
```

2B: Weaver, Chappelle, Schalk, Bridwell, Collins, Lord, Leach, Archer. 3B: Collins. Home runs: Good, Saier. SF: Archer. SH: Chappelle. DP: Sox 2. LOB: Sox 10, Cubs 6. HBP: Schulte (Russell), Chase (Cheney). BB: Cheney 4, Russell 1. Struck out: Russell 6, Scott 1, Cheney 3. Hits: Russell 11 in 7.1 innings; Scott 1 in 1.2 innings; Cheney 11 in 8 innings. WP: Russell. Umpires: O'Day, Sheridan, Orth, O'Loughlin. Time—2:03.

GAME TWO --- October 9

CUBS	AB	R	H	PO	A	E	WHITE SOX	AB	R	H	PO	A	E
Leach, cf	5	1	1	2	0	0	Weaver, ss	6	0	1	5	8	1
Evers, 2b	4	1	2	0	6	1	Lord, 3b	4	1	1	3	2	0
Schulte, lf	6	1	1	1	0	0	Chase, 1b	6	1	1	17	2	0
Zimmerman, 3b	6	2	2	0	1	1	Bodie, cf	4	2	2	1	0	0
Saier, 1b	4	0	0	22	0	0	Fournier, rf	1	0	0	0	0	0
Good, rf	6	1	1	3	1	0	Collins, rf-cf	6	1	2	3	0	0
Bridwell, ss	3	0	0	4	5	1	Chappelle, lf	6	0	2	5	1	1
Archer, c	5	0	2	7	1	0	Schalk, c	6	0	0	5	1	1
Vaughn, p	5	0	0	0	2	0	Berger, 2b	5	0	1	0	3	0
							Cicotte, p	2	0	1	0	3	0
	44	6	9	39	16	3	Benz, p	3	0	0	0	4	0
								49	5	11	39	24	3

```
CUBS   0 0 0   4 1 0   0 0 0   0 0 0   1 - 6
SOX    0 0 0   3 0 1   0 1 0   0 0 0   0 - 5
```

2B: Archer. SH: Bodie, Archer. SF: Saier. DP: Sox. LOB: Cub 8, Sox 8. BB: Cicotte 3, Benz 4, Vaughn 2. Struck out: Cicotte 2, Benz 2, Vaugh 5. Hits: Cicotte 6 in 4 innings (none out in fifth inning); Benz 3 in 9 innings. WP: Vaughn, Benz. Umpires: O'Loughlin, Orth, O'Day, Sheridan. Time—2:55.

The series opened with the Sox winning 6–4 as they pounded out five doubles and a triple among 11 hits. Rookie Ewell "Reb" Russell (22–16) went seven and a third innings for the win and bested the Cubs' Larry Cheney (21–14). Jim Scott (20–20) pitched the last inning and two-thirds in relief of Russell.

Game Two went 13 innings at Comiskey Park. The Cubs scored four in the fourth, but the Sox tallied three in the bottom of the inning. The Cubs took a 5–3 lead in the fifth, but single runs by the Sox in the sixth and eighth sent the game into extra innings. Joe Benz (7–10) relieved Eddie Cicotte (18–12) in

1913 Chicago City Championship Series

GAME THREE --- October 10

WHITE SOX	AB	R	H	PO	A	E
Weaver, ss	4	0	0	3	1	2
Lord, 3b	4	0	1	1	0	0
Chase, 1b	4	0	1	6	0	0
Bodie, cf	4	0	0	1	0	1
Collins, rf	3	0	1	3	0	1
Fournier, lf	2	0	0	1	0	0
Schalk, c	3	0	0	4	3	0
Berger, 2b	2	0	0	4	2	1
Borton, 2b	0	0	0	1	0	0
Scott, p	2	0	0	0	1	0
Lathrop, p	0	0	0	0	0	0
Easterly, ph	1	0	0	0	0	0
Chappelle, ph	1	0	1	0	0	0
	30	0	4	24	7	5

CUBS	AB	R	H	PO	A	E
Leach, cf	5	1	1	2	0	0
Evers, 2b	3	2	1	1	2	0
Schulte, lf	4	2	3	5	0	0
Zimmerman, 3b	4	1	1	0	0	0
Saier, 1b	3	1	1	8	0	0
Good, rf	4	1	2	1	0	0
Bridwell, ss	4	0	1	2	3	0
Archer, c	4	0	0	8	0	0
Humphries, p	3	0	0	0	1	0
	34	8	10	27	6	0

```
SOX   0  0  0    0  0  0    0  0  0  -  0
CUB   0  0  0    0  0  3    5  0  x  -  8
```

2B: Chase, Lord, Leach. SH: Fournier. DP: Sox. LOB: Sox 4, Cubs 6. HBP: Humphries (Scott). BB: Scott 3. Struck out: Scott 4, Humphries 7. Hits: Scott 10 in 7 innings; Lathrop 0 in 1 inning. Umpires: O'Day, Sheridan, Orth, O'Loughlin. Time—1:58.

GAME FOUR --- October 11

CUBS	AB	R	H	PO	A	E
Leach, cf	5	0	0	2	1	0
Evers, 2b	4	0	0	1	2	0
Schulte, lf	4	0	1	1	1	0
Zimmerman, 3b	5	1	1	2	1	0
Saier, 1b	3	0	1	9	0	0
Good, rf	4	0	2	1	0	0
Bridwell, ss	3	0	1	5	2	0
Archer, c	3	1	2	3	0	0
Pearce, p	3	0	0	0	5	0
Lavender, p	0	0	0	0	0	1
Smith, p	0	0	0	0	0	0
Williams, ph	1	0	0	0	0	0
	35	2	7	24	12	1

WHITE SOX	AB	R	H	PO	A	E
Weaver, ss	5	2	3	2	2	1
Lord, 3b	4	1	1	0	4	1
Chase, 1b	4	0	1	8	0	0
Bodie, cf-rf	4	0	1	0	0	0
Collins, rf-cf	4	0	1	1	0	0
Fournier, lf	3	0	2	4	0	0
Schalk, c	4	0	1	12	0	0
Berger, 2b	4	0	0	0	2	1
Cicotte, p	4	2	3	0	1	0
	36	5	13	27	9	3

```
CUB   0  1  1    0  0  0    0  0  0  -  2
SOX   0  0  0    0  1  0    3  1  x  -  5
```

2B: Zimmerman, Cicotte 2, Weaver 2. 3B: Saier. SH: Bridwell. LOB: Cubs 10, White Sox 10. BB: Cicotte 3, Pearce 3. Struck out: Cicotte 9, Pearce 2. Hits: Pearce 10 in 6 innings; Lavender 1 in 1 inning; Smith 2 in 1 inning. Umpires: O'Loughlin, Orth, Sheridan, O'Day. Time—2:20.

the fifth and gave up just two Cub hits over the next eight innings. But in the thirteenth, Heinie Zimmerman singled and Vic Saier and Al Bridwell walked. One out later, Jimmy Archer's sacrifice fly scored Zimmerman with the lead run. The White Sox failed to rally in the bottom of the inning and the series was tied. James "Hippo" Vaughn (5–1) went the distance for the Cubs and got the victory.

1913 Chicago City Championship Series

GAME FIVE --- October 12

WHITE SOX	AB	R	H	PO	A	E
Weaver, ss	5	0	1	1	3	0
Lord, 3b	4	1	2	1	3	0
Chase, 1b	4	0	0	15	0	0
Bodie, cf	5	0	1	1	0	0
Collins, rf	5	1	4	3	0	0
Fournier, lf	5	0	1	2	0	0
Schalk, c	4	0	0	9	0	0
Berger, 2b	4	0	1	1	8	0
Benz, p	4	0	0	0	2	0
	40	2	10	33	16	0

CUBS	AB	R	H	PO	A	E
Leach, cf	4	0	1	8	0	0
Evers, 2b	4	0	1	3	1	0
Schulte, lf	4	0	0	1	0	0
Zimmerman, 3b	4	0	0	1	2	0
Saier, 1b	4	0	0	13	1	0
Good, rf	4	0	0	0	0	0
Bridwell, ss	4	0	0	1	7	0
Archer, c	4	0	1	6	4	1
Cheney, p	3	0	0	0	3	0
Miller, ph	1	0	0	0	0	0
	36	0	3	33	18	1

SOX	0	0	0	0	0	0	0	0	0	0	2	-	2
CUB	0	0	0	0	0	0	0	0	0	0	0	-	0

2B: Collins 2, Evers, Berger, Lord. 3B: Lord. SH: Chase. SB: Collins, Fournier. LOB: Cub 3, Sox 7. BB: Cheney 1. Struck out: Cheney 8, Benz 9. Umpires: O'Day, Sheridan, Orth, O'Loughlin.

GAME SIX --- October 13

CUBS	AB	R	H	PO	A	E
Leach, cf	3	0	1	1	1	0
Evers, 2b	4	1	1	1	2	0
Schulte, lf	4	0	0	1	0	0
Zimmerman, 3b	4	0	0	2	0	0
Saier, 1b	3	1	2	11	1	0
Good, rf	4	0	0	4	0	0
Bridwell, ss	4	0	2	1	3	0
Archer, c	4	0	3	3	3	1
Humphries, p	1	0	0	0	2	0
Miller, ph	1	0	0	0	0	0
Lavender, p	1	0	0	0	2	0
Steward, pr	0	0	0	0	0	0
Williams, ph	1	0	0	0	0	0
Phelan, pr	0	0	0	0	0	0
	34	2	9	24	14	1

WHITE SOX	AB	R	H	PO	A	E
Weaver, ss	4	0	1	6	1	1
Lord, 3b	3	1	1	3	1	0
Chase, 1b	4	2	2	7	1	0
Bodie, rf-cf	4	1	2	2	0	0
Collins, cf-rf	4	1	2	0	0	0
Fournier, lf	4	0	3	3	0	0
Schalk, c	4	0	0	5	0	0
Berger, 2b	4	0	0	1	5	0
Scott, p	3	0	0	0	2	0
	34	5	11	27	10	1

CUB	0	0	0	1	0	0	0	0	1	-	2
SOX	0	0	0	3	2	0	0	0	x	-	5

2B: Collins, Fournier, Lord, Bodie, Leach. SB: Evers. DP: Sox 1. LOB: Cubs 7, Sox 6. BB: Scott 2, Humphries 1. Struck out: Humphries 1, Scott 5, Lavender 1. Hits: Humphries 4 in 4 innings; Lavender 7 in 4 innings. Umpires: O'Loughlin, Orth, Sheridan, O'Day. Time—1:53.

    The series resumed in West Side Park for Game Three and a second Cub victory. Bert Humphries (16–4) struck out seven and shut out the Sox on four hits as he coasted to an easy 8–0 win when the Cubs scored three runs in the sixth and five more in the seventh. Jim Scott (20–20) took the loss.

    Eddie Cicotte of the White Sox was the star of Game Four — on the mound and with the bat. Eddie had two doubles and a single, scored twice, and pitched a complete game as the Americans came from behind in the seventh to deliver a 5–2 loss to the Cubs. Jimmy Lavender (10–14), who pitched in relief of George Pearce (13–5), was the loser.

Game Five was a nail-biter. Both Joe Benz and Larry Cheney pitched superlative ball and after ten innings neither team had been able to score. In the eleventh, the White Sox netted two runs against Cheney and won the game. Both pitchers went the distance. Cheney allowed ten hits and Benz threw a three-hit shutout.

The White Sox claimed the championship of Chicago in Game Six. Bert Humphries was rematched with Jim Scott, but this time Scott came out on top. Jack Fournier's double in a three-run fourth put the Sox on top to stay. Scott allowed nine hits and pitched a complete game for the victory.

The 1914 St. Louis City Championship Series

St. Louis Browns defeat the St. Louis Cardinals; 4-1-1

In 1914, both the Cardinals (81–72) and Browns (71–82) improved upon their previous year's last-place finishes — the Redbirds finishing third, the Browns fifth. The Cardinals would have been favored in the postseason championship series, but for the fact that several of their ballplayers were thought to be preparing to desert their contracts for teams in the Federal League. Speculation was rife that a number of the boys were giving less than their full effort.

1914 St. Louis City Championship Series

GAME ONE --- October 6

BROWNS	AB	R	H	PO	A	E		CARDINALS	AB	R	H	PO	A	E
Shotton, cf	3	1	1	1	0	0		Dolan, lf	4	0	1	4	0	0
Austin, 3b	4	0	0	2	5	0		Huggins, 2b	3	0	0	2	2	1
Pratt, 2b	4	0	1	2	0	0		Magee, 1b	3	0	1	8	1	0
C. Walker, lf	4	0	1	0	0	0		J.Miller, ss	4	1	1	2	1	0
Williams, rf	4	0	0	4	0	0		Wilson, rf	4	0	1	3	0	0
Howard, 1b	3	0	1	10	0	0		Snyder, c	3	0	0	6	2	0
Lavan, ss	3	0	0	5	3	1		Riggert, cf	4	0	2	1	0	0
Agnew, c	3	0	0	3	4	0		Beck, 3b	3	0	1	1	2	0
Weilman, p	2	1	1	0	1	0		Doak, p	2	0	0	0	1	1
								Roche, ph	1	0	1	0	0	0
	30	2	5	27	13	1		E.Miller, pr	0	0	0	0	0	0
								Griner, p	0	0	0	0	0	0
								Nash, ph	1	0	0	0	0	0
									32	1	8	27	9	2

```
STA   0  0  2    0  0  0    0  0  0  -  2
STN   0  0  0    0  0  0    0  0  0  -  1
```

SB: Dolan, Magee. SH: Snyder, Weilman. LOB: STN 8, STA 3. DP: STA. BB: Weilman 3, Doak 1. Struck out: Weilman 2, Doak 5, Griner 1. Umpires: Johnson and O'Brien. Time—2:05.

The series opened with Carl Weilman (18–13) of the Browns out-dueling Bill Doak (20–6). Weilman held the Cardinals to eight hits and kept them from crossing home plate until the ninth inning. Doak, meanwhile limited the Browns to just five hits, but two Brownie runs in the third inning spelled his defeat. The final score was 2–1.

Game Two pitted the Cardinals' Slim Sallee (18–17) against Earl Hamilton (17–18). The Browns scored two runs in the first and second innings off Sallee

1914 St. Louis City Championship Series

GAME TWO --- October 7

CARDINALS	AB	R	H	PO	A	E
Dolan, lf	5	0	2	0	0	1
Huggins, 2b	3	1	2	1	5	0
Magee, 1b	5	0	0	8	3	0
J.Miller, ss	4	1	3	3	1	2
Wilson, rf	3	0	0	2	1	0
Snyder, c	2	0	1	4	2	0
Wingo, c	2	0	0	0	2	0
Cruise, cf	2	1	1	0	0	0
Riggert, cf	2	1	1	0	0	0
Beck, 3b	2	0	1	5	0	2
Sallee, p	0	0	0	1	2	0
Roche, ph	0	0	0	0	0	0
C.Miller, pr	0	0	0	0	0	0
Perdue, p	2	0	1	0	2	0
Dressen, ph	1	0	0	0	0	0
	33	4	12	24	18	5

BROWNS	AB	R	H	PO	A	E
Shotton, cf	4	1	2	1	0	0
Austin, 3b	3	0	0	3	0	0
Pratt, 2b	4	1	1	4	3	0
C. Walker, lf	4	2	3	0	1	0
Williams, rf	3	1	2	0	0	0
Howard, 1b	3	0	2	6	0	1
Lavan, ss	3	1	1	2	3	0
Agnew, c	4	0	2	11	4	0
Hamilton, p	1	1	0	0	0	0
Baumgardner, p	1	0	0	0	0	0
	30	7	13	27	11	1

```
STN   0  0  1    2  0  0    0  0  1  -  4
STA   2  2  0    0  0  0    0  3  x  -  7
```

2B: Pratt, Williams 2, C. Walker, Agnew, Riggert, J. Miller. 3B: Shotton. HR: C. Walker. SH: Williams, Lavan, Hamilton. SB: Austin, Huggins, J. Miller. LOB: STA 4, STN 8. DP: STA 2. BB: Hamilton 2, Sallee 1, Perdue 1, Baumgardner 4. Struck out: Hamilton 1, Perdue 1, Baumgardner 7. Umpires: O'Brien and Johnson. Time—2:10.

GAME THREE --- October 10

BROWNS	AB	R	H	PO	A	E
Shotton, cf	4	1	4	0	0	0
Austin, 3b	4	0	0	0	0	0
Pratt, 2b	4	0	0	4	2	0
C. Walker, lf	4	0	0	4	0	0
Williams, rf	4	1	2	1	0	0
Howard, 1b	4	0	3	12	0	0
Lavan, ss	4	0	1	1	5	1
Agnew, c	4	0	2	5	0	0
James, p	3	0	1	0	7	0
	35	2	13	27	14	1

CARDINALS	AB	R	H	PO	A	E
Dolan, lf	4	0	0	1	0	0
Huggins, 2b	4	0	0	2	1	0
Magee, 1b	3	0	2	12	0	0
J.Miller, ss	3	0	0	1	0	0
Wilson, rf	3	0	0	2	0	0
Wingo, c	4	0	0	8	5	0
Cruise, cf	3	0	1	0	0	0
Beck, 3b	4	0	1	1	5	0
Perritt, p	3	0	0	0	4	0
	31	0	4	27	15	0

```
STA   1  0  0    1  0  0    0  0  0  -  2
STN   0  0  0    0  0  0    0  0  0  -  0
```

2B: Shotton, Williams, Magee. SH: Austin, Shotton. SB: Williams, Howard. LOB: STA 8, STN 3. DP: STA. BB: Perritt 1, James 3. Struck out: Perritt 7, James 4. WP: Perritt. Umpires: Johnson and O'Brien. Time—2:00.

and he left for a pinch-hitter when the Redbirds scored once in the top of the third. The Cards made it a contest for a little while, scoring two runs in the fourth, but three eighth-inning runs by the Browns put the game on ice. The final score was 7–4. Sallee took the loss for the Cardinals. Hamilton enjoyed his 12-hitter and perhaps enjoyed it a little too much. After the game, he suffered injuries serious enough to force his retirement from the series when he crashed his car into a railing on the Eads Bridge.

1914 St. Louis City Championship Series

```
GAME FOUR --- October 10 (second game)
```

CARDINALS	AB	R	H	PO	A	E		BROWNS	AB	R	H	PO	A	E
Dolan, lf	2	0	0	1	0	0		Shotton, cf	1	0	0	1	0	0
Huggins, 2b	1	0	0	2	2	0		Austin, 3b	2	0	0	3	0	0
Magee, 1b	2	0	1	5	0	0		Pratt, 2b	3	0	1	2	1	0
J.Miller, ss	2	0	0	0	0	0		C. Walker, lf	2	0	1	3	0	0
Wilson, rf	1	1	0	0	0	0		Williams, rf	2	0	0	1	0	0
Snyder, c	2	0	0	5	1	0		Howard, 1b	2	0	0	1	0	0
Cruise, cf	2	1	1	1	0	0		Lavan, ss	2	0	0	0	0	0
Beck, 3b	2	0	1	1	1	0		Agnew, c	2	0	0	4	1	0
Griner, p	2	0	0	0	0	0		Baumgardner, p	1	0	1	0	0	0
	16	2	3	15	4	0			17	0	3	15	2	0

```
STN   0  0  0    0  2  -  2
STA   0  0  0    0  0  -  0
```

2B: Magee. 3B: Cruise. SH: Shotton. LOB: STA 2, STN 2. BB: Baumgardner 1. Struck out: Baumgardner 2, Griner 4. PB: Agnew. Umpires: Johnson and O'Brien. Time—1:10.

Two straight days of rain followed, so Games Three and Four were scheduled as a doubleheader on the 10th. Game Three was the first of three consecutive 2–0 shutouts, two of the decisions going to the Browns. The American Leaguers scored once in the first and fourth innings as Bill James (15–14) went the distance, shutting out the Cardinals on four hits. Losing pitcher Pol Perritt (16–13) pitched a complete game for the Redbirds and did a good job of keeping the Browns away from the plate, considering he gave up 13 hits and a walk.

The Cardinals returned the 2–0 shutout with their compliments in Game Four. Both teams had just three hits, but winning pitcher Dan Griner (9–13) stifled the Browns' offense completely. In the fifth, a walk to Owen Wilson, a triple by Walton Cruise, and a single by Zinn Beck accounted for the Cardinals' first win of the series. The losing pitcher was George Baumgardner (14–13).

Rookie manager Branch Rickey made surprise starter Harry Hoch (0–2) the sacrificial lamb in Game Five, figuring Bill Doak wouldn't be beaten twice in the same series. But Hoch chose not to be sacrificed and twirled a one-hit shutout for the Browns, the only Cardinal hit a scratch single by shortstop John "Dots" Miller. Hoch fell down fielding Miller's grounder, but if he had let third baseman Jimmy Austin handle the ball, he would have had his no-hitter. Austin and Del Pratt scored the game's only two runs in the third inning. The Browns had clinched the St. Louis City Championship, four games to one.

Immediately following the championship clinching victory, the two teams took the field again to play an exhibition contest. Carl Weilman started for the Browns against Hub Perdue (8–8). The Cardinals struck for two runs in the first, the Browns tied the game with single runs in the first and fourth, and the game was called on account of darkness at the end of seven.

1914 St. Louis City Championship Series

```
GAME FIVE --- October 11
```

CARDINALS	AB	R	H	PO	A	E		BROWNS	AB	R	H	PO	A	E
Riggert, lf	1	0	0	1	0	0		Shotton, cf	4	0	0	1	0	0
Dolan, lf	0	0	0	1	0	0		Austin, 3b	2	1	0	1	3	0
Huggins, 2b	4	0	0	2	3	1		Pratt, 2b	4	1	2	3	3	0
Magee, 1b	2	0	0	10	0	0		C. Walker, lf	4	0	2	2	0	0
J. Miller, ss	3	0	1	1	0	0		Williams, rf	4	0	0	1	0	0
Wilson, rf	3	0	0	2	0	0		Howard, 1b	4	0	0	11	1	0
Wingo, c	1	0	0	2	0	0		Lavan, ss	3	0	1	4	4	0
Snyder, c	2	0	0	4	3	0		Agnew, c	3	0	2	4	3	0
Cruise, cf	3	0	0	1	0	0		Hoch, p	3	0	0	0	4	0
Beck, 3b	2	0	0	0	3	1		Baumgardner, p	0	0	0	0	0	0
Doak, p	2	0	0	0	2	0								
Roche, ph	1	0	0	0	0	0			31	2	7	27	18	0
	24	0	1	24	11	2								

```
STN    0  0  0    0  0  0    0  0  0  -  0
STA    0  0  2    0  0  0    0  0  x  -  2
```

SB: Williams, Walker. LOB: STN 2, STA 7. DP: STA 1, STN 1. BB: Hoch 5, Doak 2. Struck out: Hoch 3, Doak 6, Baumgardner 1. Umpires: O'Brien and Johnson. Time—2:15.

```
GAME SIX --- October 11 (second game)
```

BROWNS	AB	R	H	PO	A	E		CARDINALS	AB	R	H	PO	A	E
Shotton, cf	3	1	1	1	0	0		Riggert, lf	4	1	1	2	0	0
Austin, 3b	3	1	1	2	3	0		Nash, 2b	4	1	3	2	2	0
Pratt, 2b	3	0	2	4	3	1		Dressen, 1b	4	0	0	12	1	0
C. Walker, lf	3	0	1	1	0	0		J. Miller, ss	3	0	1	2	3	0
Williams, rf	0	0	0	0	0	0		Wilson, rf	2	0	0	0	0	0
E. Walker, rf	2	0	1	3	0	0		Snyder, c	3	0	0	2	1	0
Howard, 1b	3	0	0	4	0	0		C. Miller, cf	0	0	0	0	0	0
Lavan, ss	3	0	1	2	2	0		Cruise, cf	2	0	0	0	0	0
Agnew, c	2	0	0	3	1	0		Roche, ph	1	0	1	0	0	0
Weilman, p	2	0	0	1	1	0		Beck, 3b	3	0	0	1	3	0
	24	2	7	21	10	1		Perdue, p	1	0	0	0	2	0
								Niehaus, p	1	0	1	0	2	0
									28	2	7	21	14	0

```
STA    1  0  0    1  0  0    0  -  2
STN    2  0  0    0  0  0    0  -  2
```

2B: Pratt, J. Miller, Austin, Lavan, Roche. SH: E. Walker. LOB: STN: 7, STA 2. BB: Weilman 1. Struck out: Weilman 1, Perdue 2. Umpires: O'Brien and Johnson. Time—1:15.

The 1914 Chicago City Championship Series

Chicago White Sox defeat Chicago Cubs; 4–3

The Cubs and White Sox played one of the most exciting city championships of all in 1914, the White Sox battling back time and again to finally prevail. The Cubs had two 20-game winners in Hippo Vaughn (21–13) and Larry Cheney (20–18), a remarkable achievement for a team which finished 16 and a half games out and only two games above .500. The series opened in Comiskey Park and alternated between Comiskey and West Side Park for each of the seven games.

1914 Chicago City Championship Series

GAME ONE --- October 7

CUBS	AB	R	H	PO	A	E		WHITE SOX	AB	R	H	PO	A	E
Leach, cf	3	2	1	1	1	0		Weaver, ss	4	0	2	3	0	0
Good, rf	4	1	3	2	2	0		Blackburne, 2b	3	0	0	1	4	0
Saier, 1b	4	0	2	9	1	0		Collins, cf	3	0	0	2	1	0
Zimmerman, 3b	4	0	1	4	3	0		Fournier, 1b	4	0	0	12	0	0
Schulte, lf	3	0	0	1	0	0		Roth, rf	3	0	1	2	1	0
Derrick, ss	3	0	1	2	2	2		Demmit, lf	1	0	1	3	0	1
Sweeney, 2b	3	0	0	1	3	0		Faber, p	1	0	0	0	1	0
Bresnahan, c	4	0	1	7	1	0		Daly, ph	1	0	0	0	0	0
Vaughn, p	4	1	0	0	6	0		Cicotte, p	0	0	0	0	0	0
								Schalk, c	4	1	2	4	0	0
	32	4	9	27	19	2		Breton, 3b	3	0	0	0	5	0
								Wolfgang, p	1	0	0	0	4	0
								Bodie, lf	3	1	2	0	0	0
									31	2	8	27	16	1

```
CUB   1 0 0   0 2 0   0 1 0 - 4
SOX   0 0 0   0 0 0   2 0 0 - 2
```

2B: Weaver, Leach, Schalk, Bodie. SH: Blackburne 2, Sweeney, Schulte. SB: Saier. LOB: Cub 5, Sox 10. DP: Cubs 2, Sox 1. BB: Wolfgang 1, Vaughn 4. Struck out: Wolfgang 1, Vaughn 7, Faber 1, Cicotte 1. PB: Bresnahan. Umpires: O'Loughlin, plate; Quigley, bases; Chill and Eason in outfield. Time—2:00.

GAME TWO --- October 8

WHITE SOX	AB	R	H	PO	A	E		CUBS	AB	R	H	PO	A	E
Weaver, ss	5	1	4	0	4	1		Leach, cf	4	0	1	1	1	1
Blackburne, 2b	4	1	1	1	5	0		Good, rf	4	0	0	0	0	0
Collins, cf	5	1	1	6	0	0		Saier, 1b	4	0	0	12	0	0
Fournier, 1b	5	0	2	14	0	0		Zimmerman, 3b	4	0	0	1	2	1
Roth, rf	4	1	1	0	0	0		Schulte, lf	4	1	1	3	0	0
Demmit, lf	5	0	2	1	0	0		Derrick, ss	4	0	0	0	6	0
Schalk, c	4	1	2	5	1	0		Sweeney, 2b	4	1	1	2	4	0
Breton, 3b	2	0	0	0	1	0		Bresnahan, c	2	0	0	8	2	0
Berger, 3b	1	0	0	0	1	0		Cheney, p	2	0	1	0	1	1
Scott, p	3	0	0	0	1	0			32	2	4	27	16	3
Bodie, ph	1	0	0	0	0	0								
	39	5	13	27	13	1								

```
SOX   0 1 0   0 0 0   0 1 3 - 5
CUB   0 2 0   0 0 0   0 0 0 - 2
```

2B: Demmit, Schulte, Fournier. SH: Blackburne. SB: Roth. BB: Cheney 2, Scott 2. Struck out: Cheney 8, Scott 4. WP: Cheney. Umpires: Eason, plate; Chill on bases; Quigley in right field, O'Loughlin in left field. Att: 12,101.

Game One pitted Vaughn against Red Faber (10–9). Vaughn pitched out of trouble often and gave up eight hits and four walks but stranded ten Sox runners when the chips were down. By the time the Americans could score, the Cubs had a 3–0 lead. Vaughn took the victory and Faber was charged with the loss.

Jim Scott (14–8) took the mound for the Sox against Larry Cheney in Game Two. Scott pitched a four-hitter, three of the Cub hits coming in the second. The fourth, off the bat of opposing pitcher Cheney, came in the seventh. Nevertheless, the game was tied at two in the ninth inning when the White Sox

1914 Chicago City Championship Series

GAME THREE --- October 9

CUBS	AB	R	H	PO	A	E		WHITE SOX	AB	R	H	PO	A	E
Leach, cf	4	0	2	1	0	0		Weaver, ss	2	0	0	0	1	0
Good, rf	3	1	1	0	0	0		Berger, ss	2	0	0	0	2	1
Saier, 1b	2	0	0	16	0	0		Blackburne, 2b	3	0	0	2	3	0
Zimmerman, 3b	3	1	1	2	4	1		Collins, cf	4	1	1	3	0	1
Schulte, lf	3	0	0	4	0	0		Fournier, 1b	4	0	1	12	1	1
Derrick, ss	4	0	0	0	5	0		Roth, rf	4	0	2	1	0	0
Sweeney, 2b	2	0	0	1	3	0		Demmit, lf	3	0	0	1	0	0
Bresnahan, c	3	0	0	3	1	0		Schalk, c	3	0	1	6	0	0
Humphries, p	4	0	0	0	3	0		Breton, 3b	3	0	0	2	1	0
								Benz, p	2	0	0	0	2	0
	28	2	4	27	16	1		Wolfgang, p	0	0	0	0	1	0
								Bodie, ph	1	0	0	0	0	0
									31	1	5	27	11	3

```
CUB   0  0  0    2  0  0    0  0  0  -  2
SOX   0  0  1    0  0  0    0  0  0  -  1
```

SB: Blackburne. SH: Schalk, Bresnahan. BB: Benz 3, Humphries 3. Struck out: Benz 3, Wolfgang 2, Humphries 3. Hits: Benz 2 in 7 innings. WP: Humphries. Umpires: Chill, plate; Eason on bases; O'Loughlin and Quigley in the field. Att: 17,377. Time—1:55.

GAME FOUR --- October 11

WHITE SOX	AB	R	H	PO	A	E		CUBS	AB	R	H	PO	A	E
Weaver, ss	5	2	2	3	4	0		Leach, cf	4	0	2	3	0	0
Blackburne, 2b	2	0	0	0	2	0		Good, rf	4	1	1	0	0	0
Collins, cf	4	0	2	2	0	0		Saier, 1b	4	0	0	17	1	0
Fournier, 1b	4	0	1	11	1	1		Zimmerman, 3b	4	1	2	0	1	0
Roth, rf	4	0	0	1	0	0		Schulte, lf	3	0	0	1	0	0
Bodie, lf	3	0	0	2	1	0		Williams, lf	1	0	1	0	0	0
Demmit, lf	1	0	0	0	0	0		Derrick, ss	4	0	0	3	3	1
Schalk, c	4	1	1	9	2	0		Sweeney, 2b	3	0	0	1	5	0
Breton, 3b	3	0	0	1	1	0		Knisely, ph	1	0	1	0	0	0
Kuhn, ph	1	0	0	0	0	0		Johnston, pr	0	1	0	0	0	0
Berger, 3b	0	0	0	0	0	0		Bresnahan, c	3	1	1	5	4	0
Cicotte, p	3	0	0	0	3	0		Vaughn, p	2	0	0	0	0	0
								Archer, ph	1	0	0	0	0	0
	34	3	6	*29	14	1		Lavender, p	0	0	0	0	2	1
								Corriden, ph	1	0	0	0	0	0
									35	4	8	30	16	2

* Two outs when winning run scored

```
SOX   1  0  0    0  0  1    0  0  0    1  -  3
CUB   0  0  0    0  0  0    0  0  2    2  -  4
```

2B: Collins, Fournier, Weaver, Zimmerman, Schalk, Knisely, Bresnahan. SH: Blackburne 2, Cicotte. DP: Sox 1. HBP: Bresnahan (Cicotte). LOB: Sox 4, Cubs 3. BB: Cicotte 1. Struck out: Cicotte 8, Vaughn 6, Lavender 1. Hits: Vaughn 5 in 8 innings, Lavender 1 in 2 innings. Balk: Lavender. Umpires: Quigley, plate; O'Loughlin on bases; Chill in left; Eason in right. Time—2:13.

struck for three runs, the big hit a two-run double by Jack Fournier which scored Buck Weaver and Lena Blackburne. Both pitchers went the distance for their decisions.

The White Sox took a second inning 1–0 lead off Bert Humphries (10–11) in Game Three when Heinie Zimmerman booted an Eddie Collins grounder for an error. Collins scored when Fournier and Robert "Braggo" Roth hit back-to-

1914 Chicago City Championship Series

GAME FIVE --- October 12

CUBS	AB	R	H	PO	A	E		WHITE SOX	AB	R	H	PO	A	E
Leach, cf	4	0	0	1	0	0		Weaver, ss	4	1	2	1	2	0
Good, rf	4	0	1	0	0	0		Blackburne, 2b	3	0	1	1	1	0
Saier, 1b	4	0	2	14	1	0		Collins, cf	4	0	1	4	0	0
Zimmerman, 3b	4	0	0	0	1	0		Fournier, 1b	3	0	1	12	0	0
Schulte, lf	2	1	1	2	0	0		Roth, rf	3	0	2	2	0	0
Derrick, ss	2	0	0	2	2	0		Demmit, lf	4	0	1	0	0	0
Sweeney, 2b	3	0	0	2	2	0		Schalk, c	3	2	2	6	0	0
Bresnahan, c	3	0	1	3	1	0		Breton, 2b	1	0	0	0	3	0
Cheney, p	2	0	0	0	4	0		Scott, p	0	0	0	0	3	0
Williams, ph	1	0	0	0	0	0		Faber, p	0	0	0	0	1	0
Knisely, ph	1	0	0	0	0	0		Bodie, ph	1	0	0	0	0	0
Johnston, pr	0	0	0	0	0	0								
	30	1	5	24	11	0			26	3	9	27	10	0

```
CUB   0  0  0   1  0  0   0  0  0  -  1
SOX   0  0  0   0  2  0   1  0  x  -  3
```

2B: Schalk. 3b: Saier, Schulte, Weaver, Roth. SB: Fournier, Roth, Leach. SH: Blackburne, Derrick 2, Scott, Breton, Faber. HBP: Schulte (Faber). BB: Cheney 3, Scott 3, Faber 1. Struck out: Cheney 2, Scott 1, Faber 4. WP: Cheney. Umpires: O'Loughlin, plate; Quigley on bases; Eason and Chill in the field. Att: 19,700. Time—1:58.

GAME SIX --- October 13

WHITE SOX	AB	R	H	PO	A	E		CUBS	AB	R	H	PO	A	E
Weaver, ss	5	1	0	0	2	1		Leach, cf	4	0	0	1	0	0
Blackburne, 2b	4	1	1	1	1	1		Good, rf	5	0	2	2	0	1
Collins, cf	4	1	0	3	0	0		Saier, 1b	5	1	3	15	0	1
Fournier, 1b	4	1	1	10	1	1		Zimmerman, 3b	5	0	1	0	5	1
Roth, rf	4	0	1	4	0	0		Schulte, lf	4	0	1	2	0	0
Demmit, lf	4	1	2	2	0	0		Derrick, ss	3	0	1	1	3	1
Schalk, c	3	0	0	5	2	0		Sweeney, 2b	4	0	1	2	2	1
Breton, 3b	4	0	0	0	2	0		Bresnahan, c	4	0	0	4	0	0
Benz, p	4	0	0	2	2	0		Vaughn, p	3	0	1	0	2	1
Cicotte, p	0	0	0	0	0	0		Zabel, p	0	0	0	0	0	0
								Johnston, pr	0	1	0	0	0	0
	36	5	5	27	10	3		Knisely, ph	0	1	0	0	0	0
									37	3	10	27	12	6

```
SOX   0  1  0   0  4  0   0  0  0  -  5
CUB   0  0  0   0  0  0   2  0  1  -  3
```

2B: Demmit. HR: Saier. SB: Zimmerman, Breton, Weaver, Blackburne, Roth, Demmit. SH: Derrick Blackburne. DP: Sox 1. BB: Vaughn 3, Benz 1. Struck out: Vaughn 3, Zabel 1, Benz 3. PB: Bresnahan 2. Umpires: Eason, plate; Chill, bases; O'Loughlin and Quigley in the field. Att: 6,601. Time—1:55.

back singles. Joe Benz (14-9) pitched an excellent game for the Sox except for some hard luck in the fourth when he walked Wilbur Good. An error by Eddie Collins sent Good to second from where he scored on Zimmerman's single. A wild throw moved Zim to third and he scored on Schulte's sacrifice fly. That was all the offense there was on the day as the Sox won, 2-1. Humphries was the winning pitcher, Benz took the loss.

Hippo Vaughn was back on the mound for the Cubs in Game Four against Eddie Cicotte (11-16). The Sox scored single runs in the first and sixth innings

1914 Chicago City Championship Series

```
GAME SEVEN --- October 15
```

CUBS	AB	R	H	PO	A	E		WHITE SOX	AB	R	H	PO	A	E
Leach, cf	3	1	0	1	0	0		Weaver, ss	4	1	0	6	4	0
Good, rf	4	1	1	0	0	0		Blackburne, 2b	4	0	0	2	2	0
Saier, 1b	4	0	2	17	0	0		Collins, cf	4	0	0	0	0	0
Zimmerman, 3b	4	0	1	1	1	0		Fournier, 1b	2	1	0	6	1	0
Schulte, lf	4	0	1	1	0	0		Roth, rf	2	1	1	3	0	0
Derrick, ss	4	0	3	1	5	1		Demmit, lf	2	0	0	2	0	0
Sweeney, 2b	3	0	0	0	4	0		Schalk, c	3	0	1	7	1	0
Archer, c	3	0	0	3	1	0		Breton, 3b	3	0	0	1	1	0
Humphries, p	1	0	0	0	2	0		Scott, p	0	0	0	0	0	0
Vaughn, p	1	0	0	0	1	0		Cicotte, p	3	0	0	0	1	0
Lavender, p	0	0	0	0	1	0								
Knisely, ph	1	0	0	0	0	0			27	3	2	27	10	0
Bresnahan, ph	1	0	0	0	0	0								
	33	2	8	24	15	1								

```
CUB   2 0 0   0 0 0   0 0 0 - 2
SOX   0 0 0   3 0 0   0 0 x - 3
```

2B: Zimmerman, Roth, Saier 2. 3B: Good. BB: Scott 1, Humphries 2, Vaughn 2. Struck out: Humphries 2, Lavender 1, Vaughn 1, Cicotte 7. Umpires: Chill, plate; Eason on bases; Quigley and O'Loughlin in the field. Time—1:58.

and had a 2–0 lead heading into the bottom of the ninth when two Cub runs sent the game into extra innings. Cicotte had only allowed five hits—four of those singles—over the first nine innings and looked to be in good shape when the White Sox scored once in the top of the tenth. In the bottom of the inning, pinch-hitter Pete Knisely doubled down the right field foul line with one out. Roger Bresnahan's double a moment later tied the game. Pinch-hitter Red Corriden made the second out of the inning, but 37-year old Tommy Leach came through with the third double of the inning and ended the game. Cicotte was tagged for the loss while Jimmy Lavender (11–11) pitched the last two innings for the victory.

Larry Cheney made his second start of the series in Game Five and was touched for a double, two triples, six singles and three runs in losing to Jim Scott who scattered five Cub hits. The final score was 3–1.

The Sox were leading 1–0 in the fifth inning of Game Six when Cubs catcher Roger Bresnahan let a third strike which would have retired the side get by him. Given a two-out reprieve, the Sox scored four times. Joe Benz was the winning pitcher, Hippo Vaughn took the loss.

Game Seven was, to mix sports metaphors, a goal-line stand for Eddie Cicotte and the White Sox. Cicotte started off weakly, allowing two Cub runs in the first. In the fourth, a two-run double by Braggo Roth scored Buck Weaver and Jack Fournier to tie the game. Ray Schalk's single brought Roth home with the lead run. Those were the only two hits the Sox made off Humphries, Vaughn, and Lavender, but they proved sufficient. Cicotte gave up eight hits, walking no one and striking out seven to record his only victory of the series.

1914 New York City Championship Series

GAME ONE --- October 8

YANKEES	AB	R	H	PO	A	E		GIANTS	AB	R	H	PO	A	E
Maisel, 3b	5	1	1	3	0	0		Bescher, lf	6	1	1	2	1	0
Hartzell, lf	5	0	3	1	0	0		Doyle, 2b	3	2	2	3	1	0
Cook, rf	5	1	1	2	0	0		Burns, rf	5	1	4	4	0	0
Cree, cf	4	1	2	3	0	0		Fletcher, ss	5	1	2	4	6	2
Mullen, 1b	3	2	1	7	0	0		Snodgrass, cf	4	0	0	0	0	0
Peckinpaugh, ss	3	0	1	2	3	0		Grant, 3b	5	0	1	2	2	0
Sweeney, c	4	0	1	6	2	1		Merkle, 1b	3	1	1	10	1	0
Boone, 2b	4	0	2	3	2	1		Meyers, c	5	0	1	5	2	0
Keating, p	4	0	0	0	1	1		Mathewson, p	5	0	1	0	5	0
	37	5	12	*27	8	3			41	6	13	30	18	2

* Snodgrass out for interference by third-base coach; one out when winning run scored

```
NYA    0  0  1     0  0  3     0  0  1     0  -  5
NYN    0  1  1     0  0  0     3  0  0     1  -  6
```

2B: Cree, Sweeney. 3B: Burns, Bescher. HR: Merkle. SH: Mullen, Peckinpaugh. SB: Burns 2, Doyle 2, Fletcher, Maisel, Mullen. CS: Meyers 2, Sweeney 1. LOB: NYN: 12, NYA 4. DP: NYN 2, NYA 1. BB: Keating 5. Struck out: Keating 5, Mathewson 2. WP: Mathewson, PB: Sweeney. Umpires: Rigler, Evans, Hart, Connolly. Att: 7,640. Time—2:17.

The 1914 New York City Championship Series

New York Giants defeat the New York Yankees; 4–1

For the first time since 1910, the two New York teams met each other in postseason exhibition play. The second-place Giants (84–70) lost the pennant to the Boston Braves by a margin of ten and one-half games, and the seventh-place Yankees, with a mirror image record of 70–84, finished a distant 30 games behind the Philadelphia Athletics. The first three games were decided in the last round of play, two of them extra inning affairs.

Game One saw 37-year old Christy Mathewson (24–13) outlast Ray Keating (7–11) in a ten-inning affair which featured a total of 25 hits and 11 runs. The Giants had a 2–1 lead when the Yankees struck for three runs in the sixth. New York came back with three of their own in the seventh, but the Yankees sent the game into extra innings with a single run in the ninth. There was one out in the bottom of the tenth when the Giants scored the winning run. Mathewson allowed 12 hits but walked no one in earning the victory. Keating, who went the distance for the Yankees, was the loser.

It was Jeff Tesreau (26–10) for the Nationals against Jack Warhop (8–15) in Game Two. Tesreau had a 1–0 lead after eight and a half innings when Roger Peckinpaugh, Jeff Sweeney, and Warhop singled to lead off the ninth, Peckinpaugh scoring to tie the game. Fritz Maisel and Roy Hartzell made out, but Doc Cook's single won the game for the Yankees.

Game Three was another nail-biter. Rube Marquard (12–22) started for the Giants against Ray Fisher (10–12) but neither pitcher was effective. The Yankees led 5–2 in the seventh when the Giants rallied on Turkey Mike Donlin's triple with two on. Bob Bescher's sacrifice fly scored pinch-runner

1914 New York City Championship Series

GAME TWO --- October 9

GIANTS	AB	R	H	PO	A	E		YANKEES	AB	R	H	PO	A	E
Bescher, lf	2	0	1	1	0	0		Maisel, 3b	4	0	0	5	1	0
Doyle, 2b	3	0	1	1	5	0		Hartzell, lf	4	0	0	3	1	0
Burns, rf	4	0	0	1	0	0		Cook, rf	4	0	3	1	2	0
Fletcher, ss	4	0	0	4	1	1		Cree, cf	3	0	1	4	0	0
Snodgrass, cf	3	1	1	2	0	0		Mullen, 1b	4	0	2	5	0	0
Grant, 3b	3	0	2	1	1	0		Peckinpaugh, ss	3	1	0	3	3	1
Merkle, 1b	3	0	1	9	0	0		Sweeney, c	4	0	1	3	2	0
Meyers, c	3	0	0	7	1	0		McHale, pr	0	1	0	0	0	0
Tesreau, p	3	0	0	0	1	0		Boone, 2b	3	0	0	3	1	0
								Warhop, p	4	0	1	0	1	0
	28	1	6	*26	9	1			33	2	8	27	11	1

* Two out when winning run scored

```
NYN     0  1  0     0  0  0     0  0  0  -  1
NYA     0  0  0     0  0  0     0  0  2  -  2
```

2B: Merkle, Grant. 3B: Cree. SB: Cook 2, Maisel, Hartzell, Snodgrass, Bescher. LOB: NYA 11, NYG 4. DP: NYA. BB: Tesreau 5, Warhop 3. Struck out: Tesreau 7, Warhop 2. WP: Tesreau. PB: Meyers. Umpires: Connolly, plate; Hart, first; Rigler, left; Evans, right; Att: 5,456. Time—1:58.

GAME THREE --- October 10

YANKEES	AB	R	H	PO	A	E		GIANTS	AB	R	H	PO	A	E
Maisel, 3b	5	1	1	0	4	0		Bescher, lf	4	0	2	4	1	0
Hartzell, lf	5	0	1	3	0	0		Doyle, 2b	5	1	2	2	4	1
Cook, rf	3	1	1	0	0	1		Burns, rf	3	0	0	0	0	0
Cree, cf	4	0	1	2	0	0		Fletcher, ss	5	0	0	1	4	0
Mullen, 1b	4	0	1	14	1	0		Snodgrass, cf	4	0	1	3	0	1
Peckinpaugh, ss	4	1	2	3	5	0		Grant, 3b	4	1	1	0	3	0
Nunamaker, c	5	1	1	6	1	0		Merkle, 1b	5	1	1	11	0	0
Boone, 2b	4	1	1	1	2	0		Meyers, c	4	0	3	6	1	1
Fisher, p	3	0	1	0	2	0		Thorpe, pr	0	1	0	0	0	0
								Johnson, c	1	0	0	3	0	0
	37	5	10	*29	15	1		Marquard, p	3	0	1	0	1	0
								Donlin, ph	1	0	1	0	0	0
								Piez, pr	0	1	0	0	0	0
								Demaree, p	1	1	1	0	1	0
									40	6	13	30	15	3

* Two out when winning run scored

```
NYA     0  0  0     1  1  0     1  2  0     0  -  5
NYN     0  1  0     0  0  0     1  3  0     1  -  6
```

2B: Hartzell, Bescher, Doyle. 3B: Maisel, Donlin. HR: Nunamaker. SH: Mullen, Cree, Fisher. SF: Bescher. SB: Snodgrass, Hartzell. LOB: NYN 10, NYA 8. DP: NYN. BB: Fisher 4, Marquard 3, Demaree 1. Struck out: Fisher 6, Marquard 3, Demaree 2. WP: Demaree. Hits: Marquard 9 in 8 innings; Demaree 1 in 2 innings. Umpires: Hart, Connolly, Evans, Rigler. Att: 11,222. Time—2:15.

Sandy Piez with the tying run. In the bottom of the tenth, Giants' pitcher Al Demaree lined a ball which fell in front of right-fielder Doc Cook then rolled to the wall for a three-base error. The Giants had their second victory of the series.

Art Fromme (9–5) pitched a five-hitter against the Yankees in Game Four and the Giants won easily, 6–1. Every Giant player except George Burns had a hit in the game. The losing pitcher was starter Marty McHale (7–16) who was touched for five hits and four runs in his five innings pitched.

1914 New York City Championship Series

GAME FOUR --- October 12

GIANTS	AB	R	H	PO	A	E		YANKEES	AB	R	H	PO	A	E
Bescher, lf	5	0	1	4	0	0		Maisel, 3b	4	0	0	1	2	0
Doyle, 2b	4	0	1	4	5	0		Hartzell, lf	4	0	2	2	0	0
Burns, rf	3	1	0	1	0	0		Cook, rf	4	0	1	4	0	0
Fletcher, ss	4	2	2	2	3	1		Cree, cf	4	0	0	2	2	0
Snodgrass, cf	4	1	1	2	0	0		Mullen, 1b	3	1	0	8	0	0
Grant, 3b	3	0	2	0	2	0		Peckinpaugh, ss	4	0	0	2	3	0
Merkle, 1b	3	0	1	12	0	0		Sweeney, c	3	0	1	6	1	1
Meyers, c	4	1	1	2	0	0		Boone, 2b	3	0	0	2	2	0
Fromme, p	4	1	1	0	2	0		McHale, p	1	0	0	0	2	1
								Daley, ph	1	0	1	0	0	0
	34	6	10	27	12	1		Keating, p	0	0	0	0	0	1
								Truesdale, ph	1	0	0	0	0	0
								Cole, p	0	0	0	0	0	0
									32	1	5	27	12	3

```
NYN   0 2 0   1 1 1   1 0 0 - 6
NYA   0 0 0   1 0 0   0 0 0 - 1
```

2B: Merkle, Snodgrass. SF: Grant, Merkle. SB: Fletcher. DP: NYN. LOB: NYN 6, NYA 6. BB: Fromme 2, McHale 1, Keating 1, Cole 1. Struck out: Fromme 2, McHale 1, Keating 3, Cole 1. Hits: McHale 5 in 5 innings; Keating 4 in 2 innings; Cole 1 in 2 innings. PB: Sweeney. Umpires: Evans, Rigle, Connolly, Hart. Att: 14,040. Time—2:00.

GAME FIVE --- October 13

YANKEES	AB	R	H	PO	A	E		GIANTS	AB	R	H	PO	A	E
Maisel, 3b	4	0	1	1	1	0		Bescher, lf	2	1	0	3	0	0
Hartzell, lf	4	0	0	1	0	0		Doyle, 2b	3	1	2	1	1	1
Cook, rf	4	0	1	4	0	0		Burns, rf	3	1	1	2	0	0
Cree, cf	4	1	2	2	0	0		Fletcher, ss	4	0	0	5	5	0
Mullen, 1b	3	0	0	9	0	0		Snodgrass, cf	3	0	0	4	1	0
Peckinpaugh, ss	4	0	0	2	0	1		Grant, 3b	3	0	1	1	1	0
Nunamaker, c	2	0	1	3	2	2		Merkle, 1b	3	0	0	8	1	0
Boone, 2b	3	0	0	2	3	0		Meyers, c	3	0	1	3	0	1
Warhop, p	3	0	0	0	1	0		Demaree, p	3	1	1	0	1	0
	31	1	5	24	7	3			27	4	6	27	10	2

```
NYA   0 1 0   0 0 0   0 0 0 - 1
NYN   0 0 0   1 0 3   0 0 x - 4
```

2B: Cree, Nunamaker, Doyle. SH: Burns, Bescher. SF: Doyle. SB: Burns, Snodgrass. DP: NYN 2. LOB: NYN 4, NYA 5. BB: Warhop 1, Demaree 1. Struck out: Warhop 2, Demaree 2. Umpires: Rigler, Evans, Connolly, Hart. Att: 1,508. Time—1:08.

The final contest was somewhat anticlimactic, the Yankees being somewhat drained from the first four games. Tied 1–1 in the sixth, the Giants scored the final three runs of the series and won, 4–1. Demaree went the route for the Giants in victory while Jack Warhop pitched a complete game loss for the Yankees.

1915 St. Louis City Championship Series

GAME ONE --- October 5

BROWNS	AB	R	H	PO	A	E		CARDINALS	AB	R	H	PO	A	E
Shotton, lf	4	2	2	2	0	0		Smith, lf	5	0	2	0	0	0
Howard, 1b	4	0	1	10	0	0		Betzel, 2b	3	1	1	1	4	0
Sisler, rf	3	0	1	1	0	0		Dolan, cf	4	0	1	2	0	0
Pratt, 2b	4	1	1	1	3	0		Miller, 1b	3	0	0	13	2	0
Walker, cf	4	0	1	1	1	0		Long, rf	4	1	2	0	0	0
Austin, 3b	3	0	0	4	5	0		Beck, 3b	4	0	0	0	3	0
Lavan, ss	3	0	0	0	2	0		Snyder, c	4	0	1	10	3	0
Agnew, c	4	0	2	8	1	1		Hornsby, ss	4	0	1	1	3	1
Weilman, p	3	0	0	0	1	1		Doak, p	3	0	0	0	1	0
								Roche, ph	1	0	0	0	0	0
	32	3	8	27	13	2			35	2	8	27	16	1

```
STA     0  0  1     0  1  0     1  0  0  -  3
STN     0  0  0     0  0  1     0  1  0  -  2
```

2B: Betzel. 3B: Long. SH: Howard, Sisler, Pratt. DP: STN. BB: Doak 4, Weilman 2. Struck out: Doak 8, Weilman 6. WP: Doak. LOB: STA 7, STN 8. Umpires: Eason and Hildebrand. Time—2:04.

GAME TWO --- October 6

BROWNS	AB	R	H	PO	A	E		CARDINALS	AB	R	H	PO	A	E
Shotton, lf	5	0	2	2	1	0		Smith, lf	5	0	0	3	1	1
Austin, 3b	5	1	1	4	3	0		Betzel, 2b	5	0	2	5	4	1
Howard, 1b	5	0	1	15	0	0		Dolan, cf	5	1	2	1	0	1
Pratt, 2b	5	1	1	0	4	0		Miller, 1b	3	0	1	17	0	0
Walker, cf	4	0	0	1	0	0		Long, rf	4	1	1	1	0	0
Jacobson, rf	5	1	2	0	0	0		Beck, 3b	4	0	1	3	3	2
Lavan, ss	4	0	1	3	2	1		Snyder, c	5	0	2	4	5	0
Agnew, c	4	0	0	11	6	0		Hornsby, ss	5	0	0	1	5	1
McCabe, p	2	0	0	0	1	0		Ames, p	4	0	0	0	5	0
Hamilton, p	1	0	0	0	1	0		Hyatt, 1b	0	0	0	1	0	0
Severeid, ph	1	0	0	0	0	0		Huggins, pr	0	1	0	0	0	0
	41	3	8	36	18	1			40	3	9	36	23	6

```
STA     0  0  0     0  1  0     0  0  1     0  0  1  -  3
STN     0  0  0     1  0  0     1  0  0     0  0  1  -  3
```

3B: Betzel, Long. SH: Beck, Miller, Walker, Lavan. DP: STN. SB: Dolan, Shotton. BB: Ames 1, McCabe 1, Hamilton 1. Struck out: McCabe 9, Ames 3, Hamilton 2. Hits: McCabe 7 in 9 innings, Hamilton 2 in 3 innings. LOB: STN 5, STA 5. Umpires: Hildebrand and Eason. Time—2:19.

The 1915 St. Louis City Championship Series

St. Louis Browns defeat St. Louis Cardinals; 4–1–1

The 1915 St. Louis Cardinals (72–81) dropped three notches to sixth place and finished nine games under .500, while the St. Louis Browns (63–91) slipped back one spot to sixth, but finished a terrible 28 games under .500 and 39½ games behind first-place Boston.

The Browns scored the first run of the game and series in the third inning of Game One, played on the fifth of October. Derrill Pratt singled, stole

1915 St. Louis City Championship Series

GAME THREE --- October 9

BROWNS	AB	R	H	PO	A	E		CARDINALS	AB	R	H	PO	A	E
Shotton, lf	4	1	2	3	0	0		Smith, lf	4	0	0	2	0	0
Austin, 3b	4	2	0	1	1	2		Betzel, 3b	4	0	0	1	1	0
Howard, 1b	4	0	1	7	1	0		Dolan, cf	3	0	0	4	0	0
Pratt, 2b	4	1	2	2	3	0		Miller, 2b	3	0	1	2	3	0
Walker, cf	4	1	2	5	0	0		Long, rf	4	0	0	0	0	0
Jacobson, rf	4	0	1	1	0	0		Hyatt, 1b	4	0	1	11	0	0
Lavan, ss	4	0	0	5	4	0		Snyder, c	4	1	2	5	2	0
Agnew, c	4	0	0	3	0	0		Hornsby, ss	4	0	1	2	5	1
Weilman, p	3	0	0	0	2	0		Sallee, p	2	0	0	0	4	1
								Niehaus, p	0	0	0	0	0	0
	35	5	8	27	11	2		Gonzalez, ph	1	0	0	0	0	0
									33	1	5	27	15	2

```
STA   4 1 0   0 0 0   0 0 0 - 5
STN   0 0 0   0 0 0   0 1 0 - 1
```

3B: Walker, Snyder. SB: Austin, Howard. DP: STA. HBP: Dolan (Weilman). BB: Weilman 1. Struck out: Weilman 3, Sallee 5. Hits: Sallee 8 and 5 runs in 7 innings. LOB: STA 3, STN 7. Umpires: Eason and Hildebrand. Time—1:45.

GAME FOUR --- October 9 (second game)

BROWNS	AB	R	H	PO	A	E		CARDINALS	AB	R	H	PO	A	E
Shotton, lf	4	0	1	3	0	0		Smith, lf	2	0	0	0	0	1
Austin, 3b	5	0	0	1	2	0		Betzel, 3b	4	0	2	3	2	1
Howard, 1b	3	0	0	7	1	0		Dolan, cf	4	1	1	4	0	0
Pratt, 2b	4	2	1	1	3	0		Miller, 2b	1	1	0	4	0	0
Walker, cf	1	1	0	2	0	0		Long, rf	3	0	0	4	0	0
Lee, rf	3	2	2	2	0	0		Hyatt, 1b	4	0	1	5	3	1
Lavan, ss	3	0	0	5	5	0		Gonzalez, c	4	0	0	4	4	1
Severeid, c	1	0	1	1	1	0		Hornsby, ss	3	0	0	3	2	1
Agnew, c	2	0	0	4	0	0		Meadows, p	3	0	1	0	4	1
Koob, p	0	0	0	0	0	0			28	2	5	27	15	6
Hoff, p	2	0	1	1	1	0								
Jacobson, ph	1	0	0	0	0	0								
Walsh, pr	0	0	0	0	0	0								
	29	6	6	27	13	0								

```
STA   0 0 0   0 1 3   1 1 0 - 6
STN   0 0 0   2 0 0   0 0 0 - 2
```

2B: Shotton. SH: Smith, Walker, Lee. SF: Long. SB: Betzel, Walker, Dolan, Miller, Shotton, Lee. DP: STA. BB: Koob 2, Meadows 7, Hoff 3. Struck out: Koob 1, Meadows 4, Hoff 4. Hits: Koob 3 and 2 runs in 4 innings. LOB: STA 3, STN 7. HBP: Hornsby (Hoff). WP: Hoff. Umpires: Hildebrand and Eason. Time—1:55.

second, and scored on Ernie Walker's base knock. The Americans added another run in the fifth on singles by Burt Shotton and Ivon Howard and a squeeze bunt by Pratt. The winning run scored in the seventh as Shotton reached on Rogers Hornsby's error, went all the way to third on Howard's sacrifice bunt, and scored on George Sisler's infield single. The final score was 3–2, Browns. Carl Weilman (18–19) got the victory, Bill Doak (16–18) the loss.

Game Two was played the next day. The Cardinals led three times and three times failed to hold the lead, the Browns tying the game for the last

1915 St. Louis City Championship Series

```
GAME FIVE --- October 10
```

CARDINALS	AB	R	H	PO	A	E		BROWNS	AB	R	H	PO	A	E
Smith, lf	4	0	2	1	0	0		Shotton, lf	3	0	0	1	0	0
Betzel, 3b	5	1	2	1	1	0		Austin, 3b	4	1	0	2	1	1
Dolan, cf	5	0	1	5	0	0		Howard, 1b	2	0	0	9	0	0
Miller, 2b	5	1	1	3	3	1		Pratt, 2b	4	0	1	4	4	0
Long, rf	4	3	2	0	0	0		Walker, cf	4	1	0	2	0	0
Hyatt, 1b	3	1	2	10	0	0		Lee, rf	4	0	1	2	1	0
Snyder, c	4	1	2	7	1	1		Lavan, ss	3	0	0	0	3	0
Hornsby, ss	4	0	0	0	2	0		Severeid, c	3	0	0	7	0	0
Doak, p	4	0	0	0	2	1		Hamilton, p	2	0	0	0	0	0
								Koob, p	0	0	0	0	0	0
	38	7	12	27	9	3		Jacobson, ph	1	0	0	0	0	0
									30	2	2	27	9	1

```
STN    0  3  0    0  0  1    3  0  0  -  7
STA    1  1  0    0  0  0    0  0  0  -  2
```

2B: Lee, Smith, Snyder, Betzel. 3B: Long. SH: Lavan. SB: Austin 2, Smith. DP: STA. BB: Hamilton 2, Doak 3, Koob 1. Struck out: Hamilton 4, Doak 6. Hits: Hamilton 10 in 7 innings; Koob 2 in 2 innings. LOB: STN 7, STA 5. Umpires: Hildebrand and Eason. Time—1:45.

```
GAME SIX --- October 10 (second game)
```

BROWNS	AB	R	H	PO	A	E		CARDINALS	AB	R	H	PO	A	E
Shotton, lf	2	1	1	2	0	0		Smith, lf	4	0	1	2	0	0
Austin, 3b	2	1	1	1	4	0		Betzel, 3b	4	0	0	1	1	0
Howard, 1b	3	1	1	9	0	0		Dolan, cf	4	0	2	1	0	0
Pratt, 2b	2	1	1	4	1	1		Miller, 2b	3	0	2	4	4	0
Walker, cf	3	0	0	2	0	0		Long, rf	4	0	0	1	0	0
Jacobson, rf	4	0	2	1	0	0		Hyatt, 1b	4	0	0	8	0	0
Lavan, ss	4	0	0	1	4	1		Gonzalez, c	3	0	1	3	3	0
Agnew, c	1	1	0	4	2	0		Hornsby, ss	3	0	0	3	3	0
McCabe, p	2	0	0	0	1	1		Boardman, p	3	0	1	0	3	0
	23	5	6	24	12	3			32	0	7	*23	14	0

* Shotton out for running into batted ball off Howard's bat in third inning

```
STA    0  0  1    0  0  0    0  4  -  5
STN    0  0  0    0  0  0    0  0  -  0
```

2B: Jacobson. SH: McCabe. SB: Dolan, Austin, Jacobson. DP: STN 2, STA 1. BB: McCabe 1, Boardman 10. Struck out: McCabe 4, Boardman 1. LOB: STA 5, STN 9. WP: Boardman. Umpires: Eason and Hildebrand. Time—2:00.

time in the ninth. After 12 innings, darkness set in and the teams retired, tied 3–3.

The next day's game was called off because of rain and since no game was scheduled for the eighth, the series resumed with a doubleheader on the ninth. The Browns won both games, 5–1 and 6–2, to take a three-games-to-none lead. In Game Three, Carl Weilman won his second decision of the series. The Browns jumped on Slim Sallee (13–17) for five runs and six hits in the first two innings. Burt Shotton opened the game with a single over Hornsby's head and when Jimmy Austin reached on an errant throw to first, Shotton went to third. After Ivon Howard rolled out, advancing Austin, Pratt singled to drive in both men. Ernie Walker tripled and rookie "Baby Doll" Jacobson followed with a single to put the Brownies up, 4-0. In the second, Shotton bunted for a single but was forced by Austin. Howard singled, sending Austin to third. Both runners then worked the double steal and the Americans led, 5-0.

The nightcap, Game Four, saw Browns rookie Ernie Koob (4-5) and Cardinal rookie Lee Meadows (13-11) go at it. The Cardinals scored twice off the southpaw in the fourth. Cozy Dolan singled and Dots Miller walked and, after a double steal, Dolan scored on Tommy Long's sacrifice fly. Ham Hyatt singled to drive in Miller, but Meadows couldn't stand prosperity and his 2-0 lead. Bill Lee started the Browns' fifth with a single — the first hit off Meadows. One out later, Hank Severeid singled and left the ball game for pinch-runner Dee Walsh. Jacobson pinch-hit for Koob and forced Walsh at second, Lee scoring. In the sixth, the Browns took the lead. With two out, Derrill Pratt lined to Jack Smith who dropped the ball. Ernie Walker coaxed a base on balls and Bill Lee singled the tying run home. Lee stole second and scored when Ham Hyatt booted John "Doc" Lavan's ground ball. Single runs in the seventh and eighth put the game safely away for the Browns. Chester Hoff (2-2), who had relieved for Koob, was the winning pitcher and Lee Meadows took the loss. Meadows allowed six hits and seven walks during his time on the mound, but his teammates made six errors behind him and effectively thwarted any chance he might have had to win the game.

The series ended the next day when the Browns took the second game of a doubleheader. In the first game, the Cardinals pounded out 13 hits against Earl Hamilton (9-17) and Ernie Koob while Bill Doak held the Browns to two hits. The Cardinals won easily, 7-2.

The Americans clinched the championship in Game Six. Browns rookie Tim McCabe (3-1), fresh from the Three-I league, shut out the Cardinals on seven hits. The Browns had one less hit but scored five more runs. The losing pitcher was Charlie Boardman (1-0).

The 1915 Chicago City Championship Series

Chicago White Sox defeat Chicago Cubs; 4-1

The third place White Sox (93-61) were heavy favorites when they met the fourth-place Cubs (73-80) in the 1915 Chicago city championship. There were no surprises in the series — unless the Cubs winning one game can be considered a surprise.

The Cubbies gave the Sox a run for their money in Game One, scoring three times in the first off Sox ace Jim Scott (24-11) and eventually increasing their lead to 5-2 at the end of six innings. But the White Sox exploded for four runs in the seventh and three in the eighth to win easily, 9-5. Reb Russell (11-10) was the winning pitcher and Hippo Vaughn (20-12) took the loss.

Game Two matched Jimmy Lavender (10-16) of the Cubs against Joe Benz (15-11). Lavender was masterful, shutting out the Sox on four hits, three of

1915 Chicago City Championship Series

```
GAME ONE --- October 6
```

CUBS	AB	R	H	PO	A	E		WHITE SOX	AB	R	H	PO	A	E
Good, rf	5	1	3	2	1	0		Murphy, rf	4	0	1	0	0	0
Fisher, ss	4	0	1	1	1	0		Weaver, ss	5	2	2	3	2	0
Schulte, lf	4	2	1	1	0	0		E. Collins, 2b	5	1	4	5	2	0
Zimmerman, 3b	4	0	1	2	1	0		Fournier, cf	1	0	0	0	0	0
Saier, 1b	3	1	1	7	0	0		Felch, cf	3	2	2	2	0	0
Williams, cf	4	0	1	1	0	0		Jackson, lf	4	0	2	4	0	0
Phelan, 2b	4	1	2	2	1	0		J. Collins, 1b	4	0	1	8	2	0
Bresnahan, c	3	0	0	8	4	0		Blackburne, 3b	4	0	1	1	2	0
Vaughn, p	3	0	1	0	3	0		Schalk, c	3	2	2	4	0	0
Humphries, p	0	0	0	0	0	0		Mayer, c	0	0	0	0	0	0
Murray, ph	1	0	0	0	0	0		Scott, p	1	0	0	0	3	0
Archer, ph	1	0	0	0	0	0		Russell, p	3	2	2	0	1	0
	36	5	11	24	11	0			37	9	17	27	12	0

```
CUB    3  0  0    1  1  0    0  0  0  -  5
SOX    0  0  0    2  0  0    4  3  x  -  9
```

2B: Williams, Phelan, E. Collins. 3B: E. Collins, Schalk, Russell, Weaver. SB: E. Collins 2, Felch 2, Zimmerman. DP: Sox. WP: Scott, Vaughn. Umpires: Connolly, home; Quigley, on bases; Orth, left field; Dineen, right field. Time—1:40.

```
GAME TWO --- October 7
```

WHITE SOX	AB	R	H	PO	A	E		CUBS	AB	R	H	PO	A	E
Murphy, rf	3	0	0	3	0	1		Good, rf	4	0	0	1	0	0
Weaver, ss	3	0	1	0	4	0		Fisher, ss	4	1	1	0	2	0
E. Collins, 2b	3	0	1	1	2	0		Schulte, lf	4	1	1	2	1	0
Felch, cf	3	0	0	5	0	0		Zimmerman, 3b	4	1	2	1	1	0
Jackson, lf	4	0	0	0	0	0		Saier, 1b	4	0	0	13	0	0
J. Collins, 1b	3	0	1	8	0	0		Williams, cf	4	0	1	2	0	0
Blackburne, 3b	2	0	0	2	0	0		Phelan, 2b	3	1	0	3	6	0
Leibold, ph	1	0	0	0	0	0		Archer, c	3	0	2	5	0	0
Johns, 3b	0	0	1	0	0	0		Lavender, p	3	0	0	0	2	0
Fournier, ph	1	0	0	0	0	0			33	4	7	27	12	0
Mayer, c	2	0	0	7	0	0								
Benz, p	2	0	0	0	0	1								
Cicotte, p	1	0	0	0	0	0								
	28	0	4	24	8	2								

```
SOX    0  0  0    0  0  0    0  0  0  -  0
CUB    0  1  0    0  0  3    0  0  x  -  4
```

2B: J. Collins, Archer. HR: Zimmerman. DP: Cub. Struck out: Lavender 4, Benz 5, Cicotte 1. Hits: Benz 5 in 6 innings, Cicotte 2 in 2 innings; Umpires: Orth, plate; Dineen on bases; Connolly, left field; Quigley, right field. Time—1:29.

them singles. A home run by Heinie Zimmerman was all the offense the Cubs needed as they won the game 4–0.

Red Faber (24–14) was enjoying the best year of his career when he went up against George Pearce (13–9) of the Cubs in Game Three. Both pitchers threw goose eggs until the White Sox struck for five runs in the eighth inning off Pearce. Faber weakened in the ninth and gave up two runs, but was the winning pitcher with a five-hitter and eight strikeouts.

1915 Chicago City Championship Series

GAME THREE --- October 8

CUBS	AB	R	H	PO	A	E		WHITE SOX	AB	R	H	PO	A	E
Good, rf	4	0	0	0	1	0		Murphy, rf	4	0	2	5	0	0
Fisher, ss	3	0	0	1	3	0		Weaver, ss	3	1	1	2	2	0
Schulte, lf	3	1	1	0	0	0		E. Collins, 2b	1	1	0	0	3	0
Zimmerman, 3b	4	1	4	1	1	0		Felch, cf	3	1	1	2	0	0
Saier, 1b	2	0	0	9	1	0		Jackson, lf	4	1	1	0	0	0
Williams, cf	4	0	0	1	0	0		J. Collins, 1b	4	0	3	7	2	1
Phelan, 2b	4	0	0	4	5	0		Blackburne, 3b	4	1	2	0	0	0
Archer, c	4	0	0	8	2	0		Schalk, c	3	0	2	9	2	0
Pearce, p	3	0	0	0	3	0		Faber, p	4	0	0	2	0	0
Zabel, p	0	0	0	0	1	0								
Murray, ph	1	0	0	0	0	0			30	5	12	27	9	1
	32	2	5	24	17	0								

```
CUB   0  0  0    0  0  0    0  0  2  -  2
SOX   0  0  0    0  0  0    0  5  x  -  5
```

2B: J. Collins, Jackson, Zimmerman. 3B: J. Collins. DP: Cubs. BB: Faber 3, Pearce 4. Struck out: Faber 8, Pearce 2, Zabel 1. Hits: Pearce 11 in 7.1 innings. WP: Pierce. Umpires: Dineen, home; Orth on bases; Connolly, left field; Quigley, right field. Time—2:13.

GAME FOUR --- October 9

WHITE SOX	AB	R	H	PO	A	E		CUBS	AB	R	H	PO	A	E
Murphy, rf	5	1	2	1	0	0		Good, rf	4	0	1	4	1	0
Weaver, ss	4	0	1	1	3	0		Fisher, ss	4	0	0	5	3	0
E. Collins, 2b	2	1	2	3	6	0		Schulte, lf	3	0	0	2	0	0
Felch, cf	3	1	1	1	0	0		Zimmerman, 3b	3	0	0	2	2	0
Jackson, lf	3	1	1	0	0	0		Saier, 1b	3	0	1	8	1	0
J. Collins, 1b	3	1	2	13	1	0		Williams, cf	3	0	1	2	0	0
Blackburne, 3b	4	0	0	1	1	0		Phelan, 2b	3	0	0	2	4	0
Schalk, c	4	0	0	7	0	0		Archer, c	3	0	0	2	1	0
Scott, p	4	0	1	0	2	0		Vaughn, p	0	0	0	0	2	0
	32	5	10	27	13	0		Adams, p	2	0	0	0	1	0
								Murray, ph	1	0	1	0	0	0
									29	0	4	27	15	0

```
SOX   0  0  5    0  0  0    0  0  0  -  5
CUB   0  0  0    0  0  0    0  0  0  -  0
```

2B: Jackson. HR: J. Collins. BB: Vaughn 3. Struck out: Scott 7. Hits: Vaughn 4 in ⅔ innings. DP: Sox 2. Umpires: Quigley, home; Connolly on bases; Orth, left field; Dineen, right field. Time—1:35.

The White Sox took a three-games-to-one lead in the series in Game Four on the strength of a five-run third inning. A bases-loaded walk from the Cubs' Hippo Vaughn forced in one run and a grand-slam home run by John Collins ended the day's scoring. Jim Scott, with a four-hit shutout, was the winning pitcher. Vaughn took the loss.

Reb Russell and Jimmy Lavender were matched for the finale, the least interesting of the five games. Tied 1–1 at the end of four, the Sox scored five in the fifth and five more in the sixth to win going away, 11–3. The Sox offensive attack included seven singles and doubles from Buck Weaver, Lena

1915 Chicago City Championship Series

GAME FIVE --- October 10

CUBS	AB	R	H	PO	A	E		WHITE SOX	AB	R	H	PO	A	E
Murray, lf	5	0	0	1	0	0		Murphy, rf	4	2	1	1	0	0
Fisher, ss	4	1	2	0	4	1		Weaver, ss	5	1	2	2	2	0
Schulte, rf	3	0	1	1	0	0		E. Collins, 2b	4	2	1	8	6	0
Zimmerman, 3b	4	0	1	2	3	2		Felch, cf	4	2	2	0	0	0
Saier, 1b	4	1	1	11	2	0		Jackson, lf	4	1	2	1	0	0
Williams, cf	4	0	3	2	0	0		J. Collins, 1b	3	0	1	6	1	1
Phelan, 2b	4	0	0	2	5	1		Blackburne, 3b	4	1	1	3	1	0
Archer, c	3	1	0	5	1	0		Schalk, c	3	2	2	6	2	0
Lavender, p	1	0	0	0	2	0		Russell, p	4	0	0	0	0	1
Pearce, p	0	0	0	0	0	0								
Schultz, ph	0	0	0	0	0	0			35	11	12	27	12	2
Standridge, p	0	0	0	0	1	0								
Hargrave, ph	1	0	0	0	0	0								
	33	3	8	24	18	4								

```
CUB   0  0  1    0  0  0    1  1  0  -   3
SOX   0  1  0    0  5  5    0  0  x  -  11
```

2B: Weaver, Blackburne, Murphy, Schulte, Schalk, E. Collins. 3B: Williams. HBP: Archer and Schulte (Russell). DP: Cub 1, Sox 1. BB: Russell 1, Lavender 1, Pearce 1. Struck out: Russell 5, Lavender 1, Pearce 1. Standridge 1. Hits: Lavender 8 in 5 innings; Pearce 4 in 1 inning. WP: Pearce. Umpires: Connolly, home; Quigley on bases; Orth, left field; Dineen, right field. Time— 1:48.

Blackburne, Eddie Murphy, Ray Schalk, and Eddie Collins. The starting pitchers took the decisions.

The 1916 St. Louis City Championship Series

St. Louis Browns defeat St. Louis Cardinals; 4–1

The 1916 St. Louis Cardinals were about to work one of the greatest Jekyll/Hyde acts in the history of baseball. After a last-place 60–93 finish in 1916, the Cards rebounded to third (82–70) in 1917, then dropped back to last (51–78) in 1918. No Cardinal club has finished last since. The 1916 Browns (79–75), meanwhile, were just a few years away from being contenders in the early seasons of the 1920s.

The series opened on October 4th and the Cardinals used three young pitchers in a vain attempt to hold back the Browns — rookies Bill Steele (5–15) and Milt Watson (4–6), and one-year veteran Rees "Steamboat" Williams (6–7). Steele got off to an inglorious start by walking the first three Browns he faced — Burt Shotton, Ward Miller, and George Sisler. Watson came on and pitched out the jam, allowing just one of the runners to score. Watson went the next seven innings and gave up ten hits and four runs of his own. Dave Davenport (12–11), just back from the Federal League where he had won 22 games, went the distance for the Browns and gave up six hits. He weakened over the last two innings when the Cardinals scored three times, but won the game, 5–3.

1916 St. Louis City Championship Series

GAME ONE --- October 4

BROWNS	AB	R	H	PO	A	E		CARDINALS	AB	R	H	PO	A	E
Shotton, lf	3	2	1	0	0	1		Bescher, lf	4	0	0	0	0	0
W. Miller, rf	4	1	1	2	1	0		Bohne, ss	4	0	0	2	1	0
Sisler, 1b	3	0	1	14	0	0		Smith, cf	4	1	1	1	0	0
Pratt, 2b	5	0	2	1	5	1		Hornsby, 3b	3	0	0	1	2	1
Rumler, cf	3	0	1	1	0	0		Wilson, rf	4	1	2	2	1	0
Austin, 3b	4	0	1	2	1	0		J. Miller, 1b	4	1	1	14	0	0
Hartley, c	4	1	1	6	0	0		Snyder, c	3	0	1	5	2	0
Lavan, ss	4	1	3	0	2	2		Betzel, 2b	4	0	1	2	3	1
Davenport, p	2	0	0	1	3	0		Steele, p	0	0	0	0	0	0
								Watson, p	2	0	0	0	3	0
	32	5	11	27	12	4		Williams, p	0	0	0	0	0	0
								Butler, ph	1	0	0	0	0	0
								Long, ph	1	0	0	0	0	0
									34	3	6	27	12	2

```
STA   1 0 0   0 3 1   0 0 0  -  5
STN   0 0 0   0 0 0   2 1 0  -  3
```

2B: Pratt. 3B: Wilson. SB: Shotton, Lavan. DP: STN. BB: Steele 3, Watson 2, Davenport 1. Struck out: Davenport 5, Watson 3, Williams 1. Hits: Steele 0 in 0 innings, Watson 10 in 7 innings. WP: Watson. Umpires: Eason and Owens.

GAME TWO --- October 5

CARDINALS	AB	R	H	PO	A	E		BROWNS	AB	R	H	PO	A	E
Bescher, lf	3	0	1	1	0	0		Shotton, lf	5	0	0	1	0	0
Bohne, ss	3	1	0	2	5	2		W. Miller, rf	3	0	1	2	0	0
Smith, cf	3	1	1	0	0	0		Sisler, 1b	4	0	0	12	1	0
Hornsby, 3b	4	0	0	0	0	0		Pratt, 2b	4	0	2	1	5	1
Wilson, rf	4	0	0	2	0	0		Rumler, cf	4	1	0	4	0	0
J. Miller, 1b	4	0	1	11	1	0		Austin, 3b	3	1	0	1	2	0
Snyder, c	3	0	0	6	2	0		Hartley, c	1	0	0	1	0	0
Betzel, 2b	3	0	0	2	4	0		Hale, c	2	1	2	2	2	0
Meadows, p	2	0	0	3	0	0		Lavan, ss	3	0	1	3	2	1
Lotz, p	0	0	0	0	1	0		Groom, p	1	1	0	0	2	0
Long, ph	1	1	0	0	0	0			30	4	6	27	14	2
	30	3	3	24	16	2								

```
STN   0 0 2   0 0 0   1 0 0  -  3
STA   0 0 1   2 0 1   0 0 x  -  4
```

2B: Pratt. 3B: Lavan, Bescher. DP: STA. SB: Snyder, Smith. BB: Groom 5, Lotz 1, Meadows 4. Hits: Meadows 4 in 7 innings. WP: Meadows. PB: Hartley, Snyder. Umpires: Owens and Eason.

Game Two matched Bob Groom (13–9) and Lee Meadows (12–23). The Cards took a 2–0 lead in the third but saw the Browns score once in the bottom of the inning and twice in the fourth to move ahead to stay. The clubs traded single runs later in the game and the final score was 4–3, Browns. Groom went the distance, giving up three hits and five walks. Tommy Long pinch-hit for losing pitcher Meadows in the seventh and Joe Lotz (0–3), suffering through his only year in the major leagues, pitched the final two innings for the Cardinals.

Bill Steele was back on the mound for the Cardinals in Game Three after an off-day and lasted a bit longer than his three-batter stint in Game One. His

1916 St. Louis City Championship Series

```
GAME THREE --- October 7
```

BROWNS	AB	R	H	PO	A	E
Shotton, lf	5	1	1	2	0	0
Austin, 3b	2	1	2	1	1	1
Sisler, 1b	3	0	0	1	0	0
Pratt, 2b	4	1	2	4	2	0
Rumler, cf	4	0	1	1	0	0
Paulette, 1b	4	1	3	7	2	0
Hale, c	2	0	0	4	5	0
Lavan, ss	4	0	2	4	1	2
Davenport, p	3	0	0	0	2	1
Borton, ph	1	0	0	0	0	0
Tobin, ph	1	0	1	0	0	0
Miller, ph	1	0	0	0	0	0
	34	4	12	24	13	4

CARDINALS	AB	R	H	PO	A	E
Bescher, lf	4	1	2	1	0	0
Bohne, ss	3	0	0	1	2	0
Smith, cf	4	0	2	1	0	0
Hornsby, 3b-ss	3	1	1	0	5	0
Wilson, rf	3	1	2	2	0	0
J. Miller, 1b-2b	3	1	1	15	1	0
Gonzalez, c	2	0	1	3	1	0
Betzel, 2b-3b	3	1	0	1	3	0
Steele, p	1	0	0	1	2	0
Ames, p	1	0	0	0	0	0
Snyder, 1b	0	0	0	2	0	0
	27	5	9	27	14	0

```
STA    1  0  0    1  0  0    0  2  0  -  4
STN    0  0  1    2  0  0    1  1  x  -  5
```

2B: Paulette, Wilson. 3B: Miller. SB: Betzel, Austin, Pratt, Shotton. DP: STN 1. BB: Steele 1. Struck out: Davenport 4, Steele 3. Hits: Steele 9 in 7.1 innings. Umpires: Eason and Owens.

```
GAME FOUR --- October 8
```

CARDINALS	AB	R	H	PO	A	E
Bescher, lf	5	1	1	4	0	0
Bohne, ss	4	0	1	1	3	0
Smith, cf	3	0	1	2	0	0
Hornsby, 3b	4	0	0	4	1	0
Long, rf	4	0	1	1	0	0
J. Miller, 1b	3	1	1	11	2	0
Gonzalez, c	4	0	2	1	0	0
Betzel, 2b	4	0	0	1	4	0
Watson, p	4	0	0	0	3	1
Wilson, cf	0	0	0	4	0	0
Butler, ph	0	0	0	0	0	0
	35	2	7	*29	13	1

BROWNS	AB	R	H	PO	A	E
Shotton, lf	3	1	2	0	0	0
Austin, 3b	4	0	1	2	3	1
Sisler, cf	4	0	1	4	0	0
Pratt, 2b	4	0	0	2	4	0
Rumler, rf	3	0	0	3	1	0
Paulette, 1b	4	0	0	13	1	0
Hale, c	4	0	0	3	2	0
Lavan, ss	2	0	0	3	1	0
E. Plank, p	2	2	1	0	3	0
	30	3	5	30	15	1

```
*   Two out when winning run scored.
```

```
STN    0  0  1    0  0  0    1  0  0    0  -  2
STA    0  0  1    0  0  0    1  0  0    1  -  3
```

2B: Sisler, Smith, Miller, Plank. HR: Bescher. DP: STN. BB: Plank 2, Watson 7. Struck out: Plank 3, Watson 1. Umpires: Owens and Eason.

luck was better, too. The Cardinals batted Davenport around for nine hits in eight innings and had a 5–2 lead into the ninth when Steele weakened and gave up two runs. But Red Ames (9–3 with the Cards) relieved Steele and got the final two outs of the game, the only Cardinal victory of the series.

Games Four and Five were scheduled as a doubleheader on Sunday, October 8th. Eddie Plank (16–15), at the tail end of a long career, started the first game for the Browns. The teams traded runs in the third and seventh innings,

1916 St. Louis City Championship Series

GAME FIVE --- October 8 secnd ame

CARDINALS	AB	R	H	PO	A	E		BROWNS	AB	R	H	PO	A	E
Bescher, lf	3	0	2	2	0	0		Shotton, lf	4	1	3	0	0	0
Bohne, ss	4	0	0	1	2	0		Austin, 3b	4	0	0	2	2	0
Smith, cf	4	0	0	2	0	0		Sisler, cf	4	1	2	2	0	0
Hornsby, 3b	2	1	0	3	2	0		Pratt, 2b	4	1	1	0	1	0
Wilson, rf	3	0	1	2	0	0		Rumler, rf	2	1	1	0	0	0
J. Miller, 1b	3	0	1	5	2	2		Paulette, 1b	3	0	1	9	0	0
Snyder, c	2	0	1	6	1	0		Hale, c	3	0	0	8	1	0
Betzel, 2b	3	0	0	0	3	1		Lavan, ss	3	0	2	3	5	0
Meadows, p	2	0	0	0	3	0		Groom, p	3	0	0	0	3	1
Butler, ph	1	0	0	0	0	0			30	4	10	24	12	1
	27	1	5	21	13	3								

```
STN    0  1  0    0  0  0    0  0  -  1
STA    0  1  0    0  0  2    1  x  -  4
```

2B: Bescher. 3B: Shotton, Pratt. SB: Shotton, Sisler. DP: STA. BB: Groom 3, Meadows 1. Struck out: Meadows 4, Groom 5. WP: Meadows. Umpires: Eason and Owens.

but the Browns scored once off losing pitcher Milt Watson in the bottom of the tenth to win the game, 3–2. Plank helped his cause at the plate, scoring two of his team's three runs and driving in another.

The Americans took the series in the second game of the doubleheader, winning a darkness-shortened seven and a half inning game, 4–1. Bob Groom stifled the Cardinal offense on five hits while the Browns rapped out ten hits against loser Lee Meadows.

The 1916 Chicago City Championship Series

Chicago White Sox defeat Chicago Cubs; 4-0

The second-place White Sox (89–65), managed by Pants Rowland, were heavy favorites to take the fifth-place Cubs (67–86) in the 1916 city championship and take the Cubs they did, in a four game sweep. The White Sox were never seriously challenged and used only 12 players in the series.

The series opened Wednesday, October 4th, before 17,250 fans at Comiskey Park, White Sox ace Reb Russell (18–11) against Cubs' ace Hippo Vaughn (17–14). Vaughn out-dueled his opponent over the first six innings before being relieved in the seventh. Trailing 2–1 when Vaughn left the game, the White Sox struck for five runs off a battered Claude Hendrix (8–16) in the seventh. Two more runs in the eighth made the final score 8–2. Oddly enough, the Sox were outhit, 10–9.

Game Two featured Jimmy Lavender (10–14) of the Cubs against Red Faber (17–9). Although the Cubs outhit the Sox again, this time by a margin of nine to eight, the Nationals came away on the short end of a 3–1 score.

1916 Chicago City Championship Series

GAME ONE --- October 4

CUBS	AB	R	H	PO	A	E
Flack, rf	4	0	0	0	0	0
Mann, lf	4	0	2	0	0	0
Saier, 1b	4	1	1	8	0	0
Kelly, cf	3	1	0	2	0	0
Wilson, c	4	0	1	7	5	0
Yerkes, 2b	3	0	2	3	2	0
Zeider, 3b	3	0	2	2	1	0
Wortman, ss	4	0	2	2	2	1
Vaughn, p	2	0	0	0	1	1
Hendrix, p	1	0	0	0	0	0
	32	2	10	24	11	2

WHITE SOX	AB	R	H	PO	A	E
J. Collins, rf	4	0	1	0	0	0
Weaver, 3b	3	1	2	2	0	0
E. Collins, 2b	3	1	1	4	2	0
Jackson, lf	3	2	0	4	0	0
Felsch, cf	2	1	1	4	0	0
Ness, 1b	4	1	2	6	0	0
Terry, ss	4	1	1	1	4	0
Schalk, c	3	1	1	6	2	0
Russell, p	2	0	0	0	3	0
	28	8	9	27	11	0

```
CUB   0  0  0    0  0  2    0  0  0  -  2
SOX   0  0  1    0  0  0    5  2  x  -  8
```

2B: Wilson, Saier, Ness, Zeider. SB: Kelly, Wortman, Weaver, Jackson, Zeider. DP: Sox 1. BB: Russell 1, Vaughn 3. Struck out: Russell 6, Vaughn 3, Hendrix 3. Hits: Vaughn 5 in 6 innings. Umpires: Evans, plate; Orth on bases; Byron in right, Hildebrand in left. Att: 17,250.

GAME TWO --- October 5

WHITE SOX	AB	R	H	PO	A	E
J. Collins, rf	5	0	2	3	0	0
Weaver, 3b	5	0	0	0	3	0
E. Collins, 2b	3	1	1	2	4	0
Jackson, lf	3	0	1	1	0	0
Felsch, cf	4	1	2	0	1	0
Ness, 1b	4	1	1	13	0	0
Terry, ss	4	0	1	2	1	1
Schalk, c	3	0	0	6	1	0
Faber, p	4	0	0	0	4	0
	35	3	8	27	14	2

CUBS	AB	R	H	PO	A	E
Flack, rf	4	0	0	0	0	0
Mann, lf	5	1	2	0	1	0
Saier, 1b	5	0	2	13	0	0
F. Williams, cf	4	0	1	2	0	0
Wilson, c	4	0	1	8	0	0
Yerkes, 2b	3	0	1	3	4	0
Zeider, 3b	3	0	0	0	1	0
Wortman, ss	4	0	2	1	6	1
Lavender, p	1	0	0	0	1	0
Mollwitz, ph	1	0	0	0	0	0
Packard, p	1	0	0	0	0	0
Archer, ph	1	0	0	0	0	0
	36	1	9	27	13	1

```
SOX   0  0  0    3  0  0    0  0  0  -  3
CUB   0  0  0    0  1  0    0  0  0  -  1
```

2B: Wortman, Saier, Mann, J. Collins. 3B: Felsch. SB: Saier, E. Collins, Felsch. DP: Cub 1, Sox 1. BB: Faber 3, Lavender 2, Packard 1. Hits: Lavender 5 in 4 innings. Struck out: Faber 6, Lavender 3, Packard 5. Umpires: Byron, plate; Hildebrand on bases; Evans in right; Orth in left. Att: 11,649.

Lavender gave up five hits and three runs in four innings to take the loss, while Faber went the distance for the Sox. The Cubs' only run came in the fifth.

The third game pitted Claude "Lefty" Williams (13–7), enjoying his first full season in the majors, against the Cubs' Mike Prendergast (6–11). Prendergast was a veteran of the Federal League, having worked his freshman and sophomore seasons for the Chicago Whales. Williams went all the way for the Sox, pitching a six-hit shutout and striking out eight. Prendergast gave up single runs in the second, third, and sixth and lost the game, 3–0. The hitting star of the day was "Shoeless Joe" Jackson with three doubles in four times at bat.

1916 Chicago City Championship Series

GAME THREE --- October 6

CUBS	AB	R	H	PO	A	E		WHITE SOX	AB	R	H	PO	A	E
Flack, rf	2	0	1	1	0	0		J. Collins, rf	4	0	0	1	0	0
F. Williams, cf	1	0	0	1	0	0		Weaver, 3b	4	0	2	1	1	0
Mann, lf	3	0	1	0	2	0		E. Collins, 2b	3	1	1	4	1	0
Saier, 1b	2	0	0	8	0	0		Jackson, lf	4	2	3	3	0	0
Mollwitz, 1b	2	0	1	4	1	0		Felsch, cf	3	0	1	2	0	0
Kelly, cf-rf	4	0	0	0	0	0		Ness, 1b	4	0	0	6	0	0
Wilson, c	4	0	1	5	0	0		Terry, ss	2	0	1	2	1	0
Yerkes, 2b	3	0	1	0	0	1		Schalk, c	3	0	0	8	3	0
Zeider, 3b	3	0	0	3	4	0		C. Williams, p	3	0	0	0	1	0
Wortman, ss	3	0	1	2	6	1								
M. Prendergast, p	2	0	0	0	2	0			30	3	8	27	7	0
Archer, ph	1	0	0	0	0	0								
McConnell, p	0	0	0	0	1	0								
	30	0	6	24	16	2								

```
CUB   0 0 0   0 0 0   0 0 0  -  0
SOX   0 1 1   0 0 1   0 0 x  -  3
```

2B: Jackson 3, Felsch. 3B: Weaver. SB: Black, Schalk, Mann, J. Collins. DP: Sox 1, Cubs 1. BB: Prendergast 2, C. Williams 1, McConnell 1. Struck out: C. Williams 8, Prendergast 3, McConnell 1. Hits: Prendergast 8 in 7 innings. Umpires: Hildebrand, home; Byron on bases; Orth in left; Evans in right. Att: 10,916.

GAME FOUR --- October 7

WHITE SOX	AB	R	H	PO	A	E		CUBS	AB	R	H	PO	A	E
J. Collins, rf	5	1	1	3	0	1		F. Williams, cf	4	2	3	1	0	0
Weaver, 3b	4	0	0	0	2	0		Mann, lf	4	1	2	4	0	0
E. Collins, 2b	2	2	1	3	3	0		Saier, 1b	4	0	2	7	0	0
Jackson, lf	4	2	3	3	0	0		Kelly, rf	4	0	0	0	0	0
Felsch, cf	4	0	2	2	1	0		Wilson, c	4	0	0	6	3	0
Ness, 1b	4	0	0	6	1	0		Yerkes, 2b	1	0	1	0	1	1
Terry, ss	3	0	1	2	1	0		Knabe, 2b	3	0	1	2	1	0
Schalk, c	4	0	0	8	0	0		Zeider, 3b	3	0	1	3	2	0
Cicotte, p	4	1	1	0	2	0		Wortman, ss	3	0	0	4	5	0
	34	6	9	27	10	1		Archer, ph	1	0	0	0	0	0
								Vaughn, p	1	0	0	0	0	0
								Packard, p	2	0	0	0	0	0
									34	3	10	27	12	1

```
SOX   0 0 3   0 3 0   0 0 0  -  6
CUB   1 0 1   0 1 0   0 0 0  -  3
```

2B: Saier, Zeider, Williams 2. 3B: Mann, Williams, E. Collins, Saier. HR: Jackson. SB: E. Collins, Jackson, Mann, Zeider. DP: Cub 1, Sox 2. BB: Vaughn 2, Cicotte 1. Struck out: Vaughn 2, Cicotte 6, Packard 3. Hits: Vaughn 5 in 3 innings. Umpires: Orth, plate; Evans on bases; Byron in right; Hildebrand in left. Att: 16,799.

The White Sox completed their sweep of the series on the seventh as Eddie Cicotte (15–7) paired off with Hippo Vaughn. Cicotte had been in better form, as he gave up ten hits and a walk, but he worked out of jams when it counted. Three-run innings in the third and fifth were the difference as the Sox won the game, 6–3. Joe Jackson had his second straight 3-for-4 with a home run and two singles. The big man with the bat for the Cubs was center-fielder Cy Williams with two doubles and a triple in four times at bat. The White Sox used no relief pitchers in the series as Russell, Faber, Williams, and Cicotte all pitched complete games.

No Chicago city championships were played in 1917 or 1918 because the two clubs were attending to more important matters. The White Sox won the 1917 World Series from the Giants and the Cubs lost to the Red Sox in 1918. The White Sox, it will be remembered, played the Cincinnati Reds in the 1919 World Series and were defeated five games to three. Joe Jackson, Fred McMullin, Charles "Swede" Risberg, Charles "Chick" Gandil, Oscar "Happy" Felsch, George "Buck" Weaver, Lefty Williams, and Eddie Cicotte were barred from the game for life in September of 1920 by commissioner Kenesaw Mountain Landis. As a result, the White Sox were unable to field a team at the end of the 1920 season and there was no Chicago postseason championship series until 1921.

1917 St. Louis City Series

St. Louis Cardinals defeat St. Louis Browns; 4-2-1

The St. Louis Cardinals (82–70) finished a respectable third in 1917 but were to completely collapse the following year when manager Miller Huggins was replaced by Jack Hendricks. Huggins moved on to greater success with the New York Yankees where he would win six pennants and average 89 victories a year over the next 12 seasons. The Browns (57–97), under manager Fielder Jones, had finished 43 games off the pace in seventh place, down from a better than .500 finish in 1916. The Americans narrowly escaped the cellar, due only

1917 St. Louis City Championship Series

GAME ONE --- October 3

BROWNS	AB	R	H	PO	A	E	CARDINALS	AB	R	H	PO	A	E
Shotton, lf	3	0	0	2	0	0	Long, rf	4	0	2	2	0	0
Austin, 3b	4	0	1	1	3	1	J.Smith, cf	4	0	0	1	0	0
E.Smith, cf	4	1	1	2	0	0	Miller, 2b	4	0	1	2	1	0
Severeid, c	3	0	1	7	4	1	Hornsby, ss	4	1	1	1	3	0
Demmitt, rf	3	0	0	1	0	1	Cruise, lf	3	0	0	2	1	0
Sisler, 1b	4	1	2	5	1	2	Paulette, 1b	4	0	2	8	3	0
Lavan, 2b	4	0	2	4	5	0	Baird, 3b	3	1	3	1	1	0
Gerber, ss	3	0	1	3	1	0	Snyder, c	3	1	2	7	0	0
Lowdermilk, p	4	0	0	0	0	0	Meadows, p	1	0	0	1	2	0
Rumler, ph	1	0	1	0	0	0	Packard, p	1	0	0	2	2	0
Johnson, ss	0	0	0	0	0	0	Smyth, ph	1	0	0	0	0	0
Jacobson, rf	1	0	1	0	0	0							
	34	2	10	25	14	5		32	3	11	27	13	0

One out when winning run scored

```
STA   1 0 0   0 0 0   0 0 1  -  2
STN   0 0 0   0 2 0   0 0 1  -  3
```

2B: Snyder, Lavan. 3B: E. Smith, Severeid, Sisler. SH: Cruise. DP: STN 1, STA 3. HBP: Baird (Lowdermilk). BB: Meadows 2. Struck out: Meadows 4, Lowdermilk 6, Packard 3. Hits: Meadows 6 and 1 run in 5 innings. LOB: STA 7, STN 6. Umpires: Quigley and Owens. Time—1:45.

1917 St. Louis City Championship Series

GAME TWO --- October 4

CARDINALS	AB	R	H	PO	A	E		BROWNS	AB	R	H	PO	A	E
Long, rf	5	2	3	1	0	0		Shotton, lf	4	0	1	3	0	1
J.Smith, cf	4	0	1	1	0	0		Austin, 3b	4	0	1	1	1	0
Miller, 2b	4	0	2	6	4	0		E.Smith, cf	4	1	0	0	0	0
Hornsby, ss	3	1	0	0	3	0		Sisler, 1b	1	0	1	0	1	0
Cruise, lf	3	0	0	0	0	0		Jacobson, 1b	3	0	2	8	1	1
Paulette, 1b	4	0	2	14	1	1		Severeid, c	2	0	0	8	2	0
Baird, 3b	2	0	0	1	3	0		Demmitt, rf	2	0	0	0	0	0
Snyder, c	3	0	0	4	1	0		Lavan, 2b	2	0	0	6	1	1
Doak, p	4	0	0	0	5	0		Gerber, ss	2	0	1	1	3	2
	32	3	8	27	17	1		Johnson, ss	0	0	0	0	0	0
								Davenport, p	1	0	0	0	4	0
								Sothoron, p	0	0	0	0	1	0
STN	0 0 0	1 1 0	0 0 1	-	3			Rumler, ph	1	0	0	0	0	0
STA	0 0 0	0 0 0	1 0 0	-	1			Sloan, p	1	0	0	0	0	0
									27	1	6	27	14	5

2B: Long. SH; Baird, Cruise, Davenport, Severeid, J. Smith, Miller. DP: STN 2. WP: Doak. Balk: Davenport 2. BB: Davenport 4, Doak 2. Struck out: Davenport 5, Doak 3. Hits: Davenport 7 and 2 runs in 8 innings. LOB: STN 9, STA 3. Umpires: Owens and Quigley. Time—1:45.

GAME THREE --- October 6

BROWNS	AB	R	H	PO	A	E		CARDINALS	AB	R	H	PO	A	E
Shotton, lf	4	1	2	0	0	0		Long, rf	5	0	1	1	1	0
Austin, 3b	4	0	1	2	2	0		J.Smith, cf	5	0	0	2	1	0
E.Smith, cf	5	1	1	2	0	0		Miller, 2b	5	1	2	3	3	1
Sisler, 1b	5	1	2	13	1	1		Hornsby, ss	5	0	0	1	3	0
Severeid, c	2	0	1	3	0	0		Cruise, lf	5	0	1	2	0	0
Demmitt, rf	4	0	0	2	0	0		Paulette, 1b	3	1	0	3	1	0
Lavan, 2b-ss	3	1	1	2	4	1		Baird, 3b	3	0	1	2	2	0
Gerber, ss-2b	3	1	0	3	2	1		Snyder, c	2	1	1	13	1	1
Groom, p	3	0	0	0	2	0		Horstman, p	0	0	0	0	0	0
Lowdermilk, p	0	0	0	0	2	0		Ames, p	1	0	0	0	2	0
Hartley, c	3	0	1	3	1	0		Goodwin, p	0	0	0	0	0	0
Johnson, 2b	0	0	0	0	2	0		Packard, p	0	0	0	1	1	0
Jacobson, rf	1	0	0	0	0	0		Gonzalez, c	1	0	1	2	0	0
Rumler, ph	0	0	0	0	0	0		Smyth, ph	0	0	0	0	0	0
	37	5	9	30	16	3		Brock, ph	1	0	0	0	0	0
								Betzel, pr	0	1	0	0	0	0
									36	4	7	30	15	2
STA	2 2 0	0 0 0	0 0 0	1	- 5									
STN	0 0 1	0 0 0	2 1 0	0	- 4									

2B: Miller. 3B: Sisler, Hartley. SH: Austin. SB: Long. DP: STN 1, STA 1. WP: Groom. BB: Horstman 3, Ames 1, Groom 2. Struck out: Ames 1, Goodwin 1, Groom 3. Hits: Horstman 2 and 4 runs in 1 inning (none out in second); Ames 5 and 0 runs in 6 innings; Goodwin 0 hits and 0 runs in 2 innings; Groom 4 hits and 4 runs in 8 innings. LOB: STA 7, STN 7. Umpires: Quigley and Quinn. Time—2:55.

to the efforts of the recently gutted Philadelphia Athletics (55–98), losers of 100 or more games for the previous two years. The Cardinals were prohibitive favorites in the series, yet the Browns managed to salvage two wins and a tie from the seven games. The tie and one of the victories, however, came in truly spectacular fashion.

Game One opened on the 3rd of October at Robinson Field, the Cardinals'

1917 St. Louis City Championship Series

GAME FOUR --- October 6 (second game)

BROWNS	AB	R	H	PO	A	E	CARDINALS	AB	R	H	PO	A	E
Shotton, lf	3	0	1	0	0	0	Long, rf	2	2	1	2	0	0
Austin, 3b	1	0	0	0	2	0	J.Smith, cf	3	2	2	2	0	0
E.Smith, cf	2	0	1	1	0	0	Miller, 2b	3	0	2	1	2	1
Sisler, 1b	3	0	0	7	1	0	Hornsby, ss	3	1	1	1	1	0
Hartley, c	3	0	0	4	0	0	Cruise, lf	2	0	0	0	0	0
Demmitt, rf	1	0	0	1	1	0	Paulette, 1b	2	0	1	5	1	0
Lavan, ss	2	0	0	2	1	1	Baird, 3b	2	0	0	0	1	0
Johnson, 2b	2	1	1	0	3	0	Gonzalez, c	2	0	0	4	0	0
Sothoron, p	2	0	0	0	0	0	Meadows, p	2	1	0	0	0	0
	19	1	3	15	8	1		21	6	7	15	5	1

```
STA    0  0  0    0  1  -  1
STN    3  0  1    0  2  -  6
```

2B: Paulette. 3B: Hornsby. HR: Long. DP: STA. PB: Hartley. HBP: Demmitt (Meadows). BB: Meadows 3, Sothoron 2. Struck out: Meadows 4, Sothoron 4. LOB: STN 2, STA 7. Umpires: Owens and Quigley. Time—1:10.

Lee Meadows (15–9) pitted against Grover Lowdermilk (2–1). The Americans broke on top in the series with a run in the first as Earl Smith and Hank Severeid hit back-to-back triples after two were out. The Cardinals moved ahead in the fifth as Gene Paulette singled and raced to third on a wild relay throw from the outfield. With the infield in, Frank Snyder grounded to Jimmy Austin at third. Austin bobbled the ball just long enough to miss the play at the plate, then pivoted and unloaded a wild throw to George Sisler at first. Snyder went to third and Tommy Long's single put the Cardinals up, 2–1. The Browns tied the game in the ninth, but in the bottom of the inning Rogers Hornsby reached on a Baltimore chop, went to second on Walton Cruise's sacrifice bunt, and to third on Paulette's infield single. Doug Baird then launched a drive over center-fielder Earl Smith's head which rolled to the wall, good enough for what would have been an inside-the-park home run in any other inning. The ball went for a single and the Cardinals had won the first game of the series, Lowdermilk taking the loss. Gene Packard (9–6), who worked the last four innings in relief of Meadows, got the victory.

Spitballer Bill Doak (16–20) was on the mound for the Redbirds in Game Two as the series shifted to Sportsman's Park. Doak's luck during the regular season left something to be desired—it's not easy to have a 3.10 ERA for a third-place club and still lose 20 games—but he was on his form for this game. Despite the close score, the Cards had an easy time of it as they defeated Dave Davenport (17–17) by a 3–1 score. St. Louis scored the first run of the game with the aid of two errors in the fourth and tallied a run in the fifth when Long and Jack Smith started the trouble after two were out with bunt singles. A fastball in Jack Miller's wheelhouse was converted to a single and the Cards led, 2–0. Earl Smith scored the Browns's only run on a throwing error, a wild pitch, and a Jake "Baby Doll" Jacobson single. The Cardinals scored an insurance run off reliever Allan Sothoron (14–19) in the ninth. The Browns might have won the

1917 St. Louis City Championship Series

GAME FIVE --- October 7

CARDINALS	AB	R	H	PO	A	E		BROWNS	AB	R	H	PO	A	E
Long, rf	3	0	0	0	0	0		Shotton, lf	3	0	0	3	1	0
J.Smith, cf	4	0	1	4	0	0		Austin, 3b	3	0	0	1	0	0
Miller, 2b	4	0	1	0	5	1		E.Smith, cf	4	0	2	0	0	0
Hornsby, ss	4	0	1	3	4	1		Sisler, 1b	2	0	0	8	0	0
Cruise, lf	4	0	1	2	0	0		Hartley, c	3	1	0	7	1	0
Paulette, 1b	4	0	1	11	0	0		Demmitt, rf	4	0	0	1	0	0
Baird, 3b	4	0	0	0	1	0		Lavan, ss	4	0	2	4	5	0
Snyder, c	2	0	1	4	1	0		Johnson, 2b	3	0	0	3	3	0
Goodwin, p	1	0	0	0	1	0		Lowdermilk, p	3	1	1	0	0	0
Horstman, p	2	0	1	0	0	0								
	32	0	7	24	12	2			29	2	5	27	10	0

```
STN   0  0  0    0  0  0    0  0  0  -  0
STA   0  1  1    0  0  0    0  0  x  -  2
```

2B: Lowdermilk, E. Smith. DP: STN 2. BB: Lowdermilk 2, Horstman 4, Goodwin 2. Struck out: Lowdermilk 6, Horstman 5. Hits: Goodwin 3 and 2 runs in 2.1 innings. LOB: STA 7. Umpires: Owens and Quigley. Time—1:35.

GAME SIX --- October 7 (second game)

CARDINALS	AB	R	H	PO	A	E		BROWNS	AB	R	H	PO	A	E
Long, rf	4	0	2	2	0	0		Shotton, lf	3	0	1	3	0	0
J.Smith, cf	4	0	0	2	1	0		Austin, 3b	4	0	1	0	4	0
Miller, 2b	4	0	1	2	1	0		E.Smith, cf	4	0	2	2	0	0
Hornsby, ss	4	0	1	3	2	0		Sisler, 1b	3	0	0	12	1	1
Cruise, lf	4	0	2	0	0	0		Hartley, c	4	0	2	3	2	0
Paulette, 1b	4	0	0	10	1	0		Demmitt, rf	2	0	1	1	0	0
Baird, 3b	2	0	0	0	1	0		Lavan, ss	4	0	0	2	3	0
Gonzalez, c	3	0	1	8	3	0		Johnson, 2b	2	0	1	3	6	0
Doak, p	2	0	0	0	4	0		Lowdermilk, p	2	0	0	1	2	0
Betzel, pr	0	0	0	0	0	0								
	31	0	7	27	13	0			28	0	8	27	18	1

```
STN   0  0  0    0  0  0    0  0  0  -  0
STA   0  0  0    0  0  0    0  0  0  -  0
```

2B Shotton. SH: Baird, Demmitt, Doak. Balk: Doak. SB: Paulette, Sisler, Betzel. DP: STN. HBP: Doak (Lowdermilk). BB: Doak 5. Struck out: Doak 9, Lowdermilk 3. LOB: STA 9, STN 6. Umpires: Owens and Quigley. Time—1:45.

game had not George Sisler, already 3-for-5 in the series, been ejected in the second inning for arguing a balk call with umpire Clarence Owens.

A doubleheader was scheduled for the 6th of October as the Browns came back from the dead and won their first game of the series in the opener. Bob Groom (8–19) started for the Americans against Cardinal rookie Oscar Horstman (9–4) and had an easy time of it for the first six innings. Horstman got off to a rocky start in the first by giving up a free pass to Burt Shotton and singles to Smith and Severeid for the Browns' initial run. A wild throw scored Smith. When Horstman walked Doc Lavan and Wally Gerber to lead off the second, he was lifted in favor of reliever Red Ames (15–10). Singles by Shotton

1917 St. Louis City Championship Series

GAME SEVEN --- October 8

CARDINALS	AB	R	H	PO	A	E		BROWNS	AB	R	H	PO	A	E
Long, rf	5	0	1	3	0	0		Shotton, 1f	4	0	0	2	0	0
Smythe, rf	0	0	0	0	0	0		Austin, 3b	4	0	0	3	2	1
J. Smith, cf	5	1	2	3	0	0		E.Smith, cf	4	1	1	0	0	0
Miller, 2b	3	1	0	1	6	0		Sisler, 1b	3	0	1	6	1	0
Hornsby, ss	4	1	2	0	6	0		Hartley, c	3	0	1	8	1	0
Cruise, lf	4	1	2	0	0	0		Demmitt, rf	0	0	0	1	0	0
Paulette, 1b	3	1	0	15	0	0		Jacobson, rf	3	0	0	2	1	0
Baird, 3b	4	1	2	0	2	0		Lavan, ss	3	0	1	4	1	0
Snyder, c	4	0	0	5	0	0		Johnson, 2b	2	0	0	1	1	1
Packard, p	4	0	1	0	1	0		Gerber, 2b	0	0	0	0	0	0
	36	6	10	27	15	0		Davenport, p	2	0	0	0	2	1
								Groom, p	0	0	0	0	1	0
								Rumler, ph	1	0	0	0	0	0
								Severeid, ph	1	0	0	0	0	0
									30	1	4	27	10	4

```
STN   0  0  0    0  0  1    2  3  0  -  6
STA   0  0  0    0  0  0    1  0  0  -  1
```

2B: Long, J. Smith, Cruise, Lavan, Hartley, Hornsby. 3B: Packard. DP: STN. SB: Miller, Baird. BB: Davenport 2. Struck out: Davenport 6, Packard 4. Hits: Davenport 10 and 6 runs in 8 innings. LOB: STN 5, STA 2. Umpires: Owens and Quigley. Time—1:40.

and Lavan gave the Brownies a 4–0 lead. The Cardinals battled back, however, scoring one in the third, two in the seventh, and tying the game in the eighth. Grover Lowdermilk was the pitcher of record when Sisler and Grover Hartley hit back-to-back triples in the tenth to win the game, 5–4.

The nightcap went just five innings before darkness set in. Three Redbird runs in the first were all that Lee Meadows needed as the Cardinals won easily, 6–1. Allan Sothoron took the loss.

Grover Lowdermilk pleased and amazed the crowd at Sportsman's Park on the seventh by shutting out the Cardinals in both ends of a doubleheader. Only the fact that the Browns were unable to score in the nightcap kept Grover from winning both games. With the Cardinals needing one victory to close out the series, Lowdermilk's work was all the more noteworthy. Not since September 26, 1908, when Ed Reulbach of the Cubs threw 5–0 and 3–0 shutouts on the same day had a pitcher accomplished such a feat. (Reulbach's twin whitewash, in fact, is the only case on record of a pitcher winning two complete-game shutouts in a doubleheader during the regular season.) Both American League runs were Cardinal gifts. In the second, Hartley drew a pass from losing rookie pitcher Marv Goodwin (6–4) and Ray Demmitt was safe when Jack Miller bobbled a sure double-play grounder. Doc Lavan's single scored Hartley with the only run Lowdermilk needed. Grover singled and scored on Earl Smith's double in the third to provide some insurance.

In the nightcap, Lowdermilk and Bill Doak matched each other pitch for pitch before darkness halted the game after nine innings. Doak scattered eight hits and five walks and escaped with his head as the Browns failed time and again to get the big hit with men on base. On the day, Lowdermilk pitched two seven-hitters and walked only two men, one of them intentionally. The game was the 11th tie in the history of the St. Louis city championship series.

Lowdermilk, who by this time must have been searching his contract for the combat pay clause, was to start the eighth game, but it never got that far as the Cardinals mauled Dave Davenport in Game Seven. The game was scoreless until the Redbirds broke on top with a singleton in the sixth. Jack Smith's line drive went for a double when Jacobson lost the ball in the sun. With two out, Hornsby lifted a short fly ball for what would have retired the side, but left-fielder Shotton called shortstop Lavan off on the play, then let the ball drop, Smith scoring. Pitcher Gene Packard's triple scored Paulette and Baird with the decisive runs in the seventh. Earl Smith's home run in the bottom of the inning gave the Browns their only run of the day. Three Cardinal runs off Davenport put the game and the series out of reach in the eighth.

The Cardinals received approximately $105 as the winning share. The Browns went home with an extra $59 in their pockets.

This was the last St. Louis city championship series to be played. In all, the Browns won seven series and lost three, winning 42 games, losing 31, with 11 ties. Two of the series ended in ties.

The 1917 Ohio State Championship Series

Cincinnati Reds defeat Cleveland Indians; 4–2

The first Ohio state championship series in six years matched the third-place Cleveland Indians (88–66) against Christy Mathewson's fourth-place Cincinnati Reds (78–76). Mathewson had just finished his first full year as the Reds' manager.

The best-of-seven series opened on October 4 at Crosley Field as Cincinnati ace Fred Toney (24–16) squared off against Cleveland ace Jim Bagby (23–13). Bagby kept the Indians close, but he trailed 1–0 after five innings, in and out of trouble all the way. He finally self-destructed in the sixth, and gave up six runs. His relief, Fritz Coumbe (8–6), gave up five hits and five runs himself in the seventh. The final score was 11–2. Toney pitched a complete game for the Reds, striking out five and scattering nine hits.

After an off-day, the series resumed with Cincinnati's Pete Schneider (20–19) paired off against Stan Coveleski (19–14). Both pitchers went the distance in this 13-inning affair won by Cincinnati 2–1. Cleveland broke on top in the first on a triple by Jack Graney and an RBI single by Tris Speaker. The Reds tied the game in the fifth on Tommy Griffith's triple and Dave Shean's sacrifice fly. That's where the score remained for the next seven and a half innings until Griffith and Shean got together again in the thirteenth, Griffith singling and later coming around on Shean's base knock. Schneider struck out seven and gave up ten hits, easing past Coveleski who struck out one and limited the Reds to seven hits.

Jim Bagby got his second start of the series in Game Three, going against Cincinnati's Hod Eller (10–5). Bagby was off his game again and gave up six hits and three runs in the first four innings. Fritz Coumbe relieved again and pitched well, allowing one run on four hits over the final five innings. The deciding

1917 Ohio State Championship Series

GAME ONE --- October 4

CLEVELAND	AB	H	PO	A	E		CINCINNATI	AB	H	PO	A	E
Graney, lf	4	1	0	0	0		Groh, 3b	4	2	3	2	0
Chapman, ss	3	1	2	4	1		Kopf, ss	5	2	1	4	0
Speaker, cf	4	1	1	0	0		Roush, cf	5	3	1	0	0
Roth, rf	4	2	2	0	0		Chase, 1b	5	1	12	0	0
Harris, 1b	4	1	11	1	0		Griffith, rf	3	1	0	0	0
Evans, 3b	4	1	2	0	0		Neale, lf	4	1	2	0	0
Turner, 2b	4	1	1	3	0		Shean, 2b	3	2	1	2	0
O'Neill, c	4	0	4	2	0		Wingo, c	4	2	7	1	0
Bagby, p	2	1	0	3	1		Toney, p	4	2	0	1	0
Coumbe, p	0	0	0	1	0							
Morton, p	0	0	1	0	0			37	16	27	10	0
Smith, ph	2	0	0	0	0							
Wambsganss, ph	1	0	0	0	0							
	36	9	24	14	2							

```
CLE   0  0  0    0  0  0    0  2  0  -   2
CIN   0  0  1    0  5  5    0  0  x  -  11
```

3B: Roush, Speaker. DP: CLE 2. BB: Coumbe 1. Struck out: Bagby 2, Morton 1, Toney 6. Hits: Bagby 11 in 6 innings; Coumbe 3 in 1 inning. Umpires: Harrison and Hildebrand.

GAME TWO --- October 6

CLEVELAND	AB	H	PO	A	E		CINCINNATI	AB	H	PO	A	E
Graney, lf	5	2	5	0	0		Groh, 3b	5	0	2	2	0
Chapman, ss	5	1	1	3	0		Kopf, ss	5	1	3	8	0
Speaker, cf	5	3	4	1	0		Roush, cf	5	1	1	0	0
Roth, rf	5	1	7	0	0		Chase, 1b	5	1	18	1	0
Harris, 1b	4	0	17	1	0		Griffith, rf	5	2	0	0	0
Evans, 3b	3	1	1	1	0		Neale, lf	3	0	4	2	0
Smith, ph	1	0	0	0	0		Shean, 2b	4	1	2	4	0
Turner, 2b-3b	5	1	0	10	0		Wingo, c	4	0	7	3	0
O'Neill, c	5	0	1	1	0		Schneider, p	4	1	2	4	0
Coveleski, p	4	1	0	2	0							
Wambsganss, 2b	1	0	1	0	1			40	7	39	24	0
	43	10	*37	19	2							

* One out when winning run scored

```
CLE   1  0  0    0  0  0    0  0  0    0  0  0    0  -  1
CIN   0  0  0    0  1  0    0  0  0    0  0  0    1  -  2
```

2B: Roth. 3B: Speaker, Griffith, Graney. SH: Neale. DP: CIN. BB: Schneider 2. Struck out: Schneider 7, Coveleski 1. Umpires: Hildebrand and Harrison.

Cincinnati runs scored in the fourth after two were out. Shean singled on the infield, Ivy Wingo walked, and Eller's single brought both men home. Single runs for the Indians in the seventh and eighth made the score appear closer than it was. Eller held Cleveland to just six hits for the day and came away the winner. The final score was 4-2.

The Indians rebounded and played strong ball in Game Four on the eighth. Ed Klepfer (14-4) blanked the Reds on seven hits and five strikeouts

1917 Ohio State Championship Series

GAME THREE --- October 7

CINCINNATI	AB	H	PO	A	E
Groh, 3b	3	1	4	0	0
Kopf, ss	4	1	1	3	1
Roush, cf	4	1	3	0	0
Chase, 1b	4	1	10	0	0
Griffith, rf	4	2	1	0	0
Neale, lf	3	1	0	0	0
Shean, 2b	3	1	1	5	0
Wingo, c	3	1	7	0	0
Eller, p	3	1	0	1	0
	31	10	27	9	1

CLEVELAND	AB	H	PO	A	E
Graney, lf	3	1	3	1	0
Chapman, ss	4	0	3	2	0
Speaker, cf	3	1	5	1	0
Roth, rf	4	0	2	0	0
Harris, 1b	4	2	9	3	1
Evans, 3b	3	0	0	2	1
Turner, 2b	4	1	2	1	0
O'Neill, c	2	0	2	1	0
Bagby, p	1	0	0	1	0
Coumbe, p	2	0	1	2	0
Wambsganss, ph	1	0	0	0	0
Smith, ph	1	1	0	0	0
DeBarry, ph	1	0	0	0	0
	33	6	27	14	2

```
CIN   1 0 0   2 0 0   0 1 0  -  4
CLE   0 0 0   0 0 0   1 1 0  -  2
```

2B: Turner, Harris. SB: Groh, Neale. DP: CLE 2. BB: Bagby 1, Eller 3, Coumbe 1. Struck out: Eller 7, Coumbe 1. Hits: Bagby 4 in 4 innings. Umpires: Hildebrand and Harrison.

GAME FOUR --- October 8

CINCINNATI	AB	H	PO	A	E
Groh, 3b	3	1	2	6	1
Kopf, ss	3	0	1	4	0
Roush, cf	4	1	2	1	0
Chase, 1b	4	1	11	0	1
Griffith, rf	4	0	3	0	0
Neale, lf	4	1	3	0	0
Shean, 2b	4	0	0	1	0
Wingo, c	3	2	2	1	1
H. Smith, c	1	1	0	0	0
Toney, p	1	0	0	0	0
Regan, p	2	0	0	1	0
Reuther, ph	1	0	0	0	0
	34	7	24	14	3

CLEVELAND	AB	H	PO	A	E
Graney, lf	5	2	1	0	0
Chapman, ss	5	1	2	3	0
Speaker, cf	4	4	1	0	0
Roth, rf	4	3	2	0	0
Harris, 1b	3	1	15	0	0
Evans, 3b	4	1	0	6	0
Turner, 2b	4	1	1	2	0
O'Neill, c	4	1	5	0	0
Klepfer, p	3	2	0	2	0
	36	16	27	13	0

```
CIN   0 0 0   0 0 0   0 0 0  -  0
CLE   0 2 2   2 0 1   0 1 0  -  8
```

3B: Speaker 2. SB: Speaker, Roth. BB: Toney 1, Regan 3, Klepfer 2. Struck out: Toney 1, Regan 1, Klepfer 5. Hits: Toney 7 in 2 innings. Umpires: Harrison and Hildebrand.

GAME FIVE --- October 9

CLEVELAND	AB	H	PO	A	E
Graney, lf	4	1	3	1	0
Chapman, ss	2	0	1	3	1
Speaker, cf	4	1	1	0	1
Roth, rf	5	2	2	0	0
Harris, 1b	4	2	11	0	0
Evans, 3b	4	1	2	4	0
Turner, 2b	3	2	3	4	0
O'Neill, c	3	0	3	1	0
Morton, p	0	0	0	0	0
Coveleski, p	3	0	1	1	0
	32	9	27	14	2

CINCINNATI	AB	H	PO	A	E
Groh, 3b	4	1	1	3	0
Kopf, ss	4	1	4	1	0
Roush, cf	4	3	1	1	0
Chase, 1b	4	1	8	1	0
Griffith, rf	4	1	1	0	0
Neale, lf	3	1	3	1	0
Shean, 2b	2	0	4	2	2
Wingo, c	3	0	5	3	1
Schneider, p	3	0	0	2	1
	31	8	27	14	4

```
CLE   1 0 2   0 0 0   0 1 2  -  6
CIN   2 0 0   0 0 0   0 1 0  -  3
```

2B: Turner, Speaker. 3B: Groh. SH: Chapman. SB: Roush. PB: O'Neill. BB: Schneider 7. Struck out: Schneider 5, Morton 1, Coveleski 2. Umpires: Hildebrand and Harrison.

1917 Ohio State Championship Series

```
GAME SIX --- October 10
```

CLEVELAND	AB	H	PO	A	E		CINCINNATI	AB	H	PO	A	E
Groh, 3b	4	0	2	3	0		Graney, lf	4	0	0	3	0
Kopf, ss	5	3	3	3	0		Chapman, ss	4	1	4	4	2
Roush, cf	5	3	5	0	0		Speaker, cf	4	3	5	0	0
Chase, 1b	5	1	9	1	0		Roth, rf	1	0	0	0	0
Griffith, rf	2	0	2	0	0		Smith, rf	3	1	0	0	0
Neale, lf	1	1	0	0	0		Harris, 1b	3	0	12	0	0
Magee, lf	4	1	1	0	0		Evans, 3b	3	0	0	0	0
Shean, 2b	3	1	0	3	0		Turner, 2b	3	0	1	3	0
Wingo, c	3	0	4	2	0		O'Neill, c	3	0	5	2	0
Eller, p	3	1	1	0	0		Bagby, p	0	0	0	0	0
							Coumbe, p	2	0	0	1	0
	35	11	27	12	0		Morton, p	0	0	0	0	0
							Billings, ph	1	0	0	0	0
								31	5	27	13	2

```
CIN   0  0  0    4  3  0    0  1  0  -  8
CLE   0  0  0    0  0  0    0  1  0  -  1
```

2B: Shean, Chase. 3B: Speaker. SB: Eller, Shean, Griffith, Roush. SH: Griffith. BB: Bagby 3, Coumbe 2, Morton 1. Struck out: Bagby 1, Coumbe 2, Morton 1, Eller 3. Hits: off Bagby 4 and 4 runs in 2.2 inning; Coumbe 6 and 4 runs in 5.1 innings. PB: O'Neill 2. Umpires: Hildebrand and Harrison.

as his teammates broke through for eight big runs. Cincinnati starter Fred Toney was roughed up for seven hits and six runs in the first four innings. Rookie Mike Regan (11–10) came on in relief and fared even worse, allowing nine hits and six runs over the final seven innings. Tris Speaker had two triples as he went a perfect 4-for-4 at the plate.

Game Five saw Pete Schneider in a rematch with Stan Coveleski. Schneider's wildness and errors by his teammates were responsible for the 6–3 Cleveland victory. Both teams scored in the first and Cleveland held a slim 4–3 lead when they broke through for two insurance runs off Schneider in the top of the ninth. Coveleski went eight innings for the win and was relieved in the ninth by Guy Morton (10–10).

The Reds won the series the next day at League Park in Cleveland. Hod Eller went the distance for the Reds and stifled the Cleveland offense on five hits and a run. Cincinnati struck for four runs in the third against Jim Bagby, then pounded his relief, Fritz Coumbe, for three runs in the fourth. The final score was 8–1.

This was the fourth and last Ohio state championship series ever played. The Reds had won three of the four series, and finished with a 15–13 record in games played.

The 1921 Chicago City Championship Series

Chicago White Sox defeat Chicago Cubs; 5–0

It was difficult to choose between the 1921 Cubs and White Sox. Both teams finished seventh. The Cubs had a dismal 64–89 record. The White Sox,

1921 Chicago City Championship Series

GAME ONE --- October 5

CUBS	AB	R	H	PO	A	E		WHITE SOX	AB	R	H	PO	A	E
Flack, rf	3	0	0	4	0	0		Johnson, ss	4	1	3	4	6	0
Hollocher, ss	4	0	1	1	0	0		Strunk, lf	4	0	2	2	0	0
Terry, 2b	3	0	0	2	2	1		Collins, 2b	4	0	3	3	5	0
Kelleher, 3b	4	0	0	1	4	0		Hooper, rf	4	1	2	1	0	0
Barber, lf	4	0	3	2	1	0		Sheely, 1b	4	0	0	13	1	0
Maisel, cf	4	0	0	1	0	0		Mostil, cf	4	0	0	2	0	0
Grimes, 1b	3	0	1	8	2	0		Mulligan, 3b	4	0	0	0	3	1
O'Farrell,c	3	0	0	5	0	1		Schalk, c	3	0	0	2	1	0
Alexander, p	3	0	0	0	1	0		Kerr, p	3	0	0	0	1	1
	31	0	5	24	10	2			34	2	10	27	17	2

```
CUB   0  0  0    0  0  0    0  0  0  -  0
SOX   0  0  1    0  0  1    0  0  x  -  2
```

2B: Johnson 2, Barber, Hooper. DP: Sox 2. BB: Kerr 2. Struck out: Alexander 3, Kerr 2. WP: Kerr. Umpires: Owens, Hildebrand, Klem, McCormick.

GAME TWO --- October 6

WHITE SOX	AB	R	H	PO	A	E		CUBS	AB	R	H	PO	A	E
Johnson, ss	4	1	3	1	3	0		Flack, rf	4	2	1	2	0	0
Strunk, lf	5	2	2	2	0	0		Hollocher, ss	4	1	1	4	6	1
Collins, 2b	3	2	2	1	4	0		Terry, 2b	4	1	2	2	3	1
Hooper, rf	3	0	1	1	0	0		Kelleher, 3b	5	0	1	0	3	1
Sheely, 1b	5	0	1	14	1	0		Barber, lf	4	0	1	3	0	0
Mostil, cf	4	0	2	5	0	2		Maisel, cf	4	0	0	1	0	0
Mulligan, 3b	5	1	1	0	3	0		Grimes, 1b	3	1	2	11	1	0
Schalk, c	4	1	1	1	2	0		Killefer, c	1	0	0	2	0	1
Faber, p	2	1	1	2	2	0		O'Farrell, c	1	0	0	2	0	0
McWeeny, p	0	0	0	0	0	0		Martin, p	2	0	0	0	2	1
								Freeman, p	0	0	0	0	0	0
	35	8	14	27	15	2		York, p	0	0	0	0	0	0
								Mariott, ph	1	0	1	0	0	0
								Twombly, ph	0	0	0	0	0	0
								Deal, ph	1	0	0	0	0	0
									34	5	9	27	15	5

```
CUB   1  0  0    0  0  0    1  2  1  -  5
SOX   0  0  0    0  1  1    4  1  1  -  8
```

2B: Hooper, Mulligan, Grimes, Collins, Johnson 2, Strunk. 3B: Collins. HR: Flack. SH: Schalk, Terry 2, Killefer, Faber, Hooper 2, Twombly. SB: Barber, Mostil, Mariott. HBP: Mostil (Martin). DP: Cub. BB: Faber 1, Martin 1, York 1, McWeeny 1. Struck out: Martin 1, York 2, Faber 1. Umpires: Owens, Hildebrand, Klem, McCormick.

still devastated by the loss of the eight men involved in the 1919 World Series scandal, finished a slightly more dismal 62–92. Both teams were saved from the cellar by Philadelphia ball clubs even worse than their own. One wonders why anyone at all came out to attend this best-of-nine series.

The series' opener was played on October 5th and saw Dickie Kerr (19–17) outduel Grover Cleveland Alexander (15–13). Alex was touched for ten hits and two runs and was ultimately undone by his inability to stop the top four batters in the Sox lineup, all left-handed hitters. Ernie Johnson had two doubles and a single; Amos Strunk had two singles; Eddie Collins, three singles; and Harry Hooper, formerly of the Red Sox, two doubles. Johnson and Hooper scored

1921 Chicago City Championship Series

GAME THREE --- October 8

CUB	AB	R	H	PO	A	E		WHITE SOX	AB	R	H	PO	A	E
Flack, rf	5	0	2	0	0	1		Johnson, ss	2	1	0	1	5	0
Hollocher, ss	5	1	2	4	6	0		Strunk, lf	5	1	1	2	0	0
Terry, 2b	5	1	2	0	0	0		Collins, 2b	4	0	0	3	6	1
Kelleher, 3b	3	1	0	2	5	0		Hooper, rf	4	0	1	1	0	0
Barber, lf	3	0	0	1	0	0		Sheely, 1b	3	0	0	13	0	0
Maisel, cf	5	0	1	3	0	0		Mostil, cf	2	0	0	2	0	0
Grimes, 1b	3	0	1	15	0	0		Mulligan, 3b	4	1	1	2	2	0
Killefer, c	4	0	0	4	1	0		Schalk, c	1	0	0	4	2	0
Jones, p	4	0	1	0	3	0		Yaryan, c	2	0	0	2	1	0
Freeman, p	0	0	0	0	1	0		Kerr, p	2	0	0	0	5	1
								Bratchi, ph	0	0	0	0	0	0
	37	3	9	*29	16	1		McClellan, pr	0	1	0	0	0	0
								Hodge, p	1	0	0	0	1	0
									30	4	3	30	22	2

* Two out when winning run scored

```
CUB    2 0 0   0 0 0   1 0 0  -  3
SOX    0 0 0   0 0 0   0 2 1  -  4
```

2B: Terry. 3B: Grimes. SH: Barber, Killefer, Yaryan. SB: Johnson, Grimes, Hollocher, Sheely, Barber. WP: Kerr. Umpires: Owens, Hildebrand, Klem, McCormick.

GAME FOUR --- October 9

CUB	AB	R	H	PO	A	E		WHITE SOX	AB	R	H	PO	A	E
Flack, rf	4	0	1	0	0	0		Johnson, ss	4	2	3	6	4	0
Hollocher, ss	2	0	0	6	3	0		Strunk, lf-cf	3	0	2	0	0	0
Terry, 2b	3	0	0	2	1	1		Collins, 2b	3	0	1	1	1	0
Kelleher, 3b	3	0	0	2	1	1		Hooper, rf	3	1	1	2	0	0
Barber, lf	4	1	2	2	1	0		Sheely, 1b	3	0	0	10	2	0
Twombly, cf	4	0	1	1	0	0		Mostil, cf	1	0	1	1	0	1
Grimes, 1b	4	0	1	6	1	1		Falk, lf	3	0	1	3	0	0
O'Farrell, c	3	0	1	4	3	0		Mulligan, 3b	3	0	0	3	3	0
Alexander, p	3	1	0	1	4	0		Yaryan, c	3	0	0	0	3	0
	30	2	6	24	14	3		Hodge, p	3	0	0	1	5	0
									29	3	9	27	18	1

```
CUB    0 1 0   0 1 0   0 0 0  -  2
SOX    1 0 0   0 0 1   1 0 x  -  3
```

SH: Kelleher, Sheely, Collins. DP: Cubs. BB: Hodge 3, Alexander 2. Struck out: Alexander 4. Umpires: Owens, Hildebrand, Klem, McCormick.

the two Sox runs. Kerr scattered five hits and the only Cub who gave him any real trouble on the day was Turner Barber who made three of those.

The Cubs took a first inning lead off Urban "Red" Faber (25-15) the next day in Game Two. The Sox tied the game in the fifth, took a one run lead in the sixth, and Faber had to leave the game in the eighth when he turned on his knee fielding a groundout. He was lost for the remainder of the series. The Americans then batted around for four runs and won the game. The final score was 8–5. Faber took the victory, Elwood "Speed" Martin (11-15) was the loser.

The most exciting game of the series was Game Three on the eighth. The Cubs scored twice in the first off Dickie Kerr on two hits and two errors, then

1921 Chicago City Championship Series

GAME FIVE --- October 10

WHITE SOX	AB	R	H	PO	A	E	CUBS	AB	R	H	PO	A	E
Johnson, ss	4	1	0	3	4	0	Flack, rf	5	0	1	4	0	0
Strunk, lf	4	2	2	3	0	0	Hollocher, ss	3	1	2	2	5	0
Collins, 2b	4	1	2	4	5	0	Terry, 2b	2	1	1	1	6	0
Hooper, rf	5	2	1	4	0	0	Kelleher, 3b	3	1	0	0	2	0
Sheely, 1b	4	1	2	8	0	0	Barber, lf	4	1	0	2	0	0
Falk, lf	5	0	1	3	0	0	Maisel, cf	3	0	1	2	1	0
Mulligan, 3b	5	1	1	0	1	0	Grimes, 1b	4	0	2	11	0	0
Yaryan, c	4	0	4	2	0	0	Killefer, c	3	0	0	5	1	0
Russell, p	3	1	0	0	0	0	O'Farrell, c	0	0	0	0	0	0
Kerr, p	1	0	1	0	1	0	Cheeves, p	0	1	0	0	0	0
							York, p	0	0	0	0	0	0
	39	9	14	27	11	0	Ponder, p	0	0	0	0	0	0
							Deal, ph	1	0	0	0	0	0
							Sullivan, ph	1	0	0	0	0	0
							Freeman, p	0	0	0	0	0	0
							Daly, c	1	0	0	0	0	0
								30	5	7	27	15	0

```
SOX   2 0 0   0 5 0   0 1 1 - 9
CUB   0 1 1   0 0 3   0 0 0 - 5
```

2B: Strunk, Hollocher, Yaryan. 3B: Collins, Strunk. HR: Sheely. SH: Hollocher, Terry. SB: Kelleher, Collins, Hooper. DP: Sox 2, Cub 1. BB: Russell 2, Kerr 4, Cheeves 1, Freeman 2, York 1, Ponder 1. Struck out: Cheeves 1, Ponder 1, Kerr 1. HBP: Kelleher. Umpires: Owens, Hildebrand, Klem, McCormick.

increased their lead in the eighth on two walks, a single, and two sacrifices. The Sox were ably held in check by Percy Jones (3–5), their only safety through eight innings a Harry Hooper single in the second. It looked like the Cubs were going to coast to an easy 3–0 victory until Jones walked Hervey McClellan and Ernie Johnson to lead off the ninth. Amos Strunk hit a one-hopper right back to Jones which might have gone for a double play, but certainly should have resulted in at least one out. Jones, perhaps rattled by the two walks, threw to second an instant too late and the bases were loaded. An infield groundout by Eddie Collins sent McClellan home with the first Sox run of the day. Hooper popped out and Jones began walking off the field when Earl Sheely hit a fly ball to Max Flack in right field. Unfortunately for the Cubs, Flack dropped the ball and the game was tied. Eddie Mulligan led off the bottom of the tenth for the Sox with a single and manager Bill Killefer signalled for Buck Freeman (9–10) from the bullpen. Yam Yaryan sacrificed Mulligan to second, Ernie Johnson was walked intentionally, and Amos Strunk ended the game with a single to right field. The winning pitcher was Clarence "Shovel" Hodge (6–8) who pitched a scoreless tenth against the Cubs.

The White Sox won Game Four as Pete Alexander lost for the second time in the series. Despite pitching an inning in relief the previous day, Shovel Hodge started for the Sox and was victorious for the second time in 24 hours. The Americans took a one run lead in the first, but the Cubs tied the score with an unearned run in the second when Johnny Mostil transformed a Turner Barber fly ball into a two-base error. Clarence "Babe" Twombly grounded out, but Ray Grimes's RBI single scored the run. Single runs off Alexander in the sixth and seventh decided the contest. The final score was 3–2. There were 35,000 fans in attendance, the largest crowd of the series.

The city championship was decided the next day as John Russell (2–5) and Dickie Kerr combined to defeat four Cub pitchers. Virgil Cheeves (11–12) started for the Cubs but was knocked out in the fifth when the Sox scored five times off him and reliever Jim "Lefty" York (5–9). The big hit of the inning was a three-run homer by Earl Sheely. Russell weakened in the sixth and left the bases loaded for reliever Dickie Kerr. All three baserunners scored to make the score 7–5, but that was the last gasp for the Cubs in the series. Two Sox insurance runs made the final 9–5.

With this city victory, the White Sox ran their string of city championships to seven in a row. They had also won the last 12 consecutive games played—the last three games of 1915, the four-game sweep in 1916, and the five-game sweep this year.

Attendance for the five games was 76,788, with nearly half that total coming in Game Four.

The 1922 Chicago City Championship Series

Chicago Cubs defeat Chicago White Sox; 4–3

The World Series reverted to a best-of-seven format in 1922 and the Chicago city championship series followed form. The White Sox, who hadn't lost a city series in as long as most Chicago youngsters could remember, were in for a surprise when the Cubs (80–74) emerged victorious for the first time since 1909. Both clubs finished fifth in their respective leagues, no small accomplishment for the 77–77 White Sox, still smarting from Commissioner Landis's housecleaning at the end of the 1920 season.

1922 Chicago City Championship Series

GAME ONE --- October 4

WHITE SOX	AB	H	PO	A	E	CUBS	AB	H	PO	A	E
Hooper, rf	3	1	4	3	0	Statz, cf	4	2	4	0	0
Johnson, ss	3	0	1	4	0	Hollocher, ss	3	1	3	1	0
Collins, 2b	3	0	6	2	0	Terry, 2b	4	2	4	2	0
Sheely, 1b	2	2	7	0	0	Grimes, 1b	5	1	7	1	0
Mostil, cf	4	1	3	0	0	Barber, rf	4	1	0	0	0
Falk, lf	3	1	2	0	0	Miller, lf	3	2	3	0	0
Schalk, c	3	1	2	0	0	O'Farrell, c	4	0	6	6	1
Mulligan, 3b	4	4	2	0	0	Krug, 3b	4	0	0	0	1
Faber, p	3	0	0	0	0	Aldridge, p	2	1	0	2	0
						Heathcote, ph	1	1	0	0	0
	28	10	27	9	0	Jones, p	0	0	0	0	0
						Callaghan, ph	1	0	0	0	0
							35	11	27	12	2

```
SOX   0  0  0    0  1  3    0  1  1  -  6
CUB   1  0  0    0  0  0    0  0  1  -  2
```

2B: Mulligan. 3B: Sheely, Statz. HR: Mulligan. SB: Johnson. DP: Cubs 2, Sox 1. BB: Aldridge 7, Faber 3, Jones 1. Struck out: Aldridge 2, Faber 1, Jones 3. Hits: Aldridge 6 in 7 innings. Losing pitcher: Aldridge. Umpires: Ernest Quigley, William Dineen, Hart, Nallin. Att: 17,434. Time—2:05.

1922 Chicago City Championship Series

GAME TWO --- October 5

WHITE SOX	AB	H	PO	A	E		CUBS	AB	H	PO	A	E
Hooper, rf	4	2	2	0	0		Statz, cf	6	1	1	0	0
Johnson, ss	3	1	1	3	0		Hollocher, ss	5	0	1	3	0
Collins, 2b	4	2	3	3	0		Terry, 2b	4	4	2	2	0
Sheely, 1b	4	1	5	0	0		Grimes, 1b	4	3	8	0	0
Mostil, cf	2	0	7	0	0		Barber, rf	3	2	1	1	0
Strunk, lf	2	1	0	0	0		Miller, lf	4	1	2	0	0
Mulligan, 3b	3	1	2	2	2		Krug, 3b	3	0	3	2	0
Falk, ph	1	0	0	0	0		O'Farrell, c	3	2	9	4	0
Evers, 3b	0	0	0	0	0		Osborne, p	4	1	0	2	0
Schalk, c	3	0	4	1	0							
Leverette, p	1	1	0	1	0			36	14	27	14	0
Blankenship, p	2	0	0	0	0							
Davenport, p	0	0	0	0	0							
Mack, p	0	0	0	0	0							
Yaryan, ph	1	0	0	0	0							
	30	9	24	10	2							

```
SOX   0  0  1   1  1  0   0  0  0  -  3
CUB   2  0  1   0  0  0   4  3  x  - 10
```

2B: Sheely, Grimes. HR: Collins. SB: Hooper, Sheely, O'Farrell. DP: Cubs 1, Sox 1. BB: Osborne 6, Leverette 1, Blankenship 2, Davenport 2. Struck out: Osborne 7, Blankenship 2, Mack 1. Hits: Leverette 6 in 2 innings (none out in third); Blankenship 6 in 4.2 innings; Davenport 0 in 0.2 innings (none out in eighth). HBP: Miller (Leverette); Mostil and Hooper (Osborne). Losing pitcher: Blankenship. Umpires: Dineen, Hart, Nallin, Quigley. Att: 14,516. Time—2:30.

GAME THREE --- October 11

CUBS	AB	H	PO	A	E		WHITE SOX	AB	H	PO	A	E
Statz, cf	4	0	4	0	0		Hooper, rf	3	2	1	0	0
Hollocher, ss	5	3	1	3	1		Johnson, ss	4	1	3	2	0
Terry, 2b	4	2	3	2	0		Collins, 2b	4	1	2	5	0
Grimes, 1b	4	2	6	0	0		Sheely, 1b	4	2	8	0	0
Barber, rf	4	2	2	1	0		Mostil, cf	4	0	2	0	0
Miller, lf	4	2	1	0	0		Falk, lf	3	0	3	0	0
Krug, 3b	4	0	3	1	0		Mulligan, 3b	5	2	0	0	1
O'Farrell, c	4	1	7	1	1		Schalk, c	5	0	8	2	0
Osborne, p	4	0	0	0	1		Faber, p	2	0	0	2	0
	37	12	27	8	3		Strunk, ph	0	0	0	0	0
							Blankenship, p	1	1	0	0	0
								35	9	27	11	1

```
CUB   3  0  0   0  2  0   0  3  0  -  8
SOX   2  0  1   0  0  2   0  0  0  -  5
```

2B: Miller, Collins, Sheely. HR: Hooper, Grimes. SB: Terry, Hooper, Johnson, Sheely. DP: Cubs. BB: Osborne 3, Faber 1. Struck out: Faber 4, Osborne 5, Blankenship 2. Hits: off Faber 3 hits and 5 runs in 6 innings. Losing pitcher: Blankenship. Umpires: Hart, Nallin, Quigley and Dineen. Time—2:16.

Game One, played on October 4 at Cubs' Park (Wrigley Field) saw the Cubs' Vic Aldridge (16–15) matched against Red Faber (21–17). The Cubs jumped on top in the first when a walk, a sacrifice bunt, and a scratch hit scored the first run of the series. Eddie Mulligan tied the game with a solo home run in the fourth. The White Sox took the lead for good in the next inning, the big hit a two-run double by Mulligan. Percy Jones (8–9) relieved Aldridge and

1922 Chicago City Championship Series

```
GAME FOUR --- October 12
```

CUBS	AB	H	PO	A	E		WHITE SOX	AB	H	PO	A	E
Statz, cf	5	3	0	0	1		Hooper, rf	5	3	2	0	0
Hollocher, ss	3	0	1	3	0		Johnson, ss	4	0	0	5	0
Terry, 2b	2	0	1	3	0		Collins, 2b	5	3	4	4	0
Grimes, 1b	2	1	11	2	0		Sheely, 1b	5	0	9	0	0
Barber, rf	4	2	1	0	0		Mostil, cf	3	0	3	0	0
Miller, lf	3	1	3	0	0		Falk, lf	4	1	2	0	0
Krug, 3b	2	0	0	1	1		Mulligan, 3b	4	1	0	1	0
Heathcote, ph	0	0	0	0	0		Schalk, c	4	2	7	2	0
Kelleher, 3b	0	0	1	0	0		Leverette, p	4	0	0	4	0
O'Farrell, c	3	0	6	0	0							
Alexander, p	4	0	2	3	0			38	10	27	16	0
	28	7	*26	12	2							

```
CUB    1  0  1    0  0  1    0  0  0  -  3
SOX    0  0  0    0  0  2    1  0  1  -  4
```

* Two out when winning run scored

2B: Statz, Hooper. 3B: Hooper. DP: Sox. BB: Leverette 4, Alexander 2. Struck out: Alexander 6, Leverette 4. HBP: Krug and Heathcote (Leverette). WP: Leverette. Umpires: Nallin, Quigley, Dineen and Hart. Time—2:03.

was touched for single runs in the eighth and ninth innings. Faber weakened in the ninth and allowed a triple by Jigger Statz and an RBI single by Charlie Hollocher, but went the distance for an 11-hitter and a 6–2 victory. Mulligan finished the day a perfect 4-for-4—two singles, a double and a home run. This was the thirteenth consecutive time the White Sox had beaten the Cubs, dating back to 1915.

The Sox finally saw their seven-year winning streak come to an end in Game Two when Tiny Osborne (9–5) started on the mound against the Sox's Dixie Leverette (13–10). The game was tied at three when the Cubs knocked reliever Ted Blankenship (8–10) from the box with four runs in the seventh innings. Blankenship was followed to the mound by a duo of youngsters, Lum Davenport (1–1) and Frank Mack (2–2). Osborne scattered nine hits and was only hit hard in two innings as he went all the way for the victory. Johnny Evers—assistant to Sox manager Kid Gleason, former Cubs star, and former Cubs manager—replaced Eddie Mulligan at third in the late innings, a move calculated to please the nearly 15,000 fans in attendance. Evers hadn't played a regular-season game since 1917 and it was his good fortune that none of the Cubs' batters hit the ball in his direction.

No game was scheduled for the 6th of October and rain prevented play for the four days after that, so the series did not resume until the 11th. When it did, Tiny Osborne was again the Cubs' starter, this time pitted against Red Faber. Osborne wasn't quite as much a mystery to the Sox this time, as he was solved for nine hits, three walks, and five runs, but his teammates supported him with eight runs and he won his second game of the series. The big blow came in the seventh inning with the score tied at five. Ted Blankenship served up a three-run homer to Ray Grimes and that was all she wrote.

1922 Chicago City Championship Series

GAME FIVE --- October 13

WHITE SOX	AB	H	PO	A	E		CUBS	AB	H	PO	A	E
Hooper, rf	4	1	2	0	1		Statz, cf	4	1	8	0	0
Johnson, ss	4	0	4	3	0		Hollocher, ss	3	2	0	0	0
Collins, 2b	4	1	1	1	0		Terry, 2b	4	0	0	4	2
Sheely, 1b	4	2	9	0	0		Grimes, 1b	4	1	10	1	0
Mostil, cf	0	0	0	0	0		Barber, rf	3	1	0	1	0
Strunk, cf	4	2	0	0	0		Heathcote, rf	1	1	0	0	0
Falk, lf	4	1	1	0	0		Miller, lf	4	1	3	1	0
Mulligan, 3b	3	0	3	4	1		Kelleher, 3b	4	0	1	0	0
Schalk, c	2	0	4	3	0		O'Farrell, c	3	2	5	2	1
Blankenship, p	2	0	0	1	0		Aldridge, p	2	0	0	2	0
Duff, p	1	0	0	1	0							
	32	7	24	13	2			32	9	27	11	3

```
SOX   0  0  0    1  0  1    0  0  0  -  2
CUB   2  0  0    0  0  5    0  0  x  -  7
```

2B: Hollocher, Falk, Sheely, Statz. 3B: Hooper, Strunk. SB: Hollocher. BB: Blankenship 1. Struck out: Aldridge 4. Hits: Blankenship 7 in 5.2 innings. WP: Blankenship 2. Losing pitcher: Blankenship. Umpires: Quigley, Dineen, Hart and Nallin. Time—1:51.

GAME SIX --- October 14

CUBS	AB	H	PO	A	E		WHITE SOX	AB	H	PO	A	E
Statz, cf	4	0	0	0	0		Hooper, rf	4	0	3	0	0
Hollocher, ss	4	1	1	2	0		Johnson, ss	4	0	2	2	0
Terry, 2b	2	0	2	2	0		Collins, 2b	3	0	3	1	0
Grimes, 1b	4	1	11	0	0		Sheely, 1b	3	0	11	0	0
Barber, rf	3	1	1	0	0		Strunk, cf	3	2	2	0	0
Miller, lf	3	0	5	0	0		Falk, lf	4	0	1	0	0
Kelleher, 3b	3	0	1	4	0		Mulligan, 3b	2	1	2	2	1
O'Farrell, c	3	0	4	1	0		Schalk, c	2	0	3	1	0
Osborne, p	3	0	0	2	0		Faber, p	3	1	0	3	0
	29	3	*25	11	0			28	4	27	9	1

```
CUB   0  0  0    0  0  0    0  0  0  -  0
SOX   0  0  0    0  0  0    0  0  1  -  1
```

* One out when winning run scored

2B: Mulligan. DP: Cubs 1, Sox 1. BB: Faber 1, Osborne 2. Struck out: Faber 3, Osborne 3. HBP: Terry (Faber), Sheely (Osborne). Umpires: Dineen, Hart, Nallin, Quigley. Time—1:47.

Game Four saw the White Sox even the series in an exciting pitcher's contest between Dixie Leverette and Grover Cleveland Alexander (16–13). The Cubs had a 3–0 lead at the end of five and a half innings, but the Sox tied the game with two in the sixth and one in the seventh. That's where the score stayed until Harry Hooper doubled with one out in the bottom of the ninth. One out later, the former Red Sox star moved to third on Eddie Collins' single, then scored the winning run on Earl Sheely's hot grounder.

Game Five saw the Cubs win their third game in convincing fashion as they handed Ted Blankenship his third loss of the series. Blankenship gave up seven hits, a walk, and made two wild pitches before being relieved by Larry Duff (1–1) with two outs in the sixth. Five Cub runs in that inning were the difference

1922 Chicago City Championship Series
GAME SEVEN --- October 15

WHITE SOX	AB	H	PO	A	E		CUBS	AB	H	PO	A	E
Hooper, rf	4	1	3	0	0		Statz, cf	4	3	1	0	0
Johnson, ss	3	2	1	6	0		Hollocher, ss	4	1	1	5	1
Collins, 2b	4	0	5	1	0		Terry, 2b	4	0	3	5	0
Sheely, 1b	4	0	8	0	0		Grimes, 1b	3	1	13	1	0
Strunk, cf	4	1	2	0	0		Barber, rf	2	1	1	1	0
Falk, lf	4	1	2	0	0		Heathcote, rf	2	2	0	0	0
Mulligan, 3b	4	1	1	2	0		Miller, lf	4	1	2	0	0
Schalk, c	4	0	2	2	0		Kelleher, 3b	3	0	3	2	0
Leverette, p	2	0	0	1	0		O'Farrell, c	3	0	3	0	0
Mostil, ph	1	1	0	0	0		Alexander, p	2	1	0	0	0
Faber, p	0	0	0	0	0							
	34	7	24	12	0			31	10	27	14	1

```
SOX   0  0  0    0  0  0    0  0  0  -  0
CUB   0  0  0    0  0  1    1  0  x  -  2
```

2B: Johnson, Statz. 3B: Barber. DP: Sox. LOB: Sox 8, Cubs 7. BB: Leverette 2, Alexander 1. Struck out: Alexander 2, Faber 1. Hits: Leverette 9 in 7 innings; Faber 1 in 1 inning. Losing pitcher: Leverette. Umpires: Hart, Nallin, Quigley, Dineen. Time—1:30.

in the game as the Nationals went on to a 7–2 victory. Vic Aldridge went all the way for the victory.

It was Faber and Osborne for Game Six, a 1–0 pitcher's duel which wasn't decided until the bottom of the ninth inning. Osborne hit Earl Sheely to start the inning and Amos Strunk followed with a single. After Bibb Falk was retired, Osborne walked Eddie Mulligan intentionally to load the bases. The strategy seemed to pay off when Ray Schalk grounded up the middle, but the ball eluded Osborne and went on through to center, winning the game for the White Sox. Faber went all the way for his victory, scattering three Cub hits.

The Cubs won the 1922 city championship the next day behind Pete Alexander who shut out the Sox and Dixie Leverette by a score of 2–0. The game was scoreless until two were out in the sixth and Leverette walked Ray Grimes. Cliff Heathcote, who entered the game when Turner Barber was dismissed for arguing a decision with Umpire Hart, singled to right and sent Grimes to third. Hack Miller's single brought Grimes home with the only run Alexander needed. The Cubs added an insurance run in the next inning.

The 1923 Chicago City Championship Series

Chicago White Sox defeat Chicago Cubs; 4–2

The Chicago Cubs had improved upon their previous year's record by three games and finished in fourth place with a record of 83–71. Favored to win the 1923 city championship, the Cubs nevertheless dropped the series to the seventh-place White Sox (69–85), four games to two.

The series opened on October 10th in North Side Park with Cubs ace Grover Cleveland Alexander (22–12) against Charlie Robertson (13–18). Game One went pretty much the way everyone had expected it to. The Cubs scored

1923 Chicago City Championship Series

GAME ONE --- October 10

WHITE SOX	AB	R	H	PO	A	E		CUBS	AB	R	H	PO	A	E
Mostil, cf	5	0	1	1	0	0		Statz, cf	3	2	3	2	0	0
Hooper, rf	5	2	1	1	0	0		Adams, ss	4	0	4	3	7	0
Collins, 2b	3	1	2	2	1	0		Grantham, 2b	5	0	0	4	8	3
Sheely, 1b	4	0	0	12	1	0		Grimes, 1b	3	0	1	12	1	1
Falk, lf	4	0	0	0	0	0		Friberg, 3b	2	1	1	0	2	0
Kamm, 3b	4	0	1	1	2	0		Miller, lf	4	1	1	0	0	0
McClellan, ss	4	1	3	2	2	0		Heathcote, rf	4	0	0	1	0	0
Schalk, c	4	0	1	4	2	0		Hartnett, c	2	3	1	5	1	0
Robertson, p	2	0	1	1	1	1		Alexander, p	3	1	0	0	0	0
Lyons, p	1	0	0	0	4	0								
Strunk, ph	1	0	1	0	0	0			30	8	11	27	19	4
	37	4	11	24	13	1								

```
SOX    0  0  1    0  2  1    0  0  0  -  4
CUB    0  0  2    4  0  1    0  1  x  -  8
```

2B: Statz, Adams 2, McClellan. 3B: Adams. HR: Collins. SB: Collins, Adams. SH: Adams, Friberg, Statz, Alexander. DP: Cubs 3. HBP: Hartnett (Robertson). LOB: Sox 9, Cubs 7. BB: Robertson 2, Alexander 3, Lyons 2. Struck out: Alexander 4, Robertson 1, Lyons 1. Hits: Robertson 8 in 3.1 innings; Lyons 3 in 4.2 innings. Losing pitcher: Robertson. Umpires: Klem, Holmes, Quigley, Ormsby. Time—1:48.

GAME TWO --- October 11

CUBS	AB	R	H	PO	A	E		WHITE SOX	AB	R	H	PO	A	E
Statz, cf	5	0	2	1	0	0		Strunk, cf	4	0	0	1	0	0
Adams, ss	4	0	0	0	1	1		Elsh, ph	0	0	0	0	0	0
Grantham, 2b	5	1	2	4	2	0		Hooper, rf	4	0	1	2	0	0
Grimes, 1b	4	0	1	8	1	0		Collins, 2b	4	1	1	4	0	1
Friberg, 3b	3	0	1	5	2	0		Sheely, 1b	4	0	0	10	0	0
Miller, lf	4	0	0	1	0	0		Falk, lf	2	0	0	3	0	0
Heathcote, rf	4	0	1	4	0	0		Barrett, lf	2	1	1	1	0	0
Hartnett, c	4	1	1	4	1	0		Kamm, 3b	4	0	2	1	7	0
Aldridge, p	4	2	2	0	2	0		McClellan, ss	4	1	1	2	5	1
Fussell, p	0	0	0	0	1	0		Schalk, c	1	0	1	1	0	0
	37	4	10	27	10	1		Crouse, c	3	0	2	2	2	0
								Thurston, p	3	0	1	0	3	0
								Mostil, ph	0	0	0	0	0	0
									35	3	10	27	17	2

```
CUB    1  0  0    2  0  1    0  0  0  -  4
SOX    0  0  0    0  0  0    1  2  0  -  3
```

2B: Grantham, Statz, Grimes, McClellan, Kamm. 3B: Hooper, Barrett. SB: Hooper, Heathcote, Grantham. SH: Adams, Friberg, Elsh. DP: Cubs 1. HBP: Grimes (Thurston). LOB: Cubs 9, Sox 9. BB: Aldridge 3. Struck out: Thurston 2, Aldridge 1. Hits: Aldridge 10 in 8 innings (none out in ninth); Fussell 0 in 1 inning. WP: Thurston. Winning pitcher: Aldridge. Umpires: Holmes, Quigley, Ormsby, Klem. Time—2:00.

twice in the third and were never headed. In the fourth inning, Alexander came to the plate with the bases loaded and one out and grounded a ball right back to Robertson. His throw home was wild and Barney Friberg and Hack Miller scored to put the Cubs up 4–1. A single by Jigger Statz and a Sparky Adams double completed the four-run inning. The final score was 8–4.

No surprises in Game Two played at Comiskey Park the next day. The

1923 Chicago City Championship Series

GAME THREE --- October 12

WHITE SOX	AB	R	H	PO	A	E		CUBS	AB	R	H	PO	A	E
Strunk, lf	3	2	2	1	0	1		Statz, cf	3	0	1	2	0	0
Barrett, lf	2	1	2	3	0	0		Adams, ss	4	0	1	2	3	0
Hooper, rf	4	0	2	1	0	0		Grantham, 2b	4	0	0	1	3	0
Collins, 2b	2	0	0	3	5	0		Grimes, 1b	4	0	1	11	0	1
Sheely, 1b	3	0	0	11	0	0		Friberg, 3b	4	1	2	1	3	0
Falk, lf	2	0	1	1	0	0		Miller, lf	4	0	0	2	0	0
Mostil, lf-cf	1	0	0	1	0	0		Heathcote, rf	3	0	0	4	0	0
Kamm, 3b	4	0	0	0	0	0		O'Farrell, c	3	1	1	4	1	0
McClellan, ss	2	0	0	2	4	0		Keen, p	0	0	0	0	0	0
Crouse, c	4	1	1	4	2	0		Fussell, p	1	0	0	0	0	0
Faber, p	3	0	0	0	4	0		Grigsby, ph-c	1	0	0	0	0	0
								Osborne, p	0	0	0	0	2	1
	30	4	8	27	15	1			31	2	6	27	12	2

```
SOX   1 0 0   0 2 0   1 0 0 - 4
CUB   0 0 1   1 0 0   0 0 0 - 2
```

2B: Statz, Crouse, Friberg. HR: Friberg. SB: Adams. SH: Collins, Keen, Faber, Hooper. DP: Sox 1. LOB: Sox 7, Cubs 4. BB: Faber 1, Keen 3, Osborne 2. Struck out: Faber 4, Keen 1, Fussell 2. Hits: Keen 6 in 4.1 innings; Fussell 1 in 2.2 innings; Osborne 1 in 2 innings. WP: Fussell. Losing pitcher: Keen. Umpires: Quigley, Ormsby, Klem, Holmes. Time—2:05.

GAME FOUR --- October 14

CUBS	AB	R	H	PO	A	E		WHITE SOX	AB	R	H	PO	A	E
Statz, cf	3	1	1	3	0	0		Barrett, cf	5	0	1	3	0	0
Adams, ss	4	0	1	1	2	1		Hooper, rf	4	2	2	3	0	0
Grantham, 2b	4	0	2	2	4	1		Collins, 2b	5	1	0	3	3	0
Grimes, 1b	2	0	0	8	1	0		Sheely, 1b	4	1	3	7	0	0
Friberg, 3b	4	0	0	3	3	0		Falk, lf	4	1	1	3	0	0
Miller, lf	4	0	1	1	1	0		Kamm, 3b	2	0	1	2	1	0
Hartnett, c	3	1	0	7	0	0		McClellan, ss	4	0	2	2	1	0
Heathcote, rf	1	0	0	0	0	0		Schalk, c	3	0	1	4	3	0
Vogel, rf	1	0	0	0	0	0		Cvengros, p	2	0	0	0	1	0
Alexander, p	1	0	0	0	5	0		Thurston, p	2	0	0	0	2	0
O'Farrell, ph	1	1	0	0	0	0								
Kaufmann, p	1	0	0	0	0	0			35	5	11	27	11	0
	29	3	5	*25	16	2								

* One out when winning run scored.

```
CUB   0 0 0   0 3 0   0 0 0 - 3
SOX   2 0 1   0 0 0   0 0 2 - 5
```

2B: Hooper, Statz, Sheely, Kamm, Grantham, Falk. HR: Sheely. SH: Schalk. LOB: Cubs 4, Sox 10. BB: Alexander 1, Cvengros 5, Kaufmann 3. Struck out: Cvengros 2, Alexander 1, Kaufmann 4, Thurston 2. Hits: Alexander 8 in 4 innings; Kaufmann 3 in 4.1 innings; Cvengros 3 in 4.2. Winning pitcher: Thurston. Losing pitcher: Kaufmann. Umpires: Ormsby, Klem, Holmes, Quigley. Time—2:19.

Nationals scored four runs off Hollis "Sloppy" Thurston (7–8) in the first six innings and held that 4–0 lead as the White Sox batted against Vic Aldridge (16–9). A double by George Grantham, a Ray Grimes groundout, and a single by Friberg accounted for the Cubs' first inning run, after which they were never headed. Aldridge weakened and allowed one run in the seventh and two in the eighth. When Aldridge walked Johnny Mostil to lead off the ninth, Cubs

1923 Chicago City Championship Series

GAME FIVE --- October 15

WHITE SOX	AB	R	H	PO	A	E	CUBS	AB	R	H	PO	A	E
Barrett, cf-1f	4	0	0	3	0	0	Statz, cf	3	0	0	1	0	0
Hooper, rf	3	1	2	4	0	0	Osborne, p	0	0	0	0	1	0
Collins, 2b	3	1	1	2	2	0	Heathcote, ph	1	0	0	0	0	0
Sheely, 1b	4	1	0	10	0	1	Dumovich, p	0	0	0	0	1	0
Falk, lf	2	1	1	0	0	0	Adams, ss	4	1	1	5	5	0
Mostil, cf	2	1	1	3	0	0	Grantham, 2b	4	0	0	0	4	0
Kamm, 3b	4	2	2	1	2	0	Grimes, 1b	4	0	0	15	1	0
McClellan, ss	3	0	0	1	5	0	Friberg, 3b	3	1	2	0	0	0
Crouse, c	2	0	0	3	0	0	Miller, lf	3	0	0	2	0	0
Robertson, p	3	0	0	0	0	0	Grigsby, rf	4	0	0	1	0	0
							O'Farrell, c	3	1	2	2	0	0
	30	7	7	27	9	1	Aldridge, p	1	0	0	0	1	0
							Fussell, p	0	0	0	0	0	0
							Vogel, cf	2	1	1	1	0	0
								32	4	6	27	13	0

```
SOX   0  0  0    5  0  2    0  0  0  -  7
CUB   0  1  0    0  0  0    1  2  0  -  4
```

2B: O'Farrell. HR: Friberg, Collins, Kamm 2, Vogel. SH: Collins, Friberg. DP: Cubs 3. LOB: Sox 7, Cubs 3. HBP: Hooper (Osborne). BB: Aldridge 3, Fussell 2, Osborne 4, Robertson 1. Struck out: Aldridge 1, Robertson 3, Osborne 1. Hits: Aldridge 4 in 3.1 innings; Fussell 3 in 2.2 innings; Osborne 0 in 2 innings; Dumovich 0 in 1 inning. WP: Robertson. Losing pitcher: Aldridge. Umpires: Klem, Holmes, Quigley, Ormsby. Time—1:57.

manager Bill Killefer replaced him with Fred Fussell (3–5). Fussell pitched the ninth without incident and the Cubs had a two-games-to-none lead in the series. Sox manager Kid Gleason lost the services of catcher Ray Schalk in the second inning for throwing dirt on umpire Ormsby.

But the Sox came back strong in the next two games to pull the championship into a tie. Red Faber (14–11) scattered six hits—one of them a home run by Barney Friberg—and pitched a complete game as the White Sox won Game Three, 4–2. Vic Keen (12–8) started for the Cubs and was relieved by Fussell with one out in the fifth when he hit a wild streak. Tiny Osborne (8–15) pitched the last two innings for for the Nationals.

The Sox tied the series in Game Four after an off-day. The largest crowd ever to see a baseball game in Chicago, 41,825 fans, got their money's worth at Comiskey Park. Alexander started his second game and was batted all around the park for eight hits and three runs in four innings. The only inning in which the Cubs were able to score was the fifth, but their three runs tied the game. The contest remained knotted until the bottom of the ninth when Earl Sheely belted a two-run homer to win the game. Sloppy Thurston got the victory and Tony Kaufmann (14–10), who relieved Alexander in the fifth, was the losing pitcher.

The White Sox took their third consecutive victory in Game Five on the 15th. The starting pitchers were Vic Aldridge for the Cubs and Charlie Robertson for the Sox, but home runs were the feature of this game. Barney Friberg and Otto Vogel hit round-trippers for the Cubs while Willie Kamm hit two and Eddie Collins one for the Sox. Five runs in the fourth and two in the sixth were all the Americans needed for a 7–4 victory. By the time the Cubs got their offense untracked, they were trailing 7–1. The starting pitchers took the decisions.

1923 Chicago City Championship Series

GAME SIX --- October 16

CUBS	AB	R	H	PO	A	E
Statz, cf	5	0	1	2	0	1
Adams, ss	5	0	2	1	0	1
Grantham, 2b	4	1	1	3	0	3
Grimes, 1b	4	1	1	6	2	0
Friberg, 3b	3	1	2	3	1	1
Miller, lf	4	0	2	6	0	0
Heathcote, rf	4	0	0	2	1	0
O'Farrell, c	3	0	0	5	2	0
Kaufmann, p	4	0	0	1	3	0
	36	3	9	29	9	6

WHITE SOX	AB	R	H	PO	A	E
Barrett, cf	5	2	3	4	0	0
Hooper, rf	5	0	3	1	0	0
Collins, 2b	4	1	1	6	2	0
Sheely, 1b	4	0	1	11	1	0
Falk, lf	5	0	0	4	0	0
Kamm, 3b	2	0	0	1	2	0
McClellan, ss	5	0	1	1	3	0
Schalk, c	2	0	0	0	2	0
Strunk, ph	1	0	0	0	0	0
Lyons, p	0	0	0	0	0	0
Mostil, ph	1	1	0	0	0	0
Leverette, p	0	0	0	0	0	0
Faber, p	2	0	0	0	3	0
Crouse, c	2	0	2	2	0	0
	38	4	9	30	13	0

* Two out when winning run scored.

```
CUB   0  0  0    1  0  1    0  0  1    0  -  3
SOX   0  0  0    0  0  0    1  0  2    1  -  4
```

2B: Adams, Friberg, Sheely. 3B: Adams, Barrett. HR: Grantham, Friberg. SB: Hooper 2, Statz. SH: Friberg, Sheely. LOB: Cubs 5, Sox 10. BB: Kaufmann 4, Faber 1. Struck out: Kaufmann 3, Leverette 1. Hits: Faber 6 in 7 innings; Lyons 3 in 2 innings; Leverette 0 in 1 inning. PB: Crouse. Winning pitcher: Leverette. Umpires: Holmes, Quigley, Ormsby, Klem. Time—2:21.

The series ended the next day with the White Sox completing their belated sweep. Tony Kaufmann started against Sox pitcher Red Faber. George Grantham and Barney Friberg hit solo home runs for the Cubs who held a 2–0 lead at the end of six. Red Faber was relieved by rookie Ted Lyons (2–1) in the seventh inning with the Sox still trailing 2–1. The Cubs scored once in the top of the ninth to widen their lead to 3–1, but the Americans tallied two of their own in the bottom of the inning to send the game into overtime. Two errors and a wild throw by Grantham gave the White Sox the game and the city championship in the next inning. Kaufmann took the loss. Gorham "Dixie" Leverette (10–13) pitched a hitless tenth for the win.

The 1924 Chicago City Championship Series

Chicago White Sox defeat Chicago Cubs; 4–2

If not for 37-year-old Grover Cleveland Alexander, the Chicago Cubs would have been swept by the White Sox in the 1924 city championship series. In yet another city championship upset, the last-place Sox (66–87) trounced their perennial whipping boys, the fifth-place Cubs (81–72) in six games.

Game One saw Pete Alexander (12–5) hang on like grim death to defeat the White Sox at Wrigley Field, 10–7. The Cubs scored a single run in the second and drove Sox starter Ted Lyons (12–11) to the shower with three more in the third on George Grantham's three-run homer. The Cubs went on a final

1924 Chicago City Championship Series

GAME ONE --- October 1

WHITE SOX	AB	H	PO	A	E
Mostil, cf	2	1	1	0	0
Archdeacon, cf	2	2	0	0	0
Hooper, rf	2	1	2	0	0
Collins, 2b	2	1	0	1	0
Sheely, 1b	5	2	9	0	0
Falk, lf	4	0	3	2	0
Kamm, 3b	4	1	1	2	0
McClellan, ss	3	0	1	0	1
W.Barrett, ph	1	0	0	2	0
Crouse, c	4	2	7	0	0
Lyons, p	1	1	0	0	0
Connally, p	0	0	0	0	0
Cvengros, p	0	0	0	0	0
Clancy, ph	1	0	0	0	0
Leverette, p	1	0	0	1	0
Elsh, ph	1	1	0	0	0
	33	12	24	8	1

CUBS	AB	H	PO	A	E
Adams, ss	4	2	2	3	0
Heathcote, cf	4	1	0	0	0
Grantham, 3b	5	2	1	3	0
Weis, rf	4	3	0	0	1
Hartnett, c	3	2	2	0	0
Grigsby, lf	4	1	2	0	0
R.Barrett, 2b	4	0	0	7	0
Cotter, 1b	4	0	19	1	0
Alexander, p	2	2	1	2	0
	34	13	27	16	1

```
SOX   0  0  0    0  0  0    2  3  2  -   7
CUB   0  1  3    5  0  0    1  0  x  -  10
```

Runs: Archdeacon, Collins, Sheely 2, Kamm, Crouse, Elsh, Adams 2, Heathcote, Grantham 2, Weis 2, Hartnett 2, Grigsby, Alexander 2. 2B: Mostil, Kamm, Cotter, Elsh. 3B: Hartnett. HR: Grantham, Weis, Sheely 2. SB: Heathcote, Grantham, Grigsby, Archdeacon, Hooper. SH: Heathcote. DP: Sox. LOB: Sox 5, Cubs 5. BB: Connally 1, Alexander 1. Struck out: Lyons 1, Cvengros 1, Leverette 1, Alexander 2. Hits: Lyons 6 in 2.1 innings; Connally 3 in 1.1 innings; Cvengros 1 in 1.1 innings; Leverette 3 in 3 innings. Losing pitcher: Lyons. Umpires: Rigler, Hildebrand, Pfirman, Moriarty. Att: 15,414. Time—1:43.

GAME TWO --- October 2

CUBS	AB	H	PO	A	E
Adams, ss	4	2	4	7	0
Heathcote, cf	5	1	1	0	1
Grantham, 3b	5	0	1	1	0
Weis, rf	4	1	1	0	0
O'Farrell, c	3	2	2	0	0
Grigsby, lf	3	1	0	0	0
Miller, ph	1	1	0	0	0
Statz, lf	1	0	0	0	0
R.Barrett, 2b	5	2	3	2	0
Cotter, 1b	3	1	10	1	0
Kaufmann, p	0	0	0	0	0
Hartnett, ph	1	1	0	0	0
Keen, p	1	0	0	0	0
Wheeler, p	1	0	0	2	0
Vogel, ph	1	1	1	0	0
Milstead, p	0	0	0	3	0
	38	13	24	16	1

WHITE SOX	AB	H	PO	A	E
Mostil, cf	4	1	3	1	0
Hooper, rf	4	3	3	1	0
Collins, 2b	3	2	3	3	0
Sheely, 1b	3	1	8	1	0
Falk, lf	4	2	4	0	0
Kamm, 3b	2	0	1	1	0
W.Barrett, ss	5	2	2	1	0
Schalk, c	4	1	3	1	0
Thurston, p	3	2	0	2	0
Cvengros, p	1	1	0	0	0
	33	15	27	11	0

```
CUB   0  0  2    0  0  2    2  1  0  -   7
SOX   1  2  0    0  5  0    2  2  x  -  12
```

Runs: Adams, Weis 2, O'Farrell, R. Barrett, Cotter, Hartnett, Collins 2, Sheely 2, Falk 1, Kamm 2, W. Barrett 2, Schalk, Thurston, Cvengros. 2B: Collins, Thurston, Hooper, Cotter, Adams 2, Cvengros, Mostil, Vogel. HR: W. Barrett. SB: R. Barrett. SH: Adams, Falk. DP; Cubs 1. LOB: Cubs 9, Sox 8. BB: Kaufmann 1, Thurston 3, Keen 2, Wheeler 2, Cvengros 1. Struck out: Thurston 1, Keen 1, Cvengrso 2. Hits: Kaufmann 5 in 2 innings; Keen 4 in 2.2 inning; Wheeler 3 in 2.2 innings; Milstead 2 in 1 inning; Thurston 10 in 6.2 innings; Cvengros 3 in 2.1 innings. HBP: Sheely (Keen), Mostil (Wheeler). WP: Keen. Winning pitcher: Thurston. Losing pitcher: Kaufmann. Umpires: Hildebrand, Pfirman, Moriarty, Rigler. Att: 16,081. Time—2:23.

1924 Chicago City Championship Series

GAME THREE --- October 3

WHITE SOX	AB	H	PO	A	E		CUBS	AB	H	PO	A	E
Mostil, cf	5	1	1	2	0		Adams, ss	4	1	2	5	0
Hooper, rf	3	1	2	0	0		Heathcote, cf	4	0	4	0	0
Collins, 2b	4	1	5	3	0		Grantham, 3b	4	3	1	2	0
Sheely, 1b	5	1	10	0	0		Weis, rf	3	1	0	0	0
Falk, lf	4	2	0	0	0		O'Farrell, c	4	2	4	1	0
Kamm, 3b	3	1	1	3	0		Grigsby, lf	4	1	2	0	0
W.Barrett, ss	4	1	1	4	1		R.Barrett, 2b	2	0	1	0	0
Schalk, c	3	0	7	3	0		Hollocher, 2b	1	0	1	0	0
Faber, p	2	0	0	2	0		Cotter, 1b	3	1	12	0	0
							Jacobs, p	1	0	0	4	0
	33	8	27	17	1		Hartnett, ph	1	0	0	0	0
							Blake, p	0	0	0	0	0
							Miller, ph	1	0	0	0	0
							Keen, p	0	0	0	1	0
								32	9	27	13	0

```
SOX   0  0  0    0  0  4    0  0  2   -  6
CUB   0  0  0    0  0  0    0  3  0   -  3
```

Runs: Hooper, Collins, Sheely, Falk, Kamm, Schalk, Grigsby, Hollocher, Cotter. 2B: W. Barrett, Hooper, Cotter. 3B: Collins. HR: Sheely. SH: Sheely. DP: Sox 3. LOB: Sox 3, Cubs 4. BB: Jacobs, Faber 2, Keen 1. Struck out: Jacobs 3, Faber 6, Blake 1. Hits: Jacobs 4 in 6 innings; Blake 3 in 2 innings; Keen 1 in 1 inning. HBP: Schalk (Keen). WP: Keen. Losing pitcher: Jacobs. Umpires: Pfirman, Moriarty, Rigler, Hildebrand. Att: 15,101. Time—1:56.

rampage in the fourth, the big hit a home run by Butch Weis, when they blasted Sarge Connally (7–13) with five additional runs to take a 9–0 lead. Alexander cruised until the seventh when Earl Sheely homered with a man on base. A three-run homer by Sheely in the eighth, after the Cubs had scored once in the seventh, cut the lead in half. The Americans rallied for two more runs in the ninth, but that was all they could get. In all, the Sox used four pitchers—Lyons, Connally, Mike Cvengros (3–12) and Dixie Leverette (2–3).

The Sox tied the series the next day, October 2, in Game Two at Comiskey Park. In this contest, it was the Cubs' turn to use four pitchers—Tony Kaufmann (16–11), Vic Keen (15–14), Rip Wheeler (3–6), and rookie George Milstead (1–1). The Sox scored a single tally off Kaufmann in the first and knocked him from the box with two in the second. The Cubs closed the gap with two against Hollis "Sloppy" Thurston (20–14) in the third, but the Sox came back with five of their own off Keen and Wheeler in the fifth to take a seemingly commanding 8–2 lead. The Cubs again closed the gap, this time to 8–6, with two runs in the sixth and two in the seventh off Thurston and reliever Mike Cvengros. Two more Sox runs in the seventh off Wheeler made the score 10–6 and a Cub tally in the top of the eighth made the score 10–7. The Sox finally took the heart out of the Cubs in the eighth when Earl Sheely singled and, with two out, Bill Barrett homered. The final score was 12–7. Thurston was the winning pitcher, Kaufmann the loser. The name of the official scorer who flipped the coin to make those two decisions has been lost to history.

The Sox made it two straight the next day at Wrigley. Spitballer Red Faber (9–11) of the Sox started against Elmer Jacobs (11–12). The game was scoreless until the Sox broke through for four runs in the sixth. After two were out, Eddie Collins walked and Earl Sheely's line drive into right field rolled under the

1924 Chicago City Championship Series

GAME FOUR --- October 4

CUBS	AB	H	PO	A	E	WHITE SOX	AB	H	PO	A	E
Adams, ss	4	1	3	3	0	Mostil, cf	3	0	2	0	0
Heathcote, cf	4	0	2	1	0	Hooper, rf	4	3	2	0	0
Grantham, 3b	4	2	1	0	1	Collins, 2b	3	2	0	2	0
Weis, rf	4	0	0	0	0	Sheely, 1b	5	2	9	0	0
O'Farrell, c	4	0	8	1	1	Falk, lf	4	3	7	0	0
Grigsby, lf	3	0	2	1	0	Kamm, 3b	5	4	0	2	0
R.Barrett, 2b	3	0	4	1	0	W.Barrett, ss	5	2	0	2	1
Cotter, 1b	3	0	4	0	0	Schalk, c	2	1	7	0	0
Kaufmann, p	0	0	0	0	0	Blankenship, p	4	1	0	1	0
Blake, p	2	1	0	1	0						
Wheeler, p	0	0	0	2	1		35	18	27	7	1
Vogel, ph	1	0	0	0	0						
Bush, p	0	0	0	1	0						
	32	4	24	11	3						

```
CUB    0  0  0     0  0  0     0  0  0   -   0
SOX    3  0  0     0  4  0     2  4  x   -  13
```

Runs: Mostil, Hooper 3, Collins 2, Sheely 2, Falk 2, Kamm 3. 2B: Kamm 2, Hooper. 3B: Falk. SB: Schalk, Collins, Falk. SH: Collins, Schalk 2, Blankenship, Falk. LOB: Cubs 5, Sox 8. BB: Kaufmann 1, Blake 2, Wheeler 1. Struck out: Blankenship 6, Blake 4, Wheeler 1, Bush 1. Hits: Kaufmann 3 in 2.1 innings; Blake 7 in 3.2 innings; Bush 5 in 1 inning. Losing pitcher: Kaufmann. Umpires: Moriarty, Rigler, Hildebrand, Pfirman. Att: 22,956. Time—2:12.

grandstands for a home run. (Today, of course, such a hit would have been a ground-rule double.) This seemed to unnerve Jacobs who gave up a single to Bibb Falk, a walk to Willie Kamm, and a two-run double to Bill Barrett. The Cubs roughed up Faber for three in the eighth to pull within one. Denver Grigsby singled, Charlie Hollocher walked, Harvey Cotter doubled both men home, and Sparky Adams singled home Cotter. That was all she wrote for the Cubs, though, and the Sox added two insurance runs in the ninth off reliever Vic Keen to make the final score 6–3.

The Sox administered an unmerciful beating to the Cubs in Game Four, blowing the Nationals out of Comiskey Park by a 13–0 score. Ted Blankenship (7–6) breezed to a four-hit shutout, all singles, and struck out six. Tony Kaufmann, who lasted just two innings in Game Two, was blasted for three runs in the first inning of this game. Relievers Sheriff Blake (6–6), Rip Wheeler, and Guy Bush (2–5) were just as unable to withstand the 18-hit assault and the Sox scored four runs in the fifth, two in the seventh, and four more in the eighth.

Pete Alexander returned to the mound for the fifth game and took his second victory of the series. Earl Sheely, who certainly appeared to have Alex's number, homered as did Bill Barrett. The Sox scored twice in the second and once again in the sixth, but the Cubs pecked away at starter Charlie Robertson (4–10) for single runs in the fourth, fifth, and sixth innings to tie the game. Robertson started the seventh but failed to retire anyone and reliever Dixie Leverette gave up two more hits and three more runs. The final score was 8–3. This wasn't an example of Alexander's best stuff as he finished with a nine-hit,

1924 Chicago City Championship Series

GAME FIVE --- October 5

WHITE SOX	AB	H	PO	A	E
Mostil, cf	3	1	2	0	0
Hooper, rf	4	1	0	0	0
Collins, 2b	4	2	3	2	0
Sheely, 1b	3	2	8	1	0
Falk, lf	4	0	5	1	1
Kamm, 3b	4	1	0	3	0
W.Barrett, ss	4	0	1	2	0
Schalk, c	2	0	4	3	0
Cruse, ph	1	1	0	0	0
Robertson, p	3	1	0	1	0
Leverette, p	0	0	0	0	0
Cvengros, p	0	0	1	0	0
Archdeacon, ph	1	0	0	0	0
	33	9	24	13	1

CUBS	AB	H	PO	A	E
Adams, ss	4	1	1	4	0
Heathcote, cf	5	3	6	0	0
Grantham, 3b	3	2	1	1	0
Weis, rf	2	0	2	0	0
Hartnett, c	2	0	0	1	0
Grigsby, lf	4	1	1	1	0
R.Barrett, 2b	4	3	3	3	1
Cotter, 1b	3	1	13	1	0
Alexander, p	4	4	0	0	0
	31	15	27	11	1

```
SOX   0 2 0   0 0 1   0 0 0 - 3
CUB   0 0 0   1 1 1   3 2 x - 8
```

Runs: Sheely, Kamm, Schalk, Heathcote 3, R. Barrett 3, Cotter 1, Alexander 1. 2B: Kamm, Mostil, Alexander. HR: R. Barrett, Sheely, Heathcote. SH: Weis 2, Hartnett 2, Mostil, Cotter. DP: Cubs 2, Sox 1. LOB: Sox 6, Cubs 6. BB: Alexander 3, Robertson 2. Struck out: Robertson 3, Alexander 1. Hits: Robertson 8 in 6 innings; Leverette 2 in 1 inning; Cvengros 5 in 1.1 innings. WP: Robertson. Losing pitcher: Robertson. Umpires: Rigler, Hildebrand, Pfirman, and Moriarty. Att: 31,207. Time—1:56.

GAME SIX --- October 6

CUBS	AB	H	PO	A	E
Adams, ss	4	1	1	5	0
Heathcote, cf	4	2	0	0	0
Grantham, 3b	4	2	0	2	0
Weis, rf	4	0	1	0	0
Hartnett, c	4	1	4	0	0
Grigsby, lf	4	1	4	0	0
R.Barrett, 2b	4	2	3	3	0
Cotter, 1b	3	0	11	3	0
Aldridge, p	1	0	0	1	0
Jacobs, p	0	0	0	0	0
Vogel, ph	1	0	0	0	0
Kaufmann, p	0	0	0	0	0
Miller, ph	1	1	0	0	0
Statz, pr	0	0	0	0	0
Blake, p	0	0	0	1	0
O'Farrell, ph	1	0	0	0	0
	35	10	24	15	0

WHITE SOX	AB	H	PO	A	E
Mostil, cf	4	2	2	0	0
Hooper, rf	4	1	2	0	0
Collins, 2b	3	0	4	6	0
Sheely, 1b	4	2	8	1	0
Falk, lf	4	0	6	0	0
Kamm, 3b	4	2	1	2	0
W.Barrett, ss	3	1	2	6	2
Schalk, c	2	0	2	1	0
Thurston, p	1	0	0	1	0
Lyons, p	1	0	0	0	0
	30	8	27	17	2

```
CUB   0 0 1   0 0 0   2 0 0 - 3
SOX   1 0 3   0 0 0   0 1 x - 5
```

Runs: Adams, Grigsby, R. Barrett, Mostil 2, Hooper, Collins, Sheely. 2B: Mostil 2, Hooper, Sheely. 3B: Kamm. SH: Thurston. DP: Sox 2. LOB: Cubs 6, Sox 4. BB: Thurston 1, Jacobs 1, Blake 1. Struck out: Aldridge 1, Kaufmann 1, Lyons 1. Hits: Aldridge 7 in 2.2 inning; Jacobs 0 in 1.1 innings; Kaufmann 0 in 2 innings; Blake 1 in 2 innings; Thurston 9 in 6 innings (none out in seventh); Lyons 1 in 3 innings. Winning pitcher: Thurston. Losing pitcher: Aldridge. Umpires: Hildebrand, Pfirman, Moriarty, Rigler. Att: 12,966. Time—1:39.

three-walk, one-strikeout victory, but it was a memorable day for Alex at the plate — four hits, including a double, in five times at bat.

Sloppy Thurston and Ted Lyons pitched the Sox to the city championship in Game Six against an ineffective Vic Aldridge (15–12) of the Cubs. The Sox broke on top in the first against Aldridge on Johnny Mostil's lead-off double and infield outs by Harry Hooper and Eddie Collins. The Cubs tied the game against Thurston in the third on three consecutive singles, but the Sox put Aldridge out of his misery in the bottom of the inning with doubles by Mostil, Hooper, and Sheely, and a triple by Willie Kamm. Before reliever Elmer Jacobs could get the final out of the inning, the Sox had scored three runs and taken a 4–1 lead. The Cubs closed to within one in the seventh on three singles and an error by Bill Barrett, but those were the last two runs of the series for the National Leaguers as Ted Lyons came on and shut the door. An insurance run off Sheriff Blake in the eighth made the final score 5–3.

The Cubs used four pitchers in the final game, the third time in the series they did so. In all, the Nationals used a total of 17 pitchers in the six games — Kaufmann and Blake three times; Alexander, Keen, Wheeler, and Jacobs twice; Bush, Aldridge, and Milstead once. The Sox used 13 pitchers — Cvengros three times; Lyons, Leverette, and Thurston twice; Connally, Faber, Blankenship, and Robertson once.

The 1925 Chicago City Championship Series

Chicago Cubs defeat White Sox; 4-1-1

The year 1925 marked only the fourth time in 15 tries that the Chicago Cubs were able to wrestle away the city championship series from the White Sox. There wasn't much to recommend either team in 1925. The Sox (79–75) finished in fifth place, 18½ games off the pace set by the Washington Senators. The Cubs (68–86) finished last, but it was a very respectable last — only 27½ games behind the league-leading Pittsburgh Pirates. A mere two and a half games separated the Cubs and the fourth-place St. Louis Cardinals.

The series made a spectacular debut at Comiskey Park on the seventh of October. Ted Blankenship (17–8) hooked up with 38-year-old Grover Cleveland Alexander (15–11) in a 19-inning pitchers' duel that ended in a 2–2 draw when it became too dark to continue play. The Sox took the lead in the third when three hits and an error by Rabbit Maranville pushed across the first two runs of the game. The Cubs cut the lead in half in the fourth when Howard Freigau's triple was followed by an RBI single off the bat of rookie outfielder Art Jahn. They tied the game in the fifth on singles by Maranville and Hartnett and a squeeze bunt by Alexander. That's where the score stayed for the next 14 innings. Blankenship got stronger as the game progressed and only gave up two hits over the final nine innings. Alexander showed signs of tiring as he allowed ten hits over the last seven, but he was tough in the clutch and the Sox stranded 16 runners due in part to four double plays. When it was all over, the Sox had racked up 20 hits, the Cubs 11. Big men with the stick included Bill Barrett with a 4-for-9, Bibb Falk with a 5-for-8, and Freigau with a 4-for-7.

1925 Chicago City Championship Series

GAME ONE --- October 7

CUBS	AB	H	PO	A	E
Adams, 2b	8	0	7	5	0
Heatocote, rf	7	0	8	0	0
Freigau, 3b	7	4	2	3	0
Jahn, lf	8	3	4	0	0
Brooks, cf	6	0	5	1	0
Grimm, 1b	7	1	19	2	0
Maranville, ss	7	1	7	6	1
Hartnett, c	7	1	5	2	0
Alexander, p	6	1	0	5	0
	63	11	57	24	1

WHITE SOX	AB	H	PO	A	E
Mostil, cf	9	1	5	0	0
Hooper, rf	7	1	3	0	0
Barrett, 2b	9	4	6	7	0
Sheely, 1b	7	1	20	1	0
Falk, lf	8	5	5	0	0
Kamm, 3b	6	0	4	5	0
Davis, ss	0	0	1	0	0
Kane, ss	8	3	3	7	1
Schalk, c	8	3	9	1	0
Blankenship, p	7	2	1	3	0
	69	20	57	24	1

```
CUB   0 0 0   1 1 0   0 0 0   0 0 0   0 0 0   0 0 0   - 2
SOX   0 0 2   0 0 0   0 0 0   0 0 0   0 0 0   0 0 0   - 2
```

Runs: Jahn, Maranville, Mostil, Blankenship. 2B: Freigau, Blankenship, Hooper, Jahn, Falk. 3B: Freigau. SH: Alexander, Brooks, Freigau, Blankenship, Hooper, Kamm. DP: Cubs 4, Sox 3. LOB: Cubs 10, Sox 16. BB: Blankenship 3, Alexander 3. Struck out: Blankenship 7, Alexander 2. Umpires: Rowland, Quigley, Ormsby, Pfirman. Time—3:03.

GAME TWO --- October 8

WHITE SOX	AB	H	PO	A	E
Mostil, cf	3	0	5	0	0
Hooper, rf	3	1	0	0	0
Barrett, 2b	4	2	3	6	0
Sheely, 1b	4	0	11	0	0
Falk, lf	4	0	3	0	0
Kamm, 3b	3	1	0	4	0
Kane, ss	3	0	1	0	1
Schalk, c	3	1	1	0	0
Lyons, p	1	0	0	1	0
Collins, ph	1	0	0	0	0
Kerr, p	0	0	0	0	0
Thurston, ph	1	0	0	0	0
	30	5	24	11	1

CUBS	AB	H	PO	A	E
Adams, 2b	4	2	4	4	0
Heatocote, rf	4	0	3	0	0
Freigau, 3b	4	1	3	0	0
Jahn, lf	3	0	1	0	0
Brooks, cf	4	2	2	0	0
Grimm, 1b	4	2	9	0	0
Maranville, ss	3	0	0	3	0
Gonzalez, c	2	0	5	1	0
Cooper, p	3	1	0	0	0
	31	8	27	8	0

```
SOX   0 0 1   0 0 0   0 0 0   - 1
CUB   1 0 0   0 0 1   0 0 x   - 2
```

Runs: Lyons, Adams, Brooks. 2B: Barrett, Brooks, Kamm. SB: Cooper. SH: Jahn. DP: Cubs. BB: Lyons 2, Cooper 3. Struck out: Cooper 4. Hits: Lyons 6 in 7 innings; Kerr 2 in 1 inning. HBP: Hooper (Cooper). Losing pitcher: Lyons. Umpires: Quigley, Ormsby, Pfirman, Rowland. Time—1:39.

The series shifted to Wrigley Field for the game on the 8th. Ted Lyons (21–11) was in the box for the Sox against Wilbur Cooper (12–14) of the Cubs. Cooper had just spent his first year in Chicago after a distinguished 13-year career with the Pirates. Although he was nearing the end of his career, he still had enough left to hand a 2–1 defeat to the White Sox on this day. The Cubs took an early lead in the bottom of the first when Earl "Sparky" Adams beat out an infield hit, went to third on Freigau's single, and scored on Jahn's sacrifice fly. The White Sox tied the score in the third after two were out with

1925 Chicago City Championship Series

GAME THREE --- October 10

WHITE SOX	AB	H	PO	A	E
Mostil, cf	2	0	4	1	1
Hooper, rf	4	1	0	0	0
Barrett, 2b	4	0	5	4	2
Sheely, 1b	4	0	8	1	0
Falk, lf	4	1	0	2	0
Kamm, 3b	4	1	1	1	0
Kane, ss	5	1	0	2	1
Schalk, c	2	0	4	1	0
Thurston, p	2	0	0	1	0
Faber, p	1	1	1	1	0
Crouse, c	1	0	1	0	1
	33	5	24	14	5

CUBS	AB	H	PO	A	E
Adams, 2b	4	4	4	3	1
Heatocote, rf	3	1	1	0	0
Freigau, 3b	5	1	0	2	0
Jahn, lf	5	2	2	0	0
Brooks, cf	3	0	3	0	0
Grimm, 1b	4	3	8	0	0
Maranville, ss	4	0	2	5	0
Hartnett, c	3	0	7	0	0
Blake, p	4	2	0	2	0
	35	13	27	12	1

```
SOX   0 0 0   0 0 1   0 0 1  -  2
CUB   4 0 0   0 2 0   0 2 x  -  8
```

Runs: Hooper, Kane, Adams 2, Heathcote, Jahn 2, Brooks, Grimm, Hartnett. 2B: Adams, Grimm. 3B: Jahn. SB: Adams, Hooper. SH: Adams, Brooks. DP: Sox. LOB: Sox 14, Cubs 8. BB: Blake 9, Faber 2, Thurston 1. Struck out: Blake 7, Faber 3, Thurston 1. Hits: Faber 9 in 5 innings; Thurston 4 in 1 inning. HBP: Kamm (Blake). Losing pitcher: Faber. Umpires: Ormsby, Pfirman, Rowland, Quigley. Time—1:52.

walks to Lyons and Johnny Mostil and a single by 17-year veteran Harry Hooper. The Cubs scored what proved to be the winning run in the sixth when, with two out, Mandy Brooks doubled in front of a diving Bibb Falk and scored on Charlie Grimm's single. (Grimm was spending his first year with the Cubs, Hooper his last year in the major leagues.) Dickie Kerr (0–1), spending his last year in majors as well, worked the final inning in relief of Lyons who got the loss. Cooper held the White Sox to five hits and struck out four in recording the victory.

The Cubs made it two in a row on the 10th when Sheriff Blake (10–18) beat Red Faber (12–11). The Nationals roughed up Faber for four runs in the very first inning, the big play an error on a sure double play ball by rookie shortstop Johnny Kane. Perhaps this muffed double play (or perhaps Kane's .179 batting average) made an impression on Sox player-manager Eddie Collins, for Kane never played another game in the major leagues. In the fifth, Barrett made two errors and Mostil one, and the Cubs came away with two more unearned runs. Hollis "Sloppy" Thurston (10–14) relieved for the White Sox in the sixth and was touched for two runs in the eighth when the Cubs bunched four hits. The Sox could only manage five hits and two runs off winning pitcher Blake who struck out seven in pitching the complete game.

Game Four was a virtual replay of the day before, only the winning team and names of the starting pitchers changing. Ted Blankenship, showing no ill effects from his 19-inning stint in Game One, was on the mound for the Sox. Percy Jones (6–6) started for the Cubs. The Sox, as had the Cubs 24 hours earlier, scored four times in the first inning. The Americans reached Jones for three hits and the same number of walks to knock Percy from the box and take a 4–0 lead which was never threatened. Guy Bush (6–13) relieved and held the

1925 Chicago City Championship Series

GAME FOUR --- October 11

CUBS	AB	H	PO	A	E		WHITE SOX	AB	H	PO	A	E
Adams, 2b	4	0	2	2	0		Mostil, cf	4	1	5	0	0
Heatocote, rf	5	2	2	0	0		Hooper, rf	4	1	2	0	0
Freigau, 3b	5	1	1	2	0		Barrett, 2b	4	2	5	2	0
Jahn, lf	4	2	1	0	0		Sheely, 1b	3	1	8	0	0
Brooks, cf	4	2	5	0	0		Falk, lf	4	3	1	0	0
Grimm, 1b	2	1	9	1	0		Kamm, 3b	4	2	0	3	0
Pittenger, ss	4	1	1	1	0		Kane, ss	3	1	1	3	1
Gonzalez, c	4	1	3	2	1		Schalk, c	4	0	5	1	0
Jones, p	0	0	0	1	0		Blankenship, p	4	0	0	2	0
Weiss, ph	1	0	0	0	0							
Bush, p	1	0	0	0	0			34	11	27	11	1
Grigsby, ph	1	0	0	0	0							
Milstead, p	1	0	0	0	0							
	36	10	24	9	1							

```
CUB   0 1 0   0 1 0   0 0 0  -  2
SOX   4 0 0   0 1 2   0 0 x  -  7
```

Runs: Heathcote, Brooks, Mostil 2, Barrett 3, Sheely, Falk. 2B: Falk 2, Heathcote, Barrett, Mostil. SB: Heathcote. DP: Sox. LOB: Cubs 10, Sox 8. BB: Jones 3, Bush 1, BLankenship 3. Struck out: Blankenship 3, Bush 2, Milstead 1. Hits: Jones 3 in 1 inning; Bush 5 in 4 innings; Milstead 3 in 3 innings; HBP: Mostil (Milstead). Losing pitcher: Jones. Umpires: Pfirman, Rowland, Quigley, Ormsby. Time—2:04.

Sox for the next three innings until they touched him for a solo run in the fifth. On came George Milstead (1–1) who coughed up two runs in his first inning of relief when he hit Mostil with a pitch then gave a double to Barrett who scored when Cuban-born Mike Gonzalez heaved the ball wildly past third base. Blankenship, who was hit almost as freely as the three Cubs' pitchers, went the distance in recording the win. Jones got the loss.

Game Five saw the Cubs take a three-games-to-one lead in the series behind the strong arm of Tony Kaufmann (13–13). Kaufmann five-hit the Sox and only gave up one run. In the eighth inning, leading 3–0, Kaufmann walked losing pitcher Ted Lyons and then hit Mostil with a pitch. Harry Hooper followed with an RBI single but Bill Barrett flied out to Art Jahn at the base of the left field wall to end the threat. The Cubs scored all the runs they needed in the fourth when Freigau singled, moved to second on Jahn's sacrifice bunt, and scored on Mandy Brooks's double. Charlie Grimm's single put them up 2–0. The Nationals added an insurance run in the seventh on Grimm's single and a double by Gabby Hartnett.

The Cubs wrapped up the series in the sixth game with their new boss for 1926, Joe McCarthy, looking on. They scored a run in the third off Red Faber and widened their lead to 4–0 with three in the sixth against Faber and reliever Sarge Connally (6–7). The White Sox pulled to within one with three runs in the bottom of the seventh off starting pitcher Wilbur Cooper, but three runs off Ted Blankenship in the eighth sealed the series as the Cubs won the game, 7–4.

1925 Chicago City Championship Series

```
GAME FIVE --- October 12
```

WHITE SOX	AB	H	PO	A	E
Mostil, cf	3	0	2	0	0
Hooper, rf	3	1	5	0	0
Barrett, 2b	4	0	6	1	0
Sheely, 1b	4	1	5	2	0
Falk, lf	3	1	3	1	0
Kamm, 3b	4	0	2	0	0
Kane, ss	2	0	1	0	0
Crouse, c	1	1	0	0	0
Schalk, c	3	1	0	1	0
Elsh, 2b	0	0	0	0	0
Lyons, p	2	0	0	2	0
	29	5	24	7	0

CUBS	AB	H	PO	A	E
Adams, 2b	3	1	4	2	0
Heatocote, rf	4	0	1	0	0
Freigau, 3b	4	3	0	3	1
Jahn, lf	3	0	3	0	0
Brooks, cf	4	1	3	0	0
Grimm, 1b	3	2	11	0	0
Pittenger, ss	2	1	4	4	0
Hartnett, c	3	1	1	2	0
Kaufmann, p	3	1	0	3	0
	29	10	27	14	1

```
SOX   0  0  0    0  0  0    0  1  0  -  1
CUB   0  0  0    2  0  0    1  0  x  -  3
```

Runs: Lyons, Freigau, Brooks, Grimm. 2B: Brooks, Pittenger, Hartnett. SH: Jahn, Adams, Pittenger. DP: Sox 1, Cubs 2. LOB: Sox 5, Cubs 5. BB: Kaufmann 3. HBP: Mostil (Kaufmann). Umpires: Rowland, Quigley, Ormsby, Pfirman. Time—1:25.

```
GAME SIX --- October 13
```

CUBS	AB	H	PO	A	E
Adams, 2b	5	0	1	2	0
Heatocote, rf	4	1	3	0	0
Freigau, 3b	4	1	1	3	1
Jahn, lf	3	0	1	0	0
Brooks, cf	4	2	4	0	0
Grimm, 1b	4	1	10	3	0
Pittenger, ss	4	1	1	2	0
Gonzalez, c	4	2	4	1	0
Cooper, p	4	2	2	3	0
	36	10	27	14	1

WHITE SOX	AB	H	PO	A	E
Mostil, cf	5	1	2	0	0
Hooper, rf	5	1	0	0	0
Barrett, 2b	2	0	3	7	0
Sheely, 1b	3	0	13	1	1
Falk, lf	4	1	0	0	0
Kamm, 3b	2	1	0	3	1
Schalk, c	4	2	1	2	0
Kane, ss	4	1	5	4	1
Faber, p	1	0	0	0	2
Connally, p	0	0	0	1	0
Grabowski, ph	1	0	0	0	0
Blankenship, p	1	0	0	0	0
	32	7	27	18	5

```
CUB   0  0  1    0  0  3    0  3  0  -  7
SOX   0  0  0    0  0  0    3  1  0  -  4
```

Runs: Heathcote, Freigau, Brooks 2, Grimm, Pittenger, Gonzalez 2, Mostil, Falk, Kamm, Kane. 2B: Cooper, Heathcote. 3B: Mostil. SH: Jahn, Freigau. DP: Sox. LOB: Cubs 4, Sox 4. BB: Cooper 5, Connally 1. Struck out: Faber 1, Cooper 2. Hits: Faber 5 in 5.1 innings: Connally 1 in 1.2 innings; Blankenship 4 in 2 innings. HBP: Sheely (Cooper). Losing pitcher: Faber. Umpires: Quigley, Ormsby, Pfirman, Rowland.

This final game was interrupted by an unusual incident in the fourth inning. Art Jahn threw his bat up to protect his face from a Red Faber fastball and when the ball hit his bat, the bat hit his forehead. Jahn went down in a heap, unconscious. Smelling salts revived him and he was back at his position in left field in the bottom of the inning.

1926 Chicago City Championship Series

GAME ONE --- September 29

WHITE SOX	AB	R	H	PO	A	E		CUBS	AB	R	H	PO	A	E
Mostil, cf	4	0	0	0	0	0		Adams, 2b	4	1	1	4	3	0
Hunnefield, 2b-ss	4	0	2	1	0	1		Heathcote, rf	4	1	2	5	0	0
Barrett, rf	3	0	0	6	0	0		Kelly, lf	4	0	2	3	0	0
Sheely, 1b	3	0	1	5	0	0		Wilson, cf	4	1	0	2	0	0
Falk, lf	4	0	1	1	0	0		Grimm, 1b	4	1	1	7	0	0
Kamm, 3b	4	0	0	2	1	0		Freigau, 3b	4	0	1	0	1	0
Schalk, c	3	0	0	6	2	0		Cooney, ss	4	1	2	5	5	0
Berg, ss	2	0	0	3	1	1		Gonzalez, c	3	0	2	1	2	0
Collins, ph	1	0	0	0	0	0		Root, p	4	1	0	0	0	0
Connally, p	0	0	0	0	0	0								
Thurston, p	0	0	0	0	0	0			35	6	11	27	11	0
Faber, p	1	0	0	0	2	0								
Morehart, 2b	1	0	0	0	1	0								
	30	0	4	24	7	2								

```
SOX   0 0 0   0 0 0   0 0 0 - 0
CUB   0 0 2   0 0 0   0 4 0 - 6
```

2B: Gonzalez. SB: Cooney. LOB: Sox 6, Cubs 6. BB: Root 3, Faber 1. Struck out: Root 2, Faber 5, Connally 1. Hits: Faber 7 in 7 innings; Connally 3 in 1.1 innings; Thurston 1 in 0.2 innings; WP: Thurston. Losing pitcher: Faber. Umpires: Quigley, Nallin, Wilson, Geisel. Att: 14,721. Time—1:36.

GAME TWO --- October 1

WHITE SOX	AB	R	H	PO	A	E		CUBS	AB	R	H	PO	A	E
Mostil, cf	5	2	0	3	0	0		Adams, 2b	5	0	0	2	7	0
Morehart, 2b	5	1	3	3	3	0		Heathcote, rf	5	1	1	1	0	0
Barrett, rf	5	3	2	1	0	0		Kelly, lf	3	1	1	2	0	0
Sheely, 1b	3	1	2	10	2	0		Wilson, cf	3	2	1	3	0	0
Falk, lf	4	2	3	2	0	0		Grimm, 1b	4	1	3	11	0	0
Kamm, 3b	4	1	2	4	1	0		Freigau, 3b	3	0	1	2	1	1
Crouse, c	4	0	1	2	0	0		Cooney, ss	4	0	2	3	2	1
Berg, ss	3	0	0	1	2	0		Hartnett, c	4	0	0	3	2	0
Lyons, p	5	0	0	1	2	0		Kaufmann, p	2	0	0	0	1	0
	38	10	13	27	10	0		Blake, p	0	0	0	0	0	0
								Stephenson, ph	1	0	0	0	0	0
								Osborn, p	0	0	0	0	1	0
								Tolson, ph	1	0	0	0	0	0
									35	5	9	27	14	2

```
SOX   2 0 0   0 0 1   4 3 0 - 10
CUB   1 0 0   0 0 2   0 2 0 -  5
```

2B: Kamm. 3B: Falk. HR: Falk, Wilson, Grimm, Barrett. SB: Barrett. SH: Sheely, Freigau. DP: Cubs. LOB: Sox 9, Cubs 6. BB: Lyons 2, Kaufmann 4, Blake 2. Struck out: Lyons 1, Osborn 1. Hits: Kaufmann 10 in 6.2 innings; Blake 1 in 0.1 inning; Osborn 2 in 2 innings. HBP: Sheely (Osborn). Losing pitcher: Kaufmann. Umpires: Nallin, Wilson, Geisel, Quigley. Att: 11,588. Time—1:51.

The 1926 Chicago City Championship Series

Chicago White Sox defeat Chicago Cubs; 4–3

The Cubs (82–72) and White Sox (81–72) were about as evenly matched as two teams could be as they began play in the 1926 Chicago city championship series. The results reflected that parity as it took the White Sox a full seven games to triumph over the Cubs. The Sox were led by player-manager Eddie

1926 Chicago City Championship Series

GAME THREE --- October 2

CUBS	AB	R	H	PO	A	E		WHITE SOX	AB	R	H	PO	A	E
Adams, 2b	4	0	0	6	7	0		Mostil, cf	4	0	1	2	0	0
Heathcote, rf	4	0	0	0	0	0		Morehart, 2b	3	0	0	1	5	1
Kelly, lf	4	0	0	1	0	0		Hunnefield, ph	1	0	0	0	0	0
Wilson, cf	4	0	0	3	0	0		Barrett, rf-ss	4	0	0	4	0	0
Grimm, 1b	4	0	1	11	0	0		Sheely, 1b	2	0	1	10	0	0
Freigau, 3b	3	0	0	0	2	0		Falk, lf	3	0	0	1	0	0
Cooney, ss	3	1	2	1	5	0		Kamm, 3b	3	0	1	0	1	0
Gonzalez, c	3	0	0	5	1	0		Schalk, c	2	0	1	3	1	0
Jones, p	3	0	2	0	2	0		Berg, ss	3	0	1	5	2	0
								Harris, rf	0	0	0	1	0	0
	32	1	5	27	17	0		Thomas, p	2	0	0	0	1	0
								Thurston, ph	1	0	0	0	0	0
								Connally, p	0	0	0	0	1	0
									28	0	5	27	11	1

```
CUB   0  0  0    0  0  0    0  1  0  -  1
SOX   0  0  0    0  0  0    0  0  0  -  0
```

DP: Cubs 2, Sox 1. LOB: Cubs 4, Sox 5. BB: Jones 2. Struck out: Jones 6, Thomas 2. Hits: Thomas 5 in 3 innings; Connally 0 in 1 inning. Losing pitcher: Thomas. Umpires: Wilson, Geisel, Quigley, Nallin. Att: 20,396. Time—1:43.

GAME FOUR --- October 3

WHITE SOX	AB	R	H	PO	A	E		CUBS	AB	R	H	PO	A	E
Mostil, cf	3	0	0	6	0	0		Adams, 2b	4	0	0	1	2	0
Morehart, 2b	5	0	0	5	4	0		Heathcote, rf	4	0	2	1	1	0
Barrett, rf	5	2	3	2	2	0		Kelly, lf	3	0	0	2	0	0
Sheely, 1b	3	1	1	9	0	0		Wilson, cf	4	0	1	1	1	0
Falk, lf	4	0	2	1	0	0		Grimm, 1b	4	0	0	11	2	0
Kamm, 3b	3	0	0	1	3	0		Freigau, 3b	4	0	2	0	3	0
McCurdy, c	3	0	0	2	0	0		Cooney, ss	3	0	1	1	2	0
Berg, ss	3	0	1	0	2	1		Hartnett, c	2	0	0	8	0	0
Blankenship, p	3	1	1	1	1	0		Stephenson, ph	1	0	0	0	0	0
								Gonzalez, c	0	0	0	1	0	0
	32	4	8	27	12	1		Bush, p	2	0	0	1	2	0
								Tolson, ph	1	0	0	0	0	0
								Blake, p	0	0	0	0	0	0
									32	0	6	27	13	0

```
SOX   0  0  0    1  0  2    1  0  0  -  4
CUB   0  0  0    0  0  0    0  0  0  -  0
```

2B: Barrett 3. SB: Sheely, Falk. SH: Mostil. DP: Cubs. LOB: Sox 8, Cubs 4. BB: Bush 4, Blake 3. Struck out: Bush 5, Blankenship 2, Blake 1. Hits: Bush 8 in 8 innings. Losing pitcher: Blake. Umpires: Geisel, Quigley, Nallin, Wilson. Time—1:30.

Collins who had improved the club's record both years at the helm. Collins would get no chance to improve that record in a third year, however, as he was traded to the Philadelphia Athletics in the off-season.

The series opened on September 29th with a shutout. Charlie Root (18–17) blanked Red Faber (4–7), George "Sarge" Connally (6–5), and the White Sox on four hits, winning easily, 6–0.

After a day off, the Sox jumped on Tony Kaufmann (9–7), Sheriff Blake (11–12), and Bob Osborn (6–5) for 10 runs and 13 hits, winning the game 10–5.

1926 Chicago City Championship Series

GAME FIVE --- October 5

CUBS	AB	R	H	PO	A	E		WHITE SOX	AB	R	H	PO	A	E
Adams, 2b	4	0	2	4	2	0		Mostil, cf	4	0	0	2	0	0
Heathcote, rf	3	0	1	4	0	0		Morehart, 2b	5	0	2	0	5	1
Kelly, lf	4	1	2	2	0	0		Barrett, rf	5	1	3	0	0	0
Wilson, cf	4	0	1	2	0	0		Sheely, 1b	3	0	0	15	1	0
Grimm, 1b	4	0	0	5	1	1		Falk, lf	5	1	1	1	0	0
Freigau, 3b	3	0	1	1	1	1		Kamm, 3b	2	1	1	0	4	0
Cooney, ss	3	0	0	2	3	0		Schalk, c	4	0	3	9	0	0
Stephenson, ph	1	0	0	0	0	0		Berg, ss	4	0	2	0	2	0
Gonzalez, c	3	0	0	4	1	0		Faber, p	1	0	1	0	2	0
Tolson, ph	1	0	0	0	0	0		Connally, p	2	0	0	0	0	0
Root, p	3	0	0	0	2	0								
	33	1	7	24	10	2			35	3	13	27	14	1

```
CUB   0  0  0    0  0  1    0  0  0  -  1
SOX   0  0  0    1  1  0    0  0  x  -  2
```

2B: Freigau, Adams, Wilson. SB: Morehart. SH: Heathcote, Sheely. LOB: Cubs 7, Sox 14. BB: Root 3, Faber 1. Struck out: Faber 2, Root 4, Connally 5. Hits: Faber 7 in 5 innings (none out in sixth). HBP: Root (Mostil). Winning pitcher: Faber. Umpires: Quigley, Nallin, Wilson, Geisel. Att: 5,770. Time—2:02.

GAME SIX --- October 6

CUBS	AB	R	H	PO	A	E		WHITE SOX	AB	R	H	PO	A	E
Adams, 2b	5	0	1	2	3	0		Mostil, cf	3	0	0	3	0	1
Heathcote, rf	3	0	0	3	0	0		Hunnefield, 2b	2	0	1	4	2	0
Kelly, lf	4	0	1	2	0	0		Barrett, rf	4	0	0	2	1	0
Wilson, cf	4	1	3	1	0	0		Sheely, 1b	2	0	0	7	0	0
Grimm, 1b	3	1	1	13	0	0		Falk, lf	3	0	2	2	0	0
Freigau, 3b	3	1	1	0	2	0		Kamm, 3b	4	0	0	1	1	0
Cooney, ss	4	1	0	3	7	0		Schalk, c	4	0	2	5	1	0
Hartnett, c	3	0	0	3	1	0		Grabowsky, c	2	0	1	5	1	0
Jones, p	3	0	1	0	4	0		Berg, ss	4	1	1	1	1	1
	32	4	8	27	17	0		Lyons, p	1	0	0	0	2	0
								Thomas, p	0	0	0	0	0	0
								Thurston, ph	0	0	0	0	0	0
								Connally, p	0	0	0	0	0	0
								Collins, p	1	0	1	0	0	0
								Harris, pr	0	0	0	0	0	0
									30	1	6	27	9	2

```
CUB   0  2  0    0  0  2    0  0  0  -  4
SOX   0  0  0    0  0  0    0  1  0  -  1
```

2B: Freigau, Wilson. SH: Freigau. DP: Sox 1, Cubs 1. LOB: Cubs 6, Sox 10. BB: Jones 6, Lyons 1, Thomas 1, Connally 1. Struck out: Jones 2, Lyons 2, Thomas 2. Hits: Lyons 7 in 6 innings; Thomas 1 in 2 innings; Connally 0 in 1 inning. HBP: Hartnett and Thurston (Jones). WP: Lyons. Losing pitcher: Lyons. Umpires: Nallin, Wilson, Geisel, Quigley. Att: 7,000. Time—1:56.

Not the runaway the score indicates, the game was tied 3–3 at the end of six innings when the White Sox exploded for four runs in the seventh and three in the eighth to win going away. The big hit was a three-run homer in the eighth by Bill Barrett which put the game out of reach for the Cubs. Ted Lyons (18–16) went the distance for the victory.

The two teams traded five-hitters in Game Three. Percy Jones (12–7) went

1926 Chicago City Championship Series

GAME SEVEN --- October 7

WHITE SOX	AB	R	H	PO	A	E		CUBS	AB	R	H	PO	A	E
Mostil, cf	2	1	0	2	1	0		Adams, 2b	5	0	3	3	3	0
Morehart, 2b	4	0	2	2	4	1		Heathcote, rf	4	0	2	3	0	0
Barrett, rf	4	0	0	3	0	0		Kelly, lf	3	0	0	2	0	0
Sheely, 1b	4	1	1	11	1	0		Wilson, cf	4	0	1	4	0	1
Falk, lf	3	0	1	0	0	0		Grimm, 1b	4	0	1	6	1	0
Kamm, 3b	3	0	1	1	2	0		Freigau, 3b	3	0	0	0	1	0
McCurdy, c	3	1	0	4	0	0		Cooney, ss	4	0	0	2	2	0
Berg, ss	3	0	2	4	2	0		Hartnett, c	2	0	0	7	2	0
Blankenship, p	3	0	0	0	4	0		Root, p	2	0	0	0	0	0
								Stephenson, ph	1	0	0	0	0	0
	29	3	7	27	14	1		Blake, p	0	0	0	0	1	0
								Scott, ph	1	0	1	0	0	0
								Tolson, ph	1	0	0	0	0	0
									34	0	8	27	10	1

```
SOX   0  0  0    1  1  0    1  0  0  -  3
CUB   0  0  0    0  0  0    0  0  0  -  0
```

2B: Berg. SB: Hunnefield, Mostil, Falk, Adams. SH: Heathcote, Freigau, Barrett, Sheely, Blankenship, Hunnefield. DP: Cubs. LOB: Sox 14, Cubs 11. BB: Root 6, Blankenship 2, Blake 4. Struck out: Root 5, Blankenship 4, Blake 1. Hits: Root 7 in 7 innings; Blake 0 in 2 innings. HBP: Mostil (Root). Losing pitcher: Root. Umpires: Wilson, Geisel, Quigley, Nallin. Time—1:39.

the distance for the Cubs while Tommy Thomas (15–12) and Sarge Connally combined for a five-hitter for the White Sox. The Cubs scored once in the eighth when Jimmy Cooney singled and Mike Gonzalez reached on an error by Ray Morehart. Percy Jones then singled in the only run of the day to give himself a 1–0 victory.

Game Four saw the White Sox return the whitewash. Ted Blankenship (13–10) stifled the Cubs' offense on six hits, while the Sox scored four runs off Guy Bush (13–9) and Sheriff Blake. The big gun in the Sox lineup was Ray Barret with three doubles in five times at bat.

The White Sox pushed ahead 3–2 in the series in Game Five as Red Faber and Sarge Connally combined to seven-hit the Cubs while allowing only one run. Single runs by the Americans in the fourth, fifth, and seventh made a loser out of Charlie Root who went the distance.

After an off-day, Percy Jones knotted the series for the Cubs in Game Six, pitching a six-hitter and allowing just an eighth-inning run. By that time, the Cubs had scored four times off Sox pitchers Ted Lyons, Tommy Thomas, and Sarge Connally. A bases-loaded walk to Earl Sheely forced in the only Sox run of the day.

The series came down to the seventh and final game and, appropriately enough, it was decided by another shutout, the fourth of the series. Ted Blankenship threw his second whitewash, this time scattering eight Cub hits over nine innings. Charlie Root and Sheriff Blake pitched for the Cubs and allowed seven hits.

1928 Chicago City Championship Series

GAME ONE --- October 3

CUBS	AB	R	H	PO	A	E	WHITE SOX	AB	R	H	PO	A	E
English, ss	3	1	0	2	1	0	Metzler, cf	4	0	0	3	0	0
Maguire, 2b	4	0	0	2	2	0	Shires, 1b	3	0	1	11	1	0
Cuyler, rf	4	1	1	3	0	0	Reynolds, rf	4	0	1	3	0	0
Wilson, cf	3	0	2	4	0	0	Falk, lf	3	0	0	1	0	0
Stephenson, lf	4	1	1	2	0	0	Kamm, 3b	3	0	0	2	1	0
Grimm, 1b	4	0	1	6	0	0	Cissell, ss	3	0	1	5	4	1
Hartnett, c	4	0	0	5	1	0	Hunnefield, 2b	4	0	1	0	4	0
Beck, 3b	3	0	1	3	3	0	Berg, c	3	0	1	0	0	0
Malone, p	3	0	0	0	0	0	Crouse, c	1	0	0	2	1	0
							Faber, p	0	0	0	0	0	0
	32	3	6	27	7	0	Adkins, p	2	0	0	0	3	0
							Connally, p	0	0	0	0	0	0
							Clancy, ph	0	0	0	0	0	0
							Swanson, pr	0	0	0	0	0	0
							Blackerby, ph	1	0	0	0	0	0
								31	0	5	27	14	1

```
CUB   3 0 0   0 0 0   0 0 0  -  3
SOX   0 0 0   0 0 0   0 0 0  -  0
```

2B: Cuyler, Grimm, Wilson, Shires. DP: Sox. BB: Faber 1, Adkins 2, Malone 4, Connally 1. Struck out: Connally 1, Malone 5. Hits: Faber 3 in 0.2 inning; Adkins 2 in 6.1 innings. WP: Malone. Losing pitcher: Faber. Umpires: Hildebrand, McCormick, Geisel, Reardon. Att: 25,885.

The 1928 Chicago City Championship Series

Chicago Cubs defeat Chicago White Sox; 4–3

The third-place Cubs (91–63), managed by Joe McCarthy, were favored to beat the fifth-place White Sox (72–82) in the 1928 Chicago city championship Series. The Cubs won, but not before the Sox rebounded from a three-games-to-one deficit to force a seventh and deciding game.

Pat Malone (18–13) easily won Game One on the third of October with a five-hit shutout of the White Sox. All the runs in the game were scored in the first as the Cubs struck three times. Red Faber (13–9) walked leadoff batter Woody English on four pitches and, one out later, Kiki Cuyler doubled to send English to third. Both men scored on Hack Wilson's single. Wilson was forced at second by Riggs Stephenson for the second out of the inning, but Charlie Grimm doubled to left for the third run. Faber was relieved by Grady Adkins (10–16) at this point. Adkins and Sarge Connally (2–5) made a game of it, holding the Cubs scoreless for the rest of the game, but the Sox were never able to mount an offensive threat.

Game Two went 14 innings before the Cubs finally took a bloody 5–3 victory. The White Sox had a 2–1 lead and Tommy Thomas (17–16) had struck out Cuyler and Wilson for the first two outs in the ninth inning before Riggs Stephenson doubled down the left field foul line. Charlie Grimm hit a ground-ball right to Art Shires at first, but in his haste to make the final putout, he dropped the ball and Stephenson scored to tie the game. In the fourteenth, Hack Wilson tripled with one out. Stephenson grounded to second baseman Bill Hunnefield who ran Wilson down. The Cubs now had a runner at second,

1928 Chicago City Championship Series

GAME TWO --- October 4

CUBS	AB	R	H	PO	A	E
English, ss	5	0	1	4	3	0
Maguire, 2b	6	0	0	5	3	0
Cuyler, rf	6	0	0	1	3	0
Wilson, cf	5	1	2	4	0	0
Stephenson, lf	6	2	1	2	0	0
Grimm, 1b	4	1	1	20	0	0
Hartnett, c	6	1	2	4	2	0
Beck, 3b	1	0	0	0	0	0
Butler, 2b	3	0	0	1	2	0
Nehf, p	2	0	0	1	1	0
Jones, p	0	0	0	0	0	0
Bush, p	3	0	0	0	3	0
Webb, ph	1	0	0	0	0	0
Heathcote, ph	1	0	1	0	0	0
	49	5	8	42	20	0

WHITE SOX	AB	R	H	PO	A	E
Mostil, cf	4	1	2	3	0	1
Falk, lf	2	0	0	3	0	0
Shires, 1b	6	1	1	12	0	1
Reynoldss, rf	6	0	0	0	0	0
Metzler, lf-cf	5	0	3	4	0	1
Kamm, 3b	6	0	2	1	1	0
Cissell, ss	5	0	0	1	2	0
Hunnefield, 2b	5	1	1	6	3	0
Berg. c	5	0	1	12	2	0
Thomas, p	4	0	2	0	2	0
Clancy, ph	1	0	0	0	0	0
	49	3	12	42	10	3

```
CUB   0 0 0   0 0 0   1 0 1   0 0 0   0 3 - 5
SOX   1 0 0   0 1 0   0 0 0   0 0 0   0 1 - 3
```

2B: Mostil, Grimm, Stephenson, English, Butler, Shires. 3B: Metzler, Wilson. DP: Cubs 2. BB: Thomas 2, Bush 1. Struck out: Thomas 12, Nehf 1, Bush 2. Hits: Nehf 7 in 6.2 innings; Jones 0 in 0.1 inning. Winning pitcher: Bush. Umpires: McCormick, Geisel, Hildebrand and Reardon. Att: 15,000.

1928 CHICAGO CITY CHAMPIONSHIP SERIES (cont'd)

GAME THREE --- October 5

WHITE SOX	AB	R	H	PO	A	E
Metzler, cf	5	1	2	1	0	0
Shires, 1b	5	2	1	10	0	0
Reynolds, rf	6	2	1	4	0	0
Blackerby, lf	3	0	1	0	0	0
Falk, lf	3	1	1	0	0	0
Kamm, 3b	1	1	0	0	1	0
Redfern, 3b	2	0	0	2	1	0
Cissell, ss	4	2	1	1	4	1
Hunnefield, 2b	5	1	2	4	6	0
Berg, c	5	1	3	5	1	0
Lyons, p	0	0	0	0	0	0
Adkins, p	1	1	1	0	0	0
Connally, p	1	0	1	0	0	0
Walsh, p	1	1	1	0	0	0
Barrett, ph	1	0	0	0	0	0
	43	13	15	27	13	1

CUBS	AB	R	H	PO	A	E
English, ss	4	3	1	0	1	1
Maguire, 2b	5	1	3	2	4	0
Cuyler, rf	5	2	3	0	0	0
Wilson, cf	6	3	3	2	0	0
Stephenson, lf	4	0	0	3	1	0
Grimm, 1b	3	0	2	13	0	0
Hartnett, c	5	0	3	7	0	1
Beck, 3b	4	0	0	0	2	0
Butler, 3b	0	0	0	0	0	0
Root, p	1	1	1	0	0	0
Carlson, p	0	0	0	0	0	0
Jones, p	2	0	0	0	0	0
Malone, p	1	1	1	0	0	0
Bush, p	0	0	0	0	0	0
Heathcote, ph	1	0	0	0	0	2
Webb, ph	1	0	1	0	0	0
	42	11	18	27	8	4

```
SOX   3 1 3   0 1 0   5 0 0 - 13
CUB   3 5 0   1 1 0   1 0 0 - 11
```

2B: Wilson 2, Adkins, Metzler, Root, Maguire. 3B: Falk, English, Malone. HR: Wilson. SB: Reynolds, Blackerby, Maguire. DP: Sox 2. BB: Lyons 2, Walsh 2, Root 2, Jones 3, Connally 1. Struck out: Root 1, Jones 3, Walsh 3, Connally 2, Malone 1. Hits: Lyons 2 in 0.2 inning; Adkins 6 in 0.2 inning; Walsh 7 in 6 innings; Root 6 in 2.2 innings; Carlson 2 in 0 innings; Jones 5 in 3.2 innings; Malone 2 in 1.2 innings. WP: Root, Lyons. Winning pitcher: Walsh. Losing pitcher: Jones. Umpires: Geisel, Reardon, Hildebrand, McCormick. Time—2:33.

1928 Chicago City Championship Series

```
GAME FOUR --- October 6
```

WHITE SOX	AB	R	H	PO	A	E		CUBS	AB	R	H	PO	A	E
Metzler, cf	4	0	1	1	0	1		English, ss	4	0	1	0	2	0
Shires, 1b	4	0	1	13	0	0		Maguire, 2b	3	0	0	1	6	0
Barrett, rf	0	0	0	0	0	0		Cuyler, rf	4	0	3	0	0	0
Reynolds, rf	3	0	0	0	0	0		Wilson, cf	3	0	1	2	0	0
Falk, lf	4	1	2	2	0	0		Stephenson, lf	4	0	2	1	0	0
Hunnefield, 2b	4	0	1	3	4	0		Grimm, 1b	4	1	1	19	0	0
Cissell, ss	2	0	1	1	5	0		Hartnett, c	3	1	0	4	1	0
Redfern, 3b	2	0	0	1	7	0		Beck, 3b	3	1	1	0	4	0
Berg, c	3	0	0	1	2	0		Blake, p	3	0	1	0	4	0
Faber, p	3	0	0	2	1	0								
Connally, p	0	0	0	0	0	0			31	3	10	27	17	0
Kamm, ph	1	1	1	0	0	0								
Clancy, ph	0	0	0	0	0	0								
Swanson, ph	1	0	1	0	0	0								
McCurdy, ph	1	0	0	0	0	0								
Blackerby, ph	1	0	0	0	0	0								
	33	2	8	24	19	1								

```
SOX   0  1  0   0  0  0   0  1  0  -  2
CUB   0  3  0   0  0  0   0  0  x  -  3
```

2B: English. HR: Falk. SB: Hunnefield, Cissell. DP: Cubs 1, Sox 2. BB: Faber 3, Blake 2. Struck out: Blake 4. Hits: Faber 10 in 7 innings. Losing pitcher: Faber. Umpires: Reardon, Hildebrand, McCormick, Geisel.

but their prospects looked drearier than a few moments earlier. Grimm was intentionally passed to get to Hartnett, 1-for-5 on the day, and Gabby doubled to right center for two runs and a Cub lead. Johnny "Trolley Line" Butler added another double and another run to the Cubs' totals. The Sox came back to score once on a double by Shires and a Willie Kamm single, but Bill Cissell fouled out to Hartnett to give the Cubs a two-game edge in the series. Art Nehf started the game for the Cubs and Percy Jones (10-6) got the win in relief. Thomas went all the way and took the loss.

The White Sox won Game Three, a barnburner, for their first victory of the series. Ted Lyons (15-14) started against Charlie Root (14-18) but neither pitcher was on his game. Lyons lasted just two-thirds of an inning and Root was unable to survive the third. The teams traded three-run first innings before the Sox scored once in the second and the Cubs scored five times in the bottom of the inning. Three Sox runs in the third made the score 8-7, Cubs. The Nationals scored single runs in the fourth and fifth to take a 10-8 lead, but the Sox struck for five runs in the seventh to go ahead, 13-10. Freddie Maguire opened the ninth inning with a double for the Cubs, trailing 13-11, but Sarge Connally struck out Cuyler and Wilson and got Riggs Stephenson on a pop fly to end the wild game. The Cubs made 15 hits; the Sox, 18. The Cubs used five pitchers in the slugfest — Root, Hal Carlson (3-2), Percy Jones, Guy Bush (15-6), and Pat Malone — while the Americans employed four — Lyons, Grady Adkins, Sarge Connally, and rookie Ed Walsh (4-7). Walsh was the son of long-time Sox pitcher Ed Walsh.

1928 Chicago City Championship Series

GAME FIVE --- October 7

WHITE SOX	AB	R	H	PO	A	E		CUBS	AB	R	H	PO	A	E
Metzler, cf	3	0	2	1	0	0		English, ss	4	0	0	3	3	0
Shires, 1b	4	1	1	7	0	0		Maguire, 2b	4	0	1	4	1	0
Reynolds, rf	4	0	1	3	0	0		Cuyler, rf	4	0	0	0	0	0
Falk, lf	2	1	1	2	0	0		Wilson, cf	4	0	1	0	0	0
Hunnefield, 3b	4	0	1	1	1	0		Stephenson, lf	3	0	1	5	0	0
Swanson, 2b	3	0	0	1	3	0		Grimm, 1b	3	0	1	7	1	0
Redfern, ss	4	0	0	2	3	0		Hartnett, c	3	0	0	7	2	0
Berg, c	3	0	0	10	0	0		Beck, 3b	2	0	0	1	2	0
Thomas, p	3	0	0	0	1	0		Butler, 3b	0	0	0	0	0	0
								Malone, p	2	0	0	0	1	0
	30	2	6	27	8	0		Root, p	0	0	0	0	0	0
								Heathcote, ph	1	0	0	0	0	0
								Webb, ph	1	0	0	0	0	0
									31	0	4	27	10	0

```
SOX   2 0 0   0 0 0   0 0 0  -  2
CUB   0 0 0   0 0 0   0 0 0  -  0
```

2B: Reynolds, Falk, Hunnefield, Grimm. DP: Cubs. BB: Malone 3, Thomas 1. Struck out· Malone 4, Thomas 7, Root 1. Hits: Malone 6 in 8 innings. Losing pitcher: Malone. Umpires: Hildebrand, McCormick, Reardon, Geisel.

GAME SIX --- October 8

CUBS	AB	R	H	PO	A	E		WHITE SOX	AB	R	H	PO	A	E
English, ss	4	0	0	1	2	0		Metzler, cf	4	2	2	1	0	0
Maguire, 2b	5	0	1	1	2	0		Shires, 1b	5	1	3	12	0	0
Cuyler, rf	4	0	1	4	0	0		Reynolds, rf	4	2	2	1	0	1
Wilson, cf	3	0	0	2	0	0		Falk, lf	4	0	0	3	0	0
Stephenson, lf	3	0	0	1	1	0		Kamm, 3b	3	1	1	2	4	0
Grimm, 1b	4	0	1	8	1	0		Hunnefield, ss	4	0	2	2	2	1
Hartnett, c	4	0	1	7	1	1		Swanson, 2b	4	0	1	0	1	0
Beck, 3b	3	0	0	0	0	0		Berg, c	4	1	2	6	0	0
Bush, p	0	0	0	0	1	0		Adkins, p	4	0	1	0	3	0
Root, p	2	0	0	0	0	0								
Carlson, p	0	0	0	0	0	0			36	7	14	27	10	2
Kelly, ph	1	0	1	0	0	0								
Webb, ph	1	0	0	0	0	0								
McMillan, pr	0	0	0	0	0	0								
Heathcote, ph	1	0	1	0	0	0								
	35	1	6	24	8	1								

```
CUB   0 0 0   0 0 1   0 0 0  -  1
SOX   3 3 1   0 0 0   0 0 x  -  7
```

2B: Maguire, Grimm, Cuyler. 3B: Shires, Hunnefield. SB: Kamm. BB: Bush 1, Adkins 3, Root 1. Struck out: Adkins 6, Root 3, Carlson 1. Hits: Bush 5 in 0.2 inning; Root 7 in 5.1 innings. Losing pitcher: Bush. Umpires: McCormick, Geisel, Reardon, Hildebrand.

Things were back to normal for Game Four when the Cubs scored early against Red Faber, then hung on for a 3–2 win and a 3–1 lead in the series. Bibb Falk's home run in the second inning gave the Sox a brief 1–0 lead, but the Cubs came back with three runs in the bottom of the inning. Stephenson singled, leading off, but was forced by Charlie Grimm. Hartnett and Beck walked to load the bases. Sheriff Blake's long fly tied the game when center-fielder Alex

1928 Chicago City Championship Series

```
GAME SEVEN --- October 9
```

CUBS	AB	R	H	PO	A	E
English, ss	5	2	1	3	4	0
Maguire, 2b	6	1	4	2	3	0
Cuyler, rf	4	3	0	2	0	0
Wilson, cf	3	2	2	3	0	0
Stephenson, lf	4	1	1	2	0	0
Grimm, 1b	4	2	3	13	1	0
Hartnett, c	5	1	1	2	1	0
Beck, 3b	4	0	2	0	2	0
Blake, p	5	1	2	0	1	0
	40	13	16	27	12	0

WHITE SOX	AB	R	H	PO	A	E
Metzler, cf	4	0	0	5	1	1
Shires, 1b	3	0	1	6	0	0
Reynolds, rf	3	0	0	1	0	0
Falk, lf	4	0	0	3	0	0
Kamm, 3b	4	1	3	1	0	0
Hunnefield, ss	4	1	1	2	4	1
Swanson, 2b	4	0	0	6	1	1
Berg, c	1	0	1	3	0	2
Connally, p	0	0	0	0	0	0
Walsh, p	0	0	0	0	0	0
Adkins, p	1	0	0	0	0	0
Cox, p	2	0	0	0	1	0
Clancy, ph	1	0	1	0	0	0
Crouse, ph	1	0	0	0	0	0
	32	2	7	27	7	5

```
CUB   6 0 0   0 6 0   1 0 0  -  13
SOX   0 0 0   0 0 0   0 0 2  -   2
```

2B: Beck, Wilson. 3B: Grimm. SB: Cuyler. DP: Cubs 2, Sox 2. BB: Connally 2, Walsh 2, Blake 5, Cox 1. Struck out: Adkins 2, Blake 2. Losing pitcher: Connally. Umpires: John Reardon, Hildebrand, McCormick, Geisel. Att: 25,000.

Metzler dropped the ball. A groundout by Woody English and a passed ball by Sox catcher Moe Berg accounted for the final two runs. Sheriff Blake pitched a complete game for the victory and, with Pat Malone on the mound for Game Five, the Cubs looked forward to winning the championship.

But Tommy Thomas had a different idea. After Art Shires and Bibb Falk reached in the first inning, Bill Hunnefield's pop fly fell between Hack Wilson and Riggs Stephenson for a double. Shires and Falk scored for the only runs Thomas needed as he threw a four-hit shutout at the Nationals. Pat Malone and Charlie Root held the Sox to three hits over the next eight innings, Root pitching a scoreless ninth, but the Cubs were unable to do anything with Thomas. In a weird sideline to the game, a Cubs fan, one George A. Peterson, dropped dead in the stands as the Cubs took the field for the final half-inning.

Game Six featured the strong work of Grady Adkins in his first start of the series. By the time the Cubs scored their first run, the White Sox were well out of danger with a 7–0 lead. Guy Bush was able to retire only two men in the first before being knocked from the box as the Sox scored three times. Three runs in the second and one more in the third off Charlie Root made the final score 7–1, Americans.

If baseball were scripted, the final game would have been a dramatic, come-from-behind victory for the underdog White Sox. Real life, unfortunately, rarely follows a script. The Cubs plastered Sarge Connally, Ed Walsh, and Grady Adkins for six runs in the first inning and were in control throughout the game. Connally started and lasted one-third of an inning before being relieved by Walsh. Walsh walked Charlie Grimm and gave up singles to Gabby Hartnett and Zinn Beck before being relieved by Grady Adkins. Adkins, weary from his complete game of the day before, was able to end the scoring in the first, but he and George Cox were blasted for six runs in the fourth to end all doubt about the outcome of the game. The Sox were unable to mount a threat until the ninth inning when they crossed the plate twice to make the final score 13–2. The Cubs' Sheriff Blake was the easy winner. Second baseman Fred Maguire was the batting star of the game with four hits in six times at bat.

The Cubs' victory was their fifth in the city championships and their first since 1925. To this point, the White Sox had won ten series.

The 1930 Chicago City Championship Series

Chicago Cubs defeat Chicago White Sox; 4–2

The 1930 Cubs, led by Kiki Cuyler, Gaby Hartnett and Hack Wilson, were a formidable club that gave the Cardinals a run for the pennant. Chicago eventually finished two games behind St. Louis with a 90–64 record, but would win it all two years later. The seventh-place White Sox, with a 62–92 record, weren't much competition in the city championship although strong pitching performances allowed them to take two of the six games of the series.

1930 Chicago City Championship Series

GAME ONE --- October 1

CUBS	AB	R	H	PO	A	E		WHITE SOX	AB	R	H	PO	A	E
Blair, 2b	3	0	2	1	5	0		Kerr, 2b	2	1	0	3	2	0
Farrell, ss	3	0	0	4	3	0		Watwood, cf	4	2	2	1	0	0
Stephenson, ph	1	0	0	0	0	0		Reynolds, rf	3	1	1	1	0	0
Beck, ss	0	0	0	1	0	0		Jolley, lf	4	0	1	3	0	0
Heathcote, ph	1	0	0	0	0	0		Cissell, ss	4	0	2	0	6	0
Cuyler, rf	4	0	0	1	0	0		Clancy, 1b	3	0	0	11	0	0
Wilson, cf	3	0	0	3	0	0		Tate, c	3	0	0	7	0	0
D.Taylor, lf	4	0	0	2	0	0		Kamm, 3b	2	0	0	1	2	1
Hartnett, c	4	0	2	3	1	0		Lyons, p	3	1	1	0	2	0
Kelly, 1b	3	1	0	8	2	0								
Bell, 3b	3	0	2	1	1	0			28	5	7	27	12	1
Malone, p	3	0	1	0	1	1								
Grimm, ph	1	0	0	0	0	0								
	33	1	7	24	13	1								

```
CUB   0  0  0    0  0  0    0  0  1  -  1
SOX   3  0  0    0  0  0    0  2  x  -  5
```

2B: Reynolds, Bell. DP: Cubs. BB: Lyons 3, Malone 3. Struck out: Lyons 3, Malone 2. WP: Malone. Umpires: Ormsby, Ernest Quigley, William McGowan, Magerkurth.

Game One on October 1st featured Ted Lyons (22–15) who shut down the Cub offense on seven hits and a run before a crowd of 33,000. The Sox jumped on Pat Malone (20–9) in the first and were never in danger thereafter. John Kerr walked and Cliff Watwood followed with a single. A double by Carl Reynolds scored both runners and Smead Jolley's single drove in the third run of the inning. The Cubs loaded the bases in the second off Lyons but were unable to score and both pitchers settled down after that. Through six innings, Lyons had allowed only two singles and Malone had given up four hits. The

1930 Chicago City Championship Series

GAME TWO --- October 2

CUBS	AB	R	H	PO	A	E	WHITE SOX	AB	R	H	PO	A	E
Blair, 2b	5	1	1	2	3	0	Kerr, 2b	4	1	0	1	6	1
English, ss	4	1	1	2	2	0	Campbell, ph	1	0	0	0	0	0
Cuyler, rf	4	1	1	1	0	0	Watwood, cf	2	0	0	1	1	0
Wilson, cf	3	1	0	1	0	0	Reynolds, rf	4	0	1	2	0	0
Stephenson, lf	4	0	3	0	0	0	Jolley, lf	4	0	0	1	0	0
Hartnett, c	4	0	0	6	2	0	Cissell, ss	3	0	1	2	5	1
Grimm, 1b	4	0	1	13	1	0	Clancy, 1b	3	1	1	14	0	0
Bell, 3b	2	0	0	1	2	1	Tate, c	4	0	1	4	0	0
Blake, p	4	0	1	1	6	0	Kamm, 3b	2	0	2	2	1	0
							Fothergill, ph	1	0	0	0	0	0
	34	4	8	27	16	1	Caraway, p	3	0	1	0	2	0
							Moore, p	0	0	0	0	0	0
							Barnes, ph	0	0	0	0	0	0
								31	2	5	27	15	2

```
CUB    0  0  0    1  0  0    0  3  0  -  4
SOX    0  0  0    0  0  1    0  0  1  -  2
```

2B: Tate. HR: Cuyler. DP: Cubs 1, Sox 1. BB: Caraway 2, Moore 1, Blake 5. Struck out: Caraway 4, Blake 4. Hits: Caraway 8 in 7.2 innings. WP: Blake. Losing pitcher: Caraway. Umpires: Ernest Quigley, William McGowan, Magerkurth and Ormsby.

GAME THREE --- October 3

WHITE SOX	AB	R	H	PO	A	E	CUBS	AB	R	H	PO	A	E
Kerr, 2b	3	0	0	3	3	0	Blair, 2b	5	2	2	1	6	0
Watwood, cf	4	0	0	0	1	0	English, ss	5	2	2	1	1	2
Reynolds, rf	4	0	1	0	0	0	Cuyler, rf	5	1	1	2	0	0
Fothergill, lf	4	0	0	0	0	0	Wilson, cf	3	3	3	3	0	0
Cissell, ss	3	1	1	2	3	1	Heathcote, cf	0	0	0	0	0	0
Clancy, 1b	3	0	0	10	3	0	Stephenson, lf	3	2	2	1	0	0
Mulleavy, ph	1	0	0	0	0	0	D.Taylor, lf	0	0	0	1	0	0
Kamm, 3b	4	0	1	2	3	0	Hartnett, c	5	0	3	5	0	0
Tate, c	2	0	0	4	1	0	Grimm, 1b	5	1	2	13	0	0
Autry, c	2	0	1	2	0	0	Bell, 3b	4	1	3	0	2	0
Faber, p	2	0	0	1	0	0	Teachout, p	2	0	0	0	3	0
Moore, p	0	0	0	0	0	0		37	12	18	27	12	2
Walsh, p	1	0	0	0	1	0							
	33	1	4	24	15	1							

```
SOX    0  0  0    0  0  0    1  0  0  -   1
CUB    0  2  0    1  2  3    2  2  x  -  12
```

2B: Blair 2, Wilson. 3B: Cuyler, Hartnett. HR: Grimm. DP: Sox. BB: Faber 2, Walsh 1, Teachout 2. Struck out: Faber 2, Walsh 1, Teachout 2. Hits: Faber 9 in 4.2 innings; Moore 4 in 1 inning. Losing pitcher: Faber. Umpires: McGowan, Magerkurth, Ormsby, Quigley.

Cubs loaded the bases after two were out in the seventh on three straight singles, but pinch-hitter Riggs Stephenson took a called strike three. The Nationals were unable to score until the ninth inning when George Kelly, Les Bell and Clarence "Footsie" Blair all hit safely for one run.

The Cubs tied the series the next day as Sheriff Blake (10–14) out-dueled Pat Caraway (10–10). With one out in the fourth, Hack Wilson walked and Riggs Stephenson singled him to third. When the relay from Bill Cissell to Willie Kamm went wild, Wilson scored the first run of the game. The White Sox tied the game in the sixth. With one out, John Kerr grounded to Les Bell at

1930 Chicago City Championship Series

GAME FOUR --- October 4

WHITE SOX	AB	R	H	PO	A	E
Kerr, 2b	4	2	2	4	5	1
Watwood, cf	3	1	1	2	0	0
Reynolds, rf	5	2	2	1	0	0
Jolley, lf	5	1	2	3	0	0
Cissell, ss	5	1	2	3	0	0
Clancy, 1b	5	0	1	8	0	0
Tate, c	5	0	2	6	1	0
Kamm, 3b	4	0	2	0	3	0
Thomas, p	3	1	0	0	1	0
	39	8	14	27	10	1

CUBS	AB	R	H	PO	A	E
Blair, 2b	5	0	3	1	6	1
English, ss	4	0	0	1	2	1
Cuyler, rf	3	0	0	1	0	0
Wilson, cf	3	0	1	2	0	0
Stephenson, lf	3	0	0	3	0	0
Hartnett, c	4	0	0	6	1	0
Grimm, 1b	3	1	0	11	1	0
Bell, 3b	4	1	2	1	1	0
Bush, p	0	0	0	0	0	0
Petty, p	2	0	0	1	0	0
Heathcote, ph	1	0	0	0	0	0
Osborn, p	0	0	0	0	1	0
D.Taylor, ph	1	0	0	0	0	0
	33	2	6	27	12	2

```
SOX   1  3  0     0  0  0     1  3  0  -  8
CUB   0  0  0     0  2  0     0  0  0  -  2
```

RBI: Cissell, Reynolds 2, Petty, Blair, Jolley 2. 2B: Watwood, Kerr, Bell, Tate, Wilson. 3B: Cissell. HR: Jolley. SH: Watwood 2, Thomas. DP: Sox 1. LOB: Sox 10, Cubs 9. BB: Bush 1, Petty 2, Thomas 5. Hits: Bush 5 in 1.2 innings; Petty 5 in 5.1 innings; Osborn 4 in 2 innings. Losing pitcher: Bush. Umpires: Magerkurth, Ormsby, Quigley, McGowan. Time—2:12.

GAME FIVE --- October 5

WHITE SOX	AB	R	H	PO	A	E
Kerr, 2b	5	1	2	1	5	0
Watwood, cf	3	0	1	1	0	0
Mulleavy, ss	1	0	0	1	1	0
Reynolds, rf-cf	4	0	1	2	0	0
Jolley, lf	5	0	3	4	0	0
Cissell, ss-3b	5	0	0	1	1	0
Clancy, 1b	3	1	2	10	0	0
Tate, c	4	1	2	2	0	0
Kamm, 3b	2	0	1	1	1	0
Barnes, ph	1	0	0	0	0	0
Moore, p	0	0	0	0	0	0
Henry, p	0	0	0	0	0	0
Campbell, ph	1	0	0	0	0	0
Faber, p	0	0	0	0	0	0
Lyons, p	1	1	0	0	2	0
Braxton, p	0	0	0	0	0	0
Fothergill, lf	2	0	0	1	0	0
	37	4	12	24	10	0

CUBS	AB	R	H	PO	A	E
Blair, 2b	5	0	0	2	5	0
English, ss	4	1	1	1	2	0
Cuyler, rf	4	1	3	2	0	0
Wilson, cf	4	3	2	3	0	0
Stephenson, lf	3	0	2	4	0	0
Hartnett, c	4	0	3	8	0	0
Grimm, 1b	4	0	0	7	0	0
Bell, 3b	4	1	1	0	2	0
Malone, p	3	0	1	0	1	0
	35	6	13	27	10	0

```
SOX   0  0  0     0  2  2     0  0  0  -  4
CUB   2  1  0     0  2  0     1  0  x  -  6
```

2B: English, Hartnett 2, Jolley, Clancy. HR: Wilson. DP: Sox. BB: Lyons 1, Moore 1, Malone 1. Struck out: Lyons 1, Faber 1, Malone 3. Hits: Lyons 10 in 4.2 innings; Braxton 0 in 0.2 innings; Moore 3 in 1.3 innings; Henry 0 in 0.2 innings. Losing pitcher: Lyons. Umpires: Ormsby, Quigley, McGowan, Magerkurth.

third. Bell fielded the ball, but threw over first baseman Charlie Grimm's head into right field. Kerr wound up on third where he scored on Carl Reynolds' single. The Cubbies struck for three more runs in the eighth and won the game, 4–2, Blake getting the win, Caraway the loss.

The Cubs delivered a crushing defeat to the Sox in Game Three, battering Red Faber (8–13) and two other Sox pitchers for 18 hits and 12 runs. Faber,

1930 Chicago City Championship Series

GAME SIX --- October 6

CUBS	AB	R	H	PO	A	E		WHITE SOX	AB	R	H	PO	A	E
Blair, 2b	4	0	1	2	2	1		Kerr, 2b	4	0	1	2	4	0
Beck, 2b	0	0	0	0	1	0		Barnes, cf	4	1	2	3	0	0
English, ss	4	1	2	1	4	2		Reynolds, rf	3	1	1	4	0	0
Cuyler, rf	5	1	2	1	0	0		Jolley, lf	3	0	0	3	0	0
Wilson, cf	4	2	2	4	0	0		Clancy, 1b	4	0	1	7	1	1
Stephenson, lf	3	1	1	0	0	0		Cissell, ss	4	0	1	4	3	0
Hartnett, c	3	1	1	6	1	0		Tate, c	3	2	3	4	0	0
Grimm, 1b	4	0	0	10	2	0		Kamm, 3b	3	0	1	0	2	1
Bell, 3b	5	0	2	1	1	0		Caraway, p	0	0	0	0	0	0
Blake, p	3	0	1	1	3	0		Braxton, p	3	0	0	0	0	0
Petty, p	0	0	0	0	0	0		Thomas, p	0	0	0	0	0	0
D.Taylor, ph	1	0	1	0	0	0		Mulleavy, ph	1	0	0	0	0	0
								Fothergill, ph	1	0	0	0	0	0
	36	6	13	27	14	4			37	4	10	27	10	2

```
CUB   0  0  0    1  1  0    0  1  3  -  6
SOX   0  0  0    0  2  1    0  1  0  -  4
```

2B: Kamm, Tate, Bell. HR: Wilson. SB: Barnes 2, Kerr. DP: Sox 3. BB: Caraway 4, Blake 4, Thomas 1. Struck out: Caraway 2, Blake 5, Braxton 1, Thomas 1. Hits: Caraway 2 in 4 innings; Blake 9 in 7.2 innings; Braxton 5 in 4.1 innings. WP: Braxton. Winning pitcher: Petty. Losing pitcher: Braxton. Umpires: Quigley, McGowan, Magerkurth, Ormsby.

pitching in his 11th city series, gave up a two-run homer to Charlie Grimm in the second and singles by Hack Wilson and Gabby Hartnett made the score 3–0 in the fourth. Faber was knocked from the box in the fifth when Woody English's single was followed by a Wilson RBI double. The fun was just beginning for the Cubs, however. Riggs Stephenson touched reliever Jim Moore (2–1) for an RBI single to put the Cubs up by 5 and Kiki Cuyler's two-run triple in the sixth sent Moore to the showers. Meanwhile, the Cubs were held to one hit by Bud Teachout (11–4) until scoring once in the seventh inning.

The White Sox returned the favor the next day by administering a pretty fair beating of their own. Tommy Thomas (5–13), recently recovered from ptomaine poisoning, held the Cubs to two runs and six hits while his teammates racked up 14 hits and eight runs off Guy Bush (15–10). Johnny Watwood doubled with one out in the first, but was thrown out at third on Carl Reynolds' grounder. Singles by Smead Jolley and Bill Cissell put the Sox on the board with their first run. The Americans knocked Bush out of the box with three second inning runs. After two were out, Thomas walked, Dickie Kerr doubled to send Thomas to third where he scored when Footsie Blair bobbled Watwood's grounder. Kerr scored on the play despite being caught in a rundown between third and home, and Watwood advanced to second. Reynolds' single made the score 4–0, Sox. Jesse Petty came on in relief and finally stopped the rally, but it was a case of too little, too late. The Cubs pulled within two in the fifth, but a White Sox run off Petty in the seventh and three against Osborn in the eighth put the game in the history books.

Game Five saw the Cubs outlast the White Sox in the friendly confines of Wrigley Field. The Nationals roughed up Ted Lyons in the first as English doubled, Cuyler and Stephenson singled, and Hartnett doubled for a 2–0 lead.

Singles by Les Bell and Kiki Cuyler added a third run in the second inning. A Cuyler double and a Hack Wilson home run made the score 5–2 Sox in the fifth. The White Sox pulled to within one in the sixth on a double by Bud Clancy and singles by Bennie Tate and Dickie Kerr, but Pat Malone held the Sox in check for the final three frames. The Cubs tallied an insurance run in the seventh off Jim Moore when Wilson singled, Stephenson walked, and Hartnett singled Wilson home. Both teams hit the ball hard, the Cubs finishing with 13 hits and the Sox with 12. Pat Malone got the victory and Ted Lyons took the loss.

The Cubs took the series in Game Six, winning 6–4 for the second day in a row. After falling behind 2–0 in the fifth, the White Sox tied the game in the bottom of the inning after two were out. Red Barnes walked, Carl Reynolds singled, and Smead Jolley walked to load the bases. Bud Clancy's single tied the game. The White Sox went ahead in the sixth on a Bennie Tate double and a Barnes single. Both teams traded runs in the eighth and the White Sox led 4–3 going into the ninth, but the Cubs scored three times to decide the series. Pinch-hitter Danny Taylor singled and was forced by Woody English. Back-to-back singles by Cuyler and Wilson scored English before Riggs Stephenson was intentionally walked. Gabby Hartnett's sacrifice fly scored Cuyler and Wilson came home on Bud Clancy's error. Jesse Petty (1–3 with the Cubs), pitching his last game for a major league team, was the winner, while Garland Braxton (4–10) took the loss. Attendance for this game was 30,204, just a couple thousand less than the first game of the World Series between the St. Louis Cardinals and the Philadelphia Athletics.

This series marked the first time the Cubs had managed to win back-to-back championships since winning in 1905 and then again in 1909.

The 1931 Chicago City Championship Series

Chicago White Sox defeat Chicago Cubs; 4–3

This was a corker of a series.

The third-place Chicago Cubs (84–70) must have been licking their chops as they prepared to meet the Chicago White Sox (56–97) in the 1931 city championship. There was no doubt as to the outcome of the series — the Cubs would win easily, their third consecutive championship, fourth of the last five. After all, the White Sox were a last place team which finished a very distant 51½ games behind the league-leading Philadelphia Athletics. Their .366 winning percentage was the lowest in Sox history, even worse than the 1921 club (62–92, .403), a team ravaged by the outster of eight players from the 1919 World Series scandal.

The only problem was that apparently no one had told the White Sox they couldn't win. So they did.

The series opened September 30 at Wrigley Field as the Sox made the most of their opponent's home field, crushing the Cubs 9–0. Charlie Root (17–14) and 43-year old Red Faber (10–14) matched each other through the first five innings. Root had only given up two hits when Lu Blue popped out to Cubs' first

1931 Chicago City Championship Series

GAME ONE --- September 30

WHITE SOX	AB	R	H	PO	A	E
Blue, 1b	6	0	3	16	0	0
Cissell, ss	5	1	1	1	4	0
Jolley, rf	4	1	2	2	0	0
Fonseca, 1f	3	1	0	0	0	0
Sullivan, 3b	3	1	1	0	2	0
Watwood, cf	5	2	1	1	0	0
Kerr, 2b	3	2	1	1	8	1
Grube, c	5	1	1	6	0	0
Faber, p	4	0	0	0	1	0
	38	9	10	27	15	1

CUBS	AB	R	H	PO	A	E
English, ss	4	0	2	1	0	0
Herman, 2b	3	0	0	1	3	0
Cuyler, cf	4	0	0	0	0	0
Bell, 3b	4	0	0	1	3	1
Barton, rf	4	0	1	3	0	0
D.Taylor, 1f	4	0	2	2	0	0
Grimm, 1b	3	0	0	15	0	0
Hartnett, c	3	0	0	4	1	1
Root, p	2	0	0	0	3	0
May, p	0	0	0	0	1	0
Warneke, p	0	0	0	0	0	0
Blair, ph	1	0	0	0	0	0
Sweetland, p	0	0	0	0	0	0
	32	0	5	27	11	2

```
SOX   0  0  0    0  0  7    2  0  0  -  9
CUB   0  0  0    0  0  0    0  0  0  -  0
```

RBIs: Jolley 2, Kerr 2, Grube, Blue 3. 2B: Blue 2, Cissell, English. HR: Jolley. SB: Barton, Watwood. SH: Herman. LOB: Sox 10, Cubs 6. BB: Root 3, May 4, Warneke 1. Struck out: Root 3, Faber 4. Hits: Root 7 in 5.1 innings; May 2 in 1.1 innings; Warneke 1 in 1.1 innings; Sweetland 0 in 1 inning. Losing pitcher: Root. Umpires: Quigley, Hildebrand, Magerkurth, Owens. Time—1:56.

GAME TWO --- October 1

WHITE SOX	AB	R	H	PO	A	E
Blue, 1b	2	0	0	11	1	2
Cissell, ss	4	0	2	3	4	0
Jolley, rf	4	0	0	2	0	0
Fonseca, 1f	2	0	1	0	0	0
Sullivan, 3b	4	0	1	0	5	0
Watwood, cf	4	0	0	3	0	0
Kerr, 2b	4	0	0	3	2	0
Grube, c	3	0	1	4	1	0
Frasier, p	3	0	1	0	1	0
	30	0	6	*26	14	2

CUBS	AB	R	H	PO	A	E
English, ss	3	0	1	3	3	0
Herman, 2b	4	0	0	1	4	0
Cuyler, cf	4	1	1	0	0	0
Bell, 3b	4	0	2	4	2	0
Barton, rf	3	0	1	2	0	0
D.Taylor, 1f	3	0	0	0	0	0
Grimm, 1b	3	0	0	8	1	0
Hemsley, c	3	0	0	7	2	0
Bush, p	3	0	0	2	2	0
	30	1	5	27	14	0

* Two out when winning run scored

```
SOX   0  0  0    0  0  0    0  0  0  -  0
CUB   0  0  0    0  0  0    0  0  1  -  1
```

RBIs: Barton. 2B: Fonseca, Cuyler. SB: Blue. DP: Sox 3. LOB: Sox 7, Cubs 5. BB: Frasier 2, Bush 7. Umpires: Hildebrand, Magerkurth, Owens, Quigley. Time—1:47.

baseman Charley Grimm to open the sixth and no one had a clue what was to come. That was the last batter Root would retire. Bill Cissell doubled to left and Smead Jolley crushed a home run into the left-center-field bleachers. Root then came completely apart, issuing walks to Lew Fonseca and Billy Sullivan and an infield single to Johnny Watwood. John Kerr singled to make the score 4–0. Frank Grube singled to make it 5–0. Red Faber reached on an error by Les Bell and the bases were loaded for the second time in the inning. Blue atoned for his popout by singling in Kerr and Grube and the Sox had a seven-run inning. Jakie May (5–5) relieved at this point and retired the side without

1931 Chicago City Championship Series

GAME THREE --- October 2

CUBS	AB	R	H	PO	A	E		WHITE SOX	AB	R	H	PO	A	E
English, ss	2	1	1	6	2	0		Watwood, cf	5	1	2	2	0	0
Herman, 2b	3	1	1	3	4	1		Cissell, ss-2b	4	0	2	1	1	1
Cuyler, cf	2	0	0	1	0	0		Jolley, rf	4	0	1	5	0	0
Bell, 3b	4	0	0	0	0	0		Fonseca, lf	4	0	1	2	0	0
Barton, rf	4	0	1	4	0	0		Blue, 1b	3	0	1	13	2	0
D.Taylor, lf	4	0	0	1	0	0		Sullivan, 3b	4	0	1	0	1	0
Grimm, 1b	4	0	0	8	2	0		Kerr, 2b	2	0	0	2	3	0
Hemsley, c	4	0	1	3	1	0		Fothergill, ph	0	0	0	0	0	0
Smith, p	3	0	2	1	2	0		Tate, c	0	0	0	0	0	0
Root, p	0	0	0	0	0	0		Grube, c	2	0	0	1	2	0
								Reynolds, ph	1	0	0	0	0	0
	30	2	6	27	11	1		Appling, ss	1	0	0	0	1	0
								Lyons, p	4	0	0	1	5	0
									34	1	8	27	15	1

```
CUB   2 0 0   0 0 0   0 0 0  -  2
SOX   0 0 0   1 0 0   0 0 0  -  1
```

RBIs: Bell, Barton, Jolley. 2B: English, Watwood. SH: Cuyler 2. DP: Cubs 2, Sox 1. LOB: Cubs 6, Sox 9. BB: Smith 2, Root 1, Lyons 3. Struck out: Smith 1, Lyons 1. Hits: Smith 8 in 8 innings (none out in ninth); Root 0 in 1 inning. WP: Smith. Winning pitcher: Smith. Umpires: Magerkurth, Owens, Quigley, Hildebrand. Att: 20,000. Time—2:00.

GAME FOUR --- October 3

CUBS	AB	R	H	PO	A	E		WHITE SOX	AB	R	H	PO	A	E
English, ss	5	1	2	2	2	0		Watwood, cf	4	1	3	2	0	0
Herman, 2b	3	1	1	4	4	0		Cissell, ss	3	1	1	2	0	1
Cuyler, cf	3	0	1	1	0	0		Jolley, rf	3	1	2	5	0	0
Bell, 3b	4	0	0	0	3	0		Fonseca, lf	4	1	1	4	0	1
Barton, rf	4	0	1	3	0	0		Blue, 1b	4	0	1	3	1	0
D.Taylor, lf	4	0	0	0	0	0		Sullivan, 3b	4	0	0	3	1	0
Grimm, 1b	3	0	1	9	2	0		Kerr, 2b	4	0	1	2	3	0
Hartnett, c	4	0	1	3	0	0		Grube, c	4	0	3	5	2	0
Teachout, pr	0	1	0	0	0	0		Thomas, p	2	0	0	1	1	0
Malone, p	2	0	0	2	2	0		Frasier, p	1	0	0	0	1	0
Blair, ph	1	0	0	0	0	0			33	4	12	27	9	2
May, p	0	0	0	0	0	0								
Hemsley, ph	1	0	0	0	0	0								
	34	3	7	24	13	0								

```
CUB   0 0 0   0 0 0   0 2 1  -  3
SOX   1 0 0   0 3 0   0 0 x  -  4
```

RBIs: Jolley, Fonseca 3, Cuyler, Bell, English. 2B: Watwood, English. HR: Fonseca. SH: Cuyler, Cissell, Thomas. DP: Cubs. LOB: Cubs 8, Sox 8. BB: Malone 1, Thomas 3. Struck out: Malone 2, May 1, Thomas 2, Frasier 1. Hits: Malone 12 in 6 innings; May 0 in 2 innings; Thomas 5 in 7 innings (none out in eighth). Winning pitcher: Thomas. Losing pitcher: Malone. Umpires: Owens, Quigley, Hildebrand, Magerkurth. Time—1:53.

further damage, but the Sox came right back at him in the seventh when Sullivan, Kerr, and Faber walked and Lu Blue doubled for two more runs. Lon Warneke (2-4) came on in relief for the Cubs with two out in the seventh and he and Les Sweetland (8-7) held the Sox scoreless for the balance of the game. Faber went the distance for the Sox, pitching a five-hit shutout, striking out four and walking no one.

1931 Chicago City Championship Series

```
GAME FIVE --- October 4
```

CUBS		AB	R	H	PO	A	E		WHITE SOX		AB	R	H	PO	A	E
English, ss		5	0	2	2	1	0		Watwood, cf		5	3	3	4	0	0
Herman, 2b		4	1	0	1	1	0		Cissell, ss		5	3	4	2	4	1
Cuyler, cf		4	1	1	3	0	0		Jolley, rf		4	3	2	0	0	0
Bell, 3b		4	1	2	1	1	0		Fonseca, lf		4	1	0	1	0	0
Barton, rf		4	0	1	2	0	0		Blue, 1b		5	0	1	13	0	0
D.Taylor, lf		4	1	1	2	0	0		Sullivan, 3b		5	0	1	3	4	0
Grimm, 1b		4	0	2	4	0	0		Kerr, 2b		3	0	0	0	6	0
Hemsley, c		4	2	1	9	1	0		Grube, c		4	2	2	4	0	0
Root, p		2	0	0	0	0	0		Faber, p		2	1	2	0	2	0
Hartnett, ph		1	0	0	0	0	0		Lyons, p		1	0	0	0	0	0
Malone, p		0	0	0	0	2	0				----	--	--	--	--	--
Smith, p		0	0	0	0	0	1				38	13	15	27	16	1
May, p		0	0	0	0	0	0									
Blair, p		1	0	0	0	0	0									
		----	--	--	--	--	--									
		37	6	10	24	6	1									

```
CUB   1 0 0   2 0 1   1 0 1  -   6
SOX   1 0 0   0 5 0   3 4 x  -  13
```

RBIs: Bell, Jolley 5, Barton, Grimm, Cissell 4, Cuyler, Hemsley, Sullivan, Blue, English. 2B: Barton, English, Jolley, Blue. HR: Jolley, Cuyler, Hemsley, Cissell. SB: D. Taylor. SH: Fonseca. DP: Sox. LOB: Cubs 5, Sox 5. BB: Faber 1, Root 2, Malone 1. Struck out: Faber 4, Root 3, Smith 1, May. 1. Hits: Faber 8 in 6.2 innings; Root 9 in 6 innings; Malone 1 in 0 innings (pitched to two men); Smith 5 in 1.2 innings; May 0 in 0. 1 innings. Winning pitcher: Faber. Losing pitcher: Root. Umpires: Quigley, Hildebrand, Magerkurth, Owens. Att: 42,000. Time—2:05.

Vic Frasier (13–15) held the Cubs to six hits the next day and ran their scoreless innings sreak to 17 before the Nationals were able to push across a lone run in the bottom of the ninth. Unfortunately for Frasier, the game had been scoreless up to that point. With one out in the ninth, Kiki Cuyler doubled to center. Les Bell fouled out for the second out of the inning, but Vince Barton's clutch single drove in Cuyler with the only run of the game. Guy Bush (16–8) went the distance for the Cubs and was the winning pitcher.

The series moved to Comiskey Park the next day for Game Three, Bob Smith (15–12) against Sox pitcher Ted Lyons (4–6). The Cubs broke on top in the first against Lyons when Woody English doubled to lead off the game, Billy Herman walked, and Cuyler sacrificed both runners over. With two out, Vince Barton's single made the score 2–0. The Sox cut the lead in half in the fourth on Watwood's double, Cissell's single, and Smead Jolley's sacrifice fly. In the ninth, the Americans loaded the bases with none out on singles by Lu Blue and Billy Sullivan and a walk to Bennie Tate. But Charlie Root came on in relief, retired Luke Appling on an infield pop, Ted Lyons on a force at the plate, and Johnny Watwood on a force at second—a money pitcher, Charlie Root.

The Sox tied the series in Game Four with the bat of Lew Fonseca and the strong arms of Tommy Thomas (10–14) and Vic Frasier. Leading 1–0 in the fifth, Fonseca's three-run homer gave the Sox a four-run margin. Thomas weakened and could retire no one in the eighth, allowing two runs, but Frasier came on to stifle the Cubs' rally. With the tying run on second and two out in the ninth, Frasier struck out Billy Herman to preserve the victory. Pat Malone

1931 Chicago City Championship Series

GAME SIX --- October 5

WHITE SOX	AB	R	H	PO	A	E		CUBS	AB	R	H	PO	A	E
Watwood, cf	2	1	2	1	0	0		English, ss	4	0	0	3	1	0
Norman, cf	1	0	0	0	0	0		Herman, 2b	4	0	1	4	6	0
Cissell, ss	4	0	0	1	1	0		Cuyler, cf	2	0	0	3	0	0
Jolley, rf	3	1	0	1	0	0		Bell, 3b	3	0	0	1	1	1
Fonseca, lf	5	0	2	4	0	0		Barton, rf	4	1	1	3	0	0
Blue, 1b	2	0	0	15	0	0		D.Taylor, lf	4	2	2	0	0	1
Sullivan, 3b	3	0	0	0	2	0		Grimm, 1b	3	0	1	7	1	0
Kerr, 2b	3	0	1	1	6	1		Hemsley, c	3	0	1	6	2	0
Grube, c	1	0	0	1	1	0		Bush, p	0	0	0	0	1	0
Tate, c	3	0	1	1	1	0		May, p	1	0	0	0	1	0
Frasier, c	4	0	0	0	2	0		Blair,, ph	1	0	0	0	0	0
								Root, p	0	0	0	0	0	0
	31	2	6*25	13	1				29	3	6	27	13	2

* One out when winning run scored

```
SOX   0 0 0   0 2 0   0 0 0  -  2
CUB   0 1 0   0 0 0   0 0 2  -  3
```

RBIs: D. Taylor, Fonseca, Kerr, Grimm 2. 2B: Fonseca, Hemsley, Watwood, Grimm. HR: D. Taylor. SH: Cuyler, Cissell, Grimm. DP: Cubs 1, Sox 1. LOB: Cubs 6, Sox 11. BB: Bush 6, Frasier 3. Struck out: Bush 3, Root 2, Frasier 2. Hits: Bush 5 in 4.2 innings; May 1 in 2.1 innings; Root 0 in 2 innings. WP: Root. Winning pitcher: Root. Umpires: Hildebrand, Magerkurth, Owens, Quigley. Time—2:00.

GAME SEVEN --- October 7

CUBS	AB	R	H	PO	A	E		WHITE SOX	AB	R	H	PO	A	E
English, ss	3	0	0	4	3	0		Cissell, ss	5	1	1	1	4	0
Herman, 2b	4	0	1	2	5	0		Sullivan, 3b	3	0	0	0	3	0
Cuyler, cf	4	1	1	4	0	0		Jolley, rf	4	1	0	2	0	0
Bell, 3b	4	0	1	2	1	1		Fonseca, lf	4	1	2	3	0	0
Barton, rf	4	0	0	2	0	0		Blue, 1b	4	1	1	16	0	0
D.Taylor, lf	3	0	0	2	1	0		Reynolds, cf	4	1	1	2	0	0
Grimm, 1b	3	1	1	10	1	0		Grube, c	2	1	1	3	0	0
Hemsley, c	3	0	0	1	1	1		Kerr, 2b	3	1	2	0	6	0
Smith, p	1	0	0	0	1	0		Thomas, p	4	0	1	0	3	0
May, p	0	0	0	0	1	0			33	7	9	27	16	0
Blair, ph	1	0	0	0	0	0								
Sweetland, p	0	0	0	0	0	0								
Hartnett, ph	1	0	0	0	0	0								
Malone, p	0	0	0	0	0	0								
	31	2	4	27	14	2								

```
SOX   0 1 0   6 0 0   0 0 0  -  7
CUB   1 0 0   0 0 0   0 1 0  -  2
```

RBIs: Bell, Kerr, Reynolds 2, Thomas, Cissell, Fonseca, Hemsley. 2B: Fonseca, Cuyler, Bell, Kerr. 3B: Grimm. SH: Grube. DP: Cubs 2. LOB: Cubs 3, Sox 4. BB: Smith 1, May 1, Malone 1, Thomas 1. Struck out: Malone 1, Thomas 2. Hits: Smith 6 in 3.1 innings; May 2 in 2.2 innings; Sweetland 1 in 2 innings. HBP: Sullivan (Smith). Losing pitcher: Smith. Umpires: Magerkurth, Owens, Quigley, Hildebrand. Time—1:31.

(16–9) gave up 12 hits and a walk in his six innings for the Cubs and was the losing pitcher. Jakie May pitched two innings of scoreless ball in relief of Malone.

The White Sox drew ahead in the series in the fifth game before 42,000 fans at Comiskey Park by plastering five Cubs' pitchers for 15 hits. Charlie Root and Red Faber were the starting pitchers and Faber again came away with a victory. The clubs exchanged runs in the first and the Cubs took a 3–1 lead in the fourth, but in the bottom of the fifth, Smead Jolley's grand-slam home run gave the Americans a 6–3 lead. The Cubs closed to within one, but the Sox struck for three in the bottom of the seventh off Pat Malone and Bob Smith. Four more insurance runs came off Smith and Jakie May in the eighth, the big hit a three-run homer by Bill Cissell. The final score was 13–6, Sox. Ted Lyons pitched the final two and a third innings to save Faber's victory.

It was Vic Frasier against Guy Bush as the Cubs evened the series in Game Six on the fifth of October. Danny Taylor's solo home run in the second put the Cubs on top 1–0, but the White Sox went ahead in the fifth. Johnny Watwood doubled and was sacrificed to third. Jolley was walked intentionally and Lew Fonseca's single drove home Watwood. Bush turned his ankle trying to turn a double play on Lu Blue and, after walking Billy Sullivan and John Kerr, had to leave the game. The walk to Kerr forced in a run and put the Sox on top, 2–1. Jakie May and Charlie Root, pitching in relief of Bush, held the Sox scoreless for the rest of the game. Vic Frasier took a four-hitter into the bottom of the ninth until Vince Barton singled with one out. Danny Taylor's ground-ball to John Kerr should have been turned for a game-ending double play, but Kerr threw wild to Cissell at second and both men were safe. Charlie Grimm's two-run double forced a seventh and deciding game.

It all came down to pitching in the finale and the Cubs didn't have any. Tommy Thomas won his second game of the series by scattering four hits and two runs as the Sox were triumphant by a 7–2 score. Back-to-back doubles by Kiki Cuyler and Les Bell put the Cubs ahead 1–0 in the first, but the Sox matched that run in the next half-inning and then exploded for six runs in the fourth off losing pitcher Bob Smith and reliever Jakie May. The final Cubs' run came in the eighth on a triple by Grimm and an out by Rollie Hemsley.

The 1933 Chicago City Championship Series

Chicago White Sox defeat Chicago Cubs; 4–0

The third-place Chicago Cubs (86–68), losers of the 1933 National League pennant by six games, met a vastly inferior sixth-place White Sox team (67–83) in the Chicago city championship series and came away second best in a stunning upset. This was the thirteenth victory for the Sox in 20 postseason meetings with their National League rivals. Cubs' president William Veeck died during the series, and this may have had some affect upon the Cubs' play.

Game One featured the six-hit pitching of "Sad Sam" Jones (10–12) as the Sox ambushed Guy Bush (20–12), scoring all three of their runs in the second

1933 Chicago City Championship Series

GAME ONE --- October 4

WHITE SOX	AB	H	PO	A	E		CUBS	AB	H	PO	A	E
Swanson, rf	4	2	2	0	0		English, 3b	4	0	1	1	0
Haas, cf	4	1	2	0	0		W.Herman, 2b	4	0	3	6	0
Dykes, 3b	4	2	0	3	0		Cuyler, cf	3	2	2	1	0
Simmons, lf	4	0	1	0	0		F.Herman, rf	4	0	5	0	0
Appling	4	1	2	4	0		Stephenson, lf	4	1	1	0	0
Kress, 1b	3	1	16	0	0		Grimm, 1b	4	1	9	0	0
Hayes, 2b	4	1	2	8	0		Hartnett, c	3	1	4	0	0
Berry, c	4	0	2	0	0		Jurges, ss	3	0	2	5	1
Jones, p	3	1	0	0	0		Bush, p	2	1	0	1	0
							Mosolf, ph	1	0	0	0	0
	34	9	27	15	0		Nelson, p	0	0	0	0	0
								32	6	27	14	1

```
SOX   0  3  0    0  0  0    0  0  0  -  3
CUB   0  0  0    1  0  0    0  0  1  -  2
```

Runs: Hayes, Berry, Jones, Cuyler, Stephenson. RBIs: Swanson 2, Haas, Stephenson, Hartnett. 2B: Cuyler, Grimm. SH: Kress. DP: Sox 1, Cubs 2. LOB: Sox 5, Cubs 4. BB: Jones 1. Struck out: Jones 2, Bush 2, Nelson 1. Hits: Bush 8 in 8 innings; Nelson 1 in 1 inning. Losing pitcher: Bush. Umpires: Rigler, Owens, Reardon, Geisel. Scorer: Simons. Att: 12,000.

GAME TWO --- October 5

WHITE SOX	AB	H	PO	A	E		CUBS	AB	H	PO	A	E
Swanson, rf	3	0	2	0	0		English, 3b	2	1	1	1	0
Haas, cf	4	1	1	0	0		W.Herman, 2b	4	1	2	4	0
Dykes, 3b	4	3	0	2	0		Cuyler, cf	4	0	2	0	0
Simmons, lf	4	2	0	0	0		F.Herman, rf	4	0	1	0	0
Appling, ss	4	0	3	8	0		Stephenson, lf	4	0	1	0	0
Kress, 1b	4	1	13	1	0		Grimm, 1b	4	0	10	1	0
Hayes, 2b	4	1	5	7	0		Hartnett, c	3	2	6	0	0
Berry, c	4	0	2	0	0		Jurges, ss	2	1	4	7	0
Faber, p	3	0	1	3	0		Warneke, p	2	0	0	1	1
							Campbell, ph	1	0	0	0	0
	34	8	27	21	0		Malone, p	0	0	0	0	0
								30	5	27	13	1

```
SOX   0  0  0    0  0  1    0  1  0  -  2
CUB   0  0  0    0  0  0    0  0  0  -  0
```

Runs: Swanson, Faber. RBIs: Simmons 2. 2B: Hartnett 2. SH: Jurges. DP: Sox 1, Cubs 2. LOB: Cub 6, Sox 7. BB: Faber 2, Warneke 2. Struck out: Faber 2, Warneke 5. Hits: Warneke 7 in 8 innings; Malone 1 in 1 inning. Losing pitcher: Warneke. Umpires: Owens, Reardon, Geisel, Rigler. Att: 12,000. Time–1:53.

inning on four singles and an error by Billy Jurges. Evar Swanson had two RBIs and Mule Haas another in the decisive inning. The Sox had nine hits, all singles.

Red Faber (3–4) never let more than one Cub baserunner reach base in any inning and shut out Lon Warneke (18–13) and Pat Malone (10–14) in Game Two. The game was scoreless until Evar Swanson walked in the sixth, went to second on Jimmy Dykes's single, and scored on a single by Al Simmons. Simmons figured in the scoring again in the eighth when he drove in Faber with a sacrifice fly. Faber allowed five hits while recording the shutout.

The Sox again shut out the Cubs in Game Three on the 7th of October.

1933 Chicago City Championship Series

GAME THREE --- October 7

CUBS	AB	H	PO	A	E		WHITE SOX	AB	H	PO	A	E
English, 3b	4	0	1	2	0		Swanson, rf	4	1	2	0	0
W.Herman, 2b	4	2	1	2	0		Haas, cf	3	0	4	0	0
Cuyler, cf	4	1	3	0	0		Dykes, 3b	5	2	1	1	0
F.Herman, rf	4	1	2	0	0		Simmons, lf	4	1	3	0	0
Stephenson, lf	4	1	1	0	0		Appling, ss	4	0	1	4	0
Grimm, 1b	4	0	7	1	0		Kress, 1b	4	3	10	0	0
Hartnett, c	3	1	6	0	0		Hayes, 2b	4	1	1	5	1
Jurges, ss	4	1	2	2	1		Berry, c	4	2	5	0	1
Root, p	2	0	0	0	0		Lyons, p	3	1	0	2	0
Tinning, p	0	0	0	1	0							
Mosolf, ph	1	0	0	0	0			35	11	27	12	2
Nelson, p	0	0	1	0	0							
	34	7	24	8	1							

```
CUB   0 0 0   0 0 0   0 0 0  -  0
SOX   0 4 0   0 4 0   1 0 x  -  9
```

Runs: Swanson, Haas, Simmons, Kress 2, Hayes 2, Berry. RBIs: Swanson, Dykes 3, Kress 2, Hayes 2, Berry. 2B: Jurges, Dykes, Hayes, Berry. HR: Kress. SH: Haas. LOB: Sox 7, Cubs 8. BB: Root 3, Lyons 1. Struck out: Root 2, Nelson 2, Lyons 4. Hits: Root 6 in 4.2 innings; Tinning 3 in 1.1 innings; Nelson 2 in 2 innings. HBP: Swanson (Root). Losing pitcher: Root. Umpires: Reardon, Geisel, Rigler, Owens. Scorer: Simons. Att: 9,152. Time—1:31.

GAME FOUR --- October 9

CUBS	AB	H	PO	A	E		WHITE SOX	AB	H	PO	A	E
English, 3b	4	1	0	5	0		Swanson, rf	5	2	2	0	0
W.Herman, 2b	4	0	3	2	0		Haas, cf	4	2	1	0	0
Cuyler, cf	4	1	1	0	0		Dykes, 3b	3	2	0	3	0
F.Herman, rf	4	1	1	0	0		Simmons, lf	3	1	2	0	0
Stephenson, lf	4	2	2	0	0		Appling, ss	3	0	1	2	0
Hendrick, 1b	3	1	10	0	0		Kress, 1b	3	0	10	1	0
Hartnett, c	4	1	7	2	0		Hayes, 2b	4	1	4	4	0
Jurges, ss	2	0	0	4	0		Berry, c	4	1	6	0	0
Koenig, ss	2	0	0	0	0		Heving, p	4	1	1	2	0
Bush, p	0	0	0	0	0							
Malone, p	3	0	0	4	0			33	10	27	12	0
	34	7	24	17	0							

```
CUB   0 0 0   0 0 0   0 0 1  -  1
SOX   2 0 0   0 0 0   1 2 x  -  5
```

Runs: Stephenson, Swanson, Haas, Dykes, Hayes, Berry. RBIs: Hendrick, Haas, Dykes, Simmons, Heving 2. 2B: Stephenson, Haas, Heving. 3B: Simmons. SB: Swanson. LOB: Sox 9, Cubs 7. BB: Malone 5. Struck out: Malone 2, Heving 5. Hits: Bush 3 in 0.1 innings; Malone 7 in 7.2 innings. HBP: Hendrick (Heving). Losing pitcher: Bush. Umpires: Geisel, Rigler, Owens, Reardon. Att: 24,321. Time—1:46.

Ted Lyons scattered seven Cub hits, Red Kress had two singles and a home run, and Jimmy Dykes had three runs batted in as Cub pitchers served up four-run innings in the second and fifth. The final score was 9–0 with Lyons the winning pitcher and Root taking the loss.

Joe Heving (7–5) went against Guy Bush of the Cubs in Game Four as the Sox completed their sweep of the series. The Americans roughed up Bush in the first for all the runs they needed when Haas doubled, Dykes singled, and Al Simmons tripled. The Sox scored three more times off reliever Pat Malone. The Cubs ran their scoreless inning streak to 26 until they finally broke through for a run against Heving in the ninth when Riggs Stephenson doubled and scored on Harvey Hendrick's infield out. The final score was 5-1.

The 1936 Chicago City Championship Series

Chicago White Sox defeat Chicago Cubs; 4-0

The Chicago Cubs (87-67) won 100 games and the pennant in 1935 and were still a very strong team the following season despite winning 13 less games. Their cross-town rivals, the Chicago White Sox (81-70), had improved to third place and a better-than-.500 record for the first time since 1926. The teams had not played a postseason championship series for three years and attendance was good for most of the games.

1936 Chicago City Championship Series

GAME ONE --- October 1

WHITE SOX	AB	R	H	PO	A	E		CUBS	AB	R	H	PO	A	E
Radcliff, lf	4	1	1	2	0	0		Galan, cf	4	0	1	2	0	0
Rosenthal, cf	4	0	2	3	0	0		Cavaretta, 1b	4	0	0	8	1	1
Haas, rf	4	0	0	3	0	0		Herman, 2b	3	0	0	2	3	0
Bonura, 1b	3	0	0	8	1	0		Demaree, rf	3	0	0	3	0	0
Appling, ss	2	1	1	5	1	0		Hack, 3b	3	0	1	0	1	0
Hayes, 2b	4	1	1	3	3	0		Hartnett, c	4	0	0	7	1	0
Dykes, 3b	3	1	1	0	1	1		Gill, lf	4	1	2	1	0	0
Sewell, c	3	1	0	3	0	0		Jurges, ss	4	0	0	3	5	0
Kennedy, p	4	0	0	0	2	0		Lee, p	1	0	0	1	1	0
								Carleton, p	1	0	0	0	0	0
	31	5	6	27	8	1		Lillard, ph	0	0	0	0	0	0
								O'Dea, ph	1	0	0	0	0	0
									32	1	4	27	12	1

```
SOX    0  0  0    0  5  0    0  0  0  -  5
CUB    0  0  0    0  0  0    0  0  1  -  1
```

2B: Rosenthal, Gill. HR: Radcliff. SH: Dykes. SB: Appling. BB: Lee 2, Carleton 2, Kennedy 5. Struck out: Lee 1, Carleton 6, Kennedy 2. Hits: Lee 4 in 5 innings. DP: Cubs. Losing pitcher: Lee. LOB: Sox 4, Cubs 9. Umpires: Barr, Stewart, McGowan, Ormsby. Time—1:37.

Game One on the 1st of October saw the White Sox land on the Cubs with five runs in the fifth inning to ruin a perfectly good pitching duel between Bill Lee (18-11) and Vern Kennedy (21-9). Luke Appling walked and Jack Hayes singled. Phil Cavaretta made an error on Jimmy Dykes's attempted sacrifice, allowing Appling to score the first run of the game. Luke Sewell was intentionally walked so that Lee might pitch to Rip Radcliff, the Sox left fielder. Radcliff spoiled the strategy in the worst way possible by belting a grand slam home run into the right field stands. Lee retired the side, but gave way to Tex Carleton (14-10) in the bottom of the inning. Kennedy was the winning pitcher, Lee the loser. The final score was 5-1.

1936 Chicago City Championship Series

GAME TWO --- October 2

CUBS	AB	R	H	PO	A	E	WHITE SOX	AB	R	H	PO	A	E
Galan, cf	4	0	0	3	0	0	Radcliff, lf	3	2	0	2	0	0
Cavaretta, 1b	4	1	2	8	1	2	Rosenthal, cf	4	2	2	3	0	0
Herman, 2b	2	0	0	4	2	0	Haas, rf	3	2	0	1	0	0
Demaree, rf	1	0	1	2	2	0	Bonura, 1b	3	1	1	12	0	0
English, 2b	4	0	1	1	0	0	Appling, ss	5	1	3	6	3	0
Hack, 2b	3	1	1	0	1	1	Hayes, 2b	4	0	0	1	7	0
Hartnett, c	3	0	2	3	0	0	Dykes, 3b	3	1	1	0	4	0
O'Dea, c	1	1	0	1	0	0	Sewell, c	5	1	1	2	0	0
Gill, lf	4	0	2	2	0	0	Stratton, p	4	1	1	0	1	0
Jurges, ss	4	0	1	0	4	0							
Warneke, p	2	0	0	0	0	1		34	11	9	27	15	0
Henshaw, p	0	0	0	0	0	0							
Bryant, p	0	0	0	0	1	0							
Allen, ph	0	0	0	0	0	0							
Root, p	0	0	0	0	1	0							
Lillard, ph	1	0	0	0	0	0							
Grimm, ph	1	0	0	0	0	0							
	34	3	10	24	12	4							

```
CUB   0  1  0   0  0  0   0  1  1  -  3
SOX   3  0  0   0  0  8   0  0  x  - 11
```

2B: Appling, English. SH: Hayes. DP: Sox 2, Cubs 2. LOB: Cubs 6, Sox 9. BB: Warneke 3, Stratton 1, Henshaw 2, Bryant 4. Struck out: Warneke 3, Stratton 1. Hits: Warneke 7 in 5.1 innings; Henshaw 0 in 0 innings (pitched to 3 batters in sixth); Bryant 1 in 1.2 innings: Root 1 in 1 inning. HBP: Herman (Stratton). Winning pitcher: Stratton. Losing pitcher: Warneke. Umpires: Ormsby, Stewart, McGowan, Barr. Time—1:58.

GAME THREE --- October 3

CUBS	AB	R	H	PO	A	E	WHITE SOX	AB	R	H	PO	A	E
Galan, cf	4	1	1	1	0	0	Radcliff, lf	3	1	0	0	0	0
Cavaretta, 1b	4	0	0	13	0	0	Rosenthal, cf	4	2	2	3	0	0
Gill, lf	4	1	2	3	0	0	Haas, rf	4	0	0	0	0	0
Demaree, rf	4	0	3	3	3	0	Bonura, 1b	3	0	0	11	0	0
Hack, 3b	3	0	0	2	0	0	Appling, ss	3	0	1	5	3	0
Hartnett, c	4	0	1	2	3	0	Hayes, 2b	3	0	0	3	9	0
English, 2b	4	0	1	1	1	1	Dykes, 3b	3	0	1	2	0	0
Jurges, ss	4	0	0	1	1	0	Sewell, c	3	1	0	3	0	0
Davis, p	1	0	1	0	0	0	Lyons, p	1	0	0	0	2	0
Lee, p	1	0	0	0	0	0							
O'Dea, ph	1	0	0	0	0	0		27	4	4	27	14	0
Root, p	0	0	0	0	0	0							
Allen, p	1	0	0	0	0	0							
	35	2	9	24	10	1							

```
CUB   0  0  1   0  1  0   0  0  0  -  2
SOX   1  0  3   0  0  0   0  0  x  -  4
```

RBI: Hack, Demaree, Rosenthal, Haas, Appling. 2B: Rosethal, Gill. SH: Lyons. DP: Sox. LOB: Cubs 7, Sox 3. BB: Davis 2, Root 1. Struck out: Lyons 2, Lee 1, Root 1. Hits: Davis 3 in 2.2 innings; Lee 0 in 3.1 innings; Root 1 in 2 innings. HBP: Hack (Lyons). WP: Davis. Losing pitcher: Davis. Umpires: Stewart, McGowan, Barr and Ormsby. Time—1:25.

1936 Chicago City Championship Series

GAME FOUR --- October 5

	AB	R	H	PO	A	E		AB	R	H	PO	A	E
Galan, cf	4	1	1	2	1	0	Radcliff, lf	4	1	2	3	0	0
Cavaretta, 1b	4	1	2	11	0	0	Rosenthal, cf	4	2	3	3	1	0
Gill, lf	4	0	1	1	0	0	Haas, rf	4	2	1	2	0	0
Demaree, rf	4	0	1	0	0	0	Bonura, 1b	5	1	5	9	1	0
Hack, 3b	2	0	0	3	0	0	Appling, ss	4	1	2	1	7	0
Hartnett, c	4	0	0	5	1	0	Hayes, 2b	5	1	2	4	5	0
English, 2b	2	0	0	0	5	0	Dykes, 3b	4	0	2	1	0	0
Jurges, ss	3	0	1	2	3	1	Sewell, c	4	0	0	2	0	0
French, p	0	0	0	0	0	0	Dietrich, p	4	0	0	2	1	0
Warneke, p	0	0	0	0	0	0							
Stainback, ph	1	0	0	0	0	0		38	8	17	27	15	0
Lee, p	1	0	0	0	2	0							
O'Dea, ph	1	0	0	0	0	0							
Davis, p	0	0	0	0	0	0							
Root, p	0	0	0	0	0	0							
	30	2	6	24	12	1							

```
CUB   1 0 0   1 0 0   0 0 0  -  2
SOX   4 0 0   0 1 0   0 0 x  -  5
```

RBI: Gill, Demaree, Bonura 4, Dykes 2, Hayes, Appling. 2B: Rosethal, Gill, Cavaretta, Bonura. 3B: Radcliff. SB: Galan. SH: Appling. DP: Sox 1, Cubs 2. LOB: Cubs 5, Sox 10. BB: Dietrich 4, Lee 3. Hits: French 5 in ⅔ inning; Warneke 2 in 1.2 innings; Lee 5 in 4 innings; Davis 4 in 1.2 innings; Root 1 in ⅓ inning. Losing pitcher: French. Umpires: McGowan, Barr, Ormsby, Steward. Time—1:47.

The Americans were right back at it the next day, drilling the Cubs 11–3. Leading 3–1 into the bottom of the sixth, the Sox raked three Cubs pitchers for eight runs to take a commanding lead. Ray Phelps (4–6) was the winning pitcher while Lon Warneke (16–13), Roy Henshaw (6–5), Clay Bryant (1–2) and Charlie Root (3–6) worked for the Cubs, Warneke taking the loss.

The White Sox made it three straight as they won Game Three behind the erratic pitching of Ted Lyons (10–13). Lyons allowed nine hits and worked out of trouble all afternoon long, but stranded seven Cub baserunners and held on for the 4–2 victory. The White Sox took a 1–0 lead in the first when Larry Rosenthal scored from first on a wild pitch. The Cubs tied the game in the third, but an error by their shortstop, Billy Jurges, set the stage for three uncarned Sox runs in the bottom of the inning. Curt Davis (11–9), Bill Lee and Charley Root pitched for the Cubs, Davis taking the loss.

The White Sox completed the sweep of the series after a day off and clinched the championship by beating the Cubs in easy fashion, 8–2. Bill Dietrich (4–4 with the Sox) threw a complete game six-hitter for the Americans. Trailing 1–0 in the bottom of the first, the White Sox scored four runs off Cubs starter Larry French (18–9). Larry Rosenthal doubled and went to third on a single by Mule Haas. Zeke Bonura's double scored both men to put the Sox on top, 2–1. Bonura was thrown out trying to advance on Luke Appling's fielder's choice, but Jack Hayes grounded an infield single off Billy Jurges' glove and when Jurges made an ill-advised throw to first, the ball went into the dugout. Appling went to third and Hayes to second. Jimmy Dykes's single drove both men in and French retired in favor of Lon Warneke. The Cubs pulled to within two on a double by Cavaretta and a single by Frank Demaree, but that was as close as they would come. Four more White Sox runs made a winner of Dietrich. French took the loss. Zeke Bonura had a perfect 5-for-5 with a double and four RBIs.

The 1937 Chicago City Championship Series

Chicago White Sox defeat Chicago Cubs; 4–3

The third-place White Sox (86–68) had their best winning percentage since 1920 and prepared to meet the second-place Cubs (93–61) in the Chicago city championship. The Cubs had narrowly lost the pennant to the New York Giants (95–57), and would not finish with a .600 winning percentage until the pennant-winning year of 1945.

1937 Chicago City Championship Series

```
GAME ONE --- October 6
```

CUBS	AB	H	PO	A	E		WHITE SOX	AB	H	PO	A	E
Hack, 3b	4	1	1	2	0		Piet, 3b	3	0	1	2	0
Herman, 2b	5	3	2	4	1		Kreevich, cf	4	0	2	0	0
Demaree, rf	5	1	1	0	0		Walker, rf	3	0	2	0	0
Hartnett, c	5	1	5	0	0		Radcliff, lf	4	2	1	0	0
Cavaretta, 1b	5	2	11	1	0		Appling, ss	3	0	2	3	0
Marty, cf	3	1	2	0	0		Bonura, 1b	4	0	14	2	0
Galan, lf	4	3	1	0	0		Hayes, 2b	3	0	3	3	0
Stainback, lf	0	0	1	0	0		Sewell, c	4	2	1	1	0
Frey, ss	4	3	2	2	0		Lyons, p	2	1	1	2	0
Carleton, p	4	0	1	3	0		Dietrich, p	1	0	0	2	0
							Rosenthal, ph	1	0	0	0	0
	39	15	27	12	1			32	5	27	15	0

```
CUB   0  0  0    0  1  3    0  3  0  -  7
SOX   0  2  0    0  0  0    0  1  0  -  3
```

Runs: Herman, Demaree, Cavaretta 2, Galan 2, Frey, Piet, Bonura, Hayes. RBIs: Demaree, Cavaretta, Marty, Galan, Frey, Carleton 2, Radcliff, Lyons 2. 2B: Hack, Demaree, Cavaretta, Galan. 3B: Frey. SB: Bonura. DP: Sox 2. LOB: Cubs 7, Sox 6. BB: Carleton 4, Dietrich 1. Struck out: Carleton 5, Lyons 1. Hits: Lyons 9 in 5.1 innings; Dietrich 6 in 2.2 innings. Losing pitcher: Lyons. Umpires: Summers, Sears, Quinn, Pinelli. Time—1:43.

The series opened October 6th at Comiskey Park with the ace of the Cubs' pitching staff, Tex Carleton (16–8), going against 36-year-old Sox veteran Ted Lyons (12–7). Carleton was touched for two Sox runs in the second when Zeke Bonura reached on an error, Jack Hayes walked, and Luke Sewell and Lyons hit back-to-back singles. But he settled down after that, retiring the Sox in order from the fourth through the seventh innings, by which time he had a comfortable 7–2 lead. The Cubs' first run came in the fifth when Augie Galan and Lonnie Frey singled and Galan scored on a double play. The Nationals sent Lyons to the showers in the next inning with three runs. Billy Herman singled, Frank Demaree and Phil Cavaretta doubled and Joe Marty and Frey singled. Three insurance runs in the eighth put the Cubs safely ahead. Carleton went

1937 Chicago City Championship Series

GAME TWO --- October 7

CUBS	AB	H	PO	A	E		WHITE SOX	AB	H	PO	A	E
Hack, 3b	4	0	0	1	0		Piet, 3b-2b	4	1	2	5	0
Herman, 2b	3	1	2	1	0		Kreevich, cf	4	1	2	0	0
Stainback, lf	1	0	1	0	0		Walker, rf	3	2	2	0	0
Demaree, rf	4	0	2	0	0		Radcliff, lf	3	1	2	0	0
Hartnett, c	1	0	3	1	1		Appling, ss	3	1	4	2	1
Cavaretta, 1b	4	0	5	1	0		Bonura, 1b	3	1	9	1	0
Marty, cf	4	0	1	0	0		Hayes, 2b	3	0	1	2	0
Galan, lf-2b	3	0	5	1	1		Rosenthal, ph	0	0	0	0	0
Frey, ss	4	2	3	4	0		Berger, 3b	0	0	0	0	0
Davis, p	2	0	2	3	0		Sewell, c	4	1	4	0	0
O'Dea, ph	0	0	0	0	0		Kennedy, p	4	1	1	2	0
Root, p	0	0	0	0	0			---	---	---	---	---
Collins, ph	1	0	0	0	0			31	9	27	12	1
	---	---	---	---	---							
	31	3	24	12	2							

```
CUB   0 0 0   0 0 0   0 1 0  -  1
SOX   0 0 0   1 0 0   0 2 x  -  3
```

Runs: Stainback, Kreevich, Walker, Bonura. RBIs: Radcliff, Sewell 2. SB: Stainback. SH: Radcliff. DP: Cubs 2. LOB: Cubs 8, Sox 9. BB: Davis 2, Root 2, Kennedy 5. Struck out: Davis 1, Kennedy 3. Hits: Davis 7 in 7 innings; Root 2 in 1 inning. Losing pitcher: Root. Umpires: Sears, Quinn, Pinelli, Summers. Time—1:44.

GAME THREE --- October 8

WHITE SOX	AB	H	PO	A	E		CUBS	AB	H	PO	A	E
Piet, 3b	4	0	1	0	0		Hack, 3b	4	1	1	5	0
Kreevich, cf	4	0	2	0	0		Herman, 2b	3	2	4	2	0
Walker, rf	4	0	1	0	0		Demaree, rf	4	2	1	0	0
Appling, ss	4	2	3	3	0		Hartnett, c	3	2	4	1	0
Radcliff, lf	2	1	3	0	0		Cavaretta, 1b	4	1	12	1	0
Bonura, 1b	3	0	10	0	1		Marty, cf	4	0	3	0	0
Hayes, 2b	3	1	0	3	0		Galan, lf	3	0	0	0	0
Sewell, c	3	0	2	1	0		Frey, ss	4	0	1	6	0
T.Lee, p	1	0	0	0	0		French, p	4	1	1	1	0
Rensa, ph	1	0	0	0	0			---	---	---	---	---
Rigney, p	0	0	0	0	0			33	11	27	16	0
Berger, ph	1	0	0	0	0							
Cain, p	0	0	0	0	0							
	---	---	---	---	---							
	30	4	24	7	1							

```
SOX   0 0 0   0 0 0   0 1 0  -  1
CUB   0 0 2   1 1 0   0 0 x  -  4
```

Runs: Hayes, Herman 2, Hartnett, Galan. RBIs: Hartnett 2, Marty, French, Hayes. 2B: Galan, Appling, Demaree. 3B: French. HR: Hartnett, Hayes. DP: Sox 1, Cubs 1. LOB: Sox 3, Cubs 9. BB: T. Lee 3, Rigney 1, French 4. Hits: T. Lee 9 in 5 innings; Rigney 2 in 2 innings; Cain 0 in 1 inning. HBP: Radcliff (French). Losing pitcher: T. Lee. Umpires: Quinn, Pinelli, Summers, Sears. Att: 10,658. Time—1:21.

the distance and scattered five hits. Bill Dietrich (8–10) pitched in relief of Lyons who took the loss.

Game Two was played the next day, Curt Davis (10–5) against Vern Kennedy (14–13). The Cubs, who had belted out 15 hits just 24 hours earlier, were limited to three safeties by Kennedy, none of which figured in the scoring. Trailing 1–0 in the top of the eighth, Tuck Stainback walked, stole second, and

1937 Chicago City Championship Series

GAME FOUR --- October 9

WHITE SOX	AB	H	PO	A	E		CUBS	AB	H	PO	A	E
Piet, 3b	4	1	0	1	2		Hack, 3b	5	1	1	2	0
Kreevich, cf	5	3	2	0	0		Herman, 2b	5	1	3	7	1
Walker, rf	4	0	5	0	0		Demaree, rf	4	0	1	0	0
Radcliff, lf	5	2	1	1	0		Hartnett, c	1	0	6	1	0
Appling, ss	3	2	3	3	1		O'Dea, c	2	0	1	1	0
Bonura, 1b	5	3	9	1	1		Cavaretta, 1b	4	4	10	0	0
Hayes, 2b	4	2	3	6	0		Marty, cf	4	0	2	0	0
Sewell, c	4	2	3	1	0		Galan, lf	4	0	1	0	0
Whitehead, p	5	1	1	2	0		Frey, ss	2	0	2	2	1
							W.Lee, p	1	0	0	0	1
	39	16	27	15	4		Bryant, p	1	1	0	0	1
							Parmelee, p	1	0	0	1	0
							Shoun, p	0	0	0	0	0
							Collins, ph	1	0	0	0	0
								35	7	27	14	4

```
SOX   0  2  3    0  4  2    0  0  3  -  14
CUB   0  1  1    0  0  0    0  0  0  -   2
```

Runs: Piet, Kreevich 3, Radcliff 3, Appling 2, Bonura 2, Hayes 2, Sewell, Demaree, Hartnett. RBIs: Kreevich, Radcliff 2, Appling, Bonura 4, Hayes 2, Sewell, Whitehead 2, Galan. 2B: Bonura, Appling, Bryant. 3B: Hayes. HR: Bonura. SB: Appling. SH: Kreevich, Walker 2. DP: Sox 2, Cubs 1. LOB: Sox 8, Cubs 9. BB: Whitehead 3, Bryant 3, Shoun 1. Struck out: Whitehead 3, W. Lee 2, Bryant 3, Shoun 1. Hits: W. Lee 5 in 2.1 innings; Bryant 7 in 3 innings; Parmelee 0 in 2.2 innings; Shoun 2 in 1 inning. HBP: Piet (Lee), Appling (Bryant), Piet (Parmelee). WP: Shoun. Balk: W. Lee. PB: O'Dea. Losing pitcher: W. Lee. Umpires: Pinelli, Summers, Sears, Quinn. Time—2:14.

GAME FIVE --- October 11

CUBS	AB	H	PO	A	E		WHITE SOX	AB	H	PO	A	E
Hack, 3b	4	1	0	1	0		Berger, 3b	2	1	2	0	0
Herman, 2b	4	0	2	3	0		Kreevich, cf	3	2	3	0	0
Demaree, rf	4	2	4	1	0		Walker, rf	4	1	1	0	0
Hartnett, c	4	2	4	1	0		Radcliff, lf	4	2	0	0	0
Cavaretta, 1b	3	0	8	2	0		Appling, ss	4	0	9	4	0
Marty, cf	4	2	2	0	0		Bonura, 1b	4	1	8	3	0
Galan, lf	3	1	1	0	0		Hayes, 2b	4	0	1	4	0
Frey, ss	4	2	3	4	1		Sewell, c	2	1	3	1	0
Carleton, p	2	1	0	1	1		Stratton, p	2	0	0	0	1
O'Dea, ph	1	0	0	0	0		Brown, p	0	0	0	0	0
Root, p	0	0	0	0	0			29	8	27	12	1
Collins, ph	1	0	0	0	0							
	34	11	24	13	2							

```
CUB   0  0  1    0  0  0    2  0  1  -  4
SOX   1  0  2    0  1  0    2  0  x  -  6
```

Runs: Marty 2, Galan, Carleton, Berger 2, Kreevich 2, Sewell, Brown. RBIs: Demaree, Marty, Frey, O'Dea, Kreevich 2, Walker 2, Radcliff 2. 2B: Hartnett. HR: Kreevich, Marty. SH: Brown, Berger. DP: Cubs 2, Sox 3. LOB: Cubs 5, Sox 4. BB: Carleton 3, Stratton 2. Struck out: Carleton 3, Stratton 1. Hits: Carleton 6 in 6 innings; Root 2 in 2 innings; Stratton 8 in 6 innings (none out in seventh); Brown 3 in 1 inning. Winning pitcher: Stratton. Losing pitcher: Carleton. Umpires: Summers, Sears, Quinn, Pinelli. Att: 11,575. Time—1:39.

1937 Chicago City Championship Series

```
GAME SIX --- October 12
```

CUBS	AB	H	PO	A	E		WHITE SOX	AB	H	PO	A	E
Hack, 3b	5	2	0	1	0		Berger, 3b	4	0	1	0	0
Herman, 2b	3	2	6	4	0		Kreevich, cf	4	2	2	0	0
Demaree, rf	5	2	1	1	0		Walker, rf	4	2	3	1	0
Hartnett, c	3	2	6	0	0		Appling, ss	3	2	3	1	0
Cavaretta, 1b	3	0	9	0	0		Radcliff, lf	3	0	3	0	0
Marty, cf	5	2	1	0	0		Bonura, 1b	3	1	5	1	0
Stainback, lf	5	2	0	0	0		Hayes, 2b	2	0	2	4	0
Frey, ss	5	1	4	7	1		Sewell, c	4	0	7	1	0
French, p	4	2	0	3	0		Kennedy, p	1	0	1	1	0
							Rensa, ph	1	0	0	0	0
	38	15	27	16	1		Brown, p	0	0	0	0	0
							Dykes, ph	1	0	0	0	0
								30	7	27	9	0

```
CUB  1 2 0   0 1 0   0 1 1 - 6
SOX  0 0 0   2 0 0   0 0 0 - 2
```

Runs: Hack, Herman, Demaree, Cavaretta, Frey, French, Walker, Appling. RBIs: Hack, Herman, Demaree 2, Marty, Stainback, Bonura 2. 2B: Demaree. 3B: Hack, Herman. SH: Hartnett. DP: Cubs 4, Sox 1. LOB: Cubs 11, Sox 7. BB: French 5, Kennedy 4, Brown 1. Struck out: French 4, Kennedy 3, Brown 1. Hits: Kennedy 8 in 7 innings; Brown 7 in 2 innings. HBP: Radcliff (French). PB: Sewell. Losing pitcher: Kennedy. Umpires: Sears, Quinn, Pinelli, Summers. Att: 4,241. Time—1:47.

scored on a two-base throwing error by Luke Appling. The Sox went on to win in their half of the inning when a single by Dixie Walker, walks to Zeke Bonura and pinch-hitter Larry Rosenthal, and a Luke Sewell single sent two runs across the plate. Davis took the loss while Charlie Root (13–5) pitched a scoreless eighth in relief.

The Cubs moved ahead in the third game as Larry French (16–10) stopped the Sox on four hits and a futile eighth-inning run. Gabby Hartnett's two-run homer in the third provided all the offense French would need. A double by Augie Galan and a triple by French in the fourth added another run and Billy Herman scored the Cubs' final run in the fifth. Thornton Lee (12–10) was the Sox starter and took the loss in his five-inning stint. Rookie Johnny Rigney (2–5) and Merritt "Sugar" Cain (4–2) worked in relief of Lee.

John Whitehead (11–8) started the fourth game and his American League teammates responded with 16 hits and five multiple-run innings, winning in a walk, 14–2. The big hitters for the Sox were Zeke Bonura with a 3-for-5 including a double, a homer, and four RBIs and Mike Kreevich, 3-for-5 with an RBI and three runs scored. Even Whitehead chipped in with a single and two runs batted in. The Sox scored twice in the second, three times in the third, four times in the fifth, twice more in the sixth, and capped it off with a three-run ninth. The only Cub batter who gave Whitehead any trouble at all was Phil Cavaretta who was a perfect 4-for-4. The Cubs used four pitchers in the slaughter — loser Bill Lee (14–15), Clay Bryant (9–3), Roy Parmalee (7–8), and Clyde Shoun (7–7).

The White Sox took a three-games-to-two lead in the fifth game, despite being outhit by an 11–8 margin. Mike Kreevich's solo home run gave winner Monte Stratton (15–5) a first-inning lead, but the Cubs tied the game in the top of the third on two hits and a Stratton error. The Sox went ahead to stay when

1937 Chicago City Championship Series

```
GAME SEVEN --- October 13
```

WHITE SOX	AB	H	PO	A	E
Berger, 3b	5	0	0	3	0
Kreevich, cf	5	1	0	0	0
Walker, rf	4	0	2	0	0
Radcliff, lf	5	2	0	0	0
Appling, ss	1	1	2	6	0
Bonura, 1b	4	2	16	0	0
Hayes, 2b	3	1	4	8	0
Sewell, c	3	0	3	1	0
Whitehead, p	4	0	0	2	0
	34	7	27	20	0

CUBS	AB	H	PO	A	E
Hack, 3b	4	2	1	2	0
Herman, 2b	4	2	4	0	0
Demaree, rf	4	3	4	0	0
Hartnett, c	4	0	5	0	1
Cavaretta, 1b	3	1	5	2	0
Marty, cf	3	0	4	0	0
Stainback, lf	3	0	1	0	0
Frey, ss	3	1	1	4	1
Davis, p	1	0	0	0	0
O'Dea, ph	1	0	0	0	0
Carleton, p	0	0	2	1	0
Collins, ph	1	0	0	0	0
	31	9	27	9	2

```
SOX   0 2 0   2 0 1   1 0 0 - 6
CUB   1 0 0   0 0 0   0 0 0 - 1
```

Runs: Kreevich, Radcliff, Appling 3, Bonura, Hack. RBIs: Kreevich, Bonura 2, Hayes 2, Sewell, Demaree. 2B: Appling, Hack, Frey. HR: Kreevich. SH: Hayes. DP: Sox 4. LOB: Sox 7, Cubs 3. BB: Davis 4, Carleton 1. Struck out: Whitehead 3, Davis 4. Hits: Davis 5 in 6 innings; Carleton 2 in 3 innings. Losing pitcher: Davis. Umpires: Quinn, Pinelli, Summers, Sears. Att: 12,457. Time—1:35.

they scored twice after two were out in the bottom half of the inning. Stratton left the game with none out and a man home in the seventh, but reliever Clint Brown (7–7) got pinch-hitter Ken O'Dea on a double play and Stan Hack on a popout. A Joe Marty home run in the ninth made the final score 6–4. Charlie Root worked in relief of Tex Carleton who took the loss.

The Cubs bounced back in Game Six and tied the series as they won easily for the second time behind Larry French. The small Comiskey crowd of 4,241 didn't have long to wait to see the visitors pull ahead. Stan Hack started the game with a triple off loser Vern Kennedy and scored on Frank Demaree's single. Kennedy was even less effective in the second, giving up singles to French and Herman and a double to Frank Demaree. The Sox pulled to within one in the fourth. Dixie Walker singled, Luke Appling walked, Rip Radcliff was hit by a pitch to load the bases, and Zeke Bonura's single drove home two runs. The Nationals scored single runs in the fifth on two walks and a Joe Marty single; in the eighth on singles by Stainback, Frey, French, and Hack; and in the ninth on a walk to Cavaretta and singles by Hartnett, Marty, and Stainback.

The series' finale saw the Sox once again support John Whitehead with some excellent batting. The 200-pound Whitehead, who had been suspended by the Sox during the regular season for ignoring training rules, was touched for the only Cubs' run of the day in the first when leadoff batter Stan Hack doubled and scored on Frank Demaree's single. The Sox went ahead to stay with two runs in the next half-inning. After encountering his difficulty in the first inning, Whitehead scattered seven hits throughout the rest of the game and was the beneficiary of four double plays, the last one closing out the game. The final score was 6–1.

This was the fourth straight win for the Sox in the city championship, and the first series to go the full seven games since 1931.

1939 Chicago City Championship Series

```
GAME ONE --- October 4
```

CUBS	AB	H	PO	A	E		WHITE SOX	AB	H	PO	A	E
Hack, 3b	6	1	1	2	1		Bejma, 2b	5	1	3	5	1
Herman, 2b	6	2	2	7	0		Kuhel, 1b	5	2	16	0	0
Galan, lf	6	3	0	0	0		Kreevich, cf	4	1	2	0	0
Leiber, cf	5	3	0	0	0		Appling, ss	3	0	2	4	0
Nicholson, rf	4	3	2	0	0		McNair, 3b	5	1	1	2	0
G.Russell, 1b	4	2	15	1	1		Walker, lf	5	2	3	0	2
Bartell, ss	3	1	3	4	0		Rosenthal, rf	4	2	1	1	0
Mancuso, c	4	1	7	0	0		Tresh, c	2	0	1	1	0
French, p	2	0	0	0	0		Radcliff, ph	1	0	0	0	0
Page, p	0	0	0	0	0		Schlueter, c	2	0	1	0	0
Gleeson, ph	1	0	0	0	0		Rigney, p	2	1	0	2	0
Passeau, p	0	0	0	0	0		Brown, p	1	1	0	1	0
J.Russell, p	0	0	0	0	0		Rensa, ph	1	0	0	0	0
Cavaretta, ph	1	1	0	0	0							
Bryant, pr	0	0	0	0	0			40	11	30	16	3
Whitehill, p	1	0	0	3	0							
	43	17	30	17	2							

```
CUB   0  1  0    1  0  2    3  0  2   1 - 10
SOX   0  0  0    0  3  0    5  1  0   0 -  9
```

RBI: Bartell, Mancuso 2, Gleeson, Galan 2, Nicholson 3, G. Russell, Rosenthal, Rigney, Kuhel 3, Walker 2. 2B: G. Russell 2, Rigney, Herman, Kuhel, Cavaretta, Brown. 3B: Nicholson. HR: Walker, Nicholson. SB: Appling. SH: G. Russell, Leiber, Appling. DP: Sox 1, Cubs 1. LOB: Cubs 9, Sox 7. BB: French 1, Passeau 4, Rigney 3. Struck out: French 2, Whitehill 2, Rigney 1. Hits: French 6 in 4.1 innings; Page 0 in 0.2 innings; Passeau 2 in 1 inning; Russell 2 in 1 inning; Whitehill 1 in 3 innings; Rigney 11 in 6.1 innings; Brown 6 in 3.2 innings. HBP: Bartell (Rigney). Winning pitcher: Whitehill. Losing pitcher: Brown. Umpires: Ball, Ballafant, Rue, Goetz. Att: 42,767. Time—2:52.

The 1939 Chicago City Championship Series

Chicago White Sox defeat Chicago Cubs; 4–3

The 1938 Cubs won the National League pennant and were swept in four games by the Yankees, thus preventing a city championship. But two evenly matched teams met in the 1939 Chicago city championship series—the fourth place White Sox (85–69) and the fourth-place Cubs (84–70). The Cubs started out like a house on fire, winning three of the first four games and leading 5–0 in the fifth with four innings to go, but the White Sox came off the mat and swept the final three games.

The series opened October 4th with a wild game at Comiskey Park. The Cubs took a 2–0 lead off Johnny Rigney (15–8) only to fall behind when the Sox scored three fifth-inning runs off Larry French (15–8). The lead changed hands again in the sixth when the Cubs scored twice to go ahead by one. Three more runs in the top of the seventh off Rigney and reliever Clint Brown (11–10) put them up 7–3. But the Sox exploded for five seventh-inning runs on the strength of Gerald Walker's three-run homer to take an 8–7 lead. A run in the eighth put the Sox on top by two with one inning to go. Hank Leiber's single and rookie Bill Nicholson's home run off Brown tied the game in the ninth. The

1939 Chicago City Championship Series

```
GAME TWO --- October 5
```

CUBS	AB	R	H	PO	A	E		WHITE SOX	AB	R	H	PO	A	E
Hack, 3b	4	0	1	1	0	0		Bejma, 2b	4	0	0	4	2	0
Herman, 2b	4	0	0	2	1	0		Kuhel, 1b	4	2	3	8	0	1
Galan, lf	2	0	0	2	0	0		Kreevich, cf	4	0	1	5	0	0
Gleeson, lf	2	0	0	0	0	0		Appling, ss	4	1	1	0	3	0
Leiber, cf	4	0	0	2	1	0		McNair, 3b	3	0	0	2	0	0
Nicholson, rf	4	0	1	2	0	0		Walker, lf	4	2	2	2	0	0
Hartnett, c	3	0	0	1	1	0		Rosenthal, rf	4	2	2	2	0	0
Garbark, c	0	0	0	3	0	0		Tresh, c	3	1	1	6	0	0
G.Russell, 1b	3	2	2	10	1	0		Lyons, p	4	1	3	0	2	0
Bartell, ss	3	0	0	1	5	0								
Root, p	0	0	0	0	0	0			34	9	13	27	9	1
Page, p	2	0	1	0	4	0								
Cavaretta, ph	1	0	0	0	0	0								
Dean, p	0	0	0	0	0	0								
	32	2	5	24	13	0								

```
CUB    0  0  1    0  1  0    0  0  0  -  2
SOX    1  3  0    2  0  0    3  0  x  -  9
```

RBI: G. Russell 2, Kuhel 3, Tresh 2, Lyons, Appling. 2B: Kuhel, Appling. 3B: Kreevich, Tresh. HR: G. Russell. DP: Sox. LOB: Cubs 3, Sox 5. BB: Page 3. Struck out: Lyons 3, Dean 3. Hits: Root 5 in 1.1 innings; Page 7 in 5.2 innings; Dean 1 in 1 inning. Losing pitcher: Root. Umpires: Ballafant, Rue, Goetz, Basil. Att: 6,131. Time—1:39.

```
GAME THREE --- October 6
```

WHITE SOX	AB	R	H	PO	A	E		CUBS	AB	R	H	PO	A	E
Bejma, 2b	4	0	0	2	0	0		Hack, 3b	4	1	2	0	4	0
Kuhel, 1b	3	1	1	6	0	0		Herman, 2b	4	0	1	2	4	0
Kreevich, cf	4	0	1	4	0	0		Galan, lf	4	1	2	1	0	0
Appling, ss	4	1	3	1	3	1		Leiber, cf	4	0	0	1	0	0
McNair, 3b	3	0	1	0	2	0		Reynolds, rf	3	0	1	2	0	0
Walker, lf	4	0	1	3	0	0		Hartnett, c	3	1	2	4	1	0
Rosenthal, rf	3	0	0	5	0	0		G.Russell, 1b	4	0	0	15	0	0
Tresh, c	3	0	0	3	1	0		Bartell, ss	4	0	1	2	5	1
Steinbacher, ph	1	0	0	0	0	0		W. Lee, p	3	1	0	0	1	0
Marcum, ph	1	0	0	0	0	0								
T. Lee, p	3	0	1	0	0	0			33	4	9	27	15	1
Dietrich, p	0	0	0	0	1	0								
	33	2	8	24	7	1								

```
SOX    1  0  0    1  0  0    0  0  0  -  2
CUB    0  0  0    0  1  1    1  1  x  -  4
```

RBI: Hack, G. Russell, Herman, Bartell, Appling, Walker. 2B: Kuhel, Reynolds, Hack. SB: Reynolds, W. Lee. DP: Sox. LOB: Sox 7, Cubs 9. BB: T. Lee 4, W. Lee 3. Struck out: T. Lee 3, W. Lee 4. Hits: T. Lee 7 in 6.1 innings; Dietrich 2 in 1.2 innings. Losing pitcher: T. Lee. Umpires: Rue, Goetz, Basil, Ballafant. Time—1:43.

Cubs touched Brown for one final run in the tenth on consecutive singles by Stan Hack, Billy Herman, and Augie Galan to win the 10–9 slugfest. When it was all over, the two clubs had banged out a total of 28 hits, the Cubs with 17 of their own, and no fewer than eight men had two hits or more.

The Sox evened the series the next day in their home park when 38-year-old Ted Lyons (14–6) held the Cubs in check on five hits. If it weren't for Glen

1939 Chicago City Championship Series

GAME FOUR --- October 7

WHITE SOX	AB	R	H	PO	A	E	CUBS	AB	R	H	PO	A	E
Bejma, 2b	4	0	1	5	3	0	Hack, 3b	4	1	3	1	2	0
Kuhel, 1b	4	0	0	6	3	0	Herman, 2b	4	1	2	1	3	0
Kreevich, cf	4	0	2	2	0	0	Galan, lf	4	1	1	2	0	0
Appling, ss	4	0	0	6	1	0	Leiber, cf	5	1	2	2	0	0
McNair, 3b	4	1	1	1	3	0	Reynolds, rf	4	0	3	4	0	0
Walker, lf	4	1	2	1	0	0	Garbark, c	0	0	0	0	0	0
Rosenthal, rf	3	0	2	1	0	0	G.Russell, 1b	3	1	2	13	0	0
Tresh, c	3	0	0	3	2	0	Bartell, ss	1	0	0	1	1	0
Marcum, ph	1	0	0	0	0	0	Mattick, ss	3	0	1	1	3	0
Schlueter, c	0	0	0	1	0	0	Mancuso, c	3	0	0	2	1	0
Smith, p	2	1	1	0	0	0	Nicholson, rf	1	0	0	0	0	0
Knott, p	0	0	0	0	0	0	French, p	2	0	0	0	0	0
							Hartnett, ph	1	0	0	0	0	0
	33	3	9	*26	12	0	J.Russell, p	0	0	0	0	1	0
							Gleeson, ph	1	0	0	0	0	0
								36	5	14	27	11	0

* Two out when winning run scored.

```
SOX    0  1  0    0  0  0    2  0  0  -  3
CUB    1  0  0    1  0  0    0  0  3  -  5
```

RBI: Reynolds, G. Russell, Leiber 3, Rosenthal, Smith 2. 2B: McNair, Rosenthal. HR: G. Russell, Smith, Leiber. SB: Kreevich. SH: G. Russell. DP: Cubs 3. LOB: Sox 5, Cubs 9. BB: Smith 3, French 1, J. Russell 1. Struck out: Smith 3, Knott 1, French 2. Hits: Smith 9 in 6.2 innings; Knott 5 in 2.1 innings; French 8 in 7 innings; J. Russell 1 in 2 innings. WP: J. Russell. Winning pitcher: J. Russell. Losing pitcher: Knott. Umpires: Goetz, Basil, Ballafant, Rue. Att: 11,468. Time—2:01.

Russell's home runs in the third and fifth, the Nationals wouldn't have scored at all. The Sox took a one-run lead in the first on Joe Kuhel's solo homer and widened the margin to 4–0 in the second off loser Charlie Root (8–8). Singles by Larry Rosenthal and Lyons and a triple by Mike Tresh off Vance Page (7–7) accounted for two more Sox runs in the fourth. A walk, an RBI double by Luke Appling, and a two-run homer from Gerald Walker pushed across the final three Sox runs in the seventh. Dizzy Dean (6–4) pitched a scoreless eighth for the Cubs and struck out the side around a Ted Lyons single.

The series moved to Wrigley Field for Game Three on the 6th of October. It was Lee (Bill, 19–15) vs. Lee (Thornton, 15–11). The Sox held a 2–0 lead before the Cubs could get to Thornton for their first run of the game in the fifth. Bill Lee walked, stole second, and scored on Stan Hack's single. In the next inning, Augie Galan's single, Carl Reynolds' double, and Glen Russell's infield out tied the game. The Cubs knocked Thornton out of the box in the seventh when Hack doubled and scored on Billy Herman's single. Bill Dietrich (7–8) took over the mound duties for the Sox and was touched for the Nationals' final run in the eighth when Gabby Hartnett singled, went to second on a groundout, and scored on Dick Bartell's single.

The Bruins made it two straight at Wrigley and took a three-games-to-one lead in the series with a come-from-behind 5–3 victory in Game Four. Larry French was clutching a slim one run lead when opposing pitcher Edgar Smith (9–11) cracked a two-run homer in the top of the seventh. French retired in favor of pinch-hitter Hartnett in the bottom of the inning and it was Jack

1939 Chicago City Championship Series

GAME FIVE --- October 8

WHITE SOX	AB	R	H	PO	A	E		CUBS	AB	R	H	PO	A	E
Bejma, 2b	4	1	1	3	2	0		Hack, 3b	5	2	2	0	0	1
Kuhel, 1b	5	2	2	7	0	0		Herman, 2b	4	0	2	0	3	0
Kreevich, cf	4	1	1	6	0	0		Galan, lf	4	1	1	4	0	0
Appling, ss	5	1	1	2	2	0		Leiber, cf	5	0	1	3	0	0
McNair, 3b	5	0	1	3	3	0		Nicholson, rf	4	0	1	3	0	0
Walker, lf	4	1	0	2	0	0		G. Russell, 1b	5	1	2	6	0	0
Rosenthal, rf	4	1	1	2	0	1		Mattick, ss	5	0	0	1	4	1
Tresh, c	2	0	0	4	1	0		Mancuso, c	4	1	2	11	0	0
Marcum, ph	1	0	0	0	0	0		Passeau, p	2	0	0	2	0	0
Schlueter, c	1	1	1	1	0	0		W. Lee, p	1	0	0	0	1	1
Rigney, p	1	0	0	0	1	0								
Radcliff, ph	1	0	0	0	0	0			39	5	11	30	8	3
Dietrich, p	3	0	0	0	2	1								
	40	8	8	30	11	2								

```
SOX   0  0  0    0  0  2    0  3  0    3  -  8
CUB   1  1  1    2  0  0    0  0  0    0  -  5
```

RBI: Galan 2, Mancuso, Hack, Herman, Kreevich 2, Appling, McNair, Rosenthal, Schlueter 2. 2B: Herman, Kuhel, Schlueter. HR: Galan, Kreevich. SB: Herman, G. Russell, Walker. SH: Galan, Passeau. LOB: Sox 7, Cubs 9. BB: Dietrich 3, Passeau 2, Lee 3. Struck out: Rigney 2, Dietrich 3, Passeau 5, Lee 3. Hits: Rigney 9 in 4 innings: Dietrich 2 in 6 innings; Passeau 5 in 7 innings; Lee 4 in 3 innings. WP: Rigney. PB: Tresh, Mancuso. Winning pitcher: Dietrich. Losing pitcher: Lee. Umpires: Basil, Ballafant, Rue, Goetz. Att: 17,227. Time—2:26.

Russell (4–3) against the Sox's Jack Knott (1–6) when the game went into the final frame. The Sox failed to put any insurance on the board and in the bottom of the ninth the Cubs struck. Knott fanned pinch-hitter Jim Gleeson to start the inning, but Hack and Herman singled to bring the winning run to the plate. Augie Galan forced Herman at second and Knott was within one out of closing out the game when Hank Leiber crashed a three-run homer and snatched victory from the jaws of defeat.

It appeared as if the Cubs would wrap up the series in five games when the two teams battled into the sixth inning the next day. Single runs in the first three innings and a two-run fourth against Johnny Rigney had given Claude Passeau (13–9) a commanding 5–0 lead. Mike Kreevich's two-run homer in the sixth narrowed the margin to 5–2, but the Sox failed to score in the seventh and Passeau had a four-hitter when he took the mound for the eighth. Disaster struck when Ollie Bejma walked and Joe Kuhel doubled. Suddenly Passeau was gone, lifted in favor of Bill Lee who walked Kreevich to load the bases. Appling grounded out and Bejma scored. Eric McNair singled and Kuhel scored. Larry Rosenthal singled and Kreevich scored. The game was tied. The Cubs went out meekly in the eighth and ninth. Bill Lee retired the first two Sox batters in the tenth before Gerald Walker walked and stole second. Rosenthal received an intentional pass, but Norm Schlueter crossed up the strategy by doubling both men home. Schlueter went to third on a passed ball and scored when Lee missed a return throw from catcher Gus Mancuso. The series was over, but no one knew it yet.

1939 Chicago City Championship Series

GAME SIX --- October 9

CUBS	AB	H	PO	A	E
Hack, 3b	4	1	4	3	0
Herman, 2b	4	0	5	2	0
Galan, lf	3	1	1	1	0
Leiber, cf	4	1	3	0	0
Nicholson, rf	3	0	0	0	0
G. Russell, 1b	3	1	8	0	1
Mattick, ss	2	0	0	4	0
Mancuso, c	3	0	3	0	0
Root, p	2	0	0	2	0
Hartnett, ph	1	0	0	0	0
Dean, p	0	0	0	1	1
	29	4	24	13	2

WHITE SOX	AB	H	PO	A	E
Bejma, 2b	3	1	2	5	0
Kuhel, 1b	4	0	9	0	0
Kreevich, cf	3	1	5	0	0
Appling, ss	3	1	3	0	0
McNair, 3b	4	2	0	2	0
Walker, lf	4	3	1	2	0
Rosenthal, rf	4	1	3	0	0
Tresh, c	3	0	4	0	0
T. Lee, p	3	0	0	2	0
	31	9	27	11	0

```
CUB   1  0  0     0  0  0     0  0  0  -  1
SOX   0  0  0     1  1  1     0  3  x  -  6
```

RBI: G. Russell, Walker 2, Bejma, McNair 3. 2B: Appling. 3B: Kreevich. SH: Kreevich, Tresh. DP: Sox 1, Cubs 1. LOB: Cubs 4, Sox 5. BB: Dean 2, Lee 3. Struck out: Root 3, Lee 2. Hits: Root 7 in 7 innings; Dean 2 in 1 inning. Losing pitcher: Root. Umpires: Ballafant, Goetz, Rue, Basil. Att: 26,960. Time—1:38.

GAME SEVEN --- October 10

CUBS	AB	R	H	PO	A	E
Hack, 3b	3	0	0	1	1	0
Herman, 2b	4	0	4	1	0	0
Galan, lf	2	1	1	1	0	0
Leiber, cf	4	0	3	5	0	0
Nicholson, rf	4	0	0	2	0	0
G.Russell, 1b	3	0	0	6	0	0
Mattick, ss	4	0	0	4	3	0
Mancuso, c	3	0	0	1	1	0
Whitehill, p	0	0	0	0	2	0
Passeau, p	2	0	0	0	0	0
Cavaretta, ph	1	0	0	0	0	0
Page, p	0	0	0	0	1	0
Gleeson, ph	1	0	0	0	0	0
	31	1	5	24	9	0

WHITE SOX	AB	R	H	PO	A	E
Bejma, 2b	5	1	2	3	3	0
Kuhel, 1b	4	0	1	9	0	0
Kreevich, cf	5	0	1	5	0	0
Appling, ss	4	1	1	0	1	0
McNair, 3b	3	1	1	1	3	0
Walker, lf	3	2	2	1	0	0
Rosenthal, rf	4	0	1	2	0	0
Tresh, c	4	1	3	6	1	0
Lyons, p	4	1	1	0	1	0
	36	7	13	27	9	0

```
CUB   0  0  0     1  0  0     0  0  0  -  1
SOX   0  4  0     0  2  0     1  0  x  -  7
```

RBI: G. Russell, Tresh 2, Lyons, Kuhel 2, Rosethal, Walker. 2B: Bejma, McNair. 3B: Tresh. SB: McNair. SH: G. Russell, Kuhel. LOB: Sox 8, Cubs 9. BB: Passeau 2, Lyons 4. Struck out: Page 2, Lyons 4. Umpires: Goetz, Rue, Basil, Ballafant. Att: 14,781.

The games moved back to Comiskey Park and the Cubs took a 1–0 lead in the first inning of Game Six off Thornton Lee on singles by Galan, Leiber, and Russell. It was the last time the Cubs led in the series. The Sox tied the game off veteran Charlie Root in the fourth when Kreevich reached on an error, moved to second on an infield out, and scored on Gerald Walker's single. In their next at-bat, Larry Rosenthal singled, went to second on Mike Tresh's sacrifice bunt, and scored on Ollie Bejma's single. The Sox scored once more off Root in the sixth and three times off reliever Dizzy Dean in the eighth to win easily, 6–1. No Cub baserunner reached second after the third and they went out in the final three innings without any hits.

A demoralized Cub team met a revitalized Sox club for the series' finale on the 10th of October. The game was over before it began. Earl Whitehill (4–7) started for the Cubs but the Sox got to him for the first run of the game in the second inning when Gerald Walker reached on a safety and Mike Tresh tripled. When Ted Lyons, Ollie Bejma, and Joe Kuhel singled in succession to make the score 4–0, Whitehill was lifted in favor of Claude Passeau. Two more runs in the fifth and one in the seventh helped the Sox gild the lily and Lyons proved worthy of his big lead by shutting the Cubs down on five hits. Their only run came in the fourth when Galan and Leiber reached on singles, Galan went to third on an infield out and scored on Glen Russell's sacrifice fly.

The Sox were now 20–9 since 1931 and had won the last five series to be played.

The 1940 Chicago City Championship Series

Chicago White Sox defeat Chicago Cubs 4–2

Both the Cubs (75–79) and White Sox (82–72) finished fifth in their respective leagues in 1940 and the Nationals hoped to break the Sox's five-series winning streak which went back to 1931. It was not to be.

1940 Chicago City Championship Series

GAME ONE --- October 1

WHITE SOX	AB	R	H	PO	A	E		CUBS	AB	R	H	PO	A	E
Webb, 2b	5	0	1	0	4	1		Hack, 3b	5	0	3	0	4	0
Tresh, c	4	0	0	5	1	1		Herman, 2b	5	0	0	1	4	0
Kuhel, 1b	4	0	1	14	1	0		Nicholson, lf	5	1	1	0	0	0
Solters, lf	4	1	2	0	0	0		Leiber, rf	4	0	1	0	0	0
Appling, ss	3	1	0	2	3	0		Gleeson, cf	4	0	1	1	0	0
Wright, rf	4	1	1	2	0	0		Russell, 1b	4	0	1	14	0	0
Kreevich, cf	3	2	2	3	0	0		Todd, c	4	1	0	9	0	0
Kennedy, 3b	4	0	0	1	4	0		Mattick, ss	4	1	2	2	5	0
Lyons, p	4	0	3	0	1	0		Passeau, p	3	0	1	0	0	0
								Dallessandro, ph	1	0	0	0	0	0
	35	5	10	27	14	2			39	3	10	27	13	0

```
SOX   0  3  1    1  0  0    0  0  0  -  5
CUB   0  2  0    0  1  0    0  0  0  -  3
```

RBI: Solters, Kreevich, Lyons 3, Russell, Passeau 2. 2B: Kreevich, Lyons, Mattick, Passeau. HR: Solters. SB: Kreevich 2, Hack. SH: Tresh. DP: Cubs. LOB: Sox 7, Cubs 9. BB: Passeau 3. Struck out: Lyons 7, Passeau 8. Umpires: Magerkurth, Hubbard, Dunn, Pipgras. Att: 9,929. Time—2:03.

White Sox pitcher Ted Lyons (12–8) was the star of Game One on October first as he pitched and batted his way to victory at Wrigley Field. On the mound, the 39-year-old veteran scattered ten Cub hits and allowed three runs. At the plate, he drove in three of the Sox's five runs with two singles and a double in four times at-bat. The White Sox scored all their runs in the second, third

1940 Chicago City Championship Series

GAME TWO --- October 2

WHITE SOX	AB	R	H	PO	A	E
Webb, 2b	4	0	2	5	3	0
Hayes, 2b	0	0	0	0	0	0
Tresh, c	4	0	1	4	0	0
Kuhel, 1b	4	1	1	6	0	0
Solters, lf	4	1	1	2	0	0
Appling, ss	3	0	1	2	2	1
Wright, rf	4	0	0	2	0	0
Kreevich, cf	4	0	0	3	0	0
Kennedy, 3b	4	0	0	0	0	3
T.Lee, p	2	0	0	0	2	1
Appleton, p	1	0	1	0	2	0
	34	2	7	24	9	5

CUBS	AB	R	H	PO	A	E
Hack, 3b	4	2	1	0	5	0
Herman, 2b	3	2	2	1	3	1
Warstler, 2b	2	1	0	0	1	0
Nicholson, lf	4	1	0	1	0	0
Leiber, rf	4	1	2	0	0	0
Gleeson, cf	2	1	2	4	0	0
Russell, 2b	4	0	0	18	1	0
Todd, c	4	0	1	2	1	0
Mattick, ss	3	0	1	1	6	0
Olsen, p	4	0	0	0	1	0
	34	8	9	27	18	1

```
SOX   0  0  0    0  0  2    0  0  0  -  2
CUB   0  1  1    0  3  3    0  0  x  -  8
```

RBI: Solters, Appling, Herman, Leiber 2, Gleeson, Russell 2, Mattick. 3B: Solters. SB: Herman, Leiber. SH: Nicholson, Gleeson. DP: Sox 1, Cubs 1. LOB: Sox 6, Cubs 8. BB: T. Lee 3, Appleton 1, Olsen 1. Struck out: Appleton 4, Olsen 2. Hits: T. Lee 8 in 5 innings; Appleton 1 in 3 innings. WP: T. Lee. Losing pitcher: T. Lee. Umpires: Hubbard, Dunn, Pipgras, Magerkurth. Att: 6,600. Time—1:50.

GAME THREE --- October 3

CUBS	AB	R	H	PO	A	E
Hack, 3b	2	1	0	0	3	1
Warstler, 2b	4	1	1	1	1	1
Nicholson, lf	4	1	1	1	0	1
Leiber, rf	4	0	0	1	0	0
Gleeson, cf	3	0	1	2	0	0
Russell, 1b	4	0	0	10	1	0
Todd, c	4	0	0	7	2	1
Mattick, ss	4	1	1	1	2	0
French, p	2	1	2	1	2	0
Bonura, ph	1	0	0	0	0	0
Bryant, p	0	0	0	0	0	0
Page, p	0	0	0	0	1	0
	32	5	6	24	12	4

WHITE SOX	AB	R	H	PO	A	E
Webb, 2b	6	1	2	1	2	0
Tresh, c	5	1	1	6	1	0
Kuhel, 1b	4	2	2	12	0	0
Solters, lf	4	2	1	1	0	0
Appling, ss	3	3	2	3	3	0
Wright, rf	5	1	3	2	0	0
Kreevich, cf	3	0	1	2	0	0
Kennedy, 3b	4	1	2	0	3	0
Smith, p	4	0	1	0	0	0
	38	11	15	27	9	0

```
CUB   0  0  4    1  0  0    0  0  0  -   5
SOX   0  2  3    0  2  1    3  0  x  -  11
```

RBI: Warstler, Nicholson 3, French, Webb, Kuhel, Appling 2, Wright 2, Kennedy 2, Smith. 2B: Gleeson, Kuhel, Appling. 3B: Mattick, Webb, Kuhel. HR: Nicholson. SH: Kreevich. SB: Solters. DP: Cubs. LOB: Cubs 3, Sox 12. BB: French 4, Bryant 4, Smith 3. Struck out: French 2, Bryant 1, Page 1, Smith 4. Hits: French 12 in 6 innings; Bryant 2 in 0.1 innings; Page 1 in 1.2 innings. Losing pitcher: French. Umpires: Dunn, Pipgras, Magerkurth, Hubbard. Att: 39,625. Time—2:07.

and fourth innings, and were never headed. Claude Passeau (20–13) took the loss.

Rookie Vern Olsen (13-9) squared the series in Game Two as he kept the Sox at bay on seven hits and two runs. The Cubs had a 2-0 lead when they scored five runs in the fifth on four hits and two errors. A single by Joe Kuhel, a triple by Julius Solters, and an infield out accounted for two more Sox runs

1940 Chicago City Championship Series

GAME FOUR --- October 4

CUBS	AB	R	H	PO	A	E
Hack, 3b	5	1	4	0	2	0
Warstler, 2b	4	0	1	1	8	0
Nicholson, lf	4	0	1	1	0	0
Leiber, rf	4	0	1	3	0	0
Gleeson, cf	4	0	0	2	0	0
Bonura, 1b	4	1	2	14	0	0
Todd, c	4	0	1	4	0	0
Mattick, ss	4	1	2	2	3	0
W. Lee, p	4	1	1	0	2	0
	37	4	13	27	15	0

WHITE SOX	AB	R	H	PO	A	E
Webb, 2b	2	0	1	1	4	0
Tresh, c	4	0	0	3	0	0
Kuhel, 1b	4	0	1	10	2	0
Solters, lf	3	0	0	3	1	0
Appling, ss	3	0	0	3	4	3
Wright, rf	3	0	0	1	0	0
Kreevich, cf	4	0	2	3	0	0
Kennedy, 3b	4	0	1	2	1	0
Rigney, p	2	0	0	1	1	0
Rosenthal, ph	1	0	0	0	0	0
Brown, p	0	0	0	0	0	0
	30	0	5	27	13	3

```
CUB   0  0  1    1  0  0    1  0  1  -  4
SOX   0  0  0    0  0  0    0  0  0  -  0
```

RBI: Hack, Nicholson, Todd. 2B: Nicholson, Hack. 3B: Mattick. SB: Hack. DP: Cubs 2, Sox 2. LOB: Cubs 7, Sox 8. BB: W. Lee 5, Rigney 1. Struck out: W. Lee 3, Rigney 3. Hits: Rigney 11 in 8 innings; Brown 2 in 1 inning. Losing pitcher: Rigney. Umpires: Pipgras, Magerkurth, Hubbard, Dunn. Att: 4,789. Time—1:45.

GAME FIVE --- October 5

CUBS	AB	R	H	PO	A	E
Hack, 3b	4	0	0	1	1	0
Warstler, 2b	3	0	0	2	5	1
Herman, ph	0	0	0	0	0	0
Bryant, pr	0	1	0	0	0	0
Russell, 2b	0	0	0	0	0	0
Nicholson, lf	4	1	3	1	0	0
Leiber, rf	4	0	1	3	0	0
Gleeson, cf	4	0	0	3	1	0
Bonura, 1b	4	0	1	10	0	0
Todd, c	3	0	0	6	0	0
Mattick, ss	3	0	0	0	2	1
Passeau, p	2	0	0	0	1	0
Dallessandro, ph	1	0	0	0	0	0
Raffensberger, p	0	0	0	0	0	0
	32	2	5	*26	10	2

WHITE SOX	AB	R	H	PO	A	E
Webb, 2b	5	0	0	2	2	1
Tresh, c	5	2	2	2	1	0
Kuhel, 1b	5	0	3	8	3	0
Solters, lf	5	0	2	3	0	0
Appling, ss	3	0	1	5	4	2
Wright, rf	4	0	0	1	1	0
Rosenthal, cf	4	0	2	2	0	0
Kennedy, 3b	4	0	0	3	1	0
Dietrich, p	3	1	2	1	0	0
	38	3	12	27	12	3

* Two out when winning run scored

```
CUB   0  0  0    0  0  0    1  0  1  -  2
SOX   0  0  1    0  0  0    1  0  1  -  3
```

RBI: Leiber, Bonura, Kuhel, Solters 2. SB: Kuhel. DP: Cubs 1, Sox 2. LOB: Cubs 4, Sox 11. BB: Passeau 2, Dietrich 1. Struck out: Passeau 4, Dietrich 2. Hits: Passeau 9 in 7 innings; Raffensberger 3 in 1.2 innings. Losing pitcher: Raffensberger. Umpires: Magerkurth, Hubbard, Dunn, Pipgras. Att: 37,383. Time—2:00.

in the sixth. The Americans exhibited some shaky defense by contributing five errors to the Cubs' cause as the Bruins won the game, 8–2. Thornton Lee (12–13) was the losing pitcher.

The White Sox won Game Three as Larry French (14–14) lost to southpaw Edgar Smith (14–9) in a night game played at Comiskey Park before an excellent crowd of 39,625 fans. The Sox bashed French around freely, racking up

1940 Chicago City Championship Series

```
GAME SIX --- October 6
```

WHITE SOX	AB	R	H	PO	A	E	CUBS	AB	R	H	PO	A	E
Webb, 2b	5	1	2	0	5	0	Hack, 3b	5	0	0	1	2	0
Tresh, c	5	0	0	4	0	0	Warstler, 2b	4	0	0	1	2	0
Kuhel, 1b	5	1	1	19	0	0	Nicholson, lf	4	1	1	3	0	0
Solters, lf	4	2	3	4	0	0	Leiber, rf	3	1	1	1	0	0
Appling, ss	5	1	2	1	4	0	Dallessandro, lf	1	0	0	1	0	0
Wright, rf	5	0	2	1	0	0	Gleeson, cf	4	1	2	3	0	0
Kreevich, cf	4	0	0	1	0	0	Bonura, 1b	4	1	2	13	1	0
Kennedy, 3b	3	0	0	0	2	0	Todd, c	4	0	1	6	1	0
Lyons, p	4	0	0	0	6	0	Bryant, pr	0	0	0	0	0	0
							Mattick, ss	4	0	0	0	5	0
	40	5	10	30	17	0	Olsen, p	3	0	1	1	3	0
							Russell, ph	0	0	0	0	0	0
								36	4	7	30	14	0

```
SOX   0 0 0   0 0 0   2 0 1   2 - 5
CUB   0 1 0   2 0 0   0 0 0   1 - 4
```

RBI: Kuhel, Appling, Wright 2, Kreevich, Nicholson, Leiber, Bonura 2. 2B: Kuhel, Solters. HR: Leiber, Bonura. LOB: Sox 7, Cubs 3. BB: Lyons 1, Olsen 2. Struck out: Lyons 3, Olsen 5. Umpires: Hubbard, Dunn, Pipgras, Magerkurth. Att: 12,075. Time—1:58.

12 hits and eight runs in his six innings. Despite French's inability, the Cubs and Sox were tied at the end of four, mainly on the strength of Bill Nicholson's three-run homer. The Sox scored in the next three innings off French and relievers Clay Bryant (0–1) and Vance Page (1–3) to put the game on ice.

The Cubs tied the series at two games apiece the next day as Bill Lee (9–17) pitched a five-hit shutout. The Cubs amassed 13 hits off losing pitcher Johnny Rigney (14–18) and reliever Clint Brown (4–6). The only run they needed came in the third when Stan Hack singled, stole second, went to third on one of Luke Appling's three errors on the day, and scored on Bill Nicholson's sacrifice fly.

The Sox took a 3–2 lead in games in Game Five. The Cubs were held to two runs and five hits by Bill Dietrich (10–6), but those two runs were sufficient to take the game into the bottom of the ninth tied at two. With two outs and no one on base, the Sox lined three straight singles off loser Ken Raffensberger (7–9) for the 3–2 victory.

The White Sox won their sixth consecutive Chicago city championship as Ted Lyons won Game Six. Lyons pitched a seven-hitter and allowed four runs. Hank Leiber put the Cubs up in the second with a solo home run, and the Nationals added two more in the fourth on singles by Bill Nicholson, Jim Gleeson, and Hank Bonura. But the Sox pulled to within one in the seventh and tied the game in the top of the ninth. Two singles and Kuhel's double put the Americans up 5–3 in the tenth. Lyons faltered with two outs in the bottom of the inning when he gave up a solo home run to Zeke Bonura, a single to Al Todd, and a walk to Glen Russell, but Stan Hack struck out to end the game.

1941 Chicago City Championship Series

GAME ONE --- October 1

WHITE SOX	AB	R	H	PO	A	E		CUBS	AB	R	H	PO	A	E
Knickerbocker, 2b	5	0	1	2	5	0		Hack, 3b	4	0	1	2	2	0
Chapman, lf	5	0	0	2	0	0		Cavaretta, cf	4	0	1	3	0	0
Kuhel, 1b	4	1	2	9	1	0		Stringer, 2b	4	0	0	4	3	0
Appling, ss	4	1	1	3	5	0		Nicholson, rf	3	0	0	0	1	0
Wright, rf	4	1	3	1	0	0		Dallesandro, lf	4	1	1	3	0	0
Kreevich, cf	4	0	3	2	0	0		Dahlgren, 1b	4	0	1	12	0	0
Kennedy, 3b	4	0	0	1	0	0		McCullough, c	3	0	1	1	1	0
Tresh, c	4	1	1	6	0	0		Sturgeon, ss	3	0	0	2	7	0
Lyons, p	4	0	2	1	1	0		Passeau, p	3	0	0	0	1	0
								Pressnell, p	0	0	0	0	0	0
	38	4	13	27	12	0			32	1	5	27	15	0

```
SOX   0  0  0   0  0  0   0  0  4  -  4
CUB   0  0  0   0  0  0   1  0  0  -  1
```

RBIs: Wright, Kreevich, Lyons, Knickerbocker, Dahlgren. 2B: Dallessandro. SB: McCullough. DP: Sox 1, Cubs 1. LOB: Sox 7, Cubs 5. BB: Lyons 1. Struck out: Lyons 5, Passeau 1. Hits: Passeau 13 in 8.2 innings; Presnell 0 in 0.1 innings. Losing pitcher: Passeau. Umpires: Reardon, Summers, Jorda, Basil. Att: 7,272. Time—1:44.

The 1941 Chicago City Championship Series

Chicago White Sox defeat Chicago Cubs; 4–0

The White Sox (77–77) moved from fourth place in 1940 to third place in 1941, but their record declined from 82–72. The sixth-place Cubs (70–84), who were in the thick of the pennant race for the first week of the season, saw their won-loss record decline for the fourth straight year in 1941 and found no postseason comfort from their cross-town American League rivals. For the sixth time since the beginning of the city championships, the Cubs failed to win a game.

Game One, played at Wrigley Field on the 1st of October, saw Ted Lyons (12–10) tie the Cubs in knots over the first six innings. In the seventh, the Nationals took a brief lead when Dom Dallessandro doubled and scored on Babe Dahlgren's single. Losing pitcher Claude Passeau (14–14) took a 7-hit shutout into the ninth inning when singles by Joe Kuhel, Luke Appling, Taft Wright, and Mike Kreevich put the Sox up 2–1. Passeau got the next two men out, but Lyons and Bill Knickerbocker both singled to add two insurance runs to the Sox's sccore. Tot Presnell (5–3) got the final out of the inning, but the Cubs failed to rally in the ninth and went down to defeat, 4–1.

Game Two, at Comiskey Park on the third, was a matchup between Eddie Smith (13–17) for the Sox and Vern Olsen (10–8). The Sox blasted four Cub pitchers—Olsen, Vallie Eaves (3–3), Charlie Root (8–7), and rookie Johnny Schmitz (2–0)—for ten hits, among them homers by Wright and Bob Kennedy and a 4-for-4 performance by Bill Knickerbocker. Olsen gave up two runs in the first and two in the fourth before being relieved by Eaves in the fifth. Schmitz gave up the final two Sox runs, the last on a solo home run by Taft Wright, but the Sox won, 6–4. Smith went the distance for the victory, quelling a ninth-inning rally after the Cubs had scored twice.

1941 Chicago City Championship Series

GAME TWO --- October 3

CUBS	AB	R	H	PO	A	E
Hack, 3b	5	0	2	1	1	0
B.Olsen, cf	4	1	1	3	0	0
Stringer, 2b	5	0	0	1	4	0
Nicholson, rf	4	0	0	0	0	0
Dallessandro,lf	5	0	1	2	0	0
Dahlgren, 1b	4	0	0	12	1	0
McCullough, c	4	1	1	4	0	1
Sturgeon, ss	4	2	2	0	4	0
V.Olsen, p	2	0	1	1	0	0
Eaves, p	0	0	0	0	0	0
Hudson, ph	1	0	0	0	0	0
Schmitz, p	0	0	0	0	0	0
Root, p	0	0	0	0	0	0
Scheffing, ph	1	0	1	0	0	0
	39	4	9	24	10	1

WHITE SOX	AB	R	H	PO	A	E
Knickerbocker, 2b	4	1	4	1	0	0
Chapman, lf	3	1	1	2	0	0
Kuhel, 1b	3	0	0	8	1	0
Appling, ss	4	0	0	1	2	2
Wright, rf	4	2	2	4	0	0
Kreevich, cf	4	0	0	5	0	0
Kennedy, 3b	4	1	1	0	3	0
Tresh, c	4	1	2	5	0	0
Smith, p	4	0	0	1	4	1
	34	6	10	27	10	3

```
CUB   0  0  0    0  1  0    0  1  2   -  4
SOX   2  0  0    2  0  0    1  1  x   -  6
```

RBIs: Hack, Dallessandro, Scheffing, Kuhel, Appling, Kennedy 2, Knickerbocker, Wright. 2B: Chapman, Hack, Tresh, Dallessandro. HR: Kennedy, Wright. SB: Knickerbocker. LOB: Sox 6, Cubs 10. BB: Schmitz 2, Smith 2. Struck out: V. Olsen 2, Root 1, Smith 4. Hits: V. Olsen 6 in 4.1 innings; Eaves 0 in 1.2 innings; Schmitz 2 in 0.2 innings; Root 2 in 1.1 innings. Losing pitcher: V. Olsen. Umpires: Summers, Jorda, Basil, Reardon. Att: 27,169. Time—2:08.

GAME THREE --- October 5

WHITE SOX	AB	R	H	PO	A	E
Knickerbocker, 2b	4	0	1	2	3	0
Chapman, lf	3	1	0	1	0	0
Kuhel, 1b	5	1	2	7	1	0
Appling, ss	4	0	3	3	2	0
Wright, rf	4	0	0	3	0	0
Kreevich, cf	4	2	1	0	0	0
Kennedy, 3b	3	1	0	2	0	0
Tresh, c	4	0	2	9	0	0
Rigney, p	4	1	1	0	0	0
	35	6	10	27	6	0

CUBS	AB	R	H	PO	A	E
Hack, 3b	4	0	1	2	0	2
Cavaretta, cf	4	0	0	0	0	1
Stringer, 2b	4	0	0	3	5	0
Nicholson, rf	4	0	1	2	0	0
Dallesandro, lf	3	0	0	0	0	0
Dahlgren, 1b	3	0	0	9	3	0
Scheffing, c	1	0	1	3	0	0
McCullough, c	1	0	0	4	1	0
Sturgeon, ss	3	0	2	3	3	0
Erickson, p	0	0	0	0	1	0
W.Lee, p	1	0	0	1	1	0
Gilbert, ph	1	0	0	0	0	0
Raffensberger, p	0	0	0	0	1	0
B.Olsen, ph	1	0	0	0	0	0
Eaves, p	0	0	0	0	0	0
	30	0	5	27	15	3

```
SOX   2  2  0    2  0  0    0  0  0   -  6
CUB   0  0  0    0  0  0    0  0  0   -  0
```

RBIs: Appling 2, Rigney, Knickerbocker, Tresh. 2B: Hack, Rigney, Appling 2, Sturgeon. SB: Kreevich. SH: Kennedy. DP: Cubs. Triple play: Knickerbocker to Appling. LOB: Sox 6, Cubs 4. BB: Erickson 1, Lee 1, Eaves 1, Rigney 1. Struck out: Erickson 2, Lee 1, Raffensberger 2, Rigney 9. Hits: Erickson 6 in 2 innings; Lee 3 in 3 innings; Raffensberger 2 in 3 innings; Eaves 1 in 1 inning. WP: Lee. PB: Tresh, Scheffing. Losing pitcher: Erickson. Umpires: Jorda, Basil, Reardon, Summers. Att: 17,774. Time—2:00.

1941 Chicago City Championship Series

```
GAME FOUR --- October 7
```

CUBS	AB	R	H	PO	A	E	WHITE SOX	AB	R	H	PO	A	E
Hack, 3b	4	0	1	1	0	2	Knickerbocker, 2b	4	0	1	4	4	0
Cavaretta, cf	4	0	1	0	0	0	Chapman, lf	3	0	1	2	0	0
Stringer, 2b	4	0	0	0	6	2	Kuhel, 1b	4	0	0	12	0	0
Nicholson, rf	3	0	0	0	0	0	Appling, ss	4	0	0	1	3	0
Dahlgren, 1b	3	0	2	12	0	1	Wright, rf	4	1	1	1	0	0
McCullough, c	4	0	0	3	2	0	Kreevich, cf	2	1	1	1	0	0
B.Olsen, cf	3	0	0	6	0	0	Kennedy, 3b	3	1	2	0	4	1
Sturgeon, ss	3	0	0	2	2	0	Tresh, c	4	0	0	6	0	0
Passeau, p	3	0	0	0	1	1	Lee, p	2	0	0	0	3	0
	31	0	4	24	11	6		30	3	6	27	14	1

```
CUB   0  1  0     0  0  0     0  0  0  -  1
SOX   0  2  0     0  0  0     1  0  x  -  3
```

RBIs: Hack, Knickerbocker. 2B: Kreevich, Wright. SH: Kreevich, Lee. DP: Sox. LOB: Cubs 6, Sox 8. BB: Passeau 3, Lee 2. Struck out: Passeau 3, Lee 5. HBP: B. Olsen (Lee). PB: McCullough. Umpires: Basil, Reardon, Summes, Jorda. Att: 13,955. Time—1:51.

The third game featured a triple play and the five-hit, nine strikeout, shutout pitching of Johnny Rigney (13–13). Trailing 6–0 in the fifth, Clyde McCullough drew a base on balls, the only walk Rigney gave up. Bob Sturgeon beat out an infield hit to put men on first and second. Then pinch-hitter Charlie Gilbert lined the ball right at second baseman Bill Knickerbocker. Knickerbocker tossed the ball to Appling to force McCullough for the second out and Appling tagged Sturgeon coming into second. For the second day in a row, the Cubs used four pitchers in the game—loser Paul Erickson (5–7), Bill Lee (8–14), Ken Raffensberger (0–1), and Eaves.

The White Sox swept the series on the seventh behind the four-hit pitching of Thornton Lee (22–11). The Cubs took a 1–0 lead off Lee in the top of the second, but the White Sox struck back for two runs in the bottom of the inning off losing pitcher Claude Passeau and were never headed. The final score was 3–1.

The 1942 Chicago City Championship Series

Chicago White Sox defeat Chicago Cubs 4–2

Neither the sixth-place Cubs (68–86) nor the sixth-place White Sox (66–82) had seen their rosters raided by wartime inductions yet, so the 1942 city championship series went ahead with two whole ballclubs.

Ted Lyons (14–6) started for the Sox in Game One on September 30 and won his tenth game over the Cubs in city championship competition. In a remarkably short 78-minute contest before a remarkably small Wrigley Field crowd of 4,751, Lyons three-hit the Nationals, retiring the first 13 men he faced before Clyde McCullough singled in the fifth to break up the perfect game. The

1942 Chicago City Championship Series

GAME ONE --- September 30

WHITE SOX	AB	R	H	PO	A	E		CUBS	AB	R	H	PO	A	E
Kolloway, 1b	3	1	0	11	0	0		Hack, 3b	4	0	1	1	2	0
Moses, rf	4	0	2	3	0	0		Merullo, ss	4	0	1	4	1	0
Mueller, cf	4	1	1	4	1	0		Nicholson, rf	3	0	0	1	0	0
Appling, ss	4	1	2	0	2	0		Dallessandro, cf	3	0	0	3	0	0
Hoag, lf	4	0	1	4	0	0		McCullough, c	3	0	1	3	1	0
Lodigiani, 2b	4	0	0	1	3	0		Novikoff, lf	3	0	0	4	0	0
Kennedy, 3b	3	0	0	0	3	0		Cavaretta, 1b	3	0	0	9	1	0
Tresh, c	3	0	0	4	0	0		Sturgeon, 2b	3	0	0	1	4	0
Lyons, p	3	0	0	0	2	0		Conway, p	2	0	0	1	1	0
								Lee, p	1	0	0	0	0	0
	32	3	6	27	11	0		Russell, ph	1	0	0	0	0	0
									29	0	3	27	10	0

```
SOX   ?  0  0    0  0  0    0  0  1  -  3
CUB   0  0  0    0  0  0    0  0  0  -  0
```

RBI: Appling, Hoag, Lodigiani. 2B: Appling, Merullo. LOB: Cubs 2, Sox 4. BB: Lee 2. Struck out: Lee 1, Lyons 2. Umpires: Sears (N), Pipgras (A), Barlick (N), Passarella (A). Att: 4,751. Time—1:18.

GAME TWO --- October 1

WHITE SOX	AB	R	H	PO	A	E		CUBS	AB	R	H	PO	A	E
Kolloway, 1b	5	4	4	13	0	1		Hack, 3b	5	0	2	1	1	0
Moses, rf	5	1	3	2	0	0		Merullo, ss	5	0	1	0	3	2
Mueller, cf	3	0	0	1	0	0		Nicholson, rf	3	1	1	3	0	0
Kuhel, ph	1	0	0	0	0	0		Dallessandro, cf	4	1	0	2	0	0
Heim, lf	1	0	0	1	0	0		McCullough, c	4	2	2	5	1	0
Appling, ss	5	1	1	3	2	1		Novikoff, lf	4	0	1	0	0	0
Hoag, lf-cf	4	1	2	1	0	0		Cavaretta, 1b	3	1	0	11	1	0
Lodigiani, 2b	4	0	0	0	7	0		Sturgeon, 2b	4	0	1	4	4	0
Kennedy, 3b	3	1	1	1	3	0		Warneke, p	3	0	0	1	2	0
Tresh, c	2	0	0	4	1	0		Fleming, p	0	0	0	0	0	0
Dickey, c	0	1	0	1	0	0		Gilbert, ph	1	0	0	0	0	0
Smith, p	1	0	0	0	1	1			36	5	8	27	13	2
West, ph	1	0	0	0	0	0								
Haynes, p	2	0	0	0	1	0								
	37	9	11	27	15	3								

```
SOX   3  0  0    1  0  0    1  4  0  -  9
CUB   0  3  2    0  0  0    0  0  0  -  5
```

RBIs: Kolloway 3, Moses 2, Mueller, Kuhel, Appling, Kennedy, Hack, Novikoff. HR: Kolloway. SH: Lodigiani. DP: Sox. SB: McCullough. LOB: Sox 6, Cubs 6. BB: Smith 1. Hits: Smith 6 in 3 innings; Haynes 2 in 6 innings; Warneke 10 in 7.2 innings; Fleming 1 in 1.1 innings. Winning pitcher: Haynes. Losing pitcher: Warneke. Umpires: Pipgras (A), Barlick (N), Passarella (A), Sears (N). Att: 3,320. Time—1:57.

Cubs threatened to score in the next inning when Stan Hack singled and Lem Merullo doubled, but Hack was thrown out at the plate to retire the side. Lyons then set down the last nine Cubs he faced. The Sox, meanwhile, scored two runs in the first when Don Kolloway walked and Wally Moses singled him to third. Kolloway scored when Bill Mueller forced Moses at second. Luke Appling doubled Mueller to third and he scored on Myril Hoag's long fly ball to right. The Sox scored an insurance run in the ninth and were held to a total of six hits by losing pitcher Bill Lee (13–13).

1942 Chicago City Championship Series

GAME THREE --- October 2

CUBS	AB	R	H	PO	A	E		WHITE SOX	AB	R	H	PO	A	E
Hack, 3b	4	1	1	1	1	0		Kolloway, 1b	4	2	2	10	0	1
Merullo, ss	3	0	1	1	1	0		Moses, rf	4	1	1	4	1	0
Foxx, ph	1	0	0	0	0	0		Mueller, cf	4	0	2	5	0	0
Stringer, 2b	3	0	0	0	1	0		Appling, ss	3	0	0	0	2	1
Novikoff, lf	4	0	0	0	0	0		Hoag, lf	3	0	2	3	0	0
McCullough, c	3	0	0	3	1	0		Lodigiani, 2b	2	0	0	2	3	0
Nicholson, rf	3	1	2	2	0	0		Kennedy, 3b	3	0	0	0	4	0
Dallessandro, cf	4	0	1	3	0	0		Tresh, c	3	0	0	3	1	1
Cavaretta, 1b	3	0	1	8	1	0		Humphries, p	3	0	0	0	0	1
Sturgeon, 2b	3	0	0	2	2	0								
Passeau, p	3	0	0	4	2	0			29	3	7	27	11	4
	34	2	6	24	9	0								

```
CUB    1  0  0    1  0  0     0  0  0  -  2
SOX    1  0  2    0  0  0     0  0  x  -  3
```

RBI: McCullough, Cavaretta, Moses, Mueller 2. 2B: Hack. Kolloway. 3B: Moses. SH: McCullough DP: Sox 2. LOB: Sox 3, Cubs 4. BB: Humphries 1. Struck out: Passeau 7, Humphries. HBP: Lodigiani (Passeau). WP: Humphries. Umpires: Barlick, Passarella, Sears, Pipgras. Att: 20,819. Time—1:44.

GAME FOUR --- October 4

WHITE SOX	AB	R	H	PO	A	E		CUBS	AB	R	H	PO	A	E
Kolloway, 1b	4	0	2	16	0	0		Hack, 3b	0	0	0	2	0	0
Moses, rf	4	0	0	0	0	0		Merullo, ss	4	1	2	2	6	0
Mueller, cf	4	0	0	1	1	0		Novikoff, lf	4	0	0	1	1	0
Appling, ss	3	1	0	1	4	0		McCullough, c	4	1	0	2	0	0
Hoag, lf	4	1	1	1	0	0		Nicholson, rf	4	0	1	1	0	0
Lodigiani, 2b	4	0	1	1	4	0		Dallessandro, cf	3	1	1	1	0	0
Kennedy, 3b	4	1	1	0	3	0		Cavaretta, 1b	4	0	1	16	0	0
Tresh, c	4	0	2	4	1	0		Sturgeon, 2b	2	1	2	2	2	0
Lee, p	2	0	1	0	1	0		Bithorn, p	3	1	1	0	2	0
West, ph	1	0	0	0	0	0			28	5	8	27	11	0
Ross, p	0	0	0	0	0	0								
	34	3	8	24	14	0								

```
SOX    0  0  0    0  1  0     0  0  2  -  3
CUB    0  1  1    1  0  0     1  1  x  -  5
```

RBI: Merullo, Dallessandro, Cavaretta, Sturgeon, Lodigiani, Kennedy, Lee. 2B: Cavaretta, Bithorn, Lodigiani, Tresh. SB: Dallessandro. SH: Hack. DP: Cubs 2. LOB: Cubs 5, Sox 9. BB: Lee 4, Bithorn 4. Struck out: Bithorn 7, Lee 2. Hits: Lee 6 in 4 innings; Ross 2 in 4 innings. WP: Lee. Losing pitcher: Lee. Umpires: Passarella, Sears, Pipgras, Barlick. Att: 3,366. Time—1:48.

Before a tiny Wrigley Field crowd of 3,320, the White Sox made it two in a row the next day with a 9–5 victory. The Americans scored three in the first only to see the Cubs tie the game in the second, then take a 5–3 lead in the third by knocking out Sox starter Edgar Smith (7–20). Smith didn't lead the American League in losses for nothing. Joe Haynes (8–5) took over the pitching duties for the Sox and threw shutout ball the rest of the way. The Americans tied the game with single runs in the fourth and seventh and drove

1942 Chicago City Championship Series

```
GAME FIVE --- October 5
```

CUBS	AB	R	H	PO	A	E	WHITE SOX	AB	R	H	PO	A	E
Hack, 3b	4	0	0	1	3	0	Kolloway, 1b	5	0	0	11	0	0
Merullo, ss	4	0	0	2	1	1	Moses, rf	4	0	2	2	0	0
Novikoff, lf	4	0	1	1	0	0	Mueller, cf	5	0	0	4	0	0
McCullough, c	4	0	0	4	1	0	Appling, ss	3	1	2	5	3	0
Nicholson, rf	3	0	0	6	0	0	Hoag, lf	3	0	0	2	0	0
Dallessandro, cf	4	1	1	3	0	0	Lodigiani, 2b	4	0	1	2	2	0
Cavaretta, 1b	4	1	2	7	0	0	Kennedy, 3b	4	0	0	2	3	1
Sturgeon, 2b	4	0	1	6	1	0	Tresh, c	3	0	0	2	2	0
Passeau, p	4	0	0	0	5	0	Lyons, p	3	0	0	0	3	0
							Kuhel, ph	0	0	0	0	0	0
	35	2	5	30	11	1	Webb, pr	0	0	0	0	0	0
								34	1	5	30	13	1

```
CUB   0  0  0    0  0  0    0  1  0   1 - 2
SOX   0  0  0    0  0  0    0  0  1   0 - 1
```

RBI: Sturgeon 2, Lodigiani. 3B: Cavaretta. SH: Hoag. LOB: Cubs 4, Sox 8. BB: Passeau 3, Lyons 1. Struck out: Passeau 4, Lyons 2. HPB: Tresh (Passeau). Umpires: Sears, Pipgras, Barlick, Passarella. Att: 5,963. Time—2:06.

Lon Warneke (5-7) from the mound with four runs in the eighth. Don Kolloway led the 11-hit Sox attack with a home run, three singles, three runs batted in, and four runs scored. Hayes got the victory, Warneke the loss.

John Humphries (12-12) of the Sox shaded Claude Passeau (19-14) by a score of 3-2 in Game Three played at Comiskey Park. The teams exchanged runs in the first, but the Sox pushed across two in the third and held on for the victory. Both pitchers went the distance.

The series shifted back to Wrigley for the fourth game and the smallest crowd yet, a total of 2,366. Cubs pitcher Hi Bithorn (9-14) pitched out of trouble all day, but finally outlasted Thornton Lee (2-6) and the Sox, 5-3. The Cubs scored single runs in five of their eight innings, and withstood a two-run Sox rally in the ninth to hold on for the victory.

The Cubs looked like they were going to make the series a contest when they won Game Five. Claude Passeau went the distance for the victory against Lyons of the White Sox in this ten inning affair. The game was scoreless until Bobby Sturgeon's single drove in the Cubs' first run in the eighth. The Sox tied the game in the bottom of the ninth on an RBI single by second baseman Dario Lodigiani, but Phil Cavaretta's triple and Sturgeon's sacrifice fly gave the Cubs a 2-1 victory in the next inning.

The White Sox took their eighth consecutive city championship in Game Six, winning by a score of 4-1. Bert Humphries won his second start of the series by striking out five, walking one, and allowing just five hits. The Sox scored three of their four runs off Cubs starter and losing pitcher Lon Warneke. There were 7,599 fans at the game, bringing total attendance for the series to 45,818.

This was the final Chicago city championship series to be played. The White Sox had won 18 series, lost six, and tied one. Their record in games played was 91-60-3. The Americans' dominance of the Cubs seems to defy all

1942 Chicago City Championship Series

```
GAME SIX --- October 6
```

CUBS	AB	R	H	PO	A	E
Hack, 3b	4	0	2	1	1	0
Merullo, ss	2	0	1	1	5	0
Novikoff, lf	4	0	0	4	1	0
McCullough, c	4	0	0	5	1	1
Nicholson, rf	3	0	1	3	0	0
Dallessandro, cf	3	0	0	1	0	0
Cavaretta, 1b	3	0	0	7	0	0
Sturgeon, 2b	3	1	1	2	0	0
Warneke, p	1	0	0	0	0	1
Fleming, p	0	0	0	0	0	0
Russell, ph	1	0	0	0	0	0
Errickson, p	0	0	0	0	1	0
	28	1	5	24	9	2

WHITE SOX	AB	R	H	PO	A	E
Kolloway, 1b	4	1	1	8	1	0
Moses, rf	4	1	1	2	0	0
Mueller, cf	4	0	1	2	0	0
Appling, ss	3	1	0	2	3	0
Hoag, lf	4	0	1	1	0	0
Lodigiani, 2b	2	0	0	2	2	0
Kennedy, 3b	4	0	2	3	1	0
Tresh, c	4	0	0	6	0	0
Humphries	3	1	1	1	3	0
	32	4	7	27	10	0

```
CUB    0  0  1    0  0  0    0  0  0  -  1
SOX    0  0  0    2  1  0    1  0  x  -  4
```

RBI: Merullo, Moses, Mueller, Hoag, Kennedy. 2B: Hack, Kolloway, Hoag. 3B: Moses. SB: Moses and Merullo. SH: Merullo, Warneke. DP: Sox 2. LOB: Sox 7, Cubs 3. BB: Warneke 3, Humphries 1. Struck out: Warneke 4, Humphries 5. Hits: Warneke 3 in 5 innings; Fleming 3 in 2 innings; Errickson 1 in 1 inning. Losing pitcher: Warneke. Umpires: Pipgras, Barlick, Passarella, Sears. Att: 7,599. Time—1:46.

logic. The Cubs had a much superior regular season winning percentage in nine of these championship years—and thus, "should have won" a minimum of nine series—yet they won only three of those nine. The White Sox should have won two, and did. In the 14 "swing" series, the White Sox had an amazing record of 11–3.

The League Playoffs

Introduction

It seems incredible in retrospect, but it took 71 years for two teams to finish the regular season with the same record. Such is the marvel of baseball.

The prospect of a tie had asserted itself most strongly in the National League in 1889, 1908, 1924, and 1927 when the first-place club finished the season with less than a two-game margin. American League possibilities had occurred in 1904, 1907, 1908, 1922, 1940, 1944, and in 1945. After nearly three-quarters of a century with no playoffs at all, the two leagues very nearly saw playoffs in back-to-back seasons.

I would not presume these games have been forgotten to the degree the rest of the forgotten championships have been. Ask any knowledgeable St. Louis baseball fan about 1946 and one of the first things he will mention is the playoff series with Brooklyn. The folks in New York haven't forgotten Bobby Thomson or Ralph Branca. And try this little experiment. The next time you meet a Red Sox fan, ask him if he happens to remember the 1978 playoff game with the Yankees. Mention Bucky Dent. Mention Bob Bailey.

The average baseball fan in, say, Pittsburgh, has forgotten there were league playoffs in 1946 and 1948. He probably remembers the Miracle of Coogan's Bluff, but he's forgotten that the Dodgers have participated in four (legitimate) playoffs, losing three. He has no memory of the 1959 Milwaukee Braves being involved in a pennant playoff if, indeed, he has any memory of the Milwaukee Braves at all. There are some people, I understand, who do not know to this day that the Dodgers played in Brooklyn. Everyone remembers the split season of 1981 when Bowie Kuhn decided that miniplayoffs might be a fun idea, even if they failed to include the two teams which legitimately won pennants — the Cincinnati Reds and the St. Louis Cardinals. Fifty years into the future, however, who will remember the miniplayoffs of 1981? The Macmillan encyclopedia disdains to run so much as a line score for these games.

But I have remembered them in this book, for they may be the last in a long line of forgotten championships.

A Summary of the League Playoff Championships

1946 National League: St. Louis Cardinals defeat Brooklyn Dodgers; 2–0.
1948 American League: Cleveland Indians defeat Boston Red Sox; 1–0.

1951 National League: New York Giants defeat Brooklyn Dodgers; 2–1.
1959 National League: Los Angeles Dodgers defeat Milwaukee Braves; 2–0.
1962 National League: San Francisco Giants defeat Los Angeles Dodgers; 2–1.
1978 American League East: New York Yankees defeat Boston Red Sox; 1–0.
1981 National League East: Montreal Expos defeat Philadelphia Phillies; 3–2.
1981 National League West: Los Angeles Dodgers defeat Houston Astros; 3–2.
1981 American League East: New York Yankees defeat Milwaukee Brewers; 3–2.
1981 American League West: Oakland Athletics defeat Kansas City Royals; 3–0.

The 1946 National League Championship Playoff Series

St. Louis Cardinals defeat the Brooklyn Dodgers; 2–0

The St. Louis Cardinals and Brooklyn Dodgers reached the end of the 1946 season with identical records of 96 wins and 58 losses, precipitating an unprecedented playoff series. National League president Ford Frick talked to Cardinal owner Sam Breadon and Brooklyn manager Leo Durocher on two phones at the same time and flipped a coin to decide the home park advantage. Breadon called the toss and called it wrong. Leo the Lip wanted the series to open in St. Louis so as to give the Dodgers the second and third games in Brooklyn. Durocher would take any edge he could get, having lost 14 of the 22 regular season games to St. Louis.

Howie Pollet (21–10), torn back muscle and all, was named to pitch Game One against Ralph Branca (3–1) on October 1st in Sportsman's Park. Neither team, in fact, was completely whole. The St. Louis shortstop, Marty Marion, had a bad back, and Brooklyn's star outfielder, Pete Reiser, was sidelined with a broken ankle. In the bottom of the first, St. Louis took the lead. Red Schoendienst struck out, Terry Moore singled, Stan Musial struck out, Enos Slaughter singled, and Whitey Kurowski walked to load the bases. Rookie Joe Garagiola then grounded a ball in the hole to Pee Wee Reese and just beat the throw to first. Cards 1, Dodgers 0. Brooklyn came back to tie the game in the third on a solo home run by first baseman Howie Schultz. In the bottom of the inning, Musial walked with one out and went to third on Slaughter's single. After Stan scored on Kurowski's groundout, Garagiola and Harry "The Hat" Walker singled to put St. Louis up by two.

The score stayed 3–1 until the top of the seventh when the Dodgers made a bid to tie the game. With one out, Reese and catcher Bruce Edwards singled. Schultz singled to score Reese, but a terrific throw by right-fielder Slaughter nailed Edwards trying to go to third. In the bottom of the inning, Musial tripled and Garagiola knocked in his second run of the game with a single to put the Cards on top, 4–2. That was the final score.

Branca, showing the bad luck he would be haunted with in postseason games, was knocked out in the third inning, having allowed six hits, two walks, and three runs. Pollet was in trouble most of the day and gave up eight hits and three walks, but was the winner nonetheless — his 21st victory of the year.

1946 National League Playoffs

```
GAME ONE --- October 1 at St. Louis
```

BROOKLYN	AB	R	H	BI	PO	A	ST. LOUIS	AB	R	H	BI	PO	A
Stanky, 2b	3	0	1	0	3	2	Schoendienst, 2b	5	0	2	0	1	7
Lavagetto, 3b	3	0	0	0	2	2	Moore, cf	5	1	3	0	1	0
Medwick, lf	4	0	1	0	1	0	Musial, 1b	4	2	1	0	10	0
Tepsic, pr	0	0	0	0	0	0	Slaughter, rf	4	0	2	0	4	1
Whitman, lf	0	0	0	0	1	0	Kurowski, 3b	2	1	0	1	1	2
D.Walker, rf	4	0	0	0	0	0	Garagiola, c	4	0	3	2	2	0
Furillo, cf	4	0	0	0	5	0	H.Walker, lf	3	0	1	1	3	0
Reese, ss	4	1	2	0	2	2	Marion, ss	4	0	0	0	5	4
Edwards, c	4	0	2	0	5	1	Pollet, p	4	0	0	0	0	2
Schultz, 1b	3	1	2	2	5	0							
Branca, p	1	0	0	0	0	0		35	4	12	4	27	16
Higbe, p	0	0	0	0	0	0							
Rojek, ph	0	0	0	0	0	0							
Gregg,, p	0	0	0	0	0	0							
Ramazzotti, ph	1	0	0	0	0	0							
Lombardi, p	0	0	0	0	0	0							
Melton, p	0	0	0	0	0	0							
	31	2	8	2	24	7							

```
BKN   0 0 1   0 0 0   1 0 0  -  2
STL   1 0 2   0 0 0   1 0 x  -  4
```

Errors: Pollet. DP: STL 3. LOB: BKN 6, STL 11. 3B: Musial. HR: Schultz. SH: Schultz. WP: Melton. Umpires: Boggess, John Reardon, Lawrence Goetz, Ralph Pinelli. Att: 26,012. Time—2:48.

Pitching	IP	H	R	ER	BB	SO
Brooklyn						
Branca (L)	2.2	6	3	3	2	3
Higbe	1.1	1	0	0	0	0
Gregg	2.0	1	0	0	1	1
Lombardi	.1	1	1	1	0	0
Melton	1.2	3	0	0	1	1
St. Louis						
Pollet (W)	9.0	8	2	2	3	2

Game Two, played in Ebbets Field after an off-day for travel, was less of a contest. Murry Dickson (15–6) was the pitcher for the Cardinals while the left-hander Joe Hatten (14–11) started for Brooklyn. The Dodgers scored a run after two were out in the bottom of the first to take their only lead of the series. Augie Galan singled on the infield, Dixie Walker walked, and first baseman Ed Stevens singled up the middle to give Brooklyn a 1–0 lead. Dickson settled down after that and allowed only three more hits. St. Louis took the lead in the top of the second. Left-fielder Erv Dusak tripled to lead off the inning and scored on Marty Marion's sacrifice fly. Catcher Clyde Kluttz then singled and scored on Dickson's triple to right-center. St. Louis added three more in the fifth after two were out. Musial doubled and Kurowski was intentionally walked to get to Slaughter. But "Country" spoiled the strategy by lining a triple to deep right. A single by Dusak scored Slaughter and sent Hatten to the clubhouse.

1946 National League Playoffs

```
GAME TWO --- October 3 at Brooklyn
```

ST. LOUIS	AB	R	H	BI	PO	A		BROOKLYN	AB	R	H	BI	PO	A
Schoendienst, 2b	5	1	1	0	1	5		Stanky, 2b	5	0	0	0	3	4
Moore, cf	5	1	2	0	2	0		Whitman, lf	4	0	0	0	2	0
Musial, 1b	4	1	1	0	14	1		Schultz, ph	1	0	0	0	0	0
Kurowski, 3b	2	2	1	2	1	1		Galan, 3b	4	2	2	0	0	4
Slaughter, rf	3	1	1	2	0	0		D.Walker, rf	3	0	0	0	1	0
Dusak, lf	3	1	2	1	1	0		Stevens, 1b	4	1	2	2	11	0
H.Walker, ph	1	0	0	0	0	0		Furillo, cf	4	1	1	1	4	0
Marion, ss	3	0	1	2	4	3		Reese, ss	2	0	0	0	2	3
Kluttz, c	5	1	2	0	3	2		Edwards, c	2	0	1	1	3	1
Dickson, p	5	0	2	1	1	5		Hatten, p	1	0	0	0	0	1
Brecheen, p	0	0	0	0	0	0		Behrman, p	0	0	0	0	0	0
								Hermanski, ph	1	0	0	0	0	0
	36	8	13	8	27	17		Lombardi, p	0	0	0	0	0	1
								Higbe, p	0	0	0	0	1	0
								Melton, p	0	0	0	0	0	0
								Medwick, ph	1	0	0	0	0	0
								Taylor, p	0	0	0	0	0	0
								Lavagetto,ph	0	0	0	0	0	0
									32	4	6	4	27	14

```
STL    0  2  0    0  3  0    1  2  0  -  8
BKN    1  0  0    0  0  0    0  0  3  -  4
```

Errors: none. LOB: STL 11, BKN 7. DP: STL 1, BKN 1. 2B: Galan, Moore, Musial. 3B: Dickson, Dusak, Slaughter, Stevens. SH: Dusak, Marion. WP: Dickson. Umpires: Boggess, John Reardon, Lawrence Goetz, Ralph Pinelli. Att: 31,437. Time—2:44.

Pitching	IP	H	R	ER	BB	SO
St. Louis						
Dickson (W)	8.1	5	4	4	5	3
Brecheen (SV)	0.2	1	0	0	1	2
Brooklyn						
Hatten (L)	4.2	7	5	5	3	0
Behrman	0.1	1	0	0	0	0
Lombardi	1.1	1	1	1	2	0
Higbe	1.0	3	2	2	2	1
Melton	0.2	0	0	0	0	0
Taylor	1.0	1	0	0	0	1

    The Cardinals added another run in the seventh on a squeeze play by Marion, and two final runs in the eighth on a two-run single by Kurowski. Brooklyn's season had dwindled to six little outs and they were losing 8–1.

    The Dodgers made a go of it in the bottom of the ninth, but couldn't quite pull the trigger. Augie Galan doubled to lead off the inning and, one out later, Ed Stevens tripled him home. Center-fielder Carl Furillo singled Stevens home and when Dickson walked Reese, manager Eddie Dyer signalled to the bullpen for Harry Brecheen. But Edwards greeted Brecheen with an RBI single, pinch-hitter Cookie Lavagetto walked, and suddenly the Dodgers had the tying run at the plate with only one out. Brecheen reached back for something extra and struck out second baseman Eddie Stanky and pinch-hitter Howie Schultz to end the game. For the Dodgers, not for the first time and not for the last, it was "Wait till next year."

1948 American League Playoff

```
October 4 at Boston
```

CLEVELAND	AB	R	H	BI	PO	A
Mitchell, lf	5	0	1	0	1	0
Clark, 1b	2	0	0	0	5	0
Robinson, 1b	2	1	1	0	9	0
Boudreau, ss	4	3	4	2	3	5
Gordon, 2b	4	1	1	0	2	3
Keltner, 3b	5	1	3	3	0	6
Doby, cf	5	1	2	0	1	0
Kennedy, rf	2	0	0	0	0	0
Hegan, c	3	1	0	1	6	1
Bearden,, p	3	0	1	0	0	2
	35	8	13	6	27	17

BOSTON	AB	R	H	BI	PO	A
DiMaggio, cf	4	0	0	0	3	0
Pesky, 3b	4	1	1	0	3	4
Williams, lf	4	1	1	0	3	0
Stephens, ss	4	0	1	1	2	4
Doerr, 2b	4	1	1	2	5	2
Spence, rf	1	0	0	0	1	0
Hitchcock, ph	0	0	0	0	0	0
Wright, pr	0	0	0	0	0	0
Goodman, 1b	3	0	0	0	7	1
Tebbetts, c	4	0	1	0	3	1
Galehouse, p	0	0	0	0	0	1
Kinder, p	2	0	0	0	0	1
	30	3	5	3	27	14

```
CLE   1 0 0   4 1 0   0 1 1 - 8
BOS   1 0 0   0 0 2   0 0 0 - 3
```

Errors: Gordon, Williams. DP: CLE 3, BOS 1. LOB: CLE 7, BOS 5. 2B: Doby 2, Keltner, Pesky. HR: Boudreau 2, Doerr, Keltner. SH: Kennedy 2, Robinson. WP: Kinder. Umpires: William McGowan, William Summers, Charles Berry, Edwin Rommel. Att: 33,957. Time—2:24.

Pitching	IP	H	R	ER	BB	SO
Cleveland						
Bearden (W)	9.0	5	3	3	5	6
Boston						
Galehouse (L)	3.0	5	4	4	1	1
Kinder	6.0	8	4	3	3	2

```
Galehouse pitched to 3 batters in the fourth
```

The 1948 American League Championship Playoff

Cleveland Indians defeat the Boston Red Sox; 1-0

At the end of the last day of the 1948 American League pennant race, the Boston Red Sox and Cleveland Indians were deadlocked with identical 96-58 records. Coming two years after the first playoff series in history—the St. Louis Cardinals against the Brooklyn Dodgers—the Indians met the Red Sox for a one-game playoff before 34,000 very cold fans at Fenway Park on October 4th. Boston manager Joe McCarthy elected to start well-rested 36-year-old Denny Galehouse (8-8) in the crucial game while Indians player-manager Lou Boudreau went with knuckleballer Gene Bearden (20-7). Bearden had pitched nine innings just two days earlier.

With two out in the top of the first, Lou Boudreau parked a home run over the Green Monster in left. Boston rebounded in the bottom of the inning to tie the score on a Johnny Pesky double and a Vern Stephens single. The Indians scored all the runs they needed in the fourth and knocked Galehouse out of the box. Boudreau was the instigator again, this time with a lead-off single. Joe Gordon followed Boudreau's rap with a single and third-baseman Kenny

Keltner duplicated Boudreau's first-inning heroics by hitting a home run of his own over the left-field wall. Galehouse was relieved by Ellis Kinder who fared no better. Lary Doby doubled, was sacrificed to third by Bob Kennedy, and scored on Jim Hegan's groundout. When Boudreau hit his second home run of the day in the fifth inning, the Indians led 6–1.

Bearden had things well in hand, despite allowing two Red Sox runs in the sixth. Ted Williams reached on a single when second baseman Joe Gordon dropped his pop fly. Bobby Doerr's homer to left pulled the Sox to within three. That was all they could muster though, as Cleveland added insurance runs in the eighth and ninth. Denny Galehouse was the loser and Gene Bearden the winner, his 20th victory. Bearden went on to win one game and save another in the World Series against the Boston Braves, but he would never again win more than eight games in a regular season.

The 1951 National League Championship Playoff Series

New York Giants defeat the Brooklyn Dodgers 2–1

Many words have been written about this incredible three-game playoff between the New York Giants (98–59), winners of 52 of their last 63 games in the

1951 National League Playoffs

GAME ONE --- October 1 at Brooklyn

NEW YORK	AB	R	H	BI	PO	A		BROOKLYN	AB	R	H	BI	PO	A
Stanky, 2b	5	0	2	0	6	3		Furillo, rf	4	0	0	0	2	0
Dark, ss	4	0	1	0	0	4		Reese, ss	3	0	1	0	2	0
Mueller, rf	5	0	0	0	1	0		Snider, cf	4	0	1	0	6	0
Irvin, lf	4	2	1	1	2	0		Robinson, 2b	3	0	1	0	3	0
Lockman, 1b	4	0	1	0	10	1		Campanella, c	3	0	0	0	7	0
Thomson, 3b	2	1	1	2	2	3		Pafko, lf	3	1	1	1	2	0
Mays, cf	3	0	0	0	2	0		Hodges, 1b	2	0	0	0	2	1
Westrum, c	2	0	0	0	4	3		Cox, 3b	3	0	1	0	3	0
Hearn, p	3	0	0	0	0	1		Branca, p	2	0	0	0	0	1
								Russell, ph	1	0	0	0	0	0
	32	3	6	3	27	15		Podbielan, p	0	0	0	0	0	0
									28	1	5	1	27	2

```
NY    0  0  0    2  0  0    0  1  0  -  3
BKN   0  1  0    0  0  0    0  0  0  -  1
```

Errors: Dark, Snider. DP: NY 4. LOB: NY 10, BKN 2. 2B: Dark. HR: Irvin, Pafko, Thomson. SH: Hearn, Thompson. HBP: Irvin (Branca). Umpires: Lawrence Goetz, William Stewart, John Conlan, Jorda. Att: 30,751. Time—2:39.

Pitching	IP	H	R	ER	BB	SO
New York						
Hearn (W)	9.0	5	1	1	2	5
Brooklyn						
Branca (L)	8.0	5	3	3	5	5
Podbielan	1.0	1	0	0	0	0

1951 National League Playoffs

GAME TWO --- October 2 at New York

BROOKLYN	AB	R	H	BI	PO	A
Furillo, rf	5	0	0	0	0	0
Reese, ss	5	1	2	0	1	7
Snider, cf	4	1	2	1	2	0
Robinson, 2b	5	1	3	3	6	0
Pafko, lf	5	1	1	1	0	0
Hodges, 1b	4	2	2	1	10	0
Cox, 3b	3	2	0	0	4	4
Walker, c	5	1	3	2	4	0
Labine, p	4	1	0	0	0	1
	40	10	13	8	27	12

NEW YORK	AB	R	H	BI	PO	A
Stanky, 2b	5	0	1	0	2	4
Dark, ss	5	0	0	0	1	1
Mueller, rf	4	0	1	0	3	0
Irvin, lf	4	0	1	0	3	0
Lockman, 1b	3	0	0	0	11	?
Thomson, 3b	4	0	1	0	1	4
Mays, cf	4	0	1	0	1	0
Westrum, c	3	0	0	0	5	2
Williams, pr	0	0	0	0	0	0
Jones, p	1	0	0	0	0	1
Spencer, p	1	0	1	0	0	1
Rigney, ph	0	0	0	0	0	0
Corwin, p	0	0	0	0	0	0
Thompson, ph	1	0	0	0	0	0
	35	0	6	0	27	15

```
BKN   2 0 0   0 1 3   2 0 2  -  10
NY    0 0 0   0 0 0   0 0 0  -   0
```

Errors: Reese, Hodges, Thomson, Mays, Jones, Spencer 2. DP: NY 1. LOB: NY 11, BKN 8. 2B: Snider, Thomson. HR: Hodges, Pafko, Robinson, Walker. SH: Cox. Umpires: Lawrence Goetz, William Stewart, John Conlan, Jorda. Att: 38,609. Time—2:44.

Pitching	IP	H	R	ER	BB	SO
Brooklyn						
Labine (W)	9.0	6	0	0	3	3
New York						
Jones (L)	2.1	4	2	2	1	2
Spencer	3.2	6	4	2	1	0
Corwin	3.0	3	4	2	2	2

last weeks of the season, and the Brooklyn Dodgers (97–60), losers of six of their last ten.

The Giants' Jim Hearn (17–9) beat hard-luck Ralph Branca (13–12) by a score of 3-1 in the first game at Ebbets Field, but Brooklyn rebounded the next day at the Polo Grounds behind a Clem Labine (5–1) six-hit shutout. Sheldon Jones (6–11) took the loss. Those two contests set the stage for Branca's fall from glory and Bobby Thomson's ascension into baseball's pantheon of memories.

The Dodgers entered the bottom of the ninth with a 4–1 lead behind Don Newcombe (20–9). Lead-off hitter Al Dark singled to the infield and Don Mueller singled him to third. Monte Irvin fouled out, but Whitey Lockman doubled to left to score Dark. At this point, Brooklyn manager Charlie Dressen summoned Ralph Branca from the bullpen to face Bobby Thomson. Thomson had put the Giants ahead to stay in the first game two days earlier with a home run against Branca. Nevertheless, Dressen had confidence that Ralph could do the job. Branca's second pitch was a waist-high fastball and Thomson drove it into the left-field stands—good enough for a three-run homer and the National League pennant.

1951 National League Playoffs

```
GAME THREE --- October 3 at New York

BROOKLYN            AB  R  H BI PO  A      NEW YORK           AB  R  H BI PO  A
---------------------------------------    ---------------------------------------
Furillo, rf          5  0  0  0  0  0      Stanky, 2b          4  0  0  0  0  4
Reese, ss            4  2  1  0  2  5      Dark, ss            4  1  1  0  2  2
Snider, cf           3  1  2  0  1  0      Mueller, rf         4  0  1  0  0  0
Robinson, 2b         2  1  1  1  3  2      Hartung, pr         0  1  0  0  0  0
Pafko, lf            4  0  1  1  4  1      Irvin, lf           4  1  1  0  1  0
Hodges, 1b           4  0  0  0 11  1      Lockman, 1b         3  1  2  1 11  1
Cox, 3b              4  0  2  1  1  3      Thomson, 3b         4  1  3  4  4  1
Walker, c            4  0  1  0  2  0      Mays, cf            3  0  0  0  1  0
Newcombe, p          4  0  0  0  1  1      Westrum, c          0  0  0  0  7  1
Branca, p            0  0  0  0  0  0      Rigney, ph          1  0  0  0  0  0
                    ----------------       Noble, c            0  0  0  0  0  0
                    34  4  8  3 *25 13     Maglie, p           2  0  0  0  1  2
                                           Thompson, ph        1  0  0  0  0  0
*  One 'out when winning run scored        Jansen, p           0  0  0  0  0  0
                                                              ----------------
                                           30  5  8  5 27 11

BKN    1  0  0    0  0  0    0  3  0  -  4          30  5  8  5 27 11
NY     0  0  0    0  0  0    1  0  4  -  5
```

Errors: none. DP BKN 2. LOB: BKN 7, NY 3. 2B: Irvin, Lockman, Thomson. HR: Thomson. SH: Lockman. WP: Maglie. Umpires: Jorda, John Conlan, William Stewart, Lawrence Goetz. Att: 34,320. Time—2:28.

```
Pitching             IP   H   R  ER  BB  SO
---------------------------------------------
   Brooklyn
Newcombe            8.1   7   4   4   2   2
Branca (L)          0.0   1   1   1   0   0

   New York
Maglie              8.0   8   4   4   4   6
Jansen (W)          1.0   0   0   0   0   0
```

Branca pitched to one batter in ninth

The 1959 National League
Championship Playoff Series

Los Angeles Dodgers defeat the Milwaukee Braves; 2–0

A very small crowd turned up Monday afternoon, September 28, in Milwaukee to witness Game One of the three-game National League playoff series between the Milwaukee Braves (86–70) and the Los Angeles Dodgers (88–68). The anonymity of the starting pitchers may have had something to do with the sparse crowd but, rain and all, one has to question the Milwaukee fans' dedication to the team. Dodger manager Walter Alston picked ten-game winner Danny McDevitt and Braves manager Fred Haney chose five-game winner Carl Willey. Delayed by rain for 47 minutes, the game finally got underway. McDevitt had cause to wish the rain had never stopped.

Los Angeles jumped on top with a run in the first, but Milwaukee came back in the bottom of the second inning and knocked McDevitt out of the box. Johnny Logan walked with one out, Del Crandall and Billy Bruton singled and

1959 National League Playoffs

GAME ONE --- September 28 at Milwaukee

LOS ANGELES	AB	R	H	BI	PO	A		MILWAUKEE	AB	R	H	BI	PO	A
Gilliam, 3b	4	0	0	0	1	1		Avila, 2b	5	0	0	1	4	3
Moon, lf	5	1	3	0	3	4		Mathews, 3b	4	0	0	0	2	3
Neal, 2b	4	1	1	0	2	0		Aaron, rf	2	0	0	0	3	0
Larker, rf	4	0	3	1	0	0		Adcock, 1b	3	0	0	0	6	0
Lillis, pr	0	0	0	0	0	0		Pafko, lf	2	0	0	0	1	0
Fairly, rf	0	0	0	0	1	0		Maye, ph-lf	2	0	1	0	1	0
Hodges, 1b	3	0	1	1	7	1		Logan, ss	3	1	1	0	1	3
Demeter, cf	4	0	1	0	2	0		Crandall, c	4	1	2	0	5	0
Roseboro, c	4	1	1	1	8	0		Bruton, cf	4	0	1	1	4	0
Wills, ss	4	0	0	0	3	3		Willey, p	2	0	1	0	0	1
McDevitt, p	1	0	0	0	0	0		Slaughter, ph	1	0	0	0	0	0
Sherry, p	2	0	0	0	0	0		McMahon, p	0	0	0	0	0	0
								Torre, ph	1	0	0	0	0	0
	35	3	10	3	27	9			33	2	6	2	27	10

```
LA    1 0 1   0 0 1   0 0 0  -  3
MIL   0 2 0   0 0 0   0 0 0  -  2
```

Errors: Wills. DP: LA 1, MIL 2. LOB: LA 8, MIL 8. HR: Roseboro. Umpires: Conlan, Barlick, Boggess, Donatelli, Gorma, Jackowski. Att: 18,297. Time—2:40.

Pitching	IP	H	R	ER	BB	SO
Los Angeles						
McDevitt	1.1	2	2	2	2	2
Sherry (W)	7.2	4	0	0	2	4
Milwaukee						
Willey (L)	6.0	8	3	3	2	3
McMahon	3.0	2	0	0	1	2

Logan scored to tie the game. At this point, Alston put a rather early hook on McDevitt who had allowed two hits and two walks in an inning and a third. In came rookie Larry Sherry, 7–2 on the year. Willey grounded to Maury Wills who booted the ball for an error to load the bases. Crandall scored as Bobby Avila grounded into a forceout and the Braves led, 2–1. Sherry was never in trouble again. Consecutive singles by Charlie Neal, Norm Larker, and Gil Hodges tied the game for the Dodgers in the third and Johnny Roseboro's lead-off home run in the sixth was the deciding run. Sherry ended up the victor, allowing four hits, two walks, and no runs in the seven and two-thirds innings he pitched.

Game Two was played at the Los Angeles Memorial Coliseum before a crowd slightly more than double that of Game One in Milwaukee. The pitching aces for both teams, Lew Burdette (21–15) and Don Drysdale (17–13), were on the mound and it looked to be a pitcher's duel. It was not. In the Milwaukee first, Eddie Mathews walked, Hank Aaron doubled him to third, and Frank Torre's single scored both men to put the Braves up, 2–0. The Dodgers cut the lead in half in the bottom of the inning as Charlie Neal tripled and scored on Wally Moon's single. Milwaukee tallied another run in the second, but Neal's home run in the fourth again cut the lead to one. The Braves took their third

1959 National League Playoffs

GAME TWO --- September 29 at Los Angeles

MILWAUKEE	AB	R	H	BI	PO	A
Bruton, cf	6	0	0	0	4	0
Mathews, 3b	4	2	2	1	2	2
Aaron, rf	4	1	2	0	3	0
Torre, 1b	3	0	1	2	10	2
Maye, lf	2	0	0	0	2	0
Pafko, ph-lf	1	0	0	0	0	0
Slaughter, ph	1	0	0	0	0	0
DeMerit, lf	0	0	0	0	1	0
Spangler, ph-lf	0	0	0	0	3	0
Logan, ss	3	1	2	0	2	5
Schoendienst, 2b	1	0	0	0	0	0
Vernon, ph	1	0	0	0	0	0
Cottier, 2b	0	0	0	0	0	0
Adcock, ph	1	0	0	0	0	0
Avila, 2b	0	0	0	0	1	0
Crandall, c	6	1	1	0	6	1
Mantilla, 2b-ss	5	0	1	1	1	1
Burdette, p	4	0	1	0	0	2
McMahon, p	0	0	0	0	0	0
Spahn, p	0	0	0	0	0	0
Jay, p	1	0	0	0	0	0
Rush, p	1	0	0	0	0	0
	44	5	10	4	*35	13

LOS ANGELES	AB	R	H	BI	PO	A
Gilliam, 3b	5	0	1	0	4	3
Neal, 2b	6	2	2	1	3	2
Moon, rf-lf	6	1	3	1	3	1
Snider, cf	4	0	1	0	1	0
Lillis, pr	0	1	0	0	0	0
Williams, p	2	0	0	0	0	0
Hodges, 1b	5	2	2	0	11	0
Larker, lf	4	0	2	2	2	0
Pignatano, pr-c	1	0	1	0	3	0
Roseboro, c	3	0	0	0	5	1
Furillo, ph-rf	2	0	2	1	0	0
Wills, ss	5	0	1	0	2	5
Drysdale, p	1	0	0	0	1	1
Podres, p	1	0	0	0	0	0
Churn, p	0	0	0	0	0	1
Demeter, ph	1	0	0	0	0	0
Koufax, p	0	0	0	0	0	0
Labine, p	0	0	0	0	0	0
Essegian, ph #	0	0	0	0	0	0
Fairly, ph	2	0	0	0	1	0
	48	6	15	5	36	14

* Two out when winning run scored
\# Announced for Labine in ninth

```
MIL   2 1 0   0 1 0   0 1 0   0 0 0 - 5
LA    1 0 0   1 0 0   0 0 3   0 0 1 - 6
```

Errors: Mantilla 2, Neal, Snider. DP: LA 1, MIL 1. LOB: MIL 13, LA 11. PB: Pignatano. HBP: Pignatano (Jay). WP: Podres. 2B: Aaron. 3B: Crandall, Neal. HR: Mathews, Neal. Umpires: Barlick, Boggess, Donatelli, Conlan, Jackowski, Gorman. Att: 36,853. Time—4:06.

Pitching	IP	H	R	ER	BB	SO
Milwaukee						
Burdette	8.0	10	5	5	0	4
McMahon	0.0	1	0	0	0	0
Spahn	0.1	1	0	0	0	0
Jay	2.1	1	0	0	1	1
Rush (L)	1.0	2	1	0	1	0
Los Angeles						
Drysdale	4.1	6	4	3	2	3
Podres	2.1	3	0	0	1	1
Churn	1.1	1	1	1	0	0
Koufax	0.2	0	0	0	3	1
Labine	0.1	0	0	0	0	1
Williams (W)	3.0	0	0	0	3	3

Burdette pitched to three batters in ninth.
McMahon pitched to one batter in ninth.

two-run lead in the fifth as Eddie Mathews hit a solo home run. A triple by Crandall and sacrifice fly by Felix Mantilla put Milwaukee on top 5–2 going into the bottom of the ninth. The 1959 season was about to end for the Los Angeles Dodgers.

Alston had already used five pitchers — Drysdale, Johnny Podres (14–9), Chuck Churn (3–2), Sandy Koufax (8–6), and Clem Labine — but Milwaukee still had Lew Burdette on the mound. Lew had given up seven hits but only two runs, and no runs at all since the fourth. He tired in the ninth, however, as Wally Moon, Duke Snider, and Gil Hodges hit consecutive singles to score one run. Burdette was out, Don McMahon (5–3) was in. Norm Larker's single cut the Milwaukee lead to 5–4 and Warren Spahn (21–15) came in to try to get the last three outs of the game. Pinch-hitter Carl Furillo hit a sacrifice fly to score the tying run. A Maury Wills single sent Spahn to the clubhouse to commisserate with Burdette and McMahon, and Haney brought in Joey Jay (6–11). The inning ended, but not without incident. If not for an excellent running catch by Hank Aaron, there would have been no need for extra innings.

In the top of the 11th, reliever Stan Williams gave the partisan crowd a few anxious moments by walking three men, but he worked out of his self-made jam. Bob Rush (5–6), who got the last out for the Braves in the bottom of the 11th, took the mound for the last of the 12th. There were two men gone when Gil Hodges walked. Joey Pignatano singled Hodges to second and Furillo grounded a ball up the middle. The Braves' fine shortstop, Felix Mantilla, stopped the grounder behind second but made an ill-advised, off-balance throw to first. The ball skidded past Torre into the dugout and the Dodgers, who had finished seventh in 1958, were the National League champions of 1959.

The 1962 National League Championship Playoff Series

San Francisco Giants defeat the Los Angeles Dodgers; 2–1

Organized baseball had been in existence 71 years before the first league playoff in 1946. Yet over the next 17 years, five such playoffs would be held. In many ways, the 1962 games between the San Francisco Giants (103–62) and Los Angeles Dodgers (102–63) were the most exciting. The Dodgers had lost their last four regular season games and 10 of their last 13, blowing a four-game lead in the final week of the season. When, on the final day of the season, the Giants won and the Dodgers lost, a three-game playoff series was a reality the Dodgers did not want to face. Los Angeles had been shut out in the final two games of the season and saw nothing in the first game to allay their fears.

It was the lefthander Sandy Koufax (14–7) against Billy Pierce (16–6) in Game One at Candlestick Park. Koufax, with circulatory problems in his left index finger, was knocked from the box in the second inning after allowing three runs on four hits. The Giants banged out ten hits off six Dodger pitchers, including doubles by Felipe Alou and Jose Pagan, solo homers by Orlando Cepeda and Jim Davenport, and two home runs by Willie Mays. The Dodgers seemed resigned to defeat as they dropped the opener by a horrendous 8–0 score.

The series moved to Dodger Stadium the next day for Game Two on the 2nd of October. Things looked very dark for Los Angeles, which might explain why a crowd of only 25,321 showed up for the game. Jack Sanford (24–7) started on two days' rest for the Giants. Don Drysdale (25–9) made his fourth start in the last nine days and was scored upon once in the second, then driven from the mound with four Giant runs in the sixth. Drysdale wound up allowing seven hits, four walks, and five runs in five and one-third innings on the mound. Los Angeles was down to its last 12 outs, had not scored for 36 innings, and things looked very dark indeed.

1962 National League Playoffs

GAME ONE --- October 1 at San Francisco

LOS ANGELES	AB	R	H	BI	PO	A		SAN FRANCISCO	AB	R	H	BI	PO	A
Wills, ss,	4	0	0	0	1	2		Kuenn, lf	5	0	0	0	2	0
Gilliam, 2b	3	0	0	0	1	2		Hiller, 2b	4	0	1	0	2	0
T.Davis, lf	4	0	0	0	0	0		F.Alou, rf	4	1	1	0	5	0
Howard, rf	4	0	0	0	3	0		Mays, cf	3	3	3	3	2	0
Walls, 1b	3	0	0	0	9	0		Cepeda, 1b	4	1	1	1	6	0
Roseboro, c	3	0	0	0	4	1		Davenport, 3b	3	2	2	1	0	0
Carey, 3b	3	0	1	0	2	3		Bailey, c	2	1	1	0	6	0
W.Davis, cf	3	0	0	0	4	0		Pagan, ss	3	0	1	2	4	4
Koufax, p	0	0	0	0	0	0		Pierce, p	4	0	0	0	0	0
Roebuck, p	1	0	0	0	0	1								
McMullenn, ph	1	0	1	0	0	0			32	8	10	7	27	4
Tracewski, pr	0	0	0	0	0	0								
L.Sherry, p	0	0	0	0	0	0								
Smith, p	0	0	0	0	0	0								
Camilli, ph	1	0	1	0	0	0								
Ortega, p	0	0	0	0	0	0								
Perranoski, p	0	0	0	0	0	0								
	30	0	3	0	24	9								

```
LA    0  0  0    0  0  0    0  0  0  -  0
SF    2  1  0    0  0  2    0  3  x  -  8
```

Errors: Howard. 2B: F. Alou, Camilli, Pagan. HR: Cepeda, Davenport, Mays 2. SB: Mays. SH: Pagan. DP: LA. LOB: LA 4, SF 5. Umpires: Conlan, Boggess, Donatelli, Landes. Att: 32,652. Time—2:39.

PITCHING	IP	H	R	ER	BB	SO
Los Angeles						
Koufax (L)	1.0	4	3	3	0	0
Roebuck	4.0	1	0	0	0	2
Sherry	0.1	3	2	2	1	0
Smith	1.2	1	0	0	0	2
Ortega	0.1	0	2	2	2	0
Perranoski	0.2	1	1	0	1	0
San Francisco						
Pierce (W)	9.0	3	0	0	1	6

Koufax pitched to two batters in second.

But in the bottom of the sixth, the worm turned in a big way. The weary Jack Sanford walked Junior Gilliam to start the inning and manager Al Dark brought Stu Miller (5–8) in from the bullpen. Bad move. Duke Snider doubled and Tommy Davis hit a sacrifice fly to drive in Gilliam for the first Dodger run of the series. Wally Moon walked and Frank Howard's single scored Snider. Billy O'Dell (19–14) came in to pitch and was faced with three consecutive pinch-hitters. The first, Doug Camilli, singled to load the bases. Pinch-hitter Andy Carey was hit with a pitch, forcing in a run and making the score 5–3. Pinch-hitter Lee Walls's double to left-center emptied the bases. Unbelievably, the Dodgers led, 6–5. Don Larsen (5–4) relieved. Walls scored on a groundout as Giants' catcher Tom Haller dropped the ball. Seven runs in the inning and the Giants, who had stood as close to the National League pennant as 12 little outs, now faced a two-run deficit with only three innings to close.

1962 National League Playoffs

GAME TWO --- October 2 at Los Angeles

SAN FRANCISCO	AB	R	H	BI	PO	A
Hiller, 2b	3	1	1	1	0	3
Nieman, ph	1	0	0	0	0	0
Bowman, 2b	1	0	0	0	2	0
Davenport, 3b	6	1	2	1	1	1
Mays, cf	5	0	1	0	4	1
McCovey, lf	2	0	1	1	2	0
Miller, p	0	0	0	0	0	0
O'Dell, p	0	0	0	0	0	0
Larsen, p	0	0	0	0	0	0
Bailey, ph	1	0	1	1	0	0
Boles, pr	0	1	0	0	0	0
Bolin, p	0	0	0	0	0	0
LeMay, p	0	0	0	0	0	0
Perry, p	0	0	0	0	0	1
McCormick, p	0	0	0	0	0	0
Cepeda, 1b	5	1	1	0	6	1
F.Alou, rf	4	0	2	1	3	0
Haller, c	1	1	0	0	4	0
Orsino, c	1	0	1	1	3	1
Pagan, ss	5	1	3	0	1	1
Sanford, p	3	1	0	0	0	1
M.Alou, lf	0	0	0	0	0	0
Kuenn, ph-lf	2	0	0	0	0	0
	40	7	13	6	*26	10

LOS ANGELES	AB	R	H	BI	PO	A
Wills, ss,	4	1	0	0	3	1
Gilliam, 2b-3b	3	1	0	0	3	2
Snider, lf	3	1	1	0	2	0
Spencer, ph	0	0	0	0	0	0
T.Davis, 3b-cf	3	0	1	1	2	2
Moon, 1b	2	1	1	0	2	0
Fairly, 1b	1	0	1	1	3	0
Howard, rf	3	1	1	1	0	0
Roseboro, c	2	0	0	0	6	0
Camilli, ph-c	2	1	1	0	2	0
W.Davis, cf	2	0	0	0	3	0
Carey, ph	0	0	0	1	0	0
Burright, pr	0	1	0	0	1	1
Drysdale, p	2	0	0	0	0	2
Roebuck, p	0	0	0	0	0	0
Walls, ph	1	1	1	3	0	0
Perranoski, p	0	0	0	0	0	0
Smith, p	0	0	0	0	0	0
Williams, p	1	0	0	0	0	0
	29	8	7	7	27	8

```
SF   0  1  0    0  0  4    0  2  0  -  7
LA   0  0  0    0  0  7    0  0  1  -  8
```

Errors: Haller, Howard, Drysdale. LOB: SF 13, LA 7. 2B: F. Alou, Pagan, Snider, Walls. SB: Wills. SH: Spencer. SF: T. Davis, Fairly, Orsino. HBP: Hiller (Drysdale). Umpires: Barlick, Boggess, Donatelli, Conlan. Att: 25,321. Time—4:18.

PITCHING	IP	H	R	ER	BB	SO
San Francisco						
Sanford	5.0	2	1	1	3	4
Miller	0.1	2	3	3	1	0
O'Dell	0.0	2	3	2	0	0
Larsen	1.2	1	0	0	0	1
Bolin (L)	1.0	0	1	1	2	2
LeMay	0.0	0	0	0	1	0
Perry	0.1	0	0	0	0	0
McCormick	0.1	0	0	0	1	0
Los Angeles						
Drysdale	5.1	7	5	3	4	4
Roebuck	0.2	1	0	0	0	0
Perranoski	1.0	4	1	1	0	0
Smith	0.1	1	1	0	0	0
Williams (W)	1.2	0	0	0	1	2

Sanford pitched to one batter in sixth; O'Dell pitched to three batters in sixth; Bolin pitched to one batter in ninth; LeMay pitched to one batter in ninth; Perranoski pitched to two batters in eighth.

1962 National League Playoffs

```
GAME THREE --- October 3 at Los Angeles
```

SAN FRANCISCO	AB	R	H	BI	PO	A
Kuenn, lf	5	1	2	1	2	0
Hiller, 2b	3	0	1	0	4	1
McCovey, ph	0	0	0	0	0	0
Bowman, pr	0	1	0	0	0	0
F.Alou, rf	4	1	1	0	4	0
Mays, cf	3	1	1	1	3	0
Cepeda, 1b	4	0	1	1	8	0
Bailey, c	4	0	2	0	3	0
Davenport, 3b	4	0	1	1	2	4
Pagan, ss	5	1	2	0	1	1
Marichal, p	2	1	1	0	0	0
Larsen, p	0	0	0	0	0	1
M.Alou, ph	1	0	1	0	0	0
Nieman, ph	1	0	0	0	0	0
Pierce, p	0	0	0	0	0	0
	36	6	13	4	27	7

LOS ANGELES	AB	R	H	BI	PO	A
Wills, ss,	5	1	4	0	3	6
Gilliam, 2b-3b	5	0	0	0	3	1
Snider,, lf	3	2	2	0	2	1
Burright, 2b	1	0	0	0	4	2
Walls, ph	1	0	0	0	0	0
T.Davis, 3b-1f	3	1	2	2	1	0
Moon, 1b	3	0	0	0	7	0
Fairly, 1b-rf	0	0	0	0	2	0
Howard, rf	4	0	0	1	0	0
Harkness, 1b	0	0	0	0	0	0
Roseboro, c	3	0	0	0	3	1
W.Davis, cf	3	0	0	0	2	0
Podres, p	2	0	0	0	0	2
Roebuck, p	2	0	0	0	0	0
Williams, p	0	0	0	0	0	0
Perranoski, p	0	0	0	0	0	0
	35	4	8	3	27	14

```
SF     0  0  2     0  0  0     0  0  4  -  6
LA     0  0  0     1  0  2     1  0  0  -  4
```

Errors: Bailey, Pagan, Marichal, Gilliam, Burright, Roseboro, Podres. DP: LA 3. LOB: SF 12, LA 8. 2B: Hiller, Snider. HR: T. Davis. SB: T Davis, Wills 3. SH: Fairly, Hiller, Marichal. SF: Cepeda. WP: Williams. Umpires: Boggess, Donnatelli, Conlan, Barlick. Att: 45,693. Time—3:00.

PITCHING	IP	H	R	ER	BB	SO
San Francisco						
Marichal	7.0	8	4	3	1	2
Larsen (W)	1.0	0	0	0	2	1
Pierce (sv)	1.0	0	0	0	0	0
Los Angeles						
Podres	5.0	9	2	1	1	0
Roebuck (L)	3.1	4	4	3	3	0
Williams	0.1	0	0	0	2	0
Perranoski	0.1	0	0	0	0	1

Marichal pitched to one batter in eighth; Podres pitched to one batter in sixth.

Close they did, scoring twice in the eighth and sending the game into the bottom of the ninth tied at seven all. Three walks in the ninth inning—one to Maury Wills by Bob Bolin, one by Dick LeMay, one by Mike McCormick—a sacrifice fly by Ron Fairly, and Wills scored the run that kept the Dodgers alive in the series. Stan Williams (14–12) was the winning pitcher and Bob Bolin (7–3) the loser.

Game Three saw Juan Marichal (18–11) against Johnny Podres (15–13) before nearly 46,000 rabid fans. The game was scoreless until the third when throwing errors by Podres, Roseboro, and Gilliam allowed two Giant runs to cross the plate. The Dodgers struck once in the fourth to cut the lead in half, but were on their last legs in the top of the sixth when the Giants loaded the bases with nobody out. In strode Ed Roebuck from the bullpen. Roebuck pitched magnificently and retired the side without allowing any runs. Los

Angeles seemed to take heart from the reliever's heroics and struck for two in the bottom of the inning on Duke Snider's single and Tommy Davis's home run. The Dodgers led, 3–2, with three innings to go.

Los Angeles scored an insurance run in the bottom of the seventh and, at the end of eight, maintained a two-run lead. Then disaster struck. Pinch-hitter Matty Alou led off the Giants' ninth with a single. One out later, Willie McCovey and Felipe Alou walked to load the bases. Willie Mays lined a ball off Roebuck to make the score 4–3, bases still loaded. Stan Williams, the winner in relief 24 hours earlier, was brought on to pitch to Orlando Cepeda and Cepeda flied out for the second out of the inning, but the ball was deep enough to score McCovey with the tying run. A wild pitch moved Alou and Mays to third and second. Catcher Bob Bailey was intentionally walked, for what reason we can only guess. Williams now faced Jim Davenport and a horrified Los Angeles crowd watched as Williams lost the plate and forced in Alou with a base on balls. San Francisco led, 5–4. Ron Perranoski (6–6) relieved and got Jose Pagan to ground the ball to Larry Burright, a defensive replacement at second base. To his everlasting embarrassment, Burright booted the ball and Mays scored. The Giants now led 6–4 with three outs to go.

Billy Pierce came on in relief and got those three outs, setting the Dodgers down 1-2-3 in the bottom of the ninth. Roebuck took the loss and Larsen, who had pitched a scoreless eighth, was the winner.

The 1978 American League Championship Playoff Series

New York Yankees defeat the Boston Red Sox; 1-0

After blowing a 14-game lead over the Yankees (100–63), the 1978 Boston Red Sox (99–64) recovered and ended the season tied with the New Yorkers. The two teams met for a one-game playoff to be held in Fenway Park.

Just a few weeks earlier, the Yankees and Sox had met for four games in Fenway – a series which would forever be known as the Boston Massacre. The Yanks had won the four games by scores of 15–3, 13–2, 7–0, and 7–4. In addition to scoring 42 runs, New York had pounded out a total of 67 hits. The Boston starting pitchers had retired a grand total of 20 batters, allowing 18 hits, seven walks, and 19 runs.

The Yankees must have looked forward to the one-game playoff the way a kid looks forward to going to the candy store. Ron Guidry (25–3) was the Yankee starter, Mike Torrez (16–13) for Boston. The Red Sox jumped on top in the bottom of the second as Carl Yastrzemski lined a Guidry fastball just inside the right-field foul pole for a 1–0 lead. In the sixth, Boston padded its lead as Rick Burleson doubled and Jim Rice singled him home. The Yankees woke up in the seventh. Roy White and Chris Chambliss singled and, with two outs, Bucky Dent came to the plate. Dent had four home runs and 42 RBIs during the regular season, and Torrez quickly threw two strikes past him. On the

1978 American League Playoff

October 2, 1978 at Boston

YANKEES	AB	R	H	BI	BOSTON	AB	R	H	BI
Rivers, cf	2	1	1	0	Burleson, ss	4	1	1	0
Blair, cf	1	0	1	0	Remy, 2b	4	1	2	0
Munson, c	5	0	1	1	Rice, rf	5	0	1	1
Piniella, rf	4	0	1	0	Yastrzemski, lf	5	2	2	2
Jackson, dh	4	1	1	1	Fik, c	3	0	1	0
Nettles, 3b	4	0	0	0	Lynn, cf	4	0	1	1
Chambliss, 1b	4	1	1	0	Hobson, dh	4	0	1	0
White, lf	3	1	1	0	Scott, 1b	4	0	2	0
Thomasson, lf	0	0	0	0	Brohamer, 3b	1	0	0	0
Doyle, 2b	2	0	0	0	Bailey, ph	1	0	0	0
Spencer, ph	1	0	0	0	Duffy, 3b	0	0	0	0
Stanley, 2b	1	0	0	0	Evans, ph	1	0	0	0
Dent, ss	4	1	1	3					
	35	5	8	5		36	4	11	4

```
NY    0  0  0    0  0  0    4  1  0  -  5
BOS   0  1  0    0  0  1    0  2  0  -  4
```

LOB: NY 6, BOS 9. 2B: Rivers, Scott, Burleson, Munson, Remy. HR: Yastrzemski, Dent, Jackson. SB: Rivers 2. SH: Brohamer, Remy. PB: Munson. Att: 32,925. Time—2:52.

PITCHING	IP	H	R	ER	BB	SO
New York						
Guidry (W)	6.1	6	2	2	1	5
Gossage (sv)	2.2	5	2	2	1	2
Boston						
Torrez (L)	6.2	5	4	4	3	4
Stanley	0.1	2	1	1	0	0
Hassler	1.2	1	0	0	0	2
Drago	0.1	0	0	0	0	0

Stanley pitched to one batter in the eighth.

0–2 pitch, Bucky lofted a fly ball to left which settled into the screen above the top of the Green Monster. The Red Sox lead was gone, the Red Sox pennant chances were slipping away.

Torrez, unglued, walked Mickey Rivers and Rivers stole second. Sox manager Don Zimmer replaced Torrez with Bob Stanley (15–12), but Thurman Munson doubled to put the Yankees up by two. Rich "Goose" Gossage (10–11), the Yankees' star reliever, came on to pitch to "Beetle" Bob Bailey with one on and two out in the seventh. Three Gossage fastballs sent Bailey back to the bench. Reggie Jackson's solo home run in the top of the eighth seemed to put the game out of reach for good, but the Red Sox weren't through yet.

Jerry Remy doubled and scored on a Yastrzemski single in the eighth. When Carlton Fisk and Fred Lynn singled, Gossage was looking at a one-run lead, runners on first and second, and only one out. But Butch Hobson popped up and the one and only (to hear him tell it) George Scott struck out to end the inning. In the ninth, Boston rallied again. With one out, Rick Burleson walked. Jerry Remy jumped on a Gossage fastball and screamed it into right field. It

National League East Divisional Championship

GAME ONE --- October 7 at Montreal

PHILADELPHIA	AB	R	H	BI	E
Smith, cf	4	0	2	0	0
Rose, 1b	4	0	2	0	0
Matthews, lf	4	0	1	0	0
Schmidt, 3b	3	0	0	0	0
McBride, rf	4	0	0	0	0
Moreland, c	4	1	3	1	1
Aguayo, pr	0	0	0	0	0
Bowa, ss	3	0	0	0	0
Vuckovich, ph	1	0	1	0	0
Trillo, 2b	3	0	0	0	0
Carlton, p	2	0	1	0	0
Gross, ph	1	0	0	0	0
R. Reed, p	0	0	0	0	0
	33	1	10	1	1

MONTREAL	AB	R	H	BI	E
Cromartie, 1b	5	0	2	1	0
White, lf	4	1	1	0	0
Dawson, cf	4	0	2	0	0
Carter, c	3	0	1	1	0
Parrish, 3b	3	0	0	0	0
Wallach, rf	2	1	1	0	0
Francona, lf	0	0	0	0	0
Manuel, 2b	4	0	0	0	0
Speier, ss	1	1	1	1	0
Rogers, p	2	0	0	0	0
Reardon, p	0	0	0	0	0
	28	3	8	3	0

```
PHI   0 1 0   0 0 0   0 0 0  -  1
MTL   1 1 0   1 0 0   0 0 x  -  3
```

DP: MTL 2. LOB: MTL 10, PHI 7. 2B: Carter, Wallach, Rose Speier, Cromartie. 3B: Matthews, Dawson. HR: Moreland. SB: White 2, Dawson, Francona. SH: Rogers. WP: Carlton, R. Reed. Att: 32,327. Time—2:30.

PITCHING	IP	H	R	ER	BB	SO
Philadelphia						
Carlton (L)	6.0	7	3	3	5	6
Reed	2.0	1	0	0	2	3
Montreal						
Rogers (W)	8.2	10	1	1	0	3
Reed (S)	0.1	0	0	0	0	0

was obvious to everyone that Lou Piniella had lost the ball in the sun, obvious that is to everyone but Burleson. He thought he was being decoyed and held at first. The ball fell a few feet in front of and to the left of Piniella. Had Reggie Jackson still been in right, with his glove on his right hand instead of his left, the game might have been tied. Instead, Piniella fielded the ball, made a quick throw to the infield, and held the ever cautious Burleson at second. Jim Rice followed with what would have been a sacrifice fly to center, had Burleson been able to advance.

The entire 1978 season came down to Gossage against Yastrzemski, as it should have. And in the best tradition of the nightmarish Red Sox, Yaz took a pitch, then fouled out.

The 1981 National League East Divisional Championship

Montreal Expos defeat Philadelphia Phillies; 3–2

For seven weeks and a day in 1981, the cry of "Play ball!" was not heard in a major-league ballpark. The players' strike, the first serious strike ever in the

National League East Divisional Championship

GAME TWO --- October 8 at Montreal

PHILADELPHIA	AB	R	H	BI	E		MONTREAL	AB	R	H	BI	E
Smith, cf	4	1	0	0	0		Cromartie, 1b	4	1	2	0	0
Rose, 1b	4	0	1	1	0		White, rf	5	0	0	0	0
McBride, rf	4	0	2	0	0		Dawson, cf	4	0	1	0	0
Schmidt, 3b	3	0	0	0	1		Carter, c	4	1	1	2	0
Matthews, lf	4	0	1	0	0		Parrish, 3b	3	1	0	0	0
McGraw, p	0	0	0	0	0		Francona, lf	2	0	2	0	0
Moreland, c	3	0	0	0	0		Speier, ss	2	0	1	1	0
Bowa, ss	4	0	0	0	1		Manuel, 2b	3	0	0	0	0
Trillo, 2b	4	0	0	0	0		Gullickson, p	3	0	0	0	0
Ruthven, p	0	0	0	0	0		Reardon, p	0	0	0	0	0
Gross, ph	1	0	0	0	0							
Brusstar, p	1	0	0	0	0			30	3	7	3	0
Lyle, p	0	0	0	0	0							
Vuckovich, lf	1	0	0	0	0							
	33	1	4	1	2							

```
PHI    0  0  0    0  0  0    0  1  0  -  1
MTL    0  1  2    0  0  0    0  0  0  -  3
```

LOB: PHI 7, MTL 6. 2B: Cromartie, Smith, McBride. HR: Carter. SB: White, Francona. Att: 46,096. Time—2:33.

PITCHING	IP	H	R	ER	BB	SO
Philadelphia						
Ruthven (L)	4.0	3	2	2	1	0
Brusstar	2.0	2	0	0	1	2
Lyle	1.0	1	0	0	1	0
McGraw	1.0	1	0	0	0	0
Montreal						
Gullickson (W)	7.2	6	1	1	1	3
Reardon (S)	1.1	0	0	0	1	1

105-year history of the game, began on June 12 and cost the loss of 713 ballgames and an estimated $100 million in salaries, broadcast, ticket, and concession revenues. If anyone had told Pete Rose it would take him nearly two months to break Stan Musial's National League Record for hits he and everyone else who followed baseball would have called the idea crazy.

When the season resumed, baseball commissioner Bowie Kuhn thought it a nifty idea to revive fan interest when fan interest did not need reviving. Kuhn disdained the old advice of "If it ain't broke, don't fix it," and hit upon the ludicrous notion of a split-season with the winner of the first half in each division to play the winner of the second half in a best-of-five miniplayoff. This idea left the St. Louis Cardinals (59–43), holders of the National League East's best record, out in the cold. The Cardinals trailed the Phillies when the strike began by a game and a half. When the second half of the season ended, the Montreal Expos had run up a record of 30–23 to the Redbirds' 29–23. That the Cardinals might have tied the Expos with the opportunity of playing an extra game was of no consequence to the commissioner. That they might have tied for first place with the opportunity of playing the five additional games that

National League East Divisional Championship

GAME THREE --- October 9 at Philadelphia

MONTREAL	AB	R	H	BI	E	PHILADELPHIA	AB	R	H	BI	E
Cromartie, 1b	4	0	1	0	1	Smith, cf	4	0	0	0	0
White, rf	4	1	1	0	0	Boone, c	1	0	0	0	0
Dawson, cf	3	0	1	0	1	Rose, 1b	4	0	1	1	0
Carter, c	3	1	2	1	0	McBride, rf	4	0	0	0	0
Parrish, 3b	4	0	0	0	0	Lyle, p	0	0	0	0	0
Francona, lf	4	0	1	0	0	Gross, lf	1	0	0	0	0
Speier, ss	4	0	2	1	0	Schmidt, 3b	3	1	2	0	0
Manuel, 2b	3	0	0	0	1	Matthews, lf	4	2	3	0	0
Johnson, ph	1	0	0	0	0	Reed, p	0	0	0	0	0
Burris, p	2	0	0	0	0	Moreland, c	3	1	2	0	0
Lee, p	0	0	0	0	0	Aguayo, pr	0	1	0	0	0
Wallach, ph	0	0	0	0	0	Maddox, cf	1	0	0	0	0
Sosa, p	0	0	0	0	1	Bowa, ss	3	0	2	1	0
Milner, ph	1	0	0	0	0	Trillo, 2b	2	1	1	1	0
						Christenson, p	2	0	0	0	0
	33	2	8	2	4	Vuckovich, lf	2	0	2	1	0
							34	6	13	4	0

```
MTL   0  1  0    0  0  0    0  1  0  -  2
PHI   0  2  0    0  0  2    2  0  x  -  6
```

DP: MTL 2. LOB: MTL 7, PHI 9. 2B: Carter, Brown, Schmidt, White. SH: Bowa. SF: Carter. Att: 36,835. Time—2:45.

PITCHING	IP	H	R	ER	BB	SO
Montreal						
Burris (L)	5.1	7	4	3	4	4
Lee	0.2	2	0	0	1	0
Sosa	2.0	4	2	1	0	0
Philadelphia						
Christenson (W)	6.0	4	1	1	1	8
Lyle	1.0	2	0	0	1	0
Reed	2.0	2	1	1	0	0

Philadelphia played was of no consequence either. The Cardinal team merely went home for the winter.

Thus the counterfeit series between the Phils and the Expos opened in Montreal on the 7th of October, Steve Carlton (13-4) against Steve Rogers (12-8). Carlton gave up all three Montreal runs in the six innings he worked, allowing five walks and seven hits. The Expos' leadoff batter reached base in each inning the rangy left-hander pitched. Montreal broke on top in the first when Jerry White reached on a forceout, stole second, and scored on Gary Carter's double. Keith Moreland's home run in the next half-inning tied the score, but Chris Speier walked and came around on Warren Cromartie's double in the bottom of the second as the Expos took a 2-1 lead. The Phils lost two runners on the basepaths and had the tying runs on in the ninth inning when Terry Francona snared Manny Trillo's line drive to end the game.

The Expos took a commanding two-games-to-none lead in the series the next day when Dick Ruthven (12-7) faced Bill Gullickson (7-9). Leading 1-0 in the third, Gary Carter's two-run homer provided the margin of victory as the Expos won, 3-1.

The series moved to Philadelphia. Larry Christensen (4-7), relegated to the bullpen for the last six weeks of the season, kept the Phils' hopes alive.

340 The League Playoffs

National League East Divisional Championship

GAME FOUR --- October 10 at Philadelphia

MONTREAL	AB	R	H	BI	E		PHILADELPHIA	AB	R	H	BI	E
Cromartie, 1b	5	0	0	0	0		Smith, cf	3	0	0	0	0
White, rf	3	1	0	1	0		Maddox, cf	2	0	1	0	0
Dawson, cf	5	0	1	0	0		Rose, 1b	5	1	1	0	0
Carter, c	3	1	3	2	0		McBride, rf	3	1	1	0	0
Parrish, 3b	5	1	1	0	0		Reed, p	0	0	0	0	0
Francona, lf	4	0	0	0	0		Aviles, ph	0	0	0	0	0
Reardon, p	1	0	0	0	0		McGraw, p	0	0	0	0	0
Speier, ss	4	2	2	0	0		Vuckovich, ph	1	1	1	1	0
Manuel, 2b	1	0	1	0	1		Schmidt, 3b	3	2	1	2	0
Milner, ph	1	0	1	1	0		Matthews, lf	4	1	2	1	0
Phillips, 2b	1	0	0	0	0		Moreland, c	3	0	1	2	0
Sanderson, p	1	0	0	0	0		Boone, c	1	0	0	0	0
Bahnsen, p	0	0	0	0	0		Bowa, ss	4	0	1	0	0
Mills, ph	0	0	0	0	0		Trillo, 2b	3	0	0	0	0
Sosa, p	0	0	0	0	0		Noles, p	0	0	0	0	0
Johnson, ph	1	0	1	1	0		Brusstar, p	0	0	0	0	0
Fryman, p	0	0	0	0	0		Lyle, p	0	0	0	0	0
Wallach, lf	1	0	0	0	0		Davis, rf	2	0	0	0	0
	36	5	10	5	1			34	6	9	6	0

```
MTL   0  0  0    1  1  2    1  0  0   0 - 5
PHI   2  0  2    0  0  1    0  0  0   1 - 6
```

DP: PHI 1. LOB: PHI 6, MTL 7. 2B: Speier, Carter, Maddox. HR: Carter, Schmidt, Matthews, Vuckovich. SB: Dawson. SH: Noles. SF: White. Att: 38,818. Time—2:49.

PITCHING	IP	H	R	ER	BB	SO
Montreal						
Sanderson	2.2	4	4	4	2	2
Bahnsen	1.1	1	0	0	1	1
Sosa	1.0	0	0	0	0	1
Fryman	1.1	3	1	1	1	0
Reardon (L)	2.2	1	1	1	0	0
Philadelphia						
Noles	4.0	4	2	2	2	5
Brusstar	1.2	3	2	2	0	1
Lyle	0.1	1	0	0	0	1
Reed	1.0	1	1	1	1	0
McGraw (W)	3.0	1	0	0	0	2

(Noles pitched to three batters in fifth; Reardon pitched to one batter in tenth.)

After Montreal had taken a 1–0 lead, Expo starter Ray Burris (9–7) was touched for two runs in the second. The Phils scored twice more in the sixth, knocking in two runners who were left on base by Burris with hits off Bill Lee. Burris was tagged with the loss and Christensen, who struck out eight in his six innings of work, got the victory.

Philadelphia tied the series the next day, in a game which saw the two clubs use 30 players between them. Montreal's Scott Sanderson (9–7) started against Dickie Noles (2–2) and the Phils took a 2–0 lead in the first when, with two out, Bake McBride legged out an infield hit and Mike Schmidt crashed a home run. They extended their lead to four in the third when Pete Rose singled, Schmidt

National League East Divisional Championship

```
GAME FIVE --- October 11 at Philadelphia
```

MONTREAL	AB	R	H	BI	E		PHILADELPHIA	AB	R	H	BI	E
Cromartie, 1b	4	0	0	0	0		Smith, cf	4	0	1	0	0
White, lf	4	0	1	0	0		Rose, 1b	3	0	1	0	0
Dawson, cf	4	1	1	0	0		Vuckovich, rf	4	0	0	0	0
Carter, c	4	0	1	0	0		Reed, p	0	0	0	0	0
Parrish, 3b	4	1	2	1	0		Schmidt, 3b	4	0	1	0	0
Wallach, rf	1	0	0	0	0		Matthews, lf	4	0	1	0	0
Francona, lf	1	0	1	0	0		Trillo, 2b	4	0	2	0	0
Speier, ss	4	1	0	0	0		Bowa, ss	3	0	0	0	0
Manuel, 2b	3	0	0	0	1		Boone, c	3	0	0	0	0
Rogers, p	3	0	2	2	0		Carlton, p	2	0	0	0	0
							Gross, rf	1	0	0	0	0
	32	3	8	3	1			32	0	6	0	0

```
MTL   0  0  0    0  2  1    0  0  0  -  3
PHI   0  0  0    0  0  0    0  0  0  -  0
```

DP: MTL 1. LOB: MTL 5, PHI 6. 2B: Parrish. Att: 47,384. Time—2:15.

PITCHING	IP	H	R	ER	BB	SO
Montreal						
Rogers (W)	9.0	6	0	0	1	2
Philadelphia						
Carlton (L)	8.0	7	3	3	3	7
Reed	1.0	1	0	0	0	1

walked and, one out later, Keith Moreland singled both men home. The Expos got one of those runs back on Gary Carter's solo home run in the fourth, cut the lead to one in the fifth, and tied the game with two runs in the sixth on singles from Larry Parrish, Chris Speier, and pinch-hitters John Milner and Wallace Johnson. The Phils regained the lead when Garry Matthews homered to lead off the bottom of the sixth off reliever Woody Fryman (5–3), but Montreal tied the game in the seventh on a walk to Jerry White and a Gary Carter double. Jeff Reardon entered the game with one out in the seventh and retired all eight men he faced until pinch-hitter George Vuckovich homered in the bottom of the tenth to win the game and tie the series.

With their backs to the walls, the Expos came out the next day and won the series behind the pitching and batting of Steve Rogers. Rogers fashioned a six-hit shutout and drove in his team's first two runs with a fifth-inning single as he out-dueled loser Steve Carlton for the second time in the series.

The 1981 National League West Divisional Championship

Los Angeles Dodgers defeat Houston Astros; 3–2

Even if you had an idea as to how the St. Louis Cardinals were feeling in October in 1981, it would take a great leap of imagination to appreciate the

National League West Divisional Championship

```
GAME ONE --- October 6 at Houston

LOS ANGELES        AB   R   H  BI   E       HOUSTON           AB   R   H  BI   E
------------------------------------        ------------------------------------
Lopes, 2b           4   0   0   0   0       Puhl, rf           4   1   2   0   0
Landreaux, cf       4   0   1   0   0       Garner, 2b         3   0   0   0   0
Baker, lf           3   0   0   0   0       Scott, cf          4   0   1   1   0
Garvey, 1b          3   1   1   1   0       Cruz, lf           4   0   0   0   0
Monday, rf          2   0   0   0   0       Cedeno, 1b         4   0   2   0   0
Guerrero, 3b        3   0   0   0   0       Howe, 3b           4   0   1   0   0
Scioscia, c         3   0   0   0   0       Garcia, ss         3   0   0   0   0
Russell, ss         3   0   0   0   0       Reynolds, ph       1   0   1   0   0
Valenzuela, p       2   0   0   0   0       Ashby, c           3   1   1   2   0
Johnstone, ph       1   0   0   0   0       Ryan, p            3   1   0   0   0
Stewart, p          0   0   0   0   0                         ----------------
                   ----------------                           33   3   8   3   0
                   28   1   2   1   0

Two out when winning run scored

LA     0  0  0     0  0  0     1  0  0  -  1
HOU    0  0  0     0  0  1     0  0  2  -  3
```

DP: LA 1. LOB: LA 1, HOU 6. 2B: Cedeno. HR: Garvey, Ashby. SB: Cedeno 2. Att: 44,836. Time—2:22.

```
PITCHING          IP   H   R  ER  BB  SO
----------------------------------------
  Los Angeles
Valenzuela        8.0   6   1   1   2   6
Stewart (L)       0.2   2   2   2   0   1

  Houston
Ryan (W)          9.0   2   1   1   1   7
```

predicament of the Cincinnati Reds. The Reds finished the first half of the 1981 season in second place, trailing the Dodgers by a half game. Both teams lost 21 games but the Dodgers, with 36 victories, won the extra game they played. In the second half, the Houston Astros' record of 33–20 was good enough to leave the Reds a game and a half back, at 31–21. With a seasonal record of 66–42 and a winning percentage of .611 — easily the best in all of baseball — the Cincinnati Reds cleaned out their lockers and went home. The teams with the two best records in the National League failed to make the playoffs. Nice going, Bowie.

The Astros jumped off to a one-game lead on the 6th of October as speed-baller Nolan Ryan (11–5) shut down the Dodger offense on two hits, winning 3–1. Ryan gave up a one-out single to Ken Landreaux in the first and retired the next 16 batters he faced before Steve Garvey's solo home run tied the game in the seventh. Ryan then set down the last seven Dodgers he faced. Losing pitcher Fernando Valenzuela (13–7) matched Ryan where it counted — on the scoreboard — before retiring in favor of reliever Dave Stewart (4–3). Stewart got the first two men in the ninth before pinch-hitter Craig Reynolds singled and brought Alan Ashby to the plate. Ashby, with four home runs during the

National League West Divisional Championship

GAME TWO --- October 7 at Houston

LOS ANGELES	AB	R	H	BI	E		HOUSTON	AB	R	H	BI	E
Lopes, 2b	5	0	2	0	0		Puhl, rf	5	0	1	0	0
Marshall, ph	1	0	0	0	0		Garner, 2b	5	1	2	0	0
Stewart, p	0	0	0	0	0		Scott, cf	5	0	1	0	0
Forster, p	0	0	0	0	0		Cruz, lf	5	0	2	0	0
Niedenfeur, p	0	0	0	0	0		Cedeno, 1b	3	0	0	0	0
Landreaux, cf	4	0	1	0	0		Howe, 3b	4	0	0	0	0
Baker, lf	4	0	1	0	0		Thon, ss	4	0	2	0	0
Garvey, 1b	5	0	1	0	0		Walling, ph	1	0	1	1	0
Monday, rf	4	0	1	0	0		Pujols, c	3	0	0	0	0
Thomas, rf	1	0	0	0	0		Niekro, p	2	0	0	0	0
Guerrero, 3b	5	0	1	0	0		Woods, ph	1	0	0	0	0
Scioscia, c	4	0	1	0	0		D. Smith, p	0	0	0	0	0
Yeager, c	1	0	1	0	0		Pittman, ph	1	0	0	0	0
Russell, ss	2	0	0	0	1		Sambito, p	0	0	0	0	0
Reuss, p	4	0	0	0	0							
S. Howe, p	0	0	0	0	0			39	1	9	1	0
R. Smith, ph	1	0	0	0	0							
Sax, 2b	0	0	0	0	0							
	41	0	9	0	1							

Two out when winning run scored

```
LA   0 0 0   0 0 0   0 0 0   0 0  -  0
HOU  0 0 0   0 0 0   0 0 0   0 1  -  1
```

LOB: LA 13, HOU 10. 2B: Lopes, Yeager. SB: Cruz. SH: Landreaux, Pujols. Att: 42,398. Time—3:39.

PITCHING	IP	H	R	ER	BB	SO
Los Angeles						
Reuss	9.0	5	0	0	2	3
S. Howe	1.0	1	0	0	0	0
Stewart (L)	0.0	2	1	1	0	0
Forster	0.1	0	0	0	0	0
Niedenfeur	0.1	1	0	0	1	1
Houston						
Niekro	8.0	7	0	0	3	4
D. Smith	2.0	1	0	0	0	3
Samito (W)	1.0	1	0	0	1	2

regular season, smashed a two-run homer into the right field seats to win the game.

Los Angeles dropped behind two-games-to-none the next day when the two teams evenly divided 18 hits. Jerry Reuss (10–4) started for the Dodgers and pitched shutout ball for nine innings. Joe Niekro (9–9) was the Astros' pitcher and he went eight scoreless innings before being relieved by Dave Smith (5–3). Smith was in turn relieved by Joe Sambito (5–5), the eventual winner. In the 11th inning of a scoreless game, Denny Walling's pinch-hit bases-loaded single made a loser of reliever Dave Stewart for the second day in a row.

National League West Divisional Championship

```
GAME THREE --- October 9 at Los Angeles

HOUSTON            AB  R  H BI  E       LOS ANGELES        AB  R  H BI  E
------------------------------------    ------------------------------------
Puhl, rf            4  0  0  0  0       Lopes, 2b           3  1  1  0  0
Garner, 2b          2  0  0  0  0       Landreaux, cf       4  0  1  1  0
Scott, cf           4  0  0  0  0       Baker, lf           5  1  2  1  0
Cruz, lf            4  0  2  0  1       Garvey, 1b          4  1  2  2  0
Cedeno, 1b          4  0  0  0  1       Guerrero, 3b        3  0  1  1  0
Ashby, c            2  0  0  0  0       Monday, rf          3  0  1  0  0
Howe, 3b            2  1  1  1  0       Thomas, cf          1  1  0  0  0
Reynolds, ss        2  0  0  0  0       Yeager, c           4  1  1  0  0
Thon, ss            1  0  0  0  0       Russell, ss         4  1  1  1  0
Knepper, p          1  0  0  0  0       Hooton, p           3  0  0  0  0
Spilman, ph         1  0  0  0  0       Howe, p             0  0  0  0  0
LaCorte, p          0  0  0  0  0       R. Smith, ph        0  0  0  0  0
Woods, ph           1  0  0  0  0       Welch, p            0  0  0  0  0
Sambito, p          0  0  0  0  0                          --------------------
B. Smith, p         0  0  0  0  0                          34  6 10  6  0
                   -----------------
                   28  1  3  1  2

HOU   0  0  1   0  0  0   0  0  0  -  1
LA    3  0  0   0  0  0   0  3  x  -  6
```

DP: LA 2. LOB: HOU 4, LA 9. 2B: Cruz, Baker, Guerrero. HR: A. Howe, Garvey. SF: R. Smith. SH: Landreaux. WP: Knepper. Att: 45,820. Time—2:35.

```
PITCHING           IP   H  R ER BB SO
------------------------------------
   Houston
Knepper (L)        5.0   6  3  3  2  4
LaCorte            2.0   0  0  0  0  0
Sambito            0.2   4  3  3  1  0
B. Smith           1.1   0  0  0  0  0

   Los Angeles
Hooton (W)         7.0   3  1  1  3  2
Howe               1.0   0  0  0  0  2
Welch              1.0   0  0  0  1  1

Hooton pitched to one batter in the eighth
```

After an off-day, the series resumed in Los Angeles. Burt Hooton (11–6) limited the Astros to three hits and a single run in his seven innings of work, while relievers Steve Howe (5–3) and Bob Welch (9–5) gave up nothing over the final two innings. The Dodgers got all the runs they needed in the first off loser Bob Knepper (9–5). Davey Lopes drew a base on balls and scored on Dusty Baker's one-out double. Steve Garvey then hit a two-run homer to provide the icing on the cake. Los Angeles added three insurance runs off reliever Joe Sambito in the eighth. The Astros' only run came when third baseman Art Howe hit a solo home run in the third.

Fernando Valenzuela was back on the mound for the fourth game and pitched the Dodgers into a series tie as Pedro Guerrero's solo home run in the fifth made a loser of Vern Ruhle (4–6). Steve Garvey's single, a Rick Monday sacrifice bunt, and Bill Russell's single put the Dodgers up 2–0 in the seventh.

National League West Divisional Championship

GAME FOUR --- October 10 at Los Angeles

HOUSTON	AB	R	H	BI	E
Puhl, rf	4	1	1	0	0
Garner, 2b	4	0	0	0	0
Scott, cf	4	0	1	1	0
Cruz, lf	4	0	0	0	0
Cedeno, 1b	2	0	1	0	0
Walling, 3b	1	0	0	0	0
Howe, 3b	3	0	1	0	0
Thon, ss	2	0	0	0	0
Pujols, c	3	0	0	0	0
Ruhle, p	1	0	0	0	0
Garcia, ph	0	0	0	0	0
	28	1	4	1	0

LOS ANGELES	AB	R	H	BI	E
Lopes, 2b	3	0	0	0	0
Landreaux, cf	4	0	0	1	0
Baker, lf	3	0	0	0	0
Garvey, 1b	3	1	1	0	0
Monday, rf	2	0	0	0	0
Thomas, rf	0	0	0	0	0
Guerrero, 3b	3	1	1	1	0
Sciosia, c	2	0	0	0	0
Russell, ss	3	0	2	0	0
Valenzuela, p	2	0	0	0	0
	25	2	4	2	0

```
HOU   0  0  0    0  0  0    0  0  1  -  1
LA    0  0  0    0  1  0    1  0  x  -  2
```

LOB: HOU 3, LA 3. 2B: Puhl. HR: Guerrero. SH: Valenzuela, Monday, Ruhle. Att: 55,983. Time—2:00.

PITCHING	IP	H	R	ER	BB	SO
Houston						
Ruhle (L)	8.0	4	2	2	2	1
Los Angeles						
Valenzuela (W)	9.0	4	1	1	1	4

GAME FIVE --- October 11 at Los Angeles

HOUSTON	AB	R	H	BI	E
Puhl, rf	4	0	0	0	0
Garner, 2b	4	0	0	0	1
Scott, cf	3	0	0	0	0
A. Howe, 3b	4	0	1	0	0
Cruz, lf	3	0	2	0	0
Walling, 1b	4	0	1	0	1
Thon, ss	4	0	0	0	1
Ashby, c	4	0	0	0	0
Ryan, p	1	0	1	0	0
Pittman, ph	1	0	0	0	0
D. Smith, p	0	0	0	0	0
LaCorte, p	0	0	0	0	0
Roberts, ph	1	0	0	0	0
	33	0	5	0	3

LOS ANGELES	AB	R	H	BI	E
Lopes, 2b	5	0	1	0	0
Landreaux, cf	4	1	1	0	0
Baker, lf	3	1	0	0	0
Garvey, 1b	4	1	2	1	0
Monday, rf	3	1	1	1	0
Thomas, rf	0	0	0	0	0
Guerrero, 3b	3	0	0	0	1
Scioscia, c	4	0	1	1	0
Russell, ss	4	0	1	0	1
Reuss, p	4	0	0	0	0
	34	4	7	3	2

```
HOU   0  0  0    0  0  0    0  0  0  -  0
LA    0  0  0    0  0  3    1  0  x  -  4
```

LOB: HOU 9, LA 9. 2B: Landreaux, Russell. 3B: Garvey. SB: Puhl, Guerrero, Lopes. Att: 55,979. Time—2:52.

PITCHING	IP	H	R	ER	BB	SO
Houston						
Ryan (L)	6.0	4	3	2	2	7
D. Smith	0.1	1	1	1	0	1
LaCorte	1.2	2	0	0	1	3
Los Angeles						
Reuss (W)	9.0	5	0	0	2	4

The Astros got their only run in the ninth when Terry Puhl doubled and Tony Scott singled him home.

Just as in the National League East divisional playoff, the team which lost the first two games rebounded to win three straight and the title. In Game Five, the Dodgers' Jerry Reuss scattered five hits and two walks and won handily, 4–0. The game was scoreless until the middle of the fifth when Dodger hitters rose to the occasion at the same time the Houston defense collapsed. A walk to Dusty Baker, singles by Garvey, Monday and Mike Scioscia, and a Houston error sent three men across the plate. That was all Reuss needed as he finished the series with 18 innings of shutout ball and a 1–0 record.

The 1981 American League East Divisional Championship

New York Yankees defeat Milwaukee Brewers; 3–2

The New York Yankees won the first half of the 1981 season with a 34–22 record, then coasted to a sixth-place finish (25–26) in the second half. The

American League East Divisional Championship

GAME ONE --- October 7 at Milwaukee

NEW YORK	AB	R	H	BI	E		MILWAUKEE	AB	R	H	BI	E
Randolph, 2b	5	0	0	0	0		Molitor, rf	4	0	0	0	0
Mumphrey, cf	5	1	2	0	0		Yount, ss	2	1	1	1	1
Winfield, lf	5	0	1	0	0		Cooper, 1b	3	0	1	0	0
Jackson, rf	4	1	1	0	0		Simmons, c	4	0	1	1	1
Nettles, 3b	5	0	0	0	0		Thomas, cf	4	0	0	0	0
Gamble, dh	4	1	3	2	0		Oglivie, lf	4	0	0	0	0
Watson, 1b	4	1	3	0	0		Bando, 3b	4	1	1	0	0
Milbourne, ss	4	1	1	0	0		Moore, dh	2	0	2	1	0
Cerone, c	4	0	2	2	1		Howell, dh	2	0	1	0	0
							Gantner, 2b	4	1	1	0	1
	40	5	13	4	1			33	3	8	3	3

```
NY   0  0  0    4  0  0    0  0  1  -  5
MIL  0  1  1    0  1  0    0  0  0  -  3
```

DP: MIL. LOB: MIL 7, NY 9. 2B: Bando, Gantner, Cerone 2, Gamble. HR: Molitor. SF: Yount. Att: 35,064. Time—2:57.

PITCHING	IP	H	R	ER	BB	SO
New York						
Guidry	4.1	7	3	3	2	5
Davis (W)	2.2	0	0	0	0	4
Gossage (S)	2.0	1	0	0	0	3
Milwaukee						
Haas (L)	3.1	8	4	4	1	1
Bernard	0.2	0	0	0	0	0
McClure	1.1	3	0	0	0	0
Slaton	2.1	1	0	0	0	1
Fingers	1.1	1	1	0	0	1

American League East Divisional Championship

GAME TWO --- October 8 at Milwaukee

NEW YORK	AB	R	H	BI	E	MILWAUKEE	AB	R	H	BI	E
Randolph, 2b	4	0	2	0	0	Molitor, rf	4	0	1	0	0
Mumphrey, cf	4	0	0	0	0	Yount, ss	5	0	0	0	0
Winfield, lf	4	1	3	0	0	Cooper, 1b	4	0	1	0	0
Jackson, rf	4	1	1	2	0	Simmons, c	3	0	1	0	0
Piniella, dh	4	1	1	1	0	Thomas, cf	3	0	0	0	0
Nettles, 3b	4	0	0	0	0	Oglivie, lf	4	0	0	0	0
Watson, 1b	3	0	0	0	0	Bando, 3b	4	0	3	0	0
Milbourne, ss	3	0	0	0	0	Moore, dh	2	0	0	0	0
Cerone, c	3	0	0	0	0	Howell, ph	0	0	0	0	0
						Bosley, pr	0	0	0	0	0
	33	3	7	3	0	Money, dh	1	0	0	0	0
						Gantner, 2b	4	0	1	0	0
							34	0	7	0	0

```
NY    0  0  0    1  0  0    0  0  2  -  3
MIL   0  0  0    0  0  0    0  0  0  -  0
```

DP: MIL. LOB: NY 3, MIL 11. 2B: Bando 2, Winfield. HR: Piniella, Jackson. WP: Davis. Att: 36,385. Time—2:35.

PITCHING	IP	H	R	ER	BB	SO
New York						
Righetti (W)	6.0	4	0	0	2	10
Davis	0.1	1	0	0	2	0
Gossage (S)	2.2	2	0	0	0	4
Milwaukee						
Caldwell (L)	8.1	7	3	3	0	4
Slaton	0.2	0	0	0	0	0

GAME THREE --- October 9 at New York

MILWAUKEE	AB	R	H	BI	E	NEW YORK	AB	R	H	BI	E
Molitor, rf	4	1	3	1	0	Randolph, 2b	5	0	1	1	0
Yount, ss	4	1	1	0	0	Mumphrey, cf	4	0	0	0	0
Cooper, 1b	4	1	1	0	0	Winfield, lf	3	1	2	0	0
Simmons, c	3	1	2	3	0	Jackson, rf	4	0	0	0	0
Thomas, cf	4	1	1	0	0	Piniella, dh	3	0	0	0	0
Oglivie, lf	3	0	0	0	0	Gamble, ph	1	0	1	0	0
Bando, 3b	4	0	1	1	0	Nettles, 3b	2	0	0	0	0
Moore, dh	2	0	0	0	0	Watson, 1h	2	1	2	1	1
Edwards, rf	1	0	0	0	0	Murcer, ph	1	0	0	0	0
Gantner, 2b	3	0	0	0	0	Revering, 1b	0	0	0	0	0
						Milbourne, ss	4	1	1	0	0
	32	5	9	5	0	Cerone, c	4	0	1	1	0
						May, p	0	0	0	0	1
							33	3	8	3	2

```
MIL   0  0  0    0  0  0    3  2  0  -  5
NY    0  0  0    1  0  0    2  0  0  -  3
```

DP: NY 1. LOB: MIL 3, NY 7. 2B: Winfield, Simmons. HR: Simmons, Molitor. SH: Oglivie. WP: May. Att: 54,171. Time—2:30.

PITCHING	IP	H	R	ER	BB	SO
Milwaukee						
Lerch	6.0	3	1	1	4	3
Fingers (W)	3.0	5	2	2	0	4
New York						
John (L)	7.0	8	5	5	2	0
May	2.0	1	0	0	0	1

John pitched to two batters in the eighth

American League East Divisional Championship

GAME FOUR --- October 10 at New York

MILWAUKEE	AB	R	H	BI	E		NEW YORK	AB	R	H	BI	E
Molitor, rf	4	1	1	0	0		Randolph, 2b	3	0	0	0	0
Yount, ss	3	1	1	0	0		Mumphrey, cf	4	1	0	0	0
Cooper, 1b	3	0	0	1	1		Winfield, lf	4	0	1	0	0
Simmons, c	4	0	0	0	0		Jackson, rf	4	0	1	0	0
Oglivie, lf	3	0	1	1	0		Gamble, dh	1	0	0	0	0
Thomas, cf	3	0	0	0	0		Piniella, dh	2	0	0	0	0
Edwards, cf	0	0	0	0	0		Nettles, 3b	3	0	0	0	0
Howell, dh	3	0	1	0	0		Watson, 1b	3	0	1	0	0
Bando, 3b	3	0	0	0	0		Brown, pr	0	0	0	0	0
Gantner, 2b	3	0	0	0	1		Revering, 1b	0	0	0	0	0
							Foote, ph	0	0	0	0	0
	29	2	4	2	2		Murcer, ph	1	0	1	1	0
							Milbourne, ss	4	0	0	0	0
MIL 0 0 0 2 0 0 0 0 0 - 2							Cerone, c	3	0	1	0	0
NY 0 0 0 0 0 1 0 0 0 - 1								32	1	5	1	0

LOB: MIL 2, NY 2. 2B: Oglivie, Winfield. SF: Cooper. WP: Vuckovich. Att: 52,077. Time—2:34.

PITCHING	IP	H	R	ER	BB	SO
Milwaukee						
Vuckovich (W)	5.0	2	1	0	3	4
Easterly	1.0	0	0	0	0	1
Slaton	1.2	2	0	0	0	1
McClure	1.0	0	0	0	0	1
Fingers (S)	0.1	1	0	0	1	1
New York						
Reuschel (L)	6.0	4	2	2	1	3
Davis	3.0	0	0	0	0	2

Vuckovich pitched to four batters in the sixth

Milwaukee Brewers had finished third behind the Yanks before the strike, but had a respectable 31–22 record for the final half to finish a game and a half in front of the Detroit Tigers. The Baltimore Orioles actually had a better record than the Yankees, but a second- and fourth-place finish sent them crying in their beer with the Cardinals and Reds.

Moose Haas (11–7) got the nod in the first appearance by the Brewers in postseason competition against Ron Guidry (11–5) in Game One. Both pitchers were watching the game from their respective dugouts by the time the fifth inning ended. Trailing 2–0, the Yankees racked up four runs off Haas in the fourth. The big hits were a two-run homer by designated hitter Oscar Gamble which tied the game, and a two-run double by Rick Cerone that put the Yankees ahead. Gamble was 0-for-27 when he came to the plate. Goose Gossage (3–2) pitched the last two innings for the save, but the big man in the bullpen for the Yanks was winning pitcher Ron Davis (4–5). Davis came on in relief of Guidry with two on and one out in the fifth and retired the next eight men he faced.

American League East Divisional Championship

GAME FIVE --- October 11 at New York

MILWAUKEE	AB	R	H	BI	E
Molitor, cf	4	0	0	0	0
Yount, ss	5	1	3	0	0
Cooper, 1b	4	0	1	2	0
Simmons, c	4	0	0	0	0
Thomas, dh	4	1	1	1	0
Oglivie, lf	4	0	2	0	0
Bando, 3b	2	0	0	0	0
Moore, rf	3	0	0	0	0
Howell, ph	0	0	0	0	0
Edwards, rf	0	0	0	0	0
Romero, 2b	2	1	1	0	0
Money, 2b	2	0	0	0	0
	34	3	8	3	0

NEW YORK	AB	R	H	BI	E
Mumphrey, cf	4	0	0	0	0
Milbourne, ss	4	2	3	0	0
Winfield, lf	4	0	0	0	0
Jackson, rf	4	2	3	2	0
Gamble, dh	3	1	1	1	0
Piniella, dh	1	0	1	1	0
Nettles, 3b	3	1	1	1	0
Watson, 1b	4	0	1	0	0
Cerone, c	3	1	2	2	0
Randolph, 2b	3	0	1	0	0
	33	7	13	7	0

```
MIL    0  1  1    0  0  0    1  0  0  -  3
NY     0  0  0    4  0  0    1  2  x  -  7
```

DP: MIL 3. LOB: MIL 9, NY 3. 2B: Milbourne, Piniella. 3B: Yount. HR: Thomas, Jackson, Gamble, Cerone. SF: Cooper, Nettles. Att: 47,505. Time—2:42.

PITCHING	IP	H	R	ER	BB	SO
Milwaukee						
Haas (L)	3.1	5	3	3	0	0
Caldwell	0.0	2	1	1	0	0
Bernhard	1.2	0	0	0	0	0
McClure	1.0	1	0	0	0	1
Slaton	1.1	3	2	2	0	0
Easterly	0.1	2	1	1	0	0
Vuckovich	0.1	0	0	0	0	0
New York						
Guidry	4.0	4	2	2	1	3
Righetti (W)	3.0	4	1	1	1	3
Gossage (S)	2.0	0	0	0	2	1

The Yankees took a two-games-to-none lead in the second game when Dave Righetti (8–4) bested Mike Caldwell (11–9). Caldwell, 9–2 in his career against the New Yorkers, gave up a solo home run to Lou Piniella in the fourth and a two-run homer to Reggie Jackson in the ninth. That was all the scoring for either team as Righetti, Davis and Gossage combined on a seven-hit shutout. Gossage earned a save for the second consecutive day.

Long-time St. Louis Cardinal Ted Simmons provided the firepower as the Brewers got on the board in the third game. Trailing 1–0 in the seventh, Simmons's two-run homer knocked in Cecil Cooper and put the Brewers ahead for the first time in 21 innings. Simmons's homer came off Tommy John (9–8). A home run by Paul Molitor and an RBI double by Simmons provided two more runs in the eighth after the Yankees had tied the game. Fingers, although bloodied, was the winning pitcher. Tommy John (9–8) took the loss.

Milwaukee looked like they were going to march off to the League Championship Series the next day as they struck for a run in the second to break on top. Gorman Thomas's solo home run in the third made the score 2–0. But the Yankees came back with four of their own in the bottom of the third. A home run by Reggie Jackson tied the game. A home run by Oscar Gamble put the Yankees ahead. Singles by Graig Nettles and Bob Watson plus a groundout by Cerone gave the Yankees their fourth run of the inning. The Brewers closed to within one in the seventh, but a solo home run by Cerone and two runs off Jamie Easterly and Pete Vuckovich in the eighth put the game in the record book. The final score was 7–3. Dave Righetti was the winning pitcher, Goose Gossage got his third save of the series, and Milwaukee starter Moose Haas was the loser.

The 1981 American League West Divisional Championship

Oakland Athletics defeat Kansas City Royals; 3–0

Billy Martin's Oakland A's finished the first half of the season in first place and dropped to second place after the strike. The Kansas City Royals, a hapless fifth-place team with a 20–30 record in the first half, rebounded to finish 30–23 after the strike, good enough for a spot in the mini-playoffs. The Royals, with an overall record of 50–53, thus became the first team with a sub-.500 record to play postseason ball. The Texas Rangers (.543) and Chicago White Sox (.509) were left to share the same fate as the Cardinals, Reds, and Orioles. This was the only series which failed to go the distance, as the A's easily out-classed the Royals in three straight games.

The first game, on the 6th of October, saw Mike Norris (12–9) slam the door in the Royals' face with a four-hit shutout. All the hits were singles, and two of those bunt singles at that. The only runs Norris needed came in the fourth when third baseman Wayne Gross banged a three-run homer off losing pitcher Dennis Leonard (13–11). The previous batter, Tony Armas, had grounded to George Brett for what looked to be the third out of the inning, but Brett threw low to first for an error, thus prolonging the inning for Gross's at bat.

Game Two wasn't much of an improvement as the A's got on the board in the first inning off loser Mike Jones (6–3). Dwayne Murphy singled, went to third on Cliff Johnson's double, and scored when right-fielder Clint Hurdle misjudged Tony Armas's fly ball which went for an RBI double. The Royals tied the game in the fifth on consecutive singles by John Wathan, U.L. Washington, and Willie Wilson. In the ninth, with Dwayne Murphy on second, Kansas City manager Dick Howser elected to pitch to Armas with first base open. The big Venezuelan promptly shot a pitch between George Brett's legs for a double to score what proved to be the winning run. Brett was 1-for-8 at the plate, but he'd driven in four runs for the other side with his glove.

The A's wrapped it all up on the 9th of October when Rick Langford (12–10) out-dueled Larry Gura (11–8). Langford gave up ten hits before

American League West Divisional Championship

GAME ONE --- October 6 at Kansas City

OAKLAND	AB	R	H	BI	E
Henderson, lf	4	0	0	0	0
Murphy, cf	3	2	2	1	0
Drumright, dh	4	0	1	0	0
Armas, rf	4	1	1	0	0
Gross, 3b	4	1	2	3	0
Spencer, 1b	4	0	1	0	0
Heath, c	4	0	0	0	0
McKay, 2b	4	0	1	0	1
Stanley, ss	4	0	0	0	0
Norris, p	0	0	0	0	1
	35	4	8	4	2

KANSAS CITY	AB	R	H	BI	E
Wilson, lf	4	0	1	0	0
White, 2b	3	0	0	0	0
Brett, 3b	4	0	0	0	1
Aikens, 1b	4	0	1	0	0
Otis, cf	4	0	0	0	0
McRae, dh	4	0	0	0	0
Hurdle, rf	3	0	1	0	0
Wathan, c	2	0	0	0	0
Washington, ss	3	0	1	0	0
	31	0	4	0	1

```
OAK   0  0  0    3  0  0    0  1  0  -  4
KC    0  0  0    0  0  0    0  0  0  -  0
```

DP: OAK 2, KC 1. LOB: OAK 5, KC 7. 2B: Spencer. HR: Gross, Murphy. Att: 40,592. Time—2:35.

PITCHING	IP	H	R	ER	BB	SO
Oakland						
Norris (W)	9.0	4	0	0	3	2
Kansas City						
Leonard (L)	8.0	7	4	1	1	3
Martin	1.0	1	0	0	0	0

GAME TWO --- October 7 at Kansas City

OAKLAND	AB	R	H	BI	E
Henderson, lf	5	0	0	0	0
Murphy, cf	4	2	2	0	0
Johnson, dh	3	0	1	0	0
Armas, rf	4	0	4	2	1
Bosetti, rf	0	0	0	0	0
Kluttz, 3b	3	0	1	0	0
K. Moore, 1b	4	0	0	0	0
McKay, 2b	4	0	1	0	0
Newman, c	3	0	0	0	0
Picciolo, ss	3	0	1	0	0
Gross, ph	1	0	0	0	0
Stanley, ss	0	0	0	0	0
	34	2	10	2	1

KANSAS CITY	AB	R	H	BI	E
Wilson, lf	5	0	1	1	0
White, 2b	4	0	0	0	0
Brett, 3b	4	0	1	0	0
Aikens, 1b	1	0	0	0	0
Geronimo, pr	0	0	0	0	0
L. May, 1b	0	0	0	0	0
Otis, cf	4	0	0	0	0
McRae, dh	3	0	0	0	0
Hurdle, rf	4	0	1	0	0
Wathan, c	4	0	2	0	0
Washington, ss	3	1	1	0	0
	32	1	6	1	0

```
OAK   1  0  0    0  0  0    0  1  0  -  2
KC    0  0  0    0  1  0    0  0  0  -  1
```

LOB: OAK 8, KC 9. 2B: Johnson, Armas 2. SB: Henderson. SH: Kluttz, Washington, Johnson, Newman. Att: 40,274. Time—2:50.

PITCHING	IP	H	R	ER	BB	SO
Oakland						
McCatty (W)	9.0	6	1	1	4	3
Kansas City						
Jones (L)	8.0	9	2	2	0	2
Quisenberry	1.0	1	0	0	0	0

American League West Divisional Championship

GAME THREE --- Ocober 9 at Oakland

KANSAS CITY	AB	R	H	BI	E	OAKLAND	AB	R	H	BI	E
Wilson, lf	4	0	2	0	0	Henderson, lf	2	3	2	0	0
White, 2b	4	1	2	0	1	Murphy, cf	4	0	2	1	0
Brett, 3b	4	0	1	0	0	Johnson, dh	4	0	1	0	0
Aikens, 1b	4	0	2	0	0	Armas, rf	3	0	1	1	0
Otis, cf	4	0	0	1	0	Kluttz, 3b	4	0	0	0	0
McRae, dh	4	0	1	0	0	Moore, 1b	4	0	0	0	0
Hurdle, rf	4	0	1	0	0	Heath, c	4	0	0	0	0
Wathan, c	4	0	1	0	1	McKay, 2b	3	1	1	1	0
Washington, ss	3	0	0	0	1	Stanley, ss	2	0	0	0	0
	35	1	10	1	3		30	4	7	3	0

```
KC    0  0  0    1  0  0    0  0  0  -  1
OAK   1  0  1    2  0  0    0  0  x  -  4
```

DP: OAK. LOB: OAK 2, KC 7. 2B: McRae, Murphy. HR: McKay. SB: Henderson. Att: 40,002. Time—2:59.

PITCHING	IP	H	R	ER	BB	SO
Kansas City						
Gura (L)	3.2	7	4	3	3	3
Martin	4.1	0	0	0	2	2
Oakland						
Langford (W)	7.2	10	1	1	0	3
Underwood	0.1	0	0	0	0	1
Beard (S)	2.0	0	0	0	0	2

departing in favor of reliever Tom Underwood (3–2) in the eighth, but no walks, three strikeouts, and a double play bailed him out of trouble along the way. Oakland center-fielder Rickey Henderson was the star of this game with a 2-for-2 performance and three runs scored. It was Henderson who brought home the first run of the game in the initial inning when he walked, stole second, and scored on an infield single by Tony Armas. It was Henderson again in the third when he singled, reached second despite being caught in a run-down, and scored on a throwing error by Frank White. A solo homer by Dave McKay in the fourth put the A's up 3–1. A Rickey Henderson single and a Dwayne Murphy double accounted for the final run of the series a few moments later. The Royals' only run came in the fourth on singles by Frank White and Willie Wilson and an infield out by Amos Otis.

Bibliography

Books

Allen, Lee. *The National League Story: The Official History.* New York: Hill & Wang, 1961.

_____. *The World Series: The Story of Baseball's Annual Championship.* New York: G. P. Putnam's, 1969.

Cohen, Richard M. and Neft, David S. *The World Series.* New York: Collier Books, 1986.

Gammons, Peter. *Beyond the Sixth Game.* Lexington, Mass.: Stephen Greene Press, 1985.

Hynd, Noel. *The Giants of the Polo Grounds: The Glorious Times of Baseball's New York Giants.* New York: Doubleday, 1988.

James, Bill. *The Bill James Historical Baseball Abstract.* New York: Villard Books, 1988.

Kaese, Harold. *The Boston Braves.* New York: G. P. Putnam's, 1948.

Kennedy, MacLean. *The Great Teams of Baseball.* St. Louis: Sporting News Pub. Co., 1988 (reprint).

Leptich, John, and Baranowski, Dave. *This Date in St. Louis Cardinals History.* New York: Stein and Day, 1983.

Levine, Peter. *A. G. Spalding and the Rise of Baseball: The Promise of an American Sport.* New York: Oxford University Press, 1985.

Lewis, Franklin. *The Cleveland Indians.* New York: G. P. Putnam's, 1949.

Lieb, Frederick G. *The Boston Red Sox.* New York: G. P. Putnam's, 1947.

_____. *The Detroit Tigers.* New York: G. P. Putnam's, 1946.

_____. *The St. Louis Cardinals: The Story of a Great Baseball Club.* New York: G. P. Putnam's, 1947.

Lowry, Phillip J. *Green Cathedrals.* Cooperstown, N.Y.: Society for American Baseball Research, 1986.

Peterson, Robert. *Only the Ball Was White.* New York: McGraw-Hill, 1984.

Reichler, Joseph L., editor. *The Baseball Encyclopedia: The Complete and Official Record of Major League Baseball,* 7th ed. New York: Macmillan, 1988.

_____. *The Great All-Time Baseball Record Book: A Unique Sourcebook of Facts, Feats, and Figures.* New York: Macmillan, 1981.

Reidenbaugh, Lowell. *100 Years of National League Baseball.* St. Louis: Sporting News Pub. Co., 1976.

Rogosin, Dan. *Invisible Men: Life in Baseball's Negro Leagues.* New York: Atheneum; 1985.

Tattersall, John C. *Baseball: The Early World Series: 1884–1890.* Privately published, 1976.

Tiemann, Robert. *Cardinal Classics.* St. Louis: Baseball Histories, Inc., 1982.
Turkin, Hy, and Thompson, S. C. *The Official Encyclopedia of Baseball.*
Voigt, David Quentin. *American Baseball.* Three volumes. University Park: Pennsylvania State University Press, 1983.
_____. *Baseball: An Illustrated History.* University Park: Pennsylvania State University Press, 1987.

Periodicals

Baseball in Cincinnati: From Wooden Fences to Astroturf. A publication of the Cincinnati Historical Society, Dottie L. Lewis, editor. Cincinnati, Ohio: 1988.
Rothe, Emil H. "History of the Chicago City Series." *Baseball Research Journal. Eighth Annual Historical and Statistical Review of the Society for American Baseball Research: 1979.*
Spalding's Official Base Ball Guides. A. G. Spalding and Bros., Chicago. 1882–   .
The New York Clipper. New York. 1882–1889.
The St. Louis Globe-Democrat. All years concerned.
The St. Louis Post-Dispatch. All years concerned.
The Sporting News. St. Louis, 1885–   .

Index

A

Aaron, Henry 329, 331
Abbaticchio, Ed 161
ABBREVIATED GAMES *see*
  DARKNESS...; FOR-
  FEITED GAMES; INCLE-
  MENT...; STALLING
Adams, Earl "Sparky"
  263, 269, 272
Adkins, Grady 280, 282,
  284
ADMISSION PRICES 19
Aldridge, Vic 259, 264,
  265, 271
Alexander, Grover Cleve-
  land 212, 255, 257, 261,
  262, 263, 265, 266, 268,
  269, 271
Allison, Mack 201
Alou, Felipe 331, 335
Alou, Matty 335
Alston, Walter 328, 329
Altizer, Dave 179
Altrock, Nick 134, 136,
  137, 156, 157
Ames, Leon "Red" 189,
  242, 249
Anderson, Dave 113, 116
Anderson, John 127
Andrews, Ed 75, 83, 96,
  102
Anson, Cap x, 5, 9, 13,
  14, 16, 17, 18
Appling, Luke 292, 297,
  299, 303, 304, 307, 308,
  313, 314, 316, 317
Archer, Jimmy 209, 221
Armas, Tony 350, 352
Ashby, Alan 342–343
Austin, Jimmy 187, 190,
  191, 192–193, 225, 236,
  237, 248
Avila, Bobby 329'

B

Bagby, Jim 251, 254
Bakely, Edward "Jersey"
  116, 117, 118
Bailey, Bill 171–172, 173
Bailey, Bob 321, 335, 336
Baird, Doug 248, 251
Baker, Johnnie "Dusty"
  344, 346
Baker Bowl 198
Baldwin, Charles "Lady"
  23, 25
Baldwin, Mark 18, 117,
  121
BALTIMORE ORIOLES 49–50
Bancroft, Frank 7
Bank Street Grounds 5,
  70
Barber, Turner 256, 257,
  262
Barkley, Sam 14, 80, 81
Barnes, Emile "Red" 289
Barrett, Bill 268, 269,
  271, 273, 274, 278, 279,
  292
Barry, Shad 140, 166, 169,
  171, 173
Bartell, Dick 307
Barton, Vince 292, 294
Baseball Encyclopedia
  (Macmillan) x, 1
**Baseball Grounds, The
  (Philadelphia)** 24, 32,
  102, 106, 107, 113
BASEBALL HALL OF FAME
  60, 127
Baskette, Jim 200–201
Bastian, Charlie 83, 103
Baumgardner, George 201,
  205, 215, 218, 219, 225
Bausewine, George 116
Beard, Ollie 124
Bearden, Gene 325, 326

Beatin, Ed 116, 117, 118,
  119
Becannon, James "Buck"
  9, 79, 88
Beck, Clyde 283, 284
Beck, Zinn 219, 225
Beckley, Jake 40, 147,
  149, 150, 151, 154, 155,
  156, 167
Beebe, Fred 163, 167, 168,
  183
Begley, Ed 79
Bejma, Ollie 308, 309, 310
Bell, Charlie 112
Bell, Les 286, 287, 289,
  290, 292, 294
Bemis, Harry 145
Bender, Charles "Chief"
  137, 138, 140, 141, 214
Bennett, Charlie 20, 23,
  24, 25, 26, 27, 49
Bennett, Justin "Pug"
  166, 167, 171, 173
Benton, John "Rube"
  199
Benz, Joe 196, 210, 219,
  223, 229, 230, 237
Berg, Moe 284
Bernhard, Bill 145
Bescher, Bob 231
BETTING 32
Bierbauer, Lou 113, 123
Bithorn, Hiram "Hi" 319
Blackburne, Russell
  "Lena" 228, 239–240
Blair, Clarence "Foot-
  sie" 286, 288
Blake, Harry 55, 58
Blake, John "Sheriff" 269,
  271, 273, 277, 279, 283,
  284, 285, 286, 287
Blakiston, Bob 68
Blanding, Fred 185, 197,
  198, 201